Sexuality

CONTEMPORARY ISSUES FROM A BIBLICAL PERSPECTIVE

BIBLICAL RESEARCH INSTITUTE
STUDIES IN BIBLICAL ETHICS

Sexuality

CONTEMPORARY ISSUES FROM A BIBLICAL PERSPECTIVE

Ekkehardt Mueller
Elias Brasil de Souza
EDITORS

Biblical Research Institute

Review and Herald Publishing Association
Silver Spring, MD 20904
2022

Sexuality: Contemporary Issues from a Biblical Perspective
[edited by] Ekkehardt Mueller and Elias Brasil de Souza
Sex in the Bible
Sex—Religious Aspects—Christianity
Sex—Religious Aspects—Seventh-day Adventists
BS680.S5M84 2022

Printed in the U.S.A. by the
Pacific Press Publishing Association
Nampa, ID 83653-5353

ISBN 978-0-925675-34-7

SEXUALITY

CONTEMPORARY ISSUES FROM A BIBLICAL PERSPECTIVE

Editors
Ekkehardt Mueller and Elias Brasil de Souza

Associate Editors
Daniel Bediako, Kwabena Donkor, and Gerhard Pfandl

Consulting Editor
Frank M. Hasel

Managing Editor
Marly Timm

Biblical Research Institute Ethics Committee (BRIEC)
Members and Guests 2015–2021

Stephen Bauer
Torben Bergland
Elias Brasil de Souza
Kwabena Donkor
Ann Gibson
Ante Jeroncic
Gregory A. King
Larry L. Lichtenwalter
Ekkehardt Mueller
Elaine Oliver
Willie Oliver
Artur A. Stele
Rahel Wells

Copy Editor
Schuyler Kline

Inside Layout
Nicol Belvedere

Cover Design
Regina Hayden

CONTENTS

About the Authors

Stephen Bauer, PhD, has been professor of theology and ethics at Southern Adventist University (Collegedale, TN) since 1999. His PhD in religion is from Andrews University (Berrien Springs, MI). His disserta tion explored some moral implications of Darwin's theory of evolution, especially regarding its impact on the concept of human dignity. Prior to becoming a professor, he served as a district pastor in the greater New York City area and in Connecticut.

Richard M. Davidson, PhD, is professor of Old Testament Interpre tation at the Seventh-day Adventist Theological Seminary at Andrews University (Berrien Springs, MI). His PhD in religion is from Andrews University. He is the author of numerous articles in theological journals and other publications, having published many books, including *Typology in Scripture: A Study of Hermeneutical τὐπος Structures*, *Hermeneuticã biblicã*, *In the Footsteps of Joshua*, and his magisterial work *Flame of Yahweh: Sexuality in the Old Testament*.

Kwabena Donkor, PhD, is a retired associate director of the Biblical Research Institute of the General Conference of Seventh-day Adventists. He earned his doctorate in systematic theology from Andrews University (Berrien Springs, MI). In 2003 he published his work *Tradition, Method, and Contemporary Protestant Theology*. He has written scholarly articles for various journals and magazines and contributed to *Reclaiming the Center: Confronting Evangelical Accommodation in Postmodern Times*, edited by Millard J. Erickson, Paul Kjoss Helseth, and Justin Taylor.

Vanderlei Dorneles, PhD, is professor of New Testament Interpretation at the Latin American Adventist Theological Seminary at Centro Universitário Adventista de São Paulo, Campus Engenheiro Coelho (Brazil). He has a doctorate in Religious Studies from the Methodist University of São Paulo (2020) and another in sciences of communication from the University of São Paulo (2009). He has written many articles for theological journals and popular magazines. His authored books include *The Last Empire: The New World Order and the Counterfeiting of God's Kingdom* and *Pelo Sangue do Cordeiro* ("By the Blood of the Lamb").

Martha D. Duah, PhD, is a senior lecturer in the Department of Theological Studies at Valley View University (Oyibi, Ghana). She earned a doctoral degree in systematic theology from Andrews University (Berrien Springs, MI) and has contributed to *Prosperity Gospel: A Biblical and Theological Evaluation*, edited by Daniel Kwame Bediako, and the *Encyclopedia of Seventh-day Adventists*, edited by D. J. B. Trim (encyclopedia.adventist.org).

Antonio Estrada, PhD, is a retired professor from the University of Montemorelos (Montemorelos, Mexico). He holds a PhD in marriage and family studies from Fuller Theological Seminary (Pasadena, CA). He earned an MA in family psychology from Las Americas University (Mexico City, Mexico). He has presented lectures around the world; published a number of books, including *Paternidade: Um Compomiso Com o Futuro* [Fatherhood: Commitment to the Future] (Portuguese); and contributed to *Child Abuse, A Global View*, edited by Beth M. Schwartz-Kenney, Michelle McCauley, and Michelle A. Epstein.

Nisim Estrada, MS, LAC, NCC, CDBT, graduated from Capella Uni versity with a master's degree in in mental health counseling. He is licensed in Arizona and nationally through the NBCC. He currently serves as clinical director at an outpatient treatment center in Scottsdale, Arizona, and has over fifteen years of clinical experience working with children, adolescents, and adults suffering from severe mental health issues.

Luiz Carlos Gondim, MA, studied philosophy at the Catholic University of Pernambuco (1982; Recife, Brazil), theology at Northeast Adventist College (1985; Bahia, Brazil), and pedagogy from the School of Human Sciences of Olinda (2002; Olinda, Brazil). He also holds a master's degree in the field of family in contemporary society from the Catholic University of Salvador (Salvador, Brazil). He worked as a local church pastor and a teacher in the territory of the Northeast Brazil and East Brazil Union Missions. Retired, he continues to lecture in the areas of pastoral and family counseling.

Laurentiu G. Ionescu, PhD, is an Old Testament scholar who has taught for several years at Adventus University (Cernica, Romania) and at Universidad Adventista del Plata (Libertador San Martín, Argentina), and is currently pastoring in Spain. He was editor of *TheoRhēma.*, a theological journal, and has published several articles. Among other publications, he authored a Hebrew-Romanian dictionary. He is a member of the Biblical Research Committee of the Inter-European Division of Seventh-day Adventists.

Johannes Kovar, MA, has been a lecturer in New Testament Studies and Greek for many years and is currently also responsible for the Ellen G. White Research Center at Bogenhofen Seminary (St. Peter am Hart, Austria). He earned his MA from Salève Adventist University (France). He has published several articles on various topics, including "Toward a Theology of the Remnant: An Adventist Ecclesiological Perspective" for the Ellen G, White Encyclopedia.

T. P. Kurian, PhD, though retired from active service since 2016, is engaged in writing and translation. He earned his PhD in systematic theology from the Adventist International Institute of Advanced Studies (Silang, Philippines) in 1999, writing his thesis on "The Rest That Remains: A Historical, Biblical, and Theological Study of God's Rest With Special Reference to Hebrews 4:1–10." He served as professor at Spicer Adventist University (Pune, India), as union president, communication director of the Southern Asia Division, and editor of *Southern Asia Tidings*.

Larry L. Lichtenwalter, PhD, is president of Middle East University (Beirut, Lebanon) and has his PhD in Christian ethics from Andrews University (Berrien Springs, MI). He is a professor, ethicist, theologian, pastor, and preacher who has authored numerous articles in theological journals and other publications. His published works include several books on biblical characters as well as on the books of Ecclesiastes and Revelation. Christian personal ethics, the book of Revelation, and Adventist perspectives on Islamic studies are focus areas of his research, teaching, and publication.

Ekkehardt Mueller, ThD, DMin, is a retired associate director of the Biblical Research Institute of the General Conference of Seventh-day Adventists. His doctoral degrees are from Andrews University (Berrien Springs, Michigan). He has written numerous articles for scholarly books, journals, and magazines as well as several books in English and German, such as *Come Boldly to the Throne: Sanctuary Themes in Hebrews* and *Der Erste und der Letzte: Studien zum Buch der Offenbarung* ("The First and the Last: Studies on the Book of Revelation"). He also lectures internationally.

Deanna Pitchford, MA, is a lecturer in the humanities and in the Avondale Seminary at Avondale University (Cooranbong, Australia). Her MA in clinical psychology is from Griffith University (Australia). She is a registered member of the Australian Psychological Society and a fellow of the College of Clinical Psychologists. She has a keen interest in the integration of theology and psychology.

Gerhard Pfandl, PhD, is a retired associate director of the Biblical Research Institute of the General Conference of Seventh-day Adventists. He earned his PhD in Old Testament studies from Andrews University (Berrien Springs, MI). He has worked as a pastor in Austria and in the United States, as professor at Bogenhofen Seminary (St. Peter am Hart, Austria), and as field secretary of the South Pacific Division in Australia. He has published many articles for scholarly and popular journals in German and English and is the author of books such as *The Gift of Prophecy* and *Daniel: God's Beloved Prophet.*

Ron du Preez, PhD, ThD, DMin, has served as professor, pastor, and college president. Besides being lead editor for scholarly volumes such as *The Cosmic Battle for Planet Earth* and *Prophetic Principles,* he has written articles for journals, magazines, Festschriften, and encyclopedias. His book *Judging the Sabbath* provides seminal research on the "sabbath/s" in Colossians 2:16. With the motto of "Fitness for Witness," he actively promotes healthy living and motivates many to participate in an abundant life in Jesus Christ.

Boubakar Sanou, DMin, PhD, is an associate professor of mission and intercultural leadership at the Seventh-day Adventist Theological Seminary at Andrews University (Berrien Springs, MI). He has a DMin in global mission leadership and a PhD in religion from Andrews University. He has published book chapters as well as peer-reviewed articles in various mission and leadership journals.

Aleksandar Santrac, PhD, DPhil, earned his PhD in dogmatics from North-West University (South Africa)/Greenwich School of Theology (Clarborough, UK), and his DPhil from the University of Belgrade (Serbia). Currently, he is pursuing a PhD in higher education at Notre Dame of Maryland University. He is the author of numerous articles in peer-reviewed journals and other publications, having published many different books, including *Witness to Life Worth Living: Ethics of Embrace of Miroslav Volf* and *An Evaluation of Alvin Plantinga's Free Will Defense: Whether Our Power to Do Bad Is Something Good.* He also serves as a senior pastor in the Chesapeake Conference, Maryland.

Dragoslava Santrac, PhD, is managing editor of the *Encyclopedia of Seventh-day Adventists* (encyclopedia.adventist.org), based at the General Conference Office of Archives, Statistics, and Research (Silver Spring, MD). She has a PhD in Old Testament Studies from NorthWest University (South Africa)/Greenwich School of Theology (Clarborough, UK). She has written articles in theological journals and magazines and has written several books, including the volume on Psalms 76–150 for the Seventh-day Adventist International Bible Commentary (forthcoming).

Demóstenes da Silva, PhD, holds a PhD in psychology from the Federal University of Bahia (Brazil), an MA in theology from Centro Universitário Adventista de São Paulo, Campus São Paulo (Brazil) and an MA in family studies from the Catholic University of Salvador (Brazil). He served as a professor at Northeast Adventist College (Brazil), where he was the coordinator of the School of Theology. He is the author and co-author of several books and articles on theology and psychology. Now retired, he remains active as a speaker at church meetings.

Elias Brasil de Souza, PhD, works as director of the Biblical Research Institute of the General Conference of Seventh-day Adventists. Previously he worked as church pastor, professor of biblical studies, and dean of the Theological Seminary at Northeast Brazil College (Brazil). He holds a BA and a MA in theology from the Latin American Adventist Theological Seminary and a PhD in Old Testament Studies from Andrews University (Berrien Springs, MI). He has authored and co-authored several academic publications in English and Portuguese, among them *The Heavenly Sanctuary/Temple Motif in the Hebrew Bible* and *The Book of Daniel.*

Alberto R. Timm, PhD, is a specialist in the development of Seventh-day Adventist doctrines and theology. He holds a PhD in Adventist Studies from Andrews University (Berrien Springs, MI) and worked as rector of the multi-campus Latin-American Adventist Theological Seminary (SALT) and Spirit of Prophecy coordinator for the South American Division. He joined the Ellen G. White Estate in 2012 as an associate director, and has published extensively in English, Portuguese, and Spanish.

Foreword

The publication of this second volume of the Biblical Research Institute Studies in Biblical Ethics series is possible thanks to the contributions and involvement of several people and entities. To start, we appreciate all the biblical scholars, theologians, psychologists, and family therapists from North America, South America, Asia, Africa, Australia, and Europe who have authored these chapters. We thank them for their participation in and commitment to this project. We also recognize the contribution of the Biblical Research Institute Ethics Committee, and express our gratitude to its members for their participation in vetting these chapters. We also acknowledge the associate editors, Daniel Bediako, Kwabena Donkor, and Gerhard Pfandl, and consulting editor, Frank M. Hasel, who have done diligent work on this volume. We express our appreciation to the administration of the General Conference of Seventh-day Adventists for providing the financial resources to fund this project.

Last but not least, we recognize the efficient contribution of our technical personnel. Marly Timm, the research assistant of the Biblical Research Institute and assistant editor of this volume, supervised the entire production process of the manuscript. Yuriem Rodriguez, the BRI office manager, took responsibility for the contracts and other legal aspects of this publication. Nicol Belvedere contributed her expertise as a graphic designer in the layout and made sure the final version was ready for the press. Schuyler Kline took charge of copyediting and cleaning the manuscript of typos and grammatical inaccuracies, pointing out issues that needed attention and correction. Regina Hayden used her creative skills to design the cover. To all of them, we extend our gratitude for their work and dedication to this project.

—The Editors

Introduction

The present volume—the second of a series of three books on sexuality, marriage, and family—addresses several topics of contemporary relevance to individual Christians and to the church across the globe. Some chapters of the present volume focus on theological and ethical principles; others tackle issues more specific to certain religious contexts and cultures; still others deal with extremely controversial and sensitive subjects. But it should be emphasized that however challenging particular chapters may have been, all of them were written with the conviction that the Bible provides the principles and teachings to evaluate and judge contemporary approaces to sexuality. This does not mean that the present volume is only interested in biblical teachings and facts produced by theology and supported by sciences and humanities. Rather, it also tries to understand the burdens individuals carry, seeking to accept all people while still maintaining a biblical understanding of sexuality and marriage.

Although the content of the chapters reflects the authors' perspectives, the positions taken in the book aimed to be faithful to biblical teachings and principles.

For the benefit of our readers, the paragraphs that follow provide a chapter-by-chapter overview of the book.

Laurentiu G. Ionescu ("Humans as Sexual Beings") opens the discussion by showing that the study of the theology of sexuality becomes more attractive if viewed from the perspective of cognitive linguistics. He demonstrates that the biblical paradigm is clearly defined at the linguistic level. The binomial terminology of "male" and "female" defines human sexuality at the ontological level. There is no space for existential choice. The noninterchangeability of the terms does not allow a free choice of gender identity.

Ekkehardt Mueller ("*Porneia:* Sexual Immorality") tackles the concept of sexual immorality by investigating the meaning of *porneia* and its cognates in the Septuagint (LXX) and the New Testament. His research shows that *porneia* describes only sexual sins and does not include issues such as spouse battering and abandonment. He also notes that although Jesus did not address these issues directly, they obviously must be rejected. However, the good news of the gospel is that God is willing to bless us with healing and forgiveness, which we in turn are asked to extend to others.

In a joint chapter, Richard M. Davidson and Ekkehardt Mueller ("Does Sexual Intercourse Constitute Marriage? The Issue of Premarital Sex") deal with the sometimes posed argument that sexual intercourse per se between two unmarried people constitutes marriage. After a careful examination of the pertinent biblical passages, they conclude that the Bible conceives of marriage as a covenant and does not leave room for any kind of legitimate premarital sexual intimacy. Indeed, having sex outside of marriage—whether as premarital or extramarital sex—is sinful. Although such a view goes against contemporary cultural trends, we must treasure God's love and wisdom on sexual matters.

Johannes Kovar ("Uncommitted Relationships: Cohabitation from a Historical and Biblical Perspective") discusses the major ethical challenge posed by couples living together outside of marriage. This study considers the question of how cohabitation has been viewed throughout antiquity and church history. It also examines biblical statements related to this topic and shows that the Bible is clearly opposed to sexual relations outside of marriage. The chapter concludes by noting some of the practical challenges related to the issue and offers practical guidance for pastors involved in ministering to people who have opted for cohabitation instead of marriage.

Gerhard Pfandl, Demóstenes da Silva, and Luiz Carlos Gondim ("Singleness and Sexuality in the Contemporary World") present a biblical and contextual approach to the topic of singleness. As they explore the individual and contextual elements related to single people and how they deal with their sexuality, they show that the Bible paints a beautiful and encouraging portrait of the single life and how to relate to sexuality. They conclude that singleness can be experienced as a blessing and a gift from God as much as marriage can.

Boubakar Sanou ("Having a Wife and a Mistress: A Global Challenge for Families") takes up one of the most serious challenges to the family—marital infidelity. More specifically, the chapter focuses on the prevalence of heterosexual marital infidelity, mainly on its occurrence among married men, both in history and contemporary society.

Sanou shows the consequences of marital infidelity for individuals and marriages and suggests ways of responding to such challenges from a Seventh-day Adventist perspective. According to the author, the Christian community can use a two-pronged approach of prevention and reparation.

Ron du Preez ("Polygamy, Scripture, and the Institution of Marriage") offers a study on polygamy—a marriage form known and practiced in many societies of the world, and which has proven to be a formidable barrier to the Christian gospel. The author investigates the biblical passages and pericopes related to plural marriage and concludes that the Bible maintains that monogamy is the only permissible and legitimate form of marriage. But rather than focusing exclusively on theoretical aspects of the issue, the author offers applicable scriptural principles and suggests some practical suggestions to deal with the challenge of polygamy.

Deanna A. Pitchford ("Reclaiming the Gift of Sexuality: A Biblical Perspective on Sexual Addiction") addresses the problem of sexual addiction. Pitchford defines sexual addiction as behavior of a sexual nature that is excessive, compulsive, often impulsive, and that dominates the thinking of an individual to such an extent that most other considerations are set aside. She focuses on internet sexual addiction and recognizes that there is no easy road out of it. However, there is a path to recovery, and she provides some practical suggestions to that effect.

Vanderlei Dorneles and T. P. Kurian ("Prostitution and Human Trafficking: Current Issues and Biblical Concerns and Principles") seek to evaluate the impact of human trafficking in the modern and postmodern worlds from a biblical and theological perspective. They show the biblical concerns and requirements for Christians as the people of God and make clear that every single person trafficked or prostituted was created in the image of God. Thus, prostitution and human trafficking are a vile business. Human trafficking is absolutely unbiblical, and Christians are to work to promote freedom in Christ.

Dragoslava Santrac and Aleksandar Santrac ("On Rape: Biblical and Theological Perspectives") tackle the sexual horror and crime of rape. In the first part of the study, they acknowledge the gravity and complexity of the problem of rape by identifying the different forms of rape and recent statistics of the prevalence of rape in various parts of the world. In the second part, they explore how rape and its related issues are addressed in Scripture. Finally, they offer a discussion of some main contributors to the prevalence of rape today and some suggestions of how to alleviate trauma that results from rape.

Martha D. Duah ("Female Genital Mutilation") explores an issue that has caught the attention of the international community and has been labelled a human crisis—the practice of female genital mutilation. In this chapter, Duah analyzes female genital mutilation and argues that it contradicts the biblical view on sexuality and deforms the sexuality of those subjected to it, depriving them of their innate freedom and robbing them of their true femaleness. She concludes by suggesting some practical steps to curb such an unbiblical and inhumane practice.

Richard M. Davidson ("Reproduction/Population Control and Abortion-Related Issues: Old Testament Foundations") surveys several methods of reproduction/population control utilized in the ancient Near East, followed by a discussion on the status of the fetus in the Old Testament. Davidson shows that biblically the fetus is human and therefore must be accorded the same protection to life granted every other human being. Human life is no more valuable outside of the womb than it is inside. God upholds the sanctity of life, and therefore prohibits the termination of life. The fetus is not the property of the human parents; it belongs to God.

Ekkehardt Mueller ("Abortion: Terminating a Pregnancy") tackles the controversial subject of abortion. The author contends that the abortion of human life contradicts biblical principles for the following reasons, among others: abortion militates against the divinely given value and sacredness of human life, it contradicts the biblical understanding of the unborn child as being fully human in each stage of development, and it goes against the will of God as expressed in the sixth commandment and elaborated by Jesus in the Sermon on the Mount. The author recognizes that abortion affects the community of believers. After all, the church stands for life, not for death. Therefore, the church must support women and couples who are confronted with the possibility of abortion and create an atmosphere of true love to provide care for struggling individuals, couples, and families.

Antonio Estrada, Nisim Estrada, and Stephen Bauer ("Child Sexual Abuse") explore the issue of child sexual abuse and show that it is utterly incompatible with God's moral character, which is grounded in self-sacrificial service to others, not in enforcing one's power and status. The Christian church and its leaders at every level must be committed to safeguarding every one of our children—not only from sexual abuse, but also from other forms of abuse and violence. Therefore, the Seventh-day Adventist Church should voice its prophetic opposition to such a heinous crime.

Stephen Bauer ("Queer Theology and Sexuality") offers a biblical analysis and evaluation of queer theology. As noted in the chapter, queer theology aims at "deconstructing" social norms and traditional Christian definitions of marriage and sexuality. Bauer addresses the complex and somewhat convoluted definition of "queer" and the problem of defining the meaning of "queer" in the current philosophical and moral setting. He also discusses how queer theology understands biblical inspiration and authority, and how it redefines the meaning of love, sin, and grace. Then, he moves on to how queer theology redefines God into erotic and sexualized images and metaphors. He discusses how some queer theologians sexualize the Trinity and cast Christ in the form of varying versions of non-normative sexualities. He also draws attention to how some even make use of the Sabbath to justify non-normative sexualities.

Ekkehardt Mueller ("Homosexuality and Scripture") deals with some important biblical passages relevant to the topic and draws implications for the church. He defines the concept of homosexuality and notes the diversity of interpretations of the biblical data. Mueller argues that some persons may assert that their sexual lifestyle is their own choice, and that the church should stay out of the debate on sexual ethics. However, this is not the biblical position. While individuals may choose what they want, the church is affected, and therefore the church must react and uphold biblical principles. The argument that sexual lifestyles should not matter to the church, Mueller points out, mistakenly assumes that morality is a private matter only.

Elias Brasil de Souza and Larry L. Lichtenwalter ("Transgenderism: Reflections from a Biblical Perspective") investigate from a biblical perspective some significant topics relevant to the issue of transgenderism. In doing so, they provide an overview of the theoretical foundations of contemporary transgender studies. Since it has been suggested that the duality of male and female is a social construct, not a universal given, this study surveys the notion of sexual complementarity in the Old and New Testaments. It also examines the basics of biblical anthropology, which is necessary in order to address the dichotomy between the self and the body that is claimed to affect transgender people.

Kwabena Donkor ("Towards an Adventist Approach to Transgenderism") discusses the transgender phenomenon from a theological perspective. Donkor shows that differing positions on sexuality are rooted in varying ideas of what it means to be human. He explores biblical principles that may contribute to clarifying the Adventist response to transgenderism on the contemporary landscape of sexuality. He views transgenderism against the backdrop of human sin and the controversy between Christ and Satan. Transgenderism, therefore, should be understood in light of the distortion of the image of God in humanity, and the disordering of the created world.

Vanderlei Dorneles ("Cybersex and Robotic Sex: Social, Psychological, and Biblical Issues"), after some introductory remarks on postmodernism and sexuality, addresses two kinds of postmodern sexual practices related to the internet and new technologies—cybersex and robotic sex—and provides an evaluation of such practices according to biblical principles. Dorneles shows that cybersex, robotic sex, and any other sexual experiences of a similar type must be seen as an artificial and selfish experience that cannot fulfill God's plan for human beings. Only when it occurs in a loving marriage between a male and female created in the divine image can sexuality be a pleasurable and fruitful experience that fulfills human nature.

Alberto R. Timm ("The Seduction of Forbidden Intimacy") examines the subject of sex outside of marriage from a biblical-moral perspective. He demonstrates that scriptural teachings and stories provide helpful suggestions on how to build affair resistant relationships. Indeed, the Bible provides abiding moral commands and helpful practical counsels on how to live a life of moral integrity. From a biblical perspective, sexual intercourse should be restricted to monogamous, heterosexual marriages. This implies that premarital, homosexual, and extramarital sexual affairs are transgressions of God's moral standards.

God has invented marriage and sexuality. These chapters discuss scriptural examples of negative usages of sexuality that demonstrate how important it is to God to preserve His gift and keep us from harming ourselves and others.

Last but no least, this volume includes an appendix containing statements, which give and overview of the theological-ethical thinking of the Seventh-day Adventist Church regarding several of the issues addressed in this volume.

Thus, we offer this volume to church members, pastors, students, and everyone else interested in a critical understanding of contemporary approaches to sexuality. We hope that this book will serve to instruct, encourage, and promote a sexual lifestyle in harmony with Scripture.

—The Editors

CHAPTER 1

Humans as Sexual Beings

Laurentiu G. Ionescu

Writing a new study about human sexuality in the Bible is a difficult task for various reasons. Since medieval times, the topic of sexuality in the Bible has been studied from different perspectives. As such, "there is nothing new under the sun" (Eccl 1:9). We cannot invent new information. Biblical information about sexuality is, in a sense, frozen into the transmitted form of the text of Scripture. The only way to discover new things is to look at the text from a different perspective.[1] An attractive solution might be to analyze sexuality from the philosophical perspective, although that perspective is speculative in nature. This study attempts a linguistic approach, from the perspective of cognitive linguistics.[2] In

[1] The theme of sexuality in the Bible has been analyzed from different perspectives. Here are some examples of approaches in ethics, sociology, linguistics, reader-response criticism, etc.: Gerald A. Larue, *Sex and the Bible* (Buffalo, NY: Prometheus, 1983); Michael Coogan, *God and Sex: What the Bible Really Says* (New York: Grand Central, 2010); Francis D. Ritter, *Sex, Lies and the Bible: The Controlling of Human Sexual Behavior Through the Corruption of the Bible* (Oceanside, CA: Candid Press, 2006); J. Harold Ellens, *Sex in the Bible: A New Consideration* (Westport, CT: Praeger, 2006); Joseph W. Smith, *Sex and Violence in the Bible: A Survey of Explicit Content in the Holy Book* (Phillipsburg, NJ: P&R, 2014); Kenneth M. Yelverton, *Sex and the Kingdom: A Biblical Portrait of Human Sexuality* (San Francisco, CA: Mac, 2012); Tom Gruber, *What the Bible Says About Sex: A New Look at Sexual Ethics from a Biblical Perspective* (Victoria, BC: Trafford, 2001); and Gail Corrington Streete, *The Strange Woman: Power and Sex in the Bible* (Louisville, KY: Westminster John Knox, 1997).

[2] "Cognitive linguistics" refers to the approach that analyzes the way in which a worldview is reflected at the language level. See, e.g., George Lakoff, *Women, Fire, and Dangerous Things: What Categories Reveal about the Mind* (Chicago, IL: University of Chicago Press, 2012). Gestalt theory affirms that our mind organizes the knowledge as images or visual structures. Gestalt is a German noun referring to image and form. See Raimo Antilla, "Dynamic Fields and Linguistic Structure: A Proposal for a Gestalt Linguistics," *Die Sprache* 23, no. 1 (1977): 1–10; and George Lakoff, "Linguistic Gestalts," in *Papers from the Thirteenth Regional Meeting of the Chicago Linguistic Society* 1977, ed. W. A. Beach et al., Chicago Linguistic Society 13 (Chicago, IL: Chicago Linguistic Society, 1977), 236–287.

recent years, cognitive linguistics has developed perspectives that can bring new tools to the understanding of the theology of sexuality in the Bible.

From the linguistic point of view, sexuality is not a special topic. The Bible takes sexuality as a matter of fact, as a source of human enjoyment and fulfillment and a staple of reality of what it means to be human—just like eating, sleeping, hunting, gathering, building, and worshipping. The topic of sexuality shares the same vocabulary, grammar, and language level as other aspects of life. The way in which the Bible organizes the world of ideas is reflected in structures and language patterns that can provide insights into the biblical worldview about sexuality. The study of the theology of sexuality becomes more attractive if viewed from the perspective of cognitive linguistics.

Sexuality: Vocabulary and Terminology

The vocabulary of sexuality in the Bible—its euphemistic nature, polysemy,[3] and subtleness—makes the object one of fascination and study for scholars of different disciplines. It lies between the ethereal dimensions of implicit connotations and the crassness of explicit denotations. It is challenging both from a diachronic[4] perspective as well as from a synchronic[5] point of view.

In biblical thinking, sexuality is defined by an interesting formula that is a binomial:[6] the Hebrew construction *zakhar uneqevah* ("male and female"). Its function is to define the sexual dimension, not the functional or relational dimension as "man and woman." The expression describes the gender distinction both for humans and animals. It is ontological in essence, because it defines sexuality as a physical dimension of human beings. The biblical writers affirm sexuality as part of our existence. As human beings we are sexual creatures, and as sexual creatures we are called to honor God with our bodies. God created human beings as male and female, both in His own image (Gen 1:27). God's glory is seen in the maleness of the man and the femaleness of the woman. Thus, gender is not a mere biological accident or social construction. Throughout the Bible, a complementary pattern of relation between man and woman, particularly within the institution of marriage, is presented as the divine intention. Within the context of the marital covenant, husband and wife are free to express physical love for each other, to experience pleasure,

---

[3] The term refers to a word or phrase with multiple, yet normally related, meanings.

[4] "Diachronic" relates to phenomena as they arise or change over a period of time.

[5] In contrast to "diachronic," the term "synchronic" describes a phenomenon at a certain time without considering its historical development.

[6] "Binomial" refers to an expression consisting of two connected terms.

and to join in the procreative act of sexual union. This is pleasing to God and is not to be a source of shame.

The other interesting Hebrew word pair is *ʾish/ʾishah*. It describes the function and type of relationship between man and woman. The proper translation is "man/woman" or "husband/wife," depending on the context. However, this pair cannot be restricted to a social relationship. The expression also includes the idea of sexuality. The union in marriage is expressed and realized through the sexual dimension. That sexuality is conveyed in the word pair *ʾish/ʾishah* is very clear in Genesis 7:2 where the author applies it to the animal kingdom. Instead of the normal formula *zakhar uneqevah* ("male and female"), the writer uses the pair *ʾish/ʾishah*. "You shall take with you seven each of every clean animal, a male and his female; two each of animals that are unclean, a male and his female" (Gen 7:2, NKJV, emphasis added). It is hardly possible to understand the expression as referring to a social relationship—male/female. The sexual connotation is embedded into the construction itself.

The existence of different binomial formulas "male/female," "man/woman," and "husband/wife" suggests that in Scripture sexuality is a union formed by two distinctive parts. The different relationships and links between these word pairs are better understood by analyzing how these terms connect to each other. The next section will depict this complex interrelationship by analyzing the function of the linguistic operators.

Sexuality and Linguistic Operators

In formal languages or generative grammar, truth functions are represented by unambiguous symbols. These symbols are called "logical connectives," "logical operators," or "propositional operators."[7] Commonly used logical connectives include AND (conjunction), NOT (negation), IS (equality), and OR (disjunction). Their function is to link elements, and to describe the nature or attributes of the combinations between elements. Logical operators are the building blocks of mental constructions in cognitive linguistics.

As we have seen, the word pair *zakhar uneqevah* ("male and female") must be understood as a binomial construction. It describes the gender-sexual dimension. The equivalent parallel word pair is *ʾish/ʾishah* ("man/woman") or *ʾadam/ʾishah* ("man/woman"). The operator AND joins the terms, forming a bipartite entity. If the intention of the author is to describe alternative possibilities, he uses the operator OR, as can be

---

[7] See Noam Chomsky, *Lectures on Government and Binding: The Pisa Lectures*, Studies in Generative Grammar, 7th ed. (Berlin: de Gruyter, 1993); and Liliane M. V. Haegeman, *Introduction to Government and Binding Theory*, Blackwell Textbooks in Linguistics 1, 2nd ed. (Oxford: B. Blackwell, 1994).

seen in the casuistic laws: "if a man or a woman..." (Num 6:2). In this case, the operator OR introduces the idea of interchangeable members. The difference between AND and OR operators is important in understanding the biblical worldview about sexuality.

The existence of the AND/OR operators and the selection of the AND operator to describe the family pattern in Genesis 1 and 2 seems to indicate that man and woman are not interchangeable concepts. The AND operator implies difference and complementarity. So from the cognitive perspective, the construct "man AND woman" is not equivalent with "man OR woman." This binomial aspect is reflected in the distributive construction in 1 Corinthians 7:2: "Each man is to have his own wife, and each woman is to have her own husband" (NKJV). The parallelism is evident in the Greek text. Again, the conjunction *kai* ("and") connects the two pairs without giving the possibility of other options or combinations.

From the cognitive perspective, the linguistic operators define some patterns linked to sexual terminology. "Man AND woman," "man NOT woman," and "man OR woman" are valid combinations, or truth formulas that define the specificity of biblical thinking. They describe the unity, distinction, and complementarity of human beings.

The contrast and complementarity between the man and the woman reveal that gender is part of the goodness of the design of God's creation. "Man IS woman" is an invalid or impossible formula. Thus, any transgender pattern stands outside of the biblical definition of sexuality. Modern efforts to redefine or redesign gender are directly contrary to the Bible's affirmation of maleness and femaleness as proper distinctions. This pattern of distinction is affirmed and enforced by liturgical orders and restrictions on dress, hair length, etc. Any effort to confuse or deny gender differences is expressly forbidden and opposed by Scripture, especially as can be seen in Old Testament legal codes.

The biblical worldview does not separate sexuality from human nature, it is linked in heterosexual marriage. This concept is the foundation of the theology of sexuality in the Bible. It is consistent throughout Scripture, independent of literary genres. In narratives, poetry, prophecy, parables, epistles, or apocalyptic literature, sexuality is linked to marriage and to the concept of unity and relationship.

The next section offers some examples of how sexuality and moral nature are interwoven into a complex construct that defines humans as sexual beings.

Literary Genres and Sexuality

Humans as sexual beings is a theme embedded into biblical discourse. The presence of the topic in all kinds of literary genres of the Bible shows us that it is an important part of the biblical worldview. From a diachronic perspective, it is interesting to see that the concept does not change. From the first story of Genesis to the last paragraph of the Apocalypse, the idea of unity and oneness of human beings is one important pattern. Both from literal and metaphorical points of view, "husband and wife" is the unique way to understand and define love. From the garden of Eden to the garden of paradise in the new Jerusalem, human sexuality faces different challenges. The next sections analyze some theological aspects of humans as well as sexuality in different literary genres of the Bible.

Sexuality in the Creation Account

The first part of the creation account describes Adam in his solitude. Adam walked alone as a species—neither vegetable nor mineral, neither God nor animal, and not an angel, either. He stood alone in all creation. He did not have the company of his own kind. He could not procreate and therefore was not assured of the continuation of his species. This was a truly silent solitude. "It was not good," the Bible tells us. It lacked an essential part.

And so, from Adam's flesh, to underline the oneness of the human essence, God created Eve. Not just "woman," but a person with a name, face, shape, and personality. One inescapable point of the creation account is that the human being is two-in-one. "Male and female" He "created them in the beginning" (Matt 19:4, NKJV).

The second point the Bible insists upon is that humans (*ʾadam*) are made "in the image of God" (Gen 1:26). While each of them reflects the image of God, it is the "man" and the "woman" who constitute *ʾadam* ("human"). This means that "male and female" together reflect God's image. Something in our maleness and femaleness together pulls back the veil on what God is like. The distinctness of our being male and female is revelatory of God's design and purpose of creation. Each gender by itself is not self-sufficient. Without the other, we are to some extent incomplete. As humans, we were designed for the communion of male with female.

The fall destroyed this "designed union." The primeval history of Genesis introduces the cruel reality of sexuality outside of the garden of Eden. The innocent stage of "nudity without shame" is replaced by a new and different type of relationship. The failed intent of "covering the nakedness" continues in a strange tradition of actions that implies submission, struggle for authority, rape and abuse, sexism, and all kinds of aberrant behaviors. Hidden behind the text, the inspired authors narrate the strange post-lapsarian experience of humans as sexual beings. Only the poetic or metaphorical language recovers the beauty and mystery of sexuality of the lost paradise.

Sexuality and Poetry

I remember my grandmother's comment about the Song of Solomon: "I don't know why God put this book into the Bible!" She did not doubt the inspiration of the book; her problem was about the purpose of the book. She is not alone. Many theologians and commentators have been puzzled by the content of Song of Songs. Induced by the demand for an ethical and religious element in its content, the oldest interpretation of the book is allegorical. The Midrash and the Targum interpret it as depicting the relations between God and Israel.

Today, the Song is taken, almost universally, to be the celebration of a marriage, there being no hint of allegory in the text. In fact, it is a collection of pieces in praise of the physical delights of wedded love. The freeness of expression (esp. in Song 7:2–10), quite offensive to some modern taste, is in accord with ancient custom (cf. Ezek 16:23; Prov 5:16–20). The Song reinforces the idea that sexuality is for marriage and marriage for sexuality. David Ribner summarizes the function of sexuality in Hebrew thinking: "In Judaism, sex has traditionally been viewed as one of God's gifts, to be appreciated as a form of devotion through joy. Jews are to approach lovemaking so as to deepen their knowledge of themselves, one another, and the sacred in the universe."[8]

Sexuality in the Legal Literature

The Bible addresses human sexuality from a wholistic perspective of God's intention and design. In contrast to pagan sex rituals, the Bible places sex within the context of human nature, happiness, and holiness. Taken out of this context, sexual anarchy reigns and sex tends to be an end in itself. The intent of legal texts is to define the boundaries of godly human sexual relationships. The legal literature achieves this objective by two formulas: 1) the prohibitive formulas, built around the deviant sexual behavior and formulated as negative imperatives; and 2) prescriptive formulas, formulated as blessings or positive prescriptive imperatives.

The biblical writers present marital sex as natural and holy. The Bible consistently links sexuality with procreation and the marital act. All other forms of sexual activity are presented as inappropriate and sinful. In addition to adultery and fornication, the Bible expressly forbids homosexuality, bestiality, incest, prostitution, rape, pederasty, and all other forms of sexual deviance and perversion (e.g., Exod 22:16–17, 19; Lev 18:6–18, 22–23; Prov 7:1–27; Rom 1:26–27; 1 Cor 5:1–13). Each of these practices is an "abomination." From a cognitive perspective, in the biblical text, the prohibitive formula defines the taboo dimension of sexuality. The biblical writers link holiness to happiness. True human happiness comes, among other things, in the fulfillment of sexual holiness.

---

[8] Todd Melby, "Sacred Sexuality," *Contemporary Sexuality* 45, no. 2 (February 2011): 4.

The attempt to enjoy sexual happiness without holiness is the root of sexual deviance.

An example of a positive, prescriptive imperative formula is found in Genesis 1:28: "And God blessed them; and God said to them, 'Be fruitful and multiply, and fill the earth'" (NASB). The idea of blessing/conception/multiplication and sexuality forms an interesting theological construct. It would be a big mistake to limit sexuality to its reproductive function. It is evident that the human desire to engage in sexual activities is not solely, nor even primarily, dictated by biological "reasons" linked to reproductive cycles in the service of species survival. Human beings' willingness and inclination to pursue sexual possibilities reveals that nothing so straightforward as reproductive cycles can provide sufficient rationale for their range, scope, and frequency. The desire to reproduce may be one instigator to sexual behavior, but it is rarely the primary one.

Pleasure is one of the goods biblically associated with sexual union. Sexual pleasure and procreation are linked in a healthy and natural approach that avoids the denial of either. Modern contraceptive technologies were unknown in the Bible, and the contemporary "contraceptive mentality" that champions sexual pleasure completely severed from procreation is foreign to the biblical worldview. For this reason, the legal literature protects and conserves both the holiness and happiness of human sexuality.

Sexuality in the Pauline Literature

Without a doubt, Paul's contribution cannot be ignored if we want to expand our understanding of the biblical concept of sexuality.

The issues regarding human sexuality must be placed within the broader concerns of the "body as a whole" and its relation to consciousness.[9] This is an important concept in the biblical worldview. This implies critiquing or negating all views that disengage the mind and body. The biblical mentality, reflected in various stories, makes plain that human consciousness is always a *corporeal* consciousness. Human beings inhabit and are living expressions of a "corporeal principle of being," which the Bible refers to as "the flesh" or "the body." The body is "the formative medium of the object and the subject."[10] Paul's declaration about the corporeal experience of sexual sin is very important to understanding the biblical worldview about sexuality: "Flee from sexual immorality. All other sins a person commits are *outside* the body, but whoever sins sexually, *sins against their own body*" (1 Cor 6:18, NIV, emphasis supplied).

---

[9] The concept of an indissoluble link between mind and body is excellently described in Maurice Merleau-Ponty, *The Primacy of Perception: And Other Essays on Phenomenological Psychology, the Philosophy of Art, History, and Politics* (Evanston, IL: Northwestern University Press, 1964).

[10] Ibid., 138.

To sustain this declaration, Paul quotes the passage of Genesis that defines the union by sexuality as the mysterious status of "one flesh" (Gen 2:24). "Or do you not know that the one who joins himself to a harlot is *one body* with her? For He says, 'The two will become one *flesh*'" (1 Cor 6:16, NAS, emphasis supplied). This aspect deserves more insight.

The wholistic perspective about human nature implies that we *have* a body and we *are* a body. This concept places us in an inescapable and irreducible relation.[11] It removes the duality of mind and body. Both are coexistent dimensions (or "polarities") of an inseparable and irreducible totality.

Considered from the primordial grounding of interrelatedness, being sexual provides a crucial configuration. We explore and engage sexuality with our entire being. Our sexual encounters provide us with a pivotal means that allows us to express simultaneously our own presence and the other's presence as revealed during the interaction. Therefore, "one who joins himself to a harlot is *one body* with her" (1 Cor 6:16).

Sexuality and Identity

Paul's perspective on sexuality as an expression of our corporeal dimension opens the possibility of a solution for one of the most controversial topics: the relation between sexuality and identity. The powerful link created between identity and sexuality provokes in some people an uneasy and unwilling reaction. This topic has incited great interest and debate among contemporaries.

The biblical concept of the wholistic human nature permits a radical transposition of an act or practice into a statement of inner experience and identity. Via this focus, the description and labeling of any sexual act becomes the primary means to identify, label, and pronounce upon the psyche of the person who engaged in that act. In doing so, a crucial process of internalization occurs: the act becomes the person. Statements regarding sexual behavior become inseparable from statements regarding personality and identity. The continuing interest in categorizing sexual acts has permitted the construction of sexual categories of identity. As Michel Foucault highlights, "homosexuality appeared as one of the forms of sexuality when it was transposed from the practice of sodomy onto a kind of interior androgyny, a *hermaphrodism* of the soul. The sodomite had been a temporary aberration; now, the homosexual is a species."[12]

---

[11] The awareness that *I am and have a body* is always simultaneous with the awareness of *other beings and having bodies*. Merleau-Ponty refers to this as "intersubjectivity."

[12] Michel Foucault, *The History of Sexuality: An Introduction* (New York: Knopf Doubleday, 1979), 43.

Today, this interweaving of sexuality and identity is not seen as the outcome of a natural or divinely determined set of circumstances. It does not reveal genuine "hardwired" differences between the various constructs (nor between the wider gender constructs of "male" and "female"). Rather, the basis for the maintenance of such constructs is nothing more or less than *existential choice.*

The existential argument raises implicit critiques surrounding matters of essence and its possible "fixedness" regarding the assumptions surrounding gender differences. The contemporary paradigm contradicts the biblical one. In brief, the general themes of discrepancy are the following: 1) defining human sexuality, 2) being sexual and existential choice, 3) being sexual as a "given" of existence, and 4) being sexual and the issue of gender.

Conclusion

The biblical paradigm is clearly defined at the linguistic level. The binomial terminology of "male/female" defines the human sexuality at the ontological level. There is no space for existential choice. The non-interchangeability of the terms excludes the possibility of variations.[13] "Male and female He created them" (Gen 1:27). Sexuality is linked with gender. This is not an option; it is an ontological construct designed by the Creator. The ideal of this design, meant to be an image of God, is perfectly described by the initial blessing: "Be fruitful, and multiply, and replenish the earth, and subdue it: and have dominion over the fish of the sea, and over the fowl of the air, and over every living thing that moves upon the earth" (Gen 1:28, KJV). The fall destroyed this ideal.

Outside of Eden the paradigm shifts. The biblical narrative describes this new reality very clearly. First appears polygamy. After that rape and incest. Sin multiplies in deviant forms. Sex may no longer be pure nor private. From the linguistic perspective, sexuality acquires new adjectives. "Abomination" is one of them. The rest of this book will analyze sexuality from the deviant perspective. Such an approach is necessary because we have lost our innocence. But it is necessary to return to the original design.

[13] The case of intersex people may be addressed here, but there is a debate concerning the intersex. The intersex condition involves genital ambiguity and combinations of chromosomal genotypes and sexual phenotypes other than XY-male and XX-female. It is difficult to decide if intersex is the result of a genetic anomaly or a normal genetic variation. Such a condition, labeled as "disorder of sex development" in the clinical setting, has been controversial since the label was introduced.

CHAPTER 2

Porneia: Sexual Immorality

Ekkehardt Mueller

Readers of the Bible occasionally encounter biblical terms that describe negative forms of sexual behavior. Saved by grace, God's chosen ones are—because of their salvation—called not to get involved in such conduct. But how should these terms be understood, especially the word *porneia* and its cognates? For instance, Paul writes to the Christians in Thessalonica, after praising and encouraging them, "May the Lord make you increase and abound in love for one another and for all, as we do for you, so that he may establish your hearts blameless in holiness before our God and Father, at the coming of our Lord Jesus with all his saints" (1 Thess 3:12–13).[1] He adds, "We ask and urge you in the Lord Jesus, that as you received from us how you ought to walk and to please God, just as you are doing, that you do so more and more. . . . For this is the will of God, your sanctification: that you abstain from sexual immorality" (1 Thess 4:1, 3). The term translated "sexual immorality" is *porneia.*

The issue of sexual immorality is repeatedly mentioned in both Old and New Testaments. The question arises as to what the term and its cognates really mean. We will focus on the Greek terms as found in the Septuagint (LXX) and the New Testament. The word family describing sexual immorality in Scripture is comprised of five Greek words—three nouns and two verbs. In alphabetical order the terms are *ekporneuō, porneia, porneuō, pornē,* and *pornos.* The lexicon definition of the noun *porneia* is "*prostitution, unchastity, fornication,* of every kind of unlawful sexual intercourse."[2] The verbs *ekporneuō* and *porneuō* can be translated "to prostitute," or "to practice prostitution or sexual immorality." A *pornē*

[1] All biblical quotations are taken from the ESV, unless otherwise indicated.

[2] William F. Arndt and F. Wilbur Gingrich, *A Greek-English Lexicon of the New Testament and Other Early Christian Literature* (Chicago, IL: University of Chicago Press, 1957), 699; cf. Walter Bauer, *Wörterbuch zum Neuen Testament,* ed. Kurt Aland and Barbara Aland, 6th ed. (Berlin: Walter de Gruyter, 1988), 1389.

is a female prostitute, a harlot. A *pornos* represents a male prostitute or a fornicator, one who practices sexual immorality. In this article "sexual immorality" is used to refer to this Greek word family, especially the term *porneia*.

Sexual Immorality in Extrabiblical Greek

In the non-Jewish Greek world a *pornē* usually was a woman would sell her body temporarily, typically to men, for sexual favors or a woman involved in illegitimate sexual intimacy for lust. The term is translated as "prostitute," "harlot," or "whore." However, a female slave who was acquired could also become a prostitute, oftentimes not by choice but by coercion. A *pornos* was a man who had intercourse with harlots or who allowed himself to be abused for money—in other words, a male prostitute. In certain contexts, the word is also translated "catamite" and "sodomite." *Porneia* is not found frequently in classical Greek. It can be rendered "fornication," "licentiousness," "prostitution," or "unchastity" and includes homosexual activity. The two verbs mentioned above and also found in extrabiblical Greek stand for committing sexually immoral acts and prostituting oneself. *Ekporneuō* seems to be stronger than *porneuō*. In addition, classical Greek has a number of composite words that refer to a brothel, a brothel keeper, being born of a harlot, etc.; synonyms for *porneia* and *pornē* that use the same root; and other related terms that belong to the same word family.[3] "In both Greece and Rome, prostitution was considered to be as necessary as the institutions of marriage, concubinage . . . , or slavery."[4]

Sexual Immorality in the Septuagint

Narratives and Legal Texts

The Greek word family *-porn-* is found approximately 147 times in the canonical books of the LXX. It is used predominantly in a symbolic way[5] and stands for turning away from the Lord and getting involved in idolatry. In Jeremiah 31:1–10 both the northern and southern kingdoms

---

[3] Cf. Friedrich Hauck and Siegfried Schulz, "πόρνη, πορνός, πορνεία, πορνεύω, ἐκπορνεύω," in *Theological Dictionary of the New Testament*, ed. Gerhard Friedrich, vol. 6 (Grand Rapids, MI: Eerdmans, 1968), 580–584; and Henry George Liddell and Robert Scott, *A Greek-English Lexicon*, revised and augmented by H. S. Jones (Oxford: Clarendon Press, 1968), 1450.

[4] John Roberts, ed., *The Oxford Dictionary of the Classical World* (Oxford: Oxford University Press, 2005), 624.

[5] See, e.g., Leviticus 17:7; 20:5; Numbers 15:39; Hosea 4:12–13.

are accused of playing the harlot with their lovers instead of being faithful to the Lord.

However, the terms are also used in a literal sense. They apply to secular as well as to so-called sacred prostitution. Tamar behaves like a prostitute, and Judah regards her as such. While pregnant she is accused of having played the harlot (Gen 38:13–24). As a widow she has sexual intercourse with a man—in this case, her father-in-law—and that is a case of sexual immorality.

Daughters are not to be made harlots by their fathers (for instance, to earn money) and are warned against sexual immorality (Lev 19:29; 21:9). At Shittim the Israelites have sexual relations with the women of Moab, which is described with the verb *ekporneuō*.

Another case is presented in Deuteronomy 22:13–21. A husband discovers that his wife was not a virgin when the couple married. Again the word family *-porn-* is used to describe what the woman had done. Obviously, this is a case of premarital sex described as "committing sexual immorality." The punishment was death by stoning.

Deuteronomy 23:17 warns Israel's daughters and sons not to function as prostitutes (*pornē* being used for daughters and the participle of the verb *porneuō* for sons). Instead of the normal Hebrew word for playing the harlot (*zānāh*), the Hebrew words *qedēšāh* and *qādēš* for a female and a male prostitute are employed. Some understand these words as pointing to cult or temple prostitutes and claim that temple prostitution was a common practice in the ancient Near East.[6] Others question this interpretation.[7] The word *zônāh*, describing a harlot, is found in the very next verse and may be used as a kind of synonym.

In Hosea 2:2–7, Hosea's experience with his wife becomes an illustration of God's experience with His people. In Hosea 2:2 harlotry and adultery are found in parallelism.[8] By committing harlotry a married woman also commits adultery. In Ezekiel, although used with a symbolic meaning, prostitution is adultery. Jerusalem played the harlot and committed adultery against God, her husband.[9] Israel and Judah, pictured as

---

[6] Cf. Francis D. Nichol, ed., *The Seventh-day Adventist Bible Commentary,* vol. 1 (Washington, DC: Review and Herald, 1953), 1034–1035; and P. C. Craigie, *The Book of Deuteronomy,* New International Commentary on the Old Testament (Grand Rapids, MI: Eerdmans, 1976), 301; see also translations such as the New American Standard Bible and the New Revised Standard Version.

[7] Cf. Karel van der Toorn, "Cultic Prostitution," in *The Anchor Bible Dictionary*, ed. D. N. Freedman, vol. 5 (New York: Doubleday, 1992), 510–513; and Elaine Adler Goodfriend, "Prostitution," in ibid., 507–509.

[8] See also Hosea 3:1 and 3:3; Hosea 6:10 and 7:4; and Hosea 4:13–14.

[9] See the entire chapter of Ezekiel 16. The word family *-porn-* occurs about seventeen times. Yet, in Ezekiel 16:32 the woman who plays the harlot (Ezek 16:30–34) is called an adulteress.

God's two wives, named Oholah and Oholibah, have multiplied their harlotry and by doing so have committed adultery.[10] In Isaiah 57:3 the terms "adulterer" and "prostitute" stand next to each other. In this case they may be used interchangeably, although one is masculine and the other feminine, just to avoid duplication of one term.

Summary

The following picture emerges in the Old Testament:

1. The word family *-porn-* depicts prostitution, playing the harlot.
2. It is predominantly used in a figurative sense, but it also has a literal meaning. Both the symbolic and the literal meanings correspond with each other and are even used in juxtaposition.
3. The word family *-porn-* is used for premarital sex.
4. Prostitution/sexual immorality can be adultery.
5. When Tamar is accused of sexual immorality (*porneia*), it is in reality a form of incest, which is prohibited by the later law in Leviticus 18.

Sexual Immorality in the New Testament

In the New Testament the word family *-porn-* occurs fifty-six times. The predominant word is the noun *porneia*, "sexual immorality," which occurs twenty-five times.[11] The word family is most often found in the

---

[10] In Ezekiel 23 (LXX) the word family *-porn-* is used about fifteen times. In Ezekiel 23:37, 43, 45 Oholibah's prostitution is adultery. In Ezekiel 23:43, both expressions are used. Three terms describe adultery: the noun *moicheia* and the verbs *moicheuō* and *moichaomai.* Adultery is mentioned in the Decalogue and repeatedly referenced in Scripture (Exod 20:1 [LXX]; Deut 5:17 [LXX]; Jer 7:9; Hos 4:2; Matt 5:27; 15:19; 19:9; Mark 7:21; 10:19; Luke 18:20; Rom 2:22; 13:9; Jas 2:11). In these cases adultery is understood literally: it is an extramarital affair in an existing marriage. But the term is also understood symbolically in the Old Testament as apostasy from God (e.g., Jer 3:8–9; 5:7; 13:27; Ezek 16:32; 23:37), and likewise perhaps once in the New Testament in addition to its metaphorical meaning (Rev 2:22; see Leon Morris, *Revelation: An Introduction and Commentary*, Tyndale New Testament Commentaries [Downers Grove, IL: InterVarsity Press, 1987], 75–76). In a literal sense it appears in narratives (e.g., Jer 29:23 [36:23 LXX]; John 8:3–4) and frequently in the context of divorce (Matt 5:32; 19:9; Mark 10:4, 12; Luke 16:18). Jesus heightens the commandment not to commit adultery by warning not to look at a woman lustfully, which by itself would mean to break the seventh commandment (Matt 5:28). On adultery see also F. Hauck, "*moicheúō* ['to commit adultery'], *moicháō* ['to commit adultery'], *moicheía* ['adultery'], *moíchos* ['adulterer'], *moichalís* ['adulteress,' 'adulterous']," in *Theological Dictionary of the New Testament*, ed. Gerhard Kittel, Gerhard Friedrich, and Geoffrey William Bromiley, abridged version (Grand Rapids, MI: Eerdmans, 1985), 605–606; and Ekkehardt Mueller, "Divorce and Remarriage in the New Testament," in *Marriage: Biblical and Theological Aspects*, ed. Ekkehardt Mueller and Elias Brasil de Souza, Biblical Research Institute Studies in Biblical Ethics 1 (Silver Spring, MD: Biblical Research Institute, 2015), 212–213, 216, 226–227.

[11] The noun *pornē* ("female prostitute") occurs twelve times, the noun *pornos* ("male prostitute") ten times, the verb *porneuō* ("to play the harlot") eight times, and the noun *ekporneuō* ("to play the harlot") once.

Pauline writings (Hebrews included), with twenty-four occurrences, followed by the Johannine writings, with twenty references.[12] This makes the book of Revelation the single work employing this word family most frequently—nineteen times—followed immediately by 1 Corinthians, which has fourteen references.[13]

Quite often, the word family has a symbolic meaning, but in the New Testament this is not the predominant understanding. Furthermore, the symbolic meaning is restricted to the book of Revelation. Yet, Revelation also uses the respective terms literally.

Symbolic Meaning

In Revelation 2:18–29, the church in Thyatira is addressed. In this church the woman Jezebel teaches and practices sexual immorality (*porneuō* and *porneia;* Rev 2:20–21). Jezebel, the wife of King Ahab, is a symbolic figure because the actual person with the same name had passed away several hundred years earlier. However, the larger passage seems to contain a definition of the term "sexual immorality." Jezebel's followers have played the harlot and committed adultery with her (Rev 2:20–22). Yet the others, who did not do that, are not described as those who have not played the harlot, but rather as those "who do not hold this teaching, who have not known the deep things of Satan" (Rev 2:24). Thus, sexual immorality is not to be understood in a literal sense in this instance, but has to do with the deliberate acceptance of false teachings and a turning away from the Lord, which, at the end, is a move toward Satan. Spiritual immorality is unfaithfulness to God who in symbolic contexts is oftentimes considered to be the husband of His people.[14] Additionally, it is very interesting to note that at least some of those whom Jezebel encourages to commit sexual immorality in Revelation 2:20,[15] who are also called the servants of God, have committed adultery (*moicheuō*) with her (Rev 2:22). Thus sexual immorality (*porneia*) clearly includes adultery (*moicheia*), even when used in a figurative context.

The address to the preceding church contains a reference to Balaam. He teaches Balak to entice the Israelites to practice sexual immorality (Rev 2:14). The respective Old Testament report must be understood

---

[12] Apart from Revelation, it is used only once in the Gospel of John. Furthermore, Acts uses it three times, James once, and Jude also once. The Synoptic Gospels have seven references, five being found in Matthew.

[13] In Revelation the highest concentration is found in chapter 17. In 1 Corinthians it occurs in chapters 5 and 6.

[14] This concept is already found in the Old Testament—e.g., Ezekiel 16.

[15] Grant R. Osborne, *Revelation*, Baker Exegetical Commentary on the New Testament (Grand Rapids, MI: Baker, 2002), 157, believes that in Revelation 2:20 "most likely" actual "immoral practices" are implied. Craig R. Koester, *Revelation*, Anchor Bible 38A (New Haven, CT: Yale University Press, 2014), 299, suggests it is "a metaphor for religious infidelity."

literally. However, those who hold the teaching of Balaam in the church of Pergamum seem to embrace spiritual immorality. Yet, the church itself did not renounce faith in Jesus (Rev 2:13). The same phrase to "eat food sacrificed to idols and practice sexual immorality" (Rev 2:14) is found in reverse order in Revelation 2:20 and seems to point to spiritual corruption.[16]

Babylon is the great harlot (Rev 17:1, 15–16; 19:2) and the mother of harlots (Rev 17:5). The kings of the earth have committed sexual immorality with her (Rev 17:2; 18:3, 9). She offers the wine (of the wrath) of her sexual immorality (Rev 14:8; 17:2; 18:3). Her cup is full of abominations and the unclean things of her immoral sexual practices (Rev 17:4). She corrupts the entire earth with her sexual immorality (Rev 19:2). Clearly, this is symbolic sexual immorality.

Literal Meaning

References to Historical Events

The New Testament contains several references to Old Testament events in which immoral sexual activity occurred. In Hebrews 12:16, Esau is called a *pornos*. Rahab the prostitute (*pornē*) is found in Hebrews 11:31. James 2:25 also refers to Rahab as a prostitute who, however, was justified. The Balaam episode has already been mentioned (Rev 2:14). In 1 Corinthians 10:8, the same incident is related. Israelite men had committed sexual immorality with Moabite women and had gotten involved in idolatry. As a result thousands were killed (Num 25:1, 9). Numbers 31:16 mentions Balaam's advice to defeat Israel by means of sexual immorality and idolatry. Sexual immorality in these cases describes sexual acts unrelated to marriage. They may be extramarital as well as premarital affairs.

Jude 1:7 talks about Sodom and Gomorrah and the Cities of the Plain. They engaged in sexual immorality and have "gone after other flesh." The latter term seems to stand for homosexual activity. The Old Testament text of Genesis 19:4–8 forms the background for Jude 1:7,[17] and it clearly implies homosexual acts. The inhabitants of Sodom wanted "to know" the men who visited Lot—that is, they wanted to have sexual intercourse with them[18]—although they were not aware that these men

---

[16] See Koester, 288; cf. Osborne, 145.

[17] *The Greek-English New Testament: Novum Testamentum Graece* [28th edition], *English Standard Version* (Wheaton, IL: Crossway, 2012), 1462, also mentions Genesis 19. This view is supported by various commentaries. Cf. Richard J. Bauckham, *Jude, 2 Peter,* Word Biblical Commentary 50 (Waco, TX: Word, 1983), 54.

[18] The same verb "to know" is found in Genesis 19:8 and clearly refers to sexual intercourse. Lot's daughters "have not known any man." Cf. Victor R. Hamilton, *The Book of Genesis Chapters 18–50*, New International Commentary on the Old Testament (Grand Rapids, MI: Eerdmans, 1995), 33–34.

were angels.[19] Because of their unrestrained homosexual lust, unknowingly they "went after other flesh."[20] Thus, in Jude the phrase "gone after other flesh" points to same-sex sexual relations, which apparently is also included in the term "sexual immorality." The same Old Testament background describes what Jude calls committing sexual immorality and going after other flesh. There is little doubt that the latter phrase more clearly describes the former.[21] If the word *kai*, normally translated "and," is used epexegetically—that is, with the meaning "namely"—then sexual immorality is equated with homosexual acts. If it is not used epexegetically, sexual immorality in Jude 1:7 would be a broader term, which in this context, however, seems still to include homosexual activity.[22]

The New Testament reports incidents of sexual immorality. In Matthew 21:31–32, Jesus talks favorably about tax collectors and prostitutes not because of what they had done in the past, but because they believed John and repented. Uniting with a prostitute (*pornē*) is discussed in 1 Corinthians 6:15–16. Possibly, church members in Corinth argued that this is permissible (1 Cor 6:12) and may have practiced it. The prodigal son is accused by his brother of having devoured his father's property with prostitutes (Luke 15:30). Thus, sexual immorality points to prostitution as it has been known from the early days of humankind until today.

A specific case of sexual immorality is related in 1 Corinthians 5, and sexually immoral persons are mentioned in verses 9–11. This passage uses the masculine noun *pornos* in contrast to the feminine form *pornē* in 1 Corinthians 6:15–16, which refers to female prostitutes (plural *pornai*).

---

[19] Even Lot did not know right away that these men were angels. They are introduced as messengers or angels in Genesis 19:1, but this information was not available to Lot and the Sodomites. Later in the chapter they are consistently called "men" (e.g. Gen 19:5, 8, 10). As such they were perceived by the inhabitants of Sodom. Only from verse 11 onward may it have dawned on Lot that these men were supernatural beings.

[20] The expression "gone after other flesh" may point to angels. In the canonical context this is not very likely (Matt 22:30). Another option would be to understand the phrase as referring to the sin of sodomy—which in this context is intercourse with persons of the same sex.

[21] Cf. Bauckham, 54; and Walter Grundmann, *Der Brief des Judas und der zwete Brief des Petrus*, Theologischer Handkommentar zum Neuen Testament (Berlin: Evangelische Verlagsanstalt, 1979), 34.

[22] Jude is the only New Testament book that uses the term *ekporneuō* ("to commit acts of sexual immorality"). Although this term is found forty-two times in the Old Testament and describes playing the harlot, the New Testament employs it only once. On the other hand, the verb *porneuō* without suffix occurs seventeen times in the Old Testament and eight times in the New Testament. Thus the predominant verb in the Old Testament to describe sexually immoral activity is *ekporneuō*, whereas the predominant verb in the NewTestament is *porneuō*. It may be significant that the term *ekporneuō* is found only in Jude, and it may have a slightly different or more comprehensive meaning. Michael Green, *2 Peter and Jude*, Tyndale New Testament Commentaries, rev. ed. (Grand Rapids, MI: Eerdmans, 1987), 180 n. 3, states, "The rare compound *ekporneuō*, 'fornicate', may suggest by the *ek* 'against the course of nature'."

However, the case that is described beginning with 1 Corinthians 5:1 implies more than prostitution. In this instance, a man commits sexual immorality by having his father's wife. The woman involved is not called his mother; she may be his stepmother. The case is very severe. It is an offense even among the Gentiles. Yet, the church seems not to be disturbed by such immorality. The act of having sexual intimacy with one's stepmother is called *porneia*. Some verses later Paul warns against sexually immoral persons in the Christian church and counsels fellow believers not to associate with them. The case of 1 Corinthians 5:1 is clearly spelled out in Leviticus 18:8. Leviticus 18 discusses unlawful sexual relations. First of all, it is evident that Paul considered Leviticus 18 as still valid for Christians. Secondly, the term *porneia* clearly stands for incestuous relations and may include all unlawful sexual activities spelled out in Leviticus 18—that is, different forms of incest, sexual relations with a woman during her period, sexual relations with the wife of another man, sexual relations of homosexuals, and sexual relations with animals.[23]

The issue of sexual immorality was discussed and decided upon at the Jerusalem Council (Acts 15:20, 29; 21:25). Gentile Christians were ordered to abstain from sexual immorality. Obviously, the Jerusalem Council did not discuss the validity of the Decalogue. The term that the members of this council dealt with was *porneia*, whereas the Ten Commandments use the verb *moicheuō*. It seems quite certain that the delegates to this Council, and especially James, had in mind Leviticus 18 and 20.[24] Paul, then, in the case of the Corinthian man, followed the decisions of the Council of Jerusalem. *Porneia* referred to a broad range of sexual deviations including prostitution as found in 1 Corinthians 6.

According to John 8:11–59 a dialogue between Jesus and the Jews focuses on the question of whether or not Abraham was more than their physical father. In John 8:41 the Jews tell Jesus, "We were not born of sexual immorality" and may be implying "but you were." If this is the case, then these people seem to stigmatize Jesus by implying that He was an illegitimate child. Consequently, the term *porneia* would include premarital sex.

Lists of Vices

---

[23] Oftentimes, the New Testament when it alludes to or quotes an Old Testament text does not only refer to the specific text but also to the entire context. When, e.g., in Revelation 12:5 the male child is mentioned, who is to rule all the nations with a rod of iron, the reference is not just to Psalm 2:9 but the entire second Psalm. This principle, so often found in the New Testament, may also apply to 1 Corinthians 5:1 and its Old Testament source, Leviticus 18.

[24] This is, e.g., supported by the margin of Nestle-Aland's Greek New Testament as well as their list of Old Testament quotations and allusions. When discussing the Jerusalem Council in Acts 15, Bruce refers back to Leviticus 18; see F. F. Bruce, *Commentary on the Book of Acts*, New International Commentary on the New Testament (Grand Rapids, MI: Eerdmans, 1966), 315.

The New Testament offers a number of lists of vices. Among the elements of these lists, sexual immorality is often found. However, sexual immorality is frequently not the only element that refers to sexual deviations.

In the long list of vices in Matthew 15:19 and Mark 7:21–22, Jesus mentions adultery (*moicheia*) and sexual immorality (*porneia*).[25] Quite often the apostle Paul uses similar enumerations. First Corinthians 6:9–10 refers to "fornicators" (sexually immoral persons; plural of *pornos*), "idolaters," "adulterers," "effeminate," "homosexuals,"[26] and others. Twice "sexual immorality" is found next to "impurity" (*akatharsia*) (Eph 5:3, 5;[27] Col 3:5[28]) and twice next to impurity" and "sensuality" (*aselgeia*) (2 Cor 12:21; Gal 5:19).[29] In the list of 1 Timothy 1:9–10, sexual immoral persons and *arsenokoitai* are mentioned again. The latter term is translated "sodomites" by the NRSV and "homosexuals" by the NASB.[30] Thus in these lists of vices sexual immorality may contain nuances other than adultery, impurity,[31] and homosexual activity, although it (*porneia*) is the overarching term. The two lists in 1 Corinthians 5:9–11 use only one sexual term, namely *porneia*. Certainly, the context of incest is very important, but *porneia* is probably used here in a wider sense which includes all sexual vices, especially since Paul had already given his

---

[25] The two terms appear in the plural.

[26] These are the terms used by the NASB. The Greek text talks about *pornoi, eidōlolatrai, moichoi, malakoi, and arse*nokoitai.

[27] While in Ephesians 5:3, sexual immorality and impurity are found, Ephesians 5:5 talks about the sexual immoral and the impure person.

[28] Other words in the respective verses may also have sexual implications.

[29] 2 Corinthians 12:21 focuses on sexual sins only. Galatians 5, on the other hand, contains a longer list that is continued in Galatians 5:20.

[30] On homosexuality, see Ekkehardt Mueller, *Homosexuality, Scripture, and the Church*, Biblical Research Institute Release 6 (Silver Spring, MD: Biblical Research Institute, 2010), 26–30. See also the chapter on homosexuality in the present volume. It differs to some extent from the aforementioned document.

[31] *Akatharsia* is translated as "impurity" or "uncleanness." It is used in the Old Testament to address the issue of purity and cult. For instance, humans become unclean if they experience a bodily discharge (Lev 15:3, 24–26, 30–31) or touch something unclean (Lev 5:3; 7:21). However, the term is also used in connection with moral issues and sexual sins (Hos 2:12)—for instance, a man taking his brother's wife (Lev 20:21). In the New Testament the word appears more often in this latter context, as previously mentioned verses indicate. Cf. F. Hauck, "*katharós* [clean, pure], *katharízō* [to cleanse, purify], *kathaírō* [to make clean], *katharótēs* [purity], *akáthartos* [unclean, impure], *akatharsía* [impurity], *katharismós* [cleansing, purification], *ekkathaírō* [to cleanse], *perikátharma* [offscouring, refuse]," in Kittel, Friedrich, and Bromiley, *Theological Dictionary of the New Testament*, 383: "*akáthartos, akatharsía*. These two terms are used for physical, cultic, and moral impurity, which are closely intertwined. The use in the LXX is mostly cultic."

admonition in a previous letter to the Corinthians (1 Cor 5:9) before the case of 1 Corinthians 5:1 was made known to him.

The book of Revelation contains three lists of vices in Revelation 9:21, 21:8, and 22:15 in which the word family *-porn-* occurs. The terms in these lists, especially those in Revelation 21 and 22, should probably be understood literally.[32] Only one sexual deviation is named among all the other sins: sexual immorality.[33] It seems that in these cases *porneia* is a broad term including all other sexual evils, because other terms pointing to sexual misconduct are absent.

Exhortations

In 1 Corinthians Paul devotes almost three entire chapters to sexual issues. The sexually immoral person of 1 Corinthians 5:1 has already been discussed, as have the lists of vices in 1 Corinthians 5:9–11. In this passage Paul calls believers to dissociate and withdraw completely from sexually immoral persons, who are church members, and not to eat with them. In this case, sexual immorality may include incest, but certainly covers more than that. Although sexual immorality can never be an option for followers of Christ, they cannot avoid all contact with people in the world who practice such a lifestyle—and obviously *should* not even do so because these people must be won to Christ.

In 1 Corinthians 6b, Paul continues his discussion of sexual topics.[34] Verses 13–18 contain five instances of the word family *-porn-*. Because the body of believers is a temple of the Holy Spirit, all sexual immorality must flee. Sexual immorality directly affects the body. Because the body is a member of Christ, it should never become one with a harlot. Joining a prostitute is not an option for one who has joined the Lord. While Paul in 1 Corinthians 5 summons Christians to dissociate from church members who practice sexual immorality, in 1 Corinthians 6 he commands them not to commit acts of sexual immorality themselves. Thus *porneia* is prostitution as well as extramarital or premarital sexual activity. In 1 Corinthians 7:2 Paul's call to men to have their own wives—that is, to be married to one woman in order to avoid sexual immorality—may define sexual immorality also as premarital sex. However, the very next verse pointing toward the mutual marital obligation of the respective couples seems to form another safeguard against sexual immorality. Thus to avoid *porneia* one may wish to marry and use the gift of sexuality in the God-given way within a heterosexual monogamous marriage. Apparently, sexual immorality refers to

---

[32] See David E. Aune, *Revelation 1–5*, Word Biblical Commentary 52A (Dallas: Word. 1997), 205.

[33] The last two lists mention *pornoi.*

[34] Yet, the list of vices in the first part of the chapter also includes sexual sins.

premarital as well as extramarital affairs.[35] The demand to avoid sexual immorality is repeated in 1 Corinthians 10:8. Since the thousands who had been killed were probably not all unmarried men, sexual immorality refers again to premarital and extramarital intercourse.

In 1 Thessalonians 4:3, Paul declares that it is the will of God to abstain from sexual immorality. This verse is part of a sentence that comprises verses 3–6. The passage includes the next two verses. It is a paragraph on God's will—namely, sanctification. It starts with God's will and "sanctification" (*hagiasmos*, 1 Thess 4:3). It concludes with the concept of God's will and the same word "sanctification" (*hagiasmos*, 1 Thess 4:7), which is found a third time in the middle of the passage (*hagiasmos*, 1 Thess 4:4).

1 Thess 4:3

God's will: sanctification → no sexual immorality (*porneia*)

1 Thess 4:7–8

God's calling: sanctification → no impurity (*akatharsia*)

This seems to indicate that at least here impurity may overlap in meaning to some extent with sexual immorality. Within the long sentence of 1 Thessalonians 4:3–6 *porneia* is mentioned first: we should abstain from sexual immorality. Then it is spelled out what that means—namely, "how to possess his own vessel[36] in sanctification and honor . . . and that no man transgress and defraud his brother in the matter" (1 Thess 4:4, 6, NASB). Thus, sexual immorality is to have intercourse with the wife of a fellow

[35] This observation does not support the view, entertained by men in the time of Jesus, that males commit sexual sins only if they have sexual relations with one or more wives of another man —if they, so to speak, break into another man's marriage—but are free to have intercourse with unmarried women as long as it is consensual, while it is sin for these women to have such a relationship. This would mean that relations bordering on polygamy are acceptable for men, but not for women. But this view is rejected in the New Testament, especially by Jesus. In His statements about the origin and nature of marriage (e.g., Matt 19:4–6, 8–9), He clearly rejects polygamy in all its forms.

[36] This term is difficult to interpret. Three options are being proposed: 1) "vessel" refers to a wife, 2) "vessel" is a euphemism for the male sexual organ, or 3) "vessel" refers to the human body. It seems that today the third option is preferred among expositors. It would mean that men and women should master their own bodies and desires in holiness, staying away from sexual immorality. Cf. Gene L. Green, *The Letters to the Thessalonians*, The Pillar New Testament Commentary (Grand Rapids, MI: Eerdmans, 2002), 191–194; Gary S. Shogren, *1 and 2 Thessalonians*, Zondervan Exegetical Commentary on the New Testament (Grand Rapids, MI: Zondervan, 2012), 162–164; Charles A. Wanamaker, *The Epistles to the Thessalonians*, The New International Greek Commentary (Grand Rapids, MI: Eerdmans, 1990), 151–153; and Jeffrey A. D. Weima, *1-2 Thessalonians*, Baker Exegetical Commentary on the New Testament (Grand Rapids, MI: Baker Academic, 2014), 268–272.

believer. This is a clear case of adultery if the sexually immoral person is married. Therefore, *porneia* would include adultery.

In Hebrews 12:16, believers are warned not to be sexually immoral persons like Esau. The context talks about holiness that believers must exhibit, because without sanctification no one will see the Lord (Heb 12:14). Hebrews 13:4 is a call to marital faithfulness, contained in a passage of different exhortations: "Marriage is to be held in honor among all, and the marriage bed is to be undefiled; for fornicators and adulterers God will judge." In this text, *porneia* is different from adultery unless *kai* is used epexegetically.[37] Adultery may refer to a married partner who has intercourse with another person than his/her spouse, while sexual immorality may refer to an unmarried person engaging in sexual activities with a married person.

In Matthew 5:32 and 19:9, Jesus warns against divorce.[38] Both verses talk about sexual immorality (*porneia*) and committing adultery (*moicheuō* and *moichaomai*). The argument in Matthew 5:32 focuses on the wife and seems to be as follows: if you divorce your wife and she has not committed sexual immorality, she becomes an adulteress by indirectly being forced to remarry, because the first marriage is still valid in God's eyes. An alternative reading would be: by divorcing your wife you stigmatize her as an adulteress. On the other hand, the argument in Matthew 19:9 concentrates on the husband: a man who gets a divorce and remarries when his wife was not involved in sexual immorality commits adultery. What does Jesus mean by the term *porneia*? Depending on its precise nature, the immoral sexual act can be adultery.[39] This might be the reason why many translations render the term *porneia* here as "adultery." But it may not be wise to limit the interpretation to adultery only. Obviously, the word *porneia* was chosen deliberately in order to differentiate it from *moicheia* (adultery) and its related verbs in Matthew 5:27–28, 32b. In Matthew 5:32 Jesus quotes Deuteronomy 24:1. This text not only mentions a certificate of divorce, but also the reason for divorce. The respective Hebrew term *'erwāh* can be rendered "nakedness," "pudenda," "shame," "something indecent," or metaphorically the "undefended areas." It is a negative term with strong sexual associations. Its predominant translation is "nakedness." The term is

---

[37] F. F. Bruce, *The Epistle to the Hebrews*, New International Commentary on the New Testament (Grand Rapids, MI: Eerdmans, 1970), 392, writes, "Fornication and adultery are not synonymous in the New Testament: adultery implies unfaithfulness by either party to the marriage vow, while the word translated 'fornication' [*porneia*] covers a wide range of sexual irregularities, including unions within bounds prohibited by law."

[38] See Mueller, "Divorce and Remarriage in the New Testament," 210–230.

[39] If, e.g., the wife was involved in incest or prostitution while married, then she had sexual relations with another man and this is also adultery.

found most frequently in the context of sexual immoralities in Leviticus 18 and 20 and in connection with *porneia* in Ezekiel and Hosea.[40] The complete phrase, translated "some indecency" (*'erwat dabar*, an indecent thing), occurs only in Deuteronomy 23:14 and 24:1. In the former text it refers to fecal matter, while in chapter 24 it obviously describes some kind of sexual misconduct.[41] In Matthew 5:32 Jesus uses *porneia* as the only legitimate reason for divorce,[42] rejecting at least the interpretation of Deuteronomy 24:1 by the school of Hillel, which permitted a husband to divorce his wife for trivial matters such as burning a dish of food.[43] In Matthew 19:9 Jesus uses a similar exception clause —"except for sexual immorality"—as Matthew 5:32 does. Since in both cases the literary context does not specify what *porneia* stands for, the New and Old Testaments' understanding of the word stem *-porn-* must be considered.[44] *Porneia*—that is, sexual relations outside of the

---

[40] The term is found fifty-four times in the Old Testament. It is used metaphorically for an undefended area in Genesis 42:9, 12. Deuteronomy 23:15 and 24:1 talk about an indecent thing. Shame seems to be the meaning in Isaiah 20:4, but in 1 Samuel 20:30 "shame" and "nakedness" are found next to each other. The term is used for Egypt, Babylon, and Jerusalem. About fifty times the word is translated with the term "nakedness." It is found thirty-two times in Leviticus and eight times in Ezekiel. The word occurs twenty-four times in Leviticus 18 and eight times in Leviticus 20, which also describes unlawful sexual practices. In Ezekiel it is found four times in chapter 16, which refers to Jerusalem as God's bride. But because Jerusalem has uncovered her nakedness in her *porneia* (Ezek 16:36), which in her case is also adultery, God will expose her nakedness (Ezek 16:37). In Ezekiel Oholah and Oholibah, representing Israel and Judah, are depicted. Again *porneia* and nakedness are connected (Ezek 23:10, 18, 29). Ezekiel 23:18 even reads, "She uncovered her *porneia*, and she uncovered her nakedness." Hosea 2:9 mentions nakedness. The context talks about harlotry/sexual immorality (Hos 2:2, 4–5). To uncover one's nakedness may point to sexual intercourse (Lev 20:21).

[41] The phrase may not include adultery because the penalty for adultery was death by stoning (Lev 20:10; John 8:5), not a letter of divorce. On the other hand, not every husband would expose his wife involved in adultery to the extreme punishment but rather get a divorce. See the case of Joseph and Mary in Matthew 1:19, where it seemed to Joseph that Mary had sexual relations with another man.

[42] Basically, there are two options: 1) Jesus is in opposition to Moses. He allows for divorce only in the case of sexual immorality. *Porneia* and "something shameful" (NIRV) of Deuteronomy 24:1 are not describing the same severe misconduct. 2) Jesus agrees with Moses. The "shameful things" are the same acts that Jesus describes with the word *porneia*. Jesus rejects the rabbinic misinterpretation and distortions of Moses.

[43] Cf. *m. Gittin* 9:10.

[44] Samuele Bacchiocchi, *The Marriage Covenant: A Biblical Study on Marriage, Divorce, and Remarriage* (Berrien Springs, MI: Biblical Perspectives, 1991), 179–189, and others argue to limit sexual immorality in the Matthean passages to incest only. Andrew Cornes, *Divorce and Remarriage: Biblical Principles and Pastoral Practice* (Grand Rapids, MI: Eerdmans, 1993), 202, and others are opposed to such a suggestion.

1. Bacchiocchi argues that if Jesus permits divorce for sexual sins other than incest, He would not be different from the school of Shammai, which, in contrast to the school of Hillel, did

biblical marriage relationship—seems to include a number of sexual sins, as indicated in the Old Testament and New Testament summary sections of this study.

Summary

With regard to the word family *-porn-* the following picture can be derived from the New Testament:

1. *Porneia* (sexual immorality) depicts prostitution—that is, playing the harlot.
2. It is predominantly used in a literal sense, but in the book of Revelation it also has a figurative meaning.
3. *Porneia* can stand for premarital sexual relations.
4. In some cases, sexual immorality is adultery or may include adultery; in others it is broader.
5. Uncleanness may in some cases partially overlap in meaning with sexual immorality.
6. Incest is sexual immorality. Obviously the sexual sins listed in Leviticus 18, including same-sex sexual relations, are included in the term *porneia*.

Conclusion

In this study we have looked at the word family *-porn-* in extrabiblical Greek literature, in the Old Testament, and in the New Testament. In

---

not allow divorce for trivial matters such as burning a dish of food, but restricted it to sexual misbehavior, and He would not do justice to His own claim that the righteousness of His disciples must surpass that of the scribes and Pharisees. This argument is unwarranted. Even the position of the conservative school of Shammai on divorce was wider and more open than that of Jesus. See Herman L. Strack and Paul Billerbeck, *Das Evangelium nach Matthäus erläutert aus Talmud und Midrasch*, Kommentar zum Neuen Testament aus Talmud und Midrasch 1 (München: C. H. Beck'sche Verlagsbuchhandlung, 1986), 304, 315–320.

2. Although not all "antitheses" of the Sermon on the Mount are antitheses in the strictest sense of the word, obviously Jesus' teachings exceed by far the prohibitions of Deuteronomy 24:1 and their interpretation during His time. Therefore, Jesus was considered radical. Even the disciples decided to side with the Pharisees' party in Matthew 19:10.

3. Apparently, the exception clause does not *require* a divorce to happen, but permits it. If *porneia* would be limited to incest, it would be difficult to understand why Jesus in this case did not insist on a divorce, especially since in this connection the Old Testament talked about being cut off from the people (Lev 18:29). Furthermore, the question must be asked if an incestuous relationship can be considered a marriage at all and therefore if it can be divorced.

4. The argument that there was greater danger among Jews than among Gentiles to get involved in incest and that therefore Matthew would contain the exception clause does not seem to be convincing. Obviously, Jews in the time of Jesus tried to obey God's laws. Incest in 1 Corinthians 5 may not have been primarily related to Jewish Christians because it was a non-issue for them. According to Acts 15 the newly converted Gentiles had to be instructed to abstain from sexual immorality as described in Leviticus 18, and this certainly included incest.

all sources, *porneia* and the related terms refer to sexual acts only, if used literally. Both the Old Testament and New Testament correspond largely when it comes to the word family. Although the Old Testament favors the figurative sense and the New Testament the literal meaning, the different aspects of *porneia* are found in both testaments. They include prostitution, premarital sexual relations, adultery, incest, and homosexual activity—in short, sexual relations outside of heterosexual monogamous marriage. Thus the Old Testament and the New Testament enlarge the understanding of *porneia* as found in the Greek world. Obviously, in Scripture sexual immorality is a broad concept describing various kinds of sexual aberrations (intercourse), but can also be used in a more restricted sense, referring to illicit sexual acts of married persons or sexual intercourse of unmarried persons. Frequently, a restricted meaning can be determined by investigating the context.

In Scripture, the terms describing sexual immorality are used in a negative way. Sexual immorality must be avoided in all its forms by God's people (Eph 5:3; Col 3:5; 1 Thess 4:3). Scripture, in contrast to the Greek world, neither condones *porneia* nor makes compromises. Those who have been or are engaged in sexual immorality are called to repent, receive forgiveness for these sins, and change their lifestyle (Rev 9:21; 1 Cor 6:9–11). Christians are particularly interested in the sayings of Jesus dealing with *porneia*. Although there are many evils in society and unfortunately also in marriages, sexual immorality describes only sexual sins and does not address issues such as spouse battering and abandonment. Jesus did not address these issues directly, although they must be rejected. However, the good news of the gospel is that God is willing to bless us with healing and forgiveness, which we in turn are asked to extend to others.

CHAPTER 3

Does Sexual Intercourse Constitute Marriage? The Issue of Premarital Sex

Richard M. Davidson and Ekkehardt Mueller

Various ideas concerning what constitutes marriage vie for attention in contemporary society. Many argue that sexual intercourse per se between two unmarried people constitutes marriage. This view has far-reaching implications. On the one hand, it is maintained by some that those who have had sexual intercourse outside of marriage are constrained to get married because their sexual union has in fact already united them as "one flesh." On the other hand, those who have engaged in sexual intercourse, especially in the setting of an ongoing relationship (cohabitation), often consider that such a sexual union already constitutes marriage and thus there is no need for them to have a formal/public wedding ceremony.

Others argue that sexual intercourse must be linked with a covenant ceremony. But there are varieties of interpretation concerning the nature of this linkage. One view suggests that sexual union may well come first, and then (if the couple finds themselves compatible with each other) they may move forward to a formal marriage ceremony to provide the legal basis for the relationship. Another view maintains that the sexual union should only come within the covenant relationship but considers that this covenant relationship may be entered into privately by the couple, without any public/formal covenant ceremony. According to this position, only God as witness to the couple's vows of fidelity is required for the marriage covenant to be valid. Still another view, the traditional and probably the majority position, insists that according to biblical evidence, the covenant relationship 1) forms the foundation for the marriage; 2) should precede the sexual union; 3) should be public in nature, involving a formal/legal ceremony; and 4) should include human witnesses as well as the divine witness.[1]

To understand the biblical testimony and its implications for this subject, the discussion that follows is divided into three main sections. The first section examines the Old Testament foundational material, the second one explores the New Testament passages, and the last section addresses the ethical deliberations on premarital sex.

Marriage and Sexuality in the Old Testament

The Edenic Model for the Constitution of Marriage[2]

Genesis 2:24 summarizes the divine plan for the constitution of marriage: "Therefore, a man leaves his father and his mother and cleaves to his wife, and they become one flesh."[3] The introductory "therefore"

---

[1] In the Garden of Eden, there were obviously no "human witnesses," since Adam and Eve were the only humans created at this time. But God was the divine witness, and Ellen G. White, *In Heavenly Places* (Washington, DC: Review and Herald, 1967), 203, provides the additional insight that "angels of God were witnesses to the ceremony." There may be situations where the "public" or "formal" nature of the covenant service may be very limited by time and circumstances (such as war, forced isolation from civilization, etc.), but some kind of public covenant ceremony still is possible. The Bible does not give precise details prescribing what the public covenant ceremony should involve, thus leaving room for time and circumstances within various cultures, while upholding the general principles set forth in the original divinely officiated wedding in Eden (Gen 2:22–24).

[2] Many of the foundational exegetical insights in this chapter are based on research presented in Richard M. Davidson, *Flame of Yahweh: Sexuality in the Old Testament* (Peabody, MA: Hendrickson, 2007), and this chapter builds upon these and other insights in framing biblical answers to the basic question regarding the relationship between sexual intercourse and marriage.

[3] All biblical quotations are from the NRSV, unless otherwise indicated. The majority of biblical commentators throughout the centuries have taken Genesis 2:24 as referring to the institution of marriage. Notable exceptions to this traditional view include Hermann Gunkel in his groundbreaking form-critical commentary on Genesis, *Genesis*, Handkommentar zum Alten Testament 1, no. 1, 3rd ed. (Göttingen: Vandenhoeck and Ruprecht, 1910), 13, 41, who sees Genesis 2:24 as an etiology, explaining the mutual sexual attraction of the male and female as the longing of the two, who had originally been one (androgynous), to become one again. Another exception is Claus Westermann, *Genesis 1–11* (Minneapolis, MN: Augsburg, 1974), 232, who argues that Genesis 2:18–24 refers to "personal community between man and woman in the broadest sense" and "is not concerned with the foundation of any sort of institution, but with the primeval event," and thus "is not talking about marriage as an institution for the begetting of descendants, but of the community of man and woman as such." However, language of formal covenant implies a marriage covenant, and the "therefore" implies the setting of a pattern for future marriage relationships. A study by Bernard F. Batto, "The Institution of Marriage in Genesis 2 and in *Atrahasis*," *Catholic Biblical Quarterly* 62 (2000): 621–631, argues forcefully that "this debate over the question whether the author of Gen 2:18–25 envisions the institution of marriage or not can now be settled in the affirmative on the basis of comparative evidence, hitherto overlooked, from the Mesopotamian myth of *Atrahasis*" (ibid., 623). Batto reviews the now widely recognized evidence that while there are significant differences

(*ʿal-kēn*) indicates that the marriage of Adam and Eve described in the previous verse is upheld as the pattern for all future human sexual relationships.[4] Several significant insights into the nature of the divine plan for marriage emerge from this verse. First, the paradigm for marriage in Genesis 2:24 highlights the element of exclusivity. The first of three actions described in this verse is that man "leaves" (*ʿāzab*). The Hebrew verb *ʿāzab* is a forceful term. It means literally "to abandon, forsake," and is employed frequently to describe Israel's blatant and open forsaking of Yahweh for false gods.[5] The "leaving" of Genesis 2:24 indicates the necessity of absolute freedom from outside interferences in the sexual relationship. Just as this freedom was essential in the garden, so it is crucial in all succeeding sexual relationships. This "leaving" is not done in a corner, in secret, but involves a public and open break from all other interferences with the relationship—a break that is apparent to all outside observers.

What is particularly striking in verse 24 is that it is the *man* who is to "leave." In the patriarchal society at the time Genesis 2 was penned, it was a matter of course that the wife left her mother and father.[6] But for

between the Genesis 2 account and the Atrahasis Epic, nonetheless the basic structural flow of the two accounts are parallel. He then shows how in the structurally parallel equivalent to Genesis 2:18–24 in the Atrahasis Epic there is reference to *uṣurāt nišī*, "regulations for humankind," specifically focusing upon the institution of marriage. Thus, Batto concludes, the narrator of Genesis 2:18–24 "surely intended v. 24 as the equivalent of *uṣurāt nišī* in *Atrahasis,* that is, as a universal law regulating the normative behavior of the sexes within a community of marriage" (ibid., 629); and as in *Atrahasis,* the Genesis 2 narrator is "positing that the institution of marriage is grounded in the very design of creation itself" (ibid., 631).

[4] See Robert B. Lawton, "Genesis 2:24: Trite or Tragic?," *Journal of Biblical Literature* 105 (1986): 97–98, for evidence that this is not just an etiological insertion to explain the common legal custom. Lawton points out that it was *not* the normal custom for the man to leave his father and mother, but rather only for the woman to leave. Therefore, the Hebrew imperfect *yāʿăzāb* in this context is best taken not as a frequentative imperfect "he [typically] leaves," but as a potential imperfect "he *should* leave." The verse thus expresses "a description of divine intention rather than of habitually observed fact" (ibid., 98.). See also Deborah F. Sawyer, *God, Gender and the Bible* (London: Routledge, 2002), 24: "The first couple provide the blueprint for normative citizenship in the theocracy proposed in the Bible's first story."

[5] See Deuteronomy 28:20; Judges 10:13; 2 Chronicles 34:25; Isaiah 1:4; and many other passages.

[6] Some have seen behind this passage a hint of a matriarchal social structure, but sufficient evidence does not exist to substantiate such an hypothesis. For modern proponents of matriarchal trends within (and behind) the biblical tradition, see, e.g., Savina J. Teubal, *Hagar the Egyptian: The Lost Traditions of the Matriarchs* (San Francisco, CA: Harper and Row, 1990); and Gerda Weiler, *Das Matriarchat im Alten Israel* (Stuttgart: W. Kohhammer, 1989). For further discussion, bibliography, and negative assessment of alleged evidence for this theory, see, e.g., Hennie J. Marsman, *Women in Ugarit and Israel: Their Social and Religious Position in the Context of the Ancient Near East* (Leiden: Brill, 2003), 101–102.

the husband to "leave" was revolutionary![7] In effect, the force of this statement is that both are to leave to cut loose from those ties that would encroach upon the independence and freedom of the relationship. The "leaving" implies not only the outward break to establish a new home, but also the inward "leaving"—the psychological break away from dependence upon parents. "Leaving" means "starting a whole new relationship in which the core loyalty is not to parents' priorities, traditions, or influence but to an entirely new family that must set its own course, form, and purpose."[8]

The "leaving" also implies the exclusiveness of the relationship: husband and wife, and no other interfering party, are bone of each other's bones, flesh of each other's flesh. This exclusivity in the marriage relationship is ultimately rooted in the monotheistic nature of God. Just as the one God (Yahweh Elohim) created the whole of humanity for fellowship with Himself, so the man and woman made in His image were to be exclusively devoted to each other in marriage.

Secondly, the Edenic paradigm for marriage in Genesis 2:24 underscores the aspect of *permanence*. The second of three actions described in this verse is that man "cleaves" (*dābaq*). The Hebrew verb *dābaq* is another robust term, signifying strong personal attachment. The original imagery of the word is that of sticking, clinging, and remaining as physically close as skin to flesh and flesh to bone. It is often used in the Old Testament as a technical covenant term for the permanent bond of Israel to the Lord.[9] As applied to the divine plan for marriage in Genesis 2:24, it clearly indicates a covenant context—that is, a marriage covenant.

The term "cleave" parallels the "oath of solidarity" and language of "covenant partnership" expressed by Adam concerning Eve in the previous verse. When Adam speaks of Eve (Gen 2:23*a*), "This is now bone of my bones and flesh of my flesh," he is expressing marriage covenant vows.[10] Furthermore, "the third person reference ['this'] in

---

[7] Samuel Terrien, *Till the Heart Sings: A Biblical Theology of Manhood and Womanhood* (Philadelphia, PA: Fortress, 1985), 14–15, rightly points out that "in the ancient Near East and most other cultures, patriarchal lineage prevailed in such a way that the primary bond of solidarity was the duty of a man toward his ancestors in general and to his progenitors in particular. To honor one's father and mother was the most sacred obligation of social responsibility (Exod 20:12; Deut 5:16). By dramatic contrast," Terrien continues, the author of Genesis 2 "scandalously upsets, even shockingly reverses, this deep-rooted principle of tribal morality. Against the cultures of his environment," the Hebrew author "declares unambiguously that man's first loyalty is to his woman."

[8] Dan B. Allender and Tremper Longman III, *Intimate Allies: Rediscovering God's Design for Marriage and Becoming Soul Mates for Life* (Wheaton, IL: Tyndale, 1995), 218.

[9] See, e.g., Deuteronomy 10:20; 11:22; 13:4; Joshua 22:5; 23:8; 2 Samuel 20:3; 2 Kings 18:6.

[10] For further discussion of the covenant language used by Adam, see Walter Brueggemann, "Of the Same Flesh and Bone (Gen 2:23a)," *Catholic Biblical Quarterly* 32 (1970): 535. Cf. John S. Grabowski, *Sex and Virtue: An Introduction to Sexual Ethics* (Washington, DC: The Catholic

Genesis 2:23, with God's presence asserted in the immediate context, implies that Adam was addressing his affirmation not to Eve, nor, presumably to himself but to God as witness."[11] Adam's statement regarding Eve addressed to God is "a solemn affirmation of his marital commitment, an elliptical way of saying something like, 'I hereby invite you, God, to hold me accountable to treat this woman as part of my own body.'"[12]

Moreover, God's presenting the woman to the man implies that God was the officiant at the solemn public covenant-making ceremony—the first garden wedding! And "therefore" (*'al-kēn*), the narrator states, as it was with Adam and Eve, so the divine intent for every husband and wife is that their marriage be formalized with a public, legal "cleaving"—a mutual commitment expressed in a formal/public covenant-making ceremony.[13] Of course, the precise form of this public covenant-making occasion may vary due to circumstances of time and culture.

But more is involved in "cleaving" than a formal covenant. The word *dābaq* also emphasizes the inward attitudinal dimensions of the covenant bond. It "implies a devotion and an unshakable faith between humans; it connotes a permanent attraction which transcends genital union, to which, nonetheless it gives meaning."[14] The word "cleave" in Genesis 2:24 encapsulates the nuances of Adam's covenant vows in the previous verse. The phrase "bone of my bones, flesh of my flesh" not only affirms the existence of a covenant, but expresses "the entire range of intermediate possibilities from the extreme of frailty [flesh] to power [bones]. . . . [It is] a formula of abiding loyalty for every changing circumstance."[15] It is the equivalent to our modern marriage vow "In sickness or in health, in adversity or prosperity." When a man clings

---

University of America Press, 2003), 33–38, for an extended treatment of "the wealth of covenant language" contained in Genesis 2, including the language used by Adam. For presentation of evidence from both Genesis 1 and 2 that marriage is set forth as covenantal, see John K. Tarwater, "The Covenantal Nature of Marriage in the Order of Creation in Genesis 1 and 2" (PhD diss., Southeastern Baptist Theological Seminary, 2002).

[11] Gordon P. Hugenberger, *Marriage as a Covenant: Biblical Law and Ethics as Developed from Malachi*, Supplements to Vetus Testamentum 52 (repr., Grand Rapids, MI: Baker, 1998), 202. There were no other human beings in existence who could be witnesses at the wedding ceremony of Adam and Eve, but Ellen G. White adds the insight that there were angels who served as witnesses, as observed in note 1 in the present chapter.

[12] Ibid., 165.

[13] Frank M. Hasel, "The Biblical Concept of Marriage in the Bible," in *Marriage: Biblical and Theological Aspects*, ed. Ekkehardt Mueller and Elias Brasil de Souza, vol. 1 (Nampa, ID: Pacific Press, 2015), 33, rightly summarizes, "This public character of marriage derives from the fact that Adam and Eve did not celebrate any private arrangement but that God Himself brought Eve to Adam."

[14] Raymond F. Collins, "The Bible and Sexuality," *Biblical Theology Bulletin* 7 (1977): 153.

[15] Brueggemann, 534–535.

to a woman in a public marriage covenant, he is vowing to remain in covenant relationship, no matter what may come. The marriage covenant is permanent; it is for keeps.

Thirdly, the divine paradigm for all future marriages as set forth in Genesis 2:24 stresses the ingredient of *intimacy.* The third of three actions described in this verse is that man and woman "shall become one flesh" (*wĕhāyû lĕbāśār 'eḥād*). The term "one flesh" has in view primarily the intimacy of sexual union, sexual intercourse, as clearly understood by Paul (1 Cor 6:16).[16] The fact that Paul could cite this expression with regard to sexual intercourse of a man with a prostitute, where the social context has nothing to do with marriage, makes evident that in the apostle's mind sexual intercourse does not automatically constitute marriage.

The physical act of coitus is the primary (although not the only) means of establishing the "innermost mystery" of oneness.[17] The one-flesh experience of marriage involves the deepest kind of intimacy, a total transparency between marriage partners, described in Genesis 2:25: "And they were both naked, the man and his wife, and *were not ashamed before each other* [*hithpael* of *bāšaš*]."

What is of particular importance for our purposes in this study is the fact that this "one-flesh" union *follows* the "cleaving." It is the covenant ceremony that formalizes the marriage, not the sexual union. The Edenic blueprint for sexual relationships underscores that the one-flesh union of sexual intercourse belongs within the context of the marriage covenant. The unitive purpose of sexuality is to find fulfillment inside the marital relationship. It is not the sexual union that constitutes the marriage, but rather, the first sexual intercourse follows the marriage that has already been constituted by the formal marriage covenant.[18]

---

[16] See the analysis of biblical data supporting this conclusion by Wayne J. H. Stuhlmiller, "'One Flesh' in the Old and New Testaments," *Consensus* 5 (1979): 3–9.

[17] Otto A. Piper, *The Biblical View of Sex and Marriage* (New York: Scribner, 1960), 52–67, explores the possible dimensions of this "inner mystery." The term *bāśār* ("flesh") in the Old Testament not only refers to one's physical body, but is also used as a term to denote human relationship. It indicates a oneness and intimacy in the total relationship of the whole person of the husband to the whole person of the wife, a harmony and union with each other in all things. Furthermore, Genesis 2:24c does not imply that the one-fleshness is an instantaneously achieved state. The phrase *wĕhāyû lĕbāśār 'eḥād* is better rendered "They shall *become* [not *be*] one flesh."

[18] This first sexual union of the couple after the wedding is frequently spoken of in modern parlance as the "consummation of the marriage." This study avoids this expression (except in citations of others) because of the ambiguity of its meaning and hence its liability to be misunderstood. This expression has been interpreted with at least two different meanings. According to the first definition, sexual union is a separate act that takes place after the marriage is constituted; it is not the sexual union that constitutes the marriage, but rather, sexual intercourse is the "consummation" of a marriage that has already been fully constituted

In the Song of Songs we come full circle in the Old Testament back to the garden of Eden. Numerous scholarly studies have penetratingly analyzed and conclusively demonstrated the intimate relationship between the early chapters of Genesis and the Song of Songs, and have suggested that the Song of Songs constitutes an inspired commentary on Genesis 1–3.[19] Within the Song we find confirmation of the major points regarding the theology of marriage that have previously been outlined in our exegesis of Genesis 2:24.[20]

As in Genesis 2 man "leaves"—he is free from all outside interferences in the love relationship—so in Song of Songs the lovers are unfettered by parental pre-arrangements. They are in love for love's sake alone. They are free for the spontaneous development of an exclusive and intimate friendship. In the freedom from outside interferences the couple may find mutual attraction in the physical beauty and inward character qualities of each other.

As in the Genesis model, where man and woman are to "cleave" to each other in a public marriage covenant, so the Song of Songs climaxes in the wedding ceremony. The symmetrical literary structure of the unified Song reveals an intricate design focused upon a central section that describes the wedding of Solomon and his bride.[21] Song of Songs 3:6–11 portrays the wedding procession of Solomon "on the day of his wedding" (Song 3:11). What follows in Song of Songs 4:1–5:1 encompasses the wedding ceremony proper (Song 4:1–7, and perhaps extending through v. 15), followed by sexual union on the wedding night (Song 4:16–5:1).

---

by the formal marriage covenant. Failure or delay to "consummate the marriage" because of impotence or other circumstances does not give grounds for divorce or annulment of the marriage. According to the second definition, prevalent especially in sacramental Roman Catholic contexts, "consummation of the marriage" by sexual union (i.e., insertion of the penis into the vagina) is an integral part of "completing" the marriage, and failure to "consummate the marriage" by sexual union provides grounds for annulment of the marriage (for Roman Catholics) or divorce (in other faith traditions). Research into Scripture finds support for the first definition and not the second. See the discussion that follows for this evidence.

[19] See, e.g., Nicholas Ayo, *Sacred Marriage: The Wisdom of the Song of Songs* (New York: Continuum, 1997), 37–53; Francis Landy, "The Song of Songs and the Garden of Eden," *Journal of Biblical Literature* 98 (1979): 513–528; Landy, *Paradoxes of Paradise: Identity and Difference in the Song of Songs* (Sheffield: Almond Press, 1983), esp. chap. 4, "Two Versions of Paradise" (183–265); William E. Phipps, *Genesis and Gender: Biblical Myths of Sexuality and Their Cultural Impact* (New York: Praeger, 1989), 90–95; Phyllis Trible, "Depatriarchalizing in Biblical Interpretation," *Journal of the American Academy of Religion* 41 (March 1973): 42–47; and Trible, *God and the Rhetoric of Sexuality*, Overtures to Biblical Theology (Philadelphia, PA: Fortress, 1978), 145–165.

[20] For substantiation and development of the major points made in the paragraphs that follow on the Song of Songs, see Davidson, *Flame of Yahweh*, 545–632.

[21] See Richard M. Davidson, "The Literary Structure of the Song of Songs *Redivivus*," *Journal of the Adventist Theological Society* 14, no. 2 (Fall 2003): 44–65.

Only in this section of the Song does Solomon address the Shulamite as his "bride" (*kāllâ*, Song 4:8–12; 5:1). The groom compares his bride to a garden (Song 4:12, 15). In the two central verses of the entire symmetrical literary structure of the Song (4:16; 5:1), the bride invites her groom to come and partake of the fruits of her (and now his!) garden (Song 4:16) and the groom accepts her invitation (Song 5:1a–d). The (divine) approbation is extended as the bride and groom "drink deeply" in the consummate experience of sexual union (Song 5:1e).[22]

As in Genesis 2:24, the "one-flesh" union follows the "cleaving," so in the Song of Songs sexual intercourse occurs only *within* the context of the marriage covenant. If one takes seriously the unity of the Song ("*The Song* of Songs," 1:1) and the testimony of the groom regarding his bride —that at the time of the wedding she is a "garden *locked*" (Song 4:12), which most commentators recognize as referring to virginity—the groom is clearly announcing that at the time for sexual intercourse in the bridal bed, his bride is still a virgin. The high point of the ceremony and of the entire Song is focalized in the invitation and acceptance on the part of bride and groom to "become one flesh" with each other through sexual intercourse, following the marriage covenant. Sexual union is thereby reserved and preserved for husband and wife within the formal covenant made in marriage. Sexual union per se does not constitute marriage.

The New Testament, as well as the Song of Songs, also gives tacit approval to the insights arising from Genesis 2:24, as both Jesus and Paul quote this passage in full and verbatim in their discussion of questions regarding marriage (Matt 19:5; Eph 5:31).

Marriage Outside the Garden

The Covenantal Nature of Marriage

In the previous section we have seen how according to the Edenic model for marriage, given by God at creation, husband and wife were to "cleave" (Heb. *dābaq*) to one another in a permanent relationship (Gen 2:24). This "cleaving" involved a lasting covenant bond between husband and wife, implied not only by the covenant term *dābaq* ("cleave"), but by the "covenant oath" made by Adam concerning Eve with God as witness: "This is bone of my bones, flesh of my flesh" (Gen 2:23).

Outside the garden, the divine plan for marriage is upheld throughout Old Testament Scripture. Marriage is set forth as a permanent

---

[22] For evidence that the voice of Song of Songs 5:1c is none other than God Himself, giving the divine approbation upon the marriage and sexual union on the wedding night, see Richard M. Davidson, "Is God Present in the Song of Songs?," *Journal of the Adventist Theological Society* 16, nos. 1–2 (2005): 143–154.

covenant bond between husband and wife. Numerous biblical passages present marriage as covenantal.[23] The most explicit passage is Malachi 2:14, appearing in the context of disputations between God and those among the returned exiles who had divorced Judean wives to marry pagans: "Because the Lord has been witness between you and the wife of your youth, with whom you have dealt treacherously [*bāgad*]; yet she is your companion and your wife by *covenant* [*bĕrît*]." This passage indicates that 1) the marriage is covenantal in nature, 2) the marriage covenant is between the husband and wife and not outside parties, and 3) Yahweh is the divine witness of the marriage vows.[24] All three of these aspects emphasize the solemn obligation to permanence in the relationship. The use of the term *bāgad* ("to deal treacherously, unfaithfully") in this passage also implies an intended permanent covenant commitment that has been broken.

Other Old Testament passages also refer to the marriage covenant between husband and wife. In Proverbs 2:17 Wisdom warns against the immoral woman "who forsakes the companion of her youth and forgets the *covenant* [*bĕrît*] of her God." Especially in the Prophets the concept of permanence becomes explicit as God likens His covenant relationship with Israel to a marriage covenant.[25] Hosea 2:16–20 (MT Hos 2:18–22) describes God's intent to reaffirm the covenant with Israel following her unfaithfulness to Him. Notice the covenant language of permanence: "I will betroth you to Me *forever*" (Hos 2:19 [MT Hos 2:21]). Isaiah, another eighth century prophet, also expresses the permanent marriage covenant between God the Husband and His bride: "For your Maker is your husband, the Lord of hosts is His name. . . . For the mountains shall depart and the hills be removed, but my kindness [*ḥesed* steadfast covenantal love] shall not depart from you, nor shall My covenant [*bĕrît*] of peace be removed" (Isa 54:5, 10).

Ezekiel 16:8 explicitly mentions Yahweh swearing an oath (His marriage vows!) when entering into a marriage covenant with Israel (at Sinai): "'Yes, I swore an oath to you and entered into a covenant [*bĕrît*] with you and you became mine,' says the Lord God." The divine oath

---

[23] For a full discussion, see Hugenberger, 280–312.

[24] Ibid., 27–47.

[25] For discussion of the intertextual linkages between the human marriage formulas and the divine covenant formulas, see Seock-Tae Sohn, "'I Will Be Your God and You Will Be My People': The Origin and Background of the Covenant Formula," in *Ki Baruch Hu: Ancient Near Eastern, Biblical, and Judaic Studies in Honor of Baruch A. Levine*, ed. Robert Chazan, William W. Hallo, and Lawrence H. Schiffman (Winona Lake, IN: Eisenbrauns, 1999), 355–372. Sohn also presents a helpful collection of ancient Near Eastern materials revealing a pervasive legal pattern for the marriage ceremony, which included the proclaiming or reciting a covenant-ratifying oath in the presence of witnesses.

is a powerful sign of permanence. Although Israel proved unfaithful (described in Ezekiel 16:15–43) and "despised the oath by breaking the covenant" (Ezek 16:59), God reiterates His intention for a permanent marriage covenant: "Nevertheless, I will remember My covenant [*bĕrît*] with you in the days of your youth, and I will establish an everlasting covenant [*bĕrît*] with you. . . . And I will establish My covenant [*bĕrît*] with you. Then you shall know that I am the Lord" (Ezek 16:60, 62).

The understanding of marriage as a covenant is not unique to the Bible; throughout the ancient Near East, marriage was regarded as a covenant or contract.[26] The ancient Near Eastern marriage contract included a number of elements, including payments, contract stipulations, and penalties incurred if the stipulations were broken. Various ancient Near Eastern laws make clear the necessity of the public ceremony and legal contract in order for there to be a marriage.[27] Contrary to what has sometimes been assumed, sexual intercourse between a man and woman, or the two living together, without a formal covenant or wedding ceremony did not thereby make them husband and wife.

Verbal affirmations between spouses may at times have been accompanied by a covenant oath in the presence of the deity that solemnized the marriage, or the verbal affirmations alone may have been regarded

---

[26] See esp. David Instone-Brewer, "The Ancient Near East: Marriage Is a Contract," chap. 1 in *Divorce and Remarriage in the Bible: The Social and Literary Context* (Grand Rapids, MI: Eerdmans, 2002), 1–19, for an excellent summary of the research on the contents and nature of the ancient Near Eastern marriage covenant. See also the exhaustive analysis of Hugenberger, 168–213, for decisive refutation of those who claim that marriage in Scripture and the ancient Near East should not be regarded as a covenant. See also Sohn, 355–372.

[27] See Davidson, *Flame of Yahweh*, 180, for a sample of ancient Near Eastern texts and discussion. For example, Middle Assyrian Law (MAL) §41, translated by Theophile J. Meek, *Ancient Near Eastern Texts Relating to the Old Testament*, ed. James B. Pritchard, 3rd ed. (Princeton, NJ: Princeton University Press, 1969), 183, states (with regard to a man's full marriage to his concubine), "If a seignior wishes to veil his concubine, he shall have five (or) six of his neighbors present (and) veil her in their presence (and) say, 'She is my wife,' (and so) she becomes his wife. A concubine who was not veiled in the presence of the men, whose husband did not say, 'She is my wife,' is not a wife; she is still a concubine." Again, in the "The Laws of Eshnunna," trans. Martha Roth, §§27–28, in William W. Hallo, and K. Lawson Younger, *Context of Scripture* (Leiden: Brill, 2000), 2.130:333–334, there is reference to the need for contract and wedding service ("nuptial feast") before a woman becomes a man's wife. So, Law §27 states: "If a man married the daughter of another man without the consent of her father and mother, and moreover does not conclude the nuptial feast and the contract for (?) her father and mother, should she reside in his house for even one full year, she is not a wife." The next law, Hallo and Younger, 2.131:344, §28, continues, "If he concludes the contract and the nuptial feast for (?) her father and mother and he marries her, she is indeed a wife." A final example comes from "The Laws of Hammurabi," §128, in Hallo and Younger, 2.131:344: "If a man marries a wife but does not establish a contract for her, that woman is not a wife."

as the equivalent of a covenant oath and, by themselves, constituted the *verba solemnia* of the wedding.[28]

We have noted how Adam's statement in Genesis 2:23 probably served as *verba solemnia*—indeed, a covenant oath before God in the Edenic wedding of the first human couple. Other Old Testament passages may contain or allude to *verba solemnia* or the covenant oath of the wedding ceremony (see esp. Hos 2:2 [MT Hos 2:4]; Hos 2:15–17 [MT Hos 2:17–19]; Prov 7:4–5; Song 2:16; 6:3; 7:10 [MT Song 7:11]).[29]

Based upon ancient Near Eastern background material in general, and in particular upon the biblical descriptions of weddings and the parabolic description of Israel/Judah's marriage to Yahweh in Ezekiel 16:8–13, Daniel Block infers the following series of elements in a typical wedding of Old Testament times:[30] 1) the groom covers the bride with his garment, symbolizing his intent to protect and provide for her in the new relationship (cf. Ruth 3:9); 2) the groom (and likely also the bride) swears an oath of fidelity, probably raising the right hand, thus invoking the deity as witness and guarantor of the marriage covenant; 3) the groom (and likely also the bride) enters into the marriage covenant with *verba solemnia*; 4) the groom bathes the bride and anoints her with oil, expressing his love and devotion to her; 5) the groom dresses the bride in the finest clothing and ornaments he can afford (cf. Ps 45; Isa 61:10); and 6) a sumptuous feast provided by the groom ensues at the groom's house (cf. Gen 29:22; Judg 14:10).

During the feast, which could last an entire week (Gen 29:27; Judg 14:12) or even two weeks,[31] there was elaborate celebration with singing and dancing, praises of the bride and groom, and a spirit of great joy (Ps 78:63; Isa 5:1; Ezek 33:32; Song 4–7; cf. Matt 9:15; Mark 2:19; Luke 5:34). The husband also seems to have worn a crown on the wedding day (Song 3:11).

The bride remained veiled until she and the groom were alone in the bridal chamber (*ḥeder*) during the first night of the feast, the night

---

[28] See Hugenberger, 168–239, for discussion and ancient Near Eastern/biblical evidence of *verba solemnia* and/or a covenant oath that solemnized the marriage. Ibid., 187–188, provides several possible ancient Near Eastern examples of "a mutual oath by which both bride and groom are bound to the terms of the contract" (187). On the other hand, Hugenberger notes that the presence of an oath in the written form of the marriage contract is not to be expected, since the written version of the contract usually states those extraordinary stipulations not normally assumed in the oral contract. "Hence," Hugenberger concludes, "the lack of an explicit stipulation of a ratifying oath in marriage need occasion no surprise" (ibid., 191).

[29] Ibid., 231–239.

[30] Daniel I. Block, "Marriage and Family in Ancient Israel," in *Marriage and Family in the Biblical World*, ed. Ken M. Campbell (Downers Grove, IL: InterVarsity, 2003), 44–45.

[31] *Tobit* 8:20–9:2; 10:7.

of the wedding, when on the canopied bridal bed they experienced sexual union (Gen 29:23; Song 3:4; 4:16; 5:1).[32] The evidence that the bride was a virgin was the sheet stained with virginal bleeding produced by the first sexual intercourse of the couple, and this was apparently kept by the bride's parents in case their daughter's virginity at the time of marriage should ever be questioned (Deut 22:13–21).

From the preceding discussion we may conclude that in Scripture, as well as in the ancient Near East, the covenant-making ceremony, not the sexual act, is the foundation of the marriage.

Sexual Intercourse and Marriage

The sexual union, by itself, apart from the formal/public covenant-making ceremony, does not make a marriage. In fact, as becomes evident in the next section, sexual intercourse outside the boundary of the marriage covenant is considered illegitimate and a distortion of the divine plan for marriage.

Patriarchal Marriages

Some interpreters point to specific Genesis narratives involving marriages in the time of the patriarchs and matriarchs (Isaac and Rebekah, Jacob and Rachel/Leah, Jacob and Bilhah/Zilpah), and suggest that it was the sexual union that constituted these marriages.

A mere surface reading of how Rebekah became Isaac's wife may lead to this conclusion. The text states, "Then Isaac brought her into his mother's tent; and he took Rebekah and she became his wife, and he loved her" (Gen 24:67). However, the lack of reference to an elaborate public wedding service according to our modern standards does not mean that there was no formal/public covenant-making that preceded the sexual union. The text bristles with indicators of the public/formal covenantal nature of this marriage. There was the formal "leaving" of Rebekah from her parents prompted by her family members: "Will you go with this man?" (Gen 24:58). When Rebekah neared Abraham's encampment and saw Isaac in the distance, "she took a veil and covered herself" (Gen 24:65), no doubt having important symbolic significance in her culture. Isaac's act of bringing Rebekah to a specific place, his mother's tent (the equivalent of the wedding "canopy") was part of the wedding ceremony (Gen 24:67). The narrator's reference that Isaac "took" (*lāqaḥ*) Rebekah (Gen 24:67) utilizes the Old Testament technical term for marriage.[33] We need not expect all the formal aspects of a

---

[32] For ancient Near Eastern and biblical evidence for the bridal chamber, see Steven C. Horine, *Interpretive Images in the Songs of Songs: From Wedding Chariots to Bridal Chambers*, Studies in the Humanities 55 (New York: Peter Lang, 2001), 73–121.

[33] See, e.g., Genesis 4:19; 12:19; 24:4; 25:1; 34:16.

typical later Israelite (or modern) wedding in order to recognize the public covenant-making context of the marriage, in which context the sexual act indeed takes place after the marriage has already been formalized by a formal, public covenant.

In the case of Jacob, his marriage in Syria clearly takes place in the context of an elaborate (week-long) wedding feast: "So Laban gathered together all the people of the place, and made a feast" (Gen 29:22). Part of the marriage ceremony involved the father of the bride bringing the veiled bride into the bridal chamber, where the newly married couple experienced sexual union (Gen 29:23). Some claim this narrative supports the conclusion that sexual union constitutes the marriage, because although Jacob had been formally wed to Rachel, he became Leah's husband because he (unwittingly) slept with her instead of Rachel, due to Laban's trickery (Gen 29:25). But the narrator explicitly gives the reason why Laban insisted that Leah be Jacob's wife before Rachel: "It must not be done so in our country, to give the younger before the firstborn" (Gen 29:26). This was a local custom, enforced by a scheming father, not the divine plan. The "rest of the story" in later chapters of Genesis makes clear that eventually God's plan is put in place: after his Jabbok conversion while wrestling with the Angel, Jacob renounces his polygamy and only has sexual relations with his original, legitimate "wife by covenant" (Mal 2:14)—Rachel.[34]

Some regard Jacob's marriage to his concubines as other examples where sexual union per se constitutes marriage. But it must be recognized, first and foremost, that from God's perspective these "marriages" were not legitimate ones. Furthermore, even in regard to these unions, there was a formal ceremony involved in the giving of the maids of Jacob's wives to be his concubines. For example, Genesis 30:3–4 describes Rachel's giving of her maid Bilhah to Jacob as a (secondary) wife: "So she said, 'Here is my maid Bilhah; go in to her, and she will *bear* a child on my knees, that I also may have children by her.' Then she gave [Heb. *nātan*] him Bilhah her maid as wife, and Jacob went in to her." The text gives explicit indicators of the then-accepted legal procedures for an infertile wife providing a

---

[34] For discussion of the biblical evidence in favor of the conclusion that Jacob returned to a monogamous relationship after his conversion at the Jabbok, and that the woman whom he (and the narrator) considered his one legitimate wife was Rachel, not Leah, see Davidson, *Flame of Yahweh*, 186–189. Note especially that before the encounter at the Jabbok, the narrative repeatedly mentions Jacob's sexual relationship with all four wives/concubines, but after this event, the only conjugal relations mentioned are with his wife Rachel (Gen 35:16–19). Whereas before Jacob's name (character) change at the Jabbok he had called both Rachel and Leah "my wives" (Gen 30:26; cf. 31:50), after the Jabbok experience, he called only Rachel "my wife" (Gen 44:27). Most telling of all, in the genealogy of Genesis 46, the narrator mentions Leah, Zilpah, and Bilhah as women who "bore to Jacob" children, but only Rachel is classified as "Jacob's wife" (Gen 46:15, 18–19, 25).

proxy (secondary) wife to her husband in order to raise up posterity for her, and furthermore, the narrator separates the prior action of Rachel legally "giving" Bilhah to Jacob as a (secondary) wife from the subsequent sexual union. Leah's action in "giving" her maid Zilpah to Jacob follows the same basic sequence (Gen 30:9–10). Even though these narratives are not related to reveal God's will for marriage (polygamy and concubinage was never condoned by God in Scripture),[35] even in these cases beyond the shadows of the divine plan for marriage, sexual intercourse per se does not constitute marriage.

The description of the marriage of Judah to Shua is perhaps the clearest biblical passage describing patriarchal marriages that indicates that the sexual union following the wedding is not part of what constitutes marriage, and thus a delay or failure to experience sexual union does not nullify the marriage. Genesis 38:2 states, "And Judah saw there a daughter of a certain Canaanite whose name *was* Shua, and he married [*lāqaḥ*] her and went in to her [i.e., had sex with her]." The act of marriage is clearly separated from the sexual union that follows.

Pentateuchal Legislation

Exodus 22:16–17 [MT Exod 22:15–16]; Deuteronomy 22:28–29. Exodus 22:16–17 (MT Exod 22:15–16) provides basic case law regarding the seduction of a single (unbetrothed) woman: "And if a man entices [*pātâ*] a virgin [*bĕtûlâ*] who is not betrothed, and lies with her, he shall surely pay the bride-money [*mōhar*] for her to be his wife. If her father utterly refuses to give her to him, he shall pay money according to the bride-money [*mōhar*] of virgins." Deuteronomy 22:28–29 is probably an extension and expansion of the same law:

> If a man finds a young woman who is a virgin [*bĕtûlâ*], who is not betrothed, and he seizes her [Heb. *tāpaś*] and lies with her, and they are found out, then the man who lay with her shall give to the young woman's father fifty shekels of silver, and she shall be his wife because he has humbled [*'ānâ*, *piel*] her; he shall not be permitted to divorce [*šālaḥ*] her all his days.

The law of Deuteronomy 22:28–29 does not consider the case of a ravisher who is already married, but the comparative evidence of the fuller treatment of punishment for ravishers found in Middle Assyrian

[35] For evidence that throughout Scripture God never condones polygamy or concubinage, see Davidson, *Flame of Yahweh*, 178–212; and Ronald A. G. du Preez, *Polygamy in the Bible* (Berrien Springs, MI: Adventist Theological Society, 1993).

Laws (from about the same time in world history) provides an exception clause[36] for the ravisher who is already married.

The law in Exodus 22:16–17 is most likely a situation of verbal persuasion or enticement (the meaning of *pātâ*), but commentators differ on whether Deuteronomy 22:28–29 describes a case of forcible rape or seduction (statutory rape).[37] This latter passage indicates that the man "seizes" (*tāpaś*) and "humbles" (*ʿānâ, piel*) the woman. The verb *tāpaś* usually implies taking hold of with force, and the verb *ʿānâ* (*piel*, "humble," or better, "mishandle, afflict, violate") is used several times elsewhere in the Old Testament to describe clear cases of forcible rape.[38] However, this passage in Deuteronomy 22 also seems to indicate that the woman had acquiesced and was a willing partner in the sexual encounter, when it notes that "they [not just he] are discovered [*wĕnimṣāʾû*—that is, caught in the act]" (Deut 22:28).

Both of these laws are probably speaking of a similar (but perhaps not identical) situation of sexual seduction (statutory rape) of a virgin (*bĕtûlâ*) who is not betrothed (*ʾāraś, pual* pf.), the former involving or emphasizing more the psychological pressure (he "seduces" *pātâ* her) and the latter the physical pressure (he "catches, takes, seizes" *tāpaś* her).[39] The two laws are complementary (the Deuteronomy passage an extension of the Exodus law) and together they give the whole picture of circumstances and legal consequences.[40] The woman in view in these case laws has never been[41] married or betrothed: the seduction involves premarital sexual intercourse. And such activity constitutes an illicit sexual encounter.

---

[36] MAL A §55 (Hallo and Younger, 2.132:359; and Meek, 185).

[37] So, e.g., Gerhard von Rad, *Deuteronomy: A Commentary*, trans. Dorothea Barton, Old Testament Library (Philadelphia, PA: Westminster, 1966), 143, labels it "rape"; in contrast, J. A. Thompson, *Deuteronomy,* Tyndale Old Testament Commentaries 5 (Downers Grove, IL: InterVarsity, 1974), 236, calls it "seduction."

[38] See Genesis 34:2 (Shechem's rape of Dinah); Judges 19:24; 20:5 (the men of Gibeah's rape of the Levite's concubine); 2 Samuel 13:12, 14, 22, 32 (Amnon's rape of Tamar).

[39] That these two laws are variants of the same case is recognized by a number of scholars. See, e.g., Carolyn Pressler, *The View of Women Found in the Deuteronomic Family Laws* (Berlin: Walter de Gruyter, 1993), 35–41; and J. Ridderbos, *Deuteronomy,* trans. Ed M. van der Maas (Grand Rapids, MI: Zondervan, 1984), 227.

[40] Raymond Westbrook, *Studies in Biblical and Cuneiform Law* (Paris: J. Gabalda, 1988), 6, clearly articulates this principle in dealing with biblical law: "It is therefore by combining the partial discussion in each of the separate codes that we are able to reconstruct the complete original problem, and we are entitled to assume prima facie that all the rules of the reconstructed problem applied in each of the systems that have contributed to it."

[41] Anthony Phillips, "Another Look at Adultery," *Journal for the Study of the Old Testament* 20 (1981): 12, points out how the use of the passive perfect rather than the passive participle in Exodus 22:16 and Deuteronomy 2:28 makes plain that the girl is one who *has never been* betrothed, not just (as the RSV renders it) one who is not (at present) betrothed.

The penalty for such distortion of the divine design for sexuality is not death or *kārēt* (being "cut off"), since there has been no breach in a relationship such as in adultery. Nonetheless the legislation makes clear the seriousness of the offense.[42] Tikva Frymer-Kensky summarizes the man's responsibility: "A man cannot just 'love her and leave her' by sleeping with her, he has assumed the obligation to marry her. And he must pay a normal bride-price: he cannot obtain a girl cheaply by first sleeping with her, thus dishonoring her, and lowering her bride-price."[43] Deuteronomy 22:29 tells us the amount of the bride-wealth—fifty shekels of silver—and adds that the man "shall not be permitted to divorce her all his days." The limitation of the man's right to divorce, as in the law of Deuteronomy 22:13–19, serves to protect the woman and provide for her social and financial security. At the same time, such a penalty—the high bride-wealth price and the knowledge that no matter how miserable one might try to make the other, they could not divorce—would certainly cause both unmarried men and women to give serious pause before engaging in premarital sex.

The crucial point in this passage for our concerns in this chapter is that sexual intercourse between the unmarried man and woman did not automatically constitute marriage. The penalty imposed was that the man would have to marry the woman—thus indicating that they were not yet considered married even after the sexual intercourse.

Exodus 22:17 strengthens this conclusion as it adds the provision that the father of the violated girl was not required to consent to his daughter getting married to her seducer, apparently in the case where he was already married to another woman (as in the ancient Near Eastern parallel containing an exception clause for the married ravisher, previously cited). Presumably this also applied to other situations where the father did not deem such a marriage wise. It should not be assumed that a girl who had been seduced and lost her virginity would not be able to marry—there is no hint of this in Scripture—but her father would not normally be able to command the full bride-wealth price. In the case described here, however, the father was still entitled to the full

---

[42] Cf. the similar treatment in other ancient Near Eastern law codes: CH ɘ130 (Hallo and Younger, 2.131:344; and Meek, 171) and MAL A §§55–56 (Hallo and Younger, 2.132:359B–360; and Meek, 185). MAL A §55, however, adds a talionic element in which "the father of the virgin shall take the wife of the virgin's ravisher and give her to be ravished." In the biblical view it seems that both the sanctity of marriage and the rights of the innocent wife preclude prescribing a *lex talionis* of equivalent ravishing.

[43] Tikva Frymer-Kensky, "Virginity in the Bible," in *Gender and Law in the Hebrew Bible and the Ancient Near East*, ed. Victor H. Matthews, Bernard M. Levinson, and Tikva Frymer-Kensky, Journal for the Study of the Old Testament Supplement Series 262 (Sheffield: Sheffield Academic Press, 1998), 91.

bride-price, which would ultimately belong to the daughter.[44] Thus the daughter was further protected from the sexual advances of a man who would try to seduce her so that she would be forced to marry him. By the same token, the law also preserved an unmarried daughter from her own immaturity by preventing her from circumventing her father's protective jurisdiction and impulsively choosing her own husband by having sex with him.

What is of particular importance about this case law for the subject at hand in this chapter is the provision that the father was not required to have his daughter marry the one who seduced her. This provision provides further evidence within Scripture for the conclusion that sexual intercourse per se does not constitute a marriage. In harmony with the divine plan set forth in Eden, the "cleaving" (or marriage covenant) was to come before the "becoming one flesh" (sexual intercourse). Even if there is sexual intercourse before the formalizing of the marriage covenant, this does not mean that the sexual partners are married. Those who have engaged in sexual intercourse before marriage are not by this act alone considered to be married.

Deuteronomy 21:10–14. This passage states, regarding a soldier who sees a beautiful woman among the war captives, "You may go in to her and be her husband, and she shall be your wife." Some have considered the legislation concerning marrying female war prisoners as evidence that sexual intercourse constitutes marriage. But a closer look at this passage in its immediate context points toward just the opposite conclusion. The straightforward reading of the Hebrew of Deuteronomy 21:10–11 indicates that the soldier has already taken the woman as his wife before the sexual union: "When you go to war against your enemies and Yahweh your God delivers them into your power and you take prisoners, and among the prisoners you see a beautiful woman, and you fall in love with her [*qāšaḥ* + *bĕ*], and you take [*lāqaḥ*] her to be your wife [*lĕʾiššâ*] and bring her home. . ." (Deut 21:10–12a, NJB). The following verses instruct that in such a situation, the man who has taken a female war captive as wife shall allow her to "spend a month's time in your house lamenting her father and mother; after that you may come to her and possess her [Heb. verb *bāʿal* + 3fs suffix; that is, experience sexual union]" (Deut 21:14, NJPS). Contrary to the reading of many modern versions, the Hebrew does not speak of a man only desiring to take a wife (but not actually taking her) in Deuteronomy 21:11. Rather, the Hebrew word *qāšaḥ* and the preposition *bĕ* indicate that the man has not just

---

[44] Because the deflowering of the virgin daughter resulted in loss of her value due to loss of virginity, which had to be compensated to her father by the seducer, this law is situated at the end of a series of laws in Exodus 22 dealing with property damage. This is not to say, however, that the daughter is considered as mere chattel, the property of her father.

desired, but has fallen in love with the slave woman,[45] and furthermore, the Hebrew word *lāqaḥ* in this verse indicates that the man not just "*wants* to take" but *has already* "taken" (that is, legally married) the woman to be his wife. As recognized by many commentators and modern versions, Deuteronomy 21:11–12a describes conditions (the protasis) that have already taken place, including the fact that the man already took her as his wife, even before the instructions (apodosis) described in Deuteronomy 21:12b–14, which include the sexual union. The force of this grammatical structure is grasped by the LXX translation, and recognized by several modern versions and noted commentators on the passage.[46] Far from supporting the thesis that sexual union constitutes marriage, this verse reveals that marriage has already occurred at the time when the man legally "takes" his wife, even if the sexual union is delayed (in this case by a whole month, Deut 21:13).

The "Marriages" in Ezra 9–10 and Nehemiah 13. The last two chapters of Ezra describe a state of affairs in which Ezra (upon returning from exile in the summer of 457 BC) confronts a number of leading Jews who had "married" pagan (Heb. *nokrî*, "foreign, alien") women.[47] This is probably the same kind of situation that was addressed by Nehemiah (see Neh 13:23–30). These unions were likely not regular legal marriages, but a kind of "live-in arrangement" or "cohabitation which may eventuate in formal marriage."[48] If such were the situation, these cases might be seen as a kind of "marriage" established by sexual intercourse during cohabitation and not by a covenant-making ceremony. This suggestion is supported by the fact that the specific terminology for both "marrying" and "divorce" in these Ezra passages is different than in any other passage in the Old Testament. Though Ezra knows and uses the ordinary Hebrew *lāqaḥ* ("to take") for marriage elsewhere in the book (Ezra 2:61), in the case of the "marriage" to the foreign women he uses other terms for marriage: *nāśā'* ("to take up," Ezra 9:2, 12; 10:44) and *yāšab* ("to give a dwelling to," Ezra 10:2, 10, 14, 17–18).[49] The latter term in

---

[45] See Ludwig Koehler, Walter Baumgartner, and Johann J. Stamm, *The Hebrew and Aramaic Lexicon of the Old Testament*, 4 vols. (Leiden: Brill, 1994–1999), s.v. חשק, which points out that this verb followed by the preposition *bĕ* does not just mean "desire," but rather "be very attached to, to love somebody."

[46] See, e.g., NIV, TNIV, NJB. Cf. the discussion by J. C. McConville, *Deuteronomy*, Abingdon Old Testament Commentaries 5 (Downers Grove, IL: InterVarsity, 2002), 329; and P. C. Craige, *The Book of Deuteronomy*, New International Commentary on the Old Testament (Grand Rapids, MI: Eerdmans, 1976), 281.

[47] For more complete discussion of these passages, see Davidson, *Flame of Yahweh*, 320–323.

[48] Allen Guenther, "A Typology of Israelite Marriage: Kinship, Socio-Economic, and Religious Factors," *Journal for the Study of the Old Testament* 29 (2005): 402, 405.

[49] The word *nāśā'* for marriage is used elsewhere in the Old Testament always to refer to

particular seems to imply some kind of cohabitation without a regular formal marriage.[50]

Also with regard to the words for divorce in these passages, both *yāṣ'ā* (*hiphil*, "to cause to go out, put away") and *bādal* (*niphal*, "to separate oneself") are used nowhere else in the biblical canon for divorce. It is possible that a different terminology was in vogue at that time, but this possibility seems weakened by the use of the appropriate technical terminology for divorce by the contemporary prophet Malachi. It seems more likely that these marriages were not considered legitimate, valid marriages. Ezra, the "scribe skilled in the law of God" (Ezra 7:6) who certainly knew the technical terminology for divorce, deliberately utilizes terminology that was out of the ordinary for both the "marrying" (*nāśā'* and *yāšab*) and the "putting away" of the wives. The "putting away" of the wives was not an actual divorce procedure, but the dissolution of invalid marriages.[51]

The swift and severe reactions of Ezra and Nehemiah against these sexual unions probably stem not only from the fact that these "marriages" were constituted by sexual intercourse without any formal marriage covenant, but also because they entailed divorce from previous wives without due cause and (especially) because they involved uniting with women who were practicing idolaters (in blatant disregard of Deuteronomy 7:1–5).[52] In any case, the one possible example in the Old Testament of sexual intercourse per se constituting marriage is rejected as contrary to God's will.

Sexual Intercourse and Betrothal (Engagement)

As shown so far, the Old Testament reserves sexual activity for marriage and marriage is not constituted by having sex. This applies also to those who are betrothed (engaged). In the ancient Near East, an

---

marriages with foreigners, multiple wives, and/or concubines (Ruth 1:4; 2 Chr 11:31; 13:21; 24:3; Neh 13:25), while *yāšab* appears with reference to marriage only here in Ezra and in Nehemiah 13:24, 27, again always with reference to foreign wives.

[50] For further discussion of cohabitation in Scripture and a critique of this practice from a biblical perspective, see Richard M. Davidson, "Does Marriage Still Matter? An Evaluation of Cohabitation in Light of Biblical Foundations," *Reflections* 27 (July 2009): 1–5.

[51] For additional supporting arguments for this conclusion, see esp. William A. Heth and Gordon J. Wenham, *Jesus and Divorce: The Problem With the Evangelical Consensus* (Nashville, TN: Thomas Nelson, 1985), 163–164. Because these were not viewed as valid marriages, it was not a matter of choosing between "the lesser of two evils," as often claimed.

[52] See the evidence summarized by Hyam Maccoby, "Holiness and Purity: The Holy People in Leviticus and Ezra-Nehemiah," in *Reading Leviticus: A Conversation With Mary Douglas*, ed. John F. A. Sawyer, Journal for the Study of the Old Testament Supplement Series 227 (Sheffield: Sheffield Academic Press, 1996), 153–170.

engaged young woman was already considered in some sense a wife.[53] According to Deuteronomy 22:23–24 the fiancée is a virgin and is called the "neighbor's/another man's/fellow wife."[54] Also, engagement was more binding in Israel and in Judaism than it is in Western societies today.[55] It meant to pledge oneself to be married to the partner to whom one was betrothed. It also meant accepting and exercising premarital faithfulness.[56] Engagement was connected to the payment of the bride price (1 Sam 18:23–25; 2 Sam 3:14). Although an engaged woman had a legal status similar to that of a wife, intimate relations between the couple were not to take place before the wedding. Genesis 19:8 records that Lot's daughters were virgins. However, the men to whom they were engaged were considered Lot's sons-in-law (Gen 19:14).[57] According to Genesis

---

[53] Walter A. Elwell and Barry J. Beitzel, "Marriage, Marriage Customs," in *Baker Encyclopedia of the Bible*, ed. Walter A. Elwell, vol. 2 (Grand Rapids, MI: Baker, 1988), 1408, write, "The betrothal had the legal status of a marriage (Dt 28:30; 2 Sm 3:14), and anyone violating a betrothed virgin would be stoned according to the law of Deuteronomy for violating his neighbor's 'wife' (Dt 22:23, 24). . . . Nevertheless, there remained a distinction between betrothing a woman and taking her to wife (Dt 20:7)." See also J. G. S. S. Thomson, "Marriage," in *New Bible Dictionary*, ed. D. R. W. Wood et al. (Downers Grove, IL: InterVarsity, 1996), 733–734.

[54] This is, e.g., reflected in ESV, KJV, NAB, NASB, NIV, NJB, NKJV, NRSV, and RSV.

[55] Avi Shveka and Avraham Faust, "Premarital Sex in Biblical Law: A Cross-Cultural Perspective," *Vetus Testamentum* 70, no. 2 (2020): 316–339, claim that in patrilocal and patrilineal cultures stern handling of premarital sex is usual. This applied also to ancient Israel. See also George B. Eager, "Marriage," in *The International Standard Bible Encyclopaedia*, ed. James Orr et al. (Chicago, IL: Howard-Severance, 1915), 1997–1998.

[56] Marten Stol, *Women in the Ancient Near East* (Berlin: Walter de Gruyter, 2016), 14, states, "While it is absolutely clear that in the Ancient Near East great value was attached to virginity in itself, we never find this expressed explicitly. . . . In a Babylonian collection of explanations of dreams we find evidence that a girl is expected to be a virgin when she marries." On page 16 he notes, "An exhaustive study by J. S. Cooper has concluded that Sumerian and Akkadian had no specific word to indicate a virgin. What happened in practice was that every girl was supposed to be a virgin before her marriage. . . . While seeking to answer the question of why a woman should enter into marriage as a virgin Cooper suggests that there may be two logical motives for such behaviour in a patriarchal society. One would be to prevent young people looking for a partner and experimenting together. The other would be that enforced chastity is good practice for chaste behaviour later in marriage. This in turn ensures that a husband can be sure that the children his wife bears are his own." "A Sumerian lawsuit gave a man the right to divorce after his wife had explained that a stranger had slept with her without anyone knowing of it. An alternating duet between Inanna ('my sister) and her lover Dumuzi ('my brother') begins and ends with exuberant praise for the physical excellence of each partner. . . . In the middle of the song Inanna insists, 'Brother, swear to me that you have never laid a hand on a strange woman.' . . . Virginity was a matter of importance also in the Middle Assyrian period" (ibid., 105).

[57] Some translations render the section of Genesis 19:14, which deals with Lot's sons-in-laws, with a future tense—namely, as those who were to marry Lot's daughters (ESV, NASB, NET, NIV, NJB, NRV, RSV)—while others use a past tense or a pluperfect indicating that they had already married the young women (KJV, NKJV). The Hebrew verb allows for both options, but the context of Genesis 19:8, which calls Lot's daughters "virgins," suggests the first option. They

29:21, Jacob served seven years for Rachel. Then he asked Laban for his wife to go in to her. Again, we notice that intimate relations were reserved for a time after the wedding ceremony.[58]

Summary

The Old Testament evidence regarding the relationship between sexual intercourse and marriage supports the following points: 1) Sexual union per se does not constitute marriage. 2) Marriage is covenantal in nature. 3) The marriage covenant is made between the husband and wife and not outside parties, with Yahweh as the divine witness of the marriage vows. 4) The marriage covenant is public in nature, not just a private agreement between two parties. 5) The marriage covenant involves a formal/legal ceremony with human witnesses, to the extent possible.[59] 6) It is the public covenant-making, not the sexual union, that provides the legal foundation for the marriage. 7) The sexual union follows a marriage that has already been constituted by the marriage covenant. 8) Even if the sexual union is delayed for a period of time or even indefinitely after the covenant ceremony, the marriage has already been constituted by the public covenant ceremony. 9) Sexual relations between an unmarried couple, even protracted in ongoing cohabitation, do not constitute marriage and are not approved by God. 10) According to the divine plan, the "one-flesh" sexual union follows the "cleaving" of the marriage covenant; sexual intercourse is not to occur before or during betrothal (engagement), but only *within* the context of the marriage covenant. That said, we turn to the New Testament to complete the biblical picture.

Marriage and Sexuality in the New Testament

The Situation in New Testament Times

While in Old Testament times cultures surrounding Israel had in some respects similar norms—especially regarding marrying a virgin—this was, to some extent, different in Greco-Roman times. While men would generally still appreciate marrying a woman who did not have premarital relations with another man, there was a double standard, as men could get involved in different forms of premarital sex. David Instone-Brewer observes, "Somehow Romans didn't recognize the absurdity of expecting

---

were already considered sons-in-laws but had not yet married. See Elwell and Beitzel, 1048; and Victor P. Hamilton, *The Book of Genesis, Chapters 18–50*, New International Commentary on the Old Testament (Grand Rapids, MI: Eerdmans, 1995), 35, 40.

[58] For detailed study of biblical legislation dealing with premarital/pre-betrothal sexual intercourse, see Davidson, *Flame of Yahweh*, 354–363.

[59] See note 1 in the present chapter.

first-time brides to be virgins while grooms were expected to gain premarital 'experience.' Of course, this double standard often still exists today."[60] He also declares,

> Paul didn't have to remind his converts that the Old Testament forbade sleeping with a girlfriend or fiancée. The law demanded 'proof' that she was *virgo intacta* on her wedding night in the form of a bloody cloth. Lack of proof resulted in her death . . . Paul didn't need to remind his readers of this because even Romans knew that women had to come to marriage as virgins.[61]

But given the general attitude toward sexuality in the Greco-Roman culture, insisting on premarital chastity was counter-cultural. Therefore, Steven Tracy suggests, "Due to the sexually permissive Greco-Roman culture, the NT gives much more specific attention to premarital sex."[62] In other words, there is a difference between living in a culture that has clearly defined rules and prohibitions on certain types of sexual behavior and living in a very permissive culture. The issue is that cultures affect believers—whether they want them to or not—and it is much more difficult to stick to biblical rules in cultures that disregard and reject them. This was the situation for some believers in the first century AD, just as it is for believers in many secular and even non-secular cultures today. The value system prevalent in certain cultures may be strongly opposed to the biblical value system, and vice versa. This creates tensions for the individual who lives "in the world" and is supposed "to be not of the world" (John 17:11, 14). "It is very difficult to withstand sexual temptation at an age when your body is screaming for fulfillment and everyone around you is 'doing it.'"[63] Yet, true believers followed God-given, biblical instructions in the past and do so also today.

The New Testament's Relation to the Old Testament

Here we pause and think about the relation between the Old and New Testaments, especially in the context of human sexuality and marriage. The question is: do sexual ethics change in the New Testament and become more liberal, are they maintained as they had been, or do they become more definite?

---

[60] David Instone-Brewer, *Moral Questions of the Bible: Timeless Truth in a Changing World, Scripture in Context* (Bellingham, WA: Lexham Press, 2019), 94.

[61] Ibid., 94.

[62] Steven Tracy, "Chastity and the Goodness of God: The Case for Premarital Sexual Abstinence," *Themelios* 31, no. 2 (2006): 59.

[63] Instone-Brewer, 95.

The Old Testament was the Bible of the earliest Christian communities, typically in the form of the Septuagint (LXX). Looking at the speeches of the apostles and other Christian leaders in the book of Acts, it is evident that they argued their case and preached their messages on the basis of the Old Testament, often using allusions to or quotations from the Old Testament. This is clearly the case with longer speeches—for instance, of Peter, Paul, and Stephen—which are found in the book of Acts.[64] After Peter and John's release from their arrest by the Jewish authorities, the entire early church in Jerusalem recited Psalm 2:1–2 (see Acts 4:25–26). When the New Testament began coming into existence, its writings were considered Scripture. In 2 Peter 3:15–16 Paul's works are included with the Scriptures of the Old Testament.[65] Since then Christianity at large has accepted the Old and New Testaments as its Bible.[66]

There is recognition that a basic continuity exists between the two Testaments, but there is also acknowledgment that the New Testament draws out implications and not fully developed principles found in the Old Testament and that some changes were happening in the New Testament due to the coming of the Messiah. Two of the reasons for these occurring changes were 1) that the people of God were no longer a nation and partially a theocracy and 2) that the sacrificial system of the Old Testament was fulfilled with the death of Jesus and became redundant. However, these changes do not affect the way humans are saved, nor do they affect God's moral commandments in the sense that they would become optional or superfluous.

Allusions to and quotations from the Old Testament in the New Testament, Old Testament messianic prophecy and typology fulfilled in the New Testament, important theological themes and teachings shared by both Testaments, the trajectory of the divine plan of salvation from the first pages of Genesis to the last pages of Revelation, and the structure of the Bible from Eden lost to Eden regained point to the close relationship of the New Testament to the Old Testament and the necessity

[64] See, e.g., Old Testament quotations 1) in Peter's speech of Acts 2:14–36 (Ps 16:8–11; 132:11; 110:1; Joel 2:28–32), 2) in Stephen's speech of Acts 7:2–53 (Gen 12:1, 7; 15:13–14; Exod 1:8; 2:14, 15; 3:1–2, 5–8; 32:1, 23; Deut 18:15; Amos 5:26–27; Isa 66:1–2), and 3) in Paul's speech of Acts 13:16–41 (1 Sam 13:14; Pss 2:7; 16:10; 89:20; Isa 55:3; Hab 1:5).

[65] See, e.g., Peter H. Davids, *The Letters of 2 Peter and Jude*, The Pillar New Testament Commentary (Grand Rapids, MI: Eerdmans, 2006), 307; and Richard J. Bauckham, *2 Peter, Jude,* Word Biblical Commentary (Dallas, TX: Word, 1983), 333.

[66] Scholars have debated the relation between the two Testaments, sometimes in radical ways, more or less discarding the Old Testament or the New Testament. See Richard M. Davidson, "Inner-Biblical Hermeneutics: The Use of Scripture by Bible Writers," in *Biblical Hermeneutics: An Adventist Approach*, ed. Frank Hasel, Biblical Research Institute Studies in Hermeneutics 3 (Silver Spring, MD: Biblical Research Institute, 2020), 233–234. But this debate does not need to concern us here.

for the Old Testament to be followed by the New Testament. One would be incomplete without the other.[67]

A study of theological themes appearing in both the Old and New Testaments reveals that, among others, the following are weighty: 1) the teachings about the Godhead, especially God's lovingkindness and holiness; 2) the sanctuary; 3) creation; 4) anthropology (human nature); 5) the problem of sin; 6) the great controversy; 7) salvation by God's grace; 8) the covenant; 9) the law, especially the Ten Commandment and the summary of the Decalogue in the two commandments to love God supremely and the neighbor as oneself; 10) ecclesiology (God's people and the remnant); 11) a lifestyle in accordance with God's nature, His will, and Jesus' example (biblical ethics), which means that believers need to uphold orthodoxy (in the positive sense) and orthopraxy; and 12) eschatology. Thus, the two Testaments are intrinsically connected and interrelated.

Marriage and Sexuality in the Old Testament and New Testament

It is very clear that the New Testament follows the Old also in regard to marriage and sexuality. The divine privileges and caveats provided by the Old Testament are still in place in the New. This is no wonder because God created humanity, a man and a woman. He created sexuality, or more precisely, He created humans as sexual beings—male and female—with responsibility for each other and for the rest of creation. Furthermore, as previously noted, He instituted marriage in the Garden of Eden on the same day Adam and Eve were created. Marriage is an institution for all of humanity and a divine gift. In addition, Adam's and Eve's marriage covenant in Eden, in which one male and one female became one in a permanent marriage relationship and in which they would be able to have children, is paradigmatic for all following generations.

However, this model was not always upheld by humanity after the fall. Already the book of Genesis reports, for instance, cases of mixed marriages (Gen 6:1–4), polygamy and surrogate motherhood (Gen 16:1–4; 29:21–35), incest (Gen 19:30–37; 49:3–4), rape (Gen 34:1–2), adultery, and incest (Gen 38:12–26; 35:22), and attempted seduction followed by false allegations (Gen 39:7–18). All these forms of sexual immorality and others are rampant today worldwide.

When at Mount Sinai God gave the Ten Commandments in written form, He addressed the issue of sexuality directly in the seventh and the tenth commandments of the Decalogue (Exod 20:14, 17), which are

[67] Davidson, "Inner-Biblical Hermeneutics," 236, lists seven categories that support a basic continuity between Old Testament and New Testament and that were originally suggested by Gerhard Hasel: "1) the continuous history of God's people, 2) quotations (and allusions), 3) key theological terms, 4) unity of major themes, 5) typology, 6) promise/prediction and fulfillment, and 7) the 'big picture" of salvation history.'" He develops them on pages 237–261.

repeated in Deuteronomy 5:18, 21: "You shall not commit adultery" and "You shall not covet your neighbor's wife."[68] However, a transgression of these commandments may easily lead to the transgression of other commandments, as Scripture reveals—the commandments to honor one's father and mother (Exod 20:12; 1 Cor 5:1),[69] not to kill (Exod 20:13; Mark 6:17–26),[70] not to steal (Exod 20:15; Mark 6:17–19),[71] and not to bear false witness (Exod 20:16).[72] Then an avalanche of evil is unleashed. But also the first table of the Decalogue is affected as people turn away from God and create their own gods.

Additional details regarding cases of sexual activity are often found in historical narratives and in prophetic writings. Further divine legislation about sexuality occurs in Leviticus 18 and 20 and elsewhere in the Old Testament. The consequences of not following the Edenic model were disastrous, as the stories of Israel and humanity at large show.[73]

The New Testament upholds the creation account and the Ten Commandments. Marriage according to the creation account is supported by Jesus and New Testament authors (Matt 19:4–6; 1 Cor 7:2–6). Jesus blessed marriage by attending a wedding and performing His first miracle in that context (John 2:1–11). While Jesus' wedding parables (Matt 22:1–12; 25:1–13; Luke 12:36–38) and Revelation's marriage of the Lamb with His bride (Rev 19:7–9) point to spiritual aspects of the kingdom of God, they are still built on God's institution of marriage at creation and indirectly affirm God's extraordinary gift presented to humanity, the marriage between a male and a female. But to remain single and live a celibate life is also clearly spelled out as a valid option in the New Testament (Matt 19:10–12; 1 Cor 7:1, 7–8, 25–28, 32–35). Remarriage after the death of a spouse is possible but should be "only in the Lord" (1 Cor 7:39).[74]

However, according to Jesus the option to give to one's wife a certificate of divorce (Deut 24:1–4) is forbidden in the kingdom of God, which

---

[68] In Deuteronomy 5:21 the coveting of a neighbor's wife even comes first, while in Exodus 20:17 it is second.

[69] See, e.g., Absalom taking his father's concubines (2 Sam 16:21–22).

[70] See, e.g., David killing Bathsheba's husband Uriah (2 Sam 11:14–17).

[71] See, e.g., David stealing Uriah's wife (2 Sam 12:1–7).

[72] See, e.g., Tamar behaving like a harlot while being Judah's daughter-in-law (Gen 38:12–26).

[73] See, e.g., Amnon's rape of his sister Tamar (2 Sam 13). David's sin with Bathsheba may to some extent have triggered Amnon's rape of Tamar, which led to Absalom's murder of Amnon, and possibly to his own rape of David's concubines and his revolt against his father. When the Israelites —following Balaam's advice (Num 31:16)—did "commit harlotry with the women of Moab" (Num 25:1), twenty-four thousand persons were killed through a plague (Num 25:9).

[74] See the respective chapters in Ekkehardt Mueller and Elias Brasil de Souza, eds., *Marriage: Biblical and Theological Aspects*, Biblical Research Institute Studies in Biblical Ethics 1 (Silver Spring, MD: Biblical Research Institute, 2015).

has arrived with Christ's incarnation. Divorce is intolerable, unless sexual immorality of one spouse has happened and reconciliation is not possible (Matt 5:31–32; 19:1–9).[75] This applies to divorce initiated either by a husband or a wife (Mark 10:11–12).[76] In fact, Jesus' teaching on marriage and divorce goes beyond some lax interpretations of the Old Testament's divorce laws.

> He sees in Gen 1:27; 2:24 evidence that God intended marriage to be permanent (Mark 10:6–9; cf. Mal 2:14–16). Only at Matt. 5:32; 19:9 is an exception to his rejection of divorce made "on the ground of unchastity" (Gk. *porneía*); otherwise, divorce itself can be regarded as the cause of adultery (5:32 par.; Mark 10:2–12 par.).[77]

Adultery is unacceptable (1 Cor 6:15; John 8:1–11). It begins even by looking lustfully at another person (Matt 5:27–30), which may be a form of coveting.

So, Jesus—and thereby the New Testament—supports the Old Testament but takes a stricter approach that rests on the creation account and does away with God's temporary accommodations for His people who came out of Egypt and after so many years of slavery had to get to know Him again and understand Him better. Polygamy has disappeared in the New Testament (Matt 19:4).[78] Incest (1 Cor 5:1–5) and a homosexual lifestyle (Rom 1:26–27; 1 Cor 6:9–10; Matt 19:4)[79] are absolutely objectionable in the New Testament, as they are in the Old Testament (Lev 18:22).

What has changed is that while the New Testament's sexual ethics are somewhat stricter than the Old Testament's, the penalties are different. There is no death penalty in the New Testament in the case of sexual immorality, but rather separation of persistent sinners from the church by a process of disfellowshipping (Matt 18:15–20). Even then, the goal is that sinners repent and be saved.[80]

The New Testament contains a number of shorter and longer vice catalogues. Sexual sins are featured prominently within them. Jesus' list

---

[75] See the context of Matthew 18:21–35.

[76] The exception clause is not found in Mark 10:1–12 and Luke 16:18, but only in Matthew. For a study on divorce, see Ekkehardt Mueller, "Divorce and Remarriage in the New Testament," in Mueller and de Souza, 203–247.

[77] Allen C. Myers, *The Eerdmans Bible Dictionary* (Grand Rapids, MI: Eerdmans, 1987), 694.

[78] See the chapter on polygamy by Ron du Preez in this volume.

[79] See the chapter on homosexuality by Ekkehardt Mueller in this volume.

[80] On Matthew 18:15–20, see Ekkehardt Mueller, "Caring for Brothers and Sisters: Matthew 18:15–20," *Reflections* 58 (May 2008): 1–5.

in Mark 7:21–23—"For from within, out of the heart of men, proceed evil thoughts, adulteries, fornications, murders, thefts, covetousness, wickedness, deceit, lewdness, an evil eye, blasphemy, pride, foolishness"—is followed by the lists of His apostles (e.g., Rom 13:13; 1 Cor 5:9–11; 6:9–11; 2 Cor 12:21; Gal 5:19–21; Eph 4:19; 5:3; Col 3:5; 1 Pet 4:3; 1 John 2:15–17; Rev 22:15).

When the early church convened for the Jerusalem Council in order to decide whether Gentile believers had to become Jews by being circumcised and keeping ceremonial/ritual laws, guided by the Old Testament and the Holy Spirit they arrived at the momentous decision that this would not be necessary. But they also decided what was necessary for Gentile Christians: "For it seemed good to the Holy Spirit, and to us, to lay upon you no greater burden than these necessary things: that you abstain from things offered to idols, from blood, from things strangled, and from sexual immorality" (Acts 15:28–29).[81] The mention of "sexual immorality" (*porneia*), which obviously includes all sexual sins, is noteworthy.[82]

Thus, the New Testament refers back to the creation account when marriage and sexuality are discussed and accepts it as normative in sexual matters. For the New Testament, the Decalogue is binding. But here we have an issue today. S. Tracy points out that neither the law of God nor the goodness of God are understood. Rather, "his commandments are so frequently misconstrued."[83] He laments that

> one of Satan's most widespread, persistent lies is that one must go outside of God's commandments to find well-being because God's interests and our best interests don't always intersect. . . . In fifteen years of pastoral ministry working with adolescents and university students, over and over again I heard young adults express the misconception that if they scrupulously followed biblical sexual guidelines, they would have a diminished life. They

[81] The moral law of the Ten Commandments was not under discussion.

[82] See the chapter on sexual immorality (*porñeia*) by Ekkehardt Mueller in this volume. Allison A. Trites and William J. Larkin, *Cornerstone Biblical Commentary*, vol 12, *The Gospel of Luke and Acts* (Carol Stream, IL: Tyndale House, 2006), 523, state, "Embedded in this practical wisdom, of course, was a universal ethical norm: abstinence from sexual immorality." It has also been suggested that a special connection to Leviticus 18 is in view. See, e.g., Philip A. Bence, *Acts: A Bible Commentary in the Wesleyan Tradition* (Indianapolis, IN: Wesleyan, 1998), 158; F. F. Bruce, *The Book of the Acts*, The New International Commentary on the New Testament (Grand Rapids, MI: Eerdmans, 1988), 299; and Mikeal C. Parsons, *Acts*, Paideia Commentaries on the New Testament (Grand Rapids, MI: Baker Academic, 2008), 219.

[83] Tracy, 54.

> assumed that they were infinitely more concerned about their emotional and sexual well-being than God was.[84]

He continues by saying, "Sadly, very few people today understand that God is a loving creator who wants to bless his creation, and thus his commandments are not capricious or inimical to our well-being."[85] The latter is what the Old Testament and New Testament affirm: Psalm 36:7 praises God's lovingkindness and 1 John 4:8 affirms that God is love. The psalmist considers God's revelation of His law and will a delight (Ps 119:24, 47, 70), loves God's law/commandments (Ps 119:48, 97, 113, 119, 127, 163), does so even exceedingly (Ps 119:167), and longs for them (Ps 119:131). Because God is good, the psalmist wants to be taught God's statutes (Ps 119:68). Furthermore, God's law is truth (Ps 119:142, 151), and he decides to keep it (Ps 119:33, 34–44). "The law of Your mouth is better to me than thousands of coins of gold and silver" (Ps 119:72). Jesus teaches that those who love Him keep His commandments (John 14:15, 21; see also 15:10). Paul affirms that "the law is holy, and the commandment holy and just and good" (Rom 7:12), and James calls God's law "the law of liberty" (Jas 2:12).[86] The law does not save us, but we keep God's law because we love God and because it is good and beneficial and is a guide to live blessed lives.

New Testament Passages and Texts on Marriage and Premarital Sex

The first part of this study argued that in the Old Testament sexual relations prior to marriage did not correspond to the will of God. If premarital sex happened anyway, it was sinful and did not constitute a marriage, but rather was either fornication by the people entangled in it or rape of one of the persons forced into such an act. It was also noted that sexual relations among engaged persons were not allowed in the Old Testament. Since sexual ethics do not become more liberal in the New Testament, all forms of sexual misconduct remain wrong in New Testament times. This also includes premarital sex. If *porneia*—sexual immorality—is not restricted in meaning by a specific context, it includes premarital sex.

---

[84] Tracy, 54.

[85] Ibid.

[86] Douglas J. Moo, *James: An Introduction and Commentary*, Tyndale New Testament Commentaries (Downers Grove, IL: InterVarsity, 1985), 101, states, "No longer is God's law a threatening, confining burden. For the will of God now confronts us as a *law of liberty*—an obligation that is discharged in the joyful knowledge that God has both 'liberated' us from the penalty of sin and given us, in his Spirit, the power to obey his will."

> The commands against sexual encounters outside marriage are unchanging from Old to New Testament, though they are not only countercultural in New Testament times. Ancient Near Eastern societies around Israel had just as strict laws forbidding adultery as Israel did. . . . However, the rule of abstaining from sex before marriage was extremely countercultural for members of the early church and clearly caused a lot of problems. That this rule was nevertheless insisted on makes it clear that this is a timeless command.[87]

Now, there are also New Testament texts and passages that address premarital sexual immorality. But first we return to the context of being engaged, which was mentioned at the end of the Old Testament section of this study.

(1) According to Matthew 1:18–20, Mary and Joseph were engaged but did not have intimate relations. When encountered by the angel Gabriel with the message that she would become the mother of the Messiah, Mary affirmed her virginity and was puzzled about how she could become pregnant. She was told that in a miraculous way the Holy Spirit would be involved in the process of Christ's incarnation and therefore in her conception of the Messiah (Luke 1:34–35). So Mary became pregnant as a virgin. The text in Luke affirms that she did not have sexual relations with her fiancé Joseph. On the other hand, when Joseph learned that Mary was pregnant, he also indicated that he had not been intimately involved with her. So he must have assumed that Mary had sex with another man and got pregnant by that person, either voluntarily or by rape. According to Old Testament law, he had the option of making this public or leaving her secretly. He had chosen the second option when an angel intervened and clarified the matter. Ulrich Luz summarizes the issue:

> Joseph and Mary are betrothed; that is, from a legal point of view they are bound to one another. A betrothal can be dissolved only with a bill of divorce. The betrothed woman lives with her parents and does not yet have sexual relations with her bridegroom. "To come together" (συνελθεῖν) most likely refers to her move to the bridegroom's house that takes place at the wedding.[88]

---

[87] Instone-Brewer, 97.

[88] Ulrich Luz, *Matthew 1–7: A Commentary on Matthew 1–7*, Hermeneia—A Critical and Historical Commentary on the Bible, rev. ed. (Minneapolis, MN: Fortress, 2007), 93–94. R. T. France, *Matthew: An Introduction and Commentary*, Tyndale New Testament Commentaries (Downers Grove, IL: InterVarsity, 1985), 82, is even a bit more detailed: "In Jewish law betrothal, which lasted about one year, was much more than our engagement. It was a binding contract,

This story involves Jesus and is important for the fulfillment of the messianic prophecy of Isaiah 7:14 and for the understanding of the nature of Christ. The incident may also set the tone for New Testament sexual ethics and continue the line of the Old Testament. There is no indication that Mary and Joseph's attitude of avoiding premarital sex was unnecessary and no longer binding in the New Testament. While Jesus would later challenge strict Jewish traditions of Sabbath keeping (Matt 12:1–14) and ceremonial washing (Matt 15:1–9), He challenged and corrected their lax attitude toward divorce (Matt 19:1–10) and did not undo or soften Old Testament legislation on adultery and premarital sex.

(2) John 8:41 mentions that the Jews accused Jesus of having been born in fornication. Obviously, they had learned that Mary gave birth to Jesus earlier than nine months after her wedding to Joseph. "While they would not have given countenance to the Christian doctrine of the Virgin Birth, the Jews may well have known that there was something unusual about the birth of Jesus and have chosen to allude to it in this way."[89] Actually, "they . . . imply that Jesus was fathered through an illegitimate act."[90] The Greek word used is *porneia*, which includes premarital intimacy—for instance, during the period of engagement, which seems to be the case here. While the Jews were wrong in their assumption and while they were offensive in discriminating against Jesus, this incident still shows that premarital sex was rejected in the first century AD.[91]

(3) However, premarital sexual intimacy is not only rejected by the Jews, but also by the New Testament in other places. Hebrews 13:4 reads, "Marriage is honorable among all, and the bed undefiled; but fornicators [*pornous*] and adulterers [*moiochous*] God will judge." F. F. Bruce comments on this text by stating, "Fornication and adultery are not synonymous in the New Testament: adultery implies unfaithfulness by either party to the marriage vow, while the word translated 'fornication'

---

terminable only by death (which left the betrothed a 'widow') or by a divorce as for a full marriage. The man was already the *husband* (v. 19), but the woman remained in her father's house. The marriage was completed when the husband took the betrothed to his home in a public ceremony (v. 24; cf. 25:1–13); thus they *came together*, and sexual intercourse could begin." See also John Nolland, *The Gospel of Matthew: A Commentary on the Greek Text, New International Greek Testament Commentary* (Grand Rapids, MI: Eerdmans, 2005), 92.

[89] Leon Morris, *The Gospel According to John*, The New International Commentary on the New Testament (Grand Rapids, MI: Eerdmans, 1995), 409.

[90] Jo-Ann A. Brant, *John*, Paideia Commentaries on the New Testament (Grand Rapids, MI: Baker Academic, 2011), 146.

[91] The problem in John 8:41 is not the Jews' acceptance of divine legislation, but their hostile attitude toward Jesus, which lead to the attempt to kill Him (John 8:59).

covers a wide range of sexual irregularities."[92] "Even the author of the book of Hebrews, which was written to a Jewish congregation, had to remind them that sex should only occur between married partners (Heb 13:4)," writes Instone-Brewer.[93] If a married person has sexual relations with someone outside of his or her marriage, it is adultery. If a non-married person has sex with a married person, it is premarital sex—fornication. Sex between two unmarried persons is also fornication.[94]

(4) Galatians 5:19–21 describes the "works of the flesh" in a catalogue of vices. As with other New Testament vice lists, sexual sins come first and are described with a number of terms to show their problematic nature. These vice lists respond to non-acceptable cultural practices. Here Paul mentions sexual immorality (*porneia*), impurity/uncleanness (*akatharsia*), and sensuality/lewdness/licentiousness (*aselgeia*).[95] The broad term *porneia* comes first. It includes premarital sex. The next term may in other contexts refer to non-sexual sins, but here it clearly refers also to sexual transgressions. *Akatharsia* is usually translated as "uncleanness." This may refer to uncleanness in a ritual sense, but also to spiritual and moral impurity. Already in Leviticus 20:21 incest is considered to be *akatharsia*. In Galatians and in other places, such as Ephesians 5:3 and Colossians 3:5, *akatharsia* is connected to the word *porneia* and points to very problematic sexual behavior. It "prevents fellowship with God" and "may refer specifically to impure conduct in sexual relations."[96] *Aselgeia* is also a broad term referring to sexual transgressions. It occurs only in the New Testament and does so regularly

---

[92] F. F. Bruce, *The Epistle to the Hebrews*, The New International Commentary on the New Testament, rev. ed. (Grand Rapids, MI: Eerdmans, 1990), 373.

[93] Instone-Brewer, 94.

[94] William L. Lane, *Hebrews 9–13*, Word Biblical Commentary (Dallas, TX: Word 1991), 516, maintains, "Respect for marriage has broad implications concerning sexual relationships, both for those who are married and for those who are not." He also quotes the Roman poet Horace of the first century BC, who writes in *Odes* 3.6: "Full of sin, our age has defiled first the marriage bed, then our children and our homes; springing from such a source, the stream of disaster has overflowed both people and nation. The young girl is eager to learn Ionian dances, and soon acquires the art of flirting; even in childhood she devises impure affairs." Gareth Lee Cockerill, *The Epistle to the Hebrews*, The New International Commentary on the New Testament (Grand Rapids, MI: Eerdmans, 2012), 684, notes, "The first of these terms [*pornos*] includes all who have sexual relations outside of the marriage bond." See also Tracy, 60: "Other passages such as Hebrews 13:4 link those who practise premarital sex ('fornicators') with adulterers, indicating that sex before marriage and sex after marriage to someone other than one's spouse are equally condemned ('God will judge')."

[95] In addition to these terms, some manuscripts use the noun "adultery" (*moicheia*). This is, e.g., reflected in the NKJV.

[96] Ronald Y. K. Fung, *The Epistle to the Galatians*, The New International Commentary on the New Testament (Grand Rapids, MI: Eerdmans, 1988), 255.

in lists of vices (Mark 7:21–22; Rom 13:13; 2 Cor 12:21; Eph 4:19; 1 Pet 4:3), but also in descriptions of questionable characters (2 Pet 2:2, 7, 19; Jude 1:4). *Aselgeia* "is such a terrible thing [because] 'it is the act of a character which has lost that which ought to be its greatest defense —its self-respect, and its sense of shame.'"[97] D. J. Moo applies the text to our modern situation by stating, "In some Jewish texts (3 Macc 2:26) as well as in the NT (Rom 13:13; 1 Pet. 4:3), it [*aselgeia*] is associated with wild living, the kind of lifestyle we would today associate with the 'party animal' (see also Mark 7:22; Eph 4:19; 2 Pet 2:2, 7, 18; Jude 4)."[98] The threefold mention of sexual sins in Galatians 5:19 obviously points to all sexual sins and highlight them, including premarital sex. This is even clearer in 2 Corinthians 12:21, where these three terms occur with only one article (*tē akatharsia kai porneia kai aselgeia*) "that binds them together in a conceptual unity."[99]

(5) In 1 Corinthians 7 Paul addresses singleness and marriage, including the problem of divorce. He recommends singleness in situations unfortunate or difficult for Christians, especially in the first century AD.[100] But he is not opposed to marriage. After his recommendation to remain single in verse 1, the apostle turns to marriage and married persons. If people get married, they should practice sexual intimacy within marriage and not deprive the spouse of this gift granted by God to married heterosexual couples (1 Cor 7:3–5). In 1 Corinthians 7:8, Paul turns to unmarried church members, singles and widows, and again suggests to remain unmarried. But he knows about the reality of life and that not everyone has the gift of celibacy. So he writes, "But if they cannot exercise self-control, let them marry. For it is better to marry than to burn with passion" (1 Cor 7:9). Paul presents only two alternatives: marrying or burning with passion. They are not 1) to marry or 2) to live together while having intimate relations—as is common today—but rather they should 1) marry or else 2) will burn with passion. Premarital sex even between an engaged couple is out of place. David E. Garland explains:

[97] Fung, 255.

[98] Douglas J. Moo, *Galatians*, Baker Exegetical Commentary on the New Testament (Grand Rapids, MI: Baker Academic, 2013), 359.

[99] Murray J. Harris, *The Second Epistle to the Corinthians: A Commentary on the Greek Text*, New International Greek Testament Commentary (Grand Rapids, MI: Eerdmans, 2005), 903.

[100] For an interpretation of 1 Corinthians 7:26 see, e.g., David E. Garland, *1 Corinthians*, Baker Exegetical Commentary on the New Testament (Grand Rapids, MI: Baker Academic, 2003), 324–325.

> What is distinctive about his [Paul's] use of the metaphor [of burning] is his conviction that romantic passion necessitated marriage. Others in the ancient world did not think that burning required marriage. Overpowering sexual desire only necessitated having sex, not marriage (Deming 1995b: 131 n. 88, citing Epictetus, *Diatr.* 3.22.76; 4.1.147). Soranus (*Gynecology* 1.7.31) reports, for example, that some virgins "have suffered more severe sexual passion than [active] women; for the only abatement of the craving is found in the use of intercourse, not in avoidance." Achilles Tatius (*Leuc. Clit.* 5.26.2) writes, "However angry you make me, I still burn with love for you. . . . Make a truce with me at least for now; pity me. . . . A single consummation will be enough. It is a small remedy I ask for so great an illness. Quench a little of my fire." For Paul, the fire is not to be doused by fleeting, illicit sexual encounters or by grim repression of natural sexual desire. It calls for marriage.[101]

(6) In a number of cases, a distinction between premarital sex and extramarital sex is not made, because neither fits the divine ideal of sexual intercourse being limited to marriage. Involvement with a prostitute can point both to premarital or extramarital sex (1 Cor 6:15–16). In either case, the perpetrator would not be married to the prostitute. A few verses earlier, adulterers (*moichos*) and fornicators (*pornos*) seem to be distinguished (1 Cor 6:9). Adulterers are clear. Fornicators may be understood in a wider sense, following the ones in 1 Corinthians 5:9–11, or in a narrower sense, referring to people involved in premarital sexual encounters. G. L. Bray presents Origen's interpretation: "Let no one say: 'I was young. Before I got married, I slept with prostitutes.' Why did you not get married instead?"[102]

---

[101] Garland, 274–275. William Baker, "1 Corinthians," in *Cornerstone Biblical Commentary: 1 Corinthians, 2 Corinthians* (Carol Stream, IL: Tyndale House, 2009), 101, notes, "The idea of maintaining a perennial celibate state for spiritual reasons might sound very appealing to both men and women who want to serve God with every ounce of their life, but the biological needs of their bodies could very well make this far more difficult at points than they ever realized. . . . It was better for them to recognize this and pursue marriage before they were drawn into sexual promiscuity, activity completely banned for a Christian." Richard B. Hays, *First Corinthians*, Interpretation: A Bible Commentary for Teaching and Preaching (Louisville, KY: Westminster John Knox, 1997), 119, explains, "Here again the specter of *porneia* looms in the background. Paul is concerned that [unmarried believers] might find themselves lured into illicit sexual activity." Tracy, 60, adds, "There is no moral loophole here for premarital sex, for Paul instead argues that marriage is the only God ordained provision for sexual needs."

[102] Gerald LeSirBray, ed., *1–2 Corinthians*, Ancient Christian Commentary on Scripture (Downers Grove, IL: InterVarsity, 1999), 53, quoting Origen, *Commentary on 1 Corinthians* 2.27.48–49.

Summary

The New Testament follows the Old in regard to sexual ethics. In a certain sense it is even stricter than the Old Testament. This is so because the Messiah has come and has not only brought about the kingdom of God and salvation, but has revealed to His followers the will of God more clearly, and this is to our benefit. Such stricter approach rests on the divine plan for sexuality and marriage set forth in the Old Testament creation account.

Ethical Deliberations on Premarital Sex

Based on the preceding considerations, the following discussion addresses two important issues. First, it describes and evaluates the challenges to the biblical position on premarital sex posed by contemporary society. Second, it argues that people who adhere to the biblical position on premarital sex are much more likely to experience a meaningful life and enjoy the blessings of sexual intimacy.

Challenges to the Biblical Position on Premarital Sex

Although from a biblical perspective the issue is quite clear, it is unintelligible to large segments of the present population, especially those living in Western countries. In 2006 Tracy wrote,

> In the past three decades there has been a dramatic shift in the western world regarding the moral acceptability of premarital sex. Most modern westerners find the biblical sexual ethic to be illogical, outdated, and utterly unacceptable. Thus, by the age of nineteen, 85% of American males and 77% of females will have had intercourse. In England and Wales, 39% of non-married adults ages 25–29 are cohabiting, as are 35% of non-married adults ages 30–34. From the outset of the sexual revolution in the 1960s, sexual expression has increasingly been viewed as a basic right that no one has a right to restrict.[103]

However, sexual intimacy is not a right, but a gift from the Creator and Giver of life, who is the God of goodness and love and who is more interested in our well-being than we ourselves are.[104] If this were not so, why would God still maintain the universe—especially planet earth, with humans who are able to do the greatest evils comprehensible?

---

[103] Tracy, 60–61.

[104] Ibid., 66, maintains, "Christians affirm that food, drink, sex, and physical comfort are all good gifts from God, but God graciously proscribes the use of those gifts. A primary way he asks singles to live out their sexuality is to abstain from this physical pleasure for the greater good."

Why would He care and have revealed Himself and sent His prophets with messages that call humans to fellowship with Him, love Him, and love their neighbors and even their enemies? Why would He have given His good law with the intention for His created beings to enjoy safe and blessed lives? Most of all, why would He have sent the Messiah, His Son, to disclose Himself even more clearly, to save humans through Christ's death on the cross, and give them eternal life? And why would Jesus have set an example of how to live life in its truest sense?

The problem with humanity today is that we do not trust God and His goodness and that we think of Him either as nonexistent, uninterested in us, or as a tough taskmaster who makes human life miserable. In addition, we are engulfed by and promote human hubris, because supposedly we know better than God does. Oftentimes, we do not accept the Lord as the Owner of all things, including ourselves, and us as His stewards. Rather, we attempt to make ourselves masters, lords, and kings and consider ourselves to be the measure of all things.

> Flowing out of the idea that unrestricted sex is a basic right, other arguments are commonly given for premarital sex. One of the most common is that sexual abstinence is unnatural and leads to psychologically unhealthy sexual repression. . . . Many argue that premarital sex strengthens future marriage by helping couples adjust to each other and by insuring that they are sexually compatible.[105]

But these arguments do not necessarily work. Christian Frei points out that with premarital sex "not only sexuality is thus separated from marriage, but also marriage from parenthood." In addition, the "liberalization of sexuality by no means results in better and more relaxed relationships. . . . 'People of our time are becoming increasingly incapable of living constant relationships and growing in them.' Social researchers observe a lack of commitment, loss of libido, and a tendency toward masturbation and pornography."[106]

Regarding the claim that premarital sex helps determine sexual compatibility and after a "positive" testing period allows for entering marriage successfully, Frei argues that marriage cannot be tried out before marriage takes place. The real thing is still different from the preliminary

---

[105] Tracy, 61.

[106] Christian Frei, "Die Ehe: eine überholte Form menschlichen Zusammenlebens? Über den Ursprung der rechtlich-öffentlichen Eheschließung und der monogamen Ehe sowie über die Gültigkeit des biblischen Eheverständnisses in der postmodernen Gesellschaft" (Diplomarbeit, Theologisches Seminar Marienhöhe, Darmstadt, 1994), 66.

sexual involvement. As birth and death cannot be tried out and then be evaluated, so also marriage cannot be tried out beforehand. Who knows prior to marriage how marriage will feel in a few months, in five, ten, or twenty years? Also, the sexual partner is not a trial object to be discarded after a negative test. "Sexual experimentation says nothing about fitness or unfitness for marriage. For the vast majority of couples, sexual adaptation develops over the course of weeks, months, or even years; thus, it requires a longer learning process."[107] Tracy agrees: "Research shows that couples that live together before marriage have higher infidelity rates, lower marital satisfaction rates, and higher divorce rates than those who don't live together before marriage."[108] "In short, living together and having sex before marriage does not prepare one for marriage, but decreases the likelihood of a future healthy marriage."[109]

But the present approach to sexuality may separate sex from the rest of the human being and reduce him or her to a need-satisfying machine.[110] Sex becomes a product or good to be consumed and thus is driven by consumerism. Children in the Western world have learned to experience instant gratification and are unable to wait for their wishes to be fulfilled. This attitude has also been transferred to teens, young adults, and even adults with regard to sexual gratification. They assume that sexual intimacy cannot be delayed but that the urge of having a sexual encounter must be fulfilled more or less immediately. Another problem is that with young people sexual maturation may precede emotional, mental, and spiritual maturity. Therefore, premarital sexual encounters may set up people for major problems.

> If the first sexual relationship breaks down, the resistance of the woman and the man to sexual intercourse decreases with each subsequent partner "and thus the readiness for the next sexual contact increases." In addition, objective assessment and opinion formation regarding the potential spouse becomes more difficult. The ability to judge is restricted and physical-sexual and also psychological dependencies occur.[111]

Tracy as well as John Feinberg and Paul Feinberg have shown that premarital sex may bring about other undesirable consequences.

---

107 Frei, 79.

108 Tracy, 62.

109 Ibid., 64.

110 Frei, 66.

111 Ibid., 80.

> When sex is practiced outside of marriage, it is inevitably expressed in a context that lacks the highest level of commitment, and this creates great potential for disrespect and selfish manipulation. It also creates much greater potential for harm and heartache. . . . According to a 2002 United States Department of Justice report on intimate partner violence, unmarried women are almost five times more likely to experience violence at the hands of their sexual partner than are married women.[112]

Sexual partners may not marry but accidentally procreate, which may lead to unwanted pregnancies, single women with children, and "fatherless children." To avoid such a situation, abortion is being considered and practiced by pregnant single mothers. "Young women who are sexually active before marriage have the most abortions."[113] It has also been suggested that out-of-wedlock births may significantly contribute to long-term poverty in America, these children dropping out of school, and other problems. "The point here is certainly not to condemn single mothers (who need and deserve compassion and assistance) but to underscore the fact that much long-term, even generational suffering is a direct result of sex outside of marriage."[114]

Finally, unprotected sexual activity—often desired or demanded by the male partner—including premarital sex, leads to the high number of sexually transmitted diseases and cause serious problems for individuals.[115] The rationalization of one's behavior in moments of strong desire—namely, that one will not be affected by adverse outcomes—is not only dangerous but oftentimes not true.

Benefits for People Adhering to a Biblical Position on Premarital Sex

However, there are not only potentially negative effects for engaging in premarital sex, but also positive effects for living a celibate life prior

---

[112] Tracy, 65.

[113] John S. Feinberg and Paul D. Feinberg, *Ethics for a Brave New World* (Wheaton, IL: Crossway Books, 1993), 159.

[114] Tracy, 68.

[115] Tracy states, "Sexually transmitted diseases (STDs) are at epidemic rates in many countries and communities, and are literally disrupting the modern world. There are more than fifty STDs. . . . In 2003 the Center for Disease Control (CDC) reported that nineteen million STD infections occur annually in the USA, with almost half of these infections occurring among the youth aged between fifteen and twenty-four. Furthermore, the CDC notes that in addition to potentially severe health consequences for the populace, STDs create a great economic burden. . . . According to the World Health Organization, STDs are 'among the most common causes of illness in the world', and have far reaching health, economic, and social consequences.' In spite of medical advances, several STDs are currently incurable, notably HIV, genital herpes, hepatitis B, and human papilloma virus (HPV)."

to marriage. These positive effects go beyond the benefits of avoiding negative consequences.

Christians who know about God's will regarding sexual intimacy and live in agreement with divine directions—in spite of sexual temptations, which most humans experience—avoid experiencing severe regret, trauma, guilt, and a bad conscience. They do not need to rationalize their behavior or reinterpret Scripture as others do to suit their own desires. Therefore, they can experience peace and an unbroken and intimate relationship with God. If they have failed and want to change, they can find forgiveness for sins and ask the Lord for power to live a life glorifying God.

Their commitment to the good and loving Creator leads them to mental and emotional stability and maturity of character. Sincere believers do not sacrifice biblical morality on the altar of egotism, thereby robbing themselves of a moral compass. They also know that the practice of sexual intercourse in marriage is not just about self-satisfaction of the individual but involves the spouse and has repercussions on the life as a married couple. In other words, these followers of Christ do not entertain a myopic perspective but know that human lives form a network and that one life influences another. While enjoying marital sexual intimacy, they accept responsibility for the well-being and happiness of the spouse and potential offspring. Staying away from premarital or extramarital sexuality, they become balanced personalities. Thus, sexual intimacy is embedded in the life of a married couple and has also implications for family and society.

Furthermore, true believers understand sexual intimacy not as an isolated physical act, but as an experience involving the entire human personality. If sexual intimacy is reserved for marriage, marriage has something unique and "marital sex gains added significance."[116] "The sex act involves the whole person, bonding physically and psychologically two individuals in a unique way. Therefore, while sex may bring gratification to two uncommitted partners, in at least some cases that pleasure is trivial and fleeting."[117] The multiple dimensions of marital intimacy, including the spiritual aspect, have already been elaborated in volume 1 of this series on marriage, sexuality, and family.[118] Biblically endorsed sexual activity is an expression of humans' wholistic personality and love in an encompassing sense. As such, it cannot be reduced to mere bodily

---

[116] Feinberg and Feinberg, 158.

[117] Ibid, 159.

[118] See Thomas Domanyi, "Sexuality and Marriage From a Theological Perspective," in Mueller and de Souza, 101–122; and Zoltán Szalos-Farkas, "Spirituality of Human Sexuality: A Theological and Anthropological Perspective," in Mueller and de Souza, 123–142.

functions. God's gift of sexuality—if rightfully used—does not create a dichotomy within us, but establishes us as fully integrated persons.

Tracy lists five major points in favor of abstinence before marriage, develops them, and includes some research done in this area. We list here mainly the headings:

> 1. Abstinence before marriage enhances personal and marital health. . . .
> 2. Abstinence before marriage increases the likelihood of being respected and treated with dignity. . . .
> 3. Abstinence before marriage helps one develop self-control and character necessary for a healthy marriage (and for life in general) . . . sexual abstinence before marriage can enhance sacrificial love and respect for one's partner. It also develops self-control that is essential for healthy personal and marital life. . . .
> 4. Abstinence before marriage guarantees that one will not have to deal with an unplanned pregnancy. . . . Since abstinence is the only 100% effective form of birth control, singles who practice abstinence will never have to deal with an unexpected pregnancy. . . .
> 5. Abstinence before marriage eliminates the threat of contracting STDs [sexually transmitted diseases].[119]

And there are more benefits to abstaining from premarital sex. But we must add a caveat here. Sincere Christians do not only stay away from biblically illicit sexual encounters because of detrimental effects for themselves or because of benefits that they may reap, but because it is the right thing to do. They are willing to do the will of God. They appreciate God's wisdom and the beauty of biblical instructions. Their obedience to God's will and their respect and love for the Lord deepen their relationship to Him. Subsequently, this attitude pays back rich dividends and makes life meaningful and blessed.

Conclusion

This chapter on what constitutes marriage and how to view premarital sex has attempted to show that the Old and New Testaments do not consider sexual intimacy before or outside of marriage as constituting marriage. The Bible conceives of marriage as a covenant and does not leave room for any kind of "legitimate" premarital sexual intimacy. Having sex outside of marriage—whether as premarital or extramarital sex—is sinful. Even if this position runs counter to cultural practices and

---

[119] Tracy, 62–71. Feinberg and Feinberg, 159, add to the last point: "In a marriage where both partners are absolutely faithful to one another, the likelihood of contracting a sexually transmitted disease is almost nonexistent."

expectations, we treasure God's love and wisdom more than human practices, deliberations, and conventions on sexual matters. But it needs to be added that there is also divine grace for those who have not followed God's will, who may feel hopeless in having failed, and who confess their shortcomings. God is more than willing to grant forgiveness (1 John 1:9).

"Biblical teaching allows sex only within marriage,"[120] writes Instone-Brewer. A premarital sexual encounter is not a marriage. "Against this backdrop, premarital abstinence is all about obeying God's statutes on sexuality, trusting that his statutes are anything but arbitrary—they're an expression of God's desire to protect the integrity of the family and to see his image-bearers experience true intimacy with each other."[121] On the other hand, the concept of marriage as a covenant places sexual activity within marriage as a most sublime gift through which the couple becomes one flesh. Someone who enters a marriage relationship with the a priori intention of having no sexual intimacy—and without previously communicating such a matter to the potential spouse—violates the unitive purpose of the marriage covenant, which, along with sexual communion, includes trust.

Jesus sanctioned and strongly upheld marriage in a time when it was under attack. He still does this today. This is no wonder because He is the One who made us and He wants us to have abundant life as singles and as married couples (John 10:10).

---

[120] Instone-Brewer, 94.

[121] "Rise of the Rebel Virgins: Why We Refrain Even When Premarital Sex Is Safe and 'Natural'" (A Christianity Today Editorial), *Christianity Today* 52, no. 6 (2008): 21.

CHAPTER 4

Uncommitted Relationships: Cohabitation from a Historical and Biblical Perspective

Johannes Kovar[1]

It is widely known that the number of couples who live together outside of marriage is steadily rising in Western society. Statistics suggest that in Sweden 90% of couples already cohabit before the marriage ceremony, while in Italy only 2% do so.[2] In the United States over 50% of all first marriages are preceded by cohabitation.[3] The reasons for this are varied.[4] Nearly universally condemned in former times, cohabitation in the Western world has lost its stigma and is viewed as common pratice. This development affects the church and raises the question of how Christians should assess this phenomenon. Data from 1994 show that cohabitation among Adventists in North America was a frequent reality; to the

---

[1] The author of this study thanks Jamie Boucher, former language student at Bogenhofen and theology student at Andrews University, for translating this paper from German into English and Julie Weigel for proofreading.

[2] Gary Jenkins, *Cohabitation: A Biblical Perspective* (Cambridge: Grove Books, 2002), 4. More statistical material can be found in Adrian Thatcher, *Living Together & Christian Ethics*, New Studies in Christian Ethics (Cambridge: Cambridge University Press, 2002).

[3] "Marriage Preparation and Cohabiting Couples, http://www.usccb.org/issues-and-action/marriage-and-family/marriage/marriage-preparation/cohabiting.cfm (accessed June 29, 2021) has useful information. For statistics in the United States, see Wikipedia, s.v. "Cohabitation in the United States," last modified December 10, 2020, http://en.wikipedia.org/wiki/Cohabitation_in_the_United_States (accessed May 7, 2021).

[4] Volker Gäckle, "'Wir lieben uns auch ohne Trauschein!' - die sexualethische Herausforderung des Individualismus," in *Was hält Christen zusammen?: Die Herausforderung des christlichen Glaubens durch Individualismus und Erlebnisgesellschaft*, ed. Eberhard Hahn (Wuppertal: R. Brockhaus Verlag, 2000), 205–228.

question "Did you and your spouse live together prior to being married?," 18% responded with "yes."[5]

The Goal of this Paper

To the author's knowledge, there is no detailed study on the topic of marriage-like partnerships in the Bible. References to this issue in Adventist literature are sparse, yet almost unanimous in their rejection of cohabitation.[6]

This study considers the question of how cohabitation has been viewed throughout antiquity and church history. All biblical statements related to this topic will be examined. Additionally, brief mention will be made of the practical challenges pastors face when dealing with the issue.

Definition of Terms

It is not easy to find appropriate terminology for unmarried couples living together. The term "concubinage" is often objected to, as it carries too many negative connotations: a concubine—particularly in antiquity—served primarily a sexual role in an asymmetrical relationship that was

---

[5] Monte and Norma Sahlin, *A New Generation of Adventist Families* (Portland, OR: Center for Creative Ministry, 1997), 120–121.

[6] Miroslav M. Kiš, "Christian Lifestyle and Behavior," in *Handbook of Seventh-day Adventist Theology*, ed. Raoul Dederen (Hagerstown, MD: Review and Herald, 2000), 675–723, esp. 695–696; Angel Manuel Rodríguez, "Cohabitation: Biblical and Ethical Concerns," Biblical Research Institute, https://adventistbiblicalresearch.org/materials/practical-christian-living/cohabitation-biblical-and-ethical-concerns (accessed May 7, 2021); Rodríguez, "What Is Wrong With Cohabitation?," Biblical Research Institute, https://adventistbiblicalresearch.org/materials/practical-christian-living/what-wrong-cohabitation (accessed May 7, 2021); Miroslav M. Kiš, "Seventh-day Adventist Position on Cohabitation," Biblical Research Institute, https://adventistbiblicalresearch.org/materials/adventist-heritage-practical-christian-living/seventh-day-adventist-position-cohabitation (accessed May 7, 2021); and Richard M. Davidson, "Does Marriage Still Matter?," Biblical Research Institute, https://adventistbiblicalresearch.org/materials/practical-christian-living/does-marriage-still-matter (accessed May 7, 2021). For a broader approach, see Alexander Vilem, "Kirchliche Ehesegnung ohne staatlichen Trauschein?" (MA thesis, Friedensau, 2003), who suggests a blessing in the church in cases where the couple signs a partnership contract. A document by the Euro-Africa Division (now Inter-European Division) dated April 24, 1985, speaks out against cohabitation, even when the general societal tendency tolerates such a union or when it is financially disadvantageous to enter into a state-recognized marriage. It is recommended to propose to the state a change of the law when it concerns financial discrimination due to marriage. A new series of articles began with Lothar Wilhelm, "Nichteheliche Lebensgemeinschaft: Biblisch-theologische Überlegungen zu einem Thema unserer Zeit," *Adventecho* 3 (2005): 24–26, https://advent-verlag.de/media/pdf/Eheaehnliche_Lebensgemeinschaften.pdf (accessed May 7, 2021). Reinder Bruinsma, "Is Cohabitation Always Wrong?," *Spectrum*, Spring 2012, 37–43, suggests cohabiting situations that may reflect the biblical ideal. In his opinion, an awareness of differing situations in different countries and in different cultures is necessary.

disadvantageous to the woman.[7] Instead of "concubinage," "nonmarital partnership" or "marriage-like partnership" is often suggested. In this paper, the term "cohabitation" will be used.

The meaning of the terms "cohabitation" and "concubinage" must first be clarified in order to clearly differentiate them from other forms of partnership or sexual union. It is commonly understood that cohabitation refers to a marriage-like partnership without formal or legal marriage.

The difference between prostitution and cohabitation lies in the fact that prostitution is an occasional one-time relationship for money, whereas cohabitation is intended to be a long-term relationship, and assumes that living together has more than sexuality as its goal.

The difference between marriage and cohabitation lies in the fact that marriage includes a legal aspect (a state ceremony at a registry office) and often a religious component (church wedding), having therefore an official and public character. Here, the boundary cannot always be easily drawn if we consider, for example, France, where it is possible for two partners to enter into a social contract that is juridically and socially somewhere between loose cohabitation and a fully valid marriage. Known in France as "PACS," this common form of partnership will not be considered in this study.[8]

Premarital and extramarital sex as well as the issue of cohabitation must also be mentioned. It is, of course, not easy to clearly distinguish between premarital intercourse[9] and cohabitation. Nevertheless, cohabitation implies long-term intentions for a partnership characterized by a joint residence, joint finances, and sexual union, whereas in premarital sex, these components may only be partially fulfilled.

It is problematic to use the same terminology for ancient and modern circumstances in their different social and cultural settings. However, although the Bible does not use the term "marriage-like partnership," it should be possible to detect whether we can find hints of the phenomenon we today would call "cohabitation."

---

[7] For questions of terminology, see Andreas Heller, *Zusammenleben von Frau und Mann: Kirche und nichteheliche Lebensgemeinschaften* (Wien: Hermagoras-Verlag, 1989), 35, 39; and Hermann Ringeling, "Die nichteheliche Lebensgemeinschaft," in *Handbuch der christlichen Ethik,* ed. Anselm Hertz et al., 3 vols. (Freiburg: Herder, 1993), 3:298–316.

[8] A law from 1999 regulates the details. In "Law number 99–944 of November 15, 1999 concerning a civil solidarity contract," the following definition is found "Cohabitation is a de facto union, characterized by a common life with a character of stability and continuity, between two persons of different sex or the same sex, who live as a couple." This law establishes a contract between two partners, but no moral commitment toward the other person.

[9] This study uses this expression, although a later marriage may not be intended at all.

Cohabitation in History

Cohabitation in Ancient Mesopotamia

We do not know much about cohabitation in this early period, and we have only a few hints from around 2000 BC that cohabitation between free citizens and slaves evidently existed.[10]

Cohabitation in Ancient Greece

Obviously, in Athens[11] in the fifth and fourth centuries BC, there were hetaeras and concubines alongside marriage, as indicated by a reference from a legal session in 340 BC: "We have hetaera [a courtesan] for desire, concubines for the daily care of our bodies, and wives to bear us legitimate children and to be faithful keepers of our homes."[12]

The Periclean Citizenship Law of 451/450 BC required that both parents be of Athenian descent for someone to be considered a citizen, although it is disputed whether the parents were required to be married.[13] Laws were issued during the fourth century placing the cohabitation of an Athenian with a non-citizen under penalty,[14] no doubt in order to prevent the offspring produced by such a union from creating legal problems.[15]

There were often men in Athens at this time, mostly young and unmarried, who entered into long-term relationships with a hetaera.[16] Whereas the hetaera did not live in the man's home, the concubine did.[17] Although our sources do not expressly state it, we can suppose that after the death of his wife, a widower often entered into a new relationship with a concubine. If there were children resulting from the earlier marriage, it was considered unthinkable to enter into a new marriage, as this normally led to inheritance disputes among the children of the different marriages. Since there was no legally valid marriage contract in the case of cohabitation, the children resulting from such a relationship were not entitled

---

[10] Hans Neumann, "Bemerkungen zu Ehe, Konkubinat und Bigamie in neusumerischer Zeit," in *La femme dans le Proche-Orient antique*, XXXIIIe International Assyriological Meeting (Paris, July 7–10, 1986), ed. J. M. Durand (Paris, 1987), 131–135.

[11] For details, see Elke Hartmann, *Heirat, Hetärentum und Konkubinat im klassischen Athen,* Campus Historische Studien 30 (Frankfurt: Campus, 2002).

[12] Pseudo-Demosthenes, *Rede gegen Neaira,* 59, 122, cited in Eckhard J. Schnabel, Der erste Brief des Paulus an die Korinther: Historisch-Theologische Auslegung (Witten: R. Brockhaus, 2006), 339.

[13] Hartmann, 52–57.

[14] Pseudo-Demosthenes, *Rede gegen Neaira*, 59.16, cited in Norman W. and Norman J. DeWitt, *Demosthenes With an English Translation* (Cambridge, MA: Harvard University Press, 1949), 16.

[15] Hartmann, 57–58.

[16] Ibid., 191.

[17] Ibid., 212–235.

to an inheritance. Concubines who did not have citizenship status (often they were emancipated slaves) took over the role of the wife—caring for the household and the sick or aged partner, and, of course, satisfying the erotic needs of her partner. It appears that in ancient Athens, such cohabitation was tolerated and not considered offensive. How often it took place is difficult to judge.

Cohabitation in the Roman Empire of the New Testament Period

Throughout the history of research, different conclusions have been drawn concerning the topic of cohabitation in the Roman Empire. What is presented here is the conclusion of the most recent research.

One can observe that in the Roman Empire, cohabitation took place relatively seldom.[18] Marriage was the common form of partnership, and deviations were found only in strongly urbanized and Romanized areas,[19] although divorces were frequent. Cohabitation, however, was entered into only when a prohibition excluded a fully valid marriage,[20] such as by soldiers[21] or among slaves. Nevertheless, one should note that inscriptions about soldiers used terms that were reserved for fully valid marriages only. Thus, these unions were placed on the same level as marriage, although they did not comply with the official laws.[22] One could refer to them as "quasi-marriages."[23]

Cohabitation was not a sign of decadence or an atmosphere of supposed sexual permissiveness in society. On the contrary, cohabitation was used by those who wished to adhere to the ideal of marriage yet were

---

[18] This was viewed differently by older research.

[19] Raimund Friedl, *Der Konkubinat im kaiserzeitlichen Rom: Von Augustus bis Septimius Severus*, Historia Einzelschriften 98 (Stuttgart: Steiner, 1996), 270. Cf. Gerhard Höppler, *Nichteheliche Lebens-gemeinschaften als Problem für das staatliche und kirchliche Recht,* Europäische Hochschulschriften Series 23: Theology 663 (Frankfurt: Peter Lang, 1999), 26–27. Similarly Lise Arends Olsen, *La femme et l'enfant dans les unions illégitimes à Rome: L'évolution du droit jusqu'au début de l'Empire* (Bern: Lang, 1999), 198–199.

[20] Friedl, 274; Martin Grosse, *Freie römische Ehe und nichteheliche Lebensgemeinschaft*, series jurisprudence 123 (Pfaffenweiler: Centaurus, 1991), 263; and R. Leonhard, "Concubinatus," in *Realencyclopädie der classischen Altertumswissenschaft*, ed. August E. Pauly and Georg Wissowa, 84 vols. (Stuttgart: Druckenmüller, 1901), 4:835–838.

[21] Marriages of soldiers were permitted for the first time by Septimius Severus in AD 197; see Friedl, 247.

[22] Ibid., 237–269.

[23] Ibid., 271.

prohibited from marrying.[24] Under the Augustan marriage laws,[25] every man between twenty-five and sixty and every woman between twenty and fifty was required to marry. This also applied to the divorced and widowed who did not have at least three children.[26] Only Roman citizens were allowed to enter into a fully validated marriage. Slaves could enter with each other or with Roman citizens into a union called a *contubernium*, which did not lead to a legal status and could be ended by the slaves' patron at any time.[27] Under Augustus, unions between free citizens and freed slaves or women of lower origin were for the first time legally defined by the term *concubinatus*. This legal status was not really desirable for the woman, because it denied her full recognition as a wife (*iustum matrimonium* and *honor matrimonii*) and deemed the children illegitimate.[28]

Today, the majority of scholars are of the opinion that the Augustan marriage laws at best only partially reached their goal and were not popular,[29] but they were probably more or less strictly applied everywhere in the Empire.[30]

Who entered into cohabitation and through what motivation? Soldiers did so because they were not allowed to marry during their time of service. Roman citizens cohabited with slaves, who after emancipation could later enter into marriage. But due to status and inheritance considerations, this did not occur very often.[31] Freed slaves also cohabited because they were restricted by a marriage prohibition of their former owner. This brought inheritance advantages to these patrons[32] by imposing

---

[24] Friedl, 275. On pages 150–165, Friedl enumerates an abundance of prohibition cases. See also Olsen, 166. Almost every author sees the real reason for cohabitation in the laws of Augustus. Also Max Kaser, *Das Römische Privatrecht*, Handbuch der Altertumswissenschaft, Abt. 10, History of Law, III.3, 3 vols. (München: Beck, 1971), 1:328–329; and Gottfried Schiemann, "Concubinatus," in *Der neue Pauly: Encyclopädie der Antike*, 19 vols. (Stuttgart: Melzer, 1997), 3:118–119.

[25] Friedl, 60–68; and Höppler, 17. The laws come from the years 18 BC (*lex Iulia de maritandis ordinibus*) and 9 BC (*lex Papia Poppaea nuptialis*). They remained effective until Constantine (AD 306–337). See also Grosse, 126–129; G. Delling, "Ehegesetze," in *Reallexikon für Antike und Christentum*, ed., T. Klauser et al., 29 vols. to date (Stuttgart: Hiersemann Verlag, 1959–), 4:677–680; and Bruce W. Winter, *Roman Wives, Roman Widows: The Appearance of New Women and the Pauline Communities* (Grand Rapids, MI: Eerdmans, 2003), 39–58.

[26] Olsen, 160–162.

[27] Grosse, 157–158.

[28] Ibid., 152–157.

[29] Ibid., 126–129.

[30] A document (*testatio*) from the year AD 145 in Egypt confirms the birth of illegitimate twins, in which the Augustan laws are referred to. This could be evidence that the Augustan laws were also respected far from Rome. See Olsen, 175.

[31] Friedl, 176–180.

[32] Ibid., 199–213, 272.

cohabitation upon the freed slaves. Voluntary cohabitation, in contrast to a fully valid marriage, cannot really be proven from our sources, as it was true only for a few emperors,[33] not for the majority of the population. The public opinion appears to have had great reservations toward cohabitation for respectable citizens.[34]

Is it possible to compare Roman times with today's circumstances?

> These fundamental constituents moved cohabitation in Roman times far from what one understands today as "non-marital partnership." Roman cohabitation was built entirely on other foundations and based on other motives. While in Rome it was primarily a forced form of cohabitation with the goal of coming as close as possible to marriage, the "non-marital partnership" of today is either a "trial marriage" or an intentional alternative to marriage. The fundamental dissimilarity between the Roman society, which took for granted the inequality of individuals, and modern society, which is committed to the ideal of equality, permits only few analogies.[35]

Since there are no comparable marriage prohibitions at present (at least in the Western world), the circumstances in Roman times cannot be compared with the present ones, because today all who wish to may enter into a fully valid marriage.

This naturally raises the question as to where, for example, Paul stood on the Augustan marriage laws. As a matter of principle, he called for the state and its legislation to be respected (Rom 13:1–7). However, in relation to the marriage question, Paul was in no way willing to impose marriage on everyone (1 Cor 7), thus standing in contrast with the intention of the Roman legislation. Since Paul liked to use legal terminology in his manner of theological expression, we can suppose that he was also aware of the

---

[33] Friedl, 170–176; and Höppler, 25–26. In the New Testament period, this applies especially to Nero, who was successively married to different women and also maintained several different relationships. After the death of his wife, Vespasian lived as emperor in cohabitation with his former mistress, who almost occupied the position of a wife.

[34] Olsen, 168–169. Albrecht Oepke, "gynē," in *Theological Dictionary of the New Testament*, ed. Gerhard Kittel, trans. G. W. Bromiley, 10 vols. (Grand Rapids, MI: Eerdmans, 1964–1974), 1:776–789. Monogamous marriage appears to have been the norm in the ancient Greek and Roman world. Although intercourse with a prostitute or slave was often not considered reprehensible, the man, as a rule, maintained a valid marriage. Satirists ridiculing someone for being married eight times in the course of five autumns (Juvenal, *The Satires of Juvenal*, trans. P. Green [London: Penguin, 1974], Satire 6, lines 229–230), show a decay of morality, but also the fact that marriage and not cohabitation was the norm.

[35] Friedl, 276 (translated by the present author); similarly Grosse, 244–245.

marriage laws. However, he classified them—obviously—as non-binding for Christians.

As a principle, we can conclude that governmental laws may demand or allow things that, from a biblical viewpoint, are not binding for Christians. If a certain society allows cohabitation as legally correct, this does not mean that Christians can choose this option, since biblical ethics forbid doing so.

Cohabitation in Post-Biblical Judaism

Marriage was obligatory for the Jewish man.[36] As Rabbi Eleazar (around AD 270) put it, "a man who has no wife is no man."[37]

We have only a few references relevant to our topic of cohabitation. If a marriage was contractually arranged, a dowry (*ketubah*) was required.[38] Should the marriage terminate, this sum of money was paid to the woman from the assets of the man at its dissolution (divorce or death of the husband). If the dowry was settled, the marriage was considered legitimate; if not, it was then considered cohabitation (Rabbi Meir called it "adulterous intercourse").[39] Later rabbis in the third century defined a concubine as a woman without a *ketubah* and without betrothal. Therefore, a marriage contract and betrothal were normal preconditions for the entrance into marriage.

Cohabitation in Church History

Due to lack of space, only a short overview can be given here. For details and literature, see the footnotes.[40]

Early Church History

In the earliest times, upper-class Christian women apparently had difficulty finding a Christian husband of the appropriate social status, and therefore either married pagans[41] or cohabited with Christians of a lower class, as a marriage was legally impossible. This led to a controversy between Bishop Callistus (AD 218–222), who permitted monogamous

---

[36] A. Oepke, "Ehe," in *Reallexikon für Antike und Christentum*, 4:650–666, esp. 656.

[37] For further quotations, see Hermann L. Strack and Paul Billerbeck, *Kommentar zum Neuen Testament aus Talmud und Midrasch*, 6 vols., 9th ed. (München: Beck, 1989), 2:373.

[38] Ibid., 2:388, 391.

[39] Ibid., 2:391.

[40] For more details and references, see Raimund Friedl, "Konkubinat," in *Reallexikon für Antike und Christentum*, 21:416–435.

[41] Höppler, 34–36. Tertullian argues against marriage with an unbeliever (*Ad uxorem* 2.3, in Alexander Roberts and James Donaldson, eds., *The Ante-Nicene Fathers*, 10 vols. [1885–1887; repr. Peabody, MA: Hendrickson, 1994], 4:45–46).

cohabitation for Christians, and Hippolytus of Rome, who protested against Callistus.[42] It seems that Callistus is the exception.[43] We know of one case in which Hippolytus gave a man living in cohabitation the advice to leave his concubine and take a wife in accordance with the law.[44]

Emperor Constantine tried in vain to abolish cohabitation.[45] However, his family legislation had private, not Christian, motives.[46]

Bishop Ambrose of Milan (AD 339–397) restricted sexuality to legitimate marriage,[47] excluding adultery and cohabitation for Christians. At the Council of Toledo (AD 400), all men who had a concubine in addition to a wife were excluded from the Sacraments, but not, however, if they only lived with a single concubine.[48] Bishop Maximus of Turin (who died before AD 423) recommended that men allow the female slaves who lived with them in cohabitation to be set free and to marry, in order to end their adulterous situation.[49]

Before his conversion, Augustine (AD 354–430) lived in two cohabitations.[50] In his old age, he portrayed sexuality in a bad light.[51] In one reference, he judges cohabitation relatively favorably, while in another he places it close to adultery.[52]

---

[42] Hippolytus, *Refutatio omnium haeresium* 9.7, in Roberts and Donaldson, 5:131. See Höppler, 36. For more details, see Hermann J. Vogt, "Die Eheschließung in der frühen Kirche," in *Eheschließung - mehr als ein rechtlich Ding?, Quaestiones Disputatae* 120, ed. Klemens Richter (Freiburg: Herder, 1989), 119–132.

[43] It seems there were no church weddings in this earliest period, according to the main conjecture among scholars today. However, the approval of a marriage was to be obtained from the bishop (Ignatius, *Ad Polykarpum* 5.2, in Roberts and Donaldson, 1:95). On the question of available sources, see G. Delling, "Eheschließung," in *Reallexikon für Antike und Christentum*, 4:719–731; and Heller, 203.

[44] Hippolytus, *Apostolic Tradition*, 16, http://www.stjohnsarlingtonva.org/Customer-Content/saintjohnsarlington/CMS/files/EFM/Apostolic_Tradition_by_Hippolytus.pdf (accessed May 7, 2021).

[45] Friedl, 33. See also Kaser, 2:183.

[46] Höppler, 28–30.

[47] Ambrose, *De Abraham* 1.7.59, quoted in Höppler, 39–40.

[48] Friedl, 34; Höppler, 47–48; and Heller, 201.

[49] Maximus, *Sermo* 88.5, quoted in Höppler, 40–41.

[50] Augustine, *Confessions* VI.15.25, in Philip Schaff, ed., *The Nicene and Post-Nicene Fathers*, Series 1, 14 vols. (1886–1889; repr. Peabody, MA: Hendrickson, 1994), 1:100; and Höppler, 41–46. See also Alfred Niebergall, *Ehe und Eheschließung in der Bibel und in der Geschichte der alten Kirche,* Marburger theologische Studien 18 (Marburg: Elwert, 1985), 192–193. For Augustine the purpose of marriage was procreation, while concubinage did not serve this goal and was therefore dissolvable (Niebergall, 196, 229).

[51] For sources, see Friedl, 34.

[52] See the discussion in Höppler, 45–46, concerning Augustine, *De bono conjugali* ["On the Good

Pope Leo I (AD 440–461) allowed Christian women to marry men who had previously lived with another woman in cohabitation. Without scruples he permitted men to put away the slaves with whom they cohabited, and to enter into a marriage with free women.[53] Later, Bishop Caesarius of Arles (AD 470–542) lamented that he could not excommunicate all men in his congregation for premarital cohabitation, simply because their number was too high.[54]

Middle Ages and the Modern Age

When we move to the time of the tenth to twelfth centuries, we observe that questions of marriage and cohabitation were not yet clarified in their final form, although most people tended to strive for a church wedding. Perhaps cohabitation was tolerated for many men, if it was not possible to enter into a marriage due to economic reasons.[55] At the church level, the First and Second Lateran Councils (1123 and 1139) prohibited cohabitation for clerics. Finally, the Council of Basel (1435) and later Pope Leo X (at the Fifth Lateran Council, 1514) issued a prohibition of lay cohabitation. At the Council of Trent (1563), marriage was proclaimed to be the only legitimate form of partnership.[56]

Cohabitation was penalized by state authorities for the first time in 1530 through the legislation of the Holy Roman Empire (*Reichspolizeiordnung*).[57] We can suppose that until the nineteenth century, only half the population could marry, as people were not in a position to prove the minimal assets necessary for a marriage, leading inevitably to many cohabitations.[58]

The Catholic Church in Recent Times

We can only very briefly touch on the last 160 years.[59] In 1852, Pope Pius IX condemned civil marriage without a church wedding as "disgraceful and disastrous cohabitation."[60]

---

of Marriage"] 5, in Schaff, 3:399–413.

[53] Leo, *Resp. ad inquis* 5, quoted in Höppler, 48–49.

[54] Caesarius, *Sermons* 32.4, 42.5, quoted in Höppler, 50–51.

[55] Höppler, 60.

[56] Friedl, 37; for more details, see Höppler, 63–70.

[57] Höppler, 75.

[58] Helga Frisch, "*Wilde Ehe*" *mit kirchlichem Segen?* (Gütersloh: Gütersloher Verlagshaus Mohn, 1990), 52–54.

[59] For a detailed discussion, see Höppler, 226–320.

[60] Pius, *Allocution Acerbissimum vom* 27.9.1852, quoted in Höppler, 226.

The most recent catechism states:

> 2390 In a so-called free union, a man and a woman refuse to give juridical and public form to a liaison involving sexual intimacy. . . . The expression covers a number of different situations: cohabitation, rejection of marriage as such, or inability to make long-term commitments. . . . The sexual act must take place exclusively within marriage. Outside of marriage it always constitutes a grave sin and excludes one from sacramental communion.[61]

In the next paragraph the catechism condemns "trial marriages." Before the Codex Iuris Canonici (CIC) 1917, lay people who lived in cohabitation could be excommunicated after three unsuccessful warnings. With the CIC 1917, they were only excluded from the sacraments and from positions of honor in the Church. According to the CIC 1983, this applies only indirectly, because the offense of "cohabitation" is no longer explicitly mentioned in the CIC. However, it can always lead to a restriction as with "public sinners" (communion, anointing of the sick, and funerals).[62] In the last few years, the necessity of pastoral counseling in cases of cohabitation has quite often been emphasized.

If retired persons or students experience financial disadvantages because of a state wedding, Catholics sometimes go around the laws of their home state by getting married in another country where a church wedding alone, without state recognition, is possible.[63] This gives one the impression that the Catholic Church still rejects cohabitation in its teachings, but wishes to appear more moderate in our modern times.

Cohabitation in the Bible

In the following pages, the topic of cohabitation in the Bible will be examined. Sometimes, the opinion is expressed that the Bible does not take a position on cohabitation,[64] many offering this as an excuse for their nonmarital cohabitations. We will see, however, that some references to nonmarital cohabitation can indeed be found in the Bible. Only that material which is relevant to our question will be mentioned. We will briefly

---

[61] *Catechism of the Catholic Church* (Mahwah, NJ: Paulist Press, 1994), 575.

[62] Severin Lederhilger, "Konkubinat," in *Lexikon für Theologie und Kirche*, 3rd ed., eds. Konrad Baumgartner, Horst Bürkle, and Klaus Ganzer, 11 vols. (Freiburg: Herder, 1997), 6:271.

[63] For details, see Höppler, 302–310. In some countries, a church wedding without the civil magistrate is possible (e.g., Italy); in other countries it is prohibited by law (e.g., Germany).

[64] See, e.g., Gary Jenkins, "Cohabitation," in *New Dictionary of Christian Ethics & Pastoral Theology*, ed. David J. Atkinson et al. (Downers Grove, IL: InterVarsity, 1995), 238–239.

touch upon the texts that in the past have been brought up in connection with the topic of cohabitation.

Cohabitation in the Old Testament

Cases of Polygamy

The Hebrew expression *pilegesh*[65] is understood to mean "cohabitation," both in the LXX (*pallakē*) and in modern Bibles ("concubine").[66] We will briefly examine this issue because it deals with polygamous relationships that are not comparable to present-day conditions.

"Concubines"[67] were considered wives of their husbands, but subordinate to the main wife. As a result, they had a lower legal status than the main wife. They were often former slaves, hence their children were not eligible for a portion of the inheritance (see Ishmael, Gen 21:10). On the other hand, the father could also leave all his sons an equal inheritance, regardless of whether they were the son of a wife or of a concubine (e.g., Jacob's sons, Gen 49).[68] Obviously, polygamy was only a privilege of the rich or ruling class, and was otherwise hardly customary.[69] The Mosaic law does not mention "concubines," which in effect indicates that polygamy was not intended in God's plan[70] and is not in harmony with the creation order.

Although some men of faith in the Old Testament also had concubines (e.g., Abraham, Jacob, David), the principle of monogamy is later clearly emphasized in the New Testament.[71] In New Testament times, Josephus and Philo also used *pallakē* and related terms in the sense of concubines, in the same manner as the LXX.[72]

---

[65] For the Old Testament, see K. Engelken, *"pilegesh," in Theological Dictionary of the Old Testament,* ed. G. Johannes Botterweck, Helmer Ringgren, and Heinz-Josef Fabry, trans. J. T. Willis, G. W. Bromiley, and D. E. Green, 17 vols. (Grand Rapids, MI: Eerdmans, 1974–2021), 11:550–551. For the issue of polygamy in the Bible, see Ronald A. G. du Preez, *Polygamy in the Bible*, ATS Dissertation Series (Berrien Springs, MI: ATS Publications, 1993).

[66] KJV, NIV, RSV, etc. and Vulgate.

[67] Here we can mention the secondary wives of Abraham (Gen 25:6), Jacob (Gen 35:22), Manasseh (1 Chr 7:14), Gideon (Judg 8:31), a Levite (Judg 19:1-2), Elkanah (1 Sam 1), Saul (2 Sam 3:7), David (2 Sam 3:1–16; 5:13; 15:16; 16:21), Solomon (1 Kgs 11:3), Rehoboam (2 Chr 11:21), or Belshazzar (Dan 5:2–3) and other pagan kings (3 Ezra 4:29; Neh 2:6 [LXX], 2 *Maccabees* 4:30).

[68] R. H. McGrath, "Concubine (in the Bible)," in *New Catholic Encyclopedia,* 15 vols. (Washington, DC: Catholic University of America, 1967), 4:121.

[69] Victor P. Hamilton, "Marriage (OT and ANE)," in *Anchor Bible Dictionary*, ed. David Noel Freedman, 6 vols. (New York: Doubleday, 1992), 4:565.

[70] Du Preez, 61–64.

[71] See, e.g., Romans 7:1–3; 1 Corinthians 7:1–4; 1 Timothy 3:2; Titus 1:6.

[72] Craig Steven de Vos, "Stepmothers, Concubines and the Case of PORNEIA in 1 Corinthians 5," *New Testament Studies* 44 (1998): 104–114, esp. 113.

Since these polygamous marriages in the Old Testament have nothing to do with our modern forms of cohabitation, we do not need to further investigate this question here. We can, however, already anticipate that *pallakē* and its cognates do not occur in the New Testament.[73] The reason for this is that in the first century AD, according to the Jewish-influenced understanding of *pallakē*, it always addressed the secondary wives, and not the concubine of an ancient Greco-Roman or modern understanding. Obviously, this Greek expression was avoided in the New Testament to prevent misunderstandings.

Ezra-Nehemiah: Dismissal of Foreign Women

The books of Ezra and Nehemiah tell of Jews who had foreign women and who were requested to send them away along with their children (Ezra 10; Neh 13:23–30). We have to raise the question as to what the legal status of these men and women was. Were they living in cohabitation, or were they married?[74] Were the wives considered secondary wives?[75] The manner of expression in the Masoretic Text or the LXX is worth noting in any case.

The verses utilizing *yashab nashim/kathizō gynaikas* are Ezra 10:2, 10, 14, 17, 18; and Nehemiah 13:23, 27. The Hebrew verb *yashab* is defined as "to sit down, to sit, to dwell" and in the *hiphil* here in Ezra and Nehemiah is said to have the meaning "to make a foreign woman a citizen, to marry,"[76] or "to let (a woman) live with oneself, in the sense of to marry,"[77] or just "marry."[78] Cognates in other languages support this meaning.[79] Literally, one could translate "to let one live with oneself."[80] In the LXX, the verb *kathizō* primarily means "to sit down, to seat oneself;" however, it has

---

[73] The Vulgate uses in the New Testament cognate terms in 1 Corinthians 6:9–10 (*masculorum concubitores*) and 1 Timothy 1:10 (*masculorum concubitoribus*).

[74] Most commentators seem to prefer valid marriages without discussing the details. For one recent commentary, see Klaus-Dieter Schunck, *Nehemia*, Biblischer Kommentar Altes Testament (Neukirchen-Vluyn: Neukirchener Verlag, 2009), 396–401.

[75] "Second wives" was the interpretation of Francis D. Nichol, ed., *The Seventh-day Adventist Bible Commentary,* 7 vols. (Washington: Review and Herald, 1976), 3:452: "…who may in many instances have been second wives."

[76] L. Koehler, W. Baumgartner, and J. J. Stamm, *The Hebrew and Aramaic Lexicon of the Old Testament,* 5 vols. (Leiden: Brill, 1999), 2:444–445.

[77] Wilhelm Gesenius, *Hebräisches und Aramäisches Handwörterbuch über das Alte Testament,* 18th ed. (Berlin: Springer, 2013), 506.

[78] David J. A. Clines, ed., *The Dictionary of Classical Hebrew,* 9 vols. (Sheffield: Sheffield Academic Press, 1998), 4:329.

[79] According to the Ethiopic *vawsaba* (Koehler, 444) and the Syrian (Gesenius, 2:506).

[80] Antonius H. J. Gunneweg, *Esra*, Kommentar zum Alten Testament (Gütersloh: Mohn, 1985), 173.

been suggested that in our texts it should be translated as "to marry."[81] The newest lexicon to the LXX judges the question more cautiously, when for Ezra 10:2 it gives the meaning "to live with a (woman)."[82]

It is not quite convincing that only Ezra and Nehemiah should offer this unexpected connotation of "to marry," since the appropriate term *gameō* (in the LXX quite seldom), or *lambanō gynaika* (frequent; also Ezra 2:61; 10:44), or only *lambanō* (also Ezra 9:2, 12) were available.

Otherwise, the verb *kathizō* is used by Ezra and Nehemiah in the usual sense of "to sit,"[83] "to settle down, dwell,"[84] "to remain,"[85] or "to appoint."[86] The meaning "to dwell" most often occurs in these two books. Is the term being used in both books in the context of foreign women, meaning "to cohabit/lie with" in the sense of sexuality, without wanting to speak of an official wedding? Some commentators consider the Jewish men not to have been living together with proper wives, but rather with prostitutes.[87] Reasons provided are that the Hebrew word translated here with "to marry" is nowhere else used with this meaning, and that the mentioned "sending away" of the women uses different expressions than the usual terms for divorce.[88] Other scholars come to the conclusion that these Jews were living in cohabitation without a valid marriage.[89]

Unfortunately, it is not very clear whether Ezra and Nehemiah are referring to cases of cohabitation or if the referenced Israelites were legally married. If it was really cohabitation in the truest sense, then we would have the first biblical indication for its rejection. But this cannot be proven

---

[81] See also Henry G. Liddell and Robert Scott, *A Greek-English Lexicon* (Oxford: Clarendon Press, 1996), 854. For this meaning only biblical texts are furnished, but no extrabiblical sources.

[82] Johann Lust, Erik Eynikel, and Katrin Hauspie, *Greek-English Lexicon of the Septuagint* (Stuttgart: Deutsche Bibelgesellschaft, 2003), 296.

[83] Ezra 10:9; Nehemiah 1:4.

[84] Ezra 2:7; Nehemiah 7:72 (LXX 7:73); 8:17; 11:1–4, 25; 13:16.

[85] Ezra 8:32.

[86] Nehemiah 6:7.

[87] H. G. M. Williamson, *Ezra, Nehemiah*, Word Biblical Commentary 16 (Waco, TX: Word, 1985), 143, 150. In other passages he speaks of marriages. F. Charles Fensham, *The Books of Ezra and Nehemiah,* New International Commentary on the Old Testament (Grand Rapids, MI: Eerdmans, 1982), 135, emphasizes the illegal character of the unions that the Jewish men entered into, but also speaks of real marriages.

[88] Cf. Gordon J. Wenham and William E. Heth, *Jesus and Divorce* (Carlisle: Paternoster, 1997), 162–164, 277.

[89] Allen Guenther, "A Typology of Israelite Marriage: Kinship, Socio-Economic, and Religious Factors," *Journal for the Study of the Old Testament* 29 (June 2005): 387–407. Richard Davidson supports this view in "Does Marriage Still Matter?" See also Davidson, *Flame of Yahweh: Sexuality in the Old Testament* (Peabody, MA: Hendrickson, 2007), 320–324, 417.

definitively.[90] More likely, these unions were not in accordance with the Mosaic law, were regarded as illegal, and could therefore be declared invalid.[91] Nevertheless, these unions were very close to cohabitation because they involved a disallowed cohabitation (see Ezra 9:2).

In any case, this story shows that although parts of society in Ezra's day did not condemn these unions, biblical ethics proclaimed by Ezra and Nehemiah was more important than public opinion.

Sexual Contact Before or Outside of Marriage

The Mosaic law classified and assessed different forms of sexuality outside of marriage (Deut 22:13–23:1). For those engaged or married, extramarital sex was regarded as a heavy offense to be punished by death. If a virgin was enticed, the man had to marry her or pay a sum of money, should her father not agree to a marriage (Exod 22:16–17; Deut 22:28–29). From this procedure it can be inferred that the Old Testament rejects relationships outside of marriage or marriage-like partnerships. It becomes clear that these laws encouraged premarital sexual purity and tried to exclude any sexual activity prior to or outside of marriage, thus holding up the ideal of virginal purity.[92] This is remarkable because, contrary to the customs of the Ancient Orient, intercourse before marriage was liable to be punished only in Israel.[93]

Cohabitation in the New Testament

Herod Antipas and Herodias

Mark 6:18 reports, "For John had been saying to Herod, 'It is not lawful for you to have [*echein*] your brother's wife'" (NIV).

Unfortunately, we do not know the exact chronological sequence of events in which this statement is embedded. Herod had been married for a long time to the daughter of King Aretas when he fell in love with Herodias, who was also married. He promised Herodias he would divorce the daughter of Aretas after his return from a trip to Rome, and marry her. Upon his return, his wife fled to her father Aretas, who declared war upon

---

[90] It seems that Ellen G. White, *Prophets and Kings* (Mountain View, CA: Pacific Press, 1950), 619–622, 673–674, has marriages in mind, although she does not enter into a discussion of this question and her statements can be interpreted either way. She uses expressions such as "unlawful alliances," "even some of the men entrusted with responsibilities were living in open sin," "intermarriage," "to intermarry with the surrounding peoples," and "many who had married idolaters."

[91] According to Wenham and Heth, 163.

[92] Duane L. Christensen, *Deuteronomy 21:10–34:12*, Word Biblical Commentary 6B (Nashville, TN: Thomas Nelson, 2002), 522–523.

[93] J. G. McConville, *Deuteronomy*, Apollos Old Testament Commentary 5 (Leicester: Apollos, 2002), 341.

Herod and defeated him in battle. Later, Josephus attributed the defeat of Herod to the murder of John the Baptist.[94]

The question arises as to whether Mark 6:18 refers to the time before or after the wedding of Herod and Herodias. Mark writes "because he had married her" (6:17, NAS), whereby it must be considered that the report concerning John from verse 14 onwards is not in strict chronological order. Theoretically, the beheading of John could have taken place before the marriage of Herod,[95] and that at that time they were still living in cohabitation. That would account for the wording "to have" her (Mark 6:18, Matt 14:4), which we will look into later. If this is correct, John was criticizing cohabitation (along with adultery). However, this cannot be proven and it appears improbable.

Bernice (Acts 25:13)

After the death of her husband, Bernice lived together with her brother Herod Agrippa II, leading to disgraceful speculations.[96] After a subsequent marriage, she entered into an affair with Titus (first in Palestine then in Rome), who wanted to officially marry her. But resistance from the Romans deterred him from doing so.[97] Since the Bible is not concerned with the details of the relationships of Bernice, a detailed discussion is not necessary.

The Samaritan Woman (John 4)

In the conversation between Jesus and the Samaritan woman, the following dialogue takes place: "He told her, 'Go, call your husband and come back.' 'I have no husband,' she replied. Jesus said to her, 'You are right when you say you have no husband. The fact is, you have had five husbands, and the man you now have is not your husband. What you have just said is quite true'" (John 4:16–18, NIV).

Later Jewish scholarly opinion allowed a woman at most three marriages,[98] although the Old Testament does not stipulate a specific number. Obviously, the Samaritan woman had experienced several divorces[99] and

---

[94] For details, see Josephus, *Antiquities of the Jews* 18.109–119, in *The Works of Josephus*, trans. William Whiston (Peabody, MA: Hendrickson, 1987), 484; and Emil Schürer, *The History of the Jewish People in the Age of Jesus Christ*, 5 vols. (Edinburgh: T&T Clark, 1973), 1:344.

[95] Robert H. Gundry, *Matthew, A Commentary on His Handbook for a Mixed Church Under Persecution,* 2nd ed. (Grand Rapids, MI: Eerdmans, 1994), 286–287.

[96] Juvenal, *Satires* 6.156–160.

[97] For details, see Schürer, 1:474–479.

[98] Strack and Billerbeck, 2:437.

[99] We do not know whether the Samaritan woman had one or several divorces. It is quite unlikely that all her former husbands died.

then lived with a man to whom she was not married.[100] Compared to her detailed answers to Jesus's questions in John 4:11–12, 15, the Samaritan woman's answer to Jesus' request to get her husband (John 4:16) is conspicuously brief: "I have no husband [*ouk echō andra*]." Troubled by a guilty conscience, her reply becomes very short. She is theoretically correct, but nevertheless misleading. The term "husband" is found at the end of her clause in Greek. Of course, Jesus knew that she did not mean she was unmarried or widowed. In His reply, He turns the word order around,[101] and in Greek the term "husband" moves to the beginning of the clause: "You have correctly said, 'I have no husband [*kalōs eipas hoti andra ouk echo*].'" Obviously, Jesus emphasizes the meaning of "husband." It is important to note that the cohabitation of the Samaritan woman did not automatically constitute a marriage, but remained an illegitimate relationship.[102]

---

[100] So the following authors, in alphabetical order: George R. Beasley-Murray, *John*, Word Biblical Commentary 36, 2nd ed. (Nashville, TN: Thomas Nelson, 1999), 61; Jürgen Becker, *Das Evangelium nach Johannes,* Ökumenischer Taschenbuchkommentar zum Neuen Testament 4.1, 3rd ed. (Gütersloh: Mohn, 1991), 204–205: "an illegitimate marriage was probably forbidden by Jews as well as by the Samaritans"; Werner de Boor, *Das Evangelium des Johannes*, Wuppertaler Studienbibel (Wuppertal: Brockhaus, 1968), 135–136; F. F. Bruce, *The Gospel of John* (Grand Rapids, MI: Eerdmans, 2001), 107; Rudolf Bultmann, *Das Evangelium des Johannes*, Kritisch-exegetischer Kommentar 2 (Göttingen: Vandenhoeck & Ruprecht, 1978), 138 n. 5: ". . . if the wife's married life is already a disgrace, even more so the present illegitimate relationship"; Ernst Haenchen, *Das Johannesevangelium: Ein Kommentar* (Tübingen: Mohr, 1980), 242; Daniel J. Harrington, *The Gospel of John,* Sacra Pagina 4 (Collegeville, MN: Michael Glazier, 1998), 127: "She regards herself as not married to the man with whom she is currently living. She has lived an irregular married life and is currently in a sinful situation"; Frédéric Godet, *Kommentar zu dem Evangelium des Johannes* (Hannover: Meyer, 1903), 188: "after five lawful ones, she lived now in an illicit union"; Gerhard Maier, *Johannes-Evangelium* 1. Teil, Edition C (Neuhausen-Stuttgart: Hänssler, 1984), 157–158; Jon Paulien, *John: Jesus Gives Life to a New Generation,* Bible Amplifier (Boise, ID: Pacific Press, 1995), 104; Rudolf Schnackenburg, *Das Johannesevangelium,* Herders Theologischer Kommentar 4.1 (Freiburg: Herder, 1979), 469–470, speaks of a sinful partnership; Johannes Schneider, *Das Evangelium nach Johannes*, Sonderband Theologischer Handkommentar Neues Testament, 2nd ed. (Berlin: Evangelische Verlagsanstalt, 1978), 112: "but now she is living with a man to whom she is not legally married. In doing so, she has sinned against the provisions of the Mosaic law that also applies to her"; Klaus Wengst, *Das Johannesevangelium: 1. Teilband: Kapitel 1–10*, Theologischer Kommentar Neues Testsment 4.1 (Stuttgart: Kohlhammer, 2004), 171–172; Ulrich Wilkens, *Das Evangelium nach Johannes*, Neues Testament Deutsch 4 (Göttingen: Vandenhoeck, 1998), 83: "the sixth time to live with a man without the protection of the marriage"; and Theodor Zahn, *Das Evangelium des Johannes* (Wuppertal: Brockhaus, 1983), 244: "she is only his concubine."

[101] William Hendriksen, *Exposition of the Gospel According to John,* New Testament Commentary (Grand Rapids, MI: Baker, 1983), 164.

[102] Barnabas Lindras, *The Gospel of John*, New Century Bible Commentary (Grand Rapids, MI: Eerdmans, 1987), 186: "The point, however, is that in Jesus' eyes, her permanent union does not constitute a true marriage." See also Gäckle, *Was hält Christen zusammen?*, 13; and Wilhelm, Adventecho 3, 26: "In the encounter with the woman at Jacob's well, Jesus makes it clear that he distinguishes between marriage and non-marital cohabitation."

> More likely, however, he is simply not her husband legally, there having been no economic transaction or ceremony. Some ancients might have justified this nonmarital union, but public opinion would have been against them; for strict Jews and Samaritans it would be almost equivalent to treating her as a concubine or as a prostitute. To illustrate the odium that would have been attached to their relationship among Samaritans with stricter moral commitments: the semantic range of the Hebrew term translated "prostitute" included adultery and probably would have also included the woman living with the man without marriage.[103]

The reaction of the Samaritan woman (John 4:19) includes no objection to Jesus' reproach to her living in an immoral condition. On the contrary, she comes to the recognition of her sin[104] and acknowledges His prophetic gift.[105] She later repeats it when she says, "He told me all the things that I have done" (John 4:39, NAS). Thus, she admits her inappropriate behavior.

Commentaries discuss the question of whether Jesus wanted to lead the Samaritan woman to a confession of her guilt, or to her recognition of His messiahship. However, these considerations are not necessarily mutually exclusive because the recognition of one's sin leads to the longing for a savior.

Why Jesus did not insist that the woman should change her living conditions remains open. Although the very short Bible narrative does not answer this question, Jesus' statement of "From now on sin no more" (John 8:11, NAS) may be also applied to the Samaritan woman. Jesus handles the situation tenderly, although He does not shrink from addressing the issue.

Affair With "His Father's Wife" (1 Cor 5)

Paul had already ordered in an earlier letter[106] that the church should take care to have no association with immoral people (*pornous,* 1 Cor 5:9). In 1 Corinthians 5 he encounters an especially blatant case of immorality

---

[103] Craig S. Keener, *The Gospel of John: A Commentary*, 2 vols. (Peabody, MA: Hendrickson, 2003), 1:608.

[104] Ellen G. White, *The Desire of Ages* (Mountain View, CA: Pacific Press, 1940), 187, writes that the Samaritan woman was brought to recognition of sin through the question of Jesus about her husband. Thus, White clearly assesses the cohabitation as not being in harmony with the teachings of the Bible.

[105] Hendriksen, 165.

[106] Our numbering considers only the canonical epistles 1 and 2 Corinthians. In addition, Paul wrote at least one other but lost letter. See Ellen G. White, *Acts of the Apostles* (Mountain View, CA: Pacific Press, 1952), 300.

(1 Cor 5:1, *porneia*).[107] In Corinth, where a church member had "his father's wife"[108] (1 Cor 5:1), Paul evidently avoids the expression "stepmother."[109] The wording "his father's wife" can be interpreted in different ways,[110] the main ones being:

- an affair with the stepmother while the father was still alive[111]
- cohabitation with the former concubine of the father[112]
- an affair with the divorced stepmother[113]
- an affair with the stepmother after the death of the father

It appears most likely that the church member was living in a marriage-like relationship—that is, in cohabitation[114]—with his widowed stepmother or the former concubine of his father.[115] If "stepmother" is what

---

[107] This expression possesses a large range of meanings and is used for all cases of extramarital or premarital intercourse. See Gerhard Dautzenberg, "*pheugete tēn porneian* (1 Kor 6, 18)," in *Neues Testament und Ethik*, Festschrift für Rudolf Schnackenburg, ed. Helmut Merklein (Freiburg: Herder, 1989), 271–298. In classical Greek, the word-group around *porneuō* could also mean "cohabitation," according to H. Reißler and K. W. Niebuhr, "*porneuō*," in Lothar Coenen and Klaus Haacker, *Theologisches Begriffslexikon zum Neuen Testament*, 2 vols. (Wuppertal: Brockhaus, 1997), 1:298.

[108] She was not his own mother. Already Leviticus 18:7–8 differentiates between mother and stepmother.

[109] The Greek language has a proper term for "stepmother" (*mētria*), but it is not used in Scripture. Paul uses the remarkable phrasing "his/your father's wife" with respect to the Old Testament (Gen 37:2; Lev 18:8, 11; 20:11; Deut 27:20) in order to allude to the Mosaic laws. Compare Wolfgang Schrage, *Der erste Brief an die Korinther*, Evangelisch-Katholischer Kommentar, 2 vols. (Neukirchen: Neukirchener Verlag, 1991), 1:369. Ellen G. White leaves the question open, but avoids the term "stepmother" and speaks of a "licentious course" (*Acts of the Apostles*, 303–304).

[110] David E. Garland, *1 Corinthians*, Baker Exegetical Commentary on the New Testament (Grand Rapids, MI: Baker, 2003), 181–182. On page 158 he leaves the question open as to how the two were related. Anthony C. Thiselton, *The First Epistle to the Corinthians*, New International Greek Testament Commentary (Grand Rapids, MI: Eerdmans, 2000), 386, thinks that it may have been cohabitation or, even more probable, an illegal marriage. Similarly, Hans Conzelmann, *Der erste Brief an die Korinther*, Kritisch-Exegetischer Kommentar, 2nd ed. (Göttingen: Vandenhoeck & Ruprecht, 1981), 123–124.

[111] This option is preferred by Joseph A. Fitzmyer, *First Corinthians: A New Translation With Introduction and Commentary*, Anchor Bible 32 (New Haven, CT: Yale University Press, 2008), 234.

[112] Already Amos 2:7 criticizes, "Father and son use the same girl and so profane my holy name. (NIV)." In the pseudepigraphical book *Testament of Reuben* 1:6 (James Charlesworth, ed., *The Old Testament Pseudepigrapha*, 2 vols. [Garden City, NY: Doubleday, 1983–1985], 1:782) the term *porneia* is used to describe the immoral relations between Ruben and the secondary wife of his father.

[113] Hans Lietzmann, *An die Korinther I/II*, Handbuch zum Neuen Testament 9 (Tübingen: Mohr, 1969), 23: "It is probably an illegitimate marriage with the runaway or divorced wife of the father who is still alive."

[114] G. Delling, "Ehehindernisse," in *Reallexikon für Antike und Christentum*, 4:687.

[115] De Vos, 104–114; and Michael Wolter, "Der Brief des so genannten Unzuchtsünders," in

is meant in 1 Corinthians 5, a double sin is presented: incest and cohabitation.[116] If it was the former concubine of his father, then cohabitation is assessed as immoral.

From a certain point of view, Paul could be thinking particularly of incest in his letter. He does not describe this condition as "illegal" in the sense of Roman law,[117] but rather as "immoral" in the sense of the Old Testament (Lev 18:7–8; Deut 23:1; 27:20).[118] Because of this understanding, he uses the expression *porneia*. In the Old Testament (Lev 18:6–8; 20:11 as well as in the Mishna,[119] incestuous unions were punishable by death. In Roman law, they were forbidden and considered abominable.[120]

Paul, however, could just as well (or additionally) be criticizing cohabitation. The following points speak in favor of it being cohabitation:

- Roman law prohibited marriages between step-relatives,[121] thus making our case very likely one of cohabitation.

Liebe, Macht und Religion, Interdisciplinary Studies on Basic Dimensions of Human Existence, Gedenkschrift für Helmut Merklein, ed. Marlies Gielen (Stuttgart: Katholisches Bibelwerk, 2003), 323–337. Similarly, Peter Arzt-Grabner et al., 1. *Korinther,* Papyrologische Kommentare zum Neuen Testament 2 (Göttingen: Vandenhoeck & Ruprecht, 2006), 197, also calls the situation a long-term, marriage-like union with the stepmother.

[116] Schrage, 1:368–371.

[117] Here de Vos, 109, sees a strong argument in favor of his thesis that the woman had been the concubine of the father. It was common practice for an older man to take a concubine after the death of his wife (de Vos, 111).

[118] Lorenz Oberlinner, "Unzucht," in *Münchener Theologisches Wörterbuch*, ed. Josef Hainz and Alexander Sand (Düsseldorf: Patmos Verlag, 1997), 363. Brian S. Rosner, *Paul, Scripture, & Ethics: A Study of 1 Corinthians 5–7* (Leiden: Brill, 1994), emphasizes how forcefully Paul's moral thinking was conditioned by the Old Testament. Roy E. Ciampa and Brian S. Rosner, *The First Letter to the Corinthians,* Pillar New Testament Commentary (Grand Rapids, MI: Eerdmans, 2010), 197–200, sees incest as the main problem, whether the union was a marriage or cohabitation.

[119] m. *Sanhedrin* 7:4. The old synagogue in the second century AD was divided on the question of whether a pagan was permitted to marry his stepmother (Strack and Billerbeck, 3:345–346): Aqiba (d. AD 135) was against this idea; Eliezer (d. c. AD 90) and Meir (d. c. AD 150) did not object to it. This question implied some consequences: a proselyte could marry his stepmother, because according to the Jewish understanding a pagan lost, with his conversion, all former relational ties (Strack and Billerbeck, 3:353–356). Such an understanding, of course, was not supported by Paul.

[120] Sources are supplied by Schrage, 1:370 n. 16. A sexual relation with the stepmother was considered extremely scandalous. See Cicero, *Pro Cluentio* (*Oration for Aulus Cluentius Habitus*) 5.27, 6.15, in Loeb Classical Library 198 (Cambridge, MA: Harvard University Press, 1927); and Catullus, "Carmina," in *Complete Gedichten*, trans. Ype de Jong (Leiden: Primavera Pers, 2018), 74, 88–90.

[121] Source in Friedl, 154–155; see also Olsen, 150–154. One refers to the Roman jurist Gaius, who around AD 161 said, "It is illegal to marry the sister of one's father or mother. Nor can I marry the woman who was earlier my mother-in-law or stepmother" (Gaius, *Institutes of Roman Law* [Oxford: Clarendon, 1904], 1.63). Apparently, all legal forms of Roman law (marriage, *concubinage, contubernium*) prohibited incestuous relationships. A relationship with the former concubine of one's father was also forbidden. This would support the supposition that father and son lived in cohabitation with the same woman.

- Corinth was a Roman colony[122] and thus Roman law applied there. If the church member was married, the authorities would have reacted with a penalty.
- One early church reference describes the cohabitation clearly as concubinage.[123]
- The verb *echō* obviously connects John 4 with 1 Corinthians 5.[124]

The form of the Greek verb (present tense) makes it clear that this condition, offensive even to Gentiles, continued for a long time.[125] We need to examine if *echō* could mean a cohabitation in concubinage, which we can unequivocally affirm.[126] In the New Testament, the connection between *anēr*, *gynē*, and *echō* can refer to a legal marriage,[127] but also to unlawful unions.[128] In the LXX, the expression stands for prohibited unions[129] as well as for a lawful marriage.[130] In any case, *echein* ("to have" or "to hold") is a euphemism for sexual intercourse.[131]

---

[122] See Thiselton, 3–5; and Garland, 1–4. These authors point to the strong Roman influence in Corinth.

[123] Wolter, 323–337. He translates and comments on a letter, of which the Greek original is lost. He considers this letter to be a forgery of the old church. In this letter, a certain Eutychus (the immoral of 1 Corinthians 5) writes to Paul in defence of his concubinage with Chariklea, who was the former concubine of his deceased father. It is clear, according to this letter, that he had already lived with her before his conversion to Christianity.

[124] Thus already Bultmann, 138; Charles Kingsley Barrett, *The Gospel According to St. John*, 2nd ed. (Philadelphia, PA: Westminster Press, 1978), 235; Conzelmann, 123; and Walter Bauer, *Das Johannesevangelium*, Handbuch zum Neuen Testament 6, 2nd ed. (Tübingen: Mohr, 1925), 66.

[125] De Vos, 104–105. The aorist participles in 1 Corinthians 5:2–3 could be understood as pointing to a marriage, but more probably indicate the entrance into cohabitation (Schrage, 1:369). Helmut Merklein, *Der erste Brief an die Korinther*, Ökumenischer Taschenkommentar, 2 vol. (Gütersloh: Verlagshaus, 2000), 2:32, "It indicates a committed relationship, not necessarily a marriage. An adulterous relationship, however, is more likely to be ruled out.." Friedrich Lang, *Die Briefe an die Korinther*, Neues Testament Deutsch 7 (Göttingen: Vandenhoeck, 1994), 71: " . . . a sexual relationship with the stepmother, perhaps even during the lifetime of the father, is more likely than a marriage."

[126] Lucian, *Dialogi meretricii (Dialogues of the Courtesans)* 8.3, mentions a man who had a prostitute exclusively for himself for eight months, without entering into a valid marriage with her (*eichen oktō holous mēnas*). Also, in this passage, the verb *echō* means an unauthorized union (quoted by Bultmann, 138 n. 5 in connection with John 4).

[127] Matthew 22:28; Mark 12:23; Luke 20:28, 33; 1 Corinthians 7:2, 12–13, 29; Galatians 4:27. In the papyri, "to have as wife" always refers to legal marriage, according to Arzt-Grabner, 197.

[128] Mark 6:18; John 4:17–18; 1 Corinthians 5:1.

[129] Deuteronomy 28:30 LXX; polygamy in 2 Chronicles 11:21.

[130] Isaiah 54:1; Tobit 3:8.

[131] Garland, 256.

In the course of 1 Corinthians 5, Paul is criticizing less the individual than the lax attitude of the church, which, although it did not legitimize fornication, certainly trivialized the situation. Since the sin was heavy, persistent, and damaging to the church's reputation, Paul called for the expulsion[132] of the brother.[133] The church should have "mourned" (1 Cor 5:2) over this lamentable condition and not simply have overlooked it. The entire church was instructed to carry out the expulsion (1 Cor 5:4, "when you are assembled"). In so doing, Paul pursued a double goal: saving the sinner and maintaining the church's standards. In any case, the goal of discipline is redemptive.

Whether or not the person involved in sexual immorality in 1 Corinthians 5 repented is dependent upon the interpretation of 2 Corinthians 2:6–8. If this passage refers back to 1 Corinthians 5, which seems quite reasonable, then the disciplinary measures had been effective.[134] In any case, 1 Corinthians 5 shows in detail how the Bible wants us to deal with persistence in sexual immorality: In the Old Testament, the penalty was customarily death (e.g., Lev 18; 20; Deut 22); in the New Testament, it was removal from church membership.

General Theological Considerations

Official Starting Point of Marriage

Fundamentally, a marriage in the Old and New Testament periods was a legal transaction between the bridegroom and the family of the bride.[135] Therefore, a dowry was required[136] and the bride officially entered into the family of the bridegroom.[137] The story in the book of Ruth illustrates

---

[132] With different wording in the course of this chapter, Paul always refers to the same thing: 1 Corinthians 5:2, "to be removed from among you"; 1 Corinthians 5:5, "to hand over to Satan" (cf. 1 Tim 1:20); 1 Corinthians 5:7, "clean out the old yeast"; 1 Corinthians 5:9, "not to associate with sexually immoral persons" ("associate, mingle together"; in the LXX, the same Greek term is utilized in order to warn against an intermingling with foreign nations [Hos 7:8]); 1 Corinthians 5:11, "not to associate with" (cf. 2 Thess 3:14–15); 1 Corinthians 5:13, "drive out the wicked person from among you" (cf. Deut 17:7; 19:19).

[133] According to most commentaries, apparently the stepmother or concubine of the father was not a church member because Paul deals only with the case of the man (Schrage, 1:371). In 1 Corinthians 5:12–13 Paul makes clear that he does not judge those outside the church.

[134] Practically all church fathers (except Tertullian), as well as Martin Luther, assume that 2 Corinthians 2 refers to the same man as 1 Corinthians 5. Most modern commentators, however, have two different persons in mind. See V. P. Furnish, *II Corinthians*, Anchor Bible 32A (Garden City, NY: Doubleday, 1984), 163–168.

[135] Niebergall, 4–12.

[136] See Genesis 34:12; Exodus 22:15–16; 1 Samuel 18:25 LXX; Joshua 16:10; *2 Maccabees* 1:14.

[137] See Genesis 29:22; Judges 14:11; Ruth 4:1–13; Psalm 45:15; Jeremiah 7:34; Tobit 8:1; Matthew 9:15; 22:2–14; John 2:1–11.

this beautifully. The same understanding was in effect after the time of the New Testament.[138] Even for the levirate, a legal marriage was essential (Matt 22:24, *epigambreuō*; Matt 22:25, *gameō*). According to Tertullian, marriages that were not performed before the church were considered suspect, and the stigma of adultery was attached to them.[139] In contrast to a marriage, the beginning point in concubinage is often difficult to define. Here is a statement concerning Matthew 19:

> Thus, Jesus confirms not only the Old Testament practice, but also the ancient practice of his time, which without exception maintained a clear distinction between marital and non-marital partnerships, as well as a clearly visible starting point for marriage. Thus, it is evident that the New Testament church knew no uncertainty regarding the starting point of a marriage (i.e., 1 Cor 7:8, 10).[140]

Statements Concerning Sexuality in 1 Corinthians 5–7

In 1 Corinthians 6:12–20, Paul disapproves of intercourse with prostitutes, which is just as much *porneia* (1 Cor 6:18) as the case in 1 Corinthians 5, where it involves a long-term intended cohabitation. He refers to the creation order in Genesis 2:24, "which was intended for legitimate and orderly sexual intercourse with only one's wife, and therefore excludes sexual relationships with a *pornē*."[141]

In 1 Corinthians 7, Paul uses the terms "husband," "wife," "virgin," and "widow" as possible descriptions for a marital status acceptable before God. The expression "life companion" is missing, because it does not correspond with the biblical understanding of permissible relationships.

Overview of 1 Corinthians 7:

Term	Greek	Context	1 Corinthians
"woman"	gynē	Wife	7:2–4, 10–14, 16, 27, 29, 33, 39
"woman"	gynē	Marriageable, but unmarried woman	7:27
"woman who is married"	he gamēsasa		7:34

[138] Regarding marriage contracts and dowries, see Strack and Billerbeck, 2:384–399.

[139] See Niebergall, 143–144.

[140] W. Neuer, "Ehe, Ehescheidung, Ehelosigkeit," in *Das große Bibellexikon,* ed. Helmut Burkhardt, 2nd ed. (Wuppertal: Brockhaus, 1990), 2:296 (translation by the present author).

[141] Oberlinner, 363 (translation by the present author).

"virgin"	parthenos	Single, unmarried	7:25, 28, 34, 36–38
"his[142] virgin"	parthenos	Engaged, but still a virgin	7:36–38
"sister"	adelphē	Divorced woman	7:15
"unmarried"	agamos	Divorced woman remaining unmarried	7:11
"unmarried woman"	he gynē he agamos	Not a virgin, but nevertheless unmarried[143]	7:34
"widow"	chēra		7:8
"husband"	anēr	Husband	7:2–4, 10–11, 13–14, 16, 34, 39
"those unmarried"	tois agamois	Masculine, but can include women	7:8
"the unmarried"	ho agamos	Unmarried man	7:32
"the married"	ho gamēsas	Married man	7:33
"the married"	tois gegamēkosin	Married men and women	7:10
"marry"	gameō		7:9, 28, 36, 39
"unmarried"	agamos		7:8

For Judaism and for Paul,[144] it is clear that marriage presents the only legitimate alternative to *porneia* (see 1 Cor 7:2) in the expression of human sexuality.[145] One is either married or not; there is no in-between. The term "marry/married" occurs eleven times in 1 Corinthians 7 and sets the criterion.[146] Until the wedding, one is a virgin (or widow); after marriage one

[142] Commentators discuss whether this refers to fathers giving their daughters into marriage, or the fiancés of these virgins. For this discussion, see Garland, 336, who opts for the second opinion.

[143] 1 Corinthians 7:34 presents a text critical problem. Evidently, a general term is envisioned, including widows, as well as divorced and separated living women (Thiselton, 509).

[144] This view was held by some pagan writers, too. For example, the Stoic philosopher Musonius Rufus (first century AD) argues that husbands and wives should practice intercourse only within marriage; see Musonius, *Discourse* 12.

[145] Dautzenberg, 293–296; and Garland, 247, 256. This view is supported by the Seventh-day Adventist Church. In a declaration of the General Conference (April 23, 1996), we read, "The monogamous union in marriage of a man and a woman is affirmed as the divinely ordained foundation of the family and social life and the only morally appropriate locus of genital or related intimate sexual expression." See Ray Dabrowski, ed., *Statements, Guidelines and Other Documents* (Washington, DC: Review and Herald, 1996), 37.

[146] The verbs *gamizō* in 1 Corinthians 7:38 (2x) and *gameō* in 1 Corinthians 7:9 (2x), 10, 28 (2x), 33–34, 36, 39.

is husband or wife (1 Cor 7:36–38). There is no room for an unmarried cohabitation.[147] In other words, life in cohabitation has no biblical basis.[148]

For Paul, *porneia* can mean the one-time intercourse with a prostitute and a long-term cohabitation in an unmarried partnership. For both he uses the term *porneia*, because according to the biblical view, only husband and wife become "one flesh" (Gen 2:24; Matt 19:5–6; 1 Cor 6:16; Eph 5:31).[149]

No Cohabitation Before Marriage: Jesus' Parents in Matthew 1

Jewish teachers taught through word and deed. Matthew wants to present Jesus as the great teacher. It is obvious that the relationship between Joseph and Mary should have model-like character. Their conduct is intended to be an example.[150]

In his account Matthew emphasizes that Mary and the "righteous" (*dikaios*, Matt 1:19) Joseph entered into no sexual relations before their wedding. They were in harmony with the Old Testament and contemporary Jewish ideas of morality, for which ample evidence can be found outside the Bible. According to these ideas, premarital sexual intercourse was taboo[151] and simply unthinkable.[152] Matthew emphasizes that it was "before they came together" (Matt 1:18) that Mary became pregnant. That means that they had no sexual intercourse and lived in separate households.[153]

---

[147] A kind of "spiritual marriage" did not exist at that time. See Garland, 339–340.

[148] Kiš, 695.

[149] Schrage, 2:27.

[150] Craig S. Keener, *A Commentary on the Gospel of Matthew*, The New International Commentary on the New Testament (Grand Rapids, MI: Eerdmans, 2007), 88–90.

[151] *Joseph and Aseneth* 21:1, "And Joseph stayed that day with Pentephretes, and he did not sleep with Aseneth, because Joseph said, 'It does not befit a man who worships God to sleep with his wife before the wedding'" (Charlesworth, 2:235). Josephus, *Against Apion* 2.199: "What are our marriage laws? The Law recognizes no sexual connection, except the natural union of man and wife, and that only for the procreation of children." Rabbi Eliezer says, "An unmarried man who has intercourse with an unmarried woman without intention of marriage makes her a prostitute" (Strack and Billerbeck, 3:343).

[152] Jacob Neusner, *A History of the Mishnaic Law of Women*, 5 vols. (Leiden: Brill, 1980), 5:266, writes, "It is beyond Mishnah's imagination for a man and a woman to live together without the benefit of a betrothal, a marriage-contract, and a consummation of the marriage. I cannot think of a single rule which takes account of the possibility of cohabitation other than under normal, legal procedures." This view was criticized, e.g., by Tal Ilan, "Premarital Cohabitation in Ancient Judea: The Evidence of the Babatha Archive and the Mishnah (Ketubbot 1.4)," *Harvard Theological Review* 86 (1993): 247–264. She reports on a marriage contract from AD 131 that may point to a couple living together before marriage. Her view, however, is not the only possible interpretation of the document in question. In fact, this document has been interpreted differently by other scholars.

[153] W. D. Davies and Dale C. Allison, *The Gospel According to Saint Matthew*, International Critical Commentary, 2 vols. (Edinburgh: T&T Clark, 1988), 1:199. After the first century AD, this

How long the two were engaged and when they married is not recorded in the biblical account. At the time of Jesus' birth, they obviously were already married. Nevertheless, they had not yet consummated the marriage (Matt 1:24–25).

In John 8:41, the opponents of Jesus say, "We were not born of fornication" (NKJV) (*hēmeis ek porneias ou gegennēmetha*). This must be interpreted as a malicious allusion to the circumstances surrounding the birth of Jesus.[154] We cannot and need not determine if the Jews had in mind premarital sexual intercourse or a lasting relationship in cohabitation. In any case, we have here the biblical evidence that Judaism in the time of Jesus equated concubinage or premarital sexual intercourse with "fornication."

Further Theological Arguments in Favor of Marriage

- Marriage, in the biblical sense, is always intended to be a lifelong union (Matt 19:8–9); in cohabitation this is not always the case.
- Marriage is the best protection against the sexual ambitions of outsiders (e.g., Abraham, Gen 12:12–20; 20).
- Biblical marriage is understood as a covenant, and serves as a comparison for the relationship between God and His people (Jer 3; Ezek 16; Hos 1–2; Eph 5:22–23; Rev 19:7). This aspect is missing in concubinage.
- Chastity and purity are regarded in the New Testament as the ideal (2 Cor 11:2; Rev 14:4), refuting the possibility of cohabitation.

Considerations for Praxis

In terms of practical application, nonmarital relationships can be considered from legal, social, and pastoral perspectives.

Legal Questions

Although jurisdiction in every country can turn out differently, the general tendency in the Western world is leaning toward making non-marital partnerships increasingly more like marital unions in a legal sense. However, depending on the country, the following disadvantages can occur for a life partnership as compared to a marriage: monetary losses resulting from inheritance laws, in the case of a partner's death, and tax laws (income tax, inheritance tax); no entitlement to alimony in cases of separation; rental property forfeiture, when only one partner is considered

rule, according to our sources, is reported especially for Galilee (cf. Strack and Billerbeck, 1:45–47; and Ilan). During New Testament times, this regulation was generally accepted and valid.

[154] Origen, *Against Celsus* 1.28 (Roberts and Donaldson, 4:408). For modern commentators, see, e.g., Barrett, 348; Raymond E. Brown, *The Gospel According to John,* Anchor Bible 29, 2 vols. (Garden City, NY: Doubleday, 1966), 1:357; and Leon Morris, *The Gospel According to John,* New International Commentary on the New Testament (Grand Rapids, MI: Eerdmans, 1987), 462. See also Nichol, 5:991.

to be the legal tenant in a previously jointly used apartment; and custody of underage children[155] (in Germany, for example, there is hardly any legal difference between children of married and children of unmarried relationships; in other countries, this may be different).

These points can be sorted out in a partnership contract—at least in part. But it immediately raises the question as to why a couple would not simply want to legally enter into marriage before the state.

Length and Commitment

When entering into a "common marriage," or simply living with a "life partner," one must be aware that this form of union has drawbacks.

The probability that cohabitation will at some point come to an end is greater than the probability that a marriage will dissolve.[156] Only a third of the unions without a marriage license exist longer than two years.[157] Studies show that "trial marriages" that later turn into marriage have less chance of survival than marriages without previous cohabitation.[158] In addition, surveys substantiate that 70% of married couples still live together when their children are sixteen years of age, while only 36% of unions without a marriage license are still together.[159] One must ask oneself the question of whether love without loyalty is truly love.[160]

Pastoral and Practical Questions

Space does not allow replicating the modern discussion, but the following is certain: cohabitation without a marriage license lacks deep security and reduces the possibility of appropriately settling a conflict.[161] Cohabitors show less psychological well-being than similar married people.[162] Research in both England and the United States shows a much higher incidence of child abuse in marriage-like unions than with married couples.[163]

---

155 Grosse, 227.

156 Heinzpeter Hempelmann, *Ehe, Ehescheidung und Wiederheirat: Eine biblisch-exegetische und praktisch-seelsorgerliche Orientierung* (Bad Liebenzell: Verlag Liebenzeller Mission, 2003), 122–123.

157 Christoph Morgner, "Ehe ohne Trauschein - eine christliche Lebensform?," in *Glauben heute*, ed. Elí Diez (Lüneburg: Advent-Verlag, 1995), 32.

158 Calvin B. Rock, "Marriage and Family," in Dederen, 736; and M. W. Mangis, "Cohabitation," in *Baker Encyclopedia of Psychology & Counseling*, ed. David G. Benner and Peter C. Hill, 2nd ed. (Grand Rapids, MI: Baker, 1999), 223.

159 Jenkins, 17.

160 Morgner, 30

161 Ibid., 28.

162 Thatcher, 15.

163 Joseph M. Champlin, "Cohabitation Before Marriage," *Catholic Update* 6 (2003).

The spiritual aspect is also to be noted: A union is stronger when the partners feel committed to God, but much weaker when this dimension is missing.[164] Research shows that people who live in cohabitation practice religion less and visit worship service more seldom than people who are married.[165] Without doubt, it is necessary in pastoral counseling to resolve the tension between biblical ideals and the failure to meet them in practice.[166]

In counseling, people living in a marriage-like partnership should be advised to separate or to marry soon.[167] In any case, during the preparation for marriage this issue is to be addressed. For the time before the wedding, a temporary separation for cohabiting couples until marriage should be considered (if there are no children).

> Church members should do all they can to help couples living in cohabitation to be united in Christian marriage. We should love and care for them in spite of the fact that we cannot approve their life-style. Most of them simply do not know yet the beauty of a true Christian home.[168]

Cohabitation Among Retired People

We have to admit that we must not only discuss the problem of a loose cohabitation with young people, but also with elderly people. Perhaps older people would like to marry, but choose not to because of negative financial implications—such as losing a widow's pension, thus resulting in a severe reduction in their income.[169] Their devotion in love may be consequently restricted by a lack of willingness to sacrifice financially.[170] Although the legal regulations in many countries discriminate against marriage, this is not a sufficient reason to marry only in the church and without state recognition.[171] The question to be asked is whether a partnership contract

---

[164] Kiš, 695–696; and Thatcher, 33–35.

[165] Heller, 48; and Mangis, 223.

[166] Heller, 154.

[167] To marry soon is suggested by Rodríguez, "Cohabitation: Biblical and Ethical Concerns."

[168] Rodriguez.

[169] See in great detail Hempelmann, 127–138.

[170] Rodríguez, "Cohabitation: Biblical and Ethical Concerns."

[171] The judicial situation (for Germany only) is discussed by Hans Hattenhauer, "Was wird aus der Ehe? Christliche Ehe und Rentnerkonkubinat," http://www.bibelarbeit.privat.t-online.de/e_ehe_renterehe_hattenhauer.pdf (accessed May 7, 2021). He suggests a church wedding without a legal marriage contract. But he cautions churches with the status of public corporation (Körperschaftsrecht) against performing such weddings. However, for theological reasons the present author cannot support this suggestion. In Italy (and some other countries), a church

could be accepted as the basis for a blessing from the Seventh-day Adventist Church.[172] However, It is problematic to blur the distinction between "wedding" and "blessing" in order to comply with laws of the state that prohibit pastors in several countries of Europe from performing weddings without previous state recognition. Does it make sense to want to be married before God (church) and simultaneously to assert before man (state) that one is not married?[173]

As a church, we should request the state to find a way that takes Christian values into consideration, and to create a better financial basis for marriage.[174] It would also be conceivable for the church to give some kind of financial assistance to disadvantaged and needy couples (cf. Acts 6:1–6; 1 Tim 5:3–16). In addition, even older people and they especially should set a good example for others regarding the importance and value of Christian marriage, including for young people.[175]

Conclusion

We may suppose that a few passages in the Bible reference cohabitation. However, only two passages are really clear and understood by the overwhelming majority of theologians in reference to what we today call cohabitation: John 4 and 1 Corinthians 5. Yet, the Bible is clearly opposed to sexual relations outside of marriage. The following can be derived from these passages and from general theological considerations:

---

wedding without marriage before a civil magistrate is possible. A major critique of the ideas of Hattenhauer can be found in Hempelmann, 133–138, who convincingly shows that behind such thinking hides the splitting of marriage into legal and religious aspects, which—actually Catholic in thinking—gives priority to a church wedding. But with Romans 13 in mind, such a splitting is not legitimate.

[172] As proposed by Vilem, 68–70. He makes reference to the German version of the minister's manual and understands a statement there to include a partnership contract (*Handbuch für Prediger* [Lüneburg: Advent-Verlag, 2002], 357). Here, we have to notice that in the context of this statement, it is a legal marriage that is always and exclusively meant. The original English of the minister's manual does not include the ambiguous statement of the German version (General Conference of Seventh-day Adventists Ministerial Association, *Seventh-day Adventist Minister's Handbook* [Silver Spring, MD: General Conference of Seventh-day Adventists Ministerial Association, 1997], 259–260). In recent times, the Baptists in Germany have considered the possibility of accepting a legally signed partnership contract, in place of marriage before a civil magistrate (see "Baptisten: Trauung ohne Trauschein," *idea-Spektrum* 50 (2004): 7). The Bund Freier evangelischer Gemeinden is against weddings without a legal marriage (see "Freikirche lehnt ‚Seniorenehe' ab," *idea-Spektrum* 7 [2005]:10).

[173] See "Jurist: Ohne Trauschein niemanden kirchlich trauen," *idea-Spektrum 51* (2004): 9.

[174] Rodríguez, "Cohabitation: Biblical and Ethical Concerns."

[175] Ibid.

1. Cohabitation is not regarded as equivalent to marriage in the biblical view. In cohabitation, a public contract at the beginning is missing and sometimes so is a desire for a lifelong partnership.
2. According to biblical understanding, all sexual activity outside of marriage is considered sinful. Thus, nonmarital cohabitation is a violation against the will of God and should be considered fornication.
3. When a case of concubinage becomes known to the church, we are called to go forth pastorally and address the problem in the light of the Bible. When, despite ongoing pastoral endeavors of the church, a church member continues to live in cohabitation, according to Paul, disciplinary measures may be necessary.
4. We are called as a church, in preaching, writing and educating our youth, to increasingly present the topic of marriage (and all problems related to it) in a biblically sound manner.[176]

---

[176] Jenkins, *Cohabitation: A Biblical Perspective*, 122–123

CHAPTER 5

Singleness and Sexuality in the Contemporary World

Gerhard Pfandl, Demóstenes da Silva, and Luiz Carlos Gondim

This chapter presents a biblical and contextual approach to the topic of singleness. It seeks to understand the individual and contextual elements related to single people and how they deal with their sexuality.[1]

Singleness is a phase of human development defined by the absence of a marital bond; it may be either temporary or permanent. Temporary singleness is a developmental and transitory phase, while permanent singleness is a social and personal condition in which the individual renounces or does not prioritize marriage. Definitions of the term "single," as well as the notion of sexuality itself, may vary according to historical and cultural contexts.

This work focuses on singleness as a personal choice or due to social circumstances or other reasons that prevent the individual from getting married (Matt 19:12). However, much of what will be said about sexuality and singleness as a relatively permanent condition also applies to temporary singleness. Sexuality in this chapter is understood as a special, intimate experience of fulfillment and pleasure, in accordance with biblical values that legitimize it in the monogamous, heterosexual, lifelong union (Heb 13:4; Matt 19:4–11).

The Bible describes the conjugal union as a response to an essential human need for intimacy (Gen 2:18). Moreover, sexuality is an experience explicitly reserved for matrimony that involves purity, love, pleasure, and fertility (Gen 1:28; Eccl 9:9; 1 Cor 7:2). It bears mention that although marriage and sexuality are viewed in a negative light in some periods of

---

[1] Several parts of this chapter have been taken from an unpublished manuscript by Keldie Paroschi titled "Singleness and Sexuality: The Biblical View for a Fulfilled Life." Used with permission.

Christian history, the Bible exalts marital sexuality—as in the Song of Solomon, for example. Since normative biblical sexuality is restricted to marriage, this chapter addresses the question of how single Christians—particularly in the context of the church, and especially those who have chosen singleness—should deal with the sexual norms of the contemporary world.

Methodologically, this article follows the historical-grammatical method in the interpretation of biblical texts. Although this research uses extrabiblical sources, it is grounded in the sexual ethics of Scripture. Other literature is used to expand the discussion, placing the biblical principles in a contemporary framework and highlighting their relevance to the experience of Christian singles.

The world today is very different from the world a hundred years ago; many things have changed. The seas and skies have been explored; distances of thousands of miles are no longer an obstacle. A world of knowledge is right at our fingertips. But changes are not limited to technology and science; society itself has changed in many ways as well. In contemporary times, sexual activity, often controversial, has been understood as a socio-historical construction, whose purpose includes reproduction and pleasure. This perspective is demonstrated in academic discussions and in the understanding of social rights groups and international organizations.

In its individual and historical-social scope, sexual activity "involves gender, sexual identity, sexual orientation, eroticism, emotional involvement, love and reproduction. It is experienced or expressed in thoughts, fantasies, desires, beliefs, attitudes, values, activities, practices, roles and relationships."[2]

In the West, new paradigms of sexuality were constructed from the end of the nineteenth century until the midle of the twentieth century.[3] These paradigms coincided with changes in conceptions of adolescence, the nuclear family, universalization of the school, and modern changes in teaching,[4] society, economy,[5] and subjectivity as central in the constitution of identity.[6]

---

[2] Miriam Abramovay, Mary Garcia Castro, and Lorena Bernadete da Silva, *Juventudes e Sexualidade* (Brasília: UNESCO Brasil, 2004), 29, http://unesdoc.unesco.org/images/0013/001339/133977por.pdf (accessed September 2, 2020).

[3] Abramovay, Castro, and Silva, 29, passim.

[4] Philippe Ariès, *Centuries of Childhood: A Social History of Family Life* (New York: Vintage Books, 1962).

[5] Anthony Giddens, *The Transformation of Intimacy: Sexuality, Love and Erotism in Modern Societies* (Stanford, CA: Stanford University Press, 1992); Maria Luiza Heilborn, "Construção de Si, Gênero e Sexualidade," in *Sexualidade: O Olhar das Ciências Sociais*, ed. Maria Luiza Heilborn (Rio de Janeiro: Editora Zahar, 1999), 40–59, http://www.clam.org.br/bibliotecadigital/uploads/publicacoes/97_1512_contrucaodesi.pdf (accessed September 2, 2020).

[6] Abramovay, Castro, and Silva, 28–31.

In this connection, an oft-neglected but significant change that has taken place in society is marriage. For example, in 1900, 95% of adults in the United States were married. Two percent were either widowed or divorced, and 3% had never been married.[7] Today, the picture has changed entirely: only around 48% of American adults are married.[8] Around 17% are either widowed or divorced, and around 33% have never been married. In other words, the number of singles has increased dramatically in the last century.[9] And although marriage rates among practicing Christians tend to be higher,[10] the reality is that even in the church singles are no longer the exception. Although this situation may be more common in Western countries, one may expect that given the pressures of globalization such trends may affect other parts of the world as well.

Singles face a number of challenges in the contemporary world. And within the church, many singles feel stigmatized by older, married members. If someone happens to

> remain single well into his or her twenties or thirties, either by choice or by circumstances, many people begin to try to diagnose the problem (be it sexual orientation, physical appearance, intellectual ability, social ineptitude, unduly high standards, or other factors) that has trapped the single person in the unnatural and undesirable condition of being unmarried.[11]

In society at large, singles are encouraged to be free, live in the moment, and pursue whatever makes them feel happy and satisfied. Hollywood's depictions of love and desire have done a particularly good job of undermining traditional family values and encouraging people to

---

[7] Albert Y. Hsu, *Singles at the Crossroads: A Fresh Perspective on Christian Singleness* (Downers Grove, IL: InterVarsity, 1997), 14–15.

[8] 2020 US Census: Marital Status in the United States. https://www.census.gov/library/visualizations/interactive/marital-status-in-united-states.html (accessed October 13, 2020).

[9] There are many factors that have led to this statistical decline of marriage in the United States. Among these factors are: societal change such as the legalization of divorce, hippie and feminist movements, the sexual revolution, women entering the workforce, and fear of divorce—Generation X "are the sons and daughters of the most-divorced generation in American history" (Hsu, 19); fear of commitment; postponement of marriage in order to pursue an education, prioritize one's career; and other factors. See also Albert Ellis, "Sexual Promiscuity in America," *The Annals of the American Academy of Political and Social Science* 378 (1968): 58–67.

[10] "New Marriage and Divorce Statistics Released," Barna Group, March 31, 2008, https://www.barna.com/research/new-marriage-and-divorce-statistics-released/ (accessed January 26, 2020).

[11] Andreas J. Köstenberger and David W. Jones, *God, Marriage, and Family: Rebuilding the Biblical Foundation* (Wheaton, IL: Crossway, 2004), 173.

live out their hidden fantasies.[12] Premarital sex, for example, is not only portrayed as non-problematic, but is reinforced as necessary in order to assess one's compatibility with his or her partner.

So how can the Christian single navigate these confusing and dissonant messages? Is there such a thing as a healthy biblical view of sexuality for singles? And what can the church do to support and encourage single members to live fulfilled lives for the glory of God? This chapter will address the topic of singleness and sexuality under three main headings: 1) biblical principles for sexual ethics, 2) singleness and sexuality, and 3) the role of church and community. Thus, the topic is approached from a biblical-theological perspective in such a way that is applicable to all singles—teenagers, unmarried youth or adults, single parents, divorcees, widows and widowers—regardless of culture or circumstance.

Biblical Principles for Sexual Ethics

Marriage was the original design for human beings at creation (Gen 1:26–28; 2:18–25). The entrance of sin (Gen 3), however, introduced the experience of singleness; these individuals are in Scripture sometimes referred to as "eunuchs" (Isa 56:4; Matt 19:12).[13] In this sense, in the post-fall reality, even the person who remains single (1 Cor 7:25–40) can perfectly serve the purposes of the Creator, since the dignity of single or married people is based on their faith.

Throughout history, singleness has had a different meaning for men and women, generally being considered a disadvantage for women and a time of adventure for men. In the cultural context in which the apostles wrote, for example, sexual practices varied according to historical and social circumstances. In Homer's day (ninth or eighth century BC), prostitutes and brothels were barely known. However, there was concubinage and occasional sexual intercourse with war slaves. With the increase of prosperity and commerce, prostitution arose. At that time, only civil marriage was protected by law and custom.[14]

Prostitution was well tolerated in Athens, Corinth, and among the Ionians, but there was strong sexual discipline among the Spartans and Dorians (fifth and fourth century AD). Among the former, prostitution

---

[12] See, e.g., David Thomson, *Sleeping With Strangers: How the Movies Shaped Desire* (New York: Vintage Books, 2020). The 2016 romantic comedy How to Be Single perfectly describes Hollywood's portrayal of the romanticized bachelor life, which includes parties and numerous romantic partners.

[13] All biblical quotations are from NKJV, unless otherwise indicated.

[14] Friedrich Hauck and Siegfried Schulz, "πόρνη, πόρνος, πορνεία, πορνεύω, ἐκπορνεύω," in *Theological Dictionary of the New Testament*, ed. Gerhard Friedrich, vol. 6 (Grand Rapids, MI: Eerdmans, 1964-74), 582.

was seen as normal, since sexual activity was considered as natural as eating and drinking. Extramarital sex was allowed for men, but prohibited for women, since the practice by men did not damage civil marriage. In addition, homosexuality spread throughout Greece; rather than being censored, it was practiced even by prominent figures.[15] On the other hand, Stoicism[16] (third century BC) presented a moderating influence. Without rejecting sexual pleasure, it condemned adultery, extramarital affairs, and excesses, even defending chastity.[17] But Greece continued with a quite permissive view of sexuality.

In some societies, while women were expected to keep themselves chaste for marriage, men experienced the period of singleness as a period of freedom and learning. Single women tended to be treated as inferior and relegated to the margins of society while men exalted the advantages of the single status, being able to date countless women without having to take note of the judgement of society.[18]

As human society changed, especially in the West, new meanings have been built around the experience of singleness. Singleness for both men and women has come to be seen as an opportunity to value individuality, subjectivity, and the equality of the sexes in sexual practices. Sex in turn is considered a need akin to human rights, disconnected from biblical principles. Sexual relations in our contemporary world, often involving free and boundless relationships, are deemed to be an indispensable part of human needs.

So, the Christian single may face difficult challenges arising from societal pressure and the individual's emotional and sexual needs. Perhaps for this reason Jesus indicated that divorced people face the lifestyle of a eunuch. Not all can accept such a teaching, as Jesus pointed out, "but only those to whom it has been given" (Matt 19:11).

For those who receive the gift of celibacy, singleness can be an advantageous way of living—even more so than many who are married or who, without the gift, "burn" with sexual desire (1 Cor 7:7–9, 32–38). In addition to Paul's example, Jesus lived a celibate life and became a model in the experience of this gift. He had no wife and children, but lived to love God and serve the world.

---

[15] Hauck and Schulz, 583.

[16] Stoicism was an ancient Greek school of philosophy that taught that virtue, the highest good, is based on knowledge. Fate and providence govern nature, and one should be indifferent to the vicissitudes of fortune, pleasure, and pain.

[17] Hauck and Schulz, 583–584.

[18] Ipojucan Dias Campos, "Solteirismo e Tempo Matrimonial, Belém (1916–1925)," *Revista Cordis* 2, no. 13 (July–December 2014): 33–48, https://revistas.pucsp.br/index.php/cordis/article/view/22712 (accessed September 2, 2020).

Some authors seem to limit celibacy to a gift but, there are other types of celibacy mentioned by Jesus in Matthew 19. Among the various types are those who are castrated by men and those who live as eunuchs for the sake of the kingdom of God (Matt 19:12). Then there are those Christians who are divorced or widowed, who must live in sexual purity without a partner. In addition to these, there are also single believers who have not yet found a spouse or who cannot be married for various social, economic, or health reasons.

For those who have the gift of celibacy, celibacy is as good as marriage, for both are gifts from God (1 Cor 7:7). But to live in sadness because you did not get married or to opt for singleness to have more time for yourself or to avoid other people would distort the biblical notion of singleness. Also, it would not be the gift of celibacy to be alone and chaste for the wrong reasons—for example, because individuals were disappoin-ted by emotional relationships, or because they did not find someone who fulfilled their requirements, or because they were abandoned for someone else and felt themselves alone and frustrated.

In this connection, it is helpful to remember that in ancient Israel, girls would marry at the beginning of puberty, around twelve or thirteen years of age, while boys would marry a few years later. There was, therefore, hardly any interval between childhood and marriage that could be considered a phase of "singleness" similar to what happens today.[19] Since marriage was usually arranged between the families, there was also no "dating" phase during which young people could spend time with each other in order to find potential compatible partners.[20] Furthermore, the emphasis on a bride's virginity in antiquity was connected to her father's economic interests in securing the full bride-price for his daughter, and to the husband's paternity concerns in assuring that any children resulting from the marriage were indeed his legitimate heirs.[21] While there certainly were singles in the Bible, singleness was mostly an undesirable and exceptional situation.[22] Still, biblical laws regarding

[19] In rabbinic Judaism, marriage was considered a duty required to be fulfilled by the age of twenty. The celibate life was considered a sin (b. *Qiddushin* 29b). See Beate Ego, "Marriage in Judaism," in *Brill's New Pauly Encyclopaedia of the Ancient World*, ed. Hubert Cancik and Helmuth Schneider, vol. 8 (Boston, MA: Brill, 2008), 391; and Köstenberger and Jones, 176.

[20] Ego, "Marriage in Judaism," 8:391–392.

[21] Richard M. Davidson, *Flame of Yahweh: Sexuality in the Old Testament* (Peabody, MA: Hendrickson, 2007), 358–361.

[22] Köstenberger and Jones, 174–177, list six categories of singles in the Old Testament: 1) widows, 2) eunuchs, 3) those who could not marry due to a disease such as leprosy, 4) those who did not marry because of a divine call, 5) divorced people, and 6) unmarried young men and women. As a woman, to be widowed, sick, or divorced meant to be left without protection, which was a very difficult situation to be in. To be a eunuch in ancient Israel meant to be in a marginalized position, excluded from the congregation of worshippers and from the priesthood (cf. Lev 21:20;

marriage and sex go beyond such practical concerns within its cultural framework. Scripture contains principles and values that transcend time and culture; they address issues of marriage, singleness, and sexuality. These principles are still relevant and essential today.[23]

Singleness and the Ideal of Marriage

According to Scripture, from the beginning biblical sexuality was limited to monogamous marriage, which was the only original and approved model of sexual union (Gen 1:26–31; 2:18–25; Matt 19:3–12; 1 Cor 7:2–5; Heb 13:4), although there was some tolerance for polygamy (1 Sam 1:1–2; 1 Kgs 11:1–3) and divorce (Deut 24:1–4).

The creation account in Genesis 2 highlights the value of marriage. The creation of man is not complete until God makes for him a suitable partner (Gen 2:18), one who is like him.[24] Man and woman, then, together in marriage constitute God's ideal for humanity.[25] The paradigm of marriage and sexuality in Genesis 2:24 includes the principles of exclusivity, permanence, and intimacy: sex is affirmed within the context of a formal and binding marriage covenant, a commitment of loyalty between a man and woman free from any outside interference.[26] To "become one flesh" denotes "the deepest, harmonious relationship that exists between people, which is the unity between husband and wife in all its dimensions, emotional, physical, and spiritual."[27] These principles are upheld by the New Testament when Jesus affirms the sacredness and permanence of marriage (cf. Matt 19:1–12).

And yet, the fact that Adam's aloneness before the creation of Eve is described as "not good" (Gen 2:18) does not mean that to be single should be viewed as "less than." Scholars point out that there is a significant difference of nuance between the Hebrew terms for "not good" and for "evil." Things described as "not good" are *not* equivalent to "evil"; instead,

---

Deut 23:1). And the only explicit example of someone who did not marry because of a divine call was Jeremiah, although the command may have been temporary or limited to that particular place (cf. Jer 16:1–4). The same categories apply to the New Testament as well, but there we also have the examples of John the Baptist, Jesus, and Paul.

[23] Roy E. Gane, *Old Testament Law for Christians: Original Context and Enduring Application* (Grand Rapids, MI: Baker Academic, 2017), 22–25.

[24] The Hebrew phrase *'ezer kenegdo,* "a helper comparable to him," implies sameness and parity as well as counterpart and difference. In other words, the marriage relationship between man and woman includes the idea of harmony and understanding as much as equality and partnership. See Jacques B. Doukhan, *Genesis,* Seventh-day Adventist International Bible Commentary (Nampa, ID: Pacific Press, 2016), 80–81.

[25] Ibid.

[26] Davidson, 43–46.

[27] Ibid., 47.

they are simply not the ideal.[28] There are, in fact, a number of examples throughout the Bible that show that God does have an ideal for humanity, but because of the reality of a sinful, imperfect world, sometimes accommodation is necessary. Paul concedes that a husband and a wife can abstain from sexual relations under special circumstances (1 Cor 7:6).[29] The same applies to marriage and singleness: while marriage is the ideal, as affirmed in the creation story and all throughout the Bible, singleness itself is not intrinsically inferior to marriage.[30] The New Testament makes this clear in stating that there are circumstances in which being single could even be good and advantageous (cf. Matt 19:12; 1 Cor 7:7–8, 32–35). That singleness does *not* in any way place one at odds with God's plan for humanity should be an important reminder for everyone who finds himself or herself unmarried, regardless of the circumstance.

Sexual Purity and Respect for Marriage

When it comes to sex, however, there are clear teachings in the Bible on what is right and what is wrong. The Bible holds highly the principles of sexual purity and respect for marriage, and these principles continue to apply today.[31] It is common to hear nowadays that there is nothing wrong with casual sex, same-sex relations, and the like, but in terms of biblical principles, there is no such thing as divine accommodation. It makes no difference that cultural changes have occurred since biblical times, that contraceptives are widely available, or that one is in a loving and committed relationship. The fact is that sex is only sanctioned within the limits of a heterosexual, monogamous marriage (cf. Gen 2:18–24).[32]

The Ten Commandments contain the key moral principles that govern one's relationship to God and to others. But the principles

---

[28] Alexandru Breja, "A Biblical Approach to Transcultural Analysis" (paper presented at the annual meeting of the Evangelical Theological Society, Atlanta, GA, November 21, 2003), 1–19, referenced in Davidson, 37 n. 91. See also Doukhan, 80.

[29] In this passage Paul uses the Greek word *suggnome*, "concession," which can be understood as "to meet someone halfway"; see Gregory J. Lockwood, *1 Corinthians,* Concordia Commentary (Saint Louis, MO: Concordia, 2000), 230.

[30] Köstenberger and Jones, 182.

[31] Gane, 22–23, defines a moral principle as "an objective, absolute, changeless truth that governs human nature and relationships." According to him, "much of OT law expresses or exemplifies absolute principles to guide human life. By seeking to persuade people to make its moral principles their own, OT law encourages them to bring their personally held values into alignment with divine principles, which are based on objective, permanent, and inherently good divine principles."

[32] Davidson, 43–47, identifies the principles of exclusivity ("absolute freedom from outside interferences"), permanence ("a formal and binding covenant commitment, and an inward attitude referring to the devotion between man and woman, binding loyalty in every circumstance"), and intimacy ("the unitive purpose of sexuality is to find fulfillment inside the marital relationship") based on the Genesis 2:24 paradigm for marriage and sexuality.

contained in them are much broader in scope than what is explicitly defined in Exodus 20 and Deuteronomy 5. Other laws in the Pentateuch supplement and elaborate on them in such a way that "the Ten Commandments and the other laws are inseparable, so it is a misunderstanding of OT law for Christians to retain the former but simply dismiss the latter."[33] The seventh commandment, "You shall not commit adultery" (Exod 20:14; Deut 5:18), explicitly prohibits married people from engaging in sexual relations with someone other than their spouse. However, this commandment also encompasses many other laws relating to sexuality, thus advocating for the principles of respect for marriage and sexual purity.[34]

Premarital sex, like adultery, goes against the biblical view of sex solely within the limits of marriage.[35] The penalties for such illicit activity in ancient Israel, even if it was consensual,[36] were serious enough to "cause the unmarried, both men and women, to give serious pause before engaging in premarital sex" (cf. Exod 22:16–17; Deut 22:28–29).[37] If a man found out that his bride was not a virgin, her punishment was equivalent to that of adultery (cf. Deut 22:13–21),[38] again showing that premarital sex is unacceptable on biblical terms. Considering all of the possible scenarios covered by Old Testament law, there are simply no circumstances under which sex outside of marriage is considered unproblematic.[39]

Sexual lust or fantasies are also transgressions of the seventh commandment: "But I say to you that everyone who looks at a woman with lustful intent has already committed adultery with her in his heart" (Matt 5:28; cf. Job 31:1; Prov 6:25; Gal 5:16–21). Therefore, harboring

---

[33] Gane, 240–241.

[34] Other laws that elaborate on the seventh commandment include laws on premarital sex, promiscuity, and homosexual activity, among other things; see ibid., 267–271.

[35] Davidson, 364.

[36] Biblical laws consistently place "full responsibility upon individuals for their own sexual behavior and equitably distinguish between consensual sex (involving an unbetrothed virgin) and the more reprehensible offense of statutory or forcible rape" (ibid., 361).

[37] Ibid., 360.

[38] "Apparently what makes the punishment equivalent to that for adultery even if the sexual intercourse took place before betrothal is that the girl *concealed* from her husband her premarital sexual activity, and in such case it was to be assumed that it was illicit sex after betrothal. The serious, but not capital, offense of premarital sex thus becomes a capital offense because of the element of deceit and false pretense to premarital chastity: she has entered into marriage without acknowledging her prior loss of virginity" (ibid., 358–359).

[39] The following quote applies to all types of extramarital sexual activities: "The accumulative effect of the legislation just mentioned was to safeguard the sanctity of sexual relationships within the marriage on the part of the husband as well as the wife. It must be concluded that 'while the law does not speak directly to the promiscuous man, neither does it leave him any legitimate partner'" (ibid., 363–364).

sexual fantasies about someone other than one's spouse, whether or not masturbation is involved, falls short of the standard set forth in the Bible.[40] Furthermore, the biblical ideal of love is "other-centered, self-sacrificial, and focused on the true inner person" (1 Cor 13; cf. Prov 31:30),[41] which leads to the question of whether self-stimulation for personal pleasure fulfills this ideal.

These biblical principles should be kept in mind, whether or not one is in a relationship. Among couples who are dating, it is important to set clear boundaries at the beginning of the relationship so that both can respect each other in a way that is pleasing to God. Deciding not to have sex before marriage is essential, but if lust and sexual fantasies are also not in line with the biblical view of sexual purity, it would be important to discuss limits regarding kissing, touching, and petting as well, all of which could awaken desires that would be best to avoid. If both partners are committed to honoring God and each other, one should not be pressuring the other to go beyond those clear boundaries established together.

Likewise, outside of a relationship, it is important to be conscious of how one engages in flirtation with potential suitors. Flirtation is ambiguous by nature, and it is very easy to cross the line of what is honorable and respectable. According to Caroline Simon, flirting is problematic if

> the flirt's intent is to awaken the sexual or romantic interest of another where there is no serious possibility of long-term commitment. Flirtation, even as a part of dating behavior among the unmarried, can entice lust. Flirtation can raise expectations that the flirt has no intention of acting upon. Yet flirtation as a sincere exploration of possibilities that might lead to commitments may be allowed.[42]

It is noteworthy that the first half of the Song of Songs reveals the sexual anticipation between two lovers who are not yet married. The sexual tension and suggestive language is certainly there; yet, in line with the biblical view of sex only within the boundaries of marriage, the sexual imagery is much more restrained than in the latter half of the book, following the wedding.[43] While this shows that it is normal to feel desire for

---

[40] Davidson, 324–325.

[41] Köstenberger and Jones, 185.

[42] Caroline J. Simon, *Bringing Sex Into Focus: The Quest for Sexual Integrity* (Downers Grove, IL: InterVarsity, 2012), 89.

[43] Davidson, 596–597, says, "There appears to be a consistent pattern of more restrained sexual imagery, without reference to sexual intercourse, in the scenes before the wedding and of an intensification of sexual imagery with frequent allusions to intercourse after the wedding. For example, in sections A and B (1:2–2:7 and 2:8–17) of my proposed symmetrical structure of

one's spouse, the Song of Songs also emphasizes the principle of restraint before marriage: "I adjure, O daughters of Jerusalem, by the gazelles or the wild does: do not stir up or awaken love until it is ready" (Song 2:7; 3:5; 8:4).[44]

Nevertheless, when mistakes happen and boundaries are crossed, the Bible paints a beautiful picture of God's forgiveness and grace. He is more than willing to offer a second chance (cf. Exod 34:6–7; Isa 43:25–26; Dan 9:9; Acts 3:19; Rom 3:23–24; Eph 1:7; 1 John 1:9; etc.). Numerous stories throughout the Bible portray God's grace and the assurance of forgiveness for those who sincerely repent and seek Him, no matter what the sin.[45] Among such episodes are David's adultery with Bathsheba (2 Sam 11), accompanied by his inspired prayer for forgiveness (Ps 51), and the woman in John 8, a reminder that all are sinners and that grace is available to all.

Accommodation happens in situations that are either out of our control or affected by the state of affairs of our fallen world, while principles are divine standards applicable to all, regardless of the external circumstances. There are numerous situations that could lead to singleness: lack of suitable or available partners, divorce or death of one's spouse, a personal decision to prioritize ministry or education, or others. Though marriage is God's ideal for humanity, He understands that mistakes happen. What He does unequivocally ask of His followers is that they live holy lives according to His divine principles, regardless of marital status, culture, or situation in life. These divine standards are an issue of personal responsibility and accountability, and there is no excuse for pleading ignorance or inability to follow those standards accordingly (cf. Rom 1:19–20). Although in the case of mistakes God's forgiveness and grace is readily available to those who repent, we should avoid sinning on purpose.

Singleness and Sexuality

There are many misconceptions regarding sexuality when it comes to singles. If the biblical premise is that marriage is the ideal, and sex is limited to the context of marriage, one can easily reach the conclusion

---

the book, the desire or wish (but probably not the actual experience) of the woman before the wedding focuses upon kissing (1:2), embracing (2:6), and the man's lying between her breasts (1:12), with no reference to sexual intercourse, whereas in sections B′ (7:11–8:2 [ET 7:10-8:2]) and A′ (8:3–14) the sexual experiences (both actual and desired) intensify to include the caressing of her breasts and nipples (7:8–9 [ET 7:7–8]) and a number of references to sexual intercourse."

[44] Davidson, 617

[45] Ibid., 373–374.

that any form of conversation on the topic of sexuality outside the confines of marriage are inappropriate and even wrong. This can lead not only to misinformed and unaware teenagers left to explore the topic through channels that do not share the biblical understanding of sexuality, but also to misguided views of self-identity, soteriology, and even of God Himself. Hollywood, the internet, and social media are constantly touting the liberation and freedom of sexual desires, while churches often send the opposite message in condemnatory tones.

Sexuality as a Gift from God

In order to counterbalance these opposing, yet equally detrimental, views of sexuality, it should be acknowledged that several things can be true at once. First, sexuality is a gift from God. The poetic masterpiece, that is, the Song of Songs, is entirely dedicated to presenting sexuality as "beautiful, good, and wholesome, to be celebrated and enjoyed without fear or embarrassment."[46] "Behold, you are beautiful, my love, behold, you are beautiful; your eyes are doves. Behold, you are beautiful, my beloved, truly delightful" (Song 1:15–16), the lovers say to one another. Sex is "very good," just as the rest of God's creation, and is expressed in language reminiscent of the beauty and perfection of paradise itself.[47] This is very different from depictions of sex in today's media as vulgar and cheap, or as the objectification and dehumanization of a person's body.

Additionally, biblical anthropology supports a wholistic view of human beings in which physical, mental, and spiritual capacities are integrated as essential components.[48] The same applies to sexuality: it is not limited to sexual acts such as intercourse, or arousal. Such a limited understanding leads to misguided views of sexual purity, sin, and even of what it means to be a human being. In the words of Laura Winner, "to organize one's Christian sexual ethic around virginity is to turn sexual purity and sexual sin into a light switch you can flip—one day you're sexually righteous, and the next day, after illicit loss of your virginity, you're a sinner."[49] Instead, sexuality encompasses feelings, thoughts, attractions, behaviors, and the way one presents and views himself or herself and others. It therefore applies to all, whether single or married.

---

[46] Davidson, 607.

[47] Ibid., 604–621, highlights a number of themes depicting sexuality that are reflected in the Song of Songs, such as: sexuality is beautiful, it explores and encompasses the senses in sublime ways, it is a celebration of passion and pleasure, it is an exciting adventure and an exquisite delight, it is unashamed and uninhibited, it is restrained and in good taste, it is a romantic, passionate love affair, and an awe-inspiring mystery.

[48] Aecio E. Cairus, "The Doctrine of Man," in *Handbook of Seventh-day Adventist Theology*, ed. Raoul Dederen (Hagerstown, MD: Review and Herald, 2000), 212–213.

[49] Quoted in Simon, 71.

True sexuality shows appreciation for oneself and for others: "it views the sexual qualities of the person in light of his or her personal dignity."[50] Such a healthy, biblical view of sexuality can be described as follows:

> When you meet people who have a truly integrated sexuality, a psychological and physical unity, they seem happily and robustly embodied. They aren't all fidgety, restless, self-conscious, driven, lustful. They are content, yet aware and appreciative of their own body and those of others. They are erotic without "making moves" or ogling, leering or vamping. And here's the thing: some of these people are happily married and some of these people are happily single.[51]

Another way to look at it is that sexuality is not about fulfilling a person's own sexual desires, but about setting one's own desires aside so that others may have the opportunity to experience love, wholeness, and fulfillment. The notion that sexuality is all about sex, and that those who abstain from sex are missing out on one of the greatest pleasures in the world is a misunderstanding of sexuality. Sex in itself cannot make someone whole, and cannot truly satisfy the longings and desires of the human heart. Rather, true sexuality is directed toward the flourishing of ourselves and of others, which is possible when we leave behind our "obsessive quest for individualized sexual expression" and "embody and enact our humanity in its full breadth and depth only when we direct our passions toward the other in self-giving love."[52] And again, this self-giving love can be expressed whether one is married or single.[53]

The Reality of Temptations

It is normal to have sexual desires and passions, and to face temptations. Every teenager goes through that phase when hormones are high, peer pressure is strong, and temptations are frequent. Beyond adoles-cence, temptations abound in today's hypersexualized society, whether in movies, the music and fashion industries, through social media, or interactions with people.

Nevertheless, we must recognize the fact that not all individuals are alike in this matter of marrying or not marrying. "Some prefer to remain

---

[50] Quoted in Simon, 76.

[51] Ibid., 77.

[52] Kutter Callaway, "Sex and the Single Life: Reckoning with Paul's Writings on Marriage and Celibacy," *The Christian Century* 135, no. 15 (2018): 25.

[53] For a reflection on appreciating the beauty of sexuality in the Song of Songs as a single person, see Elizabeth Gentry, "My Resounding 'Yes' to God and Embracing My Sexuality: Singleness and the Song of Songs," *Priscilla Papers* 32, no. 1 (2018): 15–17.

single, and have the ability to live a satisfactory life without marriage. Others prefer to follow the normal plan for life on this earth, and enter the married state. Both courses are approved by the Lord when carried out in harmony with His counsel."[54]

It is normal for singles to suffer temptation, just as every other Christian who struggles to live according to God's standards on a daily basis (cf. Rom 7:14–24; 1 Cor 10:12; Gal 5:17).[55]

When we accept Christ as our Savior, Satan's power in our lives is broken, but that does not mean we are fully free from sin and temptation. On the contrary, our sinful nature and the work of the Spirit in our heart create a conflict within us from which we will only be free when Christ comes again, which is why it is crucial that we surrender ourselves daily to God (Jas 4:7).[56]

Only through His power is it possible to resist the lures of the enemy: "No temptation has overtaken you that is not common to man. God is faithful, and he will not let you be tempted beyond your ability, but with the temptation he will also provide the way of escape, that you may be able to endure it" (1 Cor 10:13). The Greek word *peirasmos* also means "trial" and "testing" (Luke 8:13, NIV). When we pray, "Do not lead us into temptation, but deliver us from evil" (Matt 6:13), God will not let us experience any test we are not able to meet. So, "let no one say when he is tempted, 'I am being tempted by God'; for God cannot be tempted by evil, and He Himself does not tempt anyone" (Jas 1:13).[57]

The important thing to remember is: despite all the struggles and even failures caused by our sinful nature, God has provided the means for grace and forgiveness, such that there is "now no condemnation for those who are in Christ Jesus" (Rom 8:1).

---

[54] Francis D. Nichol, ed., *Seventh Day Adventist Bible Commentary*, vol. 6 (Washington, DC: Review and Herald, 1978), 707–708. C. Peter Wagner, *Your Spiritual Gifts Can Help Your Church Grow* (Ventura, CA: Regal, 1994), 57, defines the gift of singleness as "the special ability that God gives to some members of the body of Christ to remain single and enjoy it; to be unmarried and not suffer undue sexual temptations." Köstenberger and Jones, 178, believe "not only is celibacy a divine gift, it is also a divine calling that is both limited to the select few and freely chosen rather than foisted upon the individual by his or her circumstances or condition. . . . It takes special grace from God for individuals called to singleness for the sake of God's kingdom to recognize this calling."

[55] The inner struggle portrayed by Paul in Romans 7:14–24 reflects the conflict between natural sinful impulse and new sanctified will, between the old self and the person now led by the Spirit. On the identity of the "I" in this passage, see discussion in Michael P. Middendorf, *Romans 1–8*, Concordia Commentary (Saint Louis, MO: Concordia, 2013), 584–597.

[56] See Ivan T. Blazen, "The Grace that Justifies and Sanctifies," in *Salvation: Contours of Adventist Soteriology,* ed. Martin F. Hanna, Darius W. Jankiewicz, and John W. Reeve (Berrien Springs, MI: Andrews University Press, 2018), 311.

[57] J. F. MacArthur, *1 Corinthians* (Chicago, IL: Moody Press, 1984), 228.

Created in the Image of God

We need to keep in mind that humans were created in the image of God (Gen 1:27).[58] What this means is that, among other things, human beings are endowed with rationality, self-awareness, morality, responsibility, and accountability.[59] In terms of sexuality, this indicates that human beings are set apart from the animal world and can control their sexual drive. Today's culture tends to glorify pleasure and to say that a person's feelings are a compass for their actions. By ignoring feelings and desires, they are told they are not being true to themselves. Giving free reign to passions and desires, however, is the manner of those who "exchanged the truth about God for a lie and worshiped and served the creature rather than the Creator" (Rom 1:25–32; cf. Eph 4:17–19).

The Bible, on the other hand, sets a higher standard for followers of Christ. "Do not be conformed to this world, but be transformed by the renewal of your mind, that by testing you may discern what is the will of God, what is good and acceptable and perfect" (Rom 12:2). Not only do Christians worship the Creator, the one who formed human beings in His own image, but they also choose to surrender their lives to Him who loved the world to the point of sending His only Son to die in its stead. And those who are in Christ have freely chosen to live according to God's will, thus viewing their identity in terms of who God made them to be, what Christ has done for them, and what He will continue to do in their lives through the work of the Holy Spirit, rather than settling for who the world says they are (cf. Gal 2:20).[60] Paul writes in Galatians:

> But the fruit of the Spirit is love, joy, peace, patience, kindness, goodness, faithfulness, gentleness, self-control; against such things there is no law. And those who belong to Christ Jesus have crucified the flesh with its passions and desires. If we live by the Spirit, let us also keep in step with the Spirit. (Gal 5:22–25)

While this does not indicate that believers are completely free from sinful passions and desires, it recognizes that they are not ruled by them (cf. Rom 6:6; 7:14–24).[61] Believers understand that feelings and desires are a part of what it means to be human, that sometimes they make mistakes and give in to temptations, but that none of those things in

---

[58] See Doukhan, 61–65; and Cairus, 206–208.

[59] For a list of suggested interpretations regarding the meaning of the image of God in human beings, see W. S. Towner, "Clones of God: Genesis 1:26–28 and the Image of God in the Hebrew Bible," *Interpretation* 59, no. 4 (2005): 343.

[60] Craig S. Keener, *Romans*, New Covenant Commentary Series (Eugene, OR: Cascade Books, 2009), 143–144.

[61] Craig S. Keener, *Galatians* (Grand Rapids, MI: Baker Academic, 2019), 524–525; and Blazen, 311.

themselves actually define them. Instead, their identity is found in Christ, in whom He says they are.

This sense of self-identity in Christ is significant for singles even beyond the issue of sexuality. It is easy to question why one is single. Some singles may feel that God is unfair because the standards of happiness involving a family have not been met, leading to discontentment and feelings of resentment towards God. They may take matters into their own hands, which can lead a person to settle for a partner or spouse who is clearly not the right choice, contributing to unhappy and unhealthy relationships. Instead, studies show that the happiest marriages are formed by couples who "had not rushed into marriage to escape an un-happy home or loneliness as a single, but had first established a sense of well-being and happiness as an individual."[62] Identity should never be found in marital status; nor should it be found in education, career, or anything else. Instead, one's identity should be firmly anchored in Christ.[63] With that understanding comes the firm belief that God knows what is best, that He has only good intentions towards His children, and that by daily choosing to follow Him with heart and soul, we will "learn to find our all in Him."[64]

A healthy, biblical view of singleness and sexuality incorporates all of the above-mentioned points: sexuality as a gift from God, the reality of temptations, and the fact that humans were created in the image of God and all that it entails. The acknowledgement and integration of all of these points allow for a healthy sense of self-identity and contribute to Christian maturity, regardless of one's marital status or external circumstance. With these aspects in mind, singles can learn to live sexually aware and holistically fulfilled lives for the honor and glory of God.

The Role of Church and Community

The Genesis account reveals that another aspect of the image of God is the importance of companionship and relationship for human beings (cf. Gen 1:27; 2:18).[65] The local as well as the world church has a responsibility

---

[62] Carolyn A. Koons and Michael J. Anthony, *Single Adult Passages: Uncharted Territories* (Grand Rapids, MI: Baker, 1991), 87, quoted in Hsu, 96.

[63] Jani Ortlund, *Fearlessly Feminine: Boldly Living God's Plan for Womanhood* (Sisters, OR: Multnomah, 2000), 97–99.

[64] Ibid., 99.

[65] Commenting on Genesis 1:27, Doukhan, 65, writes, "The use of the singular 'him,' which is inclusive and refers to both the man and the woman, clearly implies that the 'image of God' concerns the human person: each individual, either male or female, was made in the image of God. The interplay between 'him and them' precludes, then, any kind of corporate interpretation suggesting that the image of God is only obtained as a couple, the man having received one part of the image of God and the woman another part." See also Gordon J. Wenham, *Genesis 1–15*

to address sexual ethics and the fact that marriage is not the only way to have deep and meaningful relationships. If one's identity is to be found in God, it is also connected to fellow Christians, who collectively constitute the body of Christ. In the church community, singles can find a place to build relationships that are fulfilling and that contribute positively towards the formation of their identity and sexuality.

Ephesians 2:12–22 expresses how sin creates division, not only between humans and God, but between us and our fellow human beings as well. The blood of Christ, however, breaks down any dividing walls that exist between us and others, bringing all believers into the family of God: "For through him we both have access in one Spirit to the Father. So then you are no longer strangers and aliens, but you are fellow citizens with the saints and members of the household of God" (Eph 2:18–19). The church, therefore, should be seen as much more than a social gathering of people with similar beliefs; it is effectively a community of brothers and sisters, all children of the same God (cf. John 1:12–13; 1 Cor 12:26; Gal 4:4–7; 1 John 3:1–2). In this sense, the life of the believers is directly connected to their experience of being a part of the church community, a place where the single person can develop meaningful, long-lasting, and fulfilling relationships.

Unfortunately, relationships built in other environments such as school or work often overshadow the church, since most of one's time and energy are spent outside the church. This also means that notions of identity and sexuality are more influenced by what singles are exposed to in these alternative environments, often clashing with principles and values cherished in the church. The church therefore needs to be intentional in establishing opportunities for community formation, creating a positive, welcoming atmosphere that fosters character development through examples, dialogues, programs, and relationships. This includes being aware that not all singles are in the same life circumstances: some are in their twenties and in school, some in their thirties and work full-time, and some are older divorcees or single parents. Being attuned to such differences allows churches to create a welcoming environment for singles.[66] Furthermore, while it is helpful to build connections with those who are of similar ages and life circumstances, part of the richness of the church community is the diversity it provides. Singles can benefit greatly from spending time with married couples and their families, and vice versa.[67]

(Waco, TX: Word, 1987), 68; Davidson, 42; and Cairus, 209–211.

[66] Hsu, 117–136.

[67] Köstenberger and Jones, 182. Christina S. Hitchcock, *The Significance of Singleness: A Theological Vision for the Future of the Church* (Grand Rapids, MI: Baker Academic, 2018), 92–93, writes that when married people and singles spend time together, it aids in having a

On their part, singles who are serious about committing their lives to God and living wholly fulfilled lives should be intentional in seeking these opportunities for building strong ties within the church community. Regardless of one's life circumstance, the church should be a place where singles can grow and mature as Christians and human beings. In such a community, singles can be affirmed in their commitment to sexual purity and interact with others who have a strong sense of personal identity, sexuality, and moral integrity.Indeed, one of Paul's counsels to Timothy is to flee youthful passions and aspire to manifest Christian virtues "along with those who call on the Lord from a pure heart" (2 Tim 2:22). Building relationships with like-minded believers helps keep one accountable in order to guard oneself from temptation. While every Christian struggles with temptation, it is not morally responsible to blame external circumstances for one's weaknesses. Instead, Christians are admonished to avoid potentially dangerous situations, even fleeing like Joseph did from Potiphar's wife, if necessary (Gen 39:12; Prov 4:14–15; Matt 26:41; 1 Cor 6:18; 10:13; etc.).[68] Building a network of support and accountability within the church is a helpful way to avoid such temptations.

Finally, as Paul writes, singles—probably with the exception of single parents—are in a position to dedicate more time and energy to ministry and outreach opportunities (1 Cor 7:32–35). By using their talents and their time for God, they can be a tremendous asset for the church and many others can be blessed through their work and dedication.

Conclusion

While it is not always easy to articulate the biblical view on a topic that is significantly different from the cultural circumstances of biblical times, still the Bible paints a beautiful and encouraging portrait of the single life and how to relate to sexuality. It is true that marriage remains God's ideal for humans, and that sex is only sanctioned within the limits of marriage. But in no way does that categorize singles as inferior

fuller understanding of what salvation is all about: "The marriage metaphor for salvation, often based on Ephesians 5, tends to emphasize that in salvation we become part of an amazing relationship, which is very true. But if we are able to pair the marriage picture with a singleness picture, we begin to see a fuller picture of salvation and all that it means. It means being called away from ourselves, our hopes and dreams, and our own self-formed identity, and being called to another. . . . Perhaps we won't be quite so surprised when God asks us to give something up for his sake if we have spent time living with and learning from those called to be single within the church."

[68] See Köstenberger and Jones, 186–196, for Scripture's specific message to young men and women, widows and widowers, and divorcees. For a summary of steps toward moral integrity based on wisdom literature, see Davidson, 375 n. 138.

to married people; nor does it negate a fulfilled life for singles. On the contrary, singleness can be experienced as a blessing and a gift from God as much as marriage can, and it can provide singles with the opportunity to develop a strong and mature sense of identity, leading to fulfilled lives and to the flourishing of others within the church community, and even paving the way towards healthier and happier marriages in the future.[69]

Instead of looking at sex and sexuality as taboo for singles, perhaps it would be best to promote what Simon calls the "virtue of chastity." Unlike laws or rules, which work around permissions and prohibitions, virtues focus on character-building. Simon defines the virtue of chastity as

> the successful integration of sexuality within a person that results in inner unity between bodily and spiritual being. Those who are chaste are fully at peace with their bodies and their sexuality. Chastity is not best seen as the ability to keep oneself from violating the sexual "rules"; rather, it is "a dynamic principle enabling one to use one's sexual powers intelligently in the pursuit of human flourishing and happiness."[70]

As a character trait, chastity is something everyone, whether single or married, can aspire to with the help of the Holy Spirit. The virtue of chastity integrates the biblical principles of sexual purity and respect for marriage with contentment, self-giving love, and a healthy view of self. And by focusing on virtues, it is easier to understand that the Christian life is a journey of spiritual and personal growth, and if mistakes happen along the way, God is ready to forgive and to aid in continuing the journey.

As Paul writes, "whatever is true, whatever is honorable, whatever is just, whatever is pure, whatever is lovely, whatever is commendable, if there is any excellence, if there is anything worthy of praise, think about these things" (Phil 4:8). By contemplating the Person of God and the gift of grace and salvation, singles are encouraged to discover the beauty of the biblical portrait of humanness and sexuality and how it applies to and enriches their own lives.

---

[69] "As with so many truths, there is a balance that is needed. One wonders how many marriages would never take place if the two parties were encouraged to grow and mature as Christians and human beings for a few years before their union. One wonders as well how many single Christians have been insulted and excluded by well-meaning (or perhaps not-so-well-meaning) comments that assume that because they are not married, there must be something wrong with them or something incomplete about them. Jesus' words mandate that holy matrimony is to endure 'so long as you both shall live' at the same time that they declare celibacy too to be a holy estate, a God-pleasing vocation for the sake of the reign of God" (Jeffrey A. Gibbs, *Matthew 11:2-20:34*, Concordia Commentary [Saint Loius, MO: Concordia, 2010], 956).

[70] Simon, 75–76.

CHAPTER 6

Having a Wife and a Mistress: A Global Challenge for Families

Boubakar Sanou

Throughout the world, families are faced with diverse challenges. One threat to the unity and well-being of every family is marital infidelity. As one of the distortions of the pre-fall ideal of human sexuality, marital infidelity is worldwide and cross-cultural in its scope. It is found on all continents, among all races, ethnicities, genders, social groups, and adherents of all religions.

Maintaining an extramarital relationship by having a mistress, either overtly or covertly, is an old practice that goes back in history. The mention of "concubine," an older designation for a mistress, in Genesis 22:24[1] indicates that concubinage existed before the dawn of the Hebrew culture and the patriarchal age.[2] Eleanor Herma proposes that "if prostitution is the world's oldest profession, then the finer art of being a mistress must be the second oldest."[3] In the ancient Near Eastern context, a concubine was a woman who was in a sexual partnership with a man but with no dowry. As such, she did not have the full status of a wife[4] and her children were not considered legitimate heirs of their father[5] unless a barren wife provided her husband with a concubine as a

---

[1] All biblical quotations are from the New King James Version, unless otherwise indicated.

[2] Louis M. Epstein, "The Institution of Concubinage Among the Jews," *American Academy for Jewish Research* 6 (1934–1935): 153.

[3] Eleanor Herman, *Sex With Kings: 500 Years of Adultery, Power, Rivalry, and Revenge* (New York: HarperCollins, 2004), 1.

[4] John H. Walton, Victor H. Matthews, and Mark W. Chavalas, eds., *The IVP Bible Background Commentary: Old Testament* (Downers Grove, IL: InterVarsity, 2000), 48, 57. In the ancient Near Eastern context, the role of concubines included childbearing.

[5] John H. Walton, *Zondervan Illustrated Bible Background Commentary*, vol. 1 (Grand Rapids, MI: Zondervan, 2009), 103. These children did not have primary rights to inherit from their

surrogate childbearer. The children born out of this contractual arrangement were regarded as belonging to the wife.[6]

Extramarital relationships have evolved and taken different forms depending on the context.[7] However, there is agreement among family and relationship therapists that marital infidelity is "one of the most damaging problems couples may present in therapy and one of the most difficult issues to treat."[8] Also, it is the most usual reason for divorce across societies.[9] Unfortunately, Christians are not immune to marital infidelity.[10]

The focus of this chapter is on the prevalence of heterosexual marital infidelity both in history and contemporary society, its correlates, consequences for individuals and marriages, and ways of responding to its challenges from a Seventh-day Adventist perspective. Although marital infidelity is not gender specific, this chapter focuses mainly on its occurrence among married men.

Prevalence of Marital Infidelity in History and Contemporary Society

Marital infidelity is not a recent phenomenon. Although generally perceived as a morally wrong practice, marital infidelity has been, to

---

father, unless one of them was designated by their father to be his heir if he and his primary wife did not have a son.

[6] John H. Walton, *Genesis*, NIV Application Commentary (Grand Rapids, MI: Zondervan, 2001), 446. Walton notes that in the ancient Near Eastern context, it was not only appropriate but at times contractually dictated for a barren wife to provide her husband with a surrogate childbearer—usually the wife's maidservant. See also Walton, Matthews, and Chavalas, 48.

[7] See Preston Sprinkle and Branson Parler, "Polyamory: The Next Sexual Frontier," *Christianity Today—Pastors* (Fall 2019): 35–38. The authors point out that the once-taboo relationships are now showing up in churches. See also Lisa Tran, *Concubines in Court Marriage and Monogamy in Twentieth-Century China* (New York: Rowman and Littlefield, 2015), 2.

[8] Dana A. Weiser et al., "Family Background and Propensity to Engage in Infidelity," *Journal of Family Issues* 38, no. 15 (2017): 2084. See also Paul R. Peluso, *A Family Systems Guide to Infidelity: Helping Couples Understand, Recover from, and Avoid Future Affairs* (New York: Routledge, 2019), 15.

[9] Lindsay T. Labrecque and Mark A. Whisman, "Attitudes Toward and Prevalence of Extra-marital Sex and Descriptions of Extramarital Partners in the 21st Century," *Journal of Family Psychology* 31, no. 7 (2017): 952; and Paul R. Amato and Denise Previti, "People's Reasons for Divorcing: Gender, Social Class, the Life Course, and Adjustment," *Journal of Family Issues* 24, no. 5 (2003): 602–626.

[10] Sprinkle and Parler, 36. They note that "roughly 24 percent of church-going people [in the United States] believe that consensual polyamorous relationships are morally permissible." See also Monte Sahlin, *Adventist Families in North America* (Milton-Freewater, OR: Center for Creative Ministry 2010), 28, who points out that "one in eight Adventist couples [13%] report that adultery has been a cause of conflict in their marriage."

varying degrees, an enduring challenge for families of all areas and contexts throughout centuries.[11] A lot of quantitative research has been conducted on the prevalence of marital infidelity, especially in North America. One of the most reliable of such studies is the General Social Survey of the University of Chicago, which has tracked Americans' opinions about social behaviors since 1972. Comparing the prevalence of marital infidelity in North America with other regions of the Global South is difficult because of the challenge of finding comparable data. Because of the shame and honor cultures in most of the Global South, marital infidelity is a taboo topic. Although there is a lack of statistics from long-term scholarly research on marital infidelity in the Global South, there are enough indications that extramarital affairs are a global phenomenon.[12]

Royal and Princely Mistresses

In royal courts throughout the world, the role of a royal mistress was considered so indispensable that it became the rule rather than the exception for many kings and princes. Besides their wives, kings also took mistresses/concubines. Even in Europe and Byzantium, where monogamy seemed to be the norm because of the influence of Christianity, kings still had mistresses.[13] While the most essential role of a queen in many royal courts was to produce sufficient heirs to guarantee male succession[14] to her husband's throne, in French royal courts, for example,

> a mistress was chosen for other purposes. A king singled her out for his own happiness, generally on the basis of a sexual attraction, obvious and remarked upon by the entire court. . . . By the seventeenth century, an official royal mistress had become

---

[11] Elizabeth S. Allen et al., "Intrapersonal, Interpersonal, and Contextual Factors in Engaging in and Responding to Extramarital Involvement," *Clinical Psychology: Science and Practice* 12, no. 2 (Summer 2005): 101.

[12] David P. Schmitt, "The Big Five Related to Risky Sexual Behaviour Across 10 World Regions: Differential Personality Associations of Sexual Promiscuity and Relationship Infidelity," *European Journal of Personality* 18, no. 4 (2004): 301–319. The world regions included in this study cover North America, South America, Western Europe, Eastern Europe, Southern Europe, the Middle East, Africa, Oceania, South Asia, and East Asia.

[13] Herman, 7; and *Encyclopaedia Britannica Online*, s.v. "Alice Perrers: English Mistress," https://www.britannica.com/biography/Alice-Perrers (accessed October 20, 2020). Alice Perrers, also known as Alice de Windsor, was mistress of Edward III of England. *Encyclopaedia Britannica* states that "she exercised great influence at the aging monarch's court from about 1369 until 1376."

[14] Kathleen Wellman, *Queens and Mistresses of Renaissance France* (New Haven, CT: Yale University Press, 2013), 4, 78, 230, 320. More children made succession more secure and more diplomatic alliances possible.

> conventional, almost a royal norm. By then, as long as the king dutifully fathered heirs, there were few constraints on his sexual behavior. A king's fidelity to his queen could even be considered dangerous or highly suspect. From the time of the first officially designated royal mistress, a king's extramarital sexual activity could point to his virility, perhaps indicating that he was manlier than ordinary men. The mistress, whom a king selected for sexual pleasure or love, buttressed his masculinity. Her beauty sanctioned his choice, even if she provoked criticism.[15]

Because of widespread princely infidelity, "Fifteenth Century Italy has been called both the 'golden age of bastards' and the 'age of golden bastards.'"[16] Princely mistresses, either single or married, gained great social notoriety and were even publicly celebrated in literature and artistic representations.[17] Some of them wielded some degree of political power. Because such liaisons were seen as advantageous, some husbands either refused to oppose their wives' affairs with princes or even donated their wives to those princes' pleasure in order to benefit from their largesse. The princes very often endowed their mistresses with considerable wealth and property.[18] Their male offspring had lucrative permanent Church appointments. Princes even had some of their male offspring with their mistresses legitimized by papal permission.[19]

In an age when women were still largely marginalized, the role of royal mistresses created new prospects for women to exercise power. In France, for example, the position of a king's mistress significantly evolved in importance over time, with Agnès Sorel becoming in 1444 "the first officially designated French royal mistress" with a "quasi-official

---

[15] Wellman, 4–5. On the presence of many women in the lives of kings as a sign of their male potency, see also Keith McMahon, *Women Shall Not Rule: Imperial Wives and Concubines in China from Han to Liao* (New York: Rowman and Littlefield, 2013), 11.

[16] Helen S. Ettlinger, "*Visibilis et Invisibilis:* The Mistress in Italian Renaissance Court Society," *Renaissance Quarterly* 47, no. 4 (Winter, 1994): 770. See also Jane Fair Bestor, "Bastardy and Legitimacy in the Formation of a Regional State in Italy: The Estense Succession," *Comparative Studies in Society and History* 38, no. 3 (July 1996): 549–585; Timothy McCall, "Visual Imagery and Historical Invisibility: Antonia Torelli, Her Husband, and His Mistress in Fifteenth-Century Parma," *Renaissance Studies* 23, no. 3 (2009): 269–287; and McMahon, *Women Shall Not Rule*, 11.

[17] Wellman, 185.

[18] Ettlinger, 770–771, 781; Luke Syson, "Consorts, Mistresses, and Exemplary Women: The Female Medallic Portrait in Fifteenth-Century Italy," in *The Sculpted Object: 1400–1700*, ed. Stuart Currie and Peta Motture (Brookfield, VT: Scholar, 1997), 43–64; and McCall, 269–287.

[19] Lauro Martines, *Power and Imagination: City-States in Renaissance Italy* (Baltimore, MD: Johns Hopkins University Press, 1988), 239.

status" that rivaled that of the queen.[20] With such privileged designation and political engagement, some mistresses assumed prominent public and diplomatic roles, often defining the kings' reigns. Françoise de Foix and Anne de Pisseleu, the two official mistresses of Francis I (1515–1547) were so prominent that they often carried out the queen's public duties.[21] These public and diplomatic roles also presented some of the kings' contemporaries new avenues to readily access their reigns, as mistresses very often inserted their supporters into the royal court hierarchy or Church offices.[22] The phenomenon of royal mistresses was not limited to Europe. Their existence is well recorded in Asia[23] (where a contemporary example has been reported in Thailand[24]), the Middle East,[25] and Africa[26] as well. One of the major exceptions in those cases was that the rulers' women were segregated in special quarters of palaces under the close supervision of eunuchs. These special quarters were administered by the ruler's main wife, to whom all secondary wives and concubines paid obedience. Having many women and concubines with a multiplicity of offspring was an assertion of a ruler's male potency and fertility.[27]

Mistresses in History and Contemporary Society

Because of the celebrity status of royals, whatever happened in royal courts often set the pace for their subjects. Thus, what was good for

---

[20] Wellman, 14, 25. Though started in France, the position of *maîtress en titre* ("titled mistress") was also found in other European royal courts. For example, in Italy it was known as *prima favorita*. There, the *prima favorita* "could have an apartment in the palace or live nearby, but she could also be kept in another town" (Ettlinger, 777).

[21] Ibid., 15.

[22] Martines, 239; and Wellman, 25.

[23] The history of imperial women in dynastic China is detailed in Keith McMahon's two volumes *Women Shall Not Rule* and *Celestial Women, Imperial Wives and Concubines in China from Song to Qing* (Lanham, MD: Rowman and Littlefield, 2016).

[24] See Jessie Yeung, "Thai King Strips 'Disloyal' Royal Consort of Titles and Military Ranks," *CNN*, October 22, 2019, https://www.cnn.com/2019/10/22/asia/thai-king-royal-consort-intl-hnk-scli/index.html (accessed October 20, 2020).

[25] Nadia Maria El Cheikh, "To Be a Prince in the Fourth/Tenth Century Abbasid Court," in *Royal Courts in Dynastic States and Empires: A Global Perspective*, ed. Jeroen Duindam, Tülay Artan, and Metin Kunt (Boston, MA: Brill, 2011), 203, points out that in the courts of Muslim rulers, "the notion of polygamy is not limited to the four legal wives but to the multiplicity of concubines who populated the caliphal harem. The concubine, once she had borne a child, became an *umm walad* and enjoyed a legally and socially enhanced position." See also Delia Cortese and Simonetta Calderini, *Women and the Fatimids in the World of Islam* (Edinburgh: Edinburgh University Press, 2006).

[26] Marte Bogen Sinderud, "Royal Concubinage in Ngaoundere, Northern Cameroon, ca. 1900–1960," *The International Journal of African Historical Studies* 46, no. 1 (2013): 1–25.

[27] Keith McMahon, *Women Shall Not Rule*, 11.

royals was also held in high regard by their subjects. As such, having mistresses became a common practice of those who could afford it. Married men could have mistresses without any social repercussions, while married women caught in such practices could face the death penalty unless they were mistresses of aristocrats.[28] The mistress phenomenon even gained popularity among the clergy. Church historians write about priestly mistresses as a custom entrenched in clerical culture throughout Europe in the late medieval period.[29]

The pervasiveness of extramarital relationships has not declined in contemporary society. It is an ever-present concern for many families throughout the world. There is a wide range of scholarly research on the prevalence of extramarital relationships. While some of the findings are based on nonrandom and often small, convenience samples, an analysis of the 2000–2016 General Social Surveys[30] estimates that "approximately 1.5–5% of ever-married individuals will have extramarital sex annually, and 22–25% of men and 11–15% of women will have had extramarital sex in their lifetime."[31] It is believed that although fairly accurate, these findings still underestimate the true prevalence of marital infidelity for two main reasons: First, because in general people still think that marital infidelity is morally wrong, the majority of people are reluctant to admit such behavior—not just to their spouses but to anyone, and especially during face-to-face interviews.[32] Second, some people narrowly define marital infidelity as sexual intercourse.[33]

Research also reveals there has been a shift in the way the general population perceives marital infidelity. Although people still generally

---

[28] Martines, 239.

[29] Michelle Armstrong-Partida, "Priestly Wives: The Role and Acceptance of Clerics' Concubines in the Parishes of Late Medieval Catalunya," *Speculum* 88, no. 1 (January 2013): 173; James Bruce Ross and Mary Martin McLaughlin, eds., *The Portable Medieval Reader* (New York: Viking Press, 1949), 78; and Paul E. Pierson, *The Dynamics of Christian Mission: History Through a Missiological Perspective* (Pasadena, CA: William Carey International University Press, 2009), 108.

[30] The aim of the GSS is to gather data on the attributes, attitudes, and behaviors of contemporary American society. The GSS involves face-to-face interviews of a multistage, stratified probability sample of the adult (eighteen years of age and older) household population of the United States.

[31] Labrecque and Whisman, 952–953.

[32] Tara Parker-Pope, "Love, Sex and the Changing Landscape of Infidelity," *The New York Times*, October 27, 2008, https://www.nytimes.com/2008/10/28/health/28well.html (accessed October 20, 2020). Parker-Pope points out that "in a study published last summer [2007] in The Journal of Family Psychology, for example, researchers from the University of Colorado and Texas A&M surveyed 4,884 married women, using face-to-face interviews and anonymous computer questionnaires. In the interviews, only 1 percent of women said they had been unfaithful to their husbands in the past year; on the computer questionnaire, more than 6 percent did."

[33] Anthony P. Thompson, "Extramarital Sexual Crisis: Common Themes and Therapy Implications," *Journal of Sex and Marriage Therapy* 10, no. 4 (1984): 36.

think that marital infidelity is wrong,[34] "there does seem to be some softening of the absolute view of infidelity as wrong." From their analysis of the General Social Survey data, Lindsay T. Labrecque and Mark A. Whisman remark that there is

> a statistically significant linear decline in the percentage of people who viewed extramarital sex as always wrong and a significant linear increase in the percentage of people who viewed it as wrong only sometimes. The percentage of people who viewed it as always wrong declined from 79.4% in 2000 to 75.8% in 2016, whereas the percentage of people who viewed it as wrong only sometimes increased from 7.1% in 2000 to 8.7% in 2016.[35]

There is, therefore, an inherent conflict between a moral ideal and actual behavior. Labrecque and Whisman's findings are consistent with prior research about men considering extramarital sex as less immoral than women and thereby more likely than women to want to engage in it.[36] Research also shows that middle-aged and older couples are not immune to extramarital relationships. In fact, another trend that has emerged from studies on marital infidelity is that "the prevalence of infidelity increases as people age."[37] From 1991 to 2006, the lifetime rate of marital infidelity for men over sixty increased from 20% to 28%, while that of women over sixty increased from 5% to 15%.[38] It is argued that this rise of marital infidelity among older couples might also be the reason why the rate of divorce has doubled among them.[39]

Although no precise statistics from long-term studies exist on the prevalence of marital infidelity among Christians—lay members and clergy alike—its occurrence is not disputed. While religiosity (e.g.,

---

[34] Peluso, 4. Extramarital relationships are not perceived with the same degree of social stigma as they were in the past, except when it concerns royals and those in public or religious offices. See also "A New Generation of Adults Bends Moral and Sexual Rules to Their Liking," Research Releases, Barna Group, October 31, 2006, https://www.barna.com/research/a-new-generation-of-adults-bends-moral-and-sexual-rules-to-their-liking/ (accessed October 20, 2020).

[35] Labrecque and Whisman, 954–955.

[36] Bram P. Buunk and Arnold B. Bakker, "Extradyadic Sex: The Role of Descriptive and Injunctive Norms," *The Journal of Sex Research* 32, no. 4 (1995): 313–318; Judith Treas and Deirdre Giesen, "Sexual Infidelity Among Married and Cohabiting Americans," *Journal of Marriage and the Family* 62, no. 1 (February 2000): 48–60; and Allen et al., 101–130.

[37] Peluso, 4.

[38] Parker-Pope.

[39] Susan L. Brown and I-Fen Lin, "The Gray Divorce Revolution: Rising Divorce Among Middle-Aged and Older Adults, 1990–2010," *Journals of Gerontology Series B: Psychological Sciences and Social Sciences* 67, no. 6 (2012): 735.

regularly attending religious services and asserting that the Bible is the literal or inspired Word of God) appears to reduce the likelihood of marital infidelity,[40] infidelity is a significant problem for many Christian couples.[41] This is illustrated by revelations of the 2015 Ashley Madison dating site scandal that 25% of Ashley Madison's customers in the United Sates identified themselves as Evangelical Christians.[42]

Potential Correlates of Marital Infidelity

In general, married couples do not go into marriage with plans to commit adultery. Extramarital affairs happen when a rationale for them is created over a period of time.[43] The seeds of infidelity get planted in a marriage when, for one reason or another, a spouse perceives their partner as less than their ideal. As a result of this entertained thought, they are tempted to believe that someone else out there is exactly what they are missing.[44] Alfred Demaris warns that "regardless of the quality of the marital relationship, temptations to be unfaithful constitute an ever-present danger for married individuals."[45]

---

[40] Loren Marks, "How Does Religion Influence Marriage? Christian, Jewish, Mormon, and Muslim Perspectives," *Marriage & Family Review* 38, no. 1 (2005): 85–111; Andrew Village, Emyr Williams, and Leslie J. Francis, "Does Religion Make a Difference? Assessing the Effects of Christian Affiliation and Practice on Marital Solidarity and Divorce in Britain, 1985–2005," *Journal of Divorce & Remarriage* 51, no. 6 (2010): 327–338; and Joshua D. Tuttle and Shannon N. Davis, "Religion, Infidelity, and Divorce: Reexamining the Effect of Religious Behavior on Divorce Among Long-Married Couples," *Journal of Divorce & Remarriage* 56, no. 6 (2015): 475–489.

[41] John W. Thoburn and Jack O. Balswick, "An Evaluation of Infidelity Among Male Protestant Clergy," *Pastoral Psychology* 42, no. 4 (1994): 285–294; Amy M. Burdette et al., "Are There Religious Variations in Marital Infidelity?," *Journal of Family Issues* 28, no. 12 (2007): 1553–1581; Corrie Cutrer, "The New Face of Infidelity: What Lures Christians to Cheat?," *Christianity Today Women*, May 24, 2016, https://www.christianitytoday.com/women/2015/november/new-face-of-adultery.html (accessed October 20, 2020); and Joe Maxwell, "Devastated by an Affair: How Churches Heal after the Pastor Commits Adultery," *Christianity Today*, December 6, 2006, https://www.christianitytoday.com/ct/2007/january/2.51.html (accessed October 20, 2020).

[42] David Robertson, "Ashley Madison: How It Reveals the Hypocrisy of Both the Church and Culture," *Christian Today,* August 28, 2015, https://christiantoday.com/article/ashley-madison-how-it-reveals-the-hypocrisy-of-both-the-church-and-culture/63193.htm (accessed October 20, 2020). Ashley Madison is an online dating site established in Canada in 2001 for the sole purpose of facilitating adultery.

[43] Joan D. Atwood and Madeline Seifer, "Extramarital Affairs and Constructed Meanings: A Social Constructionist Therapeutic Approach," *The American Journal of Family Therapy* 25, no. 1 (1997): 62; and Emily M. Brown, "The Affair as a Catalyst for Change," in *Infidelity: A Practitioner's Guide to Working With Couples in Crisis*, 149–165, ed. Paul R. Peluso (New York: Routledge, 2007), 149.

[44] Christopher Hart, "Infidelity: Why It's So Tempting," *Sunday Nation* (December 17, 2006): 4.

[45] Alfred Demaris, "Distal and Proximal Influences on the Risk of Extramarital Sex: A \Prospective Study of Longer Duration Marriages," *Journal of Sex Research* 46, no. 6 (2009): 598.

Family studies point to multiple factors that are statistically significant in relationship to infidelity, such as age, family of origin, religiosity, premarital sexual experience, gender, relationship satisfaction, opportunity to cheat, unresolved childhood issues, low self-esteem, and social context.[46] This study discusses several of these factors in three main categories: the decline in marital satisfaction, childlessness, and the influence of contextual factors.

Decline in Marital Satisfaction

According to researchers, marital satisfaction is a critical variable in the overall health of a marriage. Marital satisfaction is defined as

> a mental state that reflects the perceived benefits and costs of marriage to a particular person. The more costs a marriage partner inflicts on a person, the less satisfied one generally is with the marriage and with the marriage partner. Similarly, the greater the perceived benefits are, the more satisfied one is with the marriage and with the marriage partner.[47]

There is a reciprocal relationship between the feeling of being loved, appreciated, respected, and fulfilled and overall marital satisfaction. Another important component of marital satisfaction is related to the degree of social support spouses receive from each other and from their relationship. By providing good social support to each other, spouses contribute to their overall marital satisfaction.[48]

The point here is that the desire to be loved, appreciated, respected, and fulfilled is an existential need common to all human beings. Its absence in marriage often leads to the estrangement of marital relationships. When couples settle down from their excitement of falling in love and getting married, there comes a time when they are likely to experience emotional and motivational erosion in their relationship. The emotional erosion occurs whenever couples deal poorly with the demands and realities of their new social status or are unable to handle conflict constructively in their relationship. In addition, motivational erosion creeps in when couples cannot work in tandem towards the

---

[46] Elizabeth Crouch and Lori Dickes, "Economic Repercussions of Marital Infidelity," *International Journal of Sociology and Social Policy* 36, nos. 1–2 (2016): 56–57; and John Thoburn and Jack O. Balswick, "A Prevention Approach to Infidelity Among Male Protestant Clergy," *Pastoral Psychology* 42, no. 1 (1993): 45–51.

[47] Emily A. Stone and Todd K. Shackelford, "Marital Satisfaction," in *Encyclopedia of Social Psychology*, vol. 2, ed. Roy F. Baumeister and Kathleen D. Vohs (Thousand Oaks, CA: Sage, 2007), 541.

[48] Ibid., 542.

achievement of either their personal goals or the goals of their marriage. When that happens, instead of working to improve their relationships, some spouses simply resort to looking outside their marriage to fulfill their longing for affection and appreciation.[49] It is believed that some partners, in their desire to exit their relationship because of dissatisfaction, will even go as far as intentionally bringing their affairs out in the open as a way of forcing the other partner to end the relationship.[50] In such cases, extramarital infidelity may merely be a symptom or a way out of a marriage that is already dead.[51]

Sometimes the search for satisfaction and fulfillment in marriage is about sexual gratification or simply sexual adventure. It has been suggested from research that the

> lack of sexual fulfillment and happiness between married couples are common causes of extra-marital affairs. Sexual dissatisfaction in marriage may arise from a boring sex life, or infrequent coitus both of which could be attributed to estrangement, sexual inexperience, old age, pregnancy, childbirth, or female circumcision.[52]

Sexual dissatisfaction in some marriages is also said to be related to the midlife crisis experienced by most middle-aged and older couples. Christopher Hart argues that as human beings, "we spend most of our adult lives feeling scared about getting old. So being reassured that we're still nice enough to attract a new partner is a great boost to the ego."[53] For older married men, finding a young and beautiful mistress is a question of prestige. Thus, some men find in the search for reassurance a compelling reason to engage in extramarital affairs.[54] According to some psychologists, the search for reassurance may also be related to sexual addiction. This has to do with spouses who, because of either prolonged emotional deprivation or past sexual abuse, are dealing with their emotional neediness by multiplying sexual conquests in the hope of filling their internal emptiness and dealing with their pain. Oftentimes,

---

[49] Frank D. Fincham and Ross W. May, "Infidelity in Romantic Relationships," *Current Opinion in Psychology* 13 (2017): 71; and Collette Akoth Suda, *Formal Monogamy and Informal Polygyny in Parallel: African Family Traditions in Transition* (Nairobi: University of Nairobi, 2007), 56, 60.

[50] Peluso, 23.

[51] Denise Previti and Paul R. Amato, "Is Infidelity a Cause or a Consequence of Poor Marital Quality?," *Journal of Social and Personal Relationships* 21, no. 2 (2004): 218.

[52] Suda, 59. Similar corelates of marital infidelity are presented in Atwood and Seifer, 59.

[53] Hart, 4.

[54] Suda, 58.

the idea of breaking the rules without being caught also becomes very intoxicating for some individuals.[55]

Finally, sexual dissatisfaction may also arise either from the practice of levirate marriages or other forms of arranged marriages. For some social, religious, economic, or political reasons, a lot of marriages are still arranged in some contexts. In arranged marriages, the concerned couple very often consent to getting married without necessarily loving each other. The majority of such couples are said to be unhappy in their relationships. It is believed that those who are in such unhappy marital relationships are more vulnerable to the temptation of extramarital relationships.[56]

Childlessness

Childlessness in marriages is a major contributing factor to the prevalence of the mistress phenomenon in many contexts. For many couples in non-Western contexts, the primary purpose of marriage is intimately linked with the continuation of the family and society through procreation.[57] Because marriage and procreation have long been perceived as means of building social capital, they are regarded as compulsory in many non-Western traditional contexts.[58] In such contexts, only upon the birth of a child is marriage deemed complete.[59] Since fertility is of utmost importance in such settings,[60] whenever a

---

[55] Peluso, 21; and Emily M. Brown, *Patterns of Infidelity and Their Treatment* (Philadelphia, PA: Brunner-Routledge, 2001), 37.

[56] Nabeela Malik et al., "Causes and Consequences of Extra-Marital Relations in Married Women: A Case Study of Darulaman Sargodha," *Mediterranean Journal of Social Sciences* 5, no. 23 (November 2014): 2047. Such was also the case in many Europeans royal courts where marriages were very often arranged to cement political alliances, seal peace treaties, or advance kings' political interests. Wellman, 6, points out that in many of those cases, "the queen was frequently dismissed as dull and unattractive, but the mistress was praised as beautiful and glamorous." See also Yasmin Jahan et al., "Factors Involving Extramarital Affairs Among Married Adults in Bangladesh," *International Journal of Community Medicine and Public Health* 4, no. 5 (May 2017): 1381; and Hart, 4.

[57] Edith Turner and Pamela R. Frese, "Marriage," in *Encyclopedia of Religion*, vol. 8, 2nd ed., ed. Lindsay Jones (New York: Thompson Gale, 2005), 5724.

[58] Tabitha Kanogo, *African Womanhood in Colonial Kenya 1900–50* (Athens, OH: Ohio University Press, 2005), 53

[59] Ama Mazama, "Marriage," in *Encyclopedia of African Religion*, ed. Molefi Kete Asante and Ama Mazama (Thousand Oaks, CA: Sage, 2009), 409.

[60] Ama Mazama, "Children," in Asante and Mazama, 161–163. On the primary importance of children in a traditional African context, Mazama notes that "children fulfill two roles. First, they remember and honor their departed parents. Second, they allow departed ones to come back into the world of the living. . . . [B]eing remembered means that one is still part of one's community and still exists. Conversely, being forgotten means being excluded, which is a terrible fate as far as Africans are concerned. In that context, to die without having had the chance or time to give birth to children is a real calamity because it is one's children's primary

couple experiences difficulty with childbearing, everything humanly possible is done to maintain the procreative function of their marriage. This may include the husband fulfilling his procreative duties with a mistress if his wife is suspected of barrenness.[61] Often in these contexts, wives cannot accuse their husbands of infidelity as husbands' fidelity to their wives is not pledged, especially in cases of customary marriage. In the case of a husband's infertility, some communities make secret arrangements for his brother or one of his male relatives to step in to fulfill the necessary procreative duties on his behalf.[62]

Throughout history and cultures, men's marital infidelity has been somewhat more sanctioned than that of women. While the community tolerates extramarital affairs from men, it expects wives to remain faithful.[63] Since the preservation and transmission of life is one of the highest values in traditional religious contexts, the community explains to all its members, including Christians, that their "failure to have children signifies that one is rejecting God, whose original creative and continuous power manifests itself, among other things, through the uninterrupted birth of human beings; it is as well a rejection of humanity because the latter depends on human fertility for its perpetuation."[64] In patriarchal societies, it is not just childlessness but "sonlessness" that leads some men to extramarital affairs. If childbearing was the most essential role of European queens, their primary role was to be bearers of sons when "the crown could be inherited only through direct male succession" because "no royal daughter could inherit the crown and . . . no male heir could claim the crown by virtue of his descent from a royal daughter."[65]

Because of such strong social pressure to conform to cultural standards and the perceived spiritual obligation to have children,[66] some

---

responsibility to remember one. This is why, everywhere in Africa, marriage and procreation are of the utmost importance" (ibid., 162). See also Mazama, "Marriage," 409–411.

[61] Mazama, "Marriage," 411.

[62] See Rebecca Magorokosho, "Barrenness and Sexuality in the Ndau Community," in *African Sexualities: A Reader,* ed. Sylvia Tamale, (Cape Town, South Africa: Pambazuka Press, 2011), 247 and Ini Dorcas Dah, *Women Do More Work than Men: Birifor Women as Change Agents in the Mission and Expansion of the Church in West Africa (Burkina Faso, Côte D'Ivoire and Ghana)* (Eugene, OR: Wipf & Stock, 2018), 42.

[63] Kanogo, 65; and Allen et al., 119.

[64] Mazama, "Marriage," 409.

[65] Wellman, 7, 19, 108, 116.

[66] Mazama, "Children," 163.

Christians, out of fear of being shunned or the shame often associated with childlessness, resort to having a child with another woman.[67]

Contextual Factors

Human beings are products of their cultures and environments. This social and environmental locatedness contributes to shape every person's overall perspective on life by creating in each person a specific "lens through which a vision of life and social order is expressed, experienced, and explored."[68] In other words, this specific lens, or worldview, equips each person with a unique overall outlook on life from which they see, interpret, evaluate, and interact with what they perceive as reality. With time, this perception, which may have only been cognitive at the beginning, becomes engrained in a person to the point of influencing also the affective and evaluative dimensions of their daily life. In a sense, a person's social locatedness affects their overall reasoning about reality, which in turn programs them to believe and live in a certain way.

From the perspective of the impact of social location on how individuals live their lives, it could be argued that the meaning of extramarital sex has, for some men, been determined by their sociocultural contexts. Commenting on extramarital relationships in Africa, Collette Suda notes that "although much of the ethnographic literature indicates that heterosexual monogamy remains the statistical marriage norm," polygamy is "increasingly being re-invented, often clandestinely, mainly to suit modern urban lifestyles."[69] The cultural phenomenon of "small house" unions is one way polygamy is being reinvented in urban settings in many parts of Africa. A "small house" is a Zimbabwean colloquial term referring to an informal, secret, and long-term sexual relationship between a married man and a single woman leading to the establishment of a parallel household. The term may be understood either as the act of a married man having a long-term, secret female partner or the long-term female partner herself.[70] Procreation may be the cause for or the outcome

---

[67] Charles H. Kraft, *Worldview for Christian Witness* (Pasadena, CA: William Carey, 2008), 33.

[68] Kevin J. Vanhoozer, "What Is Everyday Theology? How and Why Christians Should Read Culture," in *Everyday Theology: How to Read Cultural Texts and Interpret Trends*, ed. Kevin J. Vanhoozer, Charles A. Anderson, and Michael J. Sleasman (Grand Rapids, MI: Baker Academic, 2007), 26.

[69] Suda, 56.

[70] Wonder Muchabaiwa, "The Small House Phenomenon and Polygyny in Zimbabwe: A Problematic Context for Child Socialisation and Development," *Africology: The Journal of Pan African Studies* 10, no. 3 (May 2017): 149–162; Muchabaiwa, "Gender Dynamics of the Small House Phenomenon in the Harare Metropolitan Province, Zimbabwe" (PhD diss., University of South Africa, 2018); and Mildred Mushinga, "The 'Small House': An Ethnographic Investigation into Economically Independent Women and Sexual Networks in Zimbabwe" (PhD diss., University of Pretoria, 2015).

of such unions.[71] It is suggested that the phrase "small house" and its corresponding terms in other countries[72] originated from cultural practices of polygyny, in which men have senior and junior wives. In contemporary discourse, a "small house" is a modern-day version of a junior wife.[73] "Small house" is used in contrast to the legal wife and her household. Small-housing (the act of having or being a small house) thus "allows the extension of the [monogamous] marriage institution into a quasi-polygamous system, in a nostalgic cultural way, creating a new form of marriage between two ideologies, that of modernity, and a cultural adherence."[74] Because the small house institution is presented as an integral part of the African cultural heritage, men and women from all social strata and religious persuasions engage in it, fully aware that it is not a socially sanctioned form of marriage.[75] With the prevalence of such a modified/veiled urban polygyny in Africa and across the world, in many contexts the concept of monogamy is upheld only nominally.

It is also apropos to mention the influence of popular culture on people's perspective on love and sex. Ana Nogales and Laura Bellotti note that "the infidelity we have experienced or witnessed in real life is often mirrored in our popular culture. From opera to blues and country songs, serious drama to Desperate Housewives, cheating frequently

---

[71] Alex Mutseta, "The 'Small House' Phenomenon in Zimbabwe's Urban Space: Study in Glen Norah-Harare," *Open Science Journal* 1, no. 2 (2016): 9, 14.

[72] Although a Zimbabwean-specific social term, the "small house" phenomenon, whereby married men have clandestine female partners, is not singular to Zimbabwe. For example, in Francophone Africa, the same practice is commonly known as *deuxième bureau* ("second office"); it is called "little wives" or "a little third" in China, where it is reported that "in Shenzhen there are 'concubine villages,' such as the one in Huizou, where hundreds perhaps thousands of young mainland women live in spacious apartments, paid for by their lovers, in high-rise complexes close enough to the border that the men can take off early from work, visit their lovers, and be home in time for dinner with their wives" ("Concubines and Misstresses [*sic*] in China," Facts and Details, updated June 2015, http://factsanddetails.com/china/cat4/sub20/item108.html [accessed April 18, 2021]).

[73] Lene Bull Christiansen, "'Respectable Women' versus 'Small Houses': Feminist Negotiations of Sexual Morality, Marriage and the Challenge of HIV/AIDS in Zimbabwe," *Journal of Southern African Studies* 39, no. 3 (2013): 515.

[74] Mutseta, 2.

[75] Ibid., 8–10. Small house unions are very often the result of personal arrangements between two secret lovers devoid of any marital rite, although Mutseta, 8, notes that often "women such as aunties and sisters play a role in establishing small house unions as they arrange for a secret-potential wife to their male relatives if they are not comfortable with the first wife or having problems with her."

gets star billing."[76] Popular culture and the media (television, popular music, movies, and the internet) thus constitute the primary gateway to many people's expectations of romantic relationships.[77] By encouraging, glorifying, and increasing the potential for multiple sexual partners, the "hook-up" and "fast food intimacy" cultures created by a variety of dating apps have popularized casual sex as an alternative for real intimacy and "given rise to young people becoming tempted to callousness, turning people [their sexual partners] into a numbers game instead of treating them like human beings."[78] As a consequence of sexual permissiveness associated with popular culture, researchers have also established that individuals who have had multiple premarital sexual experiences have an elevated risk of extramarital relationships because of their previous permissive sexual attitudes.[79]

Internet and social networking platforms have ushered the world into a new era of marital infidelity. By offering the thrill of a make-believe romance along with the added promise of anonymity, cyber cheating has increased the opportunity and potential for marital infidelity. As part of this digital sexual revolution, several dating sites offer to married individuals discreet means of engaging in infidelity.[80] The accessibility of internet pornography and infamous dating sites has warped many people's expectations of sex.[81] Married individuals whose attraction for each other has waned over time may wish to experience the romanticized relationships portrayed by the media. When they find it difficult to do so in their relationships with their spouses, they are often tempted to think that the promised discreet extramarital relationships will offer them the opportunity to cultivate and experience such romance.[82] In this way, popular culture and its media have contributed to create relational myths more than they have contributed to create healthy and fulfilling

---

[76] Ana Nogales and Laura Golden Bellotti, *Parents Who Cheat: How Children and Adults Are Affected When Their Parents Are Unfaithful* (Deerfield Beach, FL: Health Communications, 2009), 5.

[77] Atwood and Seifer, 56; and Jenny van Hooff, "An Everyday Affair: Deciphering the Sociological Significance of Women's Attitudes Towards Infidelity," *The Sociological Review* 65, no. 4 (2016): 852.

[78] Natalie Ng, "How Has Pop Culture and the Media Influenced Our Perspectives of Love and Sex?," *Meld Magazine*, September 29, 2017, https://www.meldmagazine.com.au/2017/09/love-sex-pop-culture-media/ (accessed October 20, 2020).

[79] Jahan et al., 1379; Demaris, 599; and Suda, 64–65.

[80] Jana Hackathorn et al., "From Fear and Guilt: Negative Perceptions of Ashley Madison Users," *Psychology & Sexuality* 8, nos. 1–2 (2017): 41–54.

[81] Frank D. Fincham and Ross W. May, "Infidelity in Romantic Relationships," *Current Opinion in Psychology* 13 (2017): 72.

[82] Demaris, 598.

marital relationships.

Human nature, cultural norms and expectations, the search for significance and reassurance, popular culture, and the influence of media are not excuses for engaging in marital infidelity. Part of being a disciple of Christ is the grace and the capacity He gives us to control our instincts rather than have them control us.

Consequences of Infidelity on Individuals and Marriages

The expectation of sexual fidelity is nearly a universal social norm regulating consensual monogamy. The violation of this norm of sexual exclusivity has the potential for detrimental emotional, physical, social, and even spiritual effects for both partners, their children, as well as people in their social support network. In many regards, marital infidelity is a significant public health concern. Among the commonly listed consequences of marital infidelity by family studies researchers and couples' therapists are the increased exposure to sexually transmitted diseases and HIV because of low rates of condom use with secondary partners, increased marital distress, poor mental health (depression, anxiety, and symptoms of post-traumatic stress disorder), domestic violence, divorce, decreased productivity, and increased individual and household poverty as the result of family fragmentation.[83] Some people whose partners have cheated on them also report having crippling doubts about their self-worth as they are often prone to think that something is wrong with them, thus blaming themselves for their partner's cheating.[84]

Marital infidelity can also have spiritual impacts on both the spouse having the affair and their partner. Because married individuals known to have engaged in extramarital affairs are very often stigmatized, the guilty partner may, out of embarrassment, shame, and loss of self-esteem, stop attending church to avoid inquisitive stares and

[83] Fincham and May, 70; Labrecque and Whisman, 952; Howard J. Markman, "The Prevention of Extramarital Involvement: Steps Towards 'Affair Proofing' Marriage," *Clinical Psychology: Science and Practice* 12, no. 2 (2005): 134–138; Annmarie Cano and K. Daniel O'Leary, "Infidelity and Separations Precipitate Major Depressive Episodes and Symptoms of Nonspecific Depression and Anxiety," *Journal of Consulting and Clinical Psychology* 68, no. 5 (2000): 774–781; Ann O'Leary, "Women at Risk for HIV from a Primary Partner: Balancing Risk and Intimacy," *Annual Review of Sex Research* 11, no. 1 (2000): 191–243; Elizabeth S. Allen and David C. Atkins, "The Association of Divorce and Extramarital Sex in a Representative U.S. Sample," *Journal of Family Issues* 33, no. 11 (2012): 1477–1493; Laura Betzig, "Causes of Conjugal Dissolution: A Cross-Cultural Study," *Current Anthropology* 30, no. 5 (1989): 654–676; Terri D. Conley et al., "Unfaithful Individuals Are Less Likely to Practice Safer Sex Than Openly Nonmonogamous Individuals," *The Journal of Sexual Medicine* 9, no. 6 (2012): 1559–1565; and Crouch and Dickes, 54.

[84] W. Craig Carter, "Infidelity Accounts," *International Journal of Humanities and Social Science* 4, no. 7 (May 2014): 17.

insensitive comments. The faithful spouse may feel a sense of betrayal and anger not only at their partner, but also at God. This perspective on their painful experience can impair their relationship with God.

Children are inadvertently involved in any marital infidelity tragedy. Family studies researchers have explored the impact of a variety of family-of-origin experiences on marital infidelity and noted that parental infidelity has profound adverse effects on children.[85] When a spouse breaks their pledge of sexual fidelity to the other, "they also break an unspoken promise to their children: to be part of a loving family whose members are forever loyal to each other."[86] There are painful consequences in the lives of children of any age when one parent betrays the other. First, because the family of origin is where every person first learns about "components of relationship such as love, honesty, respect, communication, attachment, and conflict,"[87] children unconsciously "learn how to develop and maintain romantic relationships based on information directly communicated and observed in their parents' relationship."[88] Negative parental role models, especially in sexual behaviors, is believed to raise adult children's susceptibility to extramarital relationships.[89] Second, when their parent's infidelity is discovered, children can be overcome by feeling of shame and humiliation even though they are not responsible for the actions of that parent. That feeling of shame and humiliation is exacerbated by inquisitive stares, insensitive

---

[85] Rhi Anna L. Platt et al., "Parental Conflict and Infidelity as Predictors of Adult Children's Attachment Style and Infidelity," *The American Journal of Family Therapy* 36, no. 2 (2008): 149–161; Allison R. Thorson, "Adult Children's Experiences With Their Parent's Infidelity: Communicative Protection and Access Rules in the Absence of Divorce," *Communication Studies* 60, no. 1 (January–March 2009): 32–48; Thorson, "Feeling Caught: Adult Children's Experiences with Parental Infidelity," *Qualitative Research Reports in Communication* 15, no. 1 (2014): 75–83; and Alexandra E. Schmidt et al., "Effects of Parental Infidelity on Adult Children's Relational Ethics With Their Partners: A Contextual Perspective," *Journal of Couple & Relationship Therapy* 15, no. 3 (2016): 193–212.

[86] Nogales and Bellotti, 1.

[87] Schmidt et al., 194; and Weiser et al., 2085.

[88] Weiser et al., 2085.

[89] Demaris, 599; Du Feng et al., "Intergenerational Transmission of Marital Quality and Marital Instability," *Journal of Marriage and Family*, 61, no. 2 (May, 1999): 451–463; Tianyi Yu and Francesca Adler-Baeder, "The Intergenerational Transmission of Relationship Quality," *Journal of Divorce and Remarriage* 47, nos. 3–4 (2007): 87–102; Paul R. Amato and Alan Booth, "The Legacy of Parents' Marital Discord: Consequences for Children's Marital Quality," *Journal of Personality and Social Psychology* 81, no. 4 (2001): 627–638; Ming Cui and Frank D. Fincham, "The Differential Effects of Parental Divorce and Marital Conflict on Young Adult Romantic Relationships," *Personal Relationships* 17 (2010): 331–343; and Sarah W. Whitton et al., "Prospective Associations from Family-of-Origin Interactions to Adult Marital Interactions and Relationship Adjustment," *Journal of Family Psychology* 22, no. 2 (2008): 274–286.

comments, or intrusive questions of friends or acquaintances. Third, because parents are role models for their children, parental infidelity creates a loss of children's trust in the betraying parent and resentment towards them. If the father is the betraying parent, his daughters can grow up with difficulties trusting men. Likewise, if the mother is the betraying parent, her sons can grow up with difficulties trusting women. Learning from parental infidelity that marriage partners can be deceitful and love can be hurtful has the potential to create in children a loss of trust in the merits of marriage.[90] It has been established that

> the children's perceptions of their parents engaging in infidelity and betraying each other's trust may result in them being wary of getting into a relationship due to fear of their partner engaging in an extradyadic relationship. Thus, parental infidelity may have an impact on the child's view of others, which will in turn impact the attachment style the child develops in adult romantic relationships. The children of parents who engage in infidelity may be more likely to have a negative view of others because they think other people have negative intentions in relationships and are not trustworthy.[91]

Fourth, as earlier stated, several studies strongly suggest that there is a link between family-of-origin experiences and the way adult children relate to their married partners.[92] Besides parental infidelity being a source of confusion, anxiety, and distress among children, adult children who have knowledge of their still-married parents' extramarital relationship have a higher likelihood of engaging in marital infidelity than those without such knowledge.[93]

Other adverse consequences of marital infidelity include damage of the couple's relationships with other people. Because marriage does not involve only a couple and their children, whenever marital infidelity happens, its ripple effects also impact all those in the couple's social support network (e.g., in-laws, friends, and church members).[94]

---

[90] Nogales and Bellotti, 6, 10, 54–59.

[91] Platt et al., 151.

[92] Ibid., 149–161; Thorson, "Adult Children's Experiences," 32–48; Thorson, "Feeling Caught," 75–83; and Schmidt et al., 193–212.

[93] Platt et al., 149. See also Feng et al., 451–463; Yu and Adler-Baeder, 87–102; Amato and Booth, 627–638; Cui and Fincham, 331–343; and Whitton et al., 274–286.

[94] Adrian J. Blow and Kelley Hartnett, "Infidelity in Committed Relationships II: A Substantive Review," *Journal of Marital and Family Therapy* 31, no. 2 (April 2005): 228.

Marriage and Marital Infidelity: A Biblical Perspective

Before dealing with a Christian response to the challenge of marital infidelity, it is important to consider an overview of marriage and marital infidelity from a biblical perspective. Genesis 1:26–28 and 2:18–24 present marriage both as part of God's pre-fall plan for humanity and also as a foundational structure of family and community life. The first requirement of Genesis 2:24 for a man to leave his father and mother upon marriage and to cling to his wife portrays marriage as a permanent covenant bond[95] intended to mirror the covenant relationship between God and His people (Eph 5:28–32). Sexual intercourse is the physical expression of the second requirement of Genesis 2:24 regarding a married couple becoming one flesh.

Because on one hand the command of Genesis 1:28 to be fruitful, multiply, and fill the earth requires conceiving children, and because on the other hand God created Eve, a woman (not multiple women or another man), as Adam's suitable helper (Gen 2:21–22), marriage is intended by God to be a lifelong, heterosexual, monogamous covenant relationship. God's original design for marriage as expressed in Genesis 1 and 2 serves as the foundation for interpreting other biblical accounts on marriage.[96] As such, the biblical accounts of polygamy (e.g., Gen 4:19; 26:34; Abraham, David, Solomon) should be viewed as descriptive accounts of the negative impact of sin on the marriage institution.

The institution and sanctity of marriage have been negatively impacted by the fall. As a way to safeguard the sanctity of marriage from complete corruption, God instituted principles to regulate it. From a broad perspective, the definition of marital infidelity in the Bible encompasses either committing adultery or coveting one's neighbor's wife. The seventh commandment, "You shall not commit adultery" (Exod 20:14; Deut 5:18), prohibits "voluntary sexual relations between a married person and someone other than his or her spouse."[97] Part of the tenth commandment, "You shall not covet your neighbor's wife" (Exod 20:17;

---

[95] Richard M. Davidson, *Flame of Yahweh: Sexuality in the Old Testament* (Peabody, MA: Hendrickson, 2007), 45, points out that to cling (*dābaq*) "is often used in the OT as a technical covenant term for the permanent bond of Israel to the Lord." See also Jacques Doukhan, *Genesis,* The Seventh-day Adventist International Bible Commentary (Mountain View, CA: Pacific Press, 2016), 85.

[96] Davidson, 15.

[97] Daniel I. Block, *Deuteronomy*, NIV Application Commentary (Grand Rapids, MI: Zondervan, 2012), 166.

Deut 5:21), "refers to an inward desire that, if fanned, will lead to action

[i.e., physical sexual relations]."[98] In other words, coveting one's neighbor's wife (a mental desire) is what will lead to adultery (physical action). It can be said that whereas the seventh commandment seeks to preserve the integrity of marriage, the tenth commandment seeks to safeguard the security of the marriage bond.[99] Together, these two commandments are an expression of God's desire for the maintenance of both the physical and mental sanctity of a marriage covenant. Because the Ten Commandments have a communal function, their injunctions deal with individuals' attitudes concerning things that would jeopardize the community's well-being.[100] As a covenant relationship, marriage imposes obligations on the spouses as well as their community. The maintenance of the sanctity of a marriage bond constitutes a vital component in maintaining social cohesion and stability.[101] As a body of marital principles to live by, the seventh and the tenth commandments are intended to ensure the creation of "a climate of trust and security within the covenant community."[102] Also, because marriage symbolizes the intimacy between God and His people,[103] failure to maintain its sanctity "was considered one of the most serious offenses because it broke the relationship that was a reflection of God and his people."[104]

If the focus of Exodus 20:14, 17 and Deuteronomy 5:18, 21 seems to technically address adultery as a physical, sexual relationship between "a married woman and any man not her husband,"[105] Jesus expanded the definition of adultery in Matthew 5:27–28: "You have heard that it was said to those of old, 'You shall not commit adultery.' But I say to you that whoever looks at a woman to lust for her has already committed adultery with her in his heart." He makes the point that mental adultery

---

[98] Peter Enns, *Exodus*, NIV Application Commentary (Grand Rapids, MI: Zondervan, 2000), 424; and Walton, Matthews, and Chavalas, 97.

[99] Block, 167.

[100] Walton, Matthews, and Chavalas, 96.

[101] Enns, 423.

[102] Block, 166.

[103] Enns, 423. Hosea 1–3 describes failure to obey God as adultery.

[104] Michael J. Wilkins, *Matthew*, NIV Application Commentary (Grand Rapids, MI: Zondervan, 2004), 244.

[105] Bruce Wells, *Exodus*, Zondervan Illustrated Bible Background Commentary 1, ed. John H. Walton (Grand Rapids, MI: Zondervan, 2009), 235; Walton, Matthews, and Chavalas, 96; Craig S. Keener, *The IVP Bible Background Commentary: New Testament*, 2nd ed. (Downers Grove, IL: IVP Academic, 2014), 58; Enns, 422; and Wilkins, 244.

(e.g., 2 Sam 11:2–3) always takes place before any actual physical sexual act (2 Sam 11:4). It is therefore not enough to only refrain from physical sexual contact. Thus, online affairs are still adulterous although they may not involve any actual physical contact. The full implications of the seventh and tenth commandments includes mental adultery, physical adultery, and any other promiscuous behavior that undermines the pursuance of an unqualified purity of a marital relationship.[106] This perspective not only reasserts the Old Testament commitment to the physical purity and unity of marriage, but also takes it to its deepest original intended meaning. For Jesus,

> it is not enough only to maintain physical purity. The purity of marriage includes exclusive devotion to one another with every aspect of their lives, and this commitment excludes wanting another person or giving oneself in any way to another person. Looking lustfully at another woman breaks the bond of oneness that a man has with his wife. . . . Adultery, therefore, is not only physical sexual intercourse but also mentally engaging in such act of unfaithfulness.[107]

The devastating impact of lust on the marriage covenant is depicted by Jesus through the following two illustrations: "If your right eye causes you to sin, pluck it out and cast it from you; for it is more profitable for you that one of your members perish, than for your whole body to be cast into hell" (Matt 5:29) and "if your right hand causes you to sin, cut it off and cast it from you; for it is more profitable for you that one of your members perish, than for your whole body to be cast into hell" (Matt 5:30). Jesus uses this graphic imagery to emphasize the seriousness of a single-hearted commitment to one's marriage partner. For Him, spouses should be willing to go to extraordinary lengths to control their urges for the sake of safeguarding the sanctity of their marriage covenant.[108]

Although there is no consensus among secular scholars as to how marital infidelity should be defined,[109] from a biblical perspective, marital

---

[106] Craig A. Evans, *Matthew*, New Cambridge Bible Commentary (New York: Cambridge University Press, 2012), 124; Keener, 58; and Wilkins, 247.

[107] Wilkins, 245.

[108] Evans, 124; and Wilkins, 245.

[109] Some scholars define infidelity as exclusively sexual, thus limiting it to "genital sexual involvement" (Thompson, 36). Allen et al., 101, note that "the definition of affair may be fairly idiosyncratic (e.g., someone who has had a casual sexual encounter may not consider this an affair). Some researchers have included a broader continuum of involvement, such as assessing all types of physical involvement (not just intercourse). Moreover, there is emerging empirical interest in 'emotional infidelity' in which emotional intimacy and sexual attraction to another

infidelity is the breaking of the promise of sexual loyalty made to a spouse in a monogamous marriage covenant. This encompasses infidelity not only as sexual intercourse, but also as extradyadic sexual activities and emotional betrayal.[110] Marital infidelity happens when a marriage partner violates their commitment regarding emotional and physical sexual exclusivity to their spouse.[111] Because it may break the relationship that is a reflection of the bond between God and His people, betrays the marital covenant, and violates the vows to loyalty publicly made, marital infidelity is a sin against God, self, spouse, and others in the community.

A Christian Response to the Challenge of Marital Infidelity

In response to the challenge of marital infidelity, a Christian community can use a two-pronged approach of prevention and reparation.

A Preventive Approach

Since it seems that no marriage is utterly safe from the potential of infidelity,[112] what can the church do to help its members protect themselves against the potential of this tragedy? First, as a preventive

person are combined with secrecy from the spouse. A growing literature demonstrates that individuals do consider a broader range of involvement, including sexualized Internet relationships, to constitute 'infidelity.'" See also Adrian J. Blow and Kelley Hartnett, "Infidelity in Committed Relationships I: A Methodological Review," *Journal of Marital and Family Therapy* 31, no. 2 (2005): 183–216, who say the definition of infidelity "can comprise a number of activities including: 'Having an affair,' 'extramarital relationship,' 'cheating,' 'sexual intercourse,' 'oral sex,' 'kissing,' 'fondling,' 'emotional connections that are beyond friendships,' 'friendships,' 'internet relationships,' 'pornography use,' and others" (Ibid., 186). They also rightly point out that "research that limits the definition of infidelity to sexual intercourse minimizes the devastating effects that other types of sexual involvement and emotional connections can have on relationships" (ibid., 220).

[110] Naomi P. Moller and Andreas Vossler, "Defining Infidelity in Research and Couple Counseling: A Quantitative Study," *Journal of Sex and Marital Therapy* 41, no. 5 (2015): 488. Their definition of extradyadic sexual activities include "masturbating in the presence of another, performing oral sex, engaging in sexual play, kissing, flirting, visiting strip clubs, watching pornography, and having sexual fantasies about a person other than the partner." They also point out that "internet behaviors that have been defined as sexual infidelity include cybersex, exchanging sexual self-images, online dating, online flirting, and using online pornography." The authors define mental infidelity to include "deep emotional attachment; falling in love with another person; feeling deeply connected; investment of romantic love, time, and attention in a person other than the primary partner; and sharing intimate details; discussing complaints about the primary partner." This deep emotional connection formed with another person outside of the marital relationship may or may not become sexual. See also Peluso, 4–6.

[111] G. R. Weeks, N. Gambescia, and R. E. Jenkins, *Treating Infidelity: Therapeutic Dilemmas and Effective Strategies* (New York: W. W. Norton, 2003); and Wilkins, 245.

[112] Demaris, 598.

approach to marital infidelity, the church in its ministries should readily invest in the wholistic discipling of its members. Regarding marital infidelity, Emily Brown explains that "what's often misunderstood is that what's wrong is not just the affair, but the issues that led to the affair that were never addressed."[113] Spiritual issues not correctly addressed in the lives of spouses affect both their relationships with God and with each other, thus having the potential to lead to marital infidelity.

Second, the church should also be resourceful in developing creative and effective ways of promoting God's design for sexuality. While on the one hand the church needs to avoid stretching its moral code to embrace a broader perspective on acceptable human sexuality, on the other hand it also needs to avoid trying to tightly control its members' sexual attitudes and behaviors. Because it has credibly been established through research that among married individuals age is not a hinderance to an individual getting involved in extramarital affairs, the church should resourcefully adapt its sex education programs to address the needs and challenges of its members in various stages of their married lives.

Third, awareness should be raised concerning various correlates of marital infidelity. Fourth, in contexts where professional counseling is looked upon with suspicion, the church should find a way of encouraging its members to seek the opinion of professional Christian counselors on issues such as sexual addiction, family-of-origin experiences, and unresolved childhood experiences.

A Reparative Approach

Both the church and couples who have experienced marital infidelity have an important role to play in rebuilding lives and relationships after the occurrence of marital infidelity. The church should be ready and able to care for families affected by marital infidelity without making their pain worse. While church discipline has its rightful place, it should be redemptive in scope. Genesis 3 is an account of how God dealt with Adam and Eve's poor choices of allowing Satan to influence them. In a redemptive way He graciously sought them (Gen 3:7–10), confronted them (Gen 3:11–13), and offered them restoration (Gen 3:14–15). In the case of the adulteress (John 8:2–11), Jesus met human frailty with compassion and restoration without infringing upon the authority of God's law.[114]

---

[113] Brown, "The Affair as a Catalyst for Change," 149.

[114] Ellen G. White, *The Ministry of Healing* (Mountain View, CA: Pacific Press, 1909), 88. She further points out that "this was to her the beginning of a new life, a life of purity and peace, devoted to God. In the uplifting of this fallen soul, Jesus performed a greater miracle than in healing the most grievous physical disease; He cured the spiritual malady which is unto death everlasting. This penitent woman became one of His most steadfast followers. With self-sacrificing love and devotion she showed her gratitude for His forgiving mercy. For this erring woman the

On the basis of Matthew 5:31–32 and 19:9, where Jesus is recorded as allowing divorce for reason of infidelity, many Christians readily assume that divorce is the only appropriate solution to marital infidelity. Although marital infidelity is cited as the most usual reason for divorce across societies,[115] "not all couples who experience marital infidelity end their relationships."[116] Couples who survive infidelity generally come to the realization that their marriage may have undergone serious trouble long before the infidelity happened. When a couple chooses to repair their marriage rather than divorce following infidelity, both partners fully commit to actively rebuilding their relationship instead of simply putting up with what happened.[117] To help such couples achieve their goal, Jill Sauerheber and Richard Ponton recommend six steps towards full restoration: recognition, confession, repentance, forgiveness, reconciliation, and redemption.[118] To enhance this six-step process, longstanding relationship issues that may have resulted in the infidelity also need to be addressed with the help of professional counseling.[119]

Conclusion

Marital infidelity is omnipresent in every social context with significant consequences for couples, their children, and all those in their social support network. As long as sin exists, marital infidelity will remain a challenge to the marriage institution and couple relationships. However, informed by Scripture and motivated by the priority of their relationship with God, Christians can be the salt of the earth by preserving the purity and sanctity of their marriages and the light of the world by refusing to go along with the crowd and against divine principles. None of the correlates of marital infidelity should be used by any Christian as an excuse for engaging in extramarital affairs.

---

world had only contempt and scorn, but the Sinless One pitied her weakness and reached to her a helping hand. While the hypocritical Pharisees denounced, Jesus bade her, 'Go, and sin no more'" (ibid., 89).

[115] Labrecque and Whisman, 952; and Amato and Previti, 602–626.

[116] Blow and Hartnett, "Infidelity in Committed Relationships II," 227.

[117] Willard F. Harley, *His Needs, Her Needs: Building an Affair-Proof Marriage* (Grand Rapids, MI: Fleming H. Revell, 1994), 166–178.

[118] Jill Duba Sauerheber and Richard F. Ponton, "Healing From Infidelity: The Role of Covenantal Forgiveness," *Journal of Psychology and Christianity* 36, no. 1 (2017): 59.

[119] Brown, "The Affair as a Catalyst for Change," 149–165; and Allen et al., 118.

CHAPTER 7

Polygamy, Scripture, and the Institution of Marriage[1]

Ron du Preez

Though polygamy is often seen as an African issue, this custom is not confined to one continent. It is a universal marriage form, known and practiced in many societies of the world,[2] and has proven to be a formidable barrier to the Christian gospel.[3] Though there is a move away from polygamy towards monogamy in urban areas in Africa, as recently as 2013 an African researcher pointed out that plural marriage still "constitutes a prime feature of rural Africa."[4] Furthermore, Islam, with close to one and a half billion adherents, does not limit the male partner in

---

[1] For an in-depth analysis of the issue of plural marriage in Scripture, see the doctoral research of the author of this article, published in its edited and expanded form as Ronald A. G. du Preez, *Polygamy in the Bible*, Adventist Theological Society Dissertation Series vol. 3 (Berrien Springs, MI: Adventist Theological Society Publications, 1993), of which this document is excerpted, summarized, and updated. For the sake of space, some footnotes have been reduced when not critical to the discussion. For seminal research on sexuality in the Scriptures (which provides additional research on plural marriage and related matters), see Richard M. Davidson, *Flame of Yahweh: Sexuality in the Old Testament* (Peabody, MA: Hendrickson, 2007).

[2] Jacques Maquet and Joan R. Rayfield, *Africanity: The Cultural Unity of Black Africa*, trans. Joan R. Rayfield (New York: Oxford University Press, 1972), 73; and Bronislaw Malinowski, *Sex, Culture, and Myth* (New York: Harcourt, Brace and World, 1962), 31.

[3] Richard W. Schwarz, *Light Bearers to the Remnant* (Mountain View, CA: Pacific Press, 1979), 362; and John A. Kisaka, "The Adventist Church's Position and Response to Socio-Cultural Issues in Africa" (DMin project report, Andrews University, 1979), 21, 57–58.

[4] Duone Ekane, "Contemporary Family Patterns in Sub-Saharan Africa" (2013), 4, http://www.diva-portal.org/smash/record.jsf?pid=diva2%3A602444&dswid=5281, (accessed June 28, 2021). About a decade earlier, in a United Nations Report, it was noted that "the much-anticipated decline in polygamous households is still far from a social reality in most African countries. In rural areas, polygyny survives . . . . but in most urban areas, polygyny, once fairly common, is becoming rare" (Betty Bigombe and Gilbert M. Khadiagala, "Major Trends Affecting Families in Sub-Saharan Africa" [United Nations report, 2002] , 7).

marriage to a single spouse.[5] Muslims are permitted to have up to four wives at one time.[6] In brief, the practice of polygamy has resulted in difficulties for Christian missionaries.

A well-known anthropologist, in discussing how to share the Adventist message with people of other cultures, highlights the thorny issue of polygamy. He alleges that monogamy is merely one of "the optional variables of Western culture,"[7] a practice that actually hampers church growth. He concludes that to refuse to baptize practicing polygamists into the Seventh-day Adventist Church, while polygamous, is a "serious example of cross-cultural confusion."[8]

A survey of literature indicates that many documents have been produced concerning the Bible and polygamy.[9] An analysis of this material reveals that over the centuries three principal, different views have been held: One position is that the Bible does not condemn the practice of

---

[5] See Lois Lamyā' Ibsen al Faruqi, "Marriage in Islam," *Journal of Ecumenical Studies* 22 (1985): 61.

[6] See *Qur'an* 4:3; and Diane D'Souza, "The Muslim Practice of Polygamy," *Bulletin of the Henry Martyn Institute of Islamic Studies* 8 (July–September 1985): 71.

[7] Borge Schantz, "One Message—Many Cultures: How Do We Cope?," *Ministry*, June 1992, 11.

[8] Ibid., 8.

[9] In contradistinction to Davidson, *Flame of Yahweh*, the following materials hold an accommodating position towards practicing polygamists—that is, that the Christian church should not require monogamy before accepting any into full membership of the body of Christ: Daniel Eshun, *Christian Marriage: How Did Polygamy Become a Sin?* (self-pub., CreateSpace, 2017), 12, 31–35, 113–127; Roy E. Gane, *Old Testament Law for Christians: Original Context and Enduring Application* (Grand Rapids, MI: Baker, 2017), 303–306, 312–315; John Witte, "Why Two in One Flesh? The Western Case for Monogamy over Polygamy," *Emory Law Journal* 64 (January 2015): 1711–1714, 1725–1726, 1735; Matilda E. Downey, "Polygamy, Divorce, and Rape: A Comparative Analysis of Sexual and Marital Ethics in Ancient Israel and the Ancient Near East" (BA honors thesis, University of Sydney, 2015), 2, 7–13; Ken Stone, "Marriage and Sexual Relations in the World of the Hebrew Bible," in *The Oxford Handbook of Theology, Sexuality, and Gender*, ed. Adrian Thatcher (Oxford University Press, 2015), http://www.doi.org/10.1093/oxfordhb/9780199664153.013.020 (accessed May 23, 2021); Tom Shipley, *Man and Woman in Biblical Law: A Patriarchal Manifesto*, Resurrecting the Biblical Family, Part 1 (Baltimore, MD: Institute for Christian Patriarchy, 2010), 147; Samuel Waje Kunhiyop, *African Christian Ethics* (Nairobi: WordAlive, 2008), 223–242; Daniel K. Bediako, "Bible and Culture: Revisiting the Question of Polygamy," 13, https://www.academia.edu/42639406/BIBLE_AND_CULTURE_REVISITING_THE_QUESTION_OF_POLYGAMY (accessed May 23, 2021); Russell Staples, "Evangelism Among Resistant Peoples With Deeply Entrenched Polygamy," *Journal of Adventist Mission Studies* 2, no. 1 (2006): 4–28; Roy E. Gane, "Some Biblical Principles Relevant to Evangelism Among Polygamous Peoples," *Journal of Adventist Mission Studies* 2, no. 1 (2006): 29–43; Stefan Höschele, "Polygamy Among the Tanzanian Maasai and the Seventh-day Adventist Church: Reflections on a Missiological and Theological Problem," *Journal of Adventist Mission Studies* 2, no. 1 (2006): 44–56; David Instone-Brewer, "Jesus' Old Testament Basis for Monogamy," in *The Old Testament in the New Testament: Essays in Honour of J. L. North*, ed. Steve Moyise (Sheffield: Sheffield Academic Press, 2000), 75–105; and Matthew Bediako, "Polygamy and the Church in West Africa" (MA thesis, Andrews University, 1971), 15–30. These documents on polygamy do not contribute anything of substance to this research.

polygamy, even though it might regulate or restrict it carefully.[10] A second position is that the Old Testament at times required polygamy, while the New Testament completely ruled it out. A third perspective on plural marriage is that monogamy is clearly promoted throughout the Bible, while polygamy is condemned.

This chapter investigates the biblical passages and pericopes related to plural marriage in order to discover all the applicable scriptural principles essential for a sound policy concerning how to deal with the challenge of polygamy.

The Genesis of Marital Form

The book of Genesis provides a concrete account of the institution of marriage. Genesis 1:27–28 and 2:18, 21–24 specifically state that God is the originator of the marriage relationship.

Genesis 2:21–24 makes it clear that this marriage took place between one man and one woman. The repeated use of singular nouns and pronouns in this passage is noteworthy. J. S. Wright and J. A. Thompson note that "monogamy is implicit in the story of Adam and Eve, since God created only one wife for Adam."[11] Another scholar remarks, "If we are correct in viewing the union of Adam and Eve of Genesis 1 and 2 as the family as God wants it to be, then there can be no doubt about the fact that the marriage held up for the emulation of ancient Israel was a *monogamous* one."[12]

Genesis 2:18 records God's words: "'I need to make a suitable partner [*kenegdo*] for him'" (CEV).[13] The Hebrew term *kenegdo* means a "counterpart,"[14] one "'corresponding to him.'"[15] This stress on equal partnership implies that for a marital relationship to be genuinely reciprocal, it would need to be monogamous.

---

[10] For example, Shipley, 147, claims that there is "no prohibition at all against polygamy *anywhere* in the Bible" (emphasis original).

[11] J. S. Wright and J. A. Thompson, "Marriage," in *The New Bible Dictionary* (Grand Rapids, MI: Eerdmans, 1962), 787.

[12] Walter Wegner, "God's Pattern for the Family in the Old Testament," in *Family Relationships and the Church: A Sociological, Historical, and Theological Study of Family Structures, Roles, and Relationships*, Marriage and Family Research Series, ed. Oscar E. Feucht (Saint Louis, MO: Concordia, 1970), 29, emphasis original.

[13] All biblical quotations are from the NKJV, unless otherwise indicated.

[14] Ludwig Koehler and Walter Baumgartner, *Lexicon in Veteris Testamenti Libros* (Leiden: E. J. Brill, 1958), 591.

[15] Gerhard von Rad, *Old Testament Theology*, vol. 1, *The Theology of Israel's Historical Traditions*, trans. D. M. G. Stalker (New York: Harper and Brothers, 1962), 149.

Even though the words in Genesis 2:24 ("Therefore a *man* shall . . . be joined to his *wife*") were evidently penned by a human (i.e., Moses), since they are the utterance of divine revelation, "Christ could quote them, therefore, as the word of God (Matt. xix. 5)."[16] Thus, since it is a clear expression of God's will, this statement is of great import for all. "It is clear from the context that God intended that the first marriage should be the model for all subsequent marriages."[17] "These words express the deepest physical and spiritual unity of man and woman, and hold up monogamy before the world as the form of marriage ordained by God."[18]

While a considerable portion of Genesis is devoted to the story of the worldwide flood,[19] it is apparent that not much is recorded about the marital status of those involved in the narrative. However, the Genesis record is clear not only that "Noah found favor in the eyes of the Lord" (Gen 6:8), but that Noah and his three sons were married to one wife each. As one scholar observes, "Noah himself as well as his three sons are described in an unambiguous way as monogamous."[20] By preserving in the ark only those who were monogamous, God was apparently conveying His divine approval on the marital pattern that He had originally established in Eden.[21] The monogamy of Noah and his sons "is very significant to an understanding of God's will and dealing with the polygamous marriage variant."[22]

---

[16] C. F. Keil and F. Delitzsch, *The Pentateuch*, 3 vols., Biblical Commentary on the Old Testament, trans. James Martin (Grand Rapids, MI: Eerdmans, 1952), 1:90. See also Merrill F. Unger, *Unger's Commentary on the Old Testament,* 2 vols. (Chicago, IL: Moody, 1981), 1:14; A. Cohen, ed., *The Soncino Chumash* (Surrey: Soncino Press, 1947), 12; Howard F. Vos, *Genesis* (Chicago, IL: Moody, 1982), 25; F. D. Nichol, ed., *Seventh-day Adventist Bible Commentary*, 7 vols., rev. ed. (Washington, DC: Review and Herald, 1976–1980), 1:227. For a more detailed study of Matthew 19:5, see du Preez, *Polygamy in the Bible*, 248–250.

[17] Rein Muhlberg, "Polygamy—An Adventist Response," TMs [photocopy], 1, Center for Adventist Research, Berrien Springs, MI.

[18] Nichol, 1:227. See also Keil and Delitzsch, 1:90.

[19] See Genesis 6–9.

[20] Tryggve Kronholm, "Polygami och Monogami I Gamla Testamentet: Med en Utblick over den Antika Judendomen och Nya Testamentet," *Svensk Exegetisk Arsbok* 47 (1982): 66.

[21] Some scholars recognize something rather unusual in connection with the Hebrew terms used to refer to the clean and unclean animals taken into the ark. In Genesis 7:2, instead of the normal words for male (*zakar*) and female (*neqebah*), the phrase *'ish we'ishto* ("a man and his wife") is used to describe the animals. It has been suggested that this phrase, "the male and his mate" (NRSV), was used by the writer to indicate that all living creatures that entered the ark, whether birds, animals, or human beings, were classified as being in a "monogamous" relationship. See Samuel H. Dresner, "Homosexuality and the Order of Creation," *Judaism* 40 (Summer 1991): 313. Cf. Umberto Cassuto, *A Commentary on the Book of Genesis,* vol. 2, *From Noah to Abraham*, trans. Israel Abrahams (Jerusalem: Magnes Press, Hebrew University, 1964), 73–74.

[22] Clifton R. Maberly, "The Polygamous Variant: The Policy and Practice of a Church," 1975,

The identical charge that God gave to the world's first couple, "Be fruitful and multiply, and fill the earth" (Gen 1:28), He repeated to Noah and his sons (Gen 9:1), all of whom were monogamous. One author posits that "in this, the pattern of Adam and Eve in the garden of Eden is replicated."[23] God was in a sense repeating history.[24] "The message seems clear: human society is meant to be composed of families, of monogamous families."[25] Ellen G. White writes,

> Noah had but one wife, and their united family discipline was blessed of God. Because Noah's sons were righteous, they were preserved in the ark with their righteous father. God has not sanctioned polygamy in a single instance. It was contrary to his will. He knew that the happiness of man would be destroyed by it.[26]

Polygamy and Old Testament Legislation

Many questions have been raised about the issue of concubinage in the Bible. The Mosaic laws make no mention of concubines. However, the narrative portions of Scripture indicate that the terms "wife" and "concubine" were sometimes used to describe distinct categories, while at other times they were used interchangeably. The difference related primarily to the more formal aspects of the marriage, while the legal status of a concubine and her children was the same as that of the wife and her children.[27] In fact, these terms are so similar that at times they are linked together to form a "wife-concubine." Only the original wife is never called a concubine. Thus, both wives and concubines formed part of the polygamous homes of certain characters of Scripture. Besides the monogamous model instituted in Genesis, there are two regulations that address the issue of polygamy directly, both of which are located in the Pentateuch.

TMs [photocopy], 5, Center for Adventist Research, Berrien Springs, MI; see also *Great Discussion! Does the Bible Sanction Polygamy!* [A Debate Between Orson Pratt and J. P. Newman], (Baltimore, MD: J. S. Dye, 1874), 15.

[23] Dresner, 313.

[24] *Great Discussion*, 15.

[25] Dresner, 313.

[26] Ellen G. White, *Spiritual Gifts*, 4 vols. (Washington, DC: Review and Herald, 1945), 3:100.

[27] Cf. Douglas E. Welch, "A Biblical Perspective on Polygamy" (MA thesis, Fuller Theological Seminary, 1977), 47; Louis M. Epstein, "The Institution of Concubinage Among the Jews," *Proceedings of the American Academy for Jewish Research* 6 (1934–1935): 168.

The Law About Marriage to Two Women

Leviticus 18:18 reads, "'You shall not marry a woman in addition to her sister as a rival while she is alive, to uncover her nakedness'" (NASB). This text "has given occasion for much dispute."[28] One scholar speculates that "the command that a man must not have two sisters as wives at the same time (Lev. XVIII. 18) implies that he may have two wives who are not sisters."[29]

Most often Leviticus 18:18 is seen as a law against incest. However, as Angelo Tosato has demonstrated, every verse from verse 7 through verse 17 begins with the same term, *'erwat* ("nakedness of"), and culminates in *lo' tegalleh ("y*ou are not to uncover"), showing that these laws belong together as anti-incestuous regulations,[30] due to "the homogeneity and peculiarity of its formation and content."[31]

In contradistinction to the above, Leviticus 18:18–23 opens with the conjunction *waw* and closes with various permanent prohibitions regularly introduced by the negative *lo'*. Tosato again indicates that the two distinct and formally unifying elements of this new list suggest that the second series of laws, although not identical, are to be considered as a unit.[32] Many scholars have recognized this.[33] Thus, since verse 18 belongs to the more general set of regulations, the interpretation of the crucial phrase, "a woman to her sister," must likewise be open to its broader sense and not be restricted to only a literal, blood relative.[34]

The very term "sister" (*'akhot*) is used in the Old Testament[35] in a variety of ways: as a blood sister (e.g., Gen 4:22), a half sister (Gen 20:12), a kinswoman (Gen 24:59–60), or in the general sense of a female fellow citizen (Num 25:18; Hos 2:1). Although most commentators understand

---

[28] John Murray, *Principles of Conduct* (Grand Rapids, MI: Eerdmans, 1957), 251.

[29] M. M. Kalisch, *A Historical and Critical Commentary on the Old Testament: Leviticus*, vol. 2 (London: Longmans, Green, Reader, and Dyer, 1872), 373.

[30] See Angelo Tosato, "The Law of Leviticus 18:18: A Reexamination," *Catholic Biblical Quarterly* 46 (1984): 199–214.

[31] Ibid., 203.

[32] Ibid., 199–214.

[33] See, e.g., J. P. Porter, *Leviticus*, The Cambridge Bible Commentary (Cambridge: Cambridge University Press, 1976), 148; S. H. Kellogg, *The Book of Leviticus*, The Expositor's Bible (New York: A. C. Armstrong and Son, 1908), 383; Christopher Wordsworth, *The Holy Bible*, vol. 1, part 2, *The Five Books of Moses: Leviticus, Numbers, Deuteronomy*, 3rd. ed. (London: Rivington's, Waterloo Place, 1869), 59; and *Great Discussion*, 31.

[34] The temporary nature of this law further differentiates it from those on incest, which are implicitly of perpetual duration.

[35] See Siegfried Horn, ed., *Seventh-day Adventist Bible Dictionary* (Washington, DC: Review and Herald, 1979), s.v. "Sister"; and K. E. Corley, "Sister," in *The International Standard Bible Encyclopedia*, ed. Geoffrey W. Bromiley, 4 vols. (Grand Rapids, MI: Eerdmans, 1979–1988), 4:534.

the term "sister" in a literal way, we concur with Tosato that *'ishshah 'el-'akhotah* carries "the broader meaning"[36] of "two women (fellow citizens) in general."[37] Interestingly, some scholars have shown that this was the very manner in which the ancient Qumran community viewed Leviticus 18:18 as a law against "taking two wives during their lifetime."[38]

Furthermore, several scholars have recognized that the linking of words together in the phrase *'ishshah 'el-'akhotah* (literally, "a woman to her sister") may require an idiomatic interpretation,[39] as this phrase or its equivalents are rendered in Scripture. In fact, Christopher Wordsworth observes that these types of phrases are never used to "designate *blood* relationships of *two sisters* or *two brothers*, but simply the addition of one person or thing to another of the same kind."[40] Therefore, for the sake of consistency, Leviticus 18:18 should likewise be translated in a figurative manner as "one in addition to another."[41]

The practices mentioned in this section "are not just destructive for Israel. They are universal abominations."[42] Gerhard Hasel notes that

---

[36] Tosato, 208.

[37] Ibid., 203. For an alternative view, see the chapter by Dragoslava Santrac and Aleksander Santrac in this volume.

[38] Louis Ginzberg, *An Unknown Jewish Sect* (New York: Jewish Theological Seminary of America, 1976), 19. See also Chaim Rabin, ed., *The Zadokite Documents* (Oxford: Clarendon Press, 1954), 17. On page 16, Rabin translates the phrase from this document as "marrying two women in their (masc.) lifetime."

[39] See, e.g., Walter C. Kaiser Jr., *Toward Old Testament Ethics* (Grand Rapids, MI: Zondervan, 1983), 116–117, 185–186; Murray, 250–256; and H. D. M. Spence and Joseph S. Exell, eds., *The Pulpit Commentary, 23 vols., Leviticus, Numbers* (Grand Rapids, MI: Eerdmans, 1977), 2:274–275.

[40] Wordsworth, 58.

[41] Kalisch notes that after the Protestant Reformation this non-reciprocal, idiomatic translation was again suggested by Old Testament translators Franciscus Junius and Emmanuel Tremellius in 1575 (see Kalisch, 397). Wordsworth indicates that the following also held to this figurative interpretation of Leviticus 18:18: Johannes Drusius (1550–1616), professor of Hebrew at Oxford; Abraham Calovius (1612–1686), professor of theology at Wittenberg; Theodore Beza (1519–1605), Old Testament translator and professor of Greek at the Academy of Lausanne; Henry Ainsworth (1560–1623), a Hebrew scholar; Henry Hammond (1605–1660), Chaplain to Charles I; and Johann Friedrich Schleusner (1759–1831), lexicographer and theology professor at Göttingen (see Wordsworth, 58). In addition to those mentioned in the text, more recent scholars who have held to the non-reciprocal, idiomatic rendition include nineteenth-century United States Senate chaplain J. P. Newman (see *Great Discussion*, 31) and Presbyterian systematic theologian John Murray (see Murray, 250–252).

[42] Richard M. Davidson, "Revelation/Inspiration in the Old Testament: A Critique of Alden Thompson's 'Incarnational' Model," in *Issues in Revelation and Inspiration*, ed. Frank Holbrook, and Leo Van Dolson, Adventist Theological Society Occasional Papers (Berrien Springs, MI: Adventist Theological Society, 1992), 121.

these laws are not ritual or cultic, and "cannot be restricted to Israelites."[43] Thus, the prohibition of polygamy in Leviticus 18:18 can be seen as a universal law applicable to all.

On the basis of the evidence, Leviticus 18:18 seems best as rendered by Young's Literal Translation: "And a woman unto another thou dost not take. . . ." Or, as the more modern New American Standard Bible alternative rendering has it: "And you shall not take a wife in addition to another to be a rival while she is alive, to uncover her nakedness."[44] This translation, as John Murray notes, is an "express condemnation" of polygamy.[45] Or, as Gordon Hugenberger concludes: Leviticus 18:18 "offers a general (ethical) prohibition of polygyny."[46] Richard Davidson concurs: "The legislation prohibiting plural marriages, like the other prohibitions of Lev 18, is ultimately rooted in creation, as it upholds the divine order of monogamous marriage (Gen 2:24)."[47] The weight of evidence thus shows that this Levitical legislation, which is directly against the practice of polygamy, is clearly in harmony with the monogamous model set up originally by God.[48]

The Law About the Marital Status of the King

The law about royal polygamy is in Deuteronomy 17:16–17:

> Moreover, he shall not multiply horses for himself, nor shall he cause the people to return to Egypt to multiply horses, since the Lord has said to you, "You shall never again return that way." Neither shall he multiply wives for himself, lest his heart turn away; nor shall he greatly increase silver and gold for himself.

What does this passage mean? First, the language and content of verse 17 show that this prohibition is not against possessing silver and gold per se, but rather against hoarding *great* amounts of wealth.[49] Second, the prohibition concerning the accumulation of animals needs analysis.

---

[43] Davidson, 104. See also Kaiser, 117–119, 196–197, on the issue of universal law in connection with sexual matters.

[44] The alternate rendering in the KJV similarly states, "Neither shalt thou take one wife to another."

[45] Murray, 253.

[46] Gordon Paul Hugenberger, *Marriage as a Covenant: A Study of Biblical Law and Ethics Governing Marriage Developed from the Perspective of Malachi*, Supplements to *Vetus Testamentum* 52 (Leiden: E. J. Brill, 1994), 115. Hugenberger provides seven exegetical arguments in favor of the conclusion he draws from the text and its context.

[47] Davidson, *Flame of Yahweh*, 198.

[48] See Murray, 253, who notes that this "interpretation would hark back to the original ordinance of monogamy."

[49] Lee Lewis Grout, *A Reply to Bishop Colenso's Remarks on the Proper Treatment of Cases of*

Other passages, such as Isaiah 31:1, shed light on this prohibition: "Woe to those who go down to Egypt for help, and rely on horses, . . . but they do not look to the Holy One of Israel, nor seek the Lord."[50] The issue here was reliance on others rather than on God.[51]

Third, Deuteronomy 17:17 states, "Neither shall he multiply [*rabah*] wives for himself, lest his heart turn away." Since linguistic study indicates that *rabah* ("increase" or "multiply") covers a range from twice as much on upwards, it appears evident that this legislation prohibits the king from becoming polygamous.[52]

Interestingly, the expectations of the king, outlined in Deuteronomy, were essentially the same for the common people.[53] Based on this biblical evidence, Patrick Miller shows that Deuteronomy 17:17 places upon the king "the obligations incumbent upon every Israelite. In that sense, Deuteronomy's primary concern was that the king *be the model Israelite*."[54] Such a broad understanding of the prohibition of polygamy is also obvious in the thinking of Ellen G. White.[55] Commenting on Solomon, who "fell into the sinful practice of other kings, of having many wives,"[56] she observes, "God commanded Moses to warn *the people* against having a plurality of wives. 'Neither shall he multiply wives to himself, that his heart turn not away.'"[57] Davidson says, "Thus, the law prohibiting royal polygamy here in Deuteronomy 17:17 serves to uphold and further emphasize the similar prohibition given to all Israel in Leviticus 18:18."[58] In short, then, the legislation in Deuteronomy

---

Polygamy as Found Already Existing in Converts from Heathenism (Pietermaritzburg: May and Davis, 1855), 16.

[50] See also Psalms 20:7; Isaiah 2:7–9; 30:1–7; Amos 2:15; 4:10; Micah 5:10–15.

[51] See also Psalms 33:17, "A horse is a false hope for victory."

[52] As David Smith puts it, "twice one are two, and this is multiplication" (David Hyrum Smith, *The Bible Versus Polygamy* [Plano, IL: Reorganized Church of Jesus Christ of Latter Day Saints, True Latter Day Saints' Herald Office, 1983], 9). See also *Great Discussion*, 50; and Grout, 16. Note, however, that the root meaning of *rabah* is "increase," and not necessarily "multiply" in the mathematical sense.

[53] Cf., e.g., Deuteronomy 17:19 with 6:5–7; 8:1; 11:1; also Deuteronomy 17:20 with 8:14; and Deuteronomy 17:17 with 8:13–17.

[54] Patrick D. Miller, *Deuteronomy*, Interpretation (Louisville, KY: John Knox, 1990), 148–149, emphasis original. See also Robert J. Hitchens, *Multiple Marriage: A Study of Polygamy in Light of the Bible* (Elkton, MD: Doulos Publishers, 1987), 128.

[55] A recent study seeks to dismiss the counsel of Ellen G. White. See Staples, "Evangelism Among Resistant Peoples," 18–23.

[56] White, 4a:100, emphasis supplied.

[57] White, 4a:100.

[58] Davidson, *Flame of Yahweh*, 200.

17:16–17 forbade kings to marry more than one spouse and, since the king was to be a model, this law also outlawed the practice of polygamy for the entire community.

Despite the clarity of the Genesis Edenic monogamous model established by God, as well as the Pentateuchal laws delineated above, certain Old Testament passages are sometimes viewed as permitting or even promoting polygamy. These are briefly addressed here.

The Rule Concerning the Female Slave

Some scholars have concluded that the stipulation of Exodus 21:7–11 supports and legalizes the practice of polygamy.[59] The Hebrew text shows that the slave master did not marry the woman (Exod 21:8)—"He hath not betrothed her" (YLT)[60]—and that he was simply to provide food, clothing, and shelter for the female servant whom he actually did not marry.[61] That being the case, Exodus 21:10 states, "If another woman he take for him, her food, her covering, and her habitation, he doth not withdraw" (YLT).[62] Thus from a linguistic perspective, this law does not seem to contradict the Edenic model of monogamy.

The Stipulation of the Firstborn's Rights

Another passage frequently referred to in the discussion on polygamy is the one relating to the true firstborn son and his legal rights, as found in Deuteronomy 21:15–17. Since the law begins with the phrase, "If a man has two wives," some allege that this passage is an indication that polygamy was regarded as a normal and legitimate practice in Israel.[63] However, Walter Kaiser notes that the Hebrew language

---

[59] See, e.g., Eugene Hillman, *Polygamy Reconsidered: African Plural Marriage and the Christian Church* (Maryknoll, NY: Orbis, 1975), 145, who states, "In the Mosaic law polygamy is clearly regarded as a normal and licit practice (cf. Exod 21:10; Lev 18:18; Deut 21:15–17)." Joseph Omoregbe, "Is Polygamy Compatible With Christianity?," *African Ecclesial Review* 21 (December 1979): 364, posits, "The Old Testament itself recognizes polygamy as a valid lawful form of marriage along with monogamy [Exod 21:10 footnoted]."

[60] The Hebrew text does say *lo'* ("not"). Nevertheless, translations and commentators generally read *lo* ("to himself") because it seems to make more sense.

[61] Even Gane, who promotes some accommodation for practicing polygamists within the church, admits that the actual Hebrew text literally "expresses the idea that the master has *not* designated her [for himself]" (Gane, *Old Testament Law for Christians*, 312 n. 3), which is contrary to popular English versions, which are not based on the original Hebrew language of this passage.

[62] The word *'onah* is a hapax legomenon. In the LXX, Targums, and Pehitta the word is translated as "conjugal rights." This is the translation adopted by most translations and commentaries, although there is no philological support. Some translate "dwelling," for which there is some etymological support from the word *ma'on* "habitation" (Deut 26:15; 2 Chron 30:27; Jer 49:33).

[63] Hillman, 145.

> is notoriously disinterested in our Western preoccupation with the tense of the verb and time in general. . . . [Thus,] it definitely is wrong to insist that both wives are living, for that would be asking the imperfect verb form (future or continuous action of the verb) to bear a load it was not meant to carry.[64]

Several scholars favor this interpretation.[65] Another possibility in line with this view is that this could be a case relating to a man who marries again after the divorce (or even death) of the first wife. Since the Mosaic regulation of Deuteronomy 24:1–4 recognizes the practice of divorce, this option is also a plausible one.[66] Kaiser observes that the concern of this law is "inheritance rights, not polygamy,"[67] and concludes that this Mosaic stipulation does not suggest even a "tacit approval of polygamy."[68]

Regulations About Sex With an Unengaged Woman

Since Deuteronomy 22:28–29 requires the man committing a sexual crime against an unengaged virgin to marry the woman, some conclude that this law would naturally require polygamy in the case of a man already married. However, a very similar law is seen in Exodus 22:16–17. As some scholars conclude, the Deuteronomic legislation is a repetition and expansion of the one in Exodus, where the guilty man is *not* required to wed the woman.[69] In brief, when these regulations regarding sexual offenses are properly seen as parallel and also explanatory, it is clear that they do not condone or command the practice of polygamy.

The Levirate Policy and Practice

In the discussion of polygamy in the Old Testament, the "levirate,"[70] as outlined in Deuteronomy 25:5–10, is frequently mentioned. Various

---

[64] Kaiser, 187, emphasis original.

[65] Among others, see Grout, 13; *Great Discussion*, 33; and James Comper Gray and George M. Adams, *The Biblical Encyclopedia*, 5 vols. (Cleveland, OH: F. M. Barton, 1903), 1:512.

[66] Jacob Rabinowitz also suggests this option, as a result of his study of a fourth-century-BC Demotic marriage contract from the reign of Alexander IV. This document discusses the treatment of a firstborn son of an unloved woman who was apparently divorced. From his research, Rabinowitz concludes that it is possible that the Egyptians borrowed this marriage legislation from the Jews. He proposes, on linguistic grounds, that Deuteronomy 21:15–17 is not discussing a polygamous situation, but rather a home in which a man has had two wives—a second after the divorce of the first. See Jacob J. Rabinowitz, "Marriage Contracts in Ancient Egypt in the Light of Jewish Sources," *Harvard Theological Review* 46 (January 1953): 91–97.

[67] See Kaiser, 187.

[68] Ibid.

[69] See, e.g., G. R. Driver and John C. Miles, eds., *The Assyrian Laws* (Oxford: Clarendon Press, 1935), 53.

[70] The word "levirate" comes from the Latin *levir*, meaning "husband's brother" or "brother-in-law." See *Webster's New World Dictionary*, 3rd ed. (1988), s.v. "Levirate."

writers concur with Eugene Hillman in his allegation that in the Bible, polygamy "is dictated by the levirate law."[71]

Pentateuchal Legislation

Deuteronomy 25:5 states, "When brothers live together and one of them dies and has no son, the wife of the deceased shall not be married outside the family to a strange man. Her husband's brother shall go in to her and take her to himself as wife and perform the duty of a husband's brother to her." Based on this verse it has been suggested that this was a compulsory law that would cause a man to become polygamous, if he were already married. However, we would argue that Deuteronomy 25:5–10 shows the stipulation is divided into two parts: one-third of the law lays down the expectation, while two-thirds explain the formal steps to be followed in case the brother-in-law declines to marry his deceased brother's wife because he may already be married. This shows that this law "allows the brother the option of refusing."[72] Moreover, as Herbert Leupold observes, the levirate system implied that "the brother of the deceased, *if unmarried*, would take the widow to wife."[73] Therefore, this law would not necessarily require polygamous unions.

The Levirate in Patriarchal Times

The Bible shows that the levirate was practiced early—centuries before the formal legislation was recorded. However, there is no evidence that any polygamy occurred in this entire narrative in Genesis 38. As Samuel Wishard states, "there is no polygamy here. It was the first marriage of each son."[74]

Practice in the Time of the Judges

There has been some debate as to whether or not the book of Ruth deals with the levirate custom. The peculiarities are probably due to the

---

[71] Hillman, 158. See also Edward Westermarck, *The History of Human Marriage*, 3 vols., 5th ed. (London: Macmillan, 1921), 3:41–42; Anatosi Katuramu, *Polygamy and the Church in Africa* (Chicago, IL: n.p., 1977), 16; Marcus Cohn, "Marriage," *The Universal Jewish Encyclopedia*, 10 vols. (New York: Ktav, 1969), 7:369–376; Bernard Haring, *Evangelization Today* (Notre Dame, IN: Fides, 1974), 153; Norman L. Geisler, *Ethics: Alternatives and Issues* (Grand Rapids, MI: Zondervan, 1971), 206; and M. D. W. Jeffreys, "Polygny [sic] in the Christian Fold," *Practical Anthropology* 19 (March–April 1972): 85.

[72] Wright and Thompson, 789.

[73] Herbert C. Leupold, *Exposition of Genesis*, 2 vols. (Grand Rapids: Baker, 1953), 2:980, emphasis supplied. Daniel Bediako, "Levirate Marriage," in Ekkehardt Mueller, Elias Brasil de Souza, and Gerhard Pfandl, eds., *Marriage and Family: Contemporary Issues* (Silver Springs, MD: Biblical Research Institute, forthcoming), does not limit it to unmarried brothers.

[74] Samuel Ellis Wishard, *The Divine Law of Marriage, or, the Bible Against Polygamy* (New York: American Tract Society, 1816), 50. See also *Great Discussion*, 34.

fact that three institutions are exemplified in this one marriage—namely, the levirate, redemption (*go'el*), and inheritance.[75] It appears as though in the book of Ruth this optional practice was similarly carried out in a monogamous manner. In short, though this seems a common claim, there is no evidence whatsoever in the biblical text that the levirate required or resulted in polygamy. W. White concurs that the biblical levirate marriages "appear to have been monogamous."[76]

Symbolism and Marital Forms

In the latter part of the Old Testament, God's relationship to His people is often described in terms of family ties. Polygamous marriage symbolism appears in Ezekiel 23, and some suggest that this shows God is not against plural marriages. Roland de Vaux cautions that this comparison "is merely to adapt the allegory of chapter 16 to the historical conditions which prevailed after the political schism."[77] In fact, if these two kingdoms were to return in faithfulness to the Lord, they would come back as one united people. Thus the illustration would end with God in a monogamous relationship with His chosen nation, just as at the first. Clearly, it is inappropriate to conclude that the use of this allegory implies that God condones or sanctions polygamy in any manner.[78]

Summary

When the crucial Old Testament passages on marital forms are contextually examined and analyzed, none of them can be seen to command or condone the practice of polygamy. On the contrary, in accord with the Edenic monogamy, the Pentateuch records specific laws that directly forbid the practice of polygamy.

Case Studies of Polygamists in the Bible

To understand the phenomenon of polygamy in the Bible, one must take into account cases of plural marriage in the Old Testament, especially where there is sufficient story line. An adequate approach to Scripture

---

[75] E. Neufeld, *Ancient Hebrew Marriage Laws* (London: Longmans, Green 1944), 38. See also Samuel Belkin, "Levirate and Agnate Marriage in Rabbinic and Cognate Literature," *The Jewish Quarterly Review* 60 (1969–1970): 285–286; Kaiser, 191; and Leviticus 25.

[76] W. White Jr., "Family," in *The Zondervan Pictorial Encyclopedia of the Bible*, ed., Merrill C. Tenney (Grand Rapids, MI: Zondervan, 1975), 498. Wishard, 50, says that *always* "the kinsman who took in the widow of the deceased kinsman was unmarried."

[77] Roland de Vaux, *Ancient Israel: Its Life and Times*, trans. John McHugh (London: Darton, Longman and Todd, 1997), 26. See also Kronholm, 70.

[78] Note that the allegory used by Jesus in Luke 16:19–31 faces similar dangers if taken literally and interpreted without a recognition of its contextual usage.

must also emphasize that any passage be understood in the light of its total context. This approach recognizes that God spoke to a specific people at a specific point in time, using "a language and other cultural symbols that carried maximum impact for communication."[79] Thus, it must be noted that God "used linguistic forms with which the receptors felt at home."[80] Based on such analyses, the following conclusions have been drawn.[81]

Lamech, the First Polygamist

Lamech's polygamy must be understood within the following context: 1) its setting in a chapter stressing alienation; 2) Lamech being listed as part of Cain's rebellious line; 3) Lamech being the seventh generation from Adam, thus representing the "climax of the self-sufficiency to which the line of Cain has been tending;"[82] 4) the distinct contrast with the righteous Enoch, seventh from Adam through Seth's line;[83] 5) murder and polygamy (Gen 4:19–24), contrasting the creation of life and the institution of monogamy in Genesis 1 and 2; and 6) the ending of the genealogical listing with Lamech's children. Davidson notes,

> By juxtaposing these two illuminating character portraits [of Enoch and Lamech] and paralleling their position of completeness and or fullness as seventh in the respective genealogical lines, the narrator succeeds in condemning the practices of Lamech just as effectively as—and perhaps even more so than—could have been accomplished by an explicit verbal denouncement.[84]

His polygamy can thus be viewed as a perversion of God's monogamous marital plan, and implicitly condemned.

Abraham: The Friend of God[85]

Several facts can be learned from the study of Abraham's polygamy (Gen 11–25). First, Abraham was monogamous when God selected him

---

[79] Welch, 21.

[80] Ibid.

[81] In du Preez, *Polygamy in the Bible*, this is by far the longest chapter, covering over a hundred pages (138–246). Those wanting the clear biblical evidence for the conclusions provided in this section should read this entire chapter 4.

[82] Marcus Dods, *The Book of Genesis*, The Expositor's Bible (New York: A. C. Armstrong and Son, 1908), 50.

[83] Ibid., 51.

[84] Davidson, *Flame of Yahweh*, 181.

[85] See James 2:23; cf. 2 Chronicles 20:7; Isaiah 41:8.

to be the head of a special people. Second, he was apparently aware of God's requirements concerning marriage, but due to a lack of trust in God he violated divine law by marrying a second wife. Third, the result of this union was discord in the family. Fourth, God did not accept this as a marriage, but insisted that Sarah was Abraham's only true wife. Fifth, God's call for the dissolving of this polygamous alliance by sending away the second "wife" and her son was not equal to divorce. As Muhlberg notes, "separation of people in an unbiblical relationship does not constitute the divorce which God forbids;"[86] rather, it is the termination of an illicit union. Sixth, only after Abraham forsook polygamy and returned to monogamy did God call on him to sacrifice and worship at the site of the future temple. Seventh, for the rest of his life Abraham appears to have refrained from polygamy, even arranging for Isaac to marry only one wife. And eighth, as a loving father, Abraham made sure that all of his children were properly cared for.

Jacob: Patriarch of the Twelve Tribes

By way of summary, many things could be said about the marital life of Jacob (Gen 28–49). First, when he was a single man, God called him to fulfill a special role. While it was Jacob's intention to marry only Rachel, he acquiesced to custom and became polygamous. The consequences of this plural marriage were strife between the wives, grief for Jacob, and discord among the children. After God's summons to return to his ancestral home, he underwent a life-changing encounter with a divine being. In agreement with Richard Davidson, we concur (based on narrative theology) that as a result of this transformation Jacob ended his polygamous relationships and lived monogamously with his original wife, Rachel.[87] Only when he had become monogamous did God invite him to worship at the "house of God." God renewed the covenant with him. Apparently, Jacob never again practiced polygamy. Nevertheless, until the day of his death he cared for and looked after his children and their mothers.

---

[86] Muhlberg, 3.

[87] Davidson, *Flame of Yahweh*, 188, explains, "Before the Jabbok wrestling, Jacob's sexual relationship with all four wives is repeatedly mentioned, but after this event the only conjugal relations are with his wife, Rachel (Gen 35:16–19). During the next decade of Jacob's life in Canaan, only Rachel gives birth to a child (35:18). Whereas Jacob called both Rachel and Leah 'my wives' (30:26; 31:50) before his name (character) change at the Jabbok, he called only Rachel 'my wife' (44:27) after the Jabbok experience. Jacob's use of terminology at the end of his life may point in this same direction. Discussing with his own sons his future burial in the cave of Machpelah, he uses the term 'wife' for both Sarah and Rebekah, who were buried there, but simply adds 'and there I buried Leah' without using the term 'wife' with reference to her (49:31). Most telling of all, in the genealogy of Gen 46, the narrator [i.e., Moses] mentions Leah, Zilpah and Bilhah as women who 'bore to Jacob' children, but only Rachel is classified as his 'wife'—'Jacob's wife Rachel' (46:15, 18–19, 25)."

Esau: Father of the Edomites

Both the Old and New Testaments point out that Esau lived his life as a godless person who despised spiritual things. Thus, Esau's polygamous marriage appears to be part of his rebellious lifestyle (Gen 26–28; Heb 12:16).

Moses: Great Deliverer of the Israelites

After he fled from Egypt, Moses married Zipporah, daughter of Jethro, the priest of Midian (Exod 2:16–3:1). Later, mention is made of "the Cushite woman whom he had married" (Num 12:1), causing some to conclude that Moses was a polygamist.[88] However, there is some biblical indication of a close link between two geographical terms. James Hoffmeier notes that in Habakkuk 3:7 the place names "Cushan" and "Midian" occur in synonymous parallelism, suggesting that the terms referred to the same place.[89] Similarly, E. G. White notes, "Though called a 'Cushite woman' (Numbers 12:1, R.V.), the wife of Moses was a Midianite, and thus a descendant of Abraham."[90] Put simply, Moses was not a polygamist.

Gideon: "Mighty Man of Valor"[91]

Gideon, a prominent man whom God used to deliver His people, was a polygamist. The context sheds light on this issue. Judges 8:27 states, "Gideon made an idol from the gold and put it in his home town, Ophrah. All the Israelites abandoned God and went there to worship the idol. It was a trap for Gideon and his family" (TEV). Significantly, three verses after this statement, the only references to his polygamy are made. After his apostasy is noted, the record notes that Gideon had many wives, in accordance with the custom in those days. Thus, the two activities clearly contrary to God's will are placed in close proximity, which brings to a close his story, negatively reflecting on his polygamy.

---

[88] William D. Summers, *Marriage: Or, The Bible and Polygamy* (n.p., 1886), 24. This view is also held by others such as Gunnar Helander, *Must We Introduce Monogamy? A Study of Polygamy as a Mission Problem in South Africa* (Pietermaritzburg: Shuter and Shooter, 1958), 24; Harry Boer, "Polygamy," *Frontier* 11 (Spring 1968): 25; and Moyenda Nosakhere, *The Path Toward Liberation: Understanding the Need for Polygamy in the African-American Christian Community* (Nashville, TN: Imani Publications, 1991), 25–26.

[89] James K. Hoffmeier, "Zipporah," in *The International Standard Bible Encyclopedia*, ed. Geoffrey W. Bromiley, 4 vols. (Grand Rapids, MI: Eerdmans, 1988), 4:1201. See also John Joseph Owen, "Numbers," in *The Broadman Bible Commentary,* vol. 2 (Nashville, TN: Broadman, 1970), 118; N. H. Snaith, *Leviticus and Numbers*, The New Century Bible (London: Thomas Nelson and Sons, 1967), 234. Although this parallel usage of Cush and Midian appears in Habakkuk, several centuries after Moses, it is possible that these terms were already synonymous in Moses' day.

[90] White, *Patriarchs and Prophets*, 383.

[91] Judges 6:12 (RSV).

Elkanah: "A Man of Wealth and Influence"[92]

During a time when all the people did as they pleased, Elkanah became polygamous, presumably in order to have offspring (1 Sam 1). Considering the suffering of his wife Hannah as she was bullied by Peninnah, the other wife, Elkanah's violation of God's marital standards provides no positive model for the issue of polygamy.

David: "A Man After God's Own Heart"

By the time David became king in Jerusalem, he had six wives. As he became more and more successful, he drifted farther from God and married more women. His life went in a cyclical pattern, with polygamy showing up when he drifted from God.[93] When David committed adultery and then killed Bathsheba's husband to cover up his crime, he remained unpunished for a while.

However, when David married Bathsheba, God sent Nathan with a message of reproof and judgment. The message in 2 Samuel 12:7–8 reveals several elements essential to a proper understanding of God's view of David's moral faults. The judgment of God was in accord with David's sins. He was to lose four of his sons, because of his adultery another would sleep with his wives, and because of his marrying Bathsheba, he would lose all his other wives. Although there is not explicit condemnation of David's polygamous relationships, David's subsequent trials clearly show the consequences of his having more than one wife.

Solomon: "Loved by the Lord"[94]

During the first approximately twenty-five years of his forty-year reign, Solomon was a God-fearing person who lived in accordance with the monogamous marital standard set up in Eden. During this time God twice appeared to him in a dream, promising blessings if Solomon would follow His requirements. Also, during this period Solomon built and dedicated the temple. However, he drifted away from God and violated the specific Deuteronomic prohibitions concerning the excessive accumulation of wealth, the obtaining of horses from Egypt, and polygamy (1 Kgs 10–11). When this happened, God brought judgments upon him. Solomon responded with sincere repentance and confession.

---

[92] White, *Patriarchs and Prophets*, 569.

[93] Intriguingly, similar to the cycles seen in the book of Judges, David repeatedly went through the cyclical pattern of, for example, servitude (1 Sam 17), supplication (1 Sam 17:46), salvation (1 Sam 17:50–54), silence (1 Sam 18), and sin (1 Sam 21). And it is repeatedly during the "sin" cycle that David's polygamy is mentioned.

[94] 2 Samuel 12:25 (NIV) reads, "And because the Lord loved him [i.e., Solomon], he sent word through Nathan the prophet to name him Jedidiah," (which means "loved by the Lord").

His last writings make a call for obedience to God and His requirements, "for this is the whole duty of man" (Eccl 12:13, NIV).

Summary

In the cases of Lamech, Esau, Gideon, and Elkanah, there appears to be no explicit verbal assessment of their polygamy. Nevertheless, the practice of this marital form by these men seems to be placed in a rather negative light. Also, as noted above, Moses was not a polygamist.

Since, according to the biblical record, Abraham, Jacob, David, and Solomon are all identified as having been set aside by God for specific purposes, their cases are considered together. These men were all called by God before they became polygamous—Abraham and Solomon being monogamous, Jacob and David being single. Only after they were selected did each man drift away and became polygamous.

Although God bore long with polygamists, none of these accounts of polygamy is placed in an attractive light. In Abraham's case, he took a second wife because he did not trust God to fulfill His promises. Jacob became polygamous due to the deceit and persuasion of his father-in-law. In the cyclical pattern of the life of David, polygamy seems to appear only during the period when he was involved in sin. The structure of the story of Solomon indicates that his polygamy was during the time when he violated other commands of God and slipped into apostasy. The results of the polygamy of these four are extensively documented. Both in Abraham's and Jacob's cases there was jealousy and disharmony between the wives. Furthermore, strife and tension arose among the children of Jacob and David. Solomon's wives turned his heart away from God and toward idolatry.

At some point, God interposed with some form of judgment, punishment, or direction to terminate the polygamous unions. In Abraham's case, God recognized only Sarah as his wife, and sanctioned the sending away of Hagar to resolve their family problems. Jacob's encounter with the divine being at the Jabbok apparently resulted in his return to a monogamous relationship with his original wife, Rachel. David accepted the predicted loss of his spouses and set them aside when he returned to power (2 Sam 20:3) as a transformed and monogamous man. Solomon, upon recognizing God's judgments, apparently ceased his practice of polygamy as well.

In almost all cases it appears that after the dissolution of the polygamous relationships, the mothers and children were properly cared for. Abraham provided for his children who were sent away. Jacob kept the members of his family together and cared for them all of his life. While nothing is said about Solomon, the record states that David protected and provided for his former spouses the rest of their lives (2 Sam 20:3).

This analysis of the lives of the major polygamists reveals that in no case is there any sanction of polygamy. When those who were called became polygamous, God interposed and brought about the cessation of this marital form. By the language of the story, and by various kinds of judgments, God conveyed His disapproval of polygamy. As Davidson notes, "narrative theology of divine disapproval often speaks even louder, and more eloquently, than explicit condemnation."[95] Davidson concludes that "the OT consistently condemns plural marriage either explicitly or implicitly, but at the same time divine grace is consistently extended to the polygamist. . . . God does not condone the sin but also does note turn away from the sinner as long as there is any hope of repentant response."[96] That God's blessing rests only on monogamy is the fundamental message conveyed in the chronicles of those who practiced polygamy in Bible times.[97]

New Testament Passages Relating to Polygamy

In view of the absence of any direct references to polygamy in the New Testament, this section considers the materials dealing with marital relationships that appear to have implications for polygamy.

Use of the Term "One Flesh"

In His discussion with the Pharisees concerning divorce (Matt 19:3–9), Jesus appeals to the passage in Genesis 2:24 as God's word concerning marriage.[98] However, in referring to this passage, Jesus does not quote from the Hebrew text. As R. C. H. Lenski puts it, "Jesus quotes Gen 2:24, using the LXX [Septuagint] which reproduces the Hebrew exactly save that *hoi duo*, 'the two,' is added in order to bring out the sense of the original."[99] Eduard Schweizer suggests that the "one flesh" concept "presupposes monogamy."[100] Several scholars have therefore concluded that this phrase "also excludes polygamy."[101]

---

[95] Davidson, *Flame of Yahweh*, 180.

[96] Ibid., 211–212.

[97] For those who desire additional information, see ibid., 177–212; and du Preez, *Polygamy in the Bible*.

[98] See Murray, 29; Keil and Delitzsch, 1:90; and R. C. H. Lenski, *The Interpretation of St. Matthew's* Gospel (Minneapolis, MN: Augsburg, 1961), 729.

[99] Lenski, 729.

[100] Eduard Schweizer, *The Good News According to Mark*, trans. Donald H. Madvig (Louisville, KY: John Knox, 1970), 203. See also Mavumilusa Makanzu, *Can the Church Accept Polygamy?* (Accra: Asempa, 1983), 62; Kronholm, 88; Godfrey E. Phillips, *The Old Testament in the World Church*, Lutterworth Library 13, Missionary Research Series 2 (London: Lutterworth Press, 1942), 124.

[101] Davidson, *Flame of Yahweh*, 638; E. Earle Ellis, "Adultery," in *Baker's Dictionary of Christian*

The Practice of the Levirate Custom

The only clear reference to this custom is recorded in Matthew 22:23–28 in a dialogue of Jesus with the Sadducees.[102] The final question posed by the Sadducees is this: "In the resurrection therefore, which one's wife will she be? For all seven had her as wife" (Luke 20:33). If the six brothers who inherited the woman had already been married, the Sadducees' question would have been moot, since it would have been obvious that the wife would have belonged to the first brother only. Thus, crucial to the argument is the assumption that this case involved "seven men with only one wife."[103] The later interpretation by the Babylonian Talmud, which indicates that the levirate was not to be practiced polygamously, provides additional support for a monogamous levirate system.[104] As Geoffrey Parrinder notes, the teaching of the rabbis was against a married man's taking a widow as a second wife.[105] Thus, as in the Old Testament, the weight of evidence in the New Testament suggests that the levirate was practiced monogamously.

The Meaning of *Porneia* in Acts 15

In a letter sent to the churches by the Jerusalem Council, which met around AD 49,[106] the apostles and elders provided instruction for the new Gentile believers. Under the guidance of the Holy Spirit (Acts 15:28),these early church leaders informed the new believers that, while they did not have to be circumcised, they needed to "abstain from things sacrificed to idols and from blood and from things strangled and from fornication [*porneia*]" (Acts 15:29). If these four prohibitions are compared with those recorded in Leviticus, it becomes evident, as J. Carl Laney states, that "when the Council formulated its decision, the restrictions were recorded in their correct order according to Leviticus 17–18."[107] Recognizing the

---

Ethics (Grand Rapids, MI: Baker, 1973), 10. See also Gray and Adams, 4:99; Kronholm, 86; and Frederick C. Grant, "Introduction and Exegesis of the Gospel According to Mark," in *The Interpreter's Bible*, eds. G. A. Buttrick, et al. 12 vols. (Nashville, TN: Abingdon, 1979), 7:796.

[102] For the parallel accounts, see Mark 12:18–27; Luke 20:27–33.

[103] Stanley M. Horton, "Matthew," in *New Testament Study Bible*, The Complete Biblical Library (Springfield, MO: Complete Biblical Library, 1986), 479.

[104] See, e.g., Babylonian Talmud *Yebamoth* 44a; 50a–b.

[105] Geoffrey Parrinder, *The Bible and Polygamy: A Study of Hebrew and Christian Teaching* (London: SPCK, 1950), 26.

[106] See Nichol, 6:304. R. C. H. Lenski, *The Interpretation of the Acts of the Apostles* (Minneapolis, MN: Augsburg, 1961), 592, notes that "Zahn dates the council in the spring of 52; others place it earlier."

[107] J. Carl Laney, *The Divorce Myth* (Minneapolis, MN: Bethany, 1981), 73.

correspondence between Acts 15 and the Levitical laws, Hans Conzelmann concludes: "These are the prohibitions of Leviticus 17–18."[108]

Conzelmann and others note that these forbidden sexual relationships include more than just the incestuous alliances in the first part of Leviticus 18.[109] They observe that the prohibited *porneia* in Acts 15 includes the various sexual relationships listed in the second part of Leviticus 18 as well. Colin Brown points out that *porneia* apparently covers "all sexual offenses listed in Lev. 18."[110] These include adultery (Lev 18:20), bestiality (Lev 18:23), homosexuality (Lev 18:22), incest (Lev 18:7–17), and polygamy (Lev 18:18).[111]

The restrictions of the laws of Leviticus 17–18 were not only for the Israelites. The concept of inclusiveness, "whether he is a native or an alien" (Lev 17:15), is repeated several times in this Levitical legislation,[112] indicating that these "are universal abominations"[113] that apply to both Israelite and non-Israelite.[114] Thus, similarly the early church, under the direct guidance of the Holy Spirit (Acts 15:28)[115] instructed the new Gentile believers that, among other things, all Christians were required to *apechomai*—that is, "abstain from" and "give up" *porneia* in all its forms (Acts 15:29), including the practice of polygamy.

Marital Form in 1 Corinthians 7:1–4

1 Corinthians 7 is the only chapter in the entire New Testament that deals virtually exclusively with marriage. After giving the reason for his instruction, Paul says, "*Let each man* have *his own wife*, and *let each*

---

[108] Hans Conzelmann, *Acts of the Apostles*, trans. James Limburg, A. Thomas Kraabel, and Donald H. Juel, Hermeneia: A Critical and Historical Commentary on the Bible (Philadelphia, PA: Fortress, 1987), 118.

[109] See ibid., 119; and Jerome Crowe, *The Acts*, New Testament Message: A Biblical-Theological Commentary (Wilmington, DE: Michael Glazier, 1979), 117. Nichol, 6:312, recognizing the connection between *porneia* in Acts 15 and the entire chapter of Leviticus 18, notes, "In regard to fornication, the Levitical law against every form of unchastity was rightly strict (Lev. 18; 20:10–21)."

[110] Colin Brown, "Separate, Divide: Divorce, Separation and Remarriage," in *The New International Dictionary of New Testament Theology*, ed. Colin Brown, 3 vols. (Grand Rapids, MI: Zondervan, 1975–1978), 3:538.

[111] Regarding Leviticus 18:18 being a law against polygamy, see Davidson, *Flame of Yahweh*, 193–198; and du Preez, *Polygamy in the Bible*, 70–81.

[112] See Leviticus 17:8, 10, 13, 15; 18:24–26.

[113] Davidson, "Revelation/Inspiration in the Old Testament," 121.

[114] Gerhard F. Hasel, "Clean and Unclean Meats in Leviticus 11: Still Relevant?," *Journal of the Adventist Theological Society* 2 (Autumn 1991): 103–104.

[115] See F. F. Bruce, *Apostle of the Heart Set Free* (Grand Rapids, MI: Eerdmans, 1977), 298; and Nichol, 6:314.

woman have *her own husband*" (1 Cor 7:2, emphasis supplied). It has been claimed that the directive that "each woman should have *her own husband* . . . is also possible in a polygamous marriage"—that is, "in *their common husband*,"[116] but, such a conclusion seems possible only if one contravenes key concepts of communication and circumvents essential exegetical procedures.

The distributive concepts "each man" (*hekastos*) and "each woman" (*hekastē*) point strongly to the fact that there is a single individual on each side of the marital relationship.[117] Paul Hamar notes that the term "each man" suggests "a monogamous marriage."[118] He adds, "This [term] was applied first to the man, then to the woman. There is to be one mate."[119] Archibald Robertson and Alfred Plummer conclude that this passage "forbids polygamy."[120]

Scholars recognize that "the use of the possessive reflexive pronoun *heautou* ["of himself"] and the adjective *idion* ["own"] imply monogamy."[121] As Lenski observes, "the two accusatives 'his own wife' and 'her own husband' clearly point to monogamy and accord with the original divine institution of marriage."[122] F. W. Grosheide states, "*Let have* implies that monogamous marriage is a commandment."[123]

Commenting on 1 Corinthians 7:3, Curtis Morrill states, "The Greek word, *homoiōs* (likewise), between the obligation of the man to the woman and of the woman to the man, stands as an equal sign. Such could never be true in a polygamous family."[124] Verse 4 states that just as the husband has authority over the wife's body, so the wife has authority over the husband's body. Christian Kling notes that "this is a reciprocity

---

[116] Eshun, 167, emphasis supplied.

[117] See Curtis G. Morrill, "The Arguments for Christian Monogamy in First Corinthians 7:2–5" (BDiv monograph, Grace Theological Seminary, 1942), 34.

[118] Paul A. Hamar, "1 Corinthians," in *New Testament Study Bible*, The Complete Biblical Library (Springfield, MO: Complete Biblical Library, 1986), 329.

[119] Hamar, 329.

[120] Archibald Robertson and Alfred Plummer, *A Critical and Exegetical Commentary on the First Epistle of St Paul to the Corinthians*, The International Critical Commentary, 2nd ed. (Edinburgh: T&T Clark, 1914), 133.

[121] William F. Orr and James Arthur Walther, *1 Corinthians*, Anchor Bible (Garden City, NY: Doubleday, 1976), 206. See also F. W. Grosheide, *Commentary on the First Epistle to the Corinthians*, The New International Commentary on the New Testament (Grand Rapids, MI: Eerdmans, 1953), 155; Norman L. Geisler, *Christian Ethics: Options and Issues* (Grand Rapids, MI: Baker, 1989), 280; and Nichol, 6:706.

[122] R. C. H. Lenski, *The Interpretation of St. Paul's First and Second Epistles to the Corinthians* (Minneapolis, MN: Augsburg, 1961), 274.

[123] Grosheide, 155. See also Hamar, 329.

[124] Morrill, 40.

whereby marriage alone receives and maintains its monogamous character."[125] On this, Morrill observes, "This gave the woman the same rights and privileges as her husband had in the sexual relation. Such a thought would be utterly impossible in a polygamous marriage."[126] Thus, it is clear that 1 Corinthians 7:1–4 "contains an accumulative and overwhelming argument in favor of monogamous marriage."[127]

The "Pauline Privilege"[128] and Polygamy

In the discussion of the treatment of newly converted polygamists, some have referred to Paul's counsel in 1 Corinthians 7:20: "Let each man remain in that condition in which he was called." They have alleged that this is "the strongest Biblical argument in favor of a responsible and considered policy of admitting families, who are converted while in the state of polygamy, to the church."[129] This "Pauline privilege" is alleged to show that a new believer does not need to break up his polygamous marriage.[130]

However, as previously pointed out, the first four verses of 1 Corinthians 7 set forth monogamous marriage as the standard for marriages for Christians. It is clear that Paul's counsel in the latter part of the chapter would not conflict with these earlier statements. A second factor that must be taken into account relates to 1 Corinthians 7:19: "Circumcision is nothing, and uncircumcision is nothing, but what matters is the keeping of the commandments of God." Thus, when it is recognized that polygamy is prohibited and monogamy enjoined in God's "law," the summons of 1 Corinthians 7:19 for the convert to keep God's commandments becomes the basis for dissolving all polygamous unions.

---

[125] Christian Friedrich Kling, *The First Epistle of Paul to the Corinthians*, trans. Daniel W. Poor, A Commentary on the Holy Scriptures: Critical, Doctrinal and Homiletical, with Special Reference to Ministers and Students (New York: Charles Scribner's Sons, 1915), 141.

[126] Morrill, 41.

[127] Ibid., 45.

[128] Generally, the term "Pauline privilege" has been understood as referring to Paul's statement that divorce is permissible when an unbelieving spouse chooses to dissolve a marriage. See, e.g., Bruce Vawter, "Divorce and the New Testament," *Catholic Biblical Quarterly* 39 (October 1977): 536–537. However, since the term "Pauline privilege" has also been used in connection with polygamy, it is considered in this framework. See Jean-Jacques Bouit, "A Christian Consideration of Polygamy" (DMin project report, Andrews University, 1981), 106.

[129] Russell Staples, "The Church and Polygamy in Sub-Saharan Africa," 1981, TMs [photocopy], 33, Center for Adventist Research, Berrien Springs, MI.

[130] Bouit, 106. Similarly, Staples, "The Church and Polygamy in Sub-Saharan Africa," 34, maintains that "the Pauline privilege may mean, by extension, that if a man is converted in a polygamous state of marriage, . . . he may be permitted to bring wives with whom he has a positive and enduring relationship into the church with him."

Robertson and Plummer point out, "What is laid down is that, unless one's external condition of life is a sinful one, no violent change in it should be made, simply because one has become a Christian."[131] As John Calvin observes, this "condition" in which one is called "means a lawful mode of life,"[132] which would appear to exclude polygamy. When all the salient aspects of 1 Corinthians 7 are taken into account, Paul teaches faithful monogamy for all believers, including new converts.

Meaning of "Husband of One Wife"

In the epistles to Timothy and Titus, Paul gives clear counsel about the kind of people to be chosen as leaders. This includes that a leader must be "the husband of one wife" (1 Tim 3:2, 12; Titus 1:6). This phrase "has been debated from ancient times,"[133] and has "caused much controversy."[134] A variety of interpretations and explanations have been suggested by various scholars and Bible commentators.[135]

The investigation of the phrase "husband of one wife" has brought to light several facts. It has been viewed as prohibiting only church leaders from polygamy while permitting laity this practice. Also, it has been interpreted as suggesting that the bishop is married to the church and therefore must remain celibate, that a church leader must be married in order to serve, and that no remarried divorcees or remarried widowers can hold leadership posts in the church. Since each of these views stands in tension with the context and text itself, none has been considered an acceptable interpretation of the contested phrase. However, valid linguistic support can be adduced for understanding the "husband of one wife" to refer to monogamous fidelity. This idea comes out in the

---

[131] Robertson and Plummer, 145. Other Bible scholars agree; see Kling, 152; and Jean Hering, *The First Epistle of Saint Paul to the Corinthians*, trans. A. W. Heathcote and P. J. Allcock (London: Epworth, 1962), 54.

[132] John Calvin, *Commentary on the Epistle of Paul the Apostle to the Corinthians*, trans. John Pringle, vol. 1 (Grand Rapids, MI: Eerdmans, 1948), 248. Paul discussed what kinds of activities are lawful and which are not lawful for the Christian. See, e.g., 1 Corinthians 6:9–11, 13; Galatians 5:19–26; Ephesians 5–6.

[133] Fred D. Gealy, "Introduction and Exegesis of the First and Second Epistles to Timothy and the Epistle to Titus," in *The Interpreter's Bible*, eds. G. A. Buttrick, et al. 12 vols., 11:410.

[134] E. K. Simpson, *The Pastoral Epistles: The Greek Text with Introduction and Commentary* (Grand Rapids, MI: Eerdmans, 1954), 50. See also Charles R. Erdman, *The Pastoral Epistles of Paul* (Philadelphia, PA: Westminster, 1943), 39.

[135] See, e.g., the views listed by the following: Nichol, 7:297–298; Gealy, 410–412; C. H. Dodd, "New Testament Translation Problems II," *The Bible Translator* 28 (January 1977): 112–116; Robert Pearson, "A Historical and Grammatical Analysis of the Phrase 'Husband of One Wife'" (ThM thesis, Western Conservative Baptist Seminary, 1972), 38–87; and Walter Lock, *A Critical and Exegetical Commentary on the Pastoral Epistles*, The International Critical Commentary (Edinburgh: T&T Clark, 1924), 36–38.

New English Bible rendition, that the leader must be "faithful to his one wife" (1 Tim 3:2). As Ralph Earle puts it, "it means monogamy—only one wife at one time—and that the overseer must be completely faithful to his wife."[136] Nothing in the text or context limits this requirement to only church leaders; indeed, just as the king (in Old Testament times) was to be a model of monogamy for the people, so this passage calls upon the spiritual leaders to similarly lead by example. In brief, the Pauline writings on marriage are consistent with the original institution in Eden. Polygamy is incompatible with Scripture. Monogamy is enjoined.

Synopsis of Principles from Divine Revelation

From a study of the original institution of marriage in the Bible, several factors significant for polygamy have been observed.

The Form of Marriage Instituted in Eden

From a scriptural point of view, marriage is not merely a societal convention. According to the Genesis account of the first human couple, marriage has God as its divine originator and author. The Creator instituted marriage as a special relationship between *one* man and *one* woman, an unquestioningly monogamous relationship. This prototype or pattern was set up by God as the "order and law"[137] for all future marriages and "re-instituted" at the worldwide flood through the example of the monogamous marriages of Noah and his three sons. Thus, the new world began just as the original one had in Eden, with monogamy as God's standard. The New Testament confirms this Old Testament view. In discussing marriage, Jesus, by His choice of words, points His listeners back to the monogamous norm established by God. The church must recognize the sanctity of the marital standard established by the Creator. Heterosexual monogamy is not just an "ideal," but rather the only permissible form of marriage.

Regulations Restricting Polygamy

A study of Leviticus 18:18 shows that, according to the structural and linguistic contexts, plural marriage was the specific target of this regulation. Leviticus 18:18 is a universal law that distinctly and deliberately prohibits polygamy for believer and non-believer alike. A similar legislation is located in Deuteronomy 17:17, among the specific commands

---

[136] Ralph Earle, "1, 2 Timothy," *The Expositor's Bible Commentary*, ed. Frank E. Gaebelein, 12 vols. (Grand Rapids, MI: Zondervan, 1978), 11:364.

[137] Ellen G. White, "The Great Controversy Between Christ and His Angels and Satan and His Angels: The Flood," *Signs of the Times*, February 27, 1879, 66.

for future rulers of the people. Since these rulers were role models for the people, this law also forbade all from practicing plural marriage.

While in the New Testament nothing is directly stated about polygamy, Acts 15 and the writings of Paul seem to refer to this practice. Among other things, Acts 15 indicates that all new Gentile converts must avoid *porneia*, which in the larger context of Leviticus 17–18 includes polygamy. Similarly, the discussion of 1 Corinthians 7, which maintains that monogamy is the standard for all, calls upon new believers to bring their lives into conformity with God's marital standards. In delineating the qualifications for church leaders, Paul calls for leaders to practice monogamous fidelity. Just as with Israel's rulers, these leaders were to be role models. Thus, this exclusion of polygamy can be seen as applying to all members.

In both the Old and New Testaments, therefore, there appears to be clear evidence forbidding the practice of polygamy. These regulations confirm and support the monogamous law as originally set up. In brief then, as Mavumilusa Makanzu states, "the whole of God's word condemns polygamy."[138]

The Cases of Practicing Polygamists

Close examination of these narratives shows that in no case was polygamy viewed positively. While in no instance was there any divine approval for this type of marital alliance, in most cases some sort of judgment or punishment is indicated.

In the cases of Abraham, Jacob, and David, their polygamy resulted in jealousy, strife, and tension in the home. In Solomon's case his wives led him into apostasy. God interposed in these four cases (Gen 21:9–14; 31:3; 2 Sam 12:1–15; 1 Kgs 11:9–13) with messages designed to bring about reformation.

In connection with these four men who were specifically called by God for a special task, it appears that all were summoned prior to becoming polygamous. While Abraham and Solomon were monogamous when God called them, Jacob and David were set aside by God while still single. Only later did they become polygamous. In fact, there is no record of God calling a polygamist into service for Him or His people.

Although God bore long with polygamists, there is no evidence that He ever approved or condoned the polygamous marriages of any Bible characters. Gleason Archer notes that "every case of polygamy or concbinage amounted to a failure to follow God's original model and plan."[139] As observed in this study, God worked at bringing all polygamists back to His standard of monogamy.

---

[138] Makanzu, 65.

[139] Gleason L. Archer, *Encyclopedia of Bible Difficulties* (Grand Rapids, MI: Zondervan, 1982), 122.

Contextualizing the Gospel in Different Cultures

These aforementioned conclusions indicate that the Bible maintains that monogamy is the only permissible and legitimate form of marriage. Furthermore, the practice of polygamy is repeatedly prohibited, both in the legislation as well as in the chronicles of Scripture. Thus the question remains: how is one to share the gospel with a practicing polygamist?

Admittedly, because missionaries bring a message that often requires radical change, they have at times been perceived as agents of destruction.[140] Therefore, all Christians should recognize that only changes essential to Christianity should be undertaken—and as constructively as possible.

To know how best to deal with polygamists who desire admission into the church, it would be well to gain an understanding of the reasons for this form of marriage. For example, polygamy provides a large pool of laborers to provide for the needs of the family. Also, John Mbiti notes that "it is instilled in the minds of African peoples that a big family earns its head great respect in the eyes of the community."[141]

In ancient times people felt that their safety lay in joining forces.[142] Chiefs or kings would marry the women of other tribes or nations, thus forming bonds of friendship, solidarity, and inter-clan loyalty.[143] This type of political alliance seems to have been the reason behind some of Solomon's marriages (1 Kgs 11:1).[144]

Makanzu observes that "polygamy ensures that every woman will be married."[145] Even the unwed mother, who, as David Gitari notes, is a disgrace to the family in most African cultures,[146] is taken in as a polygamous wife. Polygamy helps resolve the problem of the so-called surplus of women. To care for war widows and orphans the Qur'an allows a man to

---

[140] See Barry David Oliver, "Polygamy and the Seventh-day Adventist Church in Papua New Guinea," 1986, TMs [photocopy], 35, Center for Adventist Research, Berrien Springs, MI.

[141] John S. Mbiti, *African Religions & Philosophy* (New York: Frederick A. Prager, 1969), 142.

[142] S. Ananda Kumar, "Culture in the Old Testament," in *Down to Earth: Studies in Christianity and Culture*, ed. Robert T. Coote and John Stott (Grand Rapids, MI: Eerdmans, 1980), 46.

[143] See Norman A. Horner, "Polygyny Among the Bantu of French Cameroun," *International Review of Missions* 43 (1954): 176.

[144] See Darrell Lee Wise, "African Polygamy Reexamined" (MTh thesis, Southwestern Baptist Theological Seminary, 1987), 34.

[145] Makanzu, 16. See also Horner, 174.

[146] David Gitari, "The Church and Polygamy," *Transformation* 1 (January–March 1984): 7. See also James E. Karibwije, "Polygamy and the Church in Nigeria: A Study of Various Christian Positions" (MA thesis, Trinity Evangelical Divinity School, 1986), 10.

marry up to four women.[147] Generally, the women have the responsibility of "tilling the ground, planting and harvesting crops, and caring for the needs of the husband; thus, they welcome co-wives who will relieve some of the burden."[148]

Since, in many of these societies, divorce proceedings are very complicated and usually discouraged, polygamy is often seen as a better method of handling the problem of an unloved wife.[149] In some instances the first wife puts pressure on the husband to get a second wife.[150] Eugene Hillman notes that "a wife may provoke her husband to take another wife by ridiculing him and calling him 'a poor man.'"[151] Being the senior wife increases her own status and authority and gives her power to control the household and dictate work to the other wife or wives.[152] The desire to have many offspring may also relate to the African belief that "the dead continue to live through their children."[153]

In societies where children are highly valued, the barrenness of a wife could be a powerful factor motivating a husband to take another wife.[154] In some societies, where sons are preferred, a man may seek an additional wife hoping she will give birth to a son who will be his heir.[155]

In certain cultures sexual relations between a husband and his wife are taboo during pregnancy and lactation.[156] This period of abstinence from sexual relations may "last from two to six years."[157] During this time

---

[147] *Qur'an* 4:3. See also Tabish Noori, "A Comparative Study of Polygamy in Judaism, Christianity and Islam," *Review of Religions* 80 (April 1985): 27; and Ismat Mahdi, "Sanctity of Marriage in Islam," *Bulletin of the Henry Martyn Institute of Islamic Studies* 8 (July–September 1985): 62.

[148] Hitchens, 110. See also Samson Osimbo Obwa, "Polygamy Among the Southern Luo of Kenya: A Critique of Both the Practice of Polygamy and the Reaction of Mission-Founded Churches to It in the Light of Biblical Teaching" (MA thesis, Columbia Graduate School of Bible and Missions, 1978), 16; and William D. Reyburn, "Polygamy, Economy, and Christianity in the Eastern Cameroun," in *Readings in Missionary Anthropology II*, ed. William A. Smalley, rev. ed. (Pasadena, CA: William Carey Library, 1978), 259.

[149] See Gitari, 8–9; and Hitchens, 113.

[150] Hitchens, 111; and Wise, 27.

[151] Hillman, 120. See also Walter A. Trobisch, "Congregational Responsibility and the Christian Individual," *Practical Anthropology* 13 (September–October 1966): 205–207; and Reyburn, 256.

[152] Wise, 27; Hitchens, 111; Hubert Horan, "Polygamy Comes Home to Roost," *Missiology: An International Review* 4 (October 1976): 445–446; and Reyburn, 259.

[153] Hitchens, 112.

[154] See Mbiti, 143; Karibwije, 11; Wise, 21; Hitchens, 105–106; Kumar, 45; Gitari, 8; and Hillman, 115.

[155] See Obwa, 15.

[156] See, e.g., Chidawa B. Kaburuk, "Polygyny in the Old Testament and the Church in Africa" (STM thesis, Dallas Theological Seminary, 1976), 27; Karibwije, 9; Makanzu, 14; and Reyburn, 258.

[157] Hitchens, 108.

of waiting a husband may feel the need to take a second wife. A husband may feel a similar concern during his wife's prolonged visits to her faraway relatives.[158] Among some peoples, women refuse to cohabit once they reach menopause.[159] Makanzu alleges that polygamy, which provides husbands for all women, is also a deterrent from women's practice of prostitution: "With all the women married, there can be no professional prostitution."[160]

Additionally, Chidawa Kaburuk contends, "One of the reasons for practicing polygyny is the lust of the flesh and selfishness. A man who is lustful is not satisfied with one wife. When he sees another woman, especially a beautiful one, he is stimulated sexually and determines to have her."[161]

In brief, a large variety of factors contribute to the practice of polygamy. Economic and sociopolitical factors, a concern for women and children, personal and religious motivations, and sexual and reproductive reasons all form a network of relationships that contribute to making polygamy desirable. Only within this context of the system of social values can one begin to understand polygamy.[162]

The Gospel's Call for Transformation

The Great Commission of Jesus, as recorded in Matthew 28:19–20, challenges Christians to go and make disciples of all nations, "teaching them to observe all that I have commanded you." This in itself is a radical call for change. This summons is for change to take place on more than just the intellectual level. It often requires a modification of lifestyle, habits, customs, and traditional practices. As Willem Saayman remarks, "evangelisation, because it involves such a thorough-going re-orientation of the whole person, also involves culture change."[163] The only power that can successfully accomplish this effectively is the gospel of Jesus Christ. All Christians are to participate in this change since each person forms a vital part of the church, which is "God's catalyst for transforming culture through the impact of the gospel."[164]

---

[158] Hitchens, 112. See also Reyburn, 258.

[159] See Gitari, 8; and Obwa, 18.

[160] Makanzu, 17.

[161] Kaburuk, 20–21.

[162] See Masamba ma Mpolo, *Polygamy and the Status of Women in African Churches: A Psycho-Social Approach to Pastoral Theology* (n.p., 1975), 21.

[163] Willem A. Saayman, "Intercultural Evangelism," *Missionalia* 18 (November 1990): 310.

[164] Morris A. Inch, *Doing Theology Across Cultures* (Grand Rapids, MI: Baker, 1982), 93.

Universal Validity of Moral Norms

Samson Obwa notes that "a marriage that is socially or legally acceptable to a state or nation may not necessarily be according to God's pattern."[165] Thus, the biblical concept of marriage is the only norm against which the practice of polygamy is to be evaluated.[166] Indeed, as Walter Trobisch observes, "monogamy is not a western concept of marriage pertaining only to one culture. It is a biblical concept, presenting a challenge to all cultures."[167] As previously indicated, the Bible reveals that monogamy is the law that God established. On the other hand, He clearly prohibited polygamy.

Recognizing that polygamy is "incompatible with the content of genuine Christian marriage,"[168] Joseph Tomko maintains that the gospel cannot be inculturated in this regard. Rather, there must be a profound and radical conversion of peoples and cultures to Christ and to His teachings.[169] Just as the idolater or the murderer is required to discard his former way of life when accepting Christianity, so the polygamist is to be called upon to terminate what he had not realized, prior to accepting Christ, was a sinful practice, and thus live in conformity to God's universal moral norms.

Ways of Changing Cultural Practices

In connection with polygamy, appropriate change can be brought about only when the reasons contributing to its practice are properly understood and suitable functional substitutes can be provided. Thus, Saayman notes, "The people themselves, in consultation with missionaries, can indicate how their culture might have to change in the light of the gospel."[170]

One way to bring people to a sense of their need is by helping them recognize areas in which their traditional belief has not adequately lived up to desires and hopes. For example, one could point out the many problems associated with polygamy. Mbiti mentions the frequent quarrels and fights among wives and among children, the neglect of some wives while favoring others, and the great burden of educating, disciplining,

---

[165] Inch, 93.

[166] Bouit, 26–27.

[167] Walter A. Trobisch, "Here Is My Problem," in *My Wife Made Me a Polygamist* (Kehl/Rhein: Editions Trobisch, 1980), 25.

[168] Joseph Tomko, "Inculturation and African Marriage," *African Ecclesial Review* 28 (June/August 1986): 163.

[169] Ibid., 165.

[170] Saayman, 315.

and caring for the children.[171] For example, Daniel Denga's study of delinquents in Nigeria shows the incidence of juvenile delinquency is greater among polygamous than monogamous families.[172] Makanzu points out that polygamy causes financial problems, does not satisfy a woman's sexual desires, and fosters social injustice because the rich marry most of the women while the poor are forced to remain single.[173] In fact, in mid-March 2018, *The Economist* revealed that "wherever polygamy is widely practiced (in South Sudan, perhaps 40% of marriages involve multiple wives) turmoil tends to follow."[174]

When people are more acutely conscious of the inadequacy of a custom, as concluded from their own observations and based on their own proverbs, they may be more open to considering a different practice. At this point in time one of the primary tasks of the Christian worker will be to demonstrate that Christianity can best fulfill the true needs of the individual.

While all the factors noted here are useful in facilitating the transformation of a deeply ingrained cultural practice, the most essential ingredient is the power of the gospel itself. According to 2 Corinthians 5:17, "If any man be in Christ, he is a new creature: old things are passed away; behold, all things are become new" (KJV). By means of this new relationship with Christ, it is possible to "do all things" through Him (Phil 4:13). The polygamist who wants to become a Christian must recognize that the God of the Bible will provide the power for the new convert to live a monogamous lifestyle.

Some Methods and Procedures for Implementation

Regarding those new to the gospel, Helmut Thielicke postulates that "the only possible general rule would seem to be that *existing polygamous marriages* may be allowed to continue when a person is baptized."[175]

---

[171] Mbiti,143–144.

[172] Daniel I. Denga, "Juvenile Delinquency Among Polygynous Families in Nigeria," *Journal of Social Psychology* 114 (1981): 3.

[173] Makanzu, 49–52.

[174] M. B., "Why Polygamy Breeds Civil War", *The Economist*, March 19, 2018. Part of the explanation given is that "polygamy nearly always means rich men taking multiple wives. And if the top 10% of men marry four women each, then the bottom 30% cannot marry at all. This often leaves them not only sexually frustrated but also socially marginalised. In many traditional societies, a man is not considered an adult until he has found a wife and sired children. To get a wife, he must typically pay a 'brideprice' to her father. When polygamy creates a shortage of brides, it massively inflates this brideprice. In South Sudan, it can be anything from 30 to 300 cattle, far more wealth than an ill-educated young man can plausibly accumulate by legal means."

[175] Helmut Thielicke, *Theological Ethics*, vol. 3, Sex, trans. John W. Doberstein (Grand Rapids, MI:

Responding to this view, the African evangelist Makanzu comments,

> You can't preach against polygamy and at the same time accept polygamists into your midst. It is a contradiction. You can't be for and against at the same time. Neither do I believe a temporary attitude of tolerance will lead to the disappearance of polygamy. Such a policy would, on the contrary, serve to perpetuate it. . . . The church can no longer make exceptions and special cases. If it does, Christians and non-Christians alike will be confused.[176]

Relevancy of Guidelines for Different Societies

No two societies are identical. There is a large divergence of habits and marital practices, even between societies that permit polygamy.[177] Recognizing this, it is clear that any policy that attempts to establish all the specific details of how to deal with practicing polygamists who request baptism is bound to result in misapplication and difficulty. William Blum suggests that "each particular Church or diocese must examine its own situation prior to forming a relevant policy."[178] Understandably, these church policies must be based on solid biblical norms. Already these basic principles have been outlined in the previous sections of this study. Thus, in line with the findings that monogamy is the only acceptable form of marriage and that polygamy is a violation of God's law, this section will provide a few suggestions for consideration.

In deciding what approaches to take, local people ought to be involved. With guidance and support, they can decide how to put biblical principles into effect.[179] Darrell Wise notes that "in this way the policies will be their policies,"[180] and not some outsider's requirement. Because the locals better understand the true meaning of polygamy, they will be able to suggest appropriate functional substitutes.[181] Nevertheless, the cross-cultural Christian worker can make a meaningful contribution to this issue. With this in mind, various suggestions have been included in this study from the works of Africans, though not excluding cross-cultural missionaries.

Eerdmans, 1964), 181, emphasis supplied.

[176] Makanzu, 74.

[177] See George Peter Murdock, *Ethnographic Atlas* (Pittsburgh, PA: University of Pittsburgh Press, 1967), 47–48, 62–122.

[178] William G. Blum, *Forms of Marriage: Monogamy Reconsidered* (Nairobi: AMECEA Gaba, 1989), 278.

[179] Wise, 119. See also Saayman, 315.

[180] Wise, 119.

[181] Obwa, 62.

Spiritual Transformation and Mental Reeducation

William Reyburn suggests that the deep-seated emotion that lies behind the polygamist is the desire for power.[182] Thus, if this is so, then the Christian worker should "communicate a gospel that speaks to the roots of his real need and show him that Christ is the ultimate answer to the *power* problem of his heart."[183] As Samson Obwa indicates, "the Scriptures also teach that for the Christian, the matter of heir and inheritance have a higher perspective than gaining earthly inheritance or leaving an heir to continue one's lineage."[184]

In essence, if it is possible, every one of the functions fulfilled by polygamy should be appropriately replaced so that those coming out of this practice may be able to continue as normal a life as possible. These elements include prestige, certain religious beliefs, inheritance customs, family defense, widow security, the status of women, an adequate workforce, sexual practices, and sex taboo adjustments. For this task well-trained marriage counselors, pastors, and other reliable leaders must be acquainted with the customs, needs, and desires of the people.[185]

Closely allied to the concern for wealth are the issues of power, prestige, and pride.[186] Reyburn suggests that the gospel message should communicate the "power of service for others."[187] Similarly, Obwa proposes that "all Christians, including polygamists, need to be taught that true greatness lies in humility and service to others."[188] Moreover, "prestige" can be resolved, as James Karibwije notes, by recognizing that "to be called a child of God and a friend of Jesus Christ is more than the prestige one can get in this world."[189] Thus, the fulfillment provided by polygamy will be satisfied in helping others, and in acknowledging that "the prestige in Christianity is eternal while other prestige is temporary."[190]

Attitudes toward sexual issues seem to need considerable readjustment. First, the issue of childlessness needs to be addressed. While barrenness can be a problem in marriage, Karibwije notes that "it is also true that a childless marriage can be a true and good one."[191] Tied in with

---

182 Reyburn, 272.

183 Ibid., 255, emphasis original.

184 Obwa, 66.

185 See Trobisch, 40. See also Karibwije, 67.

186 Reyburn, 272.

187 Ibid., 273.

188 Obwa, 68.

189 Karibwije, 66.

190 Ibid.

191 Ibid.

this concern is the matter of who will carry on the family name and inherit the family property. Obwa suggests that the believer focus on God's promise of eternal inheritance, and on the fact that each Christian is an heir of God's kingdom.[192]

Examples of Some Practical Procedures

Francis Arinze observes that "while strict compliance with the demands of monogamy should be a condition for full communion with the Church, due consideration in charity and justice should be given to all members of the polygamous family unit that has already been built up."[193] First, the ex-wives need to be cared for.[194] One writer mentions a case of a "polygamist (with three wives), who, having applied for baptism, promptly arranged for the livelihood (food, housing, clothes) of the two wives he was leaving."[195] One denomination provided homes at every mission station where these women could go and support themselves.[196] When this is done, "Christianity will not be regarded as a religion which breaks up families when people see that the divorced women and their children are well treated."[197]

A better solution is for the dismissed wives to find husbands. According to Willard Burce, "this not only tends to prevent relapses, but helps to assure the care, support, and social integration of the wives and their children."[198] In some societies remarriage for these women is not difficult, if the dowry is properly returned.[199] Such marriages also reduce the chances of these women becoming prostitutes.[200]

Addressing the issue of childlessness, Obwa maintained that this "should not be the occasion either for divorce or to procure an additional

[192] Obwa, 66. See Romans 8:16–17; Hebrews 9:15; James 2:5; 1 Peter 1:3–4.

[193] Francis A. Arinze, "Polygamy and Childlessness," *African Ecclesial Review* 23 (February–March 1981): 98.

[194] Ian M. Hay, "A Discussion of the Problem of Polygamy in Relation to the Church in Nigeria" (MA thesis, Columbia School of Mission, Columbia Bible College, 1951), 45; and Karibwije, 62.

[195] Domus, "An African Problem: Polygamy," *African Ecclesiastical Review* 25 (April 1983): 124. This accords well with Exodus 21, as previously discussed in the present study. See also Sophie de la Haye, *Tread Upon the Lion: The Story of Tommie Titcombe* (Ontario: Sudan Interior Mission, 1973), 62–63, who records a similar case from 1912: before baptism a polygamist quit cohabiting with two extra wives, put them "in separate quarters; maintained them, meeting all their needs, but living only with his first wife."

[196] Helander, 64.

[197] Ibid.

[198] Willard Burce, "Polygamy and the Church," *Concordia Theological Monthly* 34 (April 1963): 231.

[199] See, e.g., Horner, 178.

[200] While it is true that some women might turn to prostitution, this is not always so, especially in societies where women return to their relatives. See, e.g., Helander, 15; cf. Trobisch, 36.

wife."[201] Rather, if no medical help can solve the problem, "then the couple could be advised to adopt children of their choice."[202] This practice has already succeeded in some situations.[203] On this issue of adoption, Diane D'Souza noted that polygamy is virtually unknown among Muslims in China because "infertile couples commonly adopt children to build a family."[204]

In connection with the need for an adequate workforce, Obwa comments, "To acquire a wife for her labor obviously is not a good ground for marriage. She will be no more than a slave."[205] Rather, if a man is wealthy enough to get another wife, Obwa notes he should then hire laborers to work for him.[206]

Finally, the church itself needs to provide as much support as possible through specially trained workers. Marriage counselors who understand the particular problems attending dissolved polygamous unions need to be available in every polygamous society where evangelism is being carried out. Pastors and chaplains ought to be instructed on how to deal with these issues. Legal specialists should also be available. Perhaps most importantly, the entire congregation should be instructed and encouraged to assist in loving and caring ways as each new convert seeks to adjust to a new way of living. In practical ways, every member of the converted, former polygamous family should be properly cared for.

Conclusion

Radical conversion can only happen by God's grace. As Tomko states, "acceptance of Christian marriage, in its evangelical identity, is the most concrete proof of such a conversion."[207]

Admittedly, this biblical perspective on polygamy—according to which no polygamists who continue living in plural marriage be baptized —could result in fewer accessions to the church. However, as W. T. Bartlett states in connection with polygamy,

> we aim to follow the Word of God in all respects, and even though that should hinder our work and keep many people out

---

[201] Obwa, 63.

[202] Ibid.

[203] Haring, 158.

[204] D'Souza, 78 n. 1.

[205] Obwa, 67.

[206] Ibid.

[207] Tomko, 165.

> of the church, we would rather have only a few people who are loyal to the word of God in all respects than a multitude who have come in at a compromise. At all costs we should hold to the word of God.[208]

In the final analysis, the true measure of any gospel worker's success must be the way the local Christians apply biblical principles sensitively and intelligently to their own challenges.[209] This is the goal toward which all indigenous and cross-cultural Christian workers should diligently strive, for God's glory.

---

[208] "Missions Round Table," General Conference Session, Milwaukee, WI, May 27–June 12, 1926, 2, Center for Adventist Research, Berrien Springs, MI.

[209] See Charles R. Taber, "The Missionary: Wrecker, Builder, or Catalyst?," *Practical Anthropology* 17 (July–August 1970): 152.

CHAPTER 8

Reclaiming the Gift of Sexuality: A Biblical Perspective on Sexual Addiction

Deanna A. Pitchford

Human sexuality is a gift from God. Creating humanity male and female, as an expression of His image, God endorsed sexuality as an intrinsic human quality—one that profoundly influences the way we see and experience the world.[1] The creation of the sexual differentiation of humankind, found in Genesis 1–2, underscores the fact that "to be human is to live as a sexual person."[2] This duality of humanity finds its ultimate wholeness in the coming together of a man and a woman, not only physically but also intellectually, emotionally, and spiritually. To understand and fully embrace the good gift of sexuality in a culture that alternately glorifies and debases sexuality is one of the challenges of the twenty-first century, particularly as one strives to live a God-honoring life.

Sexuality, which God designed as part of His good creation, draws us to one another with the desire to be in relationship.[3] The original creation concept envisaged the sexual relationship between a man and a woman as wholesome, exclusive, equal, and permanent.[4] "Mankind in fellowship as male and female is what it means to be made in the image of God."[5] Nowhere, then, is the image of God reflected more clearly than when a man and a woman enter into a committed relationship with one

---

[1] Judith K. Balswick and Jack O. Balswick, *Authentic Human Sexuality: An Integrated Christian Approach*, 3rd ed. (Downers Grove, IL: IVP Academic, 2019).

[2] Richard M. Davidson, *Flame of Yahweh: Sexuality in the Old Testament* (Peabody, MA: Hendrickson, 2008), 19.

[3] Balswick and Balswick.

[4] Davidson, 45.

[5] Ibid., 39.

another.[6] Scripture makes it clear that the original relationship between Adam and Eve was one of intimacy (Gen 2:25), thereby illustrating the divine purpose of sexuality to draw us into relationship with one another. It is the disregard of this "fellowship" and the neglect of relationship that makes sexual addiction such an egregious transgression.

When sin entered the garden of Eden, and introduced shame and guilt into the human experience, relationships between men and women became fraught with difficulty and the gift of sexuality in particular was blighted. The ultimate degradation of this gift is the selfish use of sexuality to gratify one's own desires and lust, rather than embracing sexuality as the ultimate bonding experience within the marital relationship.

Understanding Sexual Addiction

Definition and Description of Sexual Addiction

Sexual addiction is behavior of a sexual nature that is excessive, compulsive, often impulsive, and that dominates the thinking of an individual to such an extent that most other considerations are set aside.[7] It has also been described as a dependency on sex for its mood-altering effects in the absence of a relationship.[8]

Such an intense preoccupation with sex often causes significant distress to the person concerned, particularly if they strive to live according to biblical principles of purity and honesty.[9] This can result in psychological problems such as depression, difficulties in conducting activities of daily living, neglect of family and work responsibilities, loneliness, and ultimately behavioral dependencies such as an addiction to internet pornography.[10]

The focus of the excessive sexual behavior is either self-directed and internal, or other-directed and external. Self-directed or internal excessive sexual behavior can consist of sexual fantasies, compulsive sexual thoughts, the seeking out of pornography, and indulging in masturbation.

---

[6] Davidson, 40.

[7] Yaniv Efrati and Mario Mikulincer, "Individual-Based Compulsive Sexual Behavior Scale: Its Development and Importance in Examining Compulsive Sexual Behavior," *Journal of Sex & Marital Therapy* 44/3 (2018): 249–259.

[8] Patrick Carnes, *Out of the Shadows: Understanding Sexual Addiction*, 3rd ed. (Center City, MN: Hazelden Publishing, 2001).

[9] Joshua B. Grubbs et al., "Transgression as Addiction: Religiosity and Moral Disapproval as Predictors of Perceived Addiction to Pornography," *Archives of Sexual Behavior* 44/1 (2015): 125–136.

[10] Kit-Aun Tan, "The Effects of Personal Susceptibility and Social Support on Internet Addiction: An Application of Adler's Theory of Individual Psychology," *International Journal of Mental Health and Addiction* 17/4 (2019): 806–816.

Other-directed or external excessive sexual behavior can take the form of serial sexual conquests, "love addiction," and engagement in cybersex.[11] In this discussion of sexual addiction, special reference will be made to internet pornography addiction, a self-directed sexual behavior that can be described as a "pathological preoccupation with online sexual behaviours in an effort to create a mood-altering experience."[12]

Within the body of psychological literature, the topic of sexual addiction is somewhat controversial. Those who work with people who struggle with their sexual fantasies and behavior have no doubt that sexual addiction is problematic, but there is currently no official psychological recognition of the concept of sexual addiction.[13] For those working in the field of psychology this is difficult to understand, as there are increasing numbers of people who describe themselves as being addicted to internet pornography, for example. The fact that excessive sexual behavior is frequently associated with significant psychological distress has prompted researchers to put forward arguments for the acknowledgement of a diagnostic category called "Hypersexual Disorder."[14] This diagnosis would encompass obsessive sexually focused behavior used to make oneself "feel better." It would also include sexual behavior that is out of control, requiring an escalation of sexual behaviors to achieve the same effect, causing significant harm and distress to the individual.[15]

The question can, however, be asked: is sexual addiction really an addiction or simply the result of poor moral choices? To answer this question we need to look at the concept of addiction.

Definition and Description of "Addiction"

A broad definition of "addiction" is the "continued use (of substances or behaviours) despite adverse consequences."[16] With regard to substances such as alcohol, other drugs, and behaviors such as gambling or viewing internet pornography, "addiction" refers to a dependency on a "mood-altering" substance or experience. In addiction, this dependency becomes more important than anything else; work, family, friends, and spirituality are all neglected. In the context of sexual addiction, this

---

[11] Efrati and Mikulincer, 250.

[12] Natasha Petty Levert, "A Comparison of Christian and Non-Christian Males, Authoritarianism, and Their Relationship to Internet Pornography Addiction/Compulsion," *Sexual Addiction & Compulsivity* 14/2 (2007): 147.

[13] *Diagnostic and Statistical Manual of Mental Disorders: DSM-5*, 5th ed. (Washington, DC: American Psychiatric Association, 2013).

[14] Martin P. Kafka, "Hypersexual Disorder: A Proposed Diagnosis for DSM-V," *Archives of Sexual Behavior 39/2* (2010): 377–400.

[15] Ibid, 383.

[16] Judson Brewer, *The Craving Mind* (New Haven, CT: Yale University Press, 2017), 18.

means continuing with activities that provide sexual gratification despite the negative personal consequences of guilt and shame and the knowledge that public exposure of the behavior would come at a very high cost.

Although Scripture does not directly address the topic of addiction, the apostle Paul's anguished cry can be applied to the struggles faced by people caught in the web of addiction: "I do not understand what I do. For what I want to do I do not do, but what I hate I do" (Rom 7:15, NIV).[17] This Scripture reference gives insight into the despair experienced by many caught up in addiction and highlights the issue of compulsion that often accompanies addictive behavior.

People with a sexual addiction make frequent promises to themselves that they will no longer indulge in the activities that enslave them, but find that despite their best efforts there are recurring failures to curb or control the behavior. Sexual addiction is an "irrepressible desire and uncontrollable craving to repeat a sexual behaviour."[18] Sexual compulsivity, a component of sexual addiction, is often demonstrated in persons who are sexual risk-takers, who consistently seek out sexual sensation and have many sexual partners, and who are unable to moderate or control this behavior. Thereby they place themselves at higher risk for sexually transmitted diseases.

In addition to feeling compelled to give way to overwhelming sexual urges and fantasies, the person with a sexual addiction might also be struggling with a lack of cognitive control over their impulses, acting out certain rituals that precede the sexual behavior, making it almost impossible for them to turn away from that behavior.

In summary, it can be said that sexual addiction is the giving over of the mind to the pursuit of sexual gratification despite negative consequences.

But what are the general mechanisms of addiction, and can sexually compulsive behavior be regarded as an addiction?

Mechanisms of Addiction

Addiction to a substance can be defined as a "compulsion to seek and take a drug, loss of control in limiting intake, and the emergence of a negative emotional state when access to the drug is prevented."[19] Typically, an addiction cycle consists of three stages: a binge/intoxication stage, a withdrawal/negative affect stage, and a preoccupation/anticipation stage.[20]

---

[17] All biblical quotations are from NLT, unless otherwise indicated.

[18] J. Christopher Barrilleaux, "Sexual Addiction: Definitions and Interventions," *Journal of Social Work Practice in the Addictions* 16/4 (2016): 423.

[19] George F. Koob and Jay Schulkin, "Addiction and Stress: An Allostatic View," *Neuroscience and Biobehavioral Reviews* 106 (2019): 245.

[20] Koob and Schulkin, 245.

Sexual addiction, although a behavioral addiction, follows much the same pattern when the individual compulsively seeks out sexual experiences.

Evidence is growing that stress response and, more particularly, a chronic stress response, in the body underpins addiction.[21] We do not all respond to stress in the same way and the Adverse Childhood Experiences (ACE) study sheds some light on the reasons why this may be so.[22] Early adverse experiences are linked to negative health outcomes later in life and are also implicated in increased susceptibility to addiction.[23] Early negative experiences result in a deficient stress response (through epigenetic processes), influence the thinking of an individual to be more impulsive and focused on short-term rewards, and cause the regulation of emotions to be unstable, leading to unpleasant, negative feelings (which the individual often tries to suppress through addiction).[24]

There is now a growing body of evidence that addiction, sexual addiction included, is not always just the result of moral failure, but may also result from an interaction between environmental factors (which often lead to the initiation of addictive behavior) and a genetic predisposition to respond to stress in a maladaptive way (which maintains addictive behavior).[25]Additionally, the challenges that early adverse experiences pose to brain mechanisms leave "neuro-adaptive traces" that make relapse likely even after years of abstinence.[26]

This is not to deny the role of personal responsibility for behavior, but highlights the complexity of the addiction process. Living as we do in a sinful world, we are shaped by our early experiences (which are not always positive) as well as by our genetic inheritance creating within some a predisposition to addiction (e.g., alcoholism). This understanding should underpin a compassionate response to people struggling with addiction. Jesus said, "Do not judge, or you too will be judged" (Matt 7:1).

For the child of God, these findings do not need to be a source of discouragement, but rather a reminder of our utter dependency on the Lord and His sustaining power. Let us consider the interaction between our spiritual practices and sexual addiction.

---

[21] Koob and Schulkin, 246.

[22] V. J. Felitti et al., "Relationship of Childhood Abuse and Household Dysfunction to Many of the Leading Causes of Death in Adults: The Adverse Childhood Experiences (ACE) Study," *American Journal of Preventative Medicine* 14 (1998): 245–258.

[23] Tony W. Buchanan and William R. Lovallo, "The Role of Genetics in Stress Effects on Health and Addiction," *Current Opinion in Psychology* 27 (2019): 72–76.

[24] Ibid., 73.

[25] Ibid.

[26] Koob and Schulkin, 245.

Sexual Addiction and Religiosity

It is a well-established fact that people who profess a religious affiliation are underrepresented in the criminal population and among those who become addicted to gambling, alcohol, tobacco, and other drugs.[27] The question may well be asked if having a relationship with God is also a protective factor against the temptations of sexual addiction.

Regular viewing of pornographic material on the internet, as an example of a potentially sexually addictive behavior, is significantly lower among religious people than in the general population but it still occurs, albeit at about half the rate of non-religiously affiliated people.[28] Yet, despite the fact that religiosity is linked to disapproval of internet pornography use, when pornography sales are analyzed, purportedly more religious areas appear to purchase more pornography.[29] One study shows that approximately one-third of Christian laity and clergy have reported visiting sites that promote sexually explicit material on the internet and about 18% of clergy have visited such sites more than once.[30] Several studies have also found a positive link between religiosity and the notion of sexual (particularly pornography) addiction, with many Christian resources such as books and videos dedicated to the discussion of this perceived addiction.[31] What do we make of these facts?

There appears to be evidence that because sexual activity outside of the marriage relationship is frequently associated with shame and guilt in religious circles, individuals with a religious background are more likely to regard and report themselves as addicted to pornography as a result of the implicit message of purity found in Scripture and the moral disapproval of pornography that exists within the church.[32]

There is no doubt that the viewing of internet pornography leads to a subjectively poorer relationship with God, possibly because of the guilt and shame experienced. Yet, it must be acknowledged that it is also linked to an increase in sexual activity, a precursor to the development of a sexual addiction and the likelihood of indulging in other risky behaviors, such as drug use.

---

[27] Alina Baltazar et al., "Internet Pornography Use in the Context of External and Internal Religiosity," *Journal of Psychology and Theology* 38/1 (2010): 32–40.

[28] Ibid., 38.

[29] Grubbs et al., 126.

[30] Christine J. Gardner, "Tangled in the Worst of the Web: What Internet Porn Did to One Pastor, His Wife, His Ministry, Their Life," *Christianity Today* 45/4 (2001): 42–49. See also Jesse W. Abell, Timothy A. Steenbergh, and Michael J. Boivin, "Cyberporn Use in the Context of Religiosity," *Journal of Psychology and Theology* 34, 2 (2006): 166.

[31] Grubbs et al., 127.

[32] Ibid., 129.

Researchers have raised the question of whether viewing pornography, in the privacy of one's own home, is less objectionable to the principles of young Christian men—and to a lesser degree, young Christian women—than indulging in premarital sex.[33] The distress and inner conflict that viewing pornography might conceivably evoke highlights two issues: 1) that sexual urges are an often unacknowledged part of our humanity, especially in the lives of young people and 2) that we should talk more openly about normal sexual development and needs within a Christian context.

Types of Sexual Addiction

Sexual addiction, as mentioned previously, can be a personal, private struggle or one that involves others.[34] Outwardly focused addictive behaviors can range from those that have limited impact on others to those that can result in a criminal conviction. In reality, however, this distinction is blurred, as any addiction—sexual addiction included—feeds on an escalation of the behavior or substance, and often involves indulging in riskier behavior to achieve the same result.

In a survey of persons with sexual addiction, "compulsive masturbation" was prevalent in 70% of a sample of 206 males, with masturbation featuring as the most common form of sexual expression over the course of a lifetime, regardless of marital status. "Pornography dependence" was reported by 50% of the sample and was significantly associated with compulsive masturbation and telephone sex dependence. "Telephone sex dependence" had a 25% sample prevalence and was associated with significant financial debt, compulsive masturbation, pornography dependence, and protracted promiscuity. It was also significantly associated with telephone scatologia (obscene telephone calls). Cybersex, another sexual addiction, uses the internet to meet potential sexual partners (significantly related to acquiring sexually transmitted diseases) or to engage in "virtual sex." Internet pornography users were predominately male, chat room participants were predominantly female, and both groups reported engaging in computer-associated sex for at least one to two hours per day, seven days per week.[35]

"Protracted promiscuity" included "one night stands," engaging prostitutes or escort services, serial sexual affairs, and repetitive casual sexual encounters in massage parlors, gay cruising areas, and pick-up bars. In the sample surveyed, 50% of males engaged in this type of sexual behavior.[36]

---

[33] Abell, Steenbergh, and Boivin, 169.

[34] Efrati and Mikulincer, 250.

[35] Kafka, 386.

[36] Ibid, 387.

In all these studies, males far outnumbered females in the samples surveyed and it should be noted that there is a significant subgroup of females who seek out treatment for sexual addiction who also report sexual abuse in the past.[37] The market share of pornography is, however, growing among women, among adolescent boys in particular, and even in very young age groups.[38]

Sexual addictions are associated with serious consequences, not the least being shame, guilt, anxiety, and depression, but also the increased risk of acquiring sexually transmitted diseases, unwanted pregnancies, marital difficulties, financial hardship, and impairment in work or educational roles.[39]

Let us take a closer look at the issue of internet pornography addiction.

Internet Pornography Addiction

It can be argued that for a very long time erotic art has been available to those who want to view it, but the internet has made pornography accessible to more people than ever before. It is estimated that up to 50% of all internet traffic is related to sexuality, and that pornography is the most frequently searched online topic.[40] Internet pornography is easily accessible, very affordable (sometimes free), and can be viewed in the privacy of one's home, thereby making it virtually anonymous (the "Triple A Engine").[41] Men between the ages of eighteen and twenty-five are the most frequent consumers of internet pornography, but women also search for internet pornography and even children are exposed to it.

In the secular world skepticism surrounds the notion of sexual addiction in general and pornography addiction in particular. Yet, despite clinical skepticism, many people regard themselves as addicted to internet pornography. This includes some who have a strong faith and may even be employed in a ministerial capacity.[42] There is a relationship between perceived addiction to pornography and reported religious affiliation and practices. This robust positive relationship is unrelated to actual hours of pornography consumption.

---

[37] Kafka, 388.

[38] Gabriele Kuby, *The Global Sexual Revolution: Destruction of Freedom in the Name of Freedom* (Kettering, OH: LifeSite, 2015), 124.

[39] Kafka, 389.

[40] Mary Short, Thomas Kasper, and Chad Wetterneck, "The Relationship Between Religiosity and Internet Pornography Use," *Journal of Religion and Health* 54/2 (2015): 571–583.

[41] Al Cooper, David L. Delmonico, and Ron Burg, "Cybersex Users, Abusers, and Compulsives: New Findings and Implications," *Sexual Addiction & Compulsivity* 7/1–2 (2000): 5–29.

[42] Bernie Anderson, *Breaking the Silence: A Pastor's Story of Going Public About His Private Battle With Pornography* (Hagerstown, MD: Autumn House, 2007).

Definition and Description

Pornography can be defined as visual as well as explicit, sexually arousing text materials, including magazines, internet images, and videos. This material can be legal or illegal and include images and material relating to children, adolescents, adults, and animals.[43] Pornography is described as "poison to the soul," which the mind has no way of "unseeing" once those images have been seen.[44]

Given the lack of official recognition of the problematic use of internet pornography, most definitions have focused on either an objective description of the problem (e.g., more than eleven hours of pornography viewing per week) or subjective reports of distress and perceived lack of control.[45] Research surrounding the topic of internet pornography continues to grow, with much of the work focusing on the potential negative effects of internet pornography consumption.

Prevalence

A 2013 article in the Huffington Post highlights the vast reach of internet pornography among all age groups and levels of society when it states that "Porn Sites Get More Visitors Each Month than Netflix, Amazon, and Twitter Combined."[46]

Researchers generally find lower levels of addiction to substances and gambling among people of faith, but the studies on internet pornography consumption are mixed. Some studies show sales of pornography in more religious areas to be higher than less religious areas.[47] Other studies find that college students who regard themselves as religious are less likely to ever have viewed or to be currently viewing pornography.[48] What is undisputed, however, is that the more religious people regard themselves to be, the more likely they are to feel guilty about pornography consumption.[49] The pairing of shame and sexuality came about as a result of sin, and shame is an integral part of sexual addiction.[50]

Effects of Internet Pornography Consumption

When consuming internet pornography, the individual indulges in a type of voyeuristic behavior, looking in on strangers engaged in one

---

[43] Kafka, 383.

[44] Kuby, 121.

[45] Grubbs et al., 126.

[46] Kuby, 122.

[47] Grubbs et al., 126.

[48] Short, Kasper, and Wetterneck, 581.

[49] Grubbs et al., 127.

[50] Davidson, 51.

of life's most intimate acts. This leads to a sense of depersonalization, with the actors viewed as objects, enabling sexual arousal in whoever is watching them.[51]

There is no arguing that internet pornography is addictive and, as with all addictions, it results in a loss of freedom.[52] It enslaves those who succumb to its seduction, desensitizing them to the humanity of those they are watching and leading them into a spiral of escalation where more explicit, more risky, and often more deviant images are needed to bring about the same level of arousal.

The addiction cycle often starts with the person experiencing stress or other unpleasant emotions (trigger), which they "escape" by consuming pornography (behavior), and the sexual release they experience (reward) makes them feel temporarily better. All this happens in the brain, mediated by various chemicals such as dopamine, and is a very powerful process.[53] Once an addiction cycle has been set up, the brain is altered forever.[54]

Sexual addiction, maintained through the use of pornography, has an effect on the social, emotional, and spiritual life of an individual. Within the marriage relationship, separation and divorce are not uncommon when one partner has, in effect, had an affair with pornography.[55] A sense of separation from God is also frequently reported.[56]

Like the apostle Paul, the person caught in this web of addiction may very well cry out, "Oh, what a miserable person I am! Who will free me from this life that is dominated by sin and death?" (Rom 7:24).

Recovery from Sexual Addiction

There is no easy road out of sexual addiction. The first step has to be an acknowledgement that internet pornography or any sexual addiction is contrary to God's desire for His children: "Let there be no sexual immorality, impurity, or greed among you. Such sins have no place among God's people" (Eph 5:3). This acknowledgement should, however, be framed within the understanding that sexual integrity and purity are possible through the grace of God.

The second step is a practical one: addiction is like a fire, and if the fire is to go out one has to stop feeding it.[57] The Bible admonishes us,

---

[51] Kuby, 125.

[52] Ibid., 127.

[53] Brewer, 80.

[54] Koob and Schulkin, 245.

[55] Kuby, 132.

[56] Baltazar et al., 33.

[57] Brewer, xvii.

"But put on the Lord Jesus Christ, and make no provision for the flesh, to fulfill its lusts" (Rom 13:14, NKJV). This step, simple as it is, is probably the most challenging one for those addicted to internet pornography, and accomplishing it requires commitment to a life of purity, honesty, accountability, and a daily reliance upon the strength of the Lord.

The third step is finding an accountability partner, someone who will help one stay committed to the goal of not viewing pornography. The Bible says, "Two people are better off than one, for they can help each other succeed. If one person falls, the other can reach out and help. But someone who falls alone is in real trouble" (Eccl 4:9–10). In addition to finding an accountability partner would be the recognition that one needs all the help one can get: therefore, making use of software on the computer to block access to pornography is a sensible precaution, as would be joining an accountability group such as a fellowship that encourages honesty and openness about life's struggles among its members.

Finally, considering one's own heart and the stresses that make life difficult might help reduce the fuel that drives an addiction. Not everyone has access to a counselor, but a good friend who knows how to listen and is willing to help bear one's burdens may prove to be very helpful. "Confess your sins to each other and pray for each other so that you may be healed. The earnest prayer of a righteous person has great power and produces wonderful results" (Jas 5:16).

Summary and Conclusion

God created humankind with an intrinsic desire for sexual interaction, thereby providing the incentive for men and women to live in relationship with one another. But in our fallen world we need to recognize that there are situations that call for wisdom. Not everyone finds a life partner where sexual desire can legitimately be expressed, and the challenges of singleness and celibacy are great. Although not everyone will have this view, the apostle Paul regarded celibacy as a gift: "I wish everyone could get along without marrying, just as I do. But we are not all the same. God gives some the gift of marriage, and to others he gives the gift of singleness" (1 Cor 7:7).

In some instances, couples find there are differences in their respective desires for sexual expression and this too is a challenge. Illness, the side effects of medication, stress, and other factors can all affect one's desire for sex. Paul, in 1 Corinthians 7, does, however, admonish married couples not to deprive one another of sexual intimacy unless there is agreement between them to refrain from sexual intimacy for the purpose of giving themselves more completely to prayer. When God said "It is not good for the man to be alone" (Gen 2:18), He endorsed human sexuality

—not only for the purposes of procreation, but also for "relationship, companionship, partnership."[58]

When sexual expression, however, becomes a purely selfish act—such as in the case of sexual addiction—it does not serve its purpose of connecting us to our spouses, and God's good gift of sexuality becomes distorted.

Sexual addiction, including internet pornography addiction, is a reality in the world in which we live. With the rise of the internet has come easy, affordable, anonymous access to pornography. Due to its strong effect on the reward system in the brain and the fact that it taps into a very human desire, it is no wonder that dependency on this type of stimulation is growing, even among Christians.

Christians are not immune to the stresses of life or the allure of sexual addiction. Acknowledging our humanity and dependency on God for help is essential. Giving ourselves permission to be vulnerable with one another can be a powerful way of ensuring accountability and one of the most powerful ways of maintaining our resolve to live a life that honors God.

[58] Davidson, 42, 50.

CHAPTER 9

Prostitution and Human Trafficking: Current Issues and Biblical Principles

Vanderlei Dorneles and T. P. Kurian

Sex is a gift from God, to be enjoyed within the boundaries of the marriage bond as defined in Scripture. As such, sex gives expression to sexual intimacy and provides for the procreation of the human race. Unfortunately, what was supposed to be an exclusive union between a man and a woman within the covenant of marriage is often corrupted by the devastating effects of sin, one of which is prostitution. Inasmuch as it entails the selling of the body, prostitution also closely resembles the crime of human trafficking, whether for sex or labor.

Strikingly, more than two centuries after the advent of modernity, problems with human trafficking are increasing. Article 4 of the United Nations Universal Declaration of Human Rights states, "No one shall be held in slavery or servitude; slavery and the slave trade shall be prohibited in all their forms."[1] However, reports from the last twenty years have shown that this phenomenon is increasing, especially the trafficking of men and children. In popular imagination, slavery ended with "the dismantling of the transatlantic slave trade" and was "completely abolished in the United States with the passage of the Thirteenth Amendment in 1865." But "slavery, also known as human trafficking, is alive and well"[2]—even in Europe and America, where the modern mindset about human rights emerged.[3]

---

[1] Cf. Yvonne C. Zimmerman, *Other Dreams of Freedom: Religion, Sex, and Human Trafficking* (New York: Oxford University Press, 2013), 3.

[2] Ibid.

[3] See Laura Lederer, *Modern Slavery: A Documentary and Reference Guide* (Santa Barbara, CA: Greenwood, 2018).

This trend is connected to recent conditions of globalization and deterritorialization,[4] which have made migration a widespread phenomenon. Clearly, the "modern world is in a state of flux and turbulence,"[5] and those movements produce the phenomenon of deterritorialization, which "have a profound effect on the way we understand our sense of belonging in the world."[6] In this context, ancient social problems are returning. Traditional types of forced labor, such as chattel slavery and bonded labor, are "still with us in some areas, and past practices of this type haunt us to this day . . . [and] disturbing forms such as forced labor in connection with trafficking for human beings are now emerging almost everywhere."[7]

According to another writer, the term "globalization" describes a number of different and sometimes heterogeneous processes, such as "deregulation of work, market flexibility, privatization of previous state tasks, neo liberalization of economy, and denationalization of politics."[8] The opening of new markets and the expansion of global trade and investment create opportunities and needs for migration. However, "the geographical and social mobility of persons" is much more complex than that of goods and capital.[9] This is a greater problem for people coming from poor countries.

In poorer countries, globalization brings forth new forms of unemployment, poor distribution of income, social polarization, and major cuts to social welfare programs. Social instability "pushes young unemployed women, single mothers, women with low social and educational status, and migrant women in Western countries to seek economic shelter in the sex industry."[10] In addition to prostitution, other forms of human trafficking are part of the picture of globalization and deterritorialization. Usually, people fall into the hands of traffickers through migration that goes wrong. Traffickers offer to help migrants

---

[4] About the processes of globalization and deterritorialization and their effects on culture and the notion of identity and belonging, see Nikos Papastergiadis, *The Turbulence of Migration: Globalization, Deterritorialization and Hybridity* (Cambridge: Polity, 2007).

[5] Papastergiadis, 1.

[6] Ibid., 2.

[7] Ronaldo Munck, "Globalisation, Governance and Migration: An Introduction," in *Globalisation and Migration: New Issues, New Politics*, ed. Ronaldo Munck (New York: Routledge, 2009), 9.

[8] Maria Markantonatou, "Globalization," in *Encyclopedia of Prostitution and Sex Work*, ed. Melissa Hope Ditmore, vol. 1 (Westport, CT: Greenwood, 2006), 186.

[9] Ibid.

[10] Ibid.

cross borders and find employment in new countries.[11] "More or less legal cartels and syndicates of organized trafficking take advantage of the social vulnerability of women in economically challenged areas such as eastern Europe, the Balkans, Southeast Asia, and Africa."[12]

The prevalence of this phenomenon requires evaluation of its borders and implications in terms of Christian values and principles. This study discusses prostitution and human trafficking and their implications in society. It begins with analyses of data on prostitution and human trafficking based on reports from the United Nations and researchers in the field. This study also seeks to evaluate the impact of human trafficking in the modern and postmodern worlds from a biblical and theological perspective. The goal of the analyses is to highlight biblical concerns and requirements for Christians as the people of God in a world perverted by the presence of evil.

Prostitution and Human Trafficking in the World

Prostitution and human trafficking are closely related. In order to understand these current phenomena, one needs to define and measure them in general terms in the context of globalization. Currently, human trafficking and social problems expose people to sexual exploitation, which makes prostitution rates increase. Following this logic, the issue of human trafficking is discussed first, followed by prostitution.

The definitions of these issues are taken from the United Nations Protocol to Prevent, Suppress and Punish Trafficking in Persons, Especially Women and Children (UN Protocol on Trafficking). It is the primary international agreement addressing the issue of trafficking, or "the transport and trade in human beings for the purpose of exploitation."[13] Increases in transnational organized crime prompted an international agreement in the United Nations, and the UN Protocol on Trafficking represents "the first major international agreement on the actions states should take to combat this problem."[14]

---

[11] Cf. Elina Penttinen, *Globalization, Prostitution and Sex-Trafficking: Corporeal Politics* (New York: Routledge, 2008).

[12] Markantonatou, 1:187.

[13] Kinsey Alden Dinan, "United Nations Trafficking Protocol," in *Encyclopedia of Prostitution and Sex Work*, ed. Ditmore, 1:512. The General Assembly of the United Nations adopted the UN Protocol on Trafficking in November 2000, and it entered into force in December 2003, after reaching the "necessary forty-state ratifications" (ibid.).

[14] Ibid. According to Dinan, during the 1990s, "trafficking in persons—and particularly the traffic in women and children for sexual purposes—attracted growing attention from governments and civil society worldwide, resulting in numerous national, bilateral, and regional anti trafficking policies and programs" (Dinan, 1:512).

An important function of the UN Protocol on Trafficking is to define "trafficking in persons" in an authoritative and international way.[15] The protocol states that "trafficking in persons" means:

> The recruitment, transportation, transfer, harboring or receipt of persons, by means of the threat or use of force or other forms of coercion, of abduction, of fraud, of deception, of the abuse of power or of a position of vulnerability or of the giving or receiving of payments or benefits to achieve the consent of a person having control over another person, for the purpose of exploitation. Exploitation shall include, at a minimum, the exploitation of the prostitution of others or other forms of sexual exploitation, forced labor or services, slavery or practices similar to slavery, servitude, or the removal of organs.[16]

The dark business of trafficking in persons to exploit them for labor or sex may be one of the fastest growing areas of criminal activity. "A study by the International Labor Organization estimates that the criminal profits of human trafficking could exceed 31 billion dollars, which would make it the second largest source of illegal income worldwide after drug trafficking."[17] The US State Department has produced oft-quoted estimates of the size of the trafficked population worldwide: between eight hundred thousand and nine hundred thousand annually.

However, F. Laczko says, there are many reasons why data on trafficking is so poor, since "trafficking is a clandestine activity, and most cases probably go unreported because victims are reluctant to go to the authorities, or are unable to do so because of intimidation and fear of reprisals."[18]

The Global Report on Trafficking in Persons, launched by the United Nations Office on Drugs and Crime (UNODC) in 2016, shows that the traffic of men had increased in the previous ten years, although most human beings trafficked are still women and children. In 2006, based on data from 155 countries, the most common purpose of human

---

[15] "Earlier international conventions, such as the 1949 Convention for the Suppression of the Traffick in Persons and of the Exploitation of the Prostitution of Others and the 1979 Convention on the Elimination of All Forms of Discrimination against Women, condemn trafficking, but without explicitly defining the term" (ibid.).

[16] Frank Laczko, "Introduction," *International Migration* 43, no. 1–2 (2005): 10. Cf. Dinan, 512.

[17] Elzbieta M. Gozdziak and Micah N. Bump, *Data and Research on Human Trafficking: Bibliography of Research-Based Literature* (Washington, DC: Georgetown University, 2008), 13.

[18] Laczko, 12.

trafficking (79%) was sexual exploitation. The victims of sexual exploitation are predominantly women and girls. To the surprise of many, in 30% of the countries that provided information on the gender of traffickers, women made up the largest proportion of traffickers. Thus, in some parts of the world, women are trafficking women. Tragically, this 2006 report shows that almost 20% of all trafficking victims are children. Based on data from 158 countries, this report shows that 51% of victims were women, 21% were men, 20% were girls, and 8% were boys. The increase in male trafficking is largely for the purpose of physical labor, which means slavery. The number of children has also increased. The report shows that in 2004, 10% of the female victims were children, but in 2014 20% were. In 2004, women were 74% of victims, compared to 51% in 2014. In this same period, the percentage of men increased from 13% to 21% and the percentage of children increased from 3% to 8%.[19] The increase in male trafficking is one of the most significant data points of the last years,[20] especially for those who believe that traditional slavery is an issue of the past.[21]

According to the 2016 UNODC report, sexual exploitation and forced labor are the most prominent reasons for trafficking, with 51% occurring for sexual exploitation and 36% for forced labor. Other forms of exploitation are child soldiers, removal of organs, selling children, and forced marriage.[22] The main destinations for trafficked people are Europe, North America, and Asia. Among the male victims, 85.7% were trafficked for forced labor and 6.8% for sexual exploitation. Among female victims, 72% were trafficked for sexual exploitation and 20% for forced labor.[23]

---

[19] UNODC, *Global Report on Trafficking in Persons 2016* (New York: United Nations Office on Drugs and Crime, 2016), 23.

[20] Zimmerman, 8, remembers that "for many years the [US] State Department estimated that 80 percent of the individuals who are trafficked transnationally every year are women and girls, and that 70 percent of female victims are trafficked into the commercial sex industry, even though the veracity of those numbers could not be corroborated. Current evidence indicates that women experience human trafficking at only slightly higher than of men." Thus, "vulnerability to human trafficking is not simply a matter of an individual's gender." Human trafficking is "not essentially about sex" and sex trafficking is "not even the largest category of trafficking."

[21] The code of Hammurabi is the first document to mention slavery (1720 BC). From 700 BC on, there is evidence of an African slave trade that operated within the Saharan region and served as a trading point. In 413 BC, during the war between Greeks and Turks, the slave trade was prevalent. There is also evidence that from ancient Egypt, Babylon, Persia, Greece, and Rome to medieval times, humans have been subject to various forms of physical and sexual slavery. From the fifteenth century on, countries such as Spain, North America, Holland, France, Sweden, and Denmark became more and more active in trading slaves (Annalisa Enrile, *Ending Human Trafficking and Modern-Day Slavery: Freedom's Journey* [London: Sage, 2018], 10–15).

[22] UNODC, 8.

[23] Ibid.

Many women are sexually exploited after being drawn in by the possibility of marriage. "For some, this is a result of being taken in by advertisements on the Web for brides for Western men."[24] Easily, they believe that they are going to be married to a rich man who will care for them. However, "they soon discover that they are enslaved." Others are forced to work as prostitutes. Some women and even children are "kidnapped, while others are sold by impoverished rural families to work in city brothels." In Thailand, for example, "young girls from the north are sold by their families to agents who, in turn, sell them on to brothel owners in the cities."[25] Additionally, "a widespread but less well-known practice is to kidnap people and remove their organs, such as their kidneys, to sell for transplant purposes." In Uganda, Burma, and the Sudan, "children are taken from their families and trained as soldiers."[26]

Thus, the postmodern world has seen ancient social dramas arise again. Current human trafficking differs from the institutionalized slavery of prior historical eras, but is not confined to remote and impoverished corners of the world. "In 2011, the U.S. State Department documented cases of human trafficking in 184 countries, including the United States."[27] The International Labor Organization estimates that 12.3 million people are enslaved worldwide in forced labor, and there are projections suggesting that twenty-seven million people live in conditions of slavery.[28]

The phenomenon of human trafficking for labor or sex comes along with the increasing popularity of diverse forms of self-prostitution, including among men. Deterritorialization and loss of the sense of belonging, so common in a postmodern and globalized world, tend to accelerate disconnection from family roots and traditional values. The postmodern increase in female prostitution and the popularization of male prostitution are connected to these conditions of globalization, deterritorialization, extreme liberation, and the loss of identity and belonging.

Prostitution and sex tourism are means of survival for many women in developing countries, where globalization, neoliberalism in the economy, and technology have stronger effects in terms of unemployment. Thus, two main factors drive people to prostitution: human trafficking and the globalized economy. For example, "India's New Economic Policy has resulted in increased poverty for women, forcing many of them into

---

[24] Marion L. S. Carson, *Setting the Captives Free: The Bible and Human Trafficking* (Cambridge: Lutterworth, 2016), 14.

[25] Ibid.

[26] Ibid.

[27] Zimmerman, 4.

[28] Ibid., 5.

sex work and trafficking. Approximately 200 Indian women and girls go into prostitution each day, and the number of sex workers is increasing rapidly."[29] The United Nations has estimated that "approximately 500,000 women are trafficked into Western Europe alone. Somewhere between 200,000 and 400,000 prostitutes are thought to be in Germany, the majority of whom are foreigners."[30] Most of the women working in Europe as prostitutes come from Russia and other countries of the former Soviet Union. "A higher estimate is reached if one believes that 50,000 Russian women alone are lured every year into sex business abroad." In the United States, it has been estimated that the number of foreign sex workers "varies between 200,000 and a half a million."[31] In 1999, UNICEF estimated that "there are 800,000 child prostitutes in Thailand; 400,000 each in Indonesia and India; and 100,000 in Philippines." Moreover, the number is "300,000 for the United States, and varies between 500,000 and 2 million in Brazil."[32]

The legal status of prostitution varies from country to country, ranging from being permitted and unregulated, to an enforced or unenforced crime, or a regulated profession. The numbers for common prostitution are very high. One estimates is that there are about forty-two million prostitutes in the world. In 2009, the annual revenue generated by prostitution worldwide was estimated at $400 billion; Spain was highlighted as having about five hundred thousand prostitutes, collectively earning $54 billion annually.[33]

Although male trafficking for forced labor is more common, men are also trafficked for sexual purposes. Male prostitution has been popularized in the last few centuries. The history of male prostitution extends deep into the past, although it was much less popular than "the world's oldest profession": female prostitution.[34] Nevertheless, although records indicate the existence of male prostitution in some ancient societies, in modern and postmodern times it has become a phenomenon. The rise of "male prostitution" as a recognizable pattern of behavior has been associated with the rise of "homosexuality" as a sexual category and

---

[29] Ashish K. Vaidya, ed., "Gender and Globalization," in *Globalization: Encyclopedia of Trade, Labor, and Politics*, vol. 1 (Santa Barbara, CA: ABC-Clio, 2006), 791.

[30] Ibid.

[31] Raimo Vayrynen, "Illegal Immigration, Human Trafficking and Organized Crime," in *Poverty, International Migration and Asylum*, ed. G. Borjas and J. Crisp (New York: United Nations University, 2005), 161.

[32] Ibid., 162.

[33] Paul Hanley, *Eleven* (Victoria: Friesen, 2014), 75.

[34] Kerwin Kaye, "Male Prostitution," in *Encyclopedia of Prostitution and Sex Work*, ed. Ditmore, 1:275.

subject of study.[35] In the late 1960s, the sexual markets began to open to male prostitution, and clients started to seek this form of sex even on the streets where they already sought female prostitutes. "Gay men began selling sex to one another in much larger numbers, mostly working off the street through escort agencies and ads." The changes in male prostitution associated with gay liberation led to a "significant reworking of the meanings associated with prostitution."[36]

Meanwhile, more significant and grievous in its occurrence and effects is the phenomenon of child prostitution. It is especially common in Asia, Thailand, and the Philippines, but verifiable all over the world. Although there is a debate over the definition, extent, and nature of child prostitution, the dangers to children who work as prostitutes are many. Among others, "the body of a child is often too small to have intercourse with an adult man, and early sexual activity can be physically damaging." Besides that, "the risks of sexually transmitted diseases are high, and children's relative powerlessness means negotiating condom use is difficult."[37]

Researchers have discussed the most appropriate terms for this phenomenon. Those who consider children unable to make this choice use the term "commercial sexual exploitation of children," and others "prostituted children." Others who consider them not simply passive victims use "child sex worker" or "child prostitute."[38] There are also discussions about the age at which to consider it "child prostitution," which varies with laws about the age of responsibility for criminal acts and decisions.

Child prostitution and human trafficking are connected. There is evidence of Burmese and Chinese girls in Thailand, Nepali girls in India, Vietnamese girls in Cambodia, and Eastern European girls in Western Europe being trafficked for prostitution. In addition, "there is a form of prostitution that involves children sold or debt-bonded by their parents."[39] Many of those children or juvenile prostitutes have "a history of abuse and have run away from home or care homes and are living on the street."[40] Moreover, "not all child prostitutes are girls."[41]

Child prostitution is explicitly forbidden by international law. Article 34 of the United Nations Convention on the Rights of the Child states,

---

[35] Kaye, 1:276.

[36] Ibid., 1:280.

[37] Heather Montgomery, "Child Prostitution," in *Encyclopedia of Prostitution and Sex Work*, ed. Ditmore, 1:98.

[38] Ibid.

[39] Ibid.

[40] Ibid., 1:99.

[41] Ibid., 1:100.

"Parties undertake to protect the child from all forms of sexual exploitation and sexual abuse." The article criminalizes "the inducement or coercion of a child to engage in any unlawful sexual activity; the exploitative use of children in prostitution or other unlawful sexual practices; and the exploitative use of children in pornographic performances and materials."[42]

Obtaining "detailed information about the children who work as prostitutes, their clients, their lifestyles, or their earning parents is extremely difficult."[43] It is unknown how many child prostitutes there are in the world, but "estimates for one single country range from 20,000 to 1,000,000 in Thailand and between 3,000 and 100,000 in the Philippines."[44]

Human sex trafficking exposes people to diverse forms of exploitation, violence, fraud, and coercion. "These individuals are essentially victims of modern-day slavery and may be physically assaulted and raped repeatedly over the course of months or even years."[45] Usually, the traffickers brutalize them physically and psychologically and gain total control over them, especially women and children. They are exposed to traumatic experiences, including "verbal and psychological abuse, enforced physical and emotional isolation, lack of basic human necessities, threats, forced abortions, physical assaults and violence, and sexual violence." Women have to continue prostituting even "when they are menstruating, pregnant, or sick." They know that "their family members may be threatened or hurt as a way of pressuring them into continuing to prostitute."[46]

In general, "the abuse that is constant in prostitution, indeed endemic to it, requires dissociation from yourself and the world to survive."[47] Incest, sexual harassment, rape, verbal and physical abuse, battering, and torture are common sufferings in a continuum of violence. The physical trauma produces acute anxiety, depression, insomnia, irritability, flashbacks, emotional numbing, and a state of emotional and physical hyper-alertness.

Organized institutions, churches, and governments may not ignore these extreme conditions of abuse and exploitation of human beings equally created in the image of God. Christian communities and societies

---

[42] UN General Assembly, "Convention on the Rights of the Child," opened for signature November 20, 1989, entered into force September 2, 1990, United Nations, Treaty Series, vol. 1577, https://treaties.un.org/Pages/ViewDetails.aspx?src=IND&mtdsg_no=IV-11&chapter=4&lang=en (accessed August 30, 2020).

[43] Montgomery, 1:100.

[44] Ibid.

[45] Elizabeth K. Hopper and Jose A. Hidalgo, "Posttraumatic Stress Disorder," in *Encyclopedia of Prostitution and Sex Work*, ed. Ditmore, 1:365.

[46] Ibid.

[47] Catharine A. MacKinnon, *Butterfly Politics* (Cambridge, MA: Belknap, 2017), 170.

must take a decided position against these unjust practices. These reactions need to take into account what the Bible says about these social problems.

Prostitution in the Bible

An Old Testament Overview

Narratives with a bearing on sexuality are common in the Old Testament, some bearing witness to the fact that deviations and distortions of sexuality, such as prostitution, occurred in ancient Israel. Indeed, prostitution appears in both narrative texts and laws in the Old Testament. "The most common word for 'prostitute' is *zonah*, which refers to any woman engaging in unauthorized sexuality, be it prostitution, adultery, or premarital sex."[48] A secondary term for "prostitute" is *qedeshah* ("female") or *qedesh* ("male"), which is used for prostitution in ritual contexts. Prostitution is also common as a metaphor for idolatry, especially in the Prophets.

In Genesis 38, when Tamar disguises herself, her father-in-law Judah sees her as a *zonah* (Gen 38:15). However, his friend calls her a *qedeshah* when he carries the payment for her "service" (Gen 38:21).[49] In Genesis 34:31, Jacob's sons say that by possessing Dinah sexually and humiliating her, Shechem treated her as a prostitute (*zonah*). The verb *zanah* can refer either to "illicit sexual immorality in general or to practicing prostitution (sex for hire), depending upon the context."[50] Another scholar notes that "the label *zonah* is used for the professional prostitute who accepts payment for her services, but perhaps can also be applied simply to a woman who had sex before marriage (Lev 21:7, 14)."[51] Another writer agrees that "the root *zanah* includes the concepts of promiscuity and adultery,

---

[48] Stephanie Lynn Budin, "Ancient World," in *Encyclopedia of Prostitution and Sex Work*, ed. Ditmore, 1:35.

[49] Avaren Ipsen, "Biblical Prostitution," in *Encyclopedia of Prostitution and Sex Work*, ed. Ditmore, 1:61, considers "the basis for translating the Hebrew word *qedeshah* as 'cult prostitute'" weak because it "literally means, 'consecrated' or 'sacred.'" He says that in the story of Tamar in Genesis 38:21–22, the word for prostitute, *zonah*, was thought a synonym for the word *qedeshah*. "These texts in conjunction with Hosea 4:14 formed the basis for translating the other instances where the word *qedeshah* appears in the Bible (Deut 23:17–18; 1 Kgs 14:24; 15:12; 22:46; 2 Kgs 23:7) to mean 'sacred prostitute.' Assyriologists once thought that the cognate terms in Akkadian and Ugaritic texts also indicated that *qedeshah* meant a 'cultic prostitute,' but the new consensus is that it merely indicates 'temple personnel,' perhaps of slave status without any cultic sexual responsibilities. *Qedeshot* were perhaps in the category of unattached women able to engage in prostitution without criminal penalty."

[50] Richard M. Davidson, *Flame of Yahweh: Sexuality in the Old Testament* (Peabody, MA: Hendrickson, 2007), 302.

[51] Elaine Adler Goodfriend, "Prostitution: Old Testament," in *The Anchor Yale Bible Dictionary*, ed. David Noel Freedman, vol. 5 (New York: Doubleday, 1992), 505.

in addition to prostitution."[52] In Genesis 34, this use of *zanah* for sexual relations outside marriage and prostitution indicates that both behaviors were condemned. In Deuteronomy 22, Moses uses the term *zanah* ("whore") to condemn the behavior of a girl who had sex before marriage with another man (Deut 22:21). Thus, prostitution and adultery or fornication are equally condemned.

Another way Genesis 38 condemns prostitution or sex outside marriage is through the juxtaposition of Judah and Joseph's stories (Gen 37, 39). The narrator juxtaposes the two narratives intentionally. Joseph's tunic, wet in blood, *hides* his brothers' *crime* (Gen 37:33), as Judah's belongings serve to *expose* his sin (Gen 38:18, 25–26). The text also shows that when Judah saw Tamar, he desired her sexually (Gen 38:15), but when Potiphar's woman saw Joseph and invited him to lie with her, he decided not to take her (Gen 39:7–8). This juxtaposition contrasts "the sexual wholeness in the life of Joseph with sexual fragmentation in the experience of Judah."[53] The narrator draws a parallel between the crime of Joseph's brothers and Judah's relation with a woman who looked to him like a prostitute. In this way, through the construction of the narrative, the Bible clearly condemns prostitution and sex outside marriage just as it does the crime of Joseph's brothers.

Leviticus 21:7–9 forbids priests to marry former prostitutes, and says that priests' daughters caught in prostitution are to be burnt to death. These restrictions are applied to the house of the priesthood, not to lay people. However, Deuteronomy 23:17 directly forbids prostitution among the Israelites: "There shall be no whore [*qedeshah*] of the daughters of Israel, nor a sodomite [*qadesh*] of the sons of Israel."[54] The former usage of *zanah* and *qedeshah* in reference to Tamar (Gen 38:15, 21) being disguised as a prostitute suggests that *qedeshah* here is about any kind of prostitution, and thus should not be restricted to cultic prostitution.

The Torah makes "explicit the implicit condemnation of prostitution in the Genesis narratives."[55] God even prohibited bringing "the hire of a whore [*zanah*], or the price of a dog [*keleb*, lit., 'dog', a person who practices homosexuality], into the house of the Lord thy God for any vow: for even both these are an abomination [*to'evah*] unto the Lord thy God" (Deut 23:18).[56] Leviticus 18 uses the word "abomination" (*to'evah*) in reference

---

[52] Esther Marie Menn, *Judah and Tamar (Genesis 38) in Ancient Jewish Exegesis: Studies in Literary Form & Hermeneutics* (New York: Brill, 1997), 67.

[53] Davidson, 298.

[54] All biblical quotations are from the KJV, unless otherwise indicated.

[55] Ibid., 306.

[56] In another reading of this text, discarding the ethical implications, Carson, *Setting Captives Free*, 83, argues that the prostitute is associated with uncleanness because "all sexual activity is associated

to illicit sexual relations like incest, polygamy, adultery, homosexuality, and zoophilia. One scholar argues that "several laws prohibit 'prostitution' in the sense of noncultic sex for hire."[57] For instance, Leviticus 19:29 says, "Do not prostitute thy daughter, to cause her to be a whore [*zanah*]; lest the land fall to whoredom [*zanah*], and the land become full of wickedness [*zimmah*]." The other uses of the noun *zimmah* in this context are to reprove incest (Lev 18:7; 20:14) and the Benjamites' collective rape of the Levite's woman, who was cut into pieces and sent to the Israelites (Judg 20:6).

This law is very clear in stating that the land, the society, would be defiled by the practice of many kinds of sexual deviations because of the toleration of prostitution. It is clear also in Leviticus 19:29 that God condemns both prostitution and the person (male or female) who makes someone a prostitute. However, Mosaic law does not make prostitution a "capital crime" punished by death, aside from the case of a priest's daughter. This could be due to divine tolerance for "possible circumstances of male abuse that would virtually force a woman into prostitution, so that she would not be primarily to blame."[58]

Moreover, Judges 16:1 introduces another Old Testament narrative that mentions the topic in the context of Samson's relationship with a prostitute. The narrative starts with Samson's birth, announced by an angel, who said that he would be a "Nazirite [*nazîr*] unto God" (Judg 13:5), which means "separated" (*nazar*) "unto the Lord" (Num 6:2), "from the womb to the day of his death" (Judg 13:7). However, Samson's life was full of contrasts and paradoxes. The Spirit of the Lord was on him (Judg 13:25), but he had a descending trajectory at each step. The Bible says he "went down" to Timnah and fell in love with one "of the daughters of the Philistines" (Judg 14:1, 3). After leaving home, he took honey from the body of a dead lion (Judg 14:9), which was unclean (Lev 22:8). Samson offered a "feast" (Judg 14:10), supposedly with "wine" and "strong drink." These three things were prohibited even to his parents before his birth (Judg 13:7). Samson's relation with a "whore" at Gaza was part of his descending trajectory from the Nazirite vow to a life of uncleanness and disobedience. A marriage relationship with a prostitute was prohibited for priests, who were "holy" unto God (Lev 21:7), like Samson was.

---

with ritual impurity—bodily fluids must be washed away prior to participation in the cult." He adds, "Married couples who have sexual intercourse are considered ritually unclean until evening (Lev 15:18), as is any man who has an emission of semen." According to him, "anthropologically, the explanation for these laws may be that bodily fluids, such as semen or blood, when outside the body, are 'matter out of place,' waste material that is a source of ritual pollution." In this sense, "as a promiscuous woman, the prostitute is ritually unclean much of the time."

[57] Davidson, 306.

[58] Ibid.

Samson developed erotic relations "in the indulgence of unrestrained or unlawful sexual passions."[59] The narrative of Samson and the harlot of Gaza "records a display of physical lust outside marriage." Indeed, the erotic exploits of Samson reveal a "decadent sexuality in which the wholistic divine ideal has been hopelessly fractured," and "the spiritual dimension is ignored in the self-centered search for what 'please me well' (Judg 14:3, RSV)."[60]

Another Bible character whose story leads some interpreters to consider prostitution a non-condemned practice is Rahab of Jericho, in Joshua 2 and 6. Rahab emerges in the narrative as one who believes in God when no one else does. Her unworthy life as a prostitute stands in contrast to her faith, even before the Israelites attack Jericho. She stands out as a faithful and intelligent woman who saw a chance to escape and took advantage of it. She makes a very impressive speech to the spies: "I know that the Lord hath given you the land, and that your terror is fallen upon us, and that all the inhabitants of the land faint because of you." She adds, "For we have heard how the Lord dried up the water of the Red sea. . . . And as soon as we had heard *these* things, our hearts did melt . . . for the Lord your God, he is God in heaven above and on earth beneath" (Josh 2:9–11). In the conquest of Jericho, Joshua orders the fulfillment of the spies' promise and saves Rahab and her house. That she gives up her life of prostitution is clear in the fact that she becomes a wife of Salmon, with whom she begat Boaz, becoming an ancestor of King David and the Messiah (Matt 1:5; cf. Ruth 4:21).

One scholar highlights that nobody expected anything from Rahab —"at least not anything of moral strength, courage, or insight"—because she was a prostitute, "the lowest of the low." However, such negative expectations heighten the "sense of wonder and surprise when these expectations are not met." Rahab displays loyalty, courage, and altruism. Thus, "the outcast harlot turns out to be a heroine of faith." Indeed, "she leaves her prostitution and is embraced by the community of Israel."[61] The emphasis in this case, when Rahab is presented as "the harlot Rahab" (Heb 11:31; Jas 2:25), is clearly to highlight the power of forgiveness, in addition to the astounding attitude of faith on the part of a prostitute and pagan woman.

The Bible story of the prostitutes asking Solomon to judge their dispute about a child may indicate that "Israelite society, like modern ones, tolerated a certain amount of prostitution, but it was clearly immoral

---

59 Davidson, 309.

60 Ibid.

61 Ibid., 308.

and the sages sternly warned against it (Prov 23:27; 29:3)."[62] On the other hand, the depiction of King Ahab's disgrace after his death (1 Kgs 22:38), when prostitutes washed in his blood at the pool of Samaria, "also illustrates the dishonor of their profession."[63]

Cultic Prostitution

The connection between prostitution and idolatry is mentioned often in the Bible. Ancient Canaanite rituals used to mix feasts to the gods with feasts of the flesh. There are evidences of cultic prostitution among the Sumerians, Babylonians, Egyptians, Hittites, and Canaanites, and highlights what Davidson calls the "foundational premise encountered already in the Mesopotamian myths: the processes of nature are controlled by the relations of the gods and goddesses."[64] In particular, according to this view, the fertility of nature resulted from the sexual union of a male god and his consort, a female goddess. This view was the base of the link between prostitution and pagan religion. According to the Baal cult, "the land is fertilized by the sperm (rain) of Baal," and thus it was crucial that sexual activity was stimulated.[65]

The story of the worship of the golden calf in Exodus 32 shows that the Israelites were not exempt from this perverted practice of sexuality. The same picture appears frequently in the history of Israel.

Although the Hebrew term *zonah*, "prostitute," in certain instances appears to be a general term encompassing the cult prostitute, there is a distinct term for the cult or religious prostitute.[66] This term is *qedeshah*, "whore" or "cult prostitute." Its root is *qadash*, which means "set apart for the use of the deity." The masculine counterpart is *qadesh*, "sodomite" or "male cult prostitute." These people (men and women) considered themselves "consecrated to their gods for the purpose of religious prostitution."[67]

The inclusion of prostitution or sexual promiscuity as part of pagan rituals has to do with the role of religion in the understanding of the ancient world, which was much more focused on survival than ethics. In Canaan, the fertility cult was a central part of religion and probably in volved sexual intercourse.[68] The ancients thought that sacred prostitution

[62] William B. Nelson Jr., "Prostitution," in *Evangelical Dictionary of Biblical Theology*, Baker Reference Library (Grand Rapids, MI: Baker, 1996), 647–648.

[63] Menn, 66.

[64] Davidson, 93.

[65] Ibid.

[66] J. Oswalt, "Prostitution," in *The Zondervan Pictorial Encyclopedia of the Bible*, ed. Merril C. Tenney, vol. 4 (Grand Rapids, MI: Zondervan, 1976), 910.

[67] Nelson Jr., 648.

[68] Davidson, 310.

was a form of sympathetic magic. "As people performed sex acts with the temple harlots, this stimulated sexual activity among the gods, ensuring the fertility of the soil."[69] Additionally, "ancient man viewed the universe as a closed system, where the actions of man, nature and deity were totally interlocked."[70] From this viewpoint, every year a man was expected to engage in "copulation with a dedicated prostitute, for this would produce the desired divine result" in terms of benefits from nature.[71]

Evidently, the Old Testament writers rejected this worldview and condemned the practice of sacred prostitution. The God of Israel is the creator of nature, and He never depends on ritual to force nature to benefit human beings. Besides that, the God of Israel is ever related "to moral and ethical ways." Thus, the practice of cult prostitution is viewed in the Bible as "an abomination."[72] Nevertheless, more abominable from the Bible's viewpoint was "male cult prostitution, since this practice involved the twin horror of paganism and homosexuality. One means of expressing this abhorrence was by calling the male cult prostitute a *dog*."[73]

However, although strictly prohibited to Israel, cultic prostitution that was "prominent in the Canaanite religions" was indeed "incorporated into Israelite worship well into the period of the divided kingdom,"[74] as indicated in Hosea 4:14 and 2 Kings 23:7. This disgusting sexual behavior, in fact, at times contaminated the worship of the true God. In Exodus 32, the feast before the golden calf degenerated into a pagan celebration involving sexual promiscuity. Aaron had said that the feast would be to the "Lord" (*Yahweh*), and the people woke up very early in the next day to drink, eat, and "play" (*tsakhaq*, Exod 32:5–6), which means that they had sexual experiences as part of this celebration. God says the people had "corrupted" themselves (Exod 32:7), and "Moses saw that the people *were* naked" (Exod 32:25, KJV). Other evidence of cultic prostitution in Israel appears in connection with Josiah's reform. As the biblical narrative reports, when Josiah purified the house of the Lord, he took out "the houses of the sodomites, that *were* by the house of the Lord, where the women wove hangings for the grove" (2 Kgs 23:7, KJV).

Although the Pentateuch clearly forbids the practice of sacred prostitution (Deut 23:17), the Israelites were attracted to this idolatrous and immoral behavior connected to religion even before they entered the

---

[69] Nelson Jr., 648.

[70] Oswalt, 4:911.

[71] Ibid., 4:912.

[72] Ibid.

[73] Ibid.

[74] Ernest D. Martin, *Toward a Biblical Theology of Marriage: A Study of the Bible's Vocabulary of Marriage* (Eugene, OR: Wipf and Stock, 2010), 55.

Promised Land (Num 25:1–5). Based on 1 Samuel 2:22, some scholars argue that Eli's sons, who slept with the women who ministered at the entrance to the tabernacle, were engaged in cultic prostitution,[75] thus borrowing a Canaanite practice.[76]

Indeed, "sexual immorality linked with the pagan fertility cult rituals formed an integral part of the sin at Baal of Peor, as with the worship of the golden calf at Sinai."[77] Numbers 25:1 says that "the people [*'am, here* "men"] began to commit whoredom [*zanah*] with the daughters of Moab." What is striking on Numbers 25:1 is that "this is the only place in the Hebrew Bible where the verb *zanah* refers to the sexual activity of men, not women. *Men* are committing harlotry/prostitution."[78] By using a term elsewhere reserved to describe the sexual activity of women, the narrator clearly links the "sexual activity to the spiritual harlotry of Israel against Yahweh, a phenomenon of 'dual harlotry' (religious and carnal) that will appear again and again throughout the OT canon."[79] Thus, in Numbers 25:1 *zanah* refers to apostasy from the covenant, expressed in the form of intercourse with the Moabite women.

Prostitution as a Metaphor

Since the idolatrous festivals promoted sexual activities, it was natural to refer to them with images of prostitution. This is the third way the Bible talks about this sexual deviation: as the metaphor of "spiritual prostitution." In the Bible, the metaphorical use of prostitution designates covenant unfaithfulness.

In Exodus, Moses reports that God made a covenant with Israel and entered into a salvific relationship with them. In Exodus 6:4, God reminds Moses of His covenant with Abraham, Isaac, and Jacob. At Sinai, God says, "If ye will obey my voice indeed, and keep my covenant, then ye shall be a peculiar treasure unto me above all people; for all the earth *is* mine" (Exod 19:5). Soon after, God exhorts them to "make no covenant with them [Canaanites], nor with their gods" (Exod 23:32). In this context, a covenant relationship with pagans was tantamount to a covenant with their gods. Since Israel had their covenant with God, being His "peculiar treasure," a relationship with any other god would

---

[75] See Donald G. Schley, *Shiloh: A Biblical City in Tradition and History*, Supplement Series 63, *Journal for the Study of the Old Testament* (Sheffield: JSOT Press, 1989), 71; and Chad Brand et al., eds., "Phinehas," *Holman Illustrated Bible Dictionary* (Nashville, TN: Holman Bible Publishers, 2003), 1294–1295.

[76] Nelson Jr., 648.

[77] Davidson, 100.

[78] Ibid.

[79] Ibid.

be spiritual adultery or prostitution. Solomon loved and established covenant relationships with pagan women who were Egyptian, Moabite, Ammonite, Edomite, Zidonian, and Hittite (1 Kgs 11:1), and they led him to serve their gods (1 Kgs 11:1–2). So did King Ahab, who married Jezebel of the Zidonians, "and went and served Baal, and worshipped him" (1 Kgs 16:31).[80]

These kings broke the covenant with God and prostituted themselves in a spiritual sense. God says, "Lest thou make a covenant with the inhabitants of the land, and they go a whoring after their gods, and do sacrifice unto their gods, and *one* call thee, and thou eat of his sacrifice" (Exod 34:15). The connection between spiritual prostitution and common prostitution is clearly established: "And thou take of their daughters unto thy sons, and their daughters go a whoring [*zanah*] after their gods, and make thy sons go a whoring [*zanah*] after their gods" (Exod 34:16). In this text, the word *zanah* that usually refers to common prostitution is used in reference to spiritual prostitution.

From this perspective, the covenant relationship between Yahweh and Israel was like that of husband and wife; thus, when the Israelites went after other deities, they were prostituting themselves. The prophet Ezekiel uses female names for Samaria and Jerusalem to describe their harlotry with language that indicates an animal impulse on the part of the harlot (Ezek 23).[81] God tells Hosea to marry the harlot Gomer (Hos 1:2–3), and through this unstable relationship, marked by adultery, the infidelity of Israel is portrayed. When Gomer was unfaithful, Hosea accepted her back in love (Hos 3:1–3). In the same manner, God took Israel as His bride (Hos 2:15), but Israel prostituted herself to the Canaanite deities (Hos 2:2–13). In accepting his wife back, Hosea exemplified the mercy of God to His sinful people. Many other prophets use this metaphor (Isa 1:21; 23:15–18; Mic 1:7; Amo 7:17; Jer 3:1–10; Nah 3:4–7; Rev 17–19).

Thus, prostitution is widely used in the Old Testament as a metaphor for Israel's unfaithful behavior in its covenant with God. One scholar says that "adultery" (*na'aph*) would be more suitable for the characterization of Israel's relations outside of its "marriage bond" (the covenant)

---

[80] According to the Greek historian Herodotus, "all Babylonian maidens had to serve as prostitute in the temple of Mylitta" (Ipsen, 1:61).

[81] Davidson, 313, states that the prophets' descriptions of prostitution on the part of Israel, especially in Ezekiel 16 and 23, "contain an exaggerated emphasis upon the driving animal passions behind the physical sex act, often utilizing intentionally crude and even vulgar language to highlight the fragmented view of sexuality in prostitution, which has interest only in satisfying sensual urges." He adds that Ezekiel "paints the most lurid portrait of raw sex in prostitution, using what is perhaps the slang vocabulary in the brothels of that day. The harlot described in Ezek 16 and 23 is no ordinary harlot; she is a nymphomaniac."

than *zanah*, the legal term that applies also to premarital sex. This scholar presents five reasons for this use of *zanah* with this purpose: 1) The term *zanah* implies that the illicit activity is habitual or iterative, since the participle *zonah* describes the professional whore. 2) The motive, personal gain, is supplied. 3) *Zanah* implies a multiplicity of partners. 4) The participle *zonah* suggests a treacherous and hardened woman (Jer 3:3), and the concrete image of the whore is well suited for the personification of Israel as a woman. Finally, 5) the root *zanah* refers to illicit sex only by females, and because Israel in the covenant relationship adopts the feminine role, it is more fitting that a verb used strictly for females play a central role. She says "*na'aph*, on the other hand, refers to illicit sexual activity by both sexes—a *no'eph* is a man, whether single or married, who engages in sex with a married woman (Lev 20:10)."[82] Another scholar suggests a sixth reason for this use of *zanah*: "in prostitution . . . there is a fragmented emphasis upon the physical aspects of sex—animalpassions of raw and even vulgar sexuality —devoid of the wholistic contexts of commitment, exclusivity, and loving relationship."[83]

The consequence of exchanging God for other gods, seeking material or human benefits, is generally "a city or territory labeled 'whore' that is punished for its infidelity to God. The punishment is the invasion by conquering armies who plunder, rape, and burn."[84] Usually the enemies are former allies, or metaphorically, "lovers."

A New Testament Overview

The New Testament leaves no room for prostitution (cultic or secular) or any sexual activity outside marriage. "The term *porneia*, which LXX uses for both Hebrew words noted above [*zanah* and *qadash*], is sometimes translated as 'fornication' (which has the narrow definition of sex involving singles), but clearly it also applies to all sexual immorality."[85]

The strong language that Paul uses is justified by the popularity of prostitution in the Roman Empire. "Prostitution in ancient Rome was widespread and constituted an important aspect of the economy in terms of upper-class investment, state revenue, and female employment." Highly exploitative in nature, "it also enjoyed great symbolic importance."[86]

---

[82] Goodfriend, 5:509.

[83] Davidson, 311.

[84] Ipsen, 1:61.

[85] Martin, 56-57.

[86] Thomas A. J. McGinn, "Ancient Rome," in *Encyclopedia of Prostitution and Sex Work*, ed. Ditmore, 1:31.

Paul is very clear in stating that any sexual immorality defies sanctification. In declaring his view on prostitution, Paul argues in terms of the holiness of the body, acquired through the blood of Jesus. He says, "Know ye not that your bodies are members of Christ? Should I then take the members of Christ, and make *them* the members of an harlot? God forbid" (1 Cor 6:15). This strong language suggests that someone in the Corinthian community thought that "they could behave as they pleased (v. 12)."[87] Paul protests, "The body *is* not for fornication, but for the Lord" (v. 13). This indicates that some Corinthian believers held the dichotomy between body and spirit or mind.[88] Paul argues that believers' bodies will not be destroyed, but will be raised up at the end of time, as the Lord's body was raised up at the resurrection (1 Cor 6:14). Moreover, he states that the believers' bodies are no longer their bodies, but "members of Christ" (1 Cor 6:15). Since they were bought from sin by the blood of Jesus, they no longer belong to themselves.

As part of his argument, Paul talks about those who will enter the kingdom of God. In the list of those who will not enter, he includes the "unrighteous," "fornicators," "idolaters," "adulterers," "effeminate," and "abusers," together with thieves, covetous people, drunkards, revilers, and extorters. Paul concludes by saying that "such were some of you," but "ye are washed, but ye are sanctified, but ye are justified in the name of the Lord Jesus, and by the Spirit of our God" (1 Cor 6:9–11).

Thus, their bodies should not be prostituted or sold because they were acquired by the blood of Jesus. Christians no longer belong to themselves or to the world. They may not sell themselves or anyone else because everyone is God's particular property. This is a clear Bible statement against the practice of prostitution and human trafficking.

In this line of thought, in Paul's argument there is "no split between their bodies and their spirits [mind]." Christians are "spiritually and physically united in Christ (1 Cor 6:17)."[89] Thus, sexual involvement is much more than a mere physical experience. Paul quotes Genesis 2:24 to state that an encounter with a prostitute means that the two people become "one flesh." "And since flesh is not separate from spirit [mind], any sexual relationship must entail spiritual union."[90] One writer states

---

[87] Marion L. S. Carson, *Human Trafficking, The Bible, and the Church: An Interdisciplinary Study* (London: SCM Press, 2017), 93.

[88] Against this fragmented view of human beings, Davidson, 297, argues that in the Hebrew thinking behind the Old Testament, "human beings do not *have* souls, they are souls. Thus within the OT canon there is no room for any kind of Platonic dichotomy, no room for a compartmentalization of the things of the body and the things of the soul. Sexuality is wholistic, involving the whole being."

[89] Carson, *Human Trafficking, The Bible and the Church*, 94.

[90] Ibid., 94.

that "the view of sexuality is no longer that it is acceptable for men to get sexual satisfaction wherever they can get it. The New Testament view of the sexual drive is that it not only can be, but must be controlled."[91]

It bears noting that Jesus is depicted as habitually associating with disreputable persons such as "tax collectors and sinners" (see Mark 2:15; Luke 7:34; 15:1–2). Jesus also said that "publicans and the harlots go into the kingdom of God before" the Pharisees (Matt 21:31). Such passages, however, far from endorsing inappropriate lifestyles, show that those sinners and publicans "followed Jesus," while the scribes and Pharisees did not. This statement contrasts the two paradoxical and unexpected attitudes.

Jesus' attitude toward prostitution seems to be very clear in the story of the woman who anointed His feet at Simon's house. The text says directly that she "was a sinner" (Luke 7:37). Jesus' acceptance of her was clearly justifiable based on her repentance and forgiveness (Luke 7:43). Jesus clearly considered her life as a prostitute a sinful life. He says that her "sins, which are many, are forgiven" (Luke 7:47). At the end of the story, He says, "Thy faith hath saved thee" (Luke 7:50), which means that she converted and gave up her former life. Jesus pointed out that "harlots and tax collectors were quicker to repent, believe, and enter the kingdom of God than the proud religious leaders."[92]

The many prostitutes who accepted Jesus and followed Him, like this one who anointed His feet, highlight the very equal condition of all sinners before the grace of God. The icon of this great group is Rahab, "the prostitute." She became an Israelite by marriage with Salmon and was one of the ancestors of Jesus. Rahab is proof that former sinners can be great believers and worshippers of God. Moreover, the woman who anointed Jesus in preparation for death (John 12:7) also shows that those who repent from prostitution and believe in Jesus are received as sons and daughters in the kingdom of God.

Human Trafficking and the Bible

Human trafficking is less discussed in the Bible than prostitution. However, the Bible has a lot to say about selling or making money on human beings. The current problems of trading people for sex exploitation, organ extraction, or forced labor can also be understood from the viewpoint of creation and human value before God. As previously discussed, it is important to realize that the world today is seeing the reemergence of ancient practices like slavery and human trafficking for sex and labor. One may say the civilized world agrees that slavery is a

---

[91] Martin, 57.

[92] Nelson Jr., 648.

detestable practice that belongs to the past. However, the reality is that it is still with us, and in a stronger way. How can the Bible help the current world face this strange phenomenon?

One author notes that "the Old Testament, like the apostle Paul, receives a large measure of criticism for *tolerating* slavery." But, at the same time, this author recognizes that "slavery was such an integral part of the social, economic and institutional life of the ancient world contemporary with Old Testament Israel that it is difficult to see how Israel could have excluded it altogether or effectively abolished it."[93] Despite this, he states that "slavery in relatively small societies like Israel was qualitatively vastly different from slavery in the large imperial civilizations—the contemporary ancient Near Eastern empires, and especially the later empires of the Greeks and Romans."[94] In these cultures, slaves were captives of war and were put to degrading and dehumanizing labor.

It is clear that Israelite slavery was even more different from "the ghastly commercialized and massive-scale slave trade that Arabs, Europeans and Americans perpetrated upon Africa."[95] One writer defends that "slavery in Israel was quite different from that experienced by black slaves, and portrayed by Hollywood in such movies as *Django Unchained* (2012) and *12 Years a Slave* (2013)."[96] Moreover, the concept of slaves in the Old Testament differs from the Western concept. A slave in Israel could "love" his owner and decide to serve him even after being set free (Exod 21:5). That slave could be part of the family and receive an inheritance when there was no son (Gen 15:2). Additionally, the word "slave" is not even "the most helpful translation of the [Hebrew] word *'eved*, which basically meant a bonded worker, and in some circumstances would be a term of high office when applied to royal servants."[97]

In dealing with slavery in the Bible, one needs to consider the law in Exodus 21:1, which says that the Hebrew "servant" should serve for only six years, and then must be set free. The causes were debts and financial

---

[93] Christopher J. H. Wright, *Old Testament Ethics for the People of God* (Downers Grove, IL: InterVarsity, 2011), 333.

[94] Ibid.

[95] Ibid.

[96] Glauber S. Araujo, "Was God in Favor of Slavery?," *The Compass Magazine*, June 16, 2016, https://thecompassmagazine.com/blog/was-god-in-favor-of-slavery (accessed December 22, 2019). Araujo points out some differences between slavery in the colonial world and in the Old Testament Scriptures: 1) An Israelite was sold into slavery for only one reason: financial debt (Lev 25:39, 47). 2) A captured thief was expected to repay double what he stole (Exod 22:1–4). 3) People who owed money could also "sell themselves" (Lev 25:39, 47) as slaves, and pay their debt through work (2 Kgs 4:1), as Jacob's family did in going down to Egypt because of the famine (Gen 47:19). After paying their debts, the Israelites could go back to reclaim their lives.

[97] Wright, 333.

difficulties. Some circumstances could tie the servant to his master, such as a given wife, children, and even love and desire to serve him (Exod 21:4–5). In the case of debts, a man could sell even a daughter. In this case, she would not be set free like a male slave, but she could be a wife of the master or his son and receive the same rights as the daughters of the house (Exod 21:7–10).

Based on Exodus 21, it is noticed that "for the first time in the ancient Near East, legislation required treating servants as persons, not property."[98] P. Copan explains that in other ancient Near East cultures, "it was the *king* who was the image of their god on earth—and certainly not the slave."[99] In contrast, slaves in Israel were the very image of God for their masters. This is clear from Genesis 1:26–27, which affirms that human beings are created in the image of God, independent of their social condition as owners or slaves. "This doctrine serves as the basis for affirming the dignity and rights of every human."[100] By establishing conditions to free these slaves or servants, Mosaic law built on creation's base. Thus, "servants (slaves) in Israel, unlike their ancient Near East contemporaries, were given radical, unprecedented legal/human rights, even if not equaling that of free persons."[101] Evidently, the story of Moses commanding the Israelites, regarding the Midianite captives ("all the women children, that have not known a man by lying with him, keep alive for yourselves," Num 31:18), must be understood according to this law in Exodus 21 on the rights of female servants. There is no suggestion that those girls would be sexually exploited.

In addition, this law prescribes a penalty for violence against servants. "If a man beats his male or female servant with a rod, so that he dies under his hand, he shall surely be punished" (Exod 21:20). The maximum penalty for kidnapping and selling people was death (Heb *mut*, "to die," "kill," "have one executed," Exod 21:16; the same law is repeated in Deut 24:7). This is a key Bible law in dealing with human trafficking. The clear statement is that nobody shall be kidnapped or sold as property of anybody else.

With this law, the Old Testament affirms "the full personhood of these debt-servants," and elsewhere the Bible highlights this condition of all human beings (cf. Gen 1:26–27; Job 31:13–15; Deut 15:1–18). It thus appears that this is "a vastly different situation to that recorded of Africans fleeing from slave traders, for fear of being captured and sold into slavery."[102]

---

[98] Paul Copan, *Is God a Moral Monster?* (Grand Rapids, MI: Baker, 2011), 129.

[99] Ibid.

[100] Ibid.

[101] Ibid.

[102] Araujo.

In the book of Job, the patriarch recognizes that he and his servants have the same Maker and come from the same place—their mother's womb (Job 31:15). Amos also repudiates slavery (Amos 2:6; 8:6), and along with other prophets strongly rebukes the city of Tyre for its involvement in human trafficking (Amos 1:9; Joel 4:6; Ezek 27:13). Genesis 1:26–27 establishes once and for all the dignity and equality of all human beings. In fact, the Bible leaves no room for "trafficking humans" or treating them as chattel.

It has been aptly noted that "we have in the Bible the first appeals in the world literature to treat slaves as human beings for their own sake and not just in the interests of their masters."[103] Thus, "rather than treating slaves as objects, property, or dehumanized beings, Old Testament slave regulations elevated slaves to a level of dignity previously unknown."[104]

No Israelite should be enslaved beyond six years or after the Jubilee (Lev 25:39–43; Deut 15:12–18; Jer 34:14). The reason God gave for this prescription was that "they *are* my servants, which I brought forth out of the land of Egypt" (Lev 25:42). Since the Israelites were God's particular property (Exod 19:5), bought by the blood of the Passover (Exod 12), nobody could trade them. Although they could buy the children of the strangers, the Israelites should never enslave their brothers, because the Lord was their master. "For unto me the children of Israel *are* servants; they are my servants whom I brought forth out of the land of Egypt: I *am* the Lord your God" (Lev 25:55). The implication for today is that all people from other nations who accepted God as their master were also bought out of the world to be property of God.

Prescriptions such as the ones noted above were part of the civil law of ancient and theocratic Israel, and, of course, are not applicable this side of the cross.[105] However, it must be borne in mind that certain laws contained the theological principles that would undermine slavery. For example, in opposition to laws about slavery promulgated elsewhere

---

[103] Muhammad A. Dandamayev, "Slavery (Old Testament)," in *Anchor Bible Dictionary*, ed. David Noel Freedman, vol. 6 (New York: Doubleday, 1992), 65.

[104] Araujo.

[105] Roy Gane, *The Role of God's Moral Law, Including Sabbath, in the "New Covenant"* (Silver Spring, MD: Biblical Research Institute, 2003), 7–8, says that the traditional Christian distinctions between the "moral," "ceremonial," "civil," and "health" categories of law are interpretive classifications not explicitly stated in the Bible. However, "these categories can be quite helpful, provided that they are defined and applied carefully and accurately," although "the usual simplistic approach can lead to erroneous results with far-reaching consequences." He states that "a common approach is to regard moral laws as timeless and universal principles governing relationships with God and with other human beings. Ceremonial laws were applicable only to the Israelite ritual system. Civil laws were applicable only to ancient Israelite life under their government, especially under the theocracy. Health laws are timeless and universal because human bodies continue to function in the same way."

in the ancient Near East, according to which a runaway slave was to be returned to the master, Deuteronomy 23:15 says, "Thou shalt not deliver unto his master the servant which is escaped from his master unto thee." As one scholar aptly notes, "if consistently applied, such a prohibition would have eroded the entire institution of slavery."[106]

God's opposition to any form of slavery or human trafficking culminated in the cross, where His son died to redeem us from the slavery of sin, which entails every other kind of slavery. Thus, Christians must look to the power of the blood of Jesus over all humankind for the principles to evaluate human trafficking. In this sense, all human beings have been bought out of this world by the blood of Jesus (John 3:16; 1 Pet 1:18–21). All human beings belong to God for two main reasons: they were created by God in His image (Gen 1:26–27) and were redeemed by Christ (Col 1:20; 2 Cor 5:17). The Bible says, "The earth is the Lord's, and the fullness thereof, the world, and they that dwell therein. For he hath founded it upon the seas, and established it upon the floods" (Ps 24:1–2). God Himself proclaims that "all souls are mine; the soul of the father, so also the soul of the son is mine" (Ezek 18:4).

Since human beings are God's property, those who traffic and sell them are stupidly taking God's belongings, for whom Christ gave His life.

An illustrative text that shows the grievous nature of human trafficking in the Bible is Genesis 37, which tells why and how Joseph's brothers kidnapped and sold him. This story begins by stating that Jacob "loved Joseph more than all his brothers" (Gen 37:3). As the loved one, Joseph was "hated" by his brothers (Gen 37:4). He started to dream and told his dreams to his family. Because of that, the brothers "hated him yet the more" (Gen 37:5). His dreams continued, and his brothers "hated him yet the more for his dreams, and for his words" (Gen 37:8). Thus, a person was distinguished and separate from the others. Because of this distinction, Joseph's relations to his brothers became fragile. He came to be a kind of scapegoat, hated and worthy of death. Family relations were fragmented, and in this situation, eliminating Joseph was perceived as the only way to reestablish order. Thus, in a timely moment, "they conspired against him to slay him" (Gen 37:18). The mention of an "evil beast" (Gen 37:20) is not casual. Joseph became for his brothers a kind of alien. He was no longer like them. Although Judah said, "He *is* our brother and our flesh" (Gen 37:27), a complete separation between Joseph and his brothers is apparent in the words: "This have we found: know now whether it *be* thy son's coat or no" (Gen 37:32). Joseph was naked when he was sold to the Ishmaelites (Gen 37:23, 28). In turn, the Ishmaelites sold Joseph in Egypt

[106] Daniel C. Snell, "Slavery in the Ancient Near East," in *The Cambridge World History of Slavery*, vol. 1, *The Ancient Mediterranean World*, ed. Keith Bradley and Paul Cartledge (Cambridge: Cambridge University Press, 2011), 18.

(Gen 37:36). Using today's definition, the older brothers were guilty of human trafficking, and Joseph was a victim.

This story is full of negative feelings such as hate, guilt, and remorse. The desire to cut off the "other" from the family is very evident. When Joseph's brothers went down to Egypt in search of food, Joseph manifested himself to them, and "they were troubled at his presence" (Gen 45:3), of course, because they were conscious of the evil done to him. The story about the events after Jacob's death, involving Joseph and his brothers, is even clearer about the wickedness of hating, selling, and trading people. The brothers said, "Joseph will peradventure hate us, and will certainly require us all the evil which we did unto him" (Gen 50:15). In the narrative, selling a person is qualified as an "evil" act. This behavior is also qualified in the story twice as a "trespass" (*pesha*ʿ, "transgression," "rebellion"), once as a "sin" (*khata't*, "sinful"), and twice as an "evil" (*ra*ʿ, "bad," "injury," "distress," Gen 50:17). From the above it becomes clear that the biblical laws, narratives, and other statements leave no room for defense or tolerance of any kind of slavery or sex exploitation.

Conclusion

The Bible has a lot to teach about human value before God, especially when one considers it in the light of God's original plan for humanity. The experience of the fall, instead of giving Adam and Eve a new perspective as the tempter had suggested, drove them to a narrow view that was passed to their descendants. Becoming self-centered, human beings lost the conscience of the image of God within them. This state of ignorance led them to treat and relate to each other as mere material belongings. The original relationship between "I and thou" was replaced by the superficial and sinful relationship "I and it."[107] Without consciousness of the divine image as the essence of their being, people are willing to use or sell themselves (prostitution) and others (human trafficking) as if they were bodies without feelings, people without names, mere equipment and belongings. Thus, other people and even our own bodies are seen as means to please and serve ourselves.

Prostitution and other sexual behaviors have to be considered from the viewpoint of God's original plan for human sexuality. Behavior such as prostitution and other extramarital sexual encounters "usually reduces sexuality to a business proposition and almost always to a promiscuous focus upon the physical sex act itself."[108] These sexual experiences are

---

[107] Writing from his Hebrew background from the beginning of the twentieth century, Martin Buber, *I and Thou* (New York: Scribner, 1970), says that human life loses its meaning when relationships are artificial with the reduction of the "other" to one "thing."

[108] Davidson, 303.

"fragmented from the wholistic links of the intellectual, emotional, and especially the spiritual dimensions." Based on the Genesis story of creation, one may conclude that "the discussion of prostitution/harlotry is included under this facet, wholeness versus fragmentation, of sexual theology."[109]

In this perspective, prostitution is to be seen as a fragmentation that affects humanity in several aspects of its original creation: wholeness, dignity, holiness, and possession by the Creator. "As in Eden, wholistic sexuality not only includes the sex, but is manifested in every aspect of human existence—physical, mental, social, and spiritual."[110] Thus, prostitutes (male or female) and prostitute users (male or female) disgust God with their degrading and destructive behaviors.

According to the Seventh-day Adventist Church's statement on this issue, "sexual practices which are contrary to God's expressed will are adultery and premarital sex, as well as obsessive sexual behavior. Sexual abuse of spouses, sexual abuse of children, incest, homosexual practices and bestiality are among the obvious perversions of God's original plan."[111]

The condition of sin fragmented human beings' view of themselves, and that is the basis of every sexually perverted behavior. At the same time, it affects their view of others. Every single form of relationship is affected by the self-centered orientation of sinful humanity. People are able to use, hate, sell, and even kill their brothers, the flesh of their flesh and bones of their bones. However, although this is the condition of the sinful world, Christians must neither adopt nor condone it.

As noted above, the Bible has a lot to say about and against prostitution and human trafficking. However, a biblically informed view on these acts entails much more than mere condemnation of them. "As the redeemed people of God, Christians are no longer in thrall to the ambitions and power-struggles of the world in which we live."[112] God calls His people to defend those who belong to Him by creation and redemption. The people of God must work for the justice, dignity, and freedom of other human beings. "Human trafficking compromises the dignity of victims, perpetrators, and those who use the services they provide."[113] Trading in human beings and exploiting them is one of the most disgraceful forms of violation of God's law and human rights.

---

[109] Davidson, 303.

[110] Ibid.

[111] This statement was approved and voted on by the General Conference of Seventh-day Adventists Executive Committee at the Annual Council Session in Washington, DC, October 12, 1987.

[112] Carson, *Human Trafficking, The Bible and the Church,* 56.

[113] Ibid., 105.

Every single person trafficked or prostituted was created in the image of God, and nothing about his or her social condition can change that. Prostitution and human trafficking are a vile business. Human trafficking is absolutely unbiblical, and Bible-believing Christians are to work to promote freedom in Christ. The followers of Jesus must follow His example in proclaiming liberty to captives and freedom to prisoners, as well as forgiveness and complete restoration for those who repent from their evil behavior and accept Jesus. Thus, it is our responsibility not only to pray but also to speak out against human trafficking, and use our means and influence to restore those victimized by this tragic crime.

CHAPTER 10

On Rape: Biblical and Theological Perspectives

Dragoslava Santrac and Aleksandar Santrac

Rape is more than just forcible, non-consensual sexual intercourse. Rape is sexual horror and a crime. Although there are different cultural and religious understandings of rape, there seems to exist a prevalent view that rape is evil. Even intuitively, without the impact of formal moral education or religious instruction, most people feel that coercive and violent forms of sexual interaction must be deeply wrong. As one scholar puts it, "it is somehow wrong not to feel revulsion at rape."[1] Yet, rape and attempts of rape happen every day and in almost every part of the world.[2] This study addresses the following key questions in an attempt to tackle the issue of sexual abuse: What constitutes rape? Why is rape evil? What are the leading factors contributing to the occurrence of rape?

The first part of this study seeks to acknowledge the gravity and complexity of the problem of rape by identifying the different forms of rape and recent statistics of the prevalence of rape in various parts of the world. The second, main part of the study explores how rape and its related issues are addressed in Scripture. Finally, this study offers a discussion of some main contributors to the prevalence of rape today and some suggestions of how to alleviate trauma that results from rape. For Scripture-abiding believers, Scripture defines good practices for human flourishing and well-being, and corrects wrong ways in all human conduct, including sexual behavior (2 Tim 3:16–17).

---

[1] Simon G. Harrak, *Virtuous Passions: The Formation of Christian Character* (New York: Paulist, 1993), 2.

[2] See the section "Statistics of Rape Incidents" in this chapter.

Prevalence of Rape

The various forms of rape and recent rape statistics reveal that rape is far more prevalent than some people believe.

Forms of Rape

> A basic definition of rape describes rape as sexual penetration accomplished against a person's will by means of physical force or threat of bodily harm or when the victim is incapable of giving consent; the latter condition usually involves cases in which the victim is mentally ill, developmentally disabled, or intentionally incapacitated through the administration of intoxicating or anesthetic substances.[3]

An expanded definition includes other specific aspects of rape, including the gender of aggressors and victims to be male as well as female, the age of aggressors and victims to be underage individuals as well as adults, forced anal and oral penetration as well as vaginal intercourse, and coercion to sexual intercourse by instigating fear of losing the partner or certain privileges as well as by physical force.[4]

The definitions of rape show that rape involves not only actions (forceful sexual intercourse and physical abuse), but also attitudes that produce those actions (for example, psychological and emotional coerciveness, extortion, manipulation, and threats). In other words, rape does not occur only in the obvious cases that involve physical violence, but also in the less evident situations in which sexual favors are obtained through psychological and emotional intimidation or other kinds of non-physical pressure that coerce people to participate in the sexual act against their will.

Recent studies have revealed the prevalence of various forms of rape: acquaintance rape, college student rape, marital/spousal rape, gang rape, rape as a military weapon, and other forms.[5] Some public disclosures of rape allegations reveal the alarming fact that rape is often difficult to corroborate because some assaulters do not admit any wrongdoing and argue that sex was consensual. The apparent ambiguity of what represents full consent to sex and what does not is one of the greatest challenges for

---

[3] Neil Gilbert, "Advocacy Research Exaggerates Rape Statistics," in *Women, Men and Gender: Ongoing Debates*, ed. Mary Roth Walsh (New Haven, CT: Yale University Press, 1996), 237.

[4] Idem, "Rape: Are Rape Statistics Exaggerated?," in *Women, Men, and Gender: Ongoing Debates*, 233.

[5] For more information, see, e.g., Edward J. Bayer, *Rape Within Marriage: A Moral Analysis Delayed* (Lanham, MD: University Press of America, 1985) and Diana Fritz Cates, "Experiential Narratives of Rape and Torture," *Journal of Religious Ethics* 38, no. 1 (2010): 43–66.

the demarcation of rape. There seems to be a wrong assumption among some people that all responses other than a strict "no" are an implicit "yes."[6]

Statistics of Rape Incidents

According to the World Health Organization's (WHO) 2016 report, violence against women, particularly intimate partner violence and sexual violence, are major public health problems and violations of women's human rights. Global estimates published by WHO indicate that about one in three women, or 35 percent of women worldwide, have experienced physical and/or sexual violence in their lifetime. The pervasiveness of sexual abuse of women varies in different parts of the world. For example, according to WHO's multi-country study on women's health and domestic violence in 2005, the prevalence estimates range from approximately 15 percent of women in Japan to 71 percent of women in Ethiopia who reported physical and/or sexual violence.[7] A 2013 analysis by WHO of the existing data from over eighty countries found that worldwide the prevalence estimates range from 23.2 percent in high-income countries and 24.6 percent in the Western Pacific region to 37 percent in the Eastern Mediterranean region and 37.7 percent in the Southeast Asian region.[8]

The tragic death of Nirbhaya in December 2012, after she was gang-raped and tortured in a bus while traveling with her boyfriend, caused international and local outrage, and raised global awareness of the ongoing issue with sexual abuse and violence against women in India.[9] A woman is raped every twenty minutes in India.[10] Rape, including child rape, is increasing in South Africa. In 2002 the University of South Africa reported that one million women and children were raped

---

[6] Courtney Ray, "Wrong Is Wrong! … Right?," *Spectrum*, September 1, 2016, http://spectrum-magazine.org/article/2016/09/01/wrong-wrong-right (accessed December 29, 2019).

[7] "Violence Against Women," World Health Organization, November 29, 2017, https://www.who.int/news-room/fact-sheets/detail/violence-against-women (accessed September 16, 2020).

[8] Ibid.

[9] Anjana Kashyap, "Delhi Gangrape Victim's Friend Relives the Horrifying 84 Minutes of December 16 Night," *India Today Online*, last modified September 14, 2013, http://indiatoday.intoday.in/story/delhi-gangrape-victims-friend-relives-the-horrifying-84-minutes-of-december-16-night/1/309573.html (accessed December 29, 2019). Cases of other rapes in India have appeared in the news. E.g., Mansi Tewari, "Delhi's unknown Nirbhaya: Horrifying story of teenager who was tortured and gang-raped for days and then left for dead in Haryana," *Daily Mail*, February 7, 2014, http://www.dailymail.co.uk/indiahome/indianews/article-2554218/Delhis-unknown-Nirbhaya-Horrifying-story-teenager-tortured-gang-raped-days-left-dead.html (accessed December 29, 2019).

[10] Samantha Bresnahan, Sumnima Udas, and Ram Ramgopal, "'Nirbhaya,' victim of India gang rape fought for justice," *CNN*, last modified December 15, 2013, http://www.cnn.com/2013/12/04/world/asia/nirbhaya-india-rape (accessed December 29, 2019).

there each year. The appallingly high rate of rapes of babies in Africa since 2001, who required extensive reconstructive surgery to rebuild urinary, genital, abdominal, or tracheal systems, increased the need to address the problem socially and legally.[11]

Islamic law forbids any sexual relationships outside marriage (Quran 5:5; 24:30), yet male sexual violence against women and girls is a major problem in contemporary Muslim societies. Human and women's rights organizations and media and government reports regularly detail the occurrence of numerous forms of such violence including molestation, incest, rape, marital sexual abuse, and forced marriages.[12]

In the United States, various surveys, including Justice Department crime statistics and Centers for Disease Control and Prevention reports, reveal alarming data on sexual abuse and violence in modern America.[13]

Acquaintance rape is the most predominant form of rape in the world. According to some statistics, an estimated 75 percent of rapes occur between people who know each other. This means there is a much greater possibility of a woman being raped by someone she knows than by a stranger. Although most occurrences of rape involve intimate partner violence committed by men against women, the rates of rape that involve sexual abuse of children and men are also high. Some surveys indicate that in the college population, for example, 12 to 16 percent of male students have been forced into sexual intercourse by female dating partners, usually by verbal pressure.[14] International studies reveal that approximately 20 percent of women and 5–10 percent of men report having been victims of sexual assault as children.[15]

Adult males are not the only group contributing to the rise of rape. According to the National Center for Juvenile Justice, juveniles accounted for 14 percent of all forcible rape arrests in the United States in 2010. An estimated 67 percent of these arrests involved youth aged fifteen to seventeen. Males accounted for 98 percent of these arrests.[16]

---

[11] Eileen Meier, "Child Rape in South Africa," *Pediatric Nursing* 28, no. 5 (2002): 532–533.

[12] Hina Azam, *Sexual Violation in Islamic Law: Substance, Evidence, and Procedure* (New York: Cambridge University Press, 2015), 1–2.

[13] Matthew J. Breiding et al., "Prevalence and Characteristics of Sexual Violence, Stalking, and Intimate Partner Violence Victimization—National Intimate Partner and Sexual Violence Survey, United States, 2011," *Surveillance Summaries* 63, no. 8 (2014), https://www.cdc.gov/mmwr/preview/mmwrhtml/ss6308a1.htm (accessed December 29, 2019); and "Rape and Sexual Assault," Bureau of Justice Statistics, Office of Justice Programs, https://www.bjs.gov/index.cfm?ty=tp&tid=317 (accessed September 28, 2018).

[14] Andrea Parrot and Laurie Bechhofer, eds., *Acquaintance Rape: The Hidden Crime* (New York: Wiley, 1991), x, 165–166, 198.

[15] "Violence Against Women," World Health Organization.

[16] Melissa Sickmund and Charles Puzzanchera, eds., *Juvenile Offenders and Victims: 2014*

As devastating as they are, the current statistics of rape incidents give only a partial picture of sexual violence in the world. Most rapes are never reported due to many intricate reasons. For example, attempts by some rape victims to share their personal experiences are jeopardized by society's victim blaming, denial of rape, distortion of truth, exaggeration of numbers of false rape claims, and indifference.[17]

A brief examination of the forms and statistics of rape reveals that rape affects millions of women, children, and men worldwide. Although perpetrators and victims of rape are both men and women, statistics indisputably demonstrate that rape is predominantly a male crime. The shocking prevalence of rape yields the conclusion that for many people obtaining sexual favors through coercion and violence, inside and outside marriage, is acceptable or considered a minor offense. This conclusion leads to an important question: What are the main contributing factors to such prevalence of rape? This study argues that rape and its contributors are the results of sin and represent violation of the biblical ideal of sexuality and the value of human life.

Biblical View of Sexuality

Scripture recognizes the value of sexuality in human life, and regards sexuality as a God-created gift to be enjoyed within the confinements of marriage. Erotic dialogues and images in the Scripture, especially in the Song of Songs, show that sexual pleasure must not be a taboo, and is not only permissible but desirable in marriage. God created sexual intimacy to be a special means of generating a unique and affectionate bond between a husband and a wife (Gen 2:24), which would also bring forth posterity (Gen 1:28). Adam and Eve reflected the perfect bond ("one flesh"), which is an incentive for genuine sexual intimacy (Gen 2:23–25). Sexual identity as an integral part of the relational aspect of the image of God was designed by the Creator to be a portal into *other-centeredness*, not *self-centeredness*. In other words, the impetus for sexual intercourse

---

National Report (Pittsburgh, PA: National Center for Juvenile Justice, 2014), 127, https://www.ojjdp.gov/ojstatbb/nr2014/downloads/chapter5.pdf (accessed December 29, 2019).

[17] Jody Raphael, *Rape Is Rape: How Denial, Distortion, and Victim Blaming Are Fueling a Hidden Acquaintance Rape Crisis* (Chicago, IL: Lawrence Hill, 2013), 1–5. "According to the National Crime Victimization Survey (NCVS) in the United States, only 28.3% of rapes and other sexual assaults are reported to the police." Yet, some studies reveal that "Western countries are more likely than non-Western ones to pass anti-rape laws to protect women from sexual violence. Therefore, in comparison with women in non-Western countries, women in Western countries may have strong attitude toward gender equality and be well aware of their legal rights as sexual assault victims and, as a result, are more likely to report their experiences to the police, in search of justice" (Don Soo Chon, "Police Reporting by Sexual Assault Victims in Western and in Non-Western Countries," *Journal of Family Violence* 29, no. 8 [2014]: 859–860).

should not revolve around one's own pleasure, but rather the pleasure of the other. Sexual expression of the couple's unity is meant to enhance their emotional, physical, and spiritual bond. Hebrew *yada'*, "to know," which is commonly used to depict sexual intercourse in Scripture, conveys more than the physical sexual act driven by passion (Gen 4:1; 1 Sam 1:19). Generally *yada'* depicts knowledge, which is "experiential, emotional, and, above all, relational," and encompasses "a range of meanings that include involvement, interaction, loyalty, and obligation."[18] The emphasis of this term seems to be on the exchange of intimate, unspoken information that takes place in properly contextualized sexual activity within a marriage, as well as on love and care transmitted in that act. Sexual intercourse thus becomes a vital element in the communication between spouses.[19]

Sexual experience is a *holistic* encounter. This means that the sexual act engages the whole person—namely, the person's physical, emotional, mental, and spiritual aspects. A holistic encounter in the sexual act takes place when two persons connect and exchange pleasure on every level of their personhood, not just on the physical level. As one scholar points out, sexual intercourse is a "meeting" point, not a "mating" point.[20] The sexual encounter generates closeness, and so is not just about procreation. It is a potent bonding activity. Genesis 2:24 describes a sexual encounter between a husband and wife as an act of joining together and becoming one. The word "join" (Heb. *dabaq*) in this text describes deep affection and loyalty. It often portrays one's commitment to God (Deut 10:20), and parts of the body sticking together (Job 41:23).[21] Sexual pleasure is maximized when the two souls and minds are united and at complete rest and peace with each other.

The immediate effects of the fall were seen in the disruption of the loving relationship between the man and the woman (Gen 3:12, 16). Very early in history, sinful human beings perverted God's gift of sexuality by making lust and sensuality the main tenets of sexuality (Gen 4:19; 6:2). Coercion and violence became part of some sexual experiences, as the early accounts of rape and attempted rape in the Bible demonstrate (e.g.,

---

[18] Nahum M. Sarna, "ידעתיו (*yeda'tiw*) Genesis," *The JPS Torah Commentary* (Philadelphia, PA: The Jewish Publication Society, 1989), 31.

[19] William C. Williams, "Sexuality, Human," in *Evangelical Dictionary of Biblical Theology*, ed. Walter A. Elwell (Grand Rapids, MI: Baker Books, 1996), 733.

[20] Ray S. Anderson, *On Being Human: Essays in Theological Anthropology* (Eugene, OR: Wipf and Stock, 1991), 106.

[21] Earl S. Kalland, "דבק (*dabaq*), cleave, cling," in *Theological Wordbook of the Old Testament*, ed. Gleason L. Archer Jr., Robert Harris, and Bruce K. Waltke, 2 vols. (Chicago, IL: Moody, 1980), 1:177–178.

Gen 19:4–9, 30–36; 34:2). As the corruption of human nature brought by sin has progressed, so have sexual sins and their contributors. Deviations from the revealed biblical design always result in emptiness, misery, and pain. Rape is thus an ultimate desecration of the Creator's plan for sexual intimacy.

Since people are sinful beings with a strong tendency to self-centeredness and exploitation of the other side in any relationship, the question that should be posed is: How can one generate genuine sexual intimacy based on trust, commitment, and a sense of security? The belief here is that genuine sexual intimacy is possible when the state of mind and motives of people, and so the setting of their relationships, are restored to their original innocence and purity. In the fallen world, sexual intimacy can reach its original and satisfying potential only in the context of God's plan of redemption. In other words, the discovery of genuine sexual intimacy and joy depends on the recognition of the delightful and wondrous grace and love of God revealed through His creation act and redemptive act through Christ.

Sexuality has a relational structure. Individuals thus cannot seek to satisfy primarily themselves and their personal wants without distorting and trivializing the core experience of sexual intimacy.[22] Sexual pleasure should be always directed towards the other. Pleasing the other in love through mutual self-giving is the essence of genuine expression of sexuality (1 Cor 7:3–4). "Thus 1 Corinthians 7:4 has a strong statement on mutual submission in sexual relations: 'For the wife does not have authority over her own body, but the husband does. Likewise the husband does not have authority over his own body, but the wife does.'"[23] Coercion in sexual relations is unacceptable. Any kind of oppression violates both the *imago Dei* and the explicit divine command. The gospel "frees both spouses from the fear and/or need of dominance that threatens to limit their mutual fulfillment in a Christian marriage."[24] Ellen G. White writes,

> Neither the husband nor the wife should attempt to exercise over the other an arbitrary control. Do not try to compel each other to yield to your wishes. You cannot do this and retain each other's love. Be kind, patient, and forbearing, considerate, and courteous.

---

[22] Rowan Williams, "Sexual Intimacy," in *Moral Issues and Christian Responses*, ed. Patricia Beattie Jung and L. Shanon Jung (Minneapolis, MN: Fortress Press, 2013), 109.

[23] Roberto Badenas, "Husband and Wife in Marriage," in *Marriage: Biblical and Theological Aspects*, ed. Ekkehardt Mueller and Elias Brasil de Souza (Silver Spring, MD: Review and Herald, 2015), 98.

[24] Ibid.

By the grace of God you can succeed in making each other happy, as in your marriage vow you promised to do.[25]

Notice that the ultimate goal of marital relations is to make both husband and wife happy and to honor God. Arbitrary control of one spouse over the other and compelling a spouse to yield to wishes of the other spouse result in losing the trust and love of the spouse who is oppressed. The aggressor loses not only the abused spouse's trust but also God's blessing in life (1 Pet 3:7), and ultimately incurs God's judgment (Rev 21:8). Only when both spouses demonstrate God's grace, kindness, and patience in their relationship can their marriage be filled with love and happiness.

Rape and the Value of Human Life

The biblical concept of sexuality is closely related to the biblical idea of the value of human life. The creation of humanity is set apart from the previous acts of creation by at least two key elements: First, whereas other creatures were created "according to its kind" (Gen 1:11–12, 21, 24–25),[26] the man and woman were made in the image of God (Gen 1:26–27). The image of God conveys the incomparable nature and infinite worth of human beings and enables their distinctive relationship with God and one another, which involves intimacy (Gen 2:18–25; 3:8) and moral accountability (Gen 2:16–17; 3:9–19). Their superior distinction is due to the fact that human beings alone of all creation on earth bear the exclusive "likeness" of their Creator. Second, only human beings have been given dominion in God's creation. This dominion is expressly stated to be over all living creatures in the sky, sea, and land, but not over fellow men and women (Gen 1:28).

However, a number of scholars see in the creation account a basis for a divinely ordained superordination of man and a subordination of woman, invoking that the woman was created from the man's rib and that she was created as the man's helper.[27] However, "[t]he relationship of the woman to the 'rib' entails no subordination, any more than man's being created from the ground implies his subordination to it."[28] The

---

[25] Ellen G. White, *The Adventist Home* (Hagerstown, MD: Review and Herald, 2001), 118.

[26] All biblical quotations are from the NKJV, unless otherwise indicated.

[27] Badenas, 80–81. For a more detailed analysis of gender issues in Scripture and a critical evaluation of the main arguments supporting divinely ordained hierarchical subordination of women to men, see ibid., 73–100.

[28] T. E. Fretheim, "The Book of Genesis," *The New Interpreter's Bible*, vol. 1 (Nashville, TN: Abingdon, 1994), 352.

creation of woman from man's rib implies the close connection between them and lays the groundwork for the understanding of marriage in Genesis 2:24. White remarks, "Eve was created from a rib taken from the side of Adam, signifying that she was not to control him as the head, nor to be trampled under his feet as an inferior, but to stand by his side as an equal, to be loved and protected by him."[29] A similar notion is conveyed in the depiction of woman as "a helper" (Gen 2:18, 20). Hebrew *'ezer,* "helper," describes "one who possesses the desire and the ability or capacity to help another, a partner."[30] It generally describes God as a helper (Ps 30:10; 54:4; 121:1–2; 146:5), and so has no derogative connotation. Significantly, after the fall, the language of Genesis 1:26–27 is repeated in Genesis 5:1–2 to stress that God's original plan for humanity had not been changed, and that no person was permitted to rule over felow human beings. Genesis 5:1–2 implies that after the fall both male and female are still considered equal and precious to God, as they both bear His image. The language of the divine plan of salvation also expresses the same truth (John 3:16; Gal 3:28). Unfortunately, the history of discrimination, slavery, racism, and abuse demonstrates how sinful humanity has been audaciously defying God in this matter.

God's will for humanity, as revealed in the creation account and the plan of salvation, grants each person immense and irrevocable value, dignity, and freedom of choice. Human beings are reduced to objects when they are treated as "mere bodies," with no regard to their emotions and other conditions and qualities of their personhood, as is the case with rape. Objectified human beings are denied their integral human right to personal autonomy and self-worth, and so are treated as sub-humans. Rape infringes upon the victim's human rights in a similar way as does torture, murder, and other violations of the body and soul. Rape and the threat of rape are fundamentally wrong, because rape violates God's will that each person should be treated with the highest moral consideration as one bearing God's image. God is portrayed as the sovereign refuge and avenger of the oppressed (Deut 32:35; Ps 9:9).

Incidents of Rape in the Bible

The following sections of the study seek to understand how rape is viewed and treated practically in the Bible, focusing on the biblical terminology, biblical laws dealing with rape, and the main cases of rape.

---

[29] Ellen G. White, *Patriarchs and Prophets* (Mountain View, CA: Pacific Press, 1913), 46.

[30] R. G. Branch, "Eve," in *Dictionary of the Old Testament: Pentateuch* ed. T. Desmond Alexander and David W. Baker (Downers Grove, IL: InterVarsity, 2003), 241.

Biblical Terminology

While no technical term for rape exists in biblical Hebrew, such a translation is fitting in certain cases. Each rendering of rape, however, depends on a thorough analysis of the vocabulary utilized, word order, and other textual clues, as well as a careful balancing of the social and cultural world of the text with the need to communicate content effectively in English.[31]

All three main biblical accounts identified with rape—the taking of Dinah in Genesis 34, the mob rape of the Levite's concubine in Judges 19, and the assault of Tamar in 2 Samuel 13—use the verb *'anah* to depict the sexual offense. This Hebrew verb is generally understood to convey affliction, humiliation, and oppression, and should be distinguished from its homonyms *'anah* I, "to answer"; *'anah* II, "to occupy"; and *'anah* IV, "to sing." The primary meaning of *'anah* III is "to force" or "to try to force submission," and "to punish or inflict pain upon." The verb can be rendered as "violate" (Deut 22:29, NIV, ESV, RSV). The meaning of force is demonstrated in numerous biblical texts.

For example, *'anah* is used to depict the pain inflicted on Joseph's ankles by the fetters (Ps 105:18). It describes the agony of Egyptian oppression (Exod 1:11–12). It designates what the lawless do to the defenseless (Exod 22:22) and the physical pain brought by war (Num 24:24). As such, the verb seemed suitable to the biblical writers to depict the forcing of a woman to sexual intercourse (Judg 19:24; 2 Sam 13:12, 14).[32]

Hebrew *'anah* conveys also the meaning of being humble or humbled (Exod 10:3; Deut 8:2). Sexual violation of a young girl is thus perceived as humbling or "making low" the girl, because her loss of virginity drastically decreases her marriageability and often results in the loss of bride price (Gen 34:2; Deut 21:14). This aspect of the meaning of *'anah* is rendered in Deuteronomy 22:29 and Judges 19:24 in some English versions (NKJV). It could be argued that sexual violation resulted not only in lowering the woman's social value as "damaged goods" for prospective marriage, but also in utter humiliation of her person, especially if the Hebrew texts are read within their original context of an honor-shame culture.

The use of the Hebrew verb *khazaq*, "to seize," in some biblical narratives reporting rape stresses the use of force and physical violence against the victim (Deut 22:25; 2 Sam 13:14). "The force in question here may or may not be psychological or social or political or emotional, but

---

[31] Sandie Gravett, "Reading 'Rape' in the Hebrew Bible: A Consideration of Language," *Journal for the Study of the Old Testament* 28, no. 3 (2004): 279.

[32] Leonard J. Coppes, "ענה (*'anah*) III, Afflict, Oppress, Humble," in *Theological Wordbook of the Old Testament*, ed. Gleason L. Archer Jr., Robert Harris, and Bruce K. Waltke, 2 vols. (Chicago, IL: Moody, 1980), 2:682.

must be physical/violent."[33] Although there is no mention of physical brutality in the incident of David and Bathsheba, David obviously used his kingly status and power to have sex with Bathsheba (2 Sam 11). One scholar convincingly argues that Bathsheba was a victim of "power rape" on the part of David. He compares the intercourse between David and Bathsheba to that between an adult and a minor, even a "consenting" minor, which is today called "statutory rape." The narrative flow suggests that David was responsible for Bathsheba's coming to the palace and highlights Bathsheba's vulnerability once she was inside the palace. If she were to cry for help, no one would dare to rescue her from the designs of the king. Even if Bathsheba acquiesced to intercourse under the psychological coercion of one in power over her, her forced consent was of no consequence and she was still a victim of David's "power rape."[34] God's judgment of David demonstrates the gravity of David's sin in God's eyes (2 Sam 12). The incident of David and Bathsheba illustrates an important point: a certain action can be sanctioned by culture and custom, and so not perceived as strictly illegal by some people, yet still morally wrong if it opposes God's standards of right and wrong that are revealed in His law (Exod 20:14, 17).

In the Old Testament, rape is depicted as *nebalah*, something outrageous or foolish, which is rendered in English as "a disgraceful thing" (Gen 34:7; 2 Sam 13:12), "a wicked thing" (NIV), "an outrageous thing" (ESV), or "wanton folly" (RSV). Rape is depicted as "a thing which ought not be done" (Gen 34:7), "a thing [that] has never been seen or done" (Judg 19:30, NIV), or "no such thing should be done in Israel" (2 Sam 13:12). Rape like any other sexual offense is undoubtedly outrageous and condemned in the Bible.

Biblical Laws Dealing with Rape

Although it does not address rape directly, the Decalogue ultimately seeks to prevent and censure some of the main underlying causes of rape. For example, the seventh commandment forbids adultery, and consequently all sexual relations outside of marriage (Exod 20:14). The eight commandment prohibits stealing (Exod 20:15). This commandment could be understood to refer not only to the theft of a person's material possessions, but also to robbing the person of her or his dignity, peace, health, and freedom of choice. The tenth commandment warns against coveting another man's wife (Exod 20:17). Coveting is an expression of

---

[33] Alexander Izuchukwu Abasili, "Was It Rape? The David and Bathsheba Pericope Re-examined," *Vetus Testamentum* 61, no. 1 (2011): 6.

[34] Richard M. Davidson, "Did David Rape Bathsheba? A Case Study in Narrative Theology," *Journal of Adventist Theological Society* 17 (2006): 88–89.

greed. In the case of rape, a person is consumed with great greed and lust, and is prompted to obtain the desired person by force.

Most biblical laws dealing with rape focus on the legal and social aspects of the offense. From the ancient Near Eastern–perspective, rape is an affair between men—namely, between the offender on one side and the violated woman's father, brothers, and/or other male guardian on the other side.[35] It is more akin to theft of property than theft of persons, for whereas kidnapping a person and selling him to slavery is a capital crime (Exod 21:16; Deut 24:7), biblical law—in accordance with the cultural context of the ancient Near Eastern views rape as a lesser offense, provided that the woman is unattached.[36] However, the high view of human dignity and gender equality reflected in the creation account leaves no room for diminishing the ugliness of rape. Remarkably, the biblical laws dealing with rape showcase only rape of a woman by a man, and not vice versa or homosexual rape. This is likely the case because incidents of rape in biblical times were largely done by men against women, as is still the case today. Yet this does not mean that the biblical law condones rape of a man by a woman or homosexual rape. A sexual offense committed by a man against a woman is consistently punishable by the law (Deut 25:11–12). We can surmise from Leviticus 20:13 that a sexual assault of a man by another man warrants a severe punishment by the law. This text assumes that both men willingly participated in the homosexual act, and so both men are punished. Yet we can conjecture from the regulations dealing with rape of a woman (Deut 22:25–27) that in cases of homosexual rape also only the rapist is punished, and never the victim. Likewise, rape involving incest incurs only the punishment of the perpetrator.[37]

---

[35] It is helpful to read biblical texts against their Near Eastern patriarchal cultural background. In such a culture, an individual's legal status was merely a function of his or her gendered position within the household. Only the household patriarchs possessed full legal status, and so only they, legally speaking, could be victims. Sons could expect to assume the full legal status and position within the household upon the father's death. This was not the case, however, for daughters. A girl lived under the legal guardianship of her father until she was betrothed and eventually married, at which point she entered the guardianship of her husband. A woman could not enter legally binding contracts, unless they were approved by her father or husband (Num 30), and her rights to own property were limited (Num 27). In other words, a woman could never attain the full legal status of her male relatives, unless she was widowed or divorced, thus detaching from the houses of both father and husband. The nature and extent of a man's patriarchal authority over his family is particularly evident in his control over the sexual consent of his daughters, and his right to choose a suitable husband for her. For this reason, legal cases involving violation of women were treated as legal offenses against their male counterparts (Robert S. Kawashima, "Could a Woman Say 'No' in Biblical Israel? On the Genealogy of Legal Status in Biblical Law and Literature," *AJS Review* 35, no. 1 (2011): 8–12).

[36] William H. Propp, "Kinship in 2 Samuel 13," *The Catholic Biblical Quarterly* 55, no. 1 (1993): 41.

[37] For a study on incest, see the chapter by Dragoslava Santrac in this volume.

The law distinguishes between seduction (consensual sex) and rape, and sexual relationship with an attached and unattached woman (Exod 22:16–17; Deut 22:23–29). Sexual union with a woman who was married or betrothed was treated as seduction when the woman was suspected of complicity, especially if the incident took place in the city, where she could cry and summon help. Such offense was tantamount to adultery, and so both the man and woman were put to death (Deut 22:23–24). However, if the woman was an unattached virgin, the seducer was obligated to marry her and pay the high bride price (*mohar*) for a virgin to her father. The man forfeited his right to ever divorce the woman (Deut 22:28–29). The law permitted the father to refuse to give his daughter, and the offender still had to pay the bride price for virgins (Exod 22:16–17).

When sexual intercourse was non-consensual, which is evident in cases when the woman cried but could not summon help, only the man was executed (Deut 22:25–27). This is prescribed for the case involving a betrothed woman, because she was committed to a relationship with another man and treated as married under the law.

However, the law makes a different provision for a case involving an unattached woman, and allows the man to marry the girl (Deut 22:28–29). The law that insists that a rapist marry his victim is outrageous to most modern readers. Yet we should not be quick to impose such a conclusion on the biblical text, because there is no agreement among biblical scholars whether Deuteronomy 22:28–29 addresses seduction, like Exodus 22:16–17, or "rape" in our sense of violent, non-consensual sexual intercourse.[38] In the authors' opinion, Deuteronomy 22:28–29 most likely addresses seduction—not rape of a virgin—because it is difficult to imagine that the law would allow the father to veto the marriage in the case of seduction (Exod 22:16–17) but not in the case of his daughter's rape, since this option is not mentioned in Deuteronomy 22:28–29. Although the law does not mention it explicitly, some biblical examples permit the assumption that the girl's approval of the prospective marriage was also requested (e.g., Gen 24:57–58). If she were to deny it, which we can expect in cases of forcible rape, the law allowed her father to ban the marriage (Exod 22:16–17). The regulations in Exodus 22:16–17 and Deuteronomy 22:28–29 thus demonstrate that the law sought to protect the seduced or raped young woman, and her child who might be born as a result of the intercourse, in two ways: 1) by affirming that the man must marry her without the possibility to divorce her, and 2) by

[38] For a review of different interpretations of Deuteronomic sex laws and a useful bibliography, see, e.g., Bruce Wells, "Sex, Lies, and Virginal Rape: The Slandered Bride and False Accusation in Deuteronomy," *Journal of Biblical Literature* 124, no. 1 (2005): 41–72 and Cynthia Edenburg, "Ideology and Social Context of the Deuteronomic Women's Sex Laws (Deuteronomy 22:13–29)," *Journal of Biblical Literature* 128, no. 1 (2009): 43–60.

allowing the girl's family to ban the marriage and have the girl remain in their protective custody.

The biblical law is concerned about the disadvantaged woman's economic well-being. A woman who was not a virgin was less eligible for marriage, presumably commanding a lower bride price (Exod 22:17). In the case when the father banned the marriage and she never married in the future, the money paid by the offender was probably designed to provide for the girl's livelihood in her father's house. An additional provision is made for the woman's economic and social security in cases when the father allowed the seducer to marry his daughter: the man could never divorce her, whatever she did (Deut 22:28–29).[39] The concern for the woman is also reflected in the case of rape in the country, when the woman is presumed to have called for help, whether she did or not, and only the man is put to death (Deut 22:25–27).

Ancient Israel's laws dealing with rape represented a radical improvement toward justice for the victims and prevention of revenge, in contrast to some other laws of the ancient Near East. For example, Assyrian laws allowed the father of a violated virgin to seek retaliatory rape of the rapist's wife.[40] Although the ancient Near Eastern culture generally envisioned women to be dependent and submissive, it would be wrong to assume that females were passive and unprotected. Notice, for example, that the biblical law prevented the patriarch's abuse of his daughters and other female relatives (Lev 18:9–19; 19:29). The law also foresees the right of the woman to oppose sexual coercion and defend herself from potent assault (Deut 22:24–27), and makes provisions to protect her social and economic status. The underlying principle of ancient Israel's sex laws thus is to prevent rape and protect victims from further abuse in the given cultural context. In that way they point the fallen world toward God's original plan for humankind at creation.

Rape in the New Testament

Although there are no accounts of rape in the New Testament, the New Testament theology and ethics of sexuality command proper behavior towards the opposite sex. The New Testament maintains the Old Testament laws pertaining to human sexuality, including regulations about marriage (Matt 19:4–5), adultery (Rom 13:9), divorce (Matt 19:1–10), fornication (Heb 13:4), and other sexual offenses (1 Cor 5:1–11; 6:9–11). The New Testament texts about lust as a sinful expression of sexual desire undeline the view that sinful and coercive forms of sexual expression

---

[39] Williams, "Sexuality, Human," 732.

[40] For more information about other ancient Near Eastern sex laws, see, e.g., J. M. Sprinkle, "Sexuality, Sexual Ethics," in *Dictionary of the Old Testament: Pentateuch,* ed. T. Desmond Alexander and David W. Baker (Downers Grove, IL: InterVarsity, 2003), 746.

(actions, desires, and thoughts) are strictly forbidden (Matt 5:28; 2 Pet 2:10; 1 John 2:16). The apostle Peter instructs, "You husbands in the same way, live with your wives in an understanding way, as with someone weaker, since she is a woman; and show her honor as a fellow heir of the grace of life, so that your prayers will not be hindered" (1 Pet 3:7, NASB). He warns men not to abuse the fact that women are often physically weaker than men and sometimes socially and economically dependent on them. A man must treat a woman as his equal, as "a fellow heir" of God's kingdom. The word "fellow" implies egalitarianism and partnership (Phil 1:23–24; Rev 6:11). The misuse of power invokes divine judgment.

Likewise, the apostle Paul advises, "Husbands, love your wives, just as Christ also loved the church and gave Himself for her" (Eph 5:25). Respect, honor, love, understanding, and sacrifice are the antidotes to any form of spousal rape or any kind of coercive expression of sexual desire. The Bible points to a high standard of sexual behavior and purity.[41] The covenant people of God should be very attentive to occurrences of offensive sexual behaviors within and outside marriage and find ways to reduce them and participate in the process of healing.

Some Cases of Rape in the Bible

We do not know much about how the legal regulations concerning rape looked in practice. All the main cases of rape in the Bible—namely, the rape of Dinah (Gen 34), of the Levite's concubine (Judges 19), and of Tamar (2 Sam 13)—ended with the execution of the offenders and sometimes even of those related to them. Jacob's reaction to his sons' revenge of Dinah reveals that he disapproved of their violence as the remedy for seduction or rape, especially since the young man proposed to right the wrong and marry Dinah (Gen 34:12, 30). Biblical scholars do not agree among themselves about whether Shechem seduced or raped Dinah.[42] The biblical narrative seems to provide evidence for each view. On one hand, the plot reflects similarities with other rape stories in the Bible, reinforced by the use of *'anah* ("humiliation," "violation") (Gen 34:2; Judg 19:24; 20:5; 2 Sam 13:14, 22, 32) and the association of the noun *nebalah* ("foolishness," "disgraceful thing") with the rape (Gen 34:7; Judg 19:23; 20:6; 2 Sam 13:12). On the other hand, some elements in the text point to seduction: no mention of violence on the part of Shechem and crying on the part of Dinah (cf. Deut 22:25; 2 Sam 13:12); and

---

[41] See, e.g., Romans 1:27; 1 Corinthians 6:9; Galatians 5:19–21; and Colossians 3:5.

[42] For a review of different interpretations of Genesis 34 and a useful bibliography, see, e.g., Yael Shemesh, "Rape Is Rape Is Rape: The Story of Dinah and Shechem (Gen 34)," *Zeitschrift fur die Alttestamentliche Wissenschaft* 119, no. 1 (2007): 2–21; and Caroline Blyth, "Terrible Silence, Eternal Silence: A Feminist Re-Reading of Dinah's Voicelessness in Genesis 34," *Biblical Interpretation* 17, no. 5 (2009): 485–506.

Shechem's desire to marry Dinah, pay any required bride price, and do whatever the girl's family requested (Gen 34:4, 8, 11–12, 15–24). Shechem is depicted as "more honorable than all the household of his father" (v. 19)—a fact the biblical author would probably not highlight if Shechem was a violent person. Yet, as it was pointed out earlier in relation to the case of David and Bathsheba, psychological coercion by one in power is a form of violence and "power rape." Shechem obviously used his authority as a prince of the Canaanites to abduct Dinah (Gen 34:2). It appears, however, that the primary issue of the narrative is not the type of violation, but rather its outcome—Jacob's sons' foolish revenge that endangered the survival of the whole family in Canaan (Gen 34:30). In either case (rape or seduction), Shechem's act was *nebalah*, a disgraceful thing and a thing that ought not to be done in Israel (vol. 7). In the eyes of her brothers, Shechem treated Dinah as a prostitute (Gen 34:31) —a woman who could be claimed without the consent of her father and family. Dinah's sexuality was part of her family's structure and honor, and her consent was not sufficient even if she had willingly consented. Whether it was seduction or rape, Shechem's act was perceived as a violation and crime that should not go unpunished.

The incident in 2 Samuel 13 undoubtedly involves rape and incest. Tamar was manipulated to come to her brother's house on the pretense of her brother Amnon's illness. When Amnon revealed his intention, Tamar objected and tried to escape, but he forcefully lay with her (2 Sam 13:11–14). The combination of words that depict abuse and violence and their order in the text undoubtedly speak of rape: "However, he would not heed her voice; and being stronger (*khazaq*) than she, he forced her (*'anah*) and lay (*shakab*) with her" (2 Sam 13:14). After the incident, Amnon despised Tamar and sent her away. Tamar's reaction in verse 15, where she claims that his abandoning her was a greater evil than his act of rape, shows her utter despair over her future. In dismissing her, Amnon violated the law that required the offender to marry the unbetrothed virgin and even forfeit his right to ever divorce her (Deut 22:28–29). Tamar thus stresses that she was wronged by Amnon twice. This incident, however, is more problematic because it involves also incest between half-siblings, which was forbidden by the law (Lev 18:9, 11; 20:17). Could the ambiguity and complexity of the situation be one of the main reasons why David did nothing to address the rape of his daughter? The law required that the culprits of incest were "cut off in the sight of their people" or disfellowshipped (Lev 20:17). This would probably mean that Amnon could not inherit his father's throne as his firstborn. While we can only hypothesize that this was David's dilemma, it is certain that David's inaction wronged his daughter and initiated murder and violence in his family (2 Sam 13–18).

The potential gang rape of Lot's daughters disturbs our moral sentiments today (Gen 19:1–9). Although Lot reasoned from the perspective of hospitality and greatest sacrifice for his guests, which was normative of his culture, many readers are still appalled by Lot's suggestion to give up his daughters to the obviously violent gang of rapists. Jacques Doukhan explains, "It is because Lot had understood this threat [of homosexual offense] that he offered his daughters in exchange, thinking in his *confused set of values* that his option was less reprehensible."[43] Lot's inexcusable act of foolishness was probably influenced by the strange ways of Sodom, where he perhaps was one of the city judges (Gen 19:1; 19:9).[44] A similar incident of offering innocent females to a violent mob of sexual predators is found in Judges 19, where the father-host proposes to the men of Gibeah to violate his virgin daughter and the Levite's concubine in order to protect his guest (Judg 19:24). The father obviously spoke out of desperation and "arguably exercised his legitimate paternal power of consent over virgin daughters."[45] Yet his as well as Lot's actions do not reflect God's perfect standards, which seek to prevent the abuse of women's sexuality (Lev 19:29; Deut 22:19, 29; 24:1–4) and insist that a man should "bring happiness to his wife whom he has taken" (Deut 24:5). The incidents of Lot and the father-host show us that living under the influence of "rape culture" and exposing oneself to values that are opposite to the values of God's kingdom may result in actions unpredictably wicked and evil, or at least may initiate impure thoughts and desires, leading to different forms of compromise of sexual integrity.

Captive Women

Absalom's rape of his father's concubines reflects the ancient Near Eastern political agenda to use the rape of women in wars as proof of power and dominance over the enemy (2 Sam 16:21–22). In cultures in which women are viewed as family possessions and tenants of the family honor, rape of women is seen as a violation of the patriarch's reputation and as an assumption of his rights and place. Similar brutal practices of rape of women in wars have existed until present times.[46] "But while the ideologies which undergird rape's permissibility in our own time must be continually resisted, cultural meanings surrounding rape in a pre-modern agrarian culture such as ancient Israel cannot be automatically collapsed

[43] Jacques B. Doukhan, *Genesis*, Seventh-day Adventist International Commentary, ed. Jacques B. Doukhan (Nampa, ID: Pacific Press, 2016), 252, emphasis supplied.

[44] Ibid., 250.

[45] Kawashima, 13.

[46] See, e.g., Nazila Isgandarova, "Rape as a Tool Against Women in War: The Role of Spiritual Caregivers to Support the Survivors of an Ethnic Violence," *Cross Currents* 63, no. 2

into our own."[47] Understood against their ancient Near Eastern background, the Mosaic regulations concerning captive women demonstrate the element of mercy within the borders of God's covenant. The ancient Israelites were instructed to exercise compassion and care for their captive women (Deut 21:10–14).Once the female captive was brought to Israel, she could not be sold for money, nor treated as a sex slave, but only as a wife. She was given a full month to grieve her parents, and only then could the Israelite man approach her. The law underlines that the husband "shall not treat her brutally" (Deut 21:14), even in the case of divorce.

The custom of women slaves can perhaps be compared with the incidents of Abraham and Isaac's passing of their wives as their sisters, which endangered the women and placed them in positions where they could have been sexually assaulted (Gen 12, 20, 26). While that was probably done with the women's consent—or at least Sarah's (Gen 12:13) —the Lord's protective intervention shows that God does not approve the maltreatment of women, even when sanctioned by culture.

Some Leading Contributors to the Prevalence of Rape Today

Given the biblical concept of sexuality as an intimate and loving expression of the marital bond between husband and wife, and the biblical view of human beings as immensely valuable and endowed with free will, rape represents an ultimate distortion of God's gift of sexuality and violation of the victim's personhood.

The factors leading to the prevalence of rape are thus the result of violating God's will for humankind. They involve a combination of socio-cultural, economic, political, and legal factors that condone and encourage sexual violence. In some modern societies, fertile ground for sexual violence is provided through challenging the borders of acceptable and genuine sexual interactions and promoting the view of bodies, especially female, as instruments of swift and rapid satisfaction. Escalating violence, as well as sexually explicit movies, music videos, internet content, and television shows significantly contribute to the growing insensitivity and affinity of popular culture toward illicit sex. The deterioration of moral and family values through a widespread emphasis on materialism and self-gratification also largely leads to this same end.

Attitudes and practices that are misogynistic in nature directly contribute to the pervasiveness of sexual crime, especially when they are or appear to be condoned by religion. For example, some famous Hindu mythological stories, which shape the worldview of certain population

---

(2013): 174–184; and Donatilla Mukamana and Petra Brysiewicz, "The Lived Experience of Genocide Rape Survivors in Rwanda," *Journal of Nursing Scholarship* 40, no. 4 (2008): 379–384.

[47] Alice A. Keefe, "Rapes of Women/Wars of Men," *Semeia* 61 (1993): 79.

in India, narrate cases of rape by gods who are never punished for their crimes but are often glorified as heroes.[48] In contrast to these Hindu stories, the perpetrators of rape in the Bible are punished, and no doubt is left concerning God's strong disapproval of rape (e.g., 2 Sam 12).[49] In practice rape is almost impossible to prove under strict Islamic law (Sharia), unlike under the biblical laws.[50] The Islamic law requires either the rapist's confession or the testimony of four witnesses to verify a sexual crime (Quran 24:4, 13), and takes a woman's testimony less seriously than a man's word (Quran 2:282). The concept of spousal rape is practically non-existent in Islam, because marriage assumes a wife's consent to sexual relations with her husband (Quran 1:223).[51] Some Islamic branches sanction rape as punishment for women who do not conform to the Muslim community's rules of life.[52]

Among the risk factors contributing to high rates of rape in Africa are inadequate and violent school environments, gangs, inadequate police and legal system, social breakdown, poverty, and a culture of violence. Yet the strongest factors are the various cultural beliefs about rape in Africa, including the beliefs that men are entitled to sex, that women even enjoy being raped, and that the raping of infants/children and virgins cures AIDS.[53]

Other factors associated with an increased risk of sexual violence include low education, exposure to violence between parents, abuse during childhood, and discriminatory laws and attitudes accepting violence

---

[48] E.g., Vishnu rapes Vrinda by assuming the disguise of her husband (*Shiva Purana, Rudra Samhita 2, Yudha Khanda* 5, 23.38–45). Brihaspati, the guru of all Indian gods, rapes his pregnant sister-in-law, Mamata (*Matsya Purana*, 49.17–28).

[49] See the section "Incidents of Rape in the Bible" in this chapter.

[50] See the section "Biblical Laws Dealing with Rape" in this chapter.

[51] For more information and examples of individual cases that highlight the major challenges in the area of sexual violence toward women in contemporary Muslim societies, see Azam, 1–18, 170–237.

[52] E.g., in the 1990s working and "Westernized" women in Algeria were profiled as "prostitutes" by Islamic militants. Rape and throat slashing were often used to punish these women. In 1992 the case of the gang rape of a young Egyptian woman at a crowded bus station in Cairo was dismissed in court for lack of evidence. The Egyptian media commented that the girl deserved to be raped because she dared to leave her home unattended. As a reaction to this case, a law was proposed by the Egyptian National Assembly that blamed the families of rape victims for allowing their daughters to walk unattended outside the home. Although the law did not pass, it illustrates the strong belief of some people in certain Muslim countries that rape is not always a crime and that women are to be blamed for rape (Elyse Semerdjian, "Rape: An Overview," in *Encyclopedia of Women and Islamic Cultures: Family, Law and Politics,* ed. Suad Joseph and Afsaneh Najmabadi (Leiden: Brill, 2005): 700.

[53] Eileen Meier, "Child Rape in South Africa," *Pediatric Nursing* 28, no. 5 (2002): 532–533.

and gender inequality.[54] War and political conflicts are also associated with the increased risk of sexual violence.[55]

At the core of most contributors to the prevalence of rape are religious and cultural views that make it easier to overlook and excuse violence against women by denying women equal rights and opportunities given to men in both private and public spheres. The concern here is that any view that assumes greater rights and privileges of some people over others in practice potentially leaves room for condoning coercion and even emotional and physical violence on the part of the "greater" over the "lesser." The perpetrators of rape often "have no other agenda than to assert their authority and dominate and control women [men]."[56] Thus the main issue behind rape is power. Certain people believe they are entitled to sex regardless of the victim's feelings and will.

The power issue seems to be particularly evident in the cases of acquaintance rape and spousal rape. Acquaintance rape occurs most often when the balance of power between men and women is not righted well. For example, some men feel more entitled to sexual contact after they pay for all dating expenses. The woman's vulnerability is increased when the man controls the transportation.[57]

One of the leading causes of sexual abuse in marriage is the distorted view of the conjugal right to allot the husband power over his wife in all matters, including sexual relations. In addition, economic and social dependence of many women on their husbands renders them more vulnerable to marital abuse. The person who possesses the so-called "rights" to assume another person's compliance renders this other person's free choice inconsequential, because refusal to submit and act in accordance with their "role" is perceived as rebellion against the established order. When rape is conflated with marital rights, the situation becomes a flagrant example of discrimination against the victim who cannot produce evidence of rape. The "rights" thus give power to one person to exercise control over the other person. When fundamental freedom and equality are not guaranteed to all people, various subtle and even deliberate forms of coercion and abuse will be eventually viewed as lesser offenses, if offenses at all.[58] Marital rape has a serious impact on the

---

[54] "Violence against women," World Health Organization.

[55] E.g., during the 1994 Rwanda genocide, rape was used as a weapon to humiliate the Tutsi women, and was often carried out in front of family members. United Nations officials estimate that a quarter of a million women were raped during that civil war (Mukamana and Brysiewicz, 380).

[56] James A. Glanville and Yolanda Dreyer, "Spousal Rape: A Challenge for Pastoral Counselors," *HTS Teologiese Studies* 69, no. 1 (2013): 1–2.

[57] Parrot and Bechhofer, 165.

[58] For a profound discussion about the consequences of practices of asymmetrical power on

victim, marriage, and the family. It not only destroys the intimate and loving bond that spouses are meant to enjoy, but it introduces mistrust and terror of never knowing when a physical or sexual assault might happen again. The victim's fear, damaged self-esteem, anxiety, and resentment as well as the perpetrator's aggression, insensitivity, and egotism can poison all family relationships and threaten the well-being and future of the children, especially if the children are aware of or suspect marital abuse in their family.[59]

In the anthology *Transforming a Rape Culture*, a group of scholars defines the present challenge:

> In a rape culture, women perceive the continuum of threatened violence that ranges from sexual remarks to sexual touching to rape itself. A rape culture condones physical and emotional terrorism against women and presents it as a norm.[60]

A "rape culture," therefore, represents the overall conscious and unconscious cultural acceptance of the forbidden forms of abuse and depravation of the human rights of equality and dignity, in general, and sexual expression bordering on violence, in particular. The various tenents of "rape culture" can be found in most cultures around the world. In societies dominated by views of women and children as family assets, most rapes are never reported, and so never prosecuted—mainly to avoid the stigma of damaged family honor, which takes precedence over the right of victims to obtain justice and find healing for themselves. Rape thus has to be viewed against a broader background—namely, the issue of discriminatory human rights. Discriminatory human rights, such as gendered human rights, award greater civil liberties to one group over the other, which in practice allows the privileged group to claim its rights and puts the underprivileged group of people in danger of being mistreated and defenseless. This outcome raises questions on the fairness and justice of the whole concept of gendered rights. Gendered and other discriminatory rights violate the biblical view of the image of God and of salvation by grace, which guarantees equality of both men and women by their Creator and Savior (Gen 5:3; Col 3:11, 28).

---

gender justice and human rights, see, e.g., Rogaia Mustafa Abusharaf, "Finding Spaces for Fairness," *Journal of Women of the Middle East and the Islamic World* 9 (2011): 3–25.

[59] For more information about the impact of marital rape, see, e.g., David Finkelhor and Kersti Yllo, *License to Rape: Sexual Abuse of Wives* (New York: Free Press, 1987), 117–138.

[60] Emilie Buchwald, Pamela R. Fletcher, and Marth Roth, *Transforming a Rape Culture*, quoted in Kate Harding, *Asking for It: The Alarming Rise of Rape Culture–and What We Can Do About It* (Boston, MA: De Capo Life Long Books, 2015), 2.

Consequences of Rape

The consequences of abandoning the biblical ideal of sexuality and view of human life are manifold and far reaching. Incidents of rape recorded in Scripture caused much misery to the affected individuals, brought collapse of relationships and families, and often resulted in revenge and bloodshed.

Research done by medical and psychological professionals confirms that rape is one of the most severe of all traumas.[61] Most victims of rape suffer a combination of short-term and long-term psychological problems: lower self-esteem, mood disorders, anxiety and trauma related disorders, depression, emotional numbing, irritability, social withdrawal, and loneliness. There are serious negative effects of rape on physical health, commonly including chronic pain syndromes, gastrointestinal disorders, increased risk of cardiovascular diseases, diabetes, sleep disorders, and increased risk of alcohol intake and smoking as well as sexual dysfunction. Older adults who have experienced sexual abuse earlier in life may be especially vulnerable to additional challenes associated with the milestones of aging, such as retirement, children leaving home, or becoming ill. These milestones can often trigger past traumatic memories, and there may be a reemergence of symptoms related to earlier trauma of rape, including increased thoughts, reminiscences, and emotional responses to past traumatic experiences in the context of losses associated with aging.[62] Survivors of rape who are particularly at risk of developing chronic post-traumatic syndrome disorders include "those who were injured during the attack, were threatened by the perpetrator that they may be hurt or killed, have a history of prior assault, or have experienced negative interactions with family, peers, or law enforcement systems."[63] Sexually transmitted diseases and unwanted pregnancy are also possible consequences of rape.

Personal testimonies of rape survivors provide another powerful witness to just how terrifying and devastating sexual violence is for those who undergo it. Heather G. Wilson describes the horrific impact of rape on its victims:

---

[61] See, e.g., Natalie Sachs-Ericsson et al., "The Influence of Prior Rape on the Psychological and Physical Health Functioning of Older Adults," *Aging & Mental Health* 18, no. 6 (2014): 717–730; and Laura G. Hensley, "Treatment for Survivors of Rape: Issues and Interventions," *Journal of Mental Health and Counseling* 24, no. 4 (2002): 331–347.

[62] Sachs-Ericsson, 717–718; and Hensley, 331.

[63] Hensley, 331.

> Rape is ugliness in its basest form. It destroys innocence and replaces it with shame. It steals a sense of security and extends fear. It cultivates bitterness. It leaves no room for beauty. The overpowering emotions I experienced that awful night did not go away the next day—or the other one after that.[64]

Even the silent cries of the victims who refuse or are unable to speak about their trauma powerfully testify about their fears, pain, and struggles. The social stigma that some victims have to endure, and the often painful and humiliating legal procedures, only prolong their anguish. Some religious victims face spiritual crisis as they question God's sovereignty and love in their lives. A comprehensive definition and treatment of rape thus must include the physical, psychological, emotional, spiritual, and social implications of the violent nature of a non-consensual sexual act enforced by the use of physical or psychological power, coercion, and/or violence.

Studies reveal that victims of rape do not typically seek formal medical health services in the year following the attack but may do so eventually when their symptoms worsen or become chronic.[65] Access to services, feelings of safety when reporting crimes, and how disclosures following rape are perceived in the community greatly command whether the victim will seek help or not. In addition, cultural factors greatly shape the survivor's view of gender roles, which in turn influence how she perceives the act of rape. For example, certain cultures are inclined to blame victims for causing the rape by their behavior and dress, which are thought to have stimulated male sexuality. If the victim subscribes to such cultural beliefs, she will likely blame herself for initiating the rape, thus adding additional burden to her trauma and an obstacle to her way to recovery.[66] In cultures where men are perceived as fearless and dominant in sexual relationships, a male rape victim can feel stripped of his manliness and lose his personal sense of worth and respect of the community.

The horrendous character of rape is that rape is not just a single event or an isolated trauma in a victim's life. The experience of rape impacts the survivor's whole person and life. The consequences of rape often extend to the victim's family, friends, co-workers, and community. Their common responses vary from grieving with the victim and attempting to provide constant psychological, spiritual, and material support to rejection, feelings of shame, and blaming the victim. Some will become

---

[64] Heather Gemmen Wilson, "Calling on the Saints," *Christianity Today*, February, 2008, 51.

[65] E.g., Hensley, 331–333.

[66] Ibid.

angry and seek revenge; some will be guilt-ridden and suffer helpless despair. In each case, the lives of people close to the survivor of rape are changed. Family members and friends will often require as much support and reassurance as the victim. They will often need assistance to cope with their trauma in order to be able to support the victim.[67]

Healing in Christ

Victims of rape are often assigned stigma, which exacerbates feelings of powerlessness and shame. Sometimes they are blamed for prompting rape and are labelled as "whores." The victim who was abused by the rapist is thus subjected to continual abuse of other people who respond to rape in this and similar harmful ways. As noted by some authors, it seems that the community does not always recognize the cultural and situational context in which the rapist and the victim are embedded and does not acknowledge that the primary cause of a sexually aggressive act lies always with the aggressor.[68]

Some victims are unfairly treated as defiled and unfit for marriage. In this context it is important to understand that rape is the sin of the aggressor, not the victim, and so only the perpetrator of rape is morally defiled and guilty of the committed crime (Deut 24:16). Some people believe that victims of rape are unfit for marriage because they have been sexually united with another person. It appears to them that marriage with a victim of rape is somehow inevitably defiled. However, this view is biblically ungrounded, because the act of rape does not unite the aggressor and the victim in "one body." Two persons become "one flesh" only when they both willingly give themselves to each other in the sexual act (Gen 2:24; 1 Cor 6:16). The victim is not a participant in the sexual act, but a prey and target of abuse and aggression. Survivors of rape thus are not adulterous or promiscuous persons, and must not be denied the right to marry.

Rape, like other major crises in life, raises a number of other associated issues in the person's life that require special attention of the family and people who are close to the victim. Stigmatization, hopelessness, and helplessness merge into a vicious cycle of despair and anger that might lead even to suicide. As discussed earlier, marital and family problems, problems in sexuality, depression, and a number of physical and psychological issues can arise as after-effects of the victim's experience of rape. For this reason, it is crucial that the victim is encouraged to seek

---

[67] For more information, see, e.g., the statement by the American Academy of Pediatrics, "Rape and the Adolescent," *Pediatrics* 51, no. 4 (1988): 595–597.

[68] Parrot and Bechhofer, 171.

professional counseling and medical treatment where they are available. Regardless of their compassion and care, people who have no special training may not be able to take care of all the needs of the victim. Yet their continual psychological, spiritual, and material support can become crucial in the process of healing. Victims need unreserved acceptance, trust, and understanding of the people who are close to them. Spending time with them in silence or listening to them without trying to moralize or explain the traumatic event can benefit the victim greatly. Helping the victim find and claim the ultimate hope in the power of divine grace and restoration is vital for the victim's holistic healing. Psalm 9:9 reminds us, "The LORD also will be a refuge for the oppressed, a refuge in times of trouble." The healing power of God stems from His willingness to defend, vindicate, restore, and transform the lives of people who suffer.

Recovery from rape does not come easily. People close to the victim need to be patient and untiring in providing their constant support and care. The experience of rape seriously jeopardizes the victim's sense of freedom and personal control over her or his own life. The victim's fear is genuine. People should acknowledge the victim's feelings, and not deny them by attempting false optimism. Instead, they should depict rape as sin against the victim. Rape, like every other sin, hurts people and causes them to feel lost in life like sheep without a shepherd (Isa 53:6; Matt 9:36). Victims can regain control over their own lives only in Christ, the good Shepherd, who leads His flock to flourishing and well-being (Ps 23; John 10:11). The experience of rape leaves the survivor in the darkness of suffering and misery. Yet there is still hope in recovery, because Christ is the light of the world (John 8:12).

Wilson, a survivor of rape, writes that many blame the church or God when calamity strikes, but in the process of recovery from hurt "we'll find this communion of saints to be a source of astonishing beauty."[69] Healing starts with recognition that to blame God or the community of believers leads only to a psychological and spiritual dead end. Openness to a renewed sense of belonging within the family of faith, the church of the living Christ, and constancy of a potent spiritual presence in this community can generate a new hope in complete recovery from pain, bitterness, and the emotional and spiritual scars that remain after the experience of rape. The grace of God prevails where redemption and healing seem impossible. Memory cannot be erased fully but can be relived rightfully in the proper context of acceptance, love, faith, and hope in the divine Redeemer who experienced agonizing death, but also resurrected to new life and amazing power available to all who ask (Matt 10:27–30).

---

[69] Wilson, 51.

Church and Perpetrators of Rape

The community of faith is called to strongly condemn the sin of rape and chastise the perpetrators. The aggressor loses not only the other people's trust but also God's blessing in life (1 Pet 3:7), and ultimately incurs God's judgment (Rev 21:8). Rape must not be covered up in an attempt to preserve the reputation of the aggressor, or of the victim's family, or of the community. Failure to condemn sin and give justice to the victims is what truly damages the family and the community's good name in God's eyes and the eyes of others. The church community, along with the victims and their families, must prayerfully seek to find the best possible ways to address the crime of rape and its related consequences for the victims without compromising the victims' process of healing, right to justice, and the divine standards of truth and righteousness. In addition, in countries in which rape has legal implications, civil duty in relation to rape must not be evaded (Rom 13:4).

The church is also called to affirm hope in a sinner's possible repentance and forgiveness of sins in Christ. When possible, perpetrators of rape should be extended the Christian care that will hopefully help them acknowledge their horrific crimes and find repentance and eventually forgiveness of sins in Christ. An incident of a man committing incest with his father's wife in the church of Corinth shows how believers should reprimand and disfellowship those who commit grave sins (1 Cor 5:2, 9–13), but also exercise spiritual care for the sinners (2 Cor 2:5–8). The gospel teaches that in Christ all sinners and people affected by sin and its consequences can become "a new creation" (2 Cor 5:17).

Conclusion

Rape is a crime that threatens human flourishing and welfare, social and marital order, the meaning of true sexual intimacy, and the holy divine covenant. Growing tolerance and insensitivity toward violence in public and social media; disintegration of the family; objectification of the human body, especially female; affinity of popular culture toward illicit sex; some religious and cultural views that foster gender inequality and misogynistic practices; and a culture of violence are among the leading factors contributing to high rates of sexual crimes today.

What can the church do to help remove the causes and consequences of rape? The church can make a difference by affirming biblical values and systematically addressing what appears to be the three main avenues of the prevalence of sexual abuse today: 1) the lack of proper education in regard to rape and its related issues, including what constitutes rape, the meaning of sexuality, the value of every human being and human rights, the sinfulness and evil of rape, consequences of rape, and healing the wounds caused by rape; 2) the socio-economic reasons, including poverty, unemployment, dislocation due to war and political unrest, discrimination, family dysfunction, and victim blaming; and 3) the deficiency of some legal systems in prosecuting rape and providing support to victims of rape due to corruption and bigoted laws.

Rape must not be ignored nor treated as a taboo, nor victims of rape stigmatized in churches. On the contrary, victims of rape should feel safe and loved, and receive spiritual and emotional support from their fellow believers (2 Cor 1:3–4). The gospel of Jesus Christ "is the power of God to salvation of everyone who believes" (Rom 1:16). Its teaching about the ideal of sexual intimacy and the value of all people regardless of their gender, race, age, and socio-economic status obliges the believers to have highest moral consideration for both women and men, and to insist on zero tolerance for violence and discrimination in both public and private spheres. The gospel of Jesus Christ, when it is practically lived, positively counters "rape culture."

CHAPTER 11

Female Genital Mutilation

Martha D. Duah

Among the many issues that have caught the attention of the international community is the practice of female genital mutilation. Since the United Nations Decade for Women (1975–1985) series of conferences honoring women, there has been a surge of interest in the issue of female genital mutilation. The international community has labeled female genital mutilation a human crisis, and discussions on it among feminist and human rights organizations, legislators, medical professionals, and anthropologists have generated a large body of literature. Yet there has been little reflection among theologians on female genital mutilation and its related issues. This study analyzes female genital mutilation and evaluates it from a biblical perspective.

What Is Female Genital Mutilation?

Before we discuss the practice of female genital mutilation, we must describe what it is. It is a non-medical surgical procedure performed mostly with crude, unsterilized instruments,[1] practiced in some traditional communities and safeguarded by women of those communities.[2] Usually, it is carried out on girls between the ages of fourteen and sixteen, and sometimes on babies within the first few weeks of postnatal life. It is also carried out with consent on women from ethnic groups that do not

---

[1] Verena Schafroth, "Female Genital Mutilation in Africa: An Analysis of the Church's Response and Proposals for Change," *Missiology: An International Review* 37 (2009): 528–529.

[2] Rogaia Mustafa Abusharaf, "Revisiting Feminist Discourses on Infibulation: Responses from Sudanese Feminists," in *Female "Circumcision" in Africa: Culture, Controversy, and Change*, ed. Bettina Shell-Duncan and Ylva Hernlund (Boulder, CO: Lynne Rienner, 2000), 153; and Abusharaf, "We Have Supped So Deep in Horrors: Understanding Colonialist Emotionality and British Responses to Female Circumcision in Northern Sudan," *History and Anthropology* 17 (2006): 217–218.

practice female genital mutilation, but who marry into a community that does adhere to the practice.[3]

The procedure bears different physiognomies, classified into major types reflecting the degree and severity of the procedure. Type 1 is clitoridectomy, the removal of the prepuce with or without the removal of any part of the clitoris. Type 2 is complete or partial removal of the clitoris and labia minora (the inner lips of the vulva), with or without excision of the labia majora. Infibulation or Pharaonic female gennital mutilation, type 3 and the severest, refers to the removal of part or all of the external genitalia with the cut edges sewn together to narrow the urethra and vagina, allowing enough of an opening for the passage of urine and menstrual blood.[4] Some victims of infibulation undergo de-infibulation later in life to allow for coitus and childbirth, then re-infibulation when widowed or divorced.[5] Type 4, termed as unclassified, includes scarification of the clitoral prepuce by pricking, piercing, incising, scraping, and cauterizing the genital area.[6]

Some authors classify these non-medical surgeries on women as "female circumcision." For others, the terms "female genital cutting," "female genital surgeries," and "female genital operations"[7] respect the cultures that practice it and appropriately depict the intensity of the practice. Still others prefer the official term "female genital mutilation." After giving much consideration to the sensitivity and concerns that have arisen about the choice of terminology in describing the practice, the author of the present study adopts the term "female genital mutilation" because of this study's philosophical and theological orientation.

---

[3] Bettina Shell-Duncan and Ylva Hernlund, "Female 'Circumcision' in Africa: Dimensions of the Practice and Debates," in Shell-Duncan and Hernlund, *Female "Circumcision" in Africa*, 3.

[4] On the different classifications of female genital mutilation, see also Barbara Couden Hernandez and Caroline Nyairo, "Understanding Female Genital Cutting," in *Church and Society: Missiological Challenges for the Seventh-day Adventist Church*, ed. Rudi Maier (Berrien Springs, MI: Department of World Missions, Andrews University), 518–519.

[5] Shell-Duncan and Hernlund, "Dimensions of the Practice and Debates," 4; Schafroth, 528; World Health Organization, "Female Genital Mutilation," fact sheet apps.who.int/iris/bitstream/handle/10665/112328/WHO_RHR_14.12_eng.pdf (accessed June 8, 2021); Christopher Hughes Conn, "Female Genital Mutilation and the Moral Status of Abortion," *Public Affairs Quarterly* 15 (2001); and Efua Dorkenoo, *Cutting the Rose Female: Genital Mutilation—The Practice and Its Prevention* (London: Minority Rights Publication, 1994), 5, 10–12.

[6] World Health Organization, "Female Genital Mutilation" factsheet; and Mairo Usman Mandara, "Female Genital Cutting in Nigeria: Views of Nigerian Doctors on the Medicalization Debate," in Shell-Duncan and Hernlund, *Female "Circumcision" in Africa*, 98.

[7] Mary Nyangweso, *Female Genital Cutting in Industrialized Countries: Mutilation or Cultural Tradition?* (Santa Barbara, CA: Praeger, 2014), 25–26; and Shell-Duncan and Hernlund, "Dimensions of the Practice and Debates," 5–6.

In the early years of the colonization of Africa, efforts were made by the colonial rulers and missionaries to counteract the practice. But their efforts, though earnest, were unsympathetic in categorizing all indigenous African cultural practices as barbaric.[8] Indigenous populations perceived the attempt to ban female genital mutilation as cultural imperialism.[9] Subsequently, conflict ensued between missionaries and colonial rulers against the native population, resulting in the spreading of the practice to regions that had not known the practice.[10] The controversy was curtailed with a tolerance of the practice of female genital mutilation.[11] Among Christians, it was swept under the carpet until 2000, when female African theologians[12] picked it up from where the missionaries had left off.

Female genital mutilation is presently prevalent in about twenty-nine African countries and nine Asian countries, as well as among[13] ethnic groups in some South American countries and immigrant communities in some industrialized countries.[14] During the mid-nineteenth century, it was recommended by physicians in the United States and England as a cure for masturbation, lesbian inclinations and hysteria, and female deviance.[15]

---

[8] Rosemary Kinyanjui, "Hidden Cost of Rejecting Female Genital Mutilation," *Transformation* 19 (2002): 74; and Mary Nyangweso Wangila, *Female Circumcision: The Interplay of Religion, Culture, and Gender in Kenya* (New York: Orbis, 2007), 120.

[9] Abusharaf, "We Have Supped So Deep in Horrors," 209–228; Elizabeth Bekers, *Rising Anthills: African and African American Writing on Female Genital Excision 1960–2000* (Madison, WI: University of Wisconsin Press, 2010), 16; Stephen Muoki Joshua, "The Church and the 1929 Female Genital Mutilation (FGM) Contention in Kenya, with Special Reference to the Scottish Presbyterian Church and the Kikuyu Community," *Studia Historiae Ecclesiasticae* 35 (2009): 15–30; Lynn Thomas, "Ngaitana (I Will Circumcise Myself): Lessons from Colonial Campaigns to Ban Excision in Meru, Kenya," in Shell-Duncan and Hernlund, *Female "Circumcision" in Africa*, 129–150; and Abusharaf, "We Have Supped So Deep in Horrors," 129–150.

[10] Thomas, 137–145; and Bekers, 14.

[11] Dorkenoo, 38–39; and Schafroth, 532.

[12] Feminist theological analysis of female genital mutilation is written by Nyambura J. Njoroge, *Kiama Kia NGO: An African Christian Feminist Ethics of Resistance and Transformation* (Accra: Asempa, 2000); Wangila, Musimbi R. Kanyoro, "Cultural Hermeneutics: An African Contribution," in *Other Ways of Reading African Women and the Bible*, ed. Musa Dube (Geneva: World Council of Churches Publications, 2001), 101–113; and Ephigenia W. Gachiri, *Female Circumcision* (Nairobi: Kolbe Press, 2000).

[13] Nyangweso, *Female Genital Cutting*, 13–22; Shell-Duncan and Hernlund, "Dimensions of the Practice and Debates," 11–14; and World Health Organization, "Female Genital Mutilation" fact sheet.

[14] Nyangweso, *Female Genital Cutting*, 13–22; and Omar Sacirbey, "Religion Said to be Key to Combating Female Genital Mutilation," *Christian Century* (2012): 17.

[15] Nyangweso, *Female Genital Cutting*, 31; and Gachiri, 36.

Philosophical Theories Underpinning Female Genital Mutilation Practices

Our analysis of female genital mutilation begins with its underlying philosophy. Religion (indigenous, Christian, and Islamic) has been earmarked as the culprit for perpetuating the practice of female genital mutilation.[16] This observation necessitates an examination of the religious and/or philosophical principles that may undergird female genital mutilation practices in these religions.

Islamic Religious/Philosophical Theory

Among Muslim scholars, there are conflicting views on female genital mutilation ensuing from their interpretation of the sources of Muslim law—specifically the Qur'an and *hadith* ("tradition," the words and actions of Muhammad). Proponents argue that passages in the Qur'an[17] point to circumcision as obligatory for both male and female Muslims. Even in *hadith*, such as a conversation between Muhammad and Um Habibah,[18] Muhammad's comment on *sunnah* and *makrumah*,[19] and Sarah's jealousy of Hagar[20] are, for some, justification for female

---

[16] Wangila, 38–44, 103–111; and Nyangweso, *Female Genital Cutting*, 99–116.

[17] *Qur'an* 2:124 states, "And remember that Abraham was tried by his Lord with certain commands, which he fulfilled: He said: 'I will make thee an Imam to the Nations.' 'And also (Imams) from my offspring!' He answered: 'But My Promise is not with the reach of evil-doers.'" *Qur'an* 16:123: "So We have taught thee the inspired (Message), 'Follow the ways of Abraham the True in Faith, and he joined not gods with Allah.'"

[18] The most cited *hadith* for religious justification for the practice of female genital mutilation references a conversation between Muhammad and 'Um Atiyyat al-Ansariyyah, a woman identified as a professional exciser of female genital mutilation who migrated with the prophet from persecution. See Sami A. Aldeeb Abu-Sahlieh, "To Mutilate in the Name of Jehovah or Allah: Legitimization of Male and Female Circumcision," *Medicine and Law* 13, nos. 7–8 (July 1994): 575–622, cirp.org/library/cultural/aldeeb1 (accessed May 28, 2021). The interpretations of the *hadith* have led to varying fatwas—conflicting opinions on female genital mutilation.

[19] Another *hadith* has Muhammad saying, "Circumcision is a *sunnah* for the men and markrumah for the women." See Sami A. Aldeeb Abu-Sahlieh, "Islamic Law and Issues of Male and Female Circumcision," *Third World Legal Studies* 13 (1995); and Nawal El-Saadawi, *The Hidden Face of Eve, Women in the Arab World*, trans. and ed. Sherif Hetata (London: Zed Press, 1980), 33. *Sunnah* here, according to Abu-Sahlieh, "means that it is to conform to tradition of Muhammed himself, or simply a custom at the time of Muhammed. The term *makrumah* can be translated into a meritorious, it is better to do it although it is not obligatory from a religious point of view" ("Islamic Law," 79).

[20] An alternative narrative used in support of female genital mutilation is Sarah's jealousy of Hagar, which is told in various versions. See Sami A. Aldeeb Abu-Sahlieh, "Male and Female Circumcision: The Myth of the Difference," in *Female Circumcision*, ed. Rogaia Mustafa Abusharaf (Philadelphia, PA: University of Pennsylvania Press, 2006), 56–57; and Nyangweso, *Female Genital Cutting*, 109.

genital mutilation. It has been recognized that "in predominantly Muslim communities, the practice has been linked with Islam and the belief that every Muslim woman must be subjected to it is very strong."[21] Opponents of the practice believe that the use of the Qur'an to justify female genital mutilation is an abusive treatment of the Qur'an.[22] They stress that the Qur'an does not approve of female genital mutilation[23] and the *hadith* used to justify it have little or no credibility.[24] They insist the four daughters of Muhammad were not excised and female genital mutilation is unknown to some Islamic communities, and thus the prophet did not endorse the practice.[25] Others hold that the decision must be left to parents. Clearly, the Islamic religion has no explicit philosophical principle that sanctions the practice, except for religious leaders' conflicting opinions.

Judeo-Christian Religious/Philosophical Theory

Few Jews and Christians who practice female genital mutilation justify their practice with an assumption drawn from the divine mandate to circumcise the male population of Israel (Gen 17:1–14). Others accept a concocted narrative of Sarah's excision of Hagar as true and then contend that Sarah would not have excised Hagar had it not been a common practice among the Jews.[26] The earmarked proof of Judeo-Christian justification of female genital mutilation is an assumption without any explicit biblical statement supporting any of the forms of the practice. The biblical perspective on female genital mutilation will be clear in this study, but it suffices to briefly mention that there is no biblical principle supporting the practice.

African Philosophical Theory

Scholars debate whether there is an African philosophy regarding female genital mutilation and, if there is, about its nature. We agree with

---

[21] Ibrahim Lethome Asmani Maryam Sheikh Abdi, *De-linking Female Genital Mutilation/Cutting from Islam* (New York, Frontiers in Reproductive Health, 2008), 2.

[22] Ibid., 3.

[23] See "Female Genital Mutilation (FGM): Debates About FGM in Africa, the Middle East & Far East," Religious Tolerance, http://www.religioustolerance.org/fem_cirm.htm (accessed May 28, 2021); and Abu-Sahlieh, "Islamic Law," 79–82.

[24] Abu-Sahlieh, "To Mutilate in the Name of Jehovah or Allah"; Female Genital Mutilation (FGM); and Sacirbey, 16.

[25] Abu-Sahlieh, "To Mutilate in the Name of Jehovah or Allah"; Carla Makhlouf Obermeyer, "Female Genital Surgeries: The Known, the Unknown, and the Unknowable," *Medical Anthropology Quarterly* 13 (1999): 91; and Nyangweso, *Female Genital Cutting,* 110.

[26] Nyangweso, *Female Genital Cutting*, 106–107. The assertions may be true, but it should be kept in mind that the Jews' rebellious acts sent them into exile, where they adopted cultures and traditions that were previously unknown to them. Thus, the practice among a group or a few Jews is more likely to be a tradition borrowed from surrounding cultures (ibid. 106).

Francis E. Ekanem's assertion that "Africa has a wide array of philosophy richly embedded in her culture and tradition in oral form."[27] Underlying all African cultures and traditions are certain philosophical affinities, which we shall explore in trying to establish the ideas that foster and perpetuate female genital mutilation in Africa.

African indigenous communities cite different versions of a cosmological myth as the origin of female genital mutilation. According to one version, having created the earth, the Supreme Being approached earth to have intercourse but Earth's protruding clitoris prevented him. Only after the Supreme Being removed the barrier could intercourse take place.[28] From this ensues the assumption that every human being is born androgynous, and therefore excision is necessary for sexual intercourse. This may have initiated the practice of female genital mutilation among the practicing African cultures. However, the myth does not explain the prevalence of the practice in our contemporary world in which myths are deemed preposterous. Probing African philosophical ideas, especially African ontology, may be more fruitful.

African Ontology

For indigenous Africans, everything exists for a purpose, though the reason may not be known or mysterious. "Being" is, therefore, perceived by many as a generic term for every existing object whether animate or inanimate.[29] One scholar observes that "being," in African culture, is a universal force—the essence of all existence. It is responsible for "activating essence of particular beings and things, it also refers to the general power to act in non-ordinary, non-physical ways." It embodies humankind and all natural phenomena, which means every existence is capable of causal activity.[30] On the basis of the African concept of being, African philosophers point out that African metaphysics concerns the systematization of being and existence. It embraces a holistic and interrelated concept of reality, in which the material and the immaterial

---

[27] Francis E. Ekanem, "On the Ontology of African Philosophy," *International Journal of Humanities and Social Science Invention* 1 (2012): 54.

[28] The origin of the cosmological myth is traced back to the Egyptian Pharaonic belief in the hermaphroditic nature of their gods. See Sami A. Aldeeb Abu-Sahlieh, *Male and Female Circumcision Among Jews, Christians and Muslims Religious; Medical, Social and Legal Debate*, Marco Polo Monographs (Warren Center, PA: Shangri-La, 2001), 223; Bekers, 3; and Wangila, *Female Circumcision*, 106–107.

[29] Dominic Effiong Abakedi, "African Metaphysics: General Traits," in *Metaphysics: A Book of Readings*, ed. A. F. Uduigwomen (Calabar: Ultimate Index, 2012), 397–398.

[30] H. Minkus, "Causal Theory in Akwapim Akan Philosophy," in *African Philosophy: An Introduction*, ed. R. Wright (Washington, DC: University Press of America, 1977), 114–115.

realms are organically linked.[31] As such, to exist means "standing in a particular relationship with all there is both visible and invisible."[32] Thus, African philosophy embraces an ontological hierarchical structure with a Supreme Being at the top. Every African culture and tradition has a designated name for this Supreme Being, but among the differing names, there is a common understanding that every being owes its existence to the Supreme Being. He is "unique, wholly other and faultless and who owes His existence to no one."[33] He oversees and regulates the affairs of the universe. In descending order of the ontological hierarchy, next to the Supreme Being are deities or divinities. While some believe the deities are created beings, others claim that they are not created beings but brought into being. However, it is agreed that some of the deities are the spirits of humans who by their heroic activities were deified.[34] The divinities are subordinates to God and are pictured as personifications of activities or spirit beings in charge of natural phenomena. They function in accordance with the will of the Supreme Being and they serve as intermediaries between God and other creatures.

African traditional ontology does not discuss time and timelessness, but it is obvious that it assumes an understanding of timelessness. Emeka C. Ekeke and Chike A. Ekewpara, in discussing African ontology, chide scholars who perceive the African conception of God as an absentee landlord. They opine that in African traditional ontology the Supreme Being's transcendence and immanence are paradoxically complementary.[35] They explain that God works on His primordial level, but connects to human history through His created supernatural deities. Thus, these deities embody historic and timeless components that alone make their timeless-historic connection possible. This is a clear mark of a timelessness conception of God; that is, African traditional ontology reflects the metaphysical view that appears Platonic in structure.

In a descending order of the ontological structure are spirits, humans, animals, and plants. Our interest now is spirits and humans. Some African cultures are certain that the Supreme Being created the

---

[31] Martin Odei Ajei, "Africa's Development: The Imperatives of Indigenous Knowledge and Values" (PhD diss., University of South Africa, 2007), 168–169.

[32] E. A. Ruah and K. C. Anyanwu, eds., *African Philosophy: An Introduction to the Main Philosophical Trends in Contemporary Africa* (Rome: Catholic Book Agency, 1981), 124, quoted in Ajei, 168.

[33] J. O. Awolalu, "What Is African Traditional Religion?," *Studies in Comparative Religion* 9, no. 1 (Winter 1975), www.studiesincomparativereligion.com/Public/articles/What_is_African_Traditional_Religion-by_Joseph_Omosade_Awolalu.aspx (accessed May 28, 2021).

[34] Emeka C. Ekeke and Chike A. Ekeopara, "God, Divinities and Spirits in African Traditional Religious Ontology," *American Journal of Social and Management Sciences* 1.2 (2010): 214.

[35] Ibid.

spirits as a race like the human race. Others hold that spirits are the spirits of humans after physical death.[36] From the African notion of being, the spirit realm includes the spirits of all visible creatures after the destruction or death of their physical bodies. Whatever this level comprises, it is a sort of existence on the African ontological structure that includes spirits that are, according to one scholar, manipulated in sorcery, witchcraft, or magic for certain ends.[37] They are immaterial and invisible but capable of physical manifestation, ubiquitous, and have designated regions as their dwelling places under the earth.[38] Next, in descending order of the African ontological hierarchy, is humanity. The African indigenous worldview perceives the human person in two ways: descriptively and normatively. Out of these two perspectives arise their ethical systems.

Descriptive Concept of Personhood

Descriptively, there is considerable consensus that a person is a being embodied in the visible form of flesh and blood, capable of epistemic discourse, creation, and organization of social structure. However, philosophical debate ensues on the relationship between the component elements. The debate has resulted in dualistic, tripatistic, and even pentachotomistic (adds paternal and maternal kinship principles to body, soul, and spirit) views of personhood among African philosophers.[39] Despite the different theories, there seems to be an agreement that personhood is comprised of visible and invisible elements. The invisible and supernatural part lives on in the spirit realm of the ontological structure after the death of the physical body.

Normative Concept of Personhood

In the African context, it is community that creates a normative or moral person.[40] Indeed, scholars who study cultures of Africa agree that features of cooperative societies are the fabric of African culture. The traditional African community may be comprised of kinfolk groups from distant to close lineage, living together as a community. The community also includes the spirits of departed relatives, also termed

---

[36] John Mbiti, *African Religions and Philosophy* (London: Heinemann Educational Books, 1990), 84.

[37] Asare Opoku, *West African Traditional Religion* (Accra: FEP International, 1978), 9–10.

[38] Mbiti, 84.

[39] Ajei, 172. See Elvis Imafidon, "The Concept of Person in an African Culture and Its Implication for Social Order," *Lumina* 23, no. 2 (2012): 4–7, ejournals.ph/article.php?id=7365 (accessed May 28, 2021).

[40] G. I. Onah, "The Universal and the Particular in Wiredu's Philosophy of Human Nature," in *The Third Way in African Philosophy: Essays in Honour of Kwasi Wiredu*, ed. Olusegun Oladipo (Ibadan: Hope Publications, 2002), 78; and Mbiti, 107.

as the living-dead or ancestral spirits, who serve as intermediaries between the spirit and physical realms. The ancestral spirits are perceived as benevolent guardians of their communities and their customs and ethical norms. They punish disdain for communal practices, infringement on taboos, and disrespect of norms of acceptable behavior in their communities with misfortunes and incurable diseases.[41] Their anger against offenders is averted with pacification rituals. Thus, they are the "conduits through which morality is instilled and new ideas are received, interpreted, understood and accepted."[42] As benevolent guardians of the community, they are also seen as the source of blessing, granting bumper harvests, fertility to women of child-bearing age, good health and longevity, and social stability to their communities. The living in the communities venerate the ancestral spirits for their benefits. The belief in ancestral spirits forms an integral part of the effort of indoctrinating, mobilizing, promoting, and legitimizing communal practices.[43]

It is this kind of community that reserves the prerogative of creating normative personhood. The life of the individual in such communities is identified as a rhythm that includes birth, puberty, marriage, procreation to continue the existence of the individual's family, old age, and finally death.[44] Birth is the entering of an ontic person, intrinsically androgynous possessing both male and female souls, into the physical realm of cultural community existence. The physiological features of androgynous genitals reveal the souls. A man's prepuce represents the feminine soul and a woman's clitoris represents the masculine soul.[45] As the myth indicates, it is a belief that excision of the prepuce is necessary to rid all the feminine aspects believed to interfere with masculinity in a male child, while the excision of the clitoris essentially liberates a female child from all traces of masculinity.

Included in the community's prerogative of creating normative personhood is defining gender and sexuality. Excision, for these cultures, is essential to being a normative personhood.[46] Death is the exiting of an ontic person from the physical realm of community existence into the spirit realm. Thus, humans experience their existence in communal

---

[41] Christopher I. Ejizu, "African Traditional Religions and the Promotion of Community-Living in Africa," *Afrika World*, January 5, 2008, http://www.afrikaworld.net/afrel/community.htm (accessed May 28, 2021). See also Mbiti, 104, for more details on the family.

[42] Wangila, 40. See also Mbiti, 82.

[43] Wangila, 40; and Ejizu.

[44] Mbiti, 107–161.

[45] Abu-Sahlieh, *Male and Female Circumcision*, 223. See also Bekers, 3; and Wangila, 106–107.

[46] Fuambai Ahmadu, "Rites and Wrongs: An Insider/Outsider Reflects on Power and Excision," in Shell-Duncan and Hernlund, *Female "Circumcision" in Africa*, 297; and Wangila, 107.

relations. Writing on African philosophy, one scholar excellently summarizes the African concept of the communal person: "The individual can only say: 'I am, because we are; and since we are, therefore I am.'"[47]

Accordingly, moral personhood is a status acquired based on how well an individual internalizes and commits to the societal values and ethical conducts and practices of the cultural community. A moral person is one whose gender and sexuality have been defined by the community, gone through all the community's prescribed appropriate rites for his or her age, and has taken his or her place as a responsible community member. Perhaps Ifeanyi Menkiti succinctly articulates this idea when he remarks that normative personhood is

> attained in direct proportion as one participates in communal life through the discharge of the various obligations defined by one's stations. It is the carrying out of these obligations that transforms one from . . . early childhoods, marked by an absence of moral functions, into the person-status of later years, marked by a widened maturity of ethical sense—an ethical maturity without which [normative] personhood is conceived as eluding one.[48]

A community member is labeled morally blameworthy if his or her conduct falls short of the community's prescription.[49]

The cultural community serves as a catalyst and a prescriber of the practices, norms, and moral principles with the belief in ancestral spirits used as a means to enforce and inculcate the prescribed practices and norms.[50] Some African philosophers argue that a moral system cannot be derived from non-revealed religions, such as African traditional religion.[51] Yet we cannot dismiss the influence indigenous African religion has on its moral system: a human creation, guiding the process of shaping moral personhood in African communal context. Belief in ancestral spirits reinforces, governs, internalizes, and legitimizes the practice of female genital mutilation. Sociologists acknowledge that culture and religion

---

[47] Mbiti, 106. See also Kwame Gyekye, "Person and Community in African Thought," galerie-inter.de/kimmerle/frameText9.htm (accessed May 28, 2021).

[48] Ifeanyi A. Menkiti, "A Person and Community in African Traditional Thought," http://www2.southeastern.edu/Academics/Faculty/mrossano/gradseminar/evo%20of%20ritual/african%20traditional%20thought.pdf (accessed May 28, 2021), 176. See also *Stanford Encyclopedia of Philosophy*, Fall 2011 ed., s.v. "African Ethics," ed. Edward N. Zalta, https://plato.stanford.edu/archives/fall2011/entries/african-ethics (accessed May 28, 2021); Gyekye; and Onah, 79.

[49] *Stanford Encyclopedia of Philosophy*; and Gyekye.

[50] Gyekye.

[51] *Stanford Encyclopedia of Philosophy*.

function interdependently. The reference to ancestral spirits instills in community members fear and unwavering obedience to social values and practices, thus making the practice absolute, unchangeable, and tenacious. Hence, the communal structure, practices, and moral system are of importance to every member of the community, with the common good perceived as something that naturally and necessarily must be met. African ethical systems guiding the creation of personhood are, therefore, duty oriented, which alone ensures the survival and perpetuity of the community and its practice of female genital mutilation.

In sum, it is clear that there is no clear evidence that the Abrahamic religions are in favor of female genital mutilation. While historians disagree on the origin, they believe female genital mutilation predates Islamic and Christian religions and Judaism's male circumcision ritual.[52] Its practice among Jews, Christians, and Muslims suggests converts from the indigenous traditions brought the practice of female genital mutilation to Islam, Judaism, and Christianity, maintaining and legitimatizing the practice in their newly found faith. Evidently, the tenacity of female genital mutilation is rooted in the African indigenous ontological worldview, but it adapts to and assimilates with sociocultural changes.

Analysis of the Moral Values at Stake

The analysis of female genital mutilation continues with the moral values that practitioners associate with the practice. Rather than considering the values individually, this study classifies them into two categories: sociological and psychosexual values. We should be reminded

---

[52] Some historical records date the practice from 163 BC, while others reference 450 BC. See Nyangweso, *Female Genital Cutting*, 29–30; Sacirbey, 16; and Rossella Lorenzi, "How Did Female Genital Mutilation Begin?," seeker.com/how-did-female-gential-mutilation-begin-1766105357.html (accessed June 8, 2021). Salima Ikram, professor of Egyptology at the American University in Cairo, believes the absence of physical evidence in mummies and in artwork or literature indicates that the origin of female genital mutilation may have been in sub-Saharan Africa and was later adopted in Egypt (Lorenzi). According to historian Catherine Coquery-Vidrovitch, *African Women: A Modern History* (Boulder, CO: West View, 1997), 207, female genital mutilation may have originated from Egypt and spread to Rome. Coquery-Vidrovitche's assumption on the origin of female genital mutilation was later proven with Greek papyrus dated 163 BC that confirms female genital mutilation was practiced on girls in Egypt during that period of time. See Rosemarie Skaine, *Female Genital Mutilation: Legal, Cultural and Medical Issues* (Jefferson, NC: McFarland, 2005), 16. Alternatively, others argue that female genital mutilation originated with the ancient practice of emasculation or phallic worship among the Phoenicians and Hittites. The practice then spread to tribes along the Red Sea coastal areas and eastern Sudan and its surrounding areas through Arab traders. See Abu-Sahlieh, *Male and Female Circumcision*, 223–224; and Ahmadu, 295–296. These authors suggest female genital mutilation was practiced long before Abrahamic religions.

that these will not cover all the reasons that have been cited for the justification of the practice.[53]

Sociological Values

In the light of the African indigenous concept of moral personhood, it comes as no surprise that many of the moral reasons practitioners cite for their devotion to the practice fall under sociological concerns, such as status in a community, marriageability, and communal and/or religious identity. Cultures that attach sociological values to female genital mutilation practice it as an initiation from girlhood to womanhood and/or as a purity ritual.

The creation of womanhood involves many activities, but our attention is on the symbols embedded in the process. Although the symbols vary by culture, the basic meaning, according to one scholar, is dying and rebirth—a form of rebirth that unites the individual with the communal family. It is a process through which female individuals die to a state of girlhood and rise in a new status of womanhood, incorporating into adulthood the full privileges and responsibilities to the community.[54] Included in the creation of womanhood, the initiates receive lessons on sociocultural norms and practices like matters of housekeeping, marital relations, norms governing sexual behavior, proper behavior in communal living, and child rearing.[55] Writing against the abolishment of female genital mutilation among the Kikuyu people, one scholar emphasizes that female genital mutilation is "*condicio sine qua non* of the whole teaching of tribal law, religion, and morality."[56] Another notes the value of the lessons to initiates and their communities, stating, "Formal schools and universities in modern Africa are often the centers of even greater ignorance of these matters, so that young people go through them knowing, perhaps, how to dissect a frog but nothing about either their own procreation system and mechanism, or how to establish family life."[57] In this respect, the educational aspect of the initiation, in a quality way, prepares the youth for married life. Nevertheless, some aspects of the cultural creation of a moral personhood are very disquieting.

---

[53] In some cultures, female genital mutilation is a recent adoption by adolescents as a fashion statement. See Lori Leonard, "Adopting Female 'Circumcision' in Southern Chad: The Experience of Myabé," in Shell-Duncan and Hernlund, *Female "Circumcision" in Africa*, 181–191.

[54] Wangila, 109; and Mbiti, 118.

[55] Mbiti, 126.

[56] Jomo Kenyatta, *Facing Mount Kenya: The Traditional Life of the Gikuyu* (London: Heinemann, 1985), 133.

[57] Ibid., 132.

Part of the creation of womanhood is an examination of the status of virginity of the initiates. Traditional African cultures are particular about the preservation of virginity before marriage. While it is easy for these cultures to know the mother of a child, it is challenging for them to identify the father of a child. The only way to know the paternity of a child, for an African traditional community, depends on a woman's preservation of her virginity before marriage and her fidelity afterward. Put differently, the integrity of a family—and for that matter, the patriarchal system—depends on the faithfulness of women in the communal society.[58] Thus in this communal structure, a husband's honor and respect are tied to a chaste wife and the children she bears. A wife's socio-economic status is linked to her ability to bear and rear children and compel them to participate in the communally prescribed rituals. Subsequently, preserving virginity before marriage is equated with virtue.[59] So in the process of creating womanhood, codes are incorporated to reveal to spectators those among the initiates who have lost their virginity before their initiation. The initiate with broken virginity and her family are subject to humiliation. Thus, the victim may be disowned or commit suicide to save her family from perpetual humiliation.[60] In a situation where none of these takes place, the victim may be stigmatized as unmarriageable or less dowry may be given for her hand in marriage. This has generated many concerns about the practice.

First, the practicing culture uses the condition of the initiates' hymen to determine their virginity status. While there is no consensus on the function of the hymen,[61] it is proper to assume that similar to any body part, every female's hymen is different in shape and thickness. In children, the hymen is very prominent, but as they grow it thins out as the vaginal opening expands:[62] the "vaginal orifice and surrounding tissue

---

[58] Gerry Mackie, "Female Genital Cutting: The Beginning of the End," in Shell-Duncan and Hernlun, *Female "Circumcision" in Africa*, 262.

[59] Mackie, 262; Bettina Shell-Duncan, Walter Obungun Obiero, and Leunita Auko Muruli, "Women Without Choices: The Debate Over Medicalization of Female Genital Cutting and Its Impact on a Northern Kenyan Community," in Shell-Duncan and Hernlund, *Female "Circumcision" in Africa,* 118.

[60] Mbiti, 124–125.

[61] Some argue that the hymen protects "female children from infection, a barrier against organisms that might be introduced into the vagina through inadequate hygiene" (Mary Knight, "Curing Cut or Ritual Mutilation?: Some Remarks on the Practice of Female and Male Circumcision in Graeco-Roman Egypt" *Isis* 92 (2001): 337); others like Hanne Blank believe it is functionless, but a piece of "flesh by which the reputations, futures, and in some cases lives of millions of women have hung in the balance" (Hanne Blank, *Virgin: The Untouched History* [New York: Bloomsbury, 2008], 23, 33).

[62] Wikipedia, s.v. "Virginity," last modified May 18, 2021, https://en.wikipedia.org/wiki/Virginity (accessed May 28, 2021).

become distensible with adult levels of circulating female hormones."[63] As some authors emphasize, aside from sexual penetration, the hymen may be lacerated by diseases, injury, rigorous exercise or physical activities, and medical examination. However, some females have a resilient hymen, and it rebounds to its original condition after even coitus and childbirth.[64] Naturally, then, the hymen is not associated with virginity; therefore, the use of the state of the hymen as a determinant of virginity status during this cultural creation of womanhood is irresponsible, inappropriate, and could mar the reputation and future of many girls.

Second, considering the family structure and community relations underpinning female genital mutilation, some feminists conclude that the practice symbolizes institutionalization of patriarchal dominance over the female population and, by extension, men's control over the sexuality of women in maintaining the honor and integrity of the patriarchal structure. This painting of female genital mutilation with a broad brush of patriarchal control over women has given rise to emotionally charged debate on racism and Western imperialism, mimicking the controversy that ensued over female genital mutilation during the colonial era. African feminists, while opposed to female genital mutilation, feel most Western feminists' approach to the practice classify African women as oppressed and ignorant victims.[65] Few among Western feminists object to this patriarchal criticism, putting forth the argument that some patriarchal communities do not perform female genital mutilation and some matrilineal communal communities who have no "obsession with family virginity and chastity" practice female genital mutilation as a symbol of the "presence of powerful female society."[66] Emphasis is put on the fact that women safeguard, manage, and control the practice and pressure other women to adhere to it. Therefore, female genital mutilation is the celebration and empowerment of women; its abolishment disempowers

---

[63] Knight, 337.

[64] https://en.wikipedia.org/wiki/Virginity (accessed May 28, 2021).

[65] Christine J. Walley, "Searching for 'Voices': Feminism, Anthropology, and the Global Debate Over Female Genital Operation," *Cultural Anthropology* 12 (1997): 418–423; and Bekers, 161. Others have responded asserting that the patriarchy system extends beyond men controlling women. See Bekers, 161; Ellen Gruenbaum, *The Female Circumcision Controversy: An Anthropological Perspective* (Philadelphia, PA: University of Pennsylvania Press, 2001) 41; and Thomas, Ylva Hernlund, "Cutting Without Ritual and Ritual Without Cutting: Female 'Circumcision' and the Re-ritualization of Initiation in the Gambia", Paper presented at the 98th Annual Meeting (AAA), Chicago, November 17–21, 1999; Fuambai Ahmadu, "Rites and Wrongs: An Insider/Outsider Reflects on Power and Excision" in Shell-Duncan and Hernlund, *Female "Circumcision" in Africa* (200): 283–312.

[66] Ahmadu, 285.

women.[67] It seems both sides of the debate have some truth in their arguments. Certainly, some may take advantage of the system to coerce and abuse women, while others perceive it as women being in charge of their reproductive organ. Having said that, it is also clear that both sides ignore the complexity of the philosophy informing female genital mutilation. On the one hand, what is intended to be a woman's assurance to a man in a marriage institution and communal community is unsympathetically criticized as males' control over female sexuality. On the other hand, some tolerate the practice of female genital mutilation because of the cooperative values of cultural affinity and family connection associated with it. Thus, both sides of the debate scratch the surface of the problem, leaving untouched the philosophical ideologies grounding the practice and the real issues relating to it.

For instance, cultures that practice female genital mutilation due to sociological values claim excision, the cutting of the genitals, signifies indispensable social values. According to the moral system underlying female genital mutilation, one of the duties of adulthood in the communal society is marriage and procreation. Thus, fertility and the ability to procreate are of much concern to African traditional communities. These cultures believe that the clitoris encourages masturbation and obstructs sexual penetration. Subsequently, it prevents coitus and, therefore, inhibits fertility in females.[68] Excision of the clitoris unseals the female generative organ and invokes ancestral spirits' fertility blessing. Medical evidence, however, shows that the clitoris does not impede fertility in females.[69] Although it has been difficult for researchers to establish a direct or secondary relationship between female genital mutilation and fertility, medical literature shows that a high number of excised women experience fertility problems. A common short-term fertility problem facing excised women is that female genital mutilation inhibits coitus in the first few weeks or months of marriage, consequently increasing the interval between marriage and first birth. Generally, the mutilation of the clitoris results in infections and injuries that hinder conception and increase the risk of pregnancy wastage.[70] Thus, female genital mutilation risks life and dampens women's fertility, instead of the assumed view that it invokes ancestral fertility and, therefore, guarantees female fertility.

---

[67] See Bekers, 161; Gruenbaum, *Female Circumcision Controversy*, 41.

[68] Ahmadu, 297.

[69] Nivin Todd, "Your Guide to Female Infertility," WebMD, July 26, 2019, http://webmd.com/infertility-and-reproduction/guide/female-infertility (accessed May 28, 2021).

[70] Deborah Balk, "To Marry and Bear Children? The Demographic Consequences of Infibulation in Sudan," in Shell-Duncan and Hernlund, *Female "Circumcision" in Africa*, 57–59.

The cultures that practice female genital mutilation due to sociological values further argue that the blood shed during the mutilation of the genitals symbolically binds the individuals being excised to their respective communities or tribes and their ancestors—a pledge of solidarity with their communities.[71] This bond is adamant and oppressive. It subjects the participants to laws and mystical obligations whose requirements they cannot break without "falling in the eyes of all."[72] Jomo Kenyatta points out that "the moral code of the tribe is bound up with this custom and that it symbolizes the unification of the whole tribal organization."[73] Thus, female genital excision is necessary for this obligatory and mutual relationship between individuals and communities.

In some Muslim regions where *fatwas* encourage the practice, in addition to female genital mutilation being associated with communal identity and solidarity, it is also classified as a purity ritual. These societies believe that as women mature physically they come in contact with pollutants such as "menstrual blood flow and the blood of childbirth and bodily emissions of young children." These pollutants limit them from participating in religious activities. So female genital mutilation cleanses them from the pollution and establishes their Muslim identity and readiness to pray in the proper way.[74]

But it is scientifically proven that blood shed under unhygienic conditions reaps irreparable health damages. As already mentioned, female genital mutilation is traditionally performed with unsterilized instruments and without pain medication, antibiotics, and anesthesia. In the absence of anesthesia and pain medications, women and girls subjected to female genital mutilation are susceptible to excruciating pain and hemorrhage. As one scholar observes, "it is not uncommon for girls, who are held down by female relatives," to die from excruciating pain or suffer "shock or hemorrhaging"[75] resulting from "ruptured blood vessels in the clitoris."[76] This is often the case due to lack of medical intervention. Those who survive the hemorrhaging complications may suffer acute

---

[71] Wangila, 109; and Abu-Sahlieh, *Male and Female Circumcision,* 231.

[72] Abdou Toure, "L' Afrique traditionnelle savait éduquer ses enfants mais l'Occident est venu et tout s'est effondré," *Le Temps Stratéguique* 79 (1988): 22–23, quoted in Abu-Sahlieh, *Male and Female Circumcision*, 231.

[73] Kenyatta, 134.

[74] Michelle C. Johnson, "Becoming a Muslim, Becoming a Person: Female 'Circumcision,' Religious Identity, and Personhood in Guinea-Bissau," in Shell-Duncan and Hernlund, *Female "Circumcision" in Africa*, 219–220.

[75] Jan Goodwin, *Prince of Honor: Muslim Women Lift the Veil of Silence on the Islamic World* (London: Penguin Books, 2003), 321.

[76] Nyangweso, *Female Genital Cutting*, 58.

anemia, possible infection such as septicema and gangrene of the vulvar tissue caused by urine and fecal contamination of the wound, and urinary tract infections. Crude and unsterilized instruments, used for multiple patients, causes and/or spreads infections like tetanus, HIV/AIDS, and hepatitis B and C.[77] This has generated a debate on the medicalization of female genital mutilation to alleviate the immediate side effects. Even with medicalization, scarring of the genitalia has its own health challenges. The health risks increase with the degree of the mutilation of the female genitalia, subjecting the victims to high risks of obstetrical complications and possible maternal and neonatal death. The immediate health dangers that all forms of excision generate make the idea of practicing female genital mutilation for the purpose of sociological values offensive.

Psychosexual Values

This study has argued that practicing female genital mutilation on account of sociological values is not worth the sacrifice of the health and lives of girls and women. Values of a psychosexual nature have also been offered by practitioners of female genital mutilation,[78] who believe that when the clitoris is untouched it overgrows and becomes excessively aggressive, leading to sexual insatiability and promiscuous activities.[79] From their point of view, the solution to these issues lies in the excision of the female genital, promoting chastity and fidelity in women.

The idea of the enlarged clitoris, which stems from an assumed theory of the bisexual nature of humanity, influenced female genital mutilation in medical sectors. For example, ancient medical sources claim medical excision of women was practiced on the grounds of abnormal growth of the clitoris.[80] Without a doubt, abnormal growth of the clitoris may be possible because humans are degenerating under the weight of sin. However, the generalization that all women of the cultures that practice female genital mutilation suffer from an oversized clitoris is an overstatement. One expert agrees with this conclusion when he argues that the assumption of an enlarged clitoris must be medically false without any biological evidence.[81]

---

[77] Balk, 58–59; Nyangweso, *Female Genital Cutting*, 58–61; and Shell-Duncan, Obiero, and Muruli, 125.

[78] Wangila, 101–102.

[79] Knight, 327; and Wangila, 101–102.

[80] Knight, 327.

[81] Gerry Mackie, "Ending Footbinding and Infibulation: A Convention Account," *American Sociological Review* 2 (1996): 1005.

Activists against female genital mutilation insist that the removal of the clitoris does a great disservice to women. According to them, a woman's clitoris is the integral sensitive part of the female reproductive system, which when stimulated arouses female orgasm during sexual intercourse. As a result, they assert, any form of excision that deforms the clitoris deprives women of sexual pleasure and desire and enforces passivity before marriage and chastity in a polygynous household.[82] Fuambai Ahmadu, born and raised in the United States, who was excised in the context of Sierra Leone's Kono initiation ritual while she was in her final year of university in Washington, DC, narrating her story, forcefully refutes the claim that excision deprives women of sexual pleasure and desire.[83] Contrary to Ahmadu's story, Miriam, an immigrant Kissi woman from Kenya who was excised at a tender age, laments the absence of her sexual sensitivity, desire, and enjoyment.[84] Michelle C. Johnson's ethnographic research indicates that it is difficult to determine the relationship between inhibiting female sexual desires and consequently female conjugal faithfulness and female genital mutilation because research data suffers from many limitations. The difficulty in such research lies, in part, in the fact that research focuses entirely on African women,[85] who do not discuss their sexuality openly, and partly because women's sexuality is subjective and individually variable. Thus, an objective study of the relationship between excision and psychosexual values seems to be impossible.

That said, clinical evidence of the health consequences of infibulation, the severest form of female genital mutilation, suggests that practicing female genital mutilation for the purposes of preservation of virginity,[86] chastity, and consequently conjugal faithfulness has a high potential of negatively impacting the sexual desire of women who undergo infibulation. Infibulation, the cutting of the external genitalia and narrowing of the vaginal opening, causes severe pain during intercourse but does not necessarily preserve virginity before marriage. The healing of this type of female genital mutilation results in abnormal scarring such as the formation of fibrous tissue in the cut area, excessive growth of tissue over the cut area, and sometimes an abnormal fusion of the major and minor

---

[82] See Abusharaf, "Revisiting Feminist Discourses on Infibulation"; and Shell-Duncan and Hernlund, "Dimensions of the Practice and Debates," 21–22.

[83] Ahmadu, 289

[84] Nyangweso, *Female Genital Cutting*, 34–38.

[85] Johnson, 226–231.

[86] Ibid., 218; and Ellen Gruenbaum, "Is Female 'Circumcision' a Maladaptive Cultural Pattern?," in Shell-Duncan and Hernlund, *Female "Circumcision" in Africa*, 50.

labia. Subsequently, infibulation has the potential to cause psychosexual problems, sexual dysfunction, and loss of sexual desire.

An additional consequence of the abnormal scarring is a loss of the elasticity of the genitalia. Consequently, infibulated women go through de-infibulation to allow for the consummation of marriage and re-infibulation when divorced or widowed. In some situations, there is de-infibulation and re-infibulation during and after each childbirth. In addition to the inflicted pain and suffering through de- and re-infibulation, the women are exposed to a high risk of gynecological problems such as painful menstruation; slow urinary stream; urinary and blood retention, which causes swelling of the abdomen and, if not cured, causes cysts; and a chronic ascendance of bacteria into the urinary tract. The loss of elasticity of the genitalia results in a high risk of obstetrical complications. Clinical studies show that female genital mutilation is linked with an increased risk of caesarean section, postpartum hemorrhage from obstetric lacerations, and de-infibulation, which sometimes leads to vesico-vaginal and rectovaginal fistulae and maternal deaths, episiotomy, instrumental delivery, prolonged labor, and extended maternal hospital stay. There is also an increase in prenatal risks such as a high incidence of infant resuscitation at delivery, brain damage, intrapartum stillbirth, and neonatal death.[87] A study on the cost of female genital mutilation in six African countries (Burkina Faso, Ghana, Kenya, Nigeria, Senegal, and Sudan) shows that a fifteen-year-old girl who undergoes the severest type of female genital mutilation will lose nearly one-fourth of a year of life. It is thus estimated that out of 2.8 million fifteen-year-old girls in the six countries studied, about 130,000 years of life loss is expected, attributed to female genital mutilation-related obstetric haemorrhage.[88] The monetary loss and the lives lost in the process of attaining psychosexual moral values through female genital

[87] Women who have undergone the severest type of "FGM had "30% higher risk for delivery by caesarean section than those who had not had genital mutilation" and "70% higher risk of post-partum hemorrhage than women who had not undergone genital mutilation. The proportion of women delivering for the first time who required an episiotomy ranged from 41% of those who had not undergone genital mutilation to 88% of those who had undergone type III. Among women who had had previous deliveries, the proportions were 14% and 61%, respectively." "The rate of resuscitation was 66% higher for infants of women who had undergone type III mutilation than for those who had no female genital mutilation. The death rates among infants during and immediately after birth were higher for those born to mothers with genital mutilation than those without, being 15% higher for women with type I, 32% higher for those with type II and 55% higher for those with type III" (World Health Organization, "Female Genital Mutilation and Obstetric Outcome: Prospective Study in Six African Countries," *The Lancet* 367 [2006]: 1835–1841. See also Shell-Duncan and Hernlund, "Dimensions of the Practice and Debates," 14–18).

[88] David Bishai et al., "Estimating the Obstetric Costs of Female Genital Mutilation in Six African Countries," *Bulletin World Health Organization* 88 (2010): 281–288.

mutilation make the practice worthless. Assessments such as this are often rejected with the argument that many infibulated women are fertile and have more live births. This rebuttal is no more sensible than to say that there are more people who do not die from stroke than there are those who do, and therefore the search to find a cure is non-essential.

In summary, the analysis of female genital mutilation via the values identified for the justification of the practice shows that cultures participating in female genital mutilation use the practice as a means to an end—moral values that ensure the continuity of cooperative living societies. The moral system that the cultures live by assign authority and respect to their predecessors. It seems that these communities are more concerned about the impact their decision regarding female genital mutilation will have on the common good of the communal society (including ancestors) than the health risks that excised girls and women may encounter. Thus, the prescribed means to the common good or achieving psychosexual values or ritual purification is the norm. Questioning the practice on the basis of its risks is tantamount to disrespecting authorities. In this context, the practicing communities appear to have become vulnerable and slaves to the poor decisions of their predecessors.

Biblical Appraisal of Female Genital Mutilation

The analysis in this study has revealed that female genital mutilation, although practiced in many parts of the world, has its historical roots in the African indigenous worldview. While activists opposing the practice argue against it because of the health risks it poses to women who undergo female genital mutilation, proponents believe that due to its moral benefits it should be maintained. But what is the biblical appraisal of the practice? The need to examine female genital mutilation from the biblical perspective is paramount. This study shall do so, focusing on the ontological, sociological, and psychosexual issues relating to the practice.

Ontological Issues

As we take on the task of pursuing a biblical assessment of the practice of female genital mutilation, we need to recall that, according to the preceding analysis, the ontological idea that enforces the practice perceives humans as being born androgynous.

The idea of androgynous human beings brings to mind scholars like Phyllis Trible, who claims the biblical creation narrative suggests a sexually undifferentiated first human person. Specifically, she argues that the term *hāʾādām* refers to an undifferentiated sexual earthly creature and it is only when the woman was created (Gen 2:21–24) that a sexual distinction was made.[89] The idea of a bisexual nature of the first human has not gone unchallenged.[90] However, even if we grant Trible's view, it does not absolve the practice of female genital mutilation, since the argument identifies only the first human created as hermaphrodite. Nearly all subsequent human beings come into the world with a distinct sexual identity; therefore, it is unnecessary to create a sexual identity with female genital mutilation.

But the sexually undifferentiated first human person is not supported by Genesis' anthropology. There is no indication in the text that male and female were created simultaneously. The term *hā'ādām* is not used differently before and after the creation of the woman, signifying that no change in the physiology of the *hā 'ādām* before and after the creation of the woman had occurred.[91] Genesis' anthropology portrays humanity as in the image and likeness of God (*imago Dei*), who exists as a being who encounters and relates to Himself—an allusion to the trinity. Personhood as the *imago Dei* is constituted as sexual differentiation, male and female (Gen 1:26–27).[92] As one author puts it, "we cannot say man without saying male or female." [93] That is, sexual differentiation or gender identity expressed in terms of female or male is ontologically intrinsic to personhood (Gen 1:27; 5:2; 9:6; Matt 19:4; Mark 10:6). Humanity is fundamentally sexually differentiated and only consequentially social.[94] Sexual differentiation is oriented toward marriage only because it is fundamentally oriented towards divine covenant relationship with the source of being—God (Gen 1:26).

Consequently, gender identity and the polarity of male and female are not acquired and are not sociocultural creations. It also means that there are intrinsic biological markers that signal physiological sexual maturity and marriageability. Thus in light of biblical anthropology,

---

[89] Phyllis A. Bird, "'Male and Female He Created Them': Gen 1:27b in the Context of the Priestly Account of Creation," *Harvard Theological Review* 74 (1981): 129–159; and Bird, *God and the Rhetoric of Sexuality* (Philadelphia, PA: Fortress, 1978), 80.

[90] See Richard M. Davidson, *Flame of Yahweh: Sexuality in the Old Testament* (Peabody, MA: Hendrickson, 2007), 20–21; Richard S. Hess, "Splitting the Adam: The Usage of 'ādām in Genesis I–V," in *Studies in the Pentateuch*, ed. J. A. Emerton (New York: E. J. Brill,1990), 1–16; and Johannes C. de Moor, "The Duality in God and Man - Gen 1:26–27 as P's Interpretation of the Yahwistic Creation Account," in *Intertextuality in Ugarit and Israel*, ed. Johannes C. de Moor (Leiden: Koninklijke Brill, 1998), 112–125.

[91] Davidson, 20.

[92] All biblical quotations are from the New King James Version.

[93] Karl Barth, *Church Dogmatics*, trans. H. Knight G. W. Bromiley, J. K. S. Reid, R. H. Fuller, G. W. Bromiley and T. F. Torrance (Edinburgh: T & T Clark Ltd., 1960), 3/2:286.

[94] Ray S. Anderson, *On Being Human: Essays in Theological Anthropology* (Eugene, OR: Wipf and Stock, 2010), 51, 108–109.

without dismissing the fact that society contributes to the upbringing of a person, the traditional African philosophy is flawed in attributing the creation of sexual and gender identity to traditional African communal societies. This understanding of biblical anthropology does not deny the fact that some individuals are born with ambiguous sexuality resulting from the degeneration of sinful human nature.

Reflection on the *imago Dei* hints at another distinctive component of personhood. The God whose plurality human sexual differentiation reflects is free to be for Himself (Trinity), to create and to relate to His creatures (John 1:1; 17:24–25).[95] Inevitably, human sexual differentiation not only marks relationship but also marks human freedom oriented toward God as an eternal source of life, self, and others. But female genital mutilation infringes on this freedom, a characteristic of being an authentic selfhood. Proponents of female genital mutilation argue that all who are exposed to the practice do so of their own free will. Indeed, when female genital mutilation is perceived outside of its cultural context, this conclusion is easily reached. However, as evidenced in the analysis, the practice is forced through indoctrination, implicit or explicit threats, and persuasion. The social and economic statuses of individual members are directly or indirectly tied to cultural practices. Thus, it is almost impossible for individual community members to protect themselves against the practice. Certainly, their freedom from that which binds the self or for the other is taken away. But, from a biblical anthropological perspective, female genital mutilation ultimately dehumanizes its practitioners, to the extent that human freedom, which is the result of sexual differentiation oriented toward fellowship with God, is disoriented by female genital mutilation. Biblically, female genital mutilation deforms and tarnishes human dignity—the *imago Dei;* its practice for any reason at all is groundless and a moral failure.

Although the biblical conception of *imago Dei* discredits female genital mutilation, some proponents attempt to moralize it using Scripture. For example, Tabona Shoko avers that the three stages of the African creation of womanhood—separation, transition, and reincorporation—are similar to the three phases of Catholic initiation sacraments (baptism, confirmation, and matrimony), which are part of a maturity process. From his perspective, both the creation of womanhood and Catholic initiation sacraments are instituted to address issues of human life and

---

[95] See Warren S. Brown, "Cognitive Contributions to Soul," in *Whatever Happened to the Soul?: Scientific and Theological Portraits of Human Nature*, ed. Warren S. Brown, Nancey Murphy, and H. Newton Malony (Minneapolis, MN: Fortress, 1998), 99–125; and Richard Rice, "Are We Really Free? A Biblically Based Response to Neurophysiological Reductionism," *Andrews University Seminary Studies* 51 (2013): 82.

share some affinities. Resultantly, there is the possibility of accommodating African initiation rites, specifically *komba*, as Christian ordinances.[96]

Shoko's perceived similarities between female genital mutilation and Catholic initiation sacraments may stem from the presuppositions he brings to the two systems. It should be noted that while both female genital mutilation and Catholic initiation sacraments are maturity processes, the Catholics initiation sacraments signal spiritual life.[97] This brings us to a staggering difference between the symbolism of dying to the old state of being and rebirth in a new state as used by Christians and female genital mutilation practitioners. Biblically, baptism is described as an initiation into the life of Christ and into the corporate body of Christ (1 Cor 6:11; 12:13). It symbolizes being buried with Christ and raised into a new life in Christ. Christ is an essential factor in biblical initiation—a factor that presupposes, contrary to the ontological view underwriting female genital mutilation, that the God of the Christian initiation is a temporal-historical reality, and a personal, historical being who acts, dwells among His people, and reveals Himself in time and space without breaking the continuum. Undeniably, God Himself is the authority of Christian moral principles and practices—as opposed to female genital mutilation, which draws its authority from cultural ancestral spirits. Scripture sees the belief in the existence of ancestral spirits as delusive. Many scholars concur the Bible teaches a wholistic view of human nature.[98] From the wholistic point of view, the spiritual and bodily dimensions of a person interact and influence each other. Thus, spirit or soul does not live independently apart from the body, nor does humankind have a soul. Therefore, death is the disintegration of a living being into dust and breath of life. The dust returns to dust and the life principle that animated the dust returns to the giver (Eccl 12:7). What returns to the giver after death is not a conscious entity (Eccl 9:5–6, 10).[99]

---

[96] Tabona Shoko, "Komba: Girl's Initiation Rite and Inculturation Among the VaRemba of Zimbabwe," *Studia Historiae Ecclesiasticae* 35 (2009), 31–45.

[97] *Catechism of the Catholic Church*, 2nd ed. (Rome: Liberia Editrice Vaticana, 1997), 311–312.

[98] From the wholism point of view, the spirit or soul does not live independently apart from the body nor does humankind have a soul. The breath of life from God animated the form formed out of dust and it became a living being. This biblical description brings us to the realization that recent approaches such as physicalism, interactionism, epiphenomenalism, and parallelism to human nature are inaccurate descriptions. See Davidson, 35–42; Joel B. Green, *Body, Soul, Human Life: The Nature of Humanity in the Bible* (Grand Rapids, MI: Baker, 2008); Aecio E. Cairus, "The Doctrine of Man," in *Handbook of Seventh-day Adventist Theology*, ed. Raoul Dederen (Hagerstown, MD: Review and Herald 2000), 205–232; and Jean R. Zurcher, *The Nature and Destiny of Man: Essay on the Problem of the Soul and the Body in Relation to the Christian View of Man* (New York: Philosophical Library 1969). For details on scientific anthropological approaches, see Brown, Murphy, and Malony, eds., *Whatever Happened to the Soul?*

[99] Some portions of Scripture seem to depict death as a new conscious existence. For

Therefore, humans are mortal (1 Tim 6:16; 1 Cor 15: 36–37); death is not entering into a new realm of existence, as African ontology proposes.

Note, however, that biblical anthropology establishes the falsehood of the premise of the cultures' belief in the reality of the existence of ancestral spirit. It does not deny the reality of the forces that cultures invoke during female genital mutilation. Rather, Scripture speaks of an adversary (Ezek 28:12–19; Dan 10:13; 12:1; Rev 12:7–9; 20:2) who establishes his religion through practices that rely on the false assumption of consulting with the spirits of the dead (spiritualistic practices). This means the practice of female genital mutilation as a rite of passage falls into the category of cultic practice. This stark contrast between biblical ontology and the ontology informing female genital mutilation reveals what is only apparent at the surface: the tension between female genital mutilation and biblical teachings. Therefore, it suffices to state that female genital mutilation is a departure from biblical teachings.

Sociological Issues

While female genital mutilation is theologically incompatible with biblical teachings, Scripture is quoted to justify female genital mutilation practiced as a response to existential issues such as fertility and communal solidarity and identity. For some Christians and Muslims, the biblical command for circumcision is evidence for God's approval of female genital mutilation as a means of curtailing possible fertility and religious issues, and of establishing communal identity and solidarity. Yet, biblically, fertility is a divine blessing bestowed on married couples (Gen 1:26–28; 12:2, 7), which means that the fertility status of an individual comes to light only after marriage. For this reason, the belief that excision enhances the fertility of womanhood defies reasoning. Furthermore, the command to circumcise the male child demands it be done on the eighth day after birth,[100] implying that circumcision was never intended to

---

instance, the kings of all nations welcome the king of Babylon into their midst (Isa 14:9–10). Contrary to the lively activity, the same passage speaks of the dead who have "become weak" (Isa 14:10), and they use "maggots" for a bed and "worms" for covering (Isa 14:11). The book of Ezekiel similarly describes the dead; the kings of Egypt, Assyria, Elam, and Edom are personified and presented as speaking out of the pit (Ezek 32:17–22). These passages are metaphorical presentations conveying the utter humiliation and destruction of tyrant kings. They rather support the definition of death in Genesis.

[100] Some ancient Near Eastern cultures practiced circumcision in two ways: by slitting the foreskin so that it hangs freely and by amputating the foreskin entirely. It was performed at puberty as a rite of passage into manhood and marriage. The amputation of the foreskin of the male generative was known among the ancient Near Eastern cultures, but by the time it was initiated in Israel it was practiced by Israel alone. Contrary to the ancient Near Eastern practice, the people of Israel were required to circumcise on the eighth day after birth, which means the meaning attached to the practice is different from other ancient Near Eastern cultures (Davidson, 449, esp. n. 9).

resolve sterility issues in males nor be a solution to Sarah's barrenness. The command to "cut off" the foreskin of the generative organ did not include Sarah (Gen 17:9–14) and all her female descendants. But Sarah was included in the blessing. Following the order of Genesis 17, John Goldingay proposes that circumcision is a sign of a discipline, which the Israelites lacked, and the reality that only males bore the mark of the covenant in their flesh means that "it is males who embody spiritual and mental unfitness to belong to the people of promise." He therefore concludes that any endeavor, either in theory or practice, to include females in the practice of circumcision "has the disadvantage of robbing circumcision of its cutting edge concerning men."[101] Subsequently, any form of justification of female genital mutilation reached from a deduction drawn from the divine decree for male circumcision is unsubstantiated.

Biblically, the issue of solidarity and identity can hardly be overemphasized. One cannot deny, as many Christian practitioners of female genital mutilation have pointed out, that male circumcision was a sign that marked the Israelites as participants of the divine covenant (Gen 17:11). In the preceding discussion it was apparent that the sign of the covenant that the men bore in their flesh was a sign of their futility and waywardness, which also served as a reminder of their needed commitment to their part of the covenant. In other words, the physical sign in their flesh was not an adequate sign of the covenant; its sufficiency depended on a religious attitude toward God. Metaphoric use of circumcision in Scripture enforces this idea.[102]

The symbolical usages of circumcision in Scripture take the emphasis from physical circumcision in Genesis 17 to spiritual circumcision. By the time of the New Testament church, the once-needed male circumcision was no longer required. Under the guidance of the Holy Spirit, the church ended physical circumcision as a requirement for belonging to the body of Christ (Act 15) and put emphasis on spiritual circumcision.[103] Most important, however, is that in lieu of the blood shed on the cross for all humankind, all that is needed for a person to belong has already been provided centuries ago. Therefore, male circumcision as a divine decree has lost its validity. Consequently, female genital mutilation either for religious or communal solidarity and identity, which was never a divine injunction but justified based on an assumption drawn from

---

[101] John Goldingay, "The Significance of Circumcision," *Journal for the Study of the Old Testament* 88 (2000): 16.

[102] For instance, God is identified as one who circumcises the heart (Deut 30:6), Moses describes his inability of speech as uncircumcised lips (Exod 6:12, 30), the Israelites' disobedience is portrayed as the result of uncircumcised heart and ears (Lev 26:41; Jer 4:4, 9:26; Ezek 44:7–9), and non-Jews are classified as uncircumcised (1 Sam 17:26, 36).

[103] Romans 2:27, 29; 1 Corinthians 7:17–20; Galatians 5:6, 6:15; Colossians 3:10–14.

divine command of male circumcision, is unnecessary. It misses the mark of biblical moral standards.

Psychosexual Issues

Besides using Scripture in support of female genital mutilation as a response to sociological issues, others believe biblical teachings on sexuality influence the practice of female genital mutilation for dealing with psychosexual issues, such as preservation of virginity until marriage, chastity, and conjugal faithfulness. Hanne Blank's use of Deuteronomy 22:13–21 seems to suggest that biblical laws on sexual morality condone premarital examination of virginity and the treatment given to those who lose their virginity before marriage.[104] Indeed, biblically illicit sexual practices are discouraged. The creation account and metaphorical reference to marriage portray the divine ideal for sexual intimacy as exclusively for the marriage relationship (Gen 2:24; Prov 1–9; Song 4:12–5:1; Eph 5:3; Col 3:5; 1 Thess 4:3; Heb 13:4). Thus, Scripture extols preservation of virginity until marriage but does not support the cultural examination of virginity status. Out of three biblical laws concerning virginity (Deut 22:23–29), two of them (Deut 22:25–29) protect individuals with broken virginity under unfortunate circumstances.

Particularly, the use of Deuteronomy 22:13–21 in support of African traditional examination of virginity in association with female genital mutilation is out of place. The woman at the center of this passage was to be stoned to death, not because of pre- or post-betrothal loss of virginity, but as one scholar rightly points out, she

> *concealed* from her husband her premarital sexual activity, and in such case, it was to be assumed that it was illicit sex after betrothal. The serious, but not capital, offense of premarital sex thus becomes a capital offense because of the element of deceit and false pretense to premarital chastity: she has entered into marriage without acknowledging her prior loss of virginity.[105]

Biblically, individuals who lose their virginity under unfortunate circumstances are protected. African cultural examination of the status of virginity as part of female genital mutilation conflicts with biblical laws.

One author enumerates Christian teachings that have been used in support of female genital mutilation as the importance of preserving virginity before marriage, exemplification of sexual control, sexual

---

[104] Blank, 29–31.

[105] Davidson, 358–359, emphasis original.

intimacy exclusively for procreation, and the use of contraception.[106] But this study has discovered that biblical anthropology affirms that sexuality and gender identity are ontological characteristics fundamentally oriented toward God and secondarily to marriage. Thus, the primary purpose of marriage is companionship and subsequently to procreate and fill the earth (Gen 1:26–28) as the consequence of becoming "one flesh" (Gen 2:24). Scholars concur that becoming "one flesh" represents sexual intimacy. The leaving of the man from his parents' house to join the woman to become "one flesh" accentuates the exclusive nature of the "one flesh"—sexual intimacy. This picturesque description of marriage means sexual intimacy and procreation are in the confines of monogamous heterosexual marriage.[107] Therefore, with monogamous heterosexual marriage, sexual intimacy "may be enjoyed for its own sake, for the beauty and ecstasy, for the sheer enjoyment by the partners."[108] Sexual intimacy "provides husband and wife with a *language* which cannot be matched by words or by any other act whatsoever. Love needs language for its adequate expression and sex has its own syntax."[109] After the fall, God protected the original nature of marriage with the seventh commandment (Exod 20:14). The rest of the Old Testament celebrates this original idea of the marriage institution (Song 4:16–5:1; Prov 5:18–19). Jesus emphasizes Genesis' theology of an ideal marriage (Matt 19:4–6) and the rest of the New Testament follows Christ's example of extolling Genesis' concept of marriage and its exclusive nature of "one flesh."

If the biblical conception of sexual intimacy is fundamentally for the relationship of married couples and subsequently for procreation, then Scripture does not frown on the use of contraception for the prevention of the formation of life in a marriage context, but frowns on the use of all kinds of contraception for the prevention of pregnancy outside of marriage institutions. This further suggests that Christianity's emphasis on upholding virginity until marriage and asceticism stems from the fact that God instituted sexual intimacy and restricted it within the marriage relationship for the benefit of the relationship. Another moral value that results from the biblical concept of the exclusive nature of sexual intimacy is that abstinence is the solution for preserving virginity until the consummation of marriage. Mary, the mother of Jesus, whom most Christian practitioners of female genital mutilation use as a model to justify their

---

106 Wangila, 89, 119–120.

107 Davidson, 46–48.

108 Ibid., 453.

109 Elton and Pauline Trueblood, *The Recovery of Family Life* (New York: Harper and Brothers, 1953), 54, quoted in Henlee H. Barnette, *Introducing Christian Ethics* (Nashville, TN: Broadman Press, 1961), 117, emphasis original.

participation, confirms this. She inquired of the angel how she could be pregnant without "know[ing] a man"—sexual intimacy (Luke 1:34). This response suggests the preservation of her virginity was due to refraining from premarital sexual intimacy, and not from female genital mutilation.

It has been suggested that the use of Scripture in defending female genital mutilation emerges from the influence of dualism. Dualism has led to erroneous principles such as equating "masculinity with transcendence, rationality, and logos, and femininity with immanence, emotionality, and eros."[110] Indeed, dualism has led to contrary teachings on biblical principles, as it is a faulty presupposition and, therefore, foreign to Scripture.

Contrary to Christians with dualistic presuppositions using the Pauline writings to encourage female genital mutilation, the Pauline writings, like other books in the Bible, exalt Genesis' theology of marriage and its exclusive nature of sexual intimacy. They call for husbands and wives to allow sexual intimacy between them to prevent sexual immorality (1 Cor 7:1–6). However, while the apostle Paul makes clear his desire that all would be like him for the furtherance of the gospel work, he immediately concludes that both lifestyles are gifts from God and are equally important (1 Cor 7:7–8). His call for Christians to preserve and care for their bodies as a spiritual responsibility, with an emphasis on fleeing sexual immorality, demonstrates that the "human body as the temple of the Holy Spirit" does not preclude human sexuality. Pauline writings do not contrast human sexuality and human spiritual experience. However, their ethical principles encourage living continually in the spirit (a person in the divine-human relationship) and staying away from the lust of the flesh (Gal 5:16–26). Sexual values, then, are a way of life guided and sustained by the Holy Spirit and not ancestral spirits, which together with other elements of traditional African ontology prescribe female genital mutilation. Consequently, a true biblical view on psychosexual values should not tolerate female genital mutilation.

Conclusion

This study has analyzed the practice of female genital mutilation to discern the reason for its prevalence in the contemporary scientific and technological world. Apparently, religion (Judeo-Christian, African indigenous religion, and Islam) has been considered the main factor underwriting the prevalence of female genital mutilation. But its origin and prevalence are solely rooted in African indigenous philosophical ideologies for setting moral standards that progress and perpetuate the

[110] Wangila, 89.

social life of the practicing communities. For the practicing communities, female genital mutilation is indispensable for their advancement. Contrary to the perception of the practicing communities about female genital mutilation, ethnographical and medical research show that the practice exposes women of the practicing communities to high health risks and could mar their reputation and future. Furthermore, as a response to existential issues, female genital mutilation contradicts biblical views on those issues. It also deforms the sexuality of those subjected to it, deprives them of their innate freedom, and utmostly robs them of their humanness.

Recommendations

Based on the side effects of female genital mutilation, many strategies have been adopted to curb or eradicate the practice, such as healthcare and educational programs, programs to bridge the economic disparity between men and women in the participating communities, and alternative initiation rites without cutting. Nevertheless, the prevalence of the practice suggests the programs have not achieved their purpose.

Christian leaders failed at their initial attempt to curb this practice. However, on several grounds, biblical Christianity is the key to curtailing and subsequently eradicating this human-invented crisis. First, religion plays an important role in the social life of the African communities that practice female genital mutilation. Second, the African takes the words of religious leaders as inviolable. Third, some of the values that these cultures attempt to achieve through the practice of female genital mutilation are the values that the biblical concept of sexuality prescribes. Fourth, the Christ of Christianity is the only alternative that satisfies the religious aspects of female genital mutilation. To this end, the Seventh-day Adventist Church has declared a statement of faith in regard to female genital mutilation, calling on all departments of the church and people of goodwill to help eliminate the practice. To achieve this goal, the following practical steps are recommended:

Deconstruction

We as a people believe in religious freedom for every people group. However, when issues undermine human dignity in the name of religion and cultural practices, the quest for religious freedom allows for needed intervention. Underlying the philosophical principles perpetuating female genital mutilation are fundamental biblical truths, such as the fundamental need of personhood (Gen 1:26–28), that have been misconstrued through cultural ideologies. Unfortunately, such misapprehensions are wrapped up in these human ideologies in such a manner that only deconstruction (Matt 15:2–6; Mark 7:1–13) would seem to be the solution.

Educational Programs

Lack of formal education on sexuality and promiscuous sexual activities on screens and social media have led Africans to trust more and more in their traditional beliefs and practices when it comes to issues of sexuality. Evidence of some Christian involvement in the practice suggests the church has not done well in disseminating biblical resources on human sexuality and procreation. In light of the discussion on values attached to the practice, the biblical conception of human sexuality and procreation is the *condicio sine qua non* of eradicating the erroneous philosophy of defining human sexuality and creating gender. Therefore, the church must intensify educational programs on human sexuality and procreation—especially in regions where the practice is prevalent.

Community–Based Programs

While there is an urgent need to iterate biblical human sexuality and procreation to church members in communities that practice female genital mutilation, the African concept of relatedness necessitates community-based programs. Programs targeting the community must be held away from church premises, in community centers where every communal society member can participate if they so wish. Programs must engage the elders of the various communities who are overseers of the communities' traditions and practices. The programs must encourage discussion, reflection, and reassessment of their cultural practices.

A Place for the Detested and Disowned

We have mentioned that individuals who are bold to stand alone in defiance to female genital mutilation are considered unsuitable for marriage and ostracized, with no family to turn to and no community to belong. The church must exhibit its ecclesiological characteristics to be a place where such individuals find a family to turn to and a community to belong. There is also the need for the church to organize programs that address the psychological and emotional stress that are usually associated with such situations and help those individuals find marriage partners within the church.

Cultural Sensitivity

Insensitivity toward the cultures that practice female genital mutilation thwarts efforts to curb the practice. The good aspects of their system must be recognized and appreciated, and the elements that are detrimental to human dignity approached with love and respect—that is, being sensitive to the communities that practice it even though we do not endorse it.

CHAPTER 12

Reproduction/Population Control and Abortion-Related Issues: Old Testament Foundations

Richard M. Davidson

Reproduction/Population Control[1]

In the ancient Near East a number of methods of reproduction/population control were utilized, including sterilization/castration, celibacy, sexual abstinence, alternative intercourse, contraception (through chemical anti-spermicides), coitus *interruptus,* infanticide (through exposure at birth), and abortion.[2] Given the high regard for having "a quiver full" of children in Hebrew society (Ps 127:5), as well as elsewhere in the ancient Near East, these birth control methods were probably not widely practiced. The problems related to reproduction were not about having too many children, but rather infertility and infant mortality.[3] However, there were times when pregnancy was unwanted, unexpected, or illegal (e.g., for some of the ancient Near Eastern priestesses who took vows

[1] The present chapter is largely adapted from Richard M. Davidson, *Flame of Yahweh: Sexuality in the Old Testament* (Peabody, MA: Hendrickson, 2007), 447–501, dealing with "Procreative Sexuality versus Problems/Distortions."

[2] For further discussion of these forms of birth control in the ancient Near East, see Andrew E. Hill, "Abortion in the Ancient Near East," in *Abortion: A Christian Understanding and Response,* ed. James K. Hoffmeier (Grand Rapids, MI: Baker, 1987), 31–48.

[3] According to ancient Mesopotamian records, only an average of two to four children in a nuclear family lived beyond early childhood (K. R. Nemet-Nejat, *Daily Life in Ancient Mesopotamia* [Westport, CT: Greenwood, 1998], 126–127). Though the average total number of children born in a nuclear family is unknown, it no doubt was considerably more than this. See also the various references in ancient Near East law codes to the possibility of a miscarriage due to someone striking a pregnant woman.

that they would not have children[4]), and various birth control practices were carried out. Sexual abstinence seems to have been more the exception than the rule,[5] except for times of ritual impurity for the woman when sexual intercourse was not permitted.[6] Various alternative forms of sexual intercourse in the ancient Near East may have served (among other things) as birth control strategies, and particularly homosexual practice for the cult functionaries of the Sumerian and Babylonian religions.[7]

Brief mention may be made of mechanical contraception, found particularly among the Egyptians. Devices included exotic potions (such as a willow bark potion mixed with the burned testicles of a castrated ass) used as chemical anti-spermicidal douches, and shields inserted into the vagina (e.g., a wool swab dipped in honey).[8] Such practices may well have been familiar to the Hebrews, and the Old Testament's silence on the utilization of such mechanical contraception devices probably indicates that "either contraception of this type was never an issue with Israel because of their high regard for children . . . or that the practice was accepted as normal and not considered worth mentioning."[9] Since sexual intercourse for the Hebrews had independent value for the pleasure and sexual fulfillment of the married couple and was not subordinated to the intent to have children,[10] there appears to have been no theological impediment preventing Hebrew couples from utilizing such contraceptives if they were ever needed. But, inasmuch as large families were highly regarded in order to supply the labor force around the estate and facilitate inheritance of property, the use of contraceptives may have been for the most part a moot issue.

One ancient Near Eastern practice of population control that may have found its way into Hebrew society, especially at the royal court,

---

[4] See Michael C. Astour, "Tamar the Hierodule: An Essay in the Method of Vestigial Motifs," *Journal of Biblical Literature* 85 (1966): 188: "These priestesses were sexually active, though in a way unnatural for women. The goal of it was to prevent conception, for no women consecrated to gods were allowed to bear children, even in marriage."

[5] Some cases of sexual abstinence in Sumerian culture are inferred from Sumerian proverbs such as "Conceiving is nice; being pregnant is irksome," and another in which a husband boasts that his wife had given birth to eight sons and was still ready to have sex with him, presumably in contrast to other wives who demand sexual abstinence. See H. W. F. Saggs, *The Greatness That Was Babylon* (New York: Hawthorn, 1962), 187, 407; cf. Hill, 33.

[6] See Davidson, 325–335.

[7] See the discussion in *Davidson*, 133–176.

[8] See Hill, 34, for references.

[9] Ibid.

[10] See discussion in Davidson, 15–80. This is contra the prevailing understanding of the purpose of sexual intercourse in rabbinic and Philonic Judaism, and the early church fathers. See Charles E. Cerling, "Abortion and Contraception in Scripture," *Christian Scholar's Review 2* (1971): 44–45.

was castration. The Hebrew term *saris* is an Akkadian loanword, which in pre-exilic times referred to a court official or royal steward, with no necessary implication of castration,[11] but in exilic and postexilic times came to indicate a eunuch who was appointed as royal steward and/or harem guard.[12] The practice of castration was forbidden by pentateuchal law (Lev 21:20; Deut 23:2 [ET v. 1]). Hence the term *saris* with the meaning of "eunuch" probably refers mainly (but not exclusively) to foreigners (Assyrians, Babylonians, and Persians) or to Judean males castrated in exile.[13] The royal courts of the neo-Assyrian and neo-Babylonian and Persian Empires regularly employed eunuchs as royal attendants of the harem. The one recorded biblical example of this practice during the time of the united monarchy in Israel appears to have been during the reign of Ahab, when Queen Jezebel had eunuch-attendants (*sarisim*) who threw her down from the window of the royal palace to Jehu (2 Kgs 9:32–33). This use of intentionally castrated men underscores Jezebel's blatant disregard of the law of Yahweh. Such a practice may have been continued during the reigns of other Israelite or Judahite kings who "did evil in the eyes of Yahweh."[14] God promises the eunuch who feels like a "dry tree" that he will be specially honored in His house with a "place and a name better than that of sons and daughters" and with "an everlasting name that shall not be cut off" (Isa 56:3–5).

Another ancient Near Eastern population control method that also found its way into Israelite society was the practice of parents exposing their unwanted female babies to die.[15] This practice seems to have been quite widespread throughout ancient Mesopotamia during the entire

---

[11] Potiphar is an example of a court official called *saris* (Gen 37:36; 39:1), but clearly married and perhaps not castrated (although Jewish tradition suggests that he was indeed castrated, and this contributed to his wife's sexual attraction to Joseph). See discussion in Janet S. Everhart, "The Hidden Eunuchs of the Hebrew Bible: Uncovering an Alternate Gender" (PhD diss., The Iliff School of Theology and University of Denver, 2003), 109–114.

[12] For a full discussion of eunuchs in the Bible, see ibid., 1–236.

[13] See 2 Kings 9:32; 18:17; Esther 1:10, 12, 15; 2:3, 14–15, 21; 6:2, 14; 7:9; Daniel 1:3, 7–11, 18; and Gordon H. Johnston, סריס (*saris*), in *New International Dictionary of Old Testament Theology and Exegesis,* ed. by Willem A. VanGemeren, vol. 3 (Grand Rapids, MI: Zondervan, 1997), 288–295. As argued in Davidson, 301, it is possible, but not certain, that Daniel was a eunuch, inasmuch as the term could refer to royal officials as well as eunuchs in Babylon.

[14] There are a number of references to *sarisim* in lists of court personnel and/or relatives of the kings of Israel and Judah other than the time of Ahab and Jezebel (1 Sam 8:15; 2 Kgs 23:11; 24:12, 15; 25:19; 1 Chr 28:1; 2 Chr 18:8; Jer 29:2; 34:19; 38:7; 41:16; 52:25). Some of these occurrences (esp. pre-exilic) may only refer to a "court official" and not necessarily a eunuch, but in Jeremiah 38:7 the Hebrew construction makes certain that Ebed-Melech the Ethiopian was a eunuch.

[15] Infanticide is similar to direct birth control in that it serves the same goal. Birth control is prenatal; infanticide is postnatal. They are not far from each other. Also if birth control through abortion does not work, infanticide may be seen as a last option for parents who reject their baby.

period of biblical history. Meir Malul collects illustrations of children being exposed in various places such as the street, in the woods, on mountains, in rivers or wells, and even in swamps or puddles.[16] Most of these children were exposed immediately after birth, with their birth blood still on them.[17] Such seems to be alluded to in the allegory of Ezekiel 16, where Yahweh depicts to Israel how He found her "thrown out into the open field, when you yourself were loathed on the day you were born. And when I passed by you and saw you struggling in your own blood, I said to you in your blood, 'Live!' Yes, I said to you in your blood, 'Live!'" (Ezek 16:5–6). The divine abhorrence of such action is shown in Yahweh's response to the abandoned infant: for all children, even abandoned ones, God seeks life, not death!

Just as abhorrent to Yahweh was the practice of child sacrifice. While human sacrifice was carried out intermittently in various parts of the ancient Near East, especially in earlier periods, child sacrifice in the second millennium BC seems to have been largely limited to Canaan.[18] This practice seems to have taken place in times of national danger (such as when a Canaanite city was being besieged), but the most horrible setting for infant sacrifice was in its connection to the worship of Molech in Canaan.[19] Numerous biblical passages denounce this abominable Canaanite practice.[20] Infant sacrifice was also very prevalent in the city

---

[16] See Meir Malul, "Adoption of Foundlings in the Bible and Mesopotamian Documents: A Study of Some Legal Metaphors in Ezekiel 16:1–7," *Journal for the Study of the Old Testament* 46 (1990): 104–106.

[17] Ibid., 106.

[18] For a general discussion of infant sacrifice in the ancient Near East, see James K. Hoffmeier, "Abortion and the Old Testament Law," in Hoffmeier, *Abortion: A Christian Understanding and Response,* 50–53. See also A. R. W. Green, *The Role of Human Sacrifice in the Ancient Near East,* ASOR Dissertation Series 1 (Missoula, MT: Scholars Press, 1975). Cf. the comprehensive bibliography of recent works dealing with human (including infant) sacrifice, provided by M. Popović, "Bibliography of Recent Studies [on Gen 22]," in *The Sacrifice of Isaac: The Aqedah (Genesis 22)* and *Its Interpretations*, ed. Edward Noort and Eibert Tigchelaar (Leiden: Brill, 2002), 211, 219.

[19] For a survey of literature and a defense of the existence of Molech as a deity, related to the Ancient Near East god Malik, and the existence of child sacrifice in the Molech cult, see esp., John Day, *Molech: A God of Human Sacrifice in the Old Testament,* University of Cambridge Oriental Publications 41 (Cambridge: University Press, 1989); George C. Heider, *The Cult of Molek: A Reassessment,* Journal for the Study of the Old Testament Supplement Series 43 (Sheffield: University of Sheffield, 1985); Heider, "Molech," in *Dictionary of Deities and Demons in the Bible*, ed. Karel van der Toorn, Bob Becking, and Pieter Willem van der Horst (Leiden: Brill, 1995), 1090–1097; Heider, "Molech," in *Anchor Bible Dictionary.* ed. by David Noel Freedman, vol. 4 (New York: Doubleday, 1992), 895–898; and Edward Noort, "Genesis 22: Human Sacrifice and Theology in the Hebrew Bible," in Noort and Tigchelaar, 11–14.

[20] For references to child sacrifice, see esp. Leviticus 18:21; Deuteronomy 12:31; 18:10; 2 Kings 16:3; 17:17, 31; 21:6; 23:10; Isaiah 57:5; Jeremiah 6:11; 9:21; 18:21; 32:35; Ezekiel 16:21, 36; 20:26,

of Carthage in North Africa (ca. 750–146 BC), as evidenced by excavation of a huge cemetery filled with infant-sacrifice victims (called a *Tophet*, the same word as used for the place of similar atrocities in Jerusalem; 2 Kgs 23:10; Jer 7:31–32; 19:6, 11–14). Though infant sacrifice did not seem to have as its primary function population control in Palestine, or in the early years of Carthage, by the fourth through the third centuries BC it seems that ritual infanticide was indeed used to regulate population.[21] As will be clarified below, child sacrifice, and not abortion, was the real issue facing the Israelites in Canaan.

There is ancient Near Eastern evidence for the practice of abortion. Both cuneiform texts[22] and Egyptian sources[23] reveal that chemical concoctions were employed to end a pregnancy before full term, and it is also possible that, given the level of sophistication in surgical procedures for other medical cases, surgical methods of abortion were also employed (though these are not mentioned in extant ancient Near Eastern texts).

However, it appears that prevailing views on abortion shifted over time in the ancient Near East, as implied especially in the Mesopotamian law codes concerning miscarriage. As will be discussed further below, in dealing with miscarriage the earlier law codes such as the Sumerian Law Code and the Code of Hammurabi do not appear to regard the unborn fetus as a person, and thus, as might be expected, no prohibition of abortion appears in these earlier codes. However, by the time of the Middle Assyrian Laws (considered to represent Assyrian ideology as far back as the fifteenth century BC, and promulgated ca. 1400–1200 BC), legislation concerning miscarriage indicates that the unborn fetus was considered a person, and thus, as expected, terminating the life of the fetus by means of abortion was legally prohibited.

The Middle Assyrian Laws (MAL) (ca. 1400 BC) is the only one of the ancient Near Eastern law collections that deals with abortion. MAL A §53 explicitly prohibits abortion, and the punishment implies a radical repudiation of the practice: the woman guilty of abortion was to be impaled alive without burying her, and if she died while attempting the

31; 23:37; Psalm 106:37; 2 Chronicles 33:6.

[21] Hoffmeier, 51–53.

[22] For reference to an herb that was taken to induce miscarriage, see *The Assyrian Dictionary of the Oriental Institute of the University of Chicago* (Chicago: Oriental Institute) 1956, 11/1:79; cf. Victor H. Matthews, "Marriage and Family in the Ancient Near East," in *Marriage and Family in the Biblical World*, ed. Ken M. Campbell (Downers Grove, IL: InterVarsity, 2003), 21.

[23] See, e.g., Cyril P. Bryan, *Ancient Egyptian Medicine: The Papyrus Ebers* (Chicago, IL: Ares, 1974), 83, for a summary of the remedy given in the Ebers Papyrus (ca. 1500 BC) to bring about abortion: "Dates, Onions, and the Fruit-of-the-Acanthus, were crushed in a vessel with Honey, sprinkled on a cloth, and applied to the Vulva. It ensured abortion either in the first, second or third period."

abortion, she was still to be impaled and denied a proper burial.[24] The seriousness of this crime is indicated by the kind of punishment. G. R. Driver and J. C. Miles point out that "from the savagery of the punishment, namely impalement, and from the refusal of burial it seems certain that the act is regarded as a most heinous and presumably sacrilegious offence." They conclude that in Assyrian law impalement "is prescribed for the worst offence that a mother can commit, namely to procure the death of the unborn child in her womb." While no reason is given in the law for such revulsion, Driver and Miles suggest "as in the case of suicide, that the woman by her offence has caused the sacred blood of the family to flow and has thereby called down the wrath of heaven not only on herself but also on the whole community."[25]

As far as is presently known, abortion was not generally practiced in Canaan, which may explain why there is no explicit reference to abortion in Scripture, either in biblical law or narrative. In light of the radical denunciation and repudiation of abortion implied in the Middle Assyrian Laws from the late second millennium BC, the absence of any pentateuchal legislation dealing directly with abortion may be significant. It must be remembered that the biblical law collections, like their counterparts elsewhere in the ancient Near East, were incomplete and did not deal with every facet of life and practice.[26] David Instone-Brewer articulates a general principle regarding silence in the biblical legislation on a given practice: "Because of the similarity of the Pentateuch with other ancient Near Eastern law codes, we must assume that where the Old Testament is silent, there was broad agreement with the prevailing culture."[27] Andrew Hill applies this principle to the practice of abortion when he points out that instead of Scripture's silence concerning abortion signifying consent of the practice, "it is more probable that the Hebrews accepted and assumed this kind of antiabortion legislation to be the norm in the cultural milieu, especially since the actual practice of abortion appears to have been an exceptional activity in the ancient world. Hence, they saw no need to condemn such an obvious criminal act."[28] Meredith Kline comes to a

---

[24] MAL A §53 (*The Context of Scripture*, ed. by E. E. Hallo 3 vols. [Leiden: Brill, 1997-2002], 2.132:359; cf. Pritchard James. B, ed., Ancient Newar Eastern Text, 3rd ed. [Princeton, NJ: Princeton University Press, 1968], 185): "If a woman aborts her fetus by her own action and they then prove the charges against her and find her guilty, they shall impale her, they shall not bury her. If she dies as a result of aborting her fetus, they shall impale her, they shall not bury her."

[25] G. R. Driver and John C. Miles, *The Assyrian Laws* (Oxford: Clarendon, 1935), 116–117.

[26] For further discussion of the characteristic incompleteness of these law codes, see Raymond Westbrook, "Biblical and Cuneiform Law Codes," *Reveu Biblique* 92 (1985): 247–264.

[27] David Instone-Brewer, *Divorce and Remarriage in the Bible: The Social and Literary Context* (Grand Rapids, MI: Eerdmans, 2002), 21.

[28] Hill, 46.

similar conclusion: "It was so unthinkable that an Israelite woman should desire an abortion that there was no need to mention this offense in the criminal code."[29]

The Status of the Human Fetus and Implications for Abortion in the Old Testament[30]

Ancient Near Eastern Background

As alluded to above, the earlier law codes such as the Sumerian Law Code and the Code of Hammurabi, when dealing with possible cases of miscarriage, do not seem to give the unborn fetus the legal status of a person, since the penalty for the miscarriage is simply a monetary fine, with no mention of the principle of *lex talionis*. According to the Laws of Lipit Ishtar (ca. 1934–1924 BC), one who struck a man's daughter causing miscarriage (but not the death of the pregnant woman) was penalized thirty shekels of silver (§d),[31] and one who struck a man's slave woman causing miscarriage (but not the woman's death) must pay five shekels (§f).[32] According to the "Sumerian Laws" (ca. 1800 BC), accidental striking of a woman resulting in miscarriage carried a fine of ten shekels of silver (§1),[33] while deliberate striking causing miscarriage called for a fine of twenty shekels (§2).[34] The Code of Hammurabi (CH) (ca. 1760–1750 BC) gives similar stipulations (but graded according to high, middle, and lower class): the penalty for an aristocrat (*awilu*) causing a miscarriage in another aristocrat's daughter (but not death of the daughter) was ten shekels of silver (§209),[35] causing miscarriage in a commoner's daughter

---

[29] Meredith G. Kline, "Lex Talionis and the Human Fetus," *Journal of the Evangelical Theological Society* 20 (1977): 193.

[30] For a comprehensive annotated bibliography on the issue of abortion from a religious or moral perspective, see esp. George F. Johnston, *Abortion from the Religious and Moral Perspective: An Annotated Bibliography* (Westport, CT: Praeger, 2003).

[31] Laws of Lipit-Ishtar §d (*The Context of Scripture*, 2.154:411): "If [a . . .] strikes the daughter of a man and causes her to lose her fetus, he shall weigh and deliver 30 shekels of silver."

[32] Laws of Lipit-Ishtar §f (*The Context of Scripture*, 2.154:411): "If a . . . strikes the slave woman of a man and causes here to lose her fetus, he shall weigh and deliver 5 shekels of silver."

[33] "Sumerian Laws," trans. J. J. Finkelstein, 525), §1: "If (a man accidentally) buffeted a woman of the free-citizen class and caused her to have a miscarriage, he must pay 10 shekels of silver."

[34] "Sumerian Laws," §2 (Pritchard, 525): "If (a man deliberately) struck a woman of the free-citizen class and caused her to have a miscarriage, he must pay one-third mina of silver [i.e., twenty shekels]."

[35] Code of Hammurabi §209 (*The Context of Scripture*. Edited by E. E. Hallo. 3 vols. (Leiden: E. J. Brill, 1997–2002), 2.131:348; cf. Prichard, 175): "If an *awilu* strikes a woman of the *awilu-class* and thereby causes her to miscarry her fetus, he shall weigh and deliver 10 shekels of silver for her fetus." Note, however, that if the woman of this class dies after being struck and a

(but not the daughter's death) carried the penalty of five shekels (§211),[36] and causing miscarriage to an aristocrat's female slave (but not the slave's death) carried the penalty of two shekels (§213).[37] Finally, the Hittite Laws (ca. 1650–1500 BC) prescribe the penalty of ten shekels of silver if the miscarriage of a free woman is caused in her tenth month, and five shekels if the miscarriage is in her fifth month (§17)[38] or if it is a female slave who is caused to miscarry in her tenth month (§18).[39]

In contrast to these earlier law collections, which merely mention a monetary penalty, the Middle Assyrian Laws (ca. 1400 BC) explicitly invoke the *lex talionis* principle, thus apparently implying that the unborn fetus was given the legal status of a person, a human being. MAL A §50 specifically states that if a man strikes a woman and causes her to abort her fetus, "*they shall treat him as he treated her; he shall make full payment of a life for her fetus*"; if the husband of the woman whose fetus was aborted had no sons, then "they shall kill the assailant for her fetus."[40] MAL A §52 indicates that "if a man strikes a prostitute causing her to abort her fetus, they shall assess him *blow for blow,* he shall make *full payment of a life.*" While Raymond Westbrook may be correct that the term to "pay a life" refers to "payment of a fixed sum representing

---

miscarriage, the penalty was to kill the daughter of the assailant (Code of Hammurabi §210 [*The Context of Scripture*, 2.131:348; cf. Pritchard, 175]: "If that woman should die, they shall kill his daughter").

[36] Code of Hammurabi §211 (*The Context of Scripture*, 2.131:348; cf. Pritchard, 175): "If he should cause a woman of the commoner-class to miscarry her fetus by the beating, he shall weigh and deliver 5 shekels of silver."

[37] Code of Hammurabi §213 (*The Context of Scripture*, 2.131:348; cf. Pritchard, 175): "If he strikes an *awīlu's* slave woman and thereby causes her to miscarry her fetus, he shall weigh and deliver 2 shekels of silver."

[38] Hittite Laws §17 (*The Context of Scripture*, 2.19:108; cf. Pritchard, 190): "If any causes a free woman to miscarry, [if] it is her tenth month, he shall pay 10 shekels of silver, if it is her fifth month, he shall pay 5 shekels of silver. He shall look to his house for it." §XVI (a late version of §17) reads, "If anyone causes a free woman to miscarry, he shall pay 20 shekels of silver" (*The Context of Scripture*, 2.19:108).

[39] Hittite Laws §18 (*The Context of Scripture*, 2.19:108; cf. Pritchard, 190): "If anyone causes a female slave to miscarry, if it is her tenth month, he shall pay 5 shekels." Hittite Law §XVII (late version of §18) reads, "If anyone causes a female slave to miscarry, he shall pay 10 shekels of silver" (Hallo, 2.19:108).

[40] MAL A §50 (*The Context of Scripture*, 2.132:359; cf. Pritchard, 184): "[If a man] strikes [another man's wife thereby causing her to abort her fetus, . . .] a man's wife [. . .] and they shall treat him as he treated her; he shall make full payment of a life for her fetus. And if that woman dies, they shall kill that man; he shall make full payment of a life for her fetus. And if there is no son of that woman's husband, and his wife whom he struck aborted her fetus, they shall kill the assailant for her fetus. If her fetus was a female, he shall make full payment of a life only."

the value of a person,"[41] this does not alter the conclusion that the fetus is considered "a person" and that the *lex talionis* principle is applied in these cases involving the death of the fetus.

Exodus 21:22–25

Although no Mosaic legislation directly addresses the issue of abortion, there is one passage concerned with the most crucial question in the abortion debate: is the fetus to be considered fully a human being or not? Exodus 21:22–25 reads as follows:

> If men fight, and hurt [lit. "strike," *wenagefu*][42] a woman with child, so that she gives birth prematurely [lit. "children[43] come out," *weyatse'u yeladeha*],[44] yet no harm [*'ason*] follows, he shall surely be punished accordingly as the woman's husband imposes on him; and he shall pay as the judges determine [*biflilim*].[45] But if any

---

[41] Raymond Westbrook, "*Lex Talionis* and Exodus 21, 22–25," *Reveu Biblique* 93 (1986): 64.

[42] The verb *nagap* means "to strike or smite" (Francis Brown , S. R. Driver and Charles A. Briggs, *A Hebrew and English Lexicon of The Old Testament* [Oxford: Clarendon Press, 1951], 619), "to injure by striking" (L. Koehler, W. Baumgartner, and J. J. Stamm, *The Hebrew and Aramic Lexicon of the Old Testament,* 5 vols. [Leiden: Brill, 1999], 669), and while it implies serious (and sometimes even fatal) injury, the term cannot be necessarily equated with "death" in this passage, contra Kline, 198. Kline's reference to the use of the word in Exodus 21:35 for the "fatal attack of the goring ox" fails to recognize that in this verse the verb *nagap* indicates the "striking/hitting" of the other ox, but the death of the victim is indicated by a separate added word *wamet,* "and it died." The modern English versions that translate as "hit" (NIV), "strike" (NASB), or "hurt" (NKJV, NRSV) seem to best capture the nuance implied in this verse. The verb is in the plural ("they hit/strike/hurt") probably because it is a generic plural, referring to "one of the combatants, which ever of them it be" (Umberto Cassuto, *A Commentary on the Book of Exodus* [Jerusalem: Magnes, 1967], 275).

[43] The plural "children" in this clause should probably be taken in the sense of a generic plural, inasmuch as potentially "male or female, one or two" might be born (Cassuto, 275). Cf. Gleason L. Archer, *Encyclopedia of Bible Difficulties* (Grand Rapids, MI: Zondervan, 1982), 247: "The plural is used here because the woman might be pregnant with twins when this injury befalls her." H. Wayne House, "Miscarriage or Premature Birth: Additional Thoughts on Exodus 21:22–25," *Westminster Theological Journal* 41 (1978): 114, suggests the plural may be "to indicate natural products in an unnatural condition," since the maliciously induced premature birth involves an irregularity; here House follows a use of the plural discussed in Ronald J. Williams, *Hebrew Syntax: An Outline* (Toronto: University of Toronto Press, 1967), 8, paragraph 10.

[44] The LXX here makes a distinction between a child who comes out "not yet fully formed (*mē exeikonismenon*)" (Exod 21:22) and one that is "fully formed (*exeikonismenon*)" (Exod 21:23). In the former case there is only a fine; in the latter the guilty party is punished by the principle of *lex talionis,* "life for life." But there is no support for this distinction in the Hebrew text.

[45] In an attempt to bolster the "miscarriage" interpretation of this verse, some interpreters suggest emending this word to *banpalim,* "for the miscarriage" (see Brown, Driver, and Briggs, 1951, 813; and Karl Budde, "Bemerkungen zum Bundesbuch," *Zeitschrift für die Alttestamentliche Wissenschaft* 11 [1891]: 108–111), but there is no need to emend the text when the

harm [*ʾason*] follows, then you shall give life [*nefesh*] for life [*nefesh*], eye for eye, tooth for tooth, hand for hand, foot for foot, burn for burn, wound for wound, stripe for stripe.

A number of interpreters throughout history,[46] including some "pro-choice" advocates among Evangelicals,[47] have found in Exodus 21:22–25 support for their contention that a fetus is not a fully human person, and thus has less inherent value than an already born person. Most of these interpreters take the clause *weyatseʾu yeladeha* as a reference to a miscarried fetus—that is, a stillborn child (Exod 21:22a). Since the fetus was not fully human, only a fine was required of the offender as compensation for the loss of fetus (Exod 21:22b). Only if *fur-*

Hebrew makes sense in its canonical form. E. A. Speiser, "The Stem *PLL* in Hebrew," *Journal of Biblical Literature* 82 (1963): 301–306 (esp. 303), suggests that the root *pll* has the meaning "to estimate, assess, calculate," but Westbrook, "*Lex Talionis*," 58–61, shows how this hypothetical translation does not fit the evidence. Westbrook's own hypothesis—translating the term as "alone"—also seems forced, and in order to substantiate his entire miscarriage hypothesis (that the contrast is between whether or not the perpetrator of the miscarriage was known), Westbrook in the end must assume that the lex talionis parallel in Leviticus 24:17–21 is a later "strained" exegetical distortion of the Exodus passage (ibid., 68). Kline, 195–196, suggests that the preposition *b-* is a *bet* of equivalence and *pelili* is an adjective meaning "liability to death" (with the *-m* as an emphatic enclitic, not abstract plural), so that *biflilim* refers to payment equivalent "for his forfeited life" or "as one deserving of death" (ibid., 196). However, there does not seem to be a compelling reason to depart from the traditional understanding of *palil* as "judge, *umpire*" (Brown, Driver, and Briggs, 813) and *biflilim* as "in [the presence of or accordance with] the judges" (with the majority of modern translations).

[46] This includes even Talmudic allusions to this text, which uniformly interpret it as referring to a miscarriage, with the fetus having the value of a property loss on the part of the father. See m. *Ohalot* 7:6; and Babylonian tractate *Sanhedrin* 72b (cf. the comments of Rashi). Many modern critical commentators take Exodus 21:22 as referring to miscarriage largely because of the ancient Near Eastern laws that seem to parallel this biblical passage. The present study has examined all these laws and found that most accept a sum of money for the loss of a fetus through miscarriage. But, as will be argued, unlike the alleged ancient Near Eastern parallels, Exodus 21:22 does not deal with miscarriage but rather with premature live birth. Furthermore, the closest ancient Near Eastern parallels are the Middle Assyrian Laws, which, as previously pointed out, seem to give an unborn fetus the legal status of a human person. In the final analysis, supposed ancient Near Eastern parallels (or lack of parallels) cannot override the weight of exegetical evidence from the biblical text.

[47] See, e.g., Bruce K. Waltke, "The Old Testament and Birth Control," *Christianity Today* 13, no. 8 (8 November 1968): 3–6; Waltke, "Old Testament Texts Bearing on the Issues," in *Birth Control and the Christians*, ed. Walter O. Spitzer and Caryle L. Saylor (Wheaton, IL: Tyndale, 1969), 10–11; and Nancy Hardesty, "When Does Life Begin?," *Eternity* 22, no. 2 (February 1971): 19, 43. It should be noted, however, that Bruce Waltke, in his presidential address at the 1975 annual meeting of the Evangelical Theological Society, reversed his former position on the status of the human fetus, concluding that "the fetus is human and therefore to be accorded the same protection to life granted every other human being" (Bruce K. Waltke, "Reflections from the Old Testament on Abortion," *Journal of the Evangelical Theological Society* 19 [1976]: 13).

ther harm followed—that is, the woman herself suffered serious injury or death—was the principle of *lex talionis* (equivalent punishment) applicable.

But this interpretation fails to take seriously the precise linguistic evidence of the text. Particularly at issue are several Hebrew expressions. First, the clause *weyatse'u yeladeha* (Exod 21:22a) literally means "when children come out." The noun *yeled* "child" is the common Old Testament term for a fully human child from infancy to the age of twelve;[48] the word for "stillborn child" (not used in this passage) is *nefel*, "untimely birth," not *yeled*.[49] The verb *yatsa'*, "to go or come out," is a term regularly used to describe the ordinary live birth of children.[50] When referring to a stillbirth, the verb is always accompanied by some form of the verb *mut*, "to die";[51] this latter verb does not appear in Exodus 21:22. Furthermore, the technical word for miscarriage in the Old Testament is not *yatsa'* but *shakal*, "to miscarry,"[52] and this latter verb is employed only two chapters later in the Covenant Code of Exodus (Exod 23:26). Had Moses intended to mean "miscarriage" in this passage, he certainly would have used the technical term *shakal*, which he employs later in the same Exodus code. It is difficult to escape the conclusion that the expression *weyatse'u yeladeha* refers to a live premature birth, and not miscarriage, as is recognized by numerous commentators and exegetical studies.[53] Recent evangelical translators of the Old Testament take seriously the above lexical evidence and translate the clause as referring to premature birth.[54]

The second expression calling for more detailed analysis in context is the word *'ason*, "harm/calamity/hurt."[55] This Hebrew word is used only three other times in the Hebrew Bible outside of the two occurrences in this passage, and all three of these appear in the Joseph narrative expressing Jacob's concern that some kind of "harm" would come upon his son Benjamin if allowed to go down to Egypt (Gen 42:4, 38; 44:29).

---

[48] Brown, Driver, and Briggs, 409; cf. Archer, 247.

[49] See Job 3:16; Psalm 58:8; Ecclesiastes 6:3; and Brown, Driver, and Briggs, 658.

[50] See, e.g., Genesis 15:4; 25:25–26; 38:28–30; 46:26; 1 Kings 8:19; Job 1:21; 3:11; Ecclesiastes 5:15; Isaiah 39:7; Jeremiah 1:5; 20:18.

[51] See, e.g., Numbers 12:12; Job 3:11.

[52] Brown, Driver, and Briggs, 1013; and Brown, Driver, and Briggs, 1492. See Genesis 31:38; 2 Kings 2:19, 21; Job 21:10.

[53] See, e.g., Cassuto, 275; Jack W. Cottrell, "Abortion and the Mosaic Laws," *Christianity Today*, March 16, 1973, 7–8; Ron du Preez, "The Status of the Fetus in Mosaic Law," *Journal of the Adventist Theological Society* 1, no. 2 (Autumn 1990): 5–21; House, 110–114; and Bernard S. Jackson, "The Problem of Exod. xxi 22-25 (*Ius Talionis*)," *Vetus Testamentum* 23 (1973): 292–293.

[54] NKJV, NIV, and Updated NASB translate as "she gives birth prematurely." NLT translates "her child is born prematurely." (Note that the original NASB had the translation "miscarriage" but this was changed in the 1995 update.)

[55] Brown, Driver, and Briggs, 62; and Eugene H. Merrill, אסון (*ason*), in VanGemeren, 1:467.

The term appears to be a general one, denoting any kind of serious harm including mortal accident.[56] The pertinent issue in Exodus 21:22–23 is not so much the meaning of the word, but its referent: who is envisioned as receiving the harm? Those who interpret verse 22 as describing a miscarriage assume that harm was already done in the abortion of the fetus, and thus are forced to supply the word "further" or "other" before "harm" in verses 22–23 to indicate additional hurt done to the mother that calls for *lex talionis* punishment, even though such a word is not in the original.[57] But if what is in view is a premature live birth of the child, as argued above, then there is no need to supply the word "further" because no serious or fatal injury was incurred in the premature birth. Thus the term *ʾason*, appearing immediately after the clause "her children come out"—with no Hebrew expression *lah*, "to her," restricting the harm to the woman—is indefinite, referring at least to the prematurely born child, and probably to either mother or child.[58]

In verse 22, then, if no harm has come to either mother or child, only a fine is imposed upon the striker, presumably to compensate for physical or mental discomfort he has caused, or "because of the danger to which mother and child are exposed and the parents' distress in connection with the unnaturally premature birth."[59] In verse 23, if harm (from serious to fatal injury) has come to either mother or child, then the law of *lex talionis* comes into effect.[60]

---

[56] Westbrook, "*Lex Talionis*," 56–57, hypothesizes that *ʾason* refers to "damage caused by an unknown perpetrator"—that is, "cases where responsibility cannot be located." But such a meaning does not seem to follow from Jacob's use of this word to describe the "harm" that might come upon Benjamin: Jacob is concerned with harm in general, regardless of whether or not the perpetrator of the crime is known. As previously noted, in order to sustain his overall hypothesis, Westbrook is forced to posit a later distortion of this Exodus legislation in Leviticus 24.

[57] See, e.g., NRSV, NJB, original NASB, JPSV, NEB, and Schocken Bible (Everett Fox).

[58] Cottrell, 8, points out that the contrast in these verses is not between harm to the mother and harm to the child, but between no harm to either mother nor child and harm to either one or the other. See also Archer, 248; Cassuto, 275; John M. Frame, "Abortion from a Biblical Perspective," in *Thou Shalt Not Kill: The Christian Case Against Abortion*, ed. Richard L. Ganz (New Rochelle, NY: Arlington House, 1978), 55; House, 118; and Walter C. Kaiser Jr., *Toward Old Testament Ethics* (Grand Rapids, MI: Zondervan, 1983), 103, 172.

[59] Cottrell, 8; cf. House, "Miscarriage or Premature Birth," 120.

[60] The language of this statement of *lex talionis* is clearly formulaic, since the kinds of injuries mentioned (e.g., "burn for burn") are not the likely injuries to occur in this situation. Kline, 197, points out that this "fossilized formula" is meant "to express only the general principle that the offense must receive a just punishment." This just punishment is in contrast to the ancient Near Eastern laws where the wealthy or people in the higher social stratas simply paid fines and escaped punishment. Shalom M. Paul, *Studies in the Book of the Covenant in the Light of Cuneiform and Biblical Law* (Leiden: Brill, 1970), 75–77, shows how the *lex talionis* principle, far from being a primitive or barbaric form of punishment, as often claimed, was an important advance in the history of jurisprudence, which in the Bible served to "curb unlimited retribution,

In summary on this crucial passage, two main exegetical points emerge: 1) the clause *weyatse'u yeladeha* refers to premature live childbirth and not miscarriage, and 2) the term *'ason* includes harm to the child as well as the mother. From these two points, the conclusion is straightforward: the *lex talionis* (law of just retribution) of Exodus 21:23–24 applies to the fetus equally as much as the mother, and the fetus is therefore granted under the law the status of a full human being just as the mother.[61] And if the fetus is fully human, then the implication for abortion is also straightforward: the passage gives no support to the legitimacy of this practice. In fact, taking the life of a human fetus is considered homicide—just as is taking the life of the mother.

Other Old Testament Passages Dealing with the Status of the Human Fetus

A number of other Old Testament passages provide evidence that God considers the unborn child fully human. A whole series of passages reveals God's personal involvement in the process of the development of the fetus in the womb. Job declares that God personally fashioned each individual person in the womb:

> Your hands have made me and fashioned me,
> An intricate unity;
> Yet You would destroy me.
> Remember, I pray, that You have made me like clay.
> And will You turn me into dust again?
> Did you not pour me out like milk,

personal vendetta, and excessive retaliation" (ibid., 76) by instituting a system of equal justice and fairness for all. In the case of the "life for life" death penalty, it is also important to recognize that a ransom was probably possible. Numbers 35:31–32 forbids a ransom in the case of homicide, which seems to imply the possibility of ransom in other cases (see Jackson, 283–284). Westbrook, "*Lex Talionis,*" 64–66, suggests that "life for a life" should be understood against the background of ancient Near Eastern references: "The phrase 'pay a life' refers to the payment of a fixed sum representing the value of a person" (ibid., 64). While appealing at first glance, and probably applicable elsewhere, Westbrook's hypothesis denies the reality of the death penalty in this passage, and thus he cannot reconcile this passage with Leviticus 24:17–21, where he must admit that literal retaliation—the death penalty—is in view (ibid., 68).

[61] Kline, 193–201, arrives at the same conclusion (that the human fetus is fully human) but from a different exegetical base. According to Kline, the "striking" of Exodus 21:22a indicates that either the mother or the fetus is killed, the "harm" of verse 22b is the premature live birth of the fetus, the "harm" of verses 23–25 is a miscarriage, and the penalty of both verse 22b and verses 23–25 is the same: "death (as at least one possibility) . . . demanding a ransom for the offender's forfeited life" (ibid., 197). Contra Kline, as already noted, the verb "strike" in verse 22a does not refer to death, but a premature live birth; and the penalties between verse 22b and verses 23–25 do not appear to be essentially the same.

> And curdle me like cheese,
> Clothe me with skin and flesh,
> And knit me together with bones and sinews?
> You have granted me life and favor,
> And Your care has preserved my spirit. (Job 10:8–12)

Again, Job declares of God's part in the creation of both himself and his fellow human beings, "Did not He who made me in the womb make them? Did not the same One fashion us in the womb?" (Job 31:15).

The psalmist gives a similar inspired testimony in Psalm 139:13–16:

> For You formed my inward parts; you covered me in my mother's womb.
> I will praise You, for I am fearfully and wonderfully made;
> Marvelous are Your works, and that my soul knows very well.
> My frame was not hidden from You, when I was made in secret,
> And skillfully wrought in the lowest parts of the earth.
> Your eyes saw my embryo [or 'fetus,' *golem*],[62] being yet unformed.
> And in Your book they all were written, the days fashioned for me,
> When as yet there were none of them.

William Brown, after analyzing the motif of *creatio corporis* ("the creation of the individual") in Psalm 139, summarizes, "Every physical thread woven in secret contains the moral fiber of the psalmist's being. In conception was established both the physical and moral constitution of a human being."[63] Brown then comments on the implications of both Psalm 139 and Job 10:

> From the perspective of both authors, the womb is the home of God's creation and sustenance. It is here that the physical nature and moral nurture coalesce. The womb is a refuge, impregnable from both physical and moral harm. . . . Whether for weal or for woe, both Job and the psalmist regard creatio corporis as the sign and seal of God's unconditional pledge of support. It is God's

[62] For the meaning of *golem* as "embryo," see Brown, Driver, and Briggs, 166; Koehler, Baumgartner, and Stamm, 194; and Leslie C. Allen, *Psalms 101–150*, Word Biblical Commentary 21 (Waco, TX: Word, 1983), 252.

[63] William P. Brown, "*Creatio Corporis* and the Rhetoric of Defense in Job 10 and Psalm 139," in *God Who Creates: Essays in Honor of W. Sibley Towner*, ed. William P. Brown and S. Dean McBride Jr. (Grand Rapids, MI: Eerdmans, 2000), 114.

covenantal grant in utero.[64]

John Stott captures the thrust of Psalm 139:13–16: "The fetus is not a growth in the mother's body (which can be removed as readily as her tonsils or appendix), nor even a potential human being, but a human life who, though not yet mature, has the potentiality to grow into the fullness of the humanity he already possesses."[65]

Isaiah repeats a similar declaration as the psalmist: "Thus says the Lord, your Redeemer, And He who formed you from the womb: I am the Lord, who makes all things" (Isa 44:24). Jeremiah likewise records the divine testimony of God's personal work of creating Jeremiah from the womb: "Before I formed you in the womb I knew you; Before you were born I sanctified you; And I ordained you a prophet to the nations" (Jer 1:5).

John Davis summarizes the implication of these passages:

> All these texts indicate that God's special dealings with human beings can long precede their awareness of a personal relationship with God. God deals with human beings in an intensely personal way long before society is accustomed to treat them as persons in the "whole sense." . . . God's actions present a striking contrast to current notions of personhood.[66]

Paul Fowler adds, "God's personal involvement with the unborn provides the foundation for their personal worth. If we are persons because God has related to us in a personal way, then the unborn are also persons since God's care for them obviously begins in the womb."[67]

Scripture's references to the unborn possessing a spiritual/moral nature even before birth provide additional evidence that biblical writers consider the fetus to be human, formed by God Himself. Psalms 58:3 speaks of the sinful nature already being present in the fetus: "The wicked are estranged from the womb; they go astray as soon as they are born, speaking lies." Psalms 51:7–8 (ET vol. 5–6) in particular supports the concept that a human's spiritual/moral nature is already present in the

---

[64] Brown, 114.

[65] John R. W. Stott, "Does Life Begin Before Birth?," *Christianity Today*, September 5, 1980, 50.

[66] John J. Davis, *Abortion and the Christian: What Every Believer Should Know* (Philadelphia, PA: Presbyterian and Reformed, 1984), 49.

[67] Paul W. Fowler, *Abortion: Toward an Evangelical Consensus* (Portland, OR: Multnomah, 1987), 144. Cf. Harold O. J. Brown, *Death before Birth* (Nashville, TN: Thomas Nelson, 1977), 127, who, after surveying these passages, concludes, "In short, there can be no doubt that God clearly says the unborn child is already a human being, made in the image of God, and deserving of protection under the law."

fetus, from the moment of conception. After being confronted by Nathan regarding his adultery with Bathsheba, David confesses, "Behold, I was brought forth in iniquity, and in sin my mother conceived me." Edward Dalglish captures the implication of this verse: "In Psalm li. 7 [ET v. 5] the psalmist is relating his sinfulness to the very inception of life; he traces his development beyond his birth . . . to the genesis of his being in his mother's womb—even to the very hour of conception."[68]

Fowler summarizes the implication of these passages regarding a fetus' moral nature and the relationship with the image of God:

> Putting all this together, we may conclude that man's moral, spiritual faculty is already present in the fetus before birth. If the image of God pertains to man's moral nature, then that nature has been passed on from Adam (Genesis 5:3). It is hard to argue that someone is not a person who has moral attributes.[69]

Another set of biblical data shows that the Old Testament writers assumed a basic continuity between prenatal and postnatal human life. In Psalm 139 "David sees himself as having existed in his mother's womb (Ps 139:13ff.)."[70] As John Stott puts it regarding Psalm 139 as a whole, "the psalmist surveys his life in four stages: past (v. 1), present (vol. 2–6), future (vol. 7–12), and before birth (vol. 13–16), and in all four refers to himself as 'I.' He who is writing as a full-grown man has the same personal identity as the fetus in his mother's womb."[71] The same could be said for many other of the verses already cited, where the prophet uses personal pronouns ("I," "me," "my," etc.) to describe the fetus in the womb as well as the postnatal human life.

Especially telling is the fact that often the biblical writers used the same nouns to label prenatal and postnatal life. So, for example, the term *geber*, normally referring to a "young, strong, man,"[72] is utilized to describe the embryo at conception in Job 3:3: "May the day perish on which I was born, And the night in which it was said, 'A man [*geber*] is conceived.'"

---

[68] Edward R. Dalglish, *Psalm Fifty-One in the Light of Near Eastern Patternism* (Leiden: Brill, 1962), 121. Dalglish goes on to argue that in the next verse, the mention of "inward parts" and "hidden part" more likely refers "to the womb where the psalmist's being was initiated" than to the inner parts of the (adult) psalmist, and verse 8 is interpreted to mean "that truth and wisdom were, alas, also part of his natal endowment" (ibid., 124), thus implying that the moral nature is already present in the fetus from conception.

[69] Fowler, 142.

[70] Ibid., 144 (emphasis original).

[71] Stott, 50.

[72] Koehler, Baumgartner, and Stamm, 175; cf. Brown, Driver, and Briggs, 149.

Again, *yeled* is the Hebrew term regularly referring to a "child" from infancy to the age of twelve,[73] and this same term is used in Exodus 21:22, as previously noted in discussion of that passage. Again, the term *ben* is the normal Hebrew term for "son,"[74] and Genesis 25:22 uses this term in the plural to describe the unborn fetuses in Rebekah's womb: "But the children [*habbanim*] struggled together within her."

From this Old Testament data on the status of the unborn fetus,[75] the inescapable conclusion, also articulated by Bruce Waltke after his survey of the same data, is that "the image of God is already present in the fetus. . . . We conclude then, on both theological and exegetical grounds, that the body, the life and moral faculty of man originate simultaneously at conception." Waltke also gives a "clear statement regarding the morality of induced abortion based upon God's Word. The fetus is human and therefore to be accorded the same protection to life granted every other human being. Indeed, feticide is murder, an attack against a fellow man who owes his life to God, and a violation of the commandment, 'You shall not kill.'"[76]

The Status of the Human Fetus and Implications for Abortion in the New Testament

The New Testament upholds the same view of the status of the unborn fetus as in the Old Testament, treating it as fully human (e.g., Luke 1:15, 35, 41, 44).[77] In John 16:21, Jesus states that "when a woman is giving birth, she has sorrow because her hour has come, but when she has delivered the baby, she no longer remembers the anguish, for joy that a *human being has been born into the world*" (ESV).[78] This statement accords the fetus the status of a "human being" before birth.

The conceptions of John the Baptist and Jesus Christ are examples indicating the importance of life, even of the fetus. In his encounter with Zechariah, the angel says,

---

[73] Brown, Driver, and Briggs, 409; cf. Archer, 247.

[74] Ibid., 119; and Koehler, Baumgartner, and Stamm, 137.

[75] For an extended discussion and rebuttal of the various attempts to discount the biblical evidence previously cited by those advocating abortion rights, see Francis J. Beckwith, *Politically Correct Death: Answering Arguments for Abortion Rights* (Grand Rapids, MI: Baker, 1993), 137–150.

[76] Waltke, "Reflections," 13.

[77] See, e.g., Frame, "Abortion from a Biblical Perspective," 43–75; and John and Millie Youngberg, eds., *The Reborn and the Unborn* (Berrien Springs, MI: Marriage and Family Commitment Seminars, 1988), 23–34.

[78] Emphasis supplied.

> Do not be afraid, Zechariah, for your prayer has been heard, and your wife Elizabeth will bear you a son, and you shall call his name John. And you will have joy and gladness, and many will rejoice at his birth, for he will be great before the Lord. And he must not drink wine or strong drink, and he will be filled with the Holy Spirit, even from his mother's womb. And he will turn many of the children of Israel to the Lord their God, and he will go before him in the spirit and power of Elijah, to turn the hearts of the fathers to the children, and the disobedient to the wisdom of the just, to make ready for the Lord a people prepared. (Luke 1:13–17, ESV)

Because conception is God's gift, He recognizes prenatal life. In the same chapter, the angel speaks to Mary regarding the conception of John the Baptist: "Now indeed, Elizabeth your relative has also conceived a son in her old age; and this is now the sixth month for her who was called barren" (Luke 1:36, NKJV). Thus, God has interest in the person right from conception. Paul indicates that God set him apart from his "mother's womb" (Gal 1:15).

In some cases, God assigns special tasks to persons yet unborn—Jeremiah, John the Baptist, and Jesus Christ being examples. The angel informs Zechariah that Elizabeth's child "will be filled with the Holy Spirit, even from his mother's womb" (Luke 1:15), affirming that God treats the unborn as fully human. Because Elizabeth's unborn child is a human filled with the Holy Spirit, he can recognize the presence of the Lord, the unborn Jesus Christ, and "leap" for "joy": "For indeed, as soon as the voice of your [Mary's] greeting sounded in my ears, the babe leaped in my womb for joy. Blessed *is* she who believed, for there will be a fulfillment of those things which were told her from the Lord" (Luke 1:44–45, NKJV).

God places the greatest value on human life, whether born or unborn. Humans were created in the "image of God" (Gen 1:26). This explains why He sacrificed His Son to save humanity from sin (John 3:16). God sustains life, even from conception (Judg 13:5; Jer 1:5; Luke 1:13–17; Gal 1:15) and wishes for humans to enjoy eternal life (John 3:16).

Human life is no more valuable outside of the womb than it is inside. God upholds the sanctity of life, and therefore prohibits the termination of life. The fetus is not the property of the human parents. It belongs to God. For this reason, terminating the life of the unborn infringes upon the sanctity of life. In the Sermon on the Mount, Jesus affirms that the sixth commandment included not only actual killing, but also derogatory speech (Matt 5:21–22). This suggests that anything that destroys human life or affects that life negatively is tantamount to murder. Jesus teaches that murderers will not "escape the sentence of hell" (Matt 23:31–35). Murderers have no place in the kingdom of God (Rev 21:8; 22:15).

In the chapter that follows, Ekkehardt Mueller amply demonstrates that while there is no direct command against abortion, biblical counsel regarding the sacredness of life indicates that abortion is against God's will. God is the owner of life; He places inestimable value upon human life, and expressly prohibits its termination.

Abortion, Divine Warning, and Divine Grace

In view of the widespread disregard of the biblical evidence on the status of the unborn fetus in the church and society today, this study ends with a biblical warning cry of alarm. God's voice on this issue is clear: abortion is feticide, a violation of the sixth commandment, "Thou shalt not kill." Who among the followers of God will hear the cry of the unnumbered unborn humans whose voices are silenced in death before they even have a chance to speak? The same God who brought ancient Israel to judgment for murdering their little children by passing them through the fire to pagan gods will bring before His judgment bar the current generation who turns a deaf ear to His cry and the cry of His unborn precious ones![79]

At the same time, we emphasize the power of divine grace. God's grace is available for forgiveness and cleansing for those who have performed or undergone abortion, just as for any other person who has killed another human being. David's inspired prayer in Psalms 51 records his repentance not only from his adultery with Bathsheba, but also his "bloodguiltiness" or murder (Ps 51:16 [ET v. 14]), and the same picture of grace drawn from this psalm in reference to adultery applies to the killing of human beings.[80]

---

[79] See esp., John O. Anderson, *Cry of the Innocents: Abortion and the Race Towards Judgement* (South Plainfield, NJ: Bridge, 1984).

[80] Grace did not, however, deliver David from the consequences of his sins—losing four sons!

CHAPTER 13

Abortion: Terminating a Pregnancy

Ekkehardt Mueller

Abortion is a much discussed and controversial topic, especially in Western societies. This study, divided into six parts, attempts to examine the issue from a biblical perspective. We will start with the state of affairs, followed by a description of the variety of opinions on the subject. We will explain the approach taken in this study, and then move to the Holy Scripture and its teachings on the topic of abortion. We will deal with difficult issues too, and end with a section on implications.

The State of Affairs

In this section we begin with a short comment on pregnancy and the development of the unborn child, before continuing with aspects related to abortion.

Pregnancy

While in some societies and people groups, women—for various reasons[1]—do not necessarily consider it desirable to become pregnant and have children, in other societies women deem it a positive experience. They wish to become mothers. Although pregnancies normally have effects that may be understood as downsides, many women are willing to accept these for the joy of having their own child, especially when they are married and, together with their husband, want to not only form a couple but also become a family. In a number of cultures, not being able to have children is seen as a disgrace and disadvantage.

[1] Such reasons may include not wanting to contribute to overpopulation, enjoying life, convenience, and the personal freedom of not having to devote time, money, and energy to children.

The Old and New Testaments report that people in biblical times felt the same way. Numerous stories indirectly lament the infertility of women, beginning with Sarah, Abraham's wife (Gen 11:30); Rebekah, Isaac's wife (Gen 25:21); and Rachel, Jacob's wife (Gen 29:31). The Old Testament continues with Manoah's wife, who was barren but through God's intervention gave birth to Samson (Judg 13:2), one of the judges of Israel. Hannah's moving story is reported in 1 Samuel 1:1–20. The shame of barrenness and her exuberant joy of becoming the mother of Samuel is expressed in 1 Samuel 2. According to the New Testament, Elizabeth was also barren and, like Sarah, in her advanced age, gave birth to John the Baptist (Luke 1:7, 13). These women regarded pregnancy as a great privilege and their children as divine gifts. Indeed, their children's potential was revealed later in their lives, and they became heroes of faith. The angel told Zachariah,

> Do not be afraid, Zechariah, for your prayer has been heard, and your wife Elizabeth will bear you a son, and you shall call his name John. And you will have joy and gladness, and many will rejoice at his birth, for he will be great before the Lord. And he must not drink wine or strong drink, and he will be filled with the Holy Spirit, even from his mother's womb. And he will turn many of the children of Israel to the Lord their God, and he will go before him in the spirit and power of Elijah, to turn the hearts of the fathers to the children, and the disobedient to the wisdom of the just, to make ready for the Lord a people prepared (Luke 1:13–17).

Mary accepted her unusual pregnancy as God's will and gave birth to the Messiah, singing her inspiring Magnificat (Luke 1:46–56). These examples should not be understood as only male descendants being a blessing. Throughout both Testaments, male and female characters are praised for their faithful lives and actions.

Apart from infertile individuals who were blessed with fertility, God promised blessings of offspring for all of Israel: "None shall miscarry or be barren in your land" (Exod 23:26). God, as the helper of the needy, "gives the barren woman a home, making her the joyous mother of children. Praise the LORD" (Ps 113:9). But males can also be barren (Deut 7:14). In any case, being with child and having children is considered a great privilege and gift (Ps 17:14; 113:9; 127:3–4; 128:3, 6). And all parents and children are called to be children of the Most High (Ps 82:6).

Richard B. Hays portrays the New Testament teaching on this topic:

> Within the *symbolic* world of the New Testament, God is the creator and author of life. The prologue of John's Gospel asserts that all life comes into being through the creative power of the Logos . . . (John 1:3–5). Wherever new life begins to develop in any pregnancy, the creative power of God is at work, and Jesus Christ, who was the original agent of creation, has already died for the redemption of the incipient life *in utero*. That is why Barth can say, "The true light of the world shines already in the darkness of the mother's womb." We are privileged to participate in the creative work of God through begetting and bearing and birthing children, but there can be no new life without the generative power of God.[2]

Now, in a world seriously affected by sin, not each and every pregnancy is a joyous, problem-free event. While pregnancy is not a sickness, it still causes at least uncomfortable and taxing times for most mothers. In some cases, it can lead to serious conditions or bring the prospect and threat of death. Shortly before he passed away, Jacob blessed Joseph and then his other sons with him. In his speech, we still recognize his pain about the death of Rachel, who had passed away while giving birth to Benjamin (Gen 48:7). But apart from health challenges, a pregnant woman may face other disturbing situations that may negatively impact the pregnancy: a loved one may die, the father of the child may leave her and the unborn child, abuse may have occurred, or the fetus may have defects. But we should not forget that in the large majority of cases, "the normal response to pregnancy within the Bible's symbolic world, is one of rejoicing for God's gift—even when this gift comes unexpectedly."[3] This is so even today, in spite of birth pangs and labor. Says Jesus, "When a woman is giving birth, she has sorrow because her hour has come, but when she has delivered the baby, she no longer remembers the anguish, for joy that a human being has been born into the world" (John 16:21).[4]

The Development of a Child

The development of a child in utero is indeed amazing. Since we cannot directly see the fetus nor realize how it grows, we may tend to regard it as more of a "thing," or a being in a secondary sense, rather than a truly

[2] Richard B. Hays, *The Moral Vision of the New Testament: A Contemporary Introduction to New Testament Ethics* (San Francisco, CA: HarperSanFrancisco, 1996), 450.

[3] Hays, 450.

[4] All biblical quotations are from the ESV, unless otherwise indicated.

human person. On the other hand, seeing a newborn baby often elicits curiosity, a sense of joy, and a feeling that this little human needs protection and care. Not so much with the unborn, which may not trigger the same positive emotional response in adults that a newborn would, because we do not encounter the fetus directly. Therefore, it may be helpful to point out how a child develops in the mother's body under normal circumstances

Conception	The father's sperm penetrates the mother's egg cell. Genetic instructions from both parents interact to begin a new and unique individual who is no bigger than a grain of sugar.
Day 1	The first cell divides into two, then two into four, and so on.
Days 5–9	The new individual implants in the mother's womb. The baby's sex can already be determined.
Day 14	The mother's normal menstrual period is suppressed by a hormone produced by her child.
Day 18	The heart is forming. Soon the eyes start to develop.
Day 20	The beginnings of brain, spinal cord, and nervous system are laid.
Day 24	The heart begins to beat.
Day 28	Muscles are developing along the future spine.
Day 30	The child in utero has grown ten thousand times, to between six and seven millimeters (one-quarter inch) long. The brain has human proportions. Blood flows in the veins and is separate from the mother's blood supply.
Day 35	The pituitary gland in the brain is forming. Mouth, ears, and nose are taking shape.
Day 40	The heart's energy output is twenty percent of an adult's output.
Day 42	The skeleton is formed. The brain coordinates movement of the muscles and organs. Reflex responses have begun. The penis has begun to form in male infants. The mother misses her second period.

Day 43 (1 ½ months)	Brain waves are recorded.
Day 45	Spontaneous movements have begun, and teeth are developing.
7 Weeks	Lips are sensitive to touch, and the ears may already be taking on the family shape.
8 Weeks	The child is well proportioned: a small-scale baby is three centimeters (one and an eighth inches) sitting up, and a gram (one-thirtieth of an ounce) in weight. Every organ is present. The heart beats sturdily; the stomach produces digestive juices; the liver makes blood cells; the kidneys begin to function; the taste buds are forming.
8 ½ Weeks	Fingerprints are being engraved. They will grow larger, but they are unique and will never change. The eyelids and palms of the hands are sensitive to touch.
9 Weeks	The child bends fingers around an object placed in the palm.
10 Weeks	The body is sensitive to touch. The child squints, swallows, furrows the brows, and frowns.
11 Weeks	The baby urinates and makes complex facial expressions, and even smiles.
12 Weeks	The baby is capable of vigorous activity—kicking, turning feet, curling and fanning toes, making a fist, moving thumbs, bending wrists, turning the head, opening the mouth, and pressing lips tightly together. Breathing has begun.
13 Weeks (End of First Trimester)	The baby is prettier, and the facial expressions resemble the parents'. Movements are graceful, reflexes vigorous. The vocal cords are formed, although without air the baby cannot cry. The sex organs are apparent.
4 Months	The baby can grasp with hands, swim, and do somersaults.
4–5 Months	The mother first feels the baby move.
5 Months	Sleeping habits are noticeable. A slammed door will result in activity. The child responds to sounds in frequencies too high or low for adults to hear.

6 Months (End of Second Trimester)	Fine hair grows on eyebrows and head. Eyelash fringe appears. The baby's weight is about 640 grams (one pound, six ounces), height is twenty-three centimeters (9 inches). Babies born at this age have survived.
7 Months	Eye-teeth are present. Eyelids open and close. Eyes look around. Hands grip strongly. The mother's voice is heard and recognized.
8 Months	Weight increases by one kilogram (over two pounds), and the baby's quarters get very cramped.
9 Months	The child triggers labor, and birth occurs, usually 255–275 days after conception. Of the forty-five generations of cell divisions before adulthood, forty one have already taken place. Four more will come during the rest of childhood and adolescence.[5]

This development of a human being has been divided into different stages, and different terms are used to describe these stages:

> In the first few days the new living entity that has been created is usually referred to as a zygote. From the moment the zygote has made its way to the uterus it becomes a blastocyst. . . . By the end of the second week the "successful" blastocyst has developed to the point where it implants itself in the wall of the uterus. From this significant moment of implantation until the end of the eighth week, we speak of an embryo. After the eighth week the embryo becomes a fetus in the narrower sense of the word (even though the word is sometimes used for the entire period from conception to birth). . . . It is important to remember that this "portrayal of development in stages is artificial and unnatural."[6]

We now turn more directly to the topic of abortion and begin with definitions of the term "abortion."

---

[5] John S. Feinberg and Paul D. Feinberg, *Ethics for a Brave New World,* 2nd ed. (Wheaton, IL: Crossway, 2010), 76–78. Elmer P. Sakala, "Observations on Abortion: One Perinatologist's Viewpoint," in *Abortion: Ethical Issues and Options*, ed. David R. Larson (Loma Linda, CA: Loma Linda University Center for Christian Bioethics, 1992), 4–10, offers additional helpful and detailed insights.

[6] Reinder Bruinsma, *Matters of Life and Death* (Nampa, ID: Pacific Press, 2000), 69–70. The quotation he uses comes from Sakala, 10–11. Niels-Erik Andreasen, "A Biblical Perspective on Abortion," in Larson, 51, suggests that the Bible distinguishes between conception, gestation, and birth.

Definitions of Abortion

The term "abortion" is used in different ways today. For instance, a miscarriage is nowadays called a "spontaneous abortion," carried out by the female body independent of willful intervention by the mother or other people.

But normally an "abortion" is understood as the termination of an unborn human life in the body of a woman.[7] Walter Jeffko defines it as follows: "Abortion is the direct killing of a fetus, either by causing its death in the womb or by removing it from the womb before it is viable, that is before it can survive outside the mother's womb."[8] Abortion can be done in various ways—for example, by the use of medication that kills the fetus within a few days, or by surgical procedures. This type of abortion is what this chapter is concerned with—not "spontaneous abortion." Abortion as the willful termination of an unborn human life is further described by the following subcategories:

"Late-term abortions" are typically performed toward the end of the second trimester of pregnancy—that is, approximately after the twenty-first or twenty-fourth week. However, they are also offered up to the ninth month (thirty-sixth week).[9]

The phrase "elective abortion" refers to a voluntary abortion at the request of a pregnant woman for reasons other than health concerns.[10] Such reasons may include 1) living in poverty; 2) encountering difficult

---

[7] Wikipedia, s.v. "Abortion," last modified March 15, 2020, https://en.wikipedia.org/wiki/Abortion (accessed March 17, 2020), defines abortion as follows: "Abortion is the ending of a pregnancy by removal or expulsion of an embryo or fetus before it can survive outside the uterus. An abortion that occurs without intervention is known as a miscarriage or spontaneous abortion. When deliberate steps are taken to end a pregnancy, it is called an induced abortion, or less frequently 'induced miscarriage'. The unmodified word *abortion* generally refers to an induced abortion. A similar procedure after the fetus has potential to survive outside the womb is known as a 'late termination of pregnancy' or less accurately as a 'late term abortion'."

[8] Walter G. Jeffko, *Contemporary Ethical Issues: A Personalistic Perspective* (New York: Humanity Books, 1999), 60.

[9] See, e.g., "Overview of Abortion Care at Capital Women's Services," Capital Women's Services, https://www.capitalwomensservices.com/overviewofabortioncare.php?gclid=EAIaIQobChMIt-urkZO95AIVTwOGCh3oQwLGEAAYASAAEgI3rfD_BwE (accessed March 19, 2020). There are other voices; see, e.g., Lila Rose and Mary Davenport, "Fact: Late-Term Abortions Are Never Medically Necessary," *The Federalist*, February 26, 2019, https://thefederalist.com/2019/02/26/fact-late-term-abortions-never-medically-necessary/ (accessed March 19, 2020) and Lila Rose and Donna Harrison, "Abortion Is Never Medically Necessary," *Washington Examiner*, February 26, 2019, https://www.washingtonexaminer.com/opinion/op-eds/abortion-is-never-medically-necessary (accessed March 19, 2020).

[10] See *Encyclopedia Britannica Online*, s.v. "Elective Abortion," https://www.britannica.com/science/elective-abortion (accessed March 17, 2020): "An elective abortion is the interruption of a pregnancy before the 20th week of gestation at the woman's request for reasons other than maternal health or fetal disease."

circumstances, such as being single or living in an abusive relationship; 3) feeling the child would threaten the pursuit of her education or career; 4) not feeling ready to have a child, or another child, or simply wanting to avoid motherhood at all; or 5) wanting to avoid the shame of having become pregnant.[11] The phrase "elective abortions," the vast majority of all abortions, focuses almost exclusively on pregnant women. Physicians who perform these procedures, or persons who may force or threaten a woman to have an abortion, such as the father, family members, or human traffickers are considered secondary or tertiary. The fetus is referred to as the "product of conception"—a euphemism. Although Elmer Sakala considers terminations of pregnancy that occur earlier than implantation of the fertilized egg in the uterus to be contraception, and holds that abortions are more questionable the later the fetus is in development, he still states,

> Employment of this euphemism ["products of conception"] avoids reference to the fetus and provides a surgical context for the abortion. The expression, however, tends to downplay and obscure the striking and exquisite development of even a first trimester fetus. Even early abortions procedures do not involve formless blobs of protoplasm but delicate, finely orchestrated embryological processes following a sequence meticulously devised by the Creator Himself.[12]

This study will address "induced abortions," abortions carried out with the purpose of ending the life of the unborn for various reasons—social (elective abortions), medical, or otherwise. Medical reasons refer to issues regarding either the health of the mother or the child. They can be mild, moderate, or severe.

Another phrase using the term "abortion," which does not fit the above definition, is the "after-birth abortion." This is a euphemism for infanticide, which is not only suggested by some academics or health practitioners but may also be carried out by a parent, relative, or another person. Both "spontaneous abortions" and "after-birth abortions" do not directly concern us in this study.

Data Concerning Abortions

Abortion has been a much-debated issue for decades, and is practiced extensively. "Between 1973 and 2005 more than 45 million legal abortions

---

[11] See, e.g., Lawrence B. Finer et al., "Reasons U.S. Women Have Abortions: Quantitative and Qualitative Perspectives," *Perspectives on Sexual Health and Reproductive Health* 37, no. 3 (2005): 110–118.

[12] Sakala, 4.

were performed in the United States. . . . Figures from 1996 show that approximately 3,700 abortions occurred each day in the United States. . . . According to the Allen Guttmacher Institute . . . , nearly half of the pregnancies among American women are unintended, and four in ten of those end in abortion."[13]

In the United States, the phenomenon has been studied so widely that numbers are available on how many women in certain age groups, social classes, religious affiliations, races, and other groups have abortions. The reasons why these women chose abortions have also been investigated. "Six percent of abortions are performed because of potential health problems regarding either the mother or child. In contrast, '93% of all abortions occur for social reasons (i.e. the child is unwanted or inconvenient).'"[14] Social reasons include, as indicated already, poverty and financial difficulties; interference with education, work, or career; perceived unreadiness for a child; being unmarried; etc. A 2004 study by the Alan Guttmacher Institute on a more limited sample of participants came to the following conclusion: "Our data suggest that after carefully assessing their individual situations, women base their decisions largely on their ability to maintain economic stability and to care for children they already have."[15] Loren Seibold states,

> Having an abortion is often argued as the way to keep unwed mothers from sinking under family responsibilities. The data doesn't support that. Women who have had abortions are more likely to become pregnant again and have more abortions, and are more likely to require welfare. They have more health and emotional problems, which makes it harder to find a job, and diminishes their chance of establishing permanent relationships with a male partner—they're more likely to never marry, more likely to divorce, and more likely to go through a long string of unsuccessful relationships.[16]

---

[13] Feinberg and Feinberg, 63. This quotation is associated with the Alan Guttmacher Institute. "The Guttmacher Institute isn't affiliated with a political party, and so it is nonpartisan in the strict sense of the word. It is true that the group does work to 'ensure that all women are able to exercise their reproductive rights and responsibilities,' which puts them among advocates of abortion rights" (Wikipedia, s.v. "Guttmacher Institute," last modified March 10, 2020, https://en.wikipedia.org/wiki/Guttmacher_Institute [accessed March 17, 2020]).

[14] Feinberg and Feinberg, 65.

[15] Finer et al., 117.

[16] Loren Seibold, "Why I'm Neither Pro-Life Nor Pro-Choice," *Spectrum*, December 18, 2009, https://spectrummagazine.org/article/column/2009/12/18/why-i%25E2%2580%2599m-neither-pro-life-nor-pro-choice (accessed March 17, 2020).

"In both surveys [1987 and 2004], 1% [of the sample of abortion patients] indicated that they had been victims of rape, and less than half a percent said they became pregnant as a result of incest."[17] "Only a small proportion of women cited concerns about their own health. However, . . . these concerns encompassed not just risks to future health, but also the health burden of pregnancy itself."[18]

While the abortion rate in the United States declined between 2008 and 2014, it is still anticipated that "nearly 1 in 4 women" will "have an abortion during her reproductive years."[19]

But abortions are not limited to the United States only. "In 2003, worldwide there were nearly 42 million abortions. . . . some 48% of all abortions worldwide were considered 'unsafe.'"[20] The magnitude of the issue becomes even more pronounced as one compares the yearly number of abortions worldwide with the population of certain countries. Forty-two million aborted children represents more than the total population of Poland in 2019 (about thirty-eight million). It is about half of the population of Germany (about eighty-four million). To eradicate the entire population of a country would be a gigantic genocide. But what we encounter is a colossal feticide. From such a perspective, the problem is urgent and cannot be ignored.

Arguments used by proponents of abortion may be startling at times. This is not only with those who are not directly affected, but also with pregnant women. Here are two examples: 1) Some women regard killing the unborn as less problematic than giving away the newborn for adoption or for care by foster parents so that he/she may reach his/her full potential. "More than one-third of interview respondents said they have considered adoption and concluded that it was a morally unconscionable option because giving one's child away is wrong."[21] 2) "Although some [women] described abortion as sinful and wrong, many of those same women, and others, described the indiscriminate bearing of children as a sin, and their abortion as 'the right thing' and a 'responsible choice.'"[22] On the other hand, Tim Crosby points to an earlier study in which seventy-two percent of the pregnant women seeking abortion claimed not to be particularly religious, "but 96 percent afterwards felt that abortion was 'taking of a life'

---

[17] Finer et al., 113.

[18] Ibid., 117.

[19] See Rachel K. Jones and Jenna Jerman, "Population Group Abortion Rates and Lifetime Incidence of Abortion: United States, 2008–2014," *American Journal of Public Health* 107, no. 12 (December 2017): 1908.

[20] Feinberg and Feinberg, 66.

[21] Finer et al., 117.

[22] Ibid., 118.

or 'murder.' . . . 'A psychological price is paid.' . . . Thus psychic trauma to the mother is probably more likely to result from an abortion than from a birth."[23] Also, to claim that abortion is a sin and still maintain that it is the best option for social reasons sounds contradictory, and may appear to be a justification for behavior that the woman herself may have questions about.

The Variety of Opinions on Abortion

Opinions on abortion vary widely. These opinions depend on one's presuppositions and value system. Here is a summary of some, but by far not all, positions on the topic.

Some people argue that all types of abortions should be allowed, suggesting that the fetus is not a human person and therefore can be aborted. Peter Singer proposes,

> My suggestion, then, is that we accord the fetus no higher moral status than we give to a nonhuman animal at a similar level or rationality, self-consciousness, awareness, capacity to feel, and so on. Because no fetus is a person, no fetus has the same claim to life as a person. Until a fetus has some capacity for conscious experience, an abortion terminates an existence that is—considered as it is and not in terms of his potential—more like that of a plant than of a sentient animal like a dog or a cow.[24]

Others agree that all or most kinds of abortions must be permitted, suggesting that an abortion is an individual's decision, which no one else has the right to interfere with, and that a woman has the full right to decide what happens with and in her body. This reasoning is different from the first, placing the value of individual choice over the sanctity of human life. But the result is basically the same. Charles Bellinger discusses the position of British philosopher Soran Reader:

> The core of her argument is that a woman should be able to choose abortion-as-killing if she does not want there to be a human being alive somewhere in the world to whom she is related as mother. She should have this ability because the inhabitant

---

[23] Crosby, 66.

[24] Peter Singer, *Practical Ethics*, 3rd ed. (New York: Cambridge University Press, 2011), 74–75. See also Charles K. Bellinger, *Jesus v. Abortion: They Know Not What They Do*, Theopolitical Visions (Eugene, OR: Cascade Books, 2016), 78.

> of her womb belongs to her; it is her child, a piece of property over which she has "maternal authority."[25]

While it is certainly true that the expecting mother is most directly affected by the pregnancy, some people would suggest that an abortion should not or even cannot be decided by the pregnant woman alone, but that society, government, churches, the father, family, etc. should also have a say. "Abortion is first of all an individual matter. . . . But abortion is not only an individual matter. The church cannot ignore the issue. It must give moral guidance to its members and it must therefore take a position."[26]

Another group would suggest that some types of abortion should be allowed, but not others. Abortion cannot just be evaluated from the pregnant woman's perspective, but must also be viewed from the perspective of the child, who has as much a right to live as the mother. Still, abortion may be permitted in cases of rape and incest, congenital defects of the unborn, and threats to the mother's health or life.[27]

The last group is opposed to abortions in principle. There are some who categorically object to all abortions,[28] while there are others who allow for abortions in only the most rare and severe medical cases, such as anencephaly of the baby or when the mother's life may be lost if medical intervention does not take place. Richard Hays states,

> The New Testament teaches us to approach ethical issues not by asking "What will happen if I do x?" but rather by asking "What is the will of God?" . . . If the New Testament witness were put into practice, abortion would almost never be seen necessary within the Christian community. Furthermore, the New Testament emphatically excludes some of the patterns of reasoning commonly used in support of abortion, particularly the appeal to the "right" of individuals to make autonomous moral decisions, the "right to privacy," and the "quality of life" argument.[29]

---

[25] Bellinger, 102. If this line of argument is followed, could a man also claim that he "does not want there to be a human being alive somewhere in the world to whom [he] is related as" father, with all the consequences following from such a statement?

[26] Bruinsma, 67.

[27] See "Religious Groups' Official Positions on Abortion," Pew Research Center, January 16, 2013, https://www.pewforum.org/2013/01/16/religious-groups-official-positions-on-abortion/ (accessed March 17, 2020).

[28] E.g., the Catholic Church. See "Abortion," Know the Issues, Diocese of Phoenix, https://dphx.org/respect-life/know-the-issues/abortion/ (accessed March 17, 2020).

[29] Hays, 455–456. Pew Research came up with the following statement: "Carson has compared abortion to slavery and called for it to be banned in all circumstances, but Adventists are actually somewhat divided over abortion. About four-in-ten (42%) say abortion should be legal in all

These positions and opinions reveal a number of underlying issues. There is the question of whether the unborn is a human person who therefore must be protected, or if the unborn child is not yet a person. If it is decided that the unborn is not a human person, then—so the reasoning goes—the fetus can be aborted. A second issue is whether or not abortion is murder or killing, falling under the scope of the sixth commandment. If it is, is it problematic or not? In other words, killing might be per-missible, as some have suggested. Third, when different civil or religious rights conflict with each other, which right has priority—the right of the mother, or the right of the child? Is a child automatically considered inferior? Fourth, apart from the issue of killing, is a child the property of the mother? If so, at what age do the mother's property rights come to an end? Or do they not end as long as the mother lives? Is the child more or less a slave of the mother, and should it remain so? Finally, the question is what role the Bible has to play in the abortion debate. These and other issues need to be evaluated.

Our Approach

Attempts to provide answers to the issue of abortion depend on certain premises. The answer of an adherent to one of the world religions may be different from the answer of an atheist. Again, the answer of a Christian may, for instance, differ from the answer given by a Hindu. And the answer of a Christian who believes in God as the Creator of all life may differ from the answer of a Christian who believes in some sort of evolution.

Here are the presuppositions with which we will work:

1. God exists and has revealed Himself in various ways, particularly in special revelation through His word—that is, Scripture—and the person of Jesus Christ.
2. The Bible is the word of God and reveals to us, among other things, God's nature—as much as humans are able to comprehend it—human nature, our human predicament, God's plan to create *shalom*,[30] and God's will for humanity to live a life in harmony and peace with Him and with each other.

---

or most cases, while 54% say it should be entirely or mostly illegal. This latter group includes one-in-five Seventh-day Adventists (19%) who take Carson's view that abortion should be illegal in all cases" ("A Closer Look at Seventh-Day Adventists in America," Pew Research Center, November 3, 2015, https://www.pewresearch.org/fact-tank/2015/11/03/a-closer-look-at-seventh-day-adventists-in-america/ (accessed March 17, 2020).

[30] *Shalom*, often translated as "peace," points to wholeness and well-being in all aspects, including salvation. See Laird Harris, Gleason L. Archer Jr., and Bruce K. Waltke, "*Shālôm*," in *Theological Wordbook of the Old Testament*, vol. 2 (Chicago, IL: Moody, 1980), 931.

3. God's written word, the Bible, and God's incarnate Word, Jesus Christ—as revealed in Scripture[31]—have to be taken seriously. This applies to biblical texts and passages that must be understood according to the Bible's own way of interpretation as well as various biblical principles. Matters of life and death—and therefore also the issue of abortion—are particularly important.
4. God is the Creator of all life as well as all inanimate matter. As Creator, God has a right to us and can tell us how to deal with matters of life and death. They fall under His jurisdiction, not ours. Human life is not humans' property.
5. The Ten Commandments reflect God's will. They have to be understood as moral absolutes. As such, they are binding for all human beings.
6. Humans have the divine gift of free choice. This even includes transgressing and/or rejecting God's will as revealed in His law, thereby rejecting God Himself. One can choose to live in a close relationship with God or to remain estranged from Him. However, such choices have consequences. In the Old Testament, these consequences are described as blessings or curses, dependent on human decisions and actions (e.g., Deut 28). The New Testament connects eternal life with believing in Christ and living with Him (John 1:12; 3:16, 36).
7. A biblical ethics of abortion must begin with the issue of abortion in general before moving to challenging cases. "Important ethical issues typically have hard cases. . . . Hard cases should never be the basis for developing normative ethical principles. As the saying goes, hard cases make bad laws. That is true in law, and it is equally true in ethics."[32]

Methodologically, our approach is founded on principle-based ethics rather than utilitarian/situation ethics.[33] We are looking for biblical

---

[31] While Jesus Christ is the highest revelation of God, we know of Him through Scripture. A Jesus independent of the Bible is a human construct that may vary from one person to the next and may even be contradictory. To say something definite about Jesus, we have to go to the record of the Bible and especially—but not exclusively—to the New Testament Gospels.

[32] Feinberg and Feinberg, 125.

[33] This is what Remwil R. Tornalejo, "The Status of the Unborn and the Seventh-day Adventist Abortion Guidelines," *Journal of Asia Adventist Seminary* 16, no. 2 (2013): 126, requests. Concerning a situationist approach, Carsten Johnsen, *God, the Situation Ethicist* (Sisteron: Untold Story, n.d.), 190, maintains, "God is the Situation Ethicist par excellence. But He is also the only One who has a perfect right to be a Situationist. Why? Simply because He is the only One who perfectly knows the situation, the context in its absolute totality. . . . So for a human being to presume that he, as well, has a right to be a situation ethicist is nothing less than taking God's place. It is the presumption of self-deification."

principles to come up with a theology/ethics of abortion. It has been suggested that the Bible only indirectly discusses abortion. Supposedly even the New Testament is silent on the issue; therefore, it is argued, believers must also be silent and let each one make his or her individual decision. Michael Gorman asks the question: "Could it be that when it comes to abortion, the New Testament's silence implies neutrality, ambiguity, or even acceptance?"[34] If this were the case, this would also mean that with all other modern issues (e.g., smoking, domestic violence, environmental care and climate control, cybersex, modern forms of slavery) the Bible would not provide any guidance and thus would become largely irrelevant to people of the twenty-first century. We believe there are sufficient biblical principles to guide us as we study the issue of abortion.

Here we must pause a moment and consider Christian theology. Exegesis is the instrument that deals with the interpretation of biblical verses and passages and includes, among other things, a careful study of the historical and literary contexts of the passage. Biblical theology studies themes within biblical books and across the entire Bible. It observes trajectories, changes, and advances. Systematic theology not only discusses the major topics of the Bible, providing an overarching system of theology, but also addresses contemporary issues and questions that are not directly spelled out in the Bible, yet are indirectly found there through principles. Here Christian ethics comes in. People face four types of questions: 1) questions on biblical texts (e.g., Dan 7 or 8), 2) questions on biblical topics (e.g., the Sabbath), 3) questions on biblical concepts (e.g., the Trinity), and 4) theological and ethical questions not mentioned in Scripture (e.g., human cloning). Abortion belongs mainly to the last category, which needs to be addressed by finding biblical principles that speak to the issue.

This should not surprise us because it has been pointed out that "the thought of abortion was so foreign to Judean-Christian thought that it is not even mentioned in the Scriptures."[35] But this statement addresses explicit texts. It is true that there is no text demanding, "You shall not abort a fetus," yet through principles the Bible, and especially the New Testament, speaks clearly enough to the issue of abortion. Research has shown that "Jesus and the early Christian movement of the first three centuries practiced non-violence."[36] Gorman shows that abortion was rejected by Jews at least between 100 BC and AD 100. "No contradictory

---

[34] Gorman, 27.

[35] Richard Muller, "Abortion: A Moral Issue?," *Ministry*, January 19, 1985. See also Michael J. Gorman, "Why Is the New Testament Silent About Abortion?," *Christianity Today*, January 11, 1993, 28.

[36] Marcus Borg, "Endorsement of Every Church a Peace Church," quoted in Robert H. Brimlow,

early Jewish texts about abortion have been discovered."[37] However, in the Greco-Roman world

> [t]here were just as many unwanted babies as today. This was due to poor birth-control methods and a sexual free-for-all that makes modern societies look prudish. Abortion was rarely practiced, because it was dangerous for the mother. Instead, the solution to the problem of an unwanted child was infanticide —the baby was born normally and then killed. In Roman society the final decision on whether a child lived wasn't made by the mother, but by the head of the household—usually the mother's father, if she wasn't married. Every newborn had to be laid on the floor before him, and the custom was that if he picked it up and named it, the baby lived. If not, the child would be "exposed." . . . "exposed" originally meant leaving an unwanted baby on a hillside for the child's fate to be decided by the gods.[38]

In that cultural setting also early Christians lived and had to make their decisions. Three early Christian documents, which were considered semi-authoritative by early believers, mention abortion negatively. Didache 2:2 and the Letter of Barnabas 19:5 speak against killing a child by abortion or a newborn by infanticide. The Apocalypse of Peter threatens women with hell who have "procured abortions."[39] In agreement with Muller, Gorman reasons that the New Testament's "silence on abortion testifies to the antiabortion stance of its original Jewish-Christian writers, its compilers, and its earliest hearers and readers. In a very real sense, then, the New Testament canon did indeed speak, and still does speak, against abortion."[40]

What About Hitler? Wrestling With Jesus's Call to Nonviolence in an Evil World (Grand Rapids, MI: Brazos, 2006), 22.

[37] Gorman, 28.

[38] David Instone-Brewer, *Moral Questions of the Bible: Timeless Truth in a Changing World*, Scripture in Context (Bellingham, WA: Lexham Press, 2019), 39-40.

[39] The Apocalypse of Peter (Ethiopic), 8, reads: ". . . And the women (are) swallowed up (by this) up to their necks and are punished with great pain. These are they who have procured abortions and have ruined the work of God which he has created." The Apocalypse of Peter (Greek), 26, states: ". . . And these were those who conceived children outside marriage and who procured abortions."

[40] Gorman, 29.

Scripture and Abortion[41]

As we enter the discussion of the Bible and abortion, we remember that Scripture talks about creation, the paradise, and the fall. Everything God had made was perfect, very good. Nothing troublesome was part of human life. The issue of miscarriages, genetic defects in the fetus, threats to the life of the mother and/or child, rape, and other forms of violence were not found in the garden of Eden. The issue of abortion was nonexistent.

This changed dramatically when Adam and Eve made a decision to turn away from God and pursue their own course (Gen 3). This tragic decision introduced sin into the world, and with it human mental and emotional instability; a tendency to disregard God's law and do evil, or a kind of schizophrenia of wanting to do what is right and yet doing the opposite; addictions; fractured relationships; oppression; enslavement; violence; a sense of meaninglessness; extreme poverty; suffering; pain; bodily illness; harmful genetic mutations; a change in the entire ecosystem and its effect on humanity; numerous other consequences; and finally death (Rom 6–8).

God's plan of salvation envisions a paradise that surpasses even the original paradise—for instance, by God being constantly present and living among His people. But in the meantime, we have to struggle with minor and major—even extreme—difficulties. Future mothers/parents may find themselves in very adverse situations, considering whether to keep or abort an unborn child. Economic factors, societal pressures, and the devastating effects of sin on the human body and mind may contribute to these deliberations, making abortion appear to be an alternative to carrying a child to full term. For direction in such situations, we as followers of Christ turn to the word of God. Holy Scripture expresses God's values for life and provides guidance for prospective mothers and fathers, medical personnel, churches, and all believers in matters of faith, doctrine, ethical behavior, and lifestyle.

While the term "abortion" is not mentioned in Scripture, the concept appears occasionally. However, the following biblical principles and teachings provide guidance for the community of faith and for individuals affected by difficult choices.

---

[41] Part of the wording in this section is taken from a draft of an abortion statement written by the present author and reviewed and improved by the Biblical Research Institute Ethics Committee and the Biblical Research Institute. The final and modified statement can be found here: https://www.adventist.org/articles/statement-on-the-biblical-view-of-unborn-life-and-its-implications-for-abortion (accessed May 5, 2020).

First Principle: The Value and Sacredness of Human Life

Human life is of the greatest value to God. This is so because God created us in His image (Gen 1:27; 2:7) and has a personal interest in all people. God loves us and communicates with us, and we in turn can seek His fellowship and love Him.

Life is a gift of God, and God is the giver of life. In fact, God the Father, Jesus, and the Holy Spirit are equated with life. God the Father has life in Himself (John 5:26). In Jesus is life (John 1:4). He also has life in Himself (John 5:26). He is the life (John 14:6) and the resurrection and life (John 11:25). He provides abundant life (John 10:10), and those who have the Son have life (1 John 5:12). He is also the sustainer of life (Acts 17:25–28; Col 1:17; Heb 1:1–3). The Holy Spirit is life (Rom 8:10). God deeply cares for His creation, and especially for us humans.

Furthermore, the importance of human life is made clear by the fact that after the fall (Gen 3) God gave His Son on behalf of humanity to save us and give us the possibility of gaining eternal life (John 3:16; Rom 5:6; 1 John 4:9–10). While God could have abandoned us and terminated completely life on planet earth, He opted for life. Therefore, Christ's followers will be raised from the dead and will live as unique individuals in direct communion with God (John 11:25–26; 1 Thess 4:15–16; Rev 21:3). Thus, human life is of inestimable value. This is true for all stages of human life: the unborn, children of various ages, adolescents, adults, and seniors—independent of physical, mental, or emotional capacities. It is also true for all humans independent of sex, color, race, social status, religion, or whatever else may distinguish us from one another. This divine sanctity of life gives inviolable and equal dignity to each and every human life and requires us to treat it with the utmost respect and care.

David Gushee affirms our understanding of the value of human life with his own definition:

> The concept of the sanctity of life is the belief that all human beings, at any and every stage of life, in any and every state of consciousness or self-awareness, of any and every race, color, ethnicity, level of intelligence, religion, language, gender, character, behavior, physical ability/disability, potential, class, social status, etc., of any and every particular quality of relationship to the viewing subject, are to be perceived as persons of equal and immeasurable worth and of inviolable dignity and therefore must be treated in a manner commensurate with this moral status.[42]

[42] David P. Gushee, "The Sanctity of Life," The Center for Bioethics & Human Dignity, Trinity International University, June 15, 2006, https://cbhd.org/content/sanctity-life (accessed March 17, 2020).

He continues to state that "the sanctity of human life is essentially a conferring of God's holiness or sanctity onto the pinnacle of God's creation, human beings. Humans can have sanctity because God, their Creator and Redeemer does."[43] But he also wonders if such a concept and conviction "can survive on the basis of a secularized vision of the foundation of that sanctity."[44]

It has, for instance, been argued that life is not the ultimate good in itself,[45] probably implying that under certain circumstances one may take life. It is true that Jesus considered giving His life in order to save us to be more important than keeping and defending it. Martyrs are persons who are willing to lose or sacrifice their life for Jesus' or others' sake. John declares that true love is manifested by the willingness "to lay down [one's] lives for the brothers" (1 John 3:16). However, it is ironic when this concept is twisted into an argument that it may be right to take someone else's life, including the life of a fetus. To let go of one's own life for a higher good is a decision that individuals have to make voluntarily. It is dependent on the martyr's consent. However, an abortion happens without the consent of the unborn child. The argument of the higher good does not apply here. We have no right to decide to terminate another's life. Giving one's life for others must be a choice freely made by that person.

Second Principle: The Unborn Child as Fully Human

The Bible mentions prenatal life in the Old Testament as well as the New Testament, and even describes God's knowledge of people before they were conceived. Prenatal life is in God's hands and is led by Him. David recounts the human situation: "For you formed my inward parts; you knitted me together in my mother's womb. . . . Your eyes saw my unformed substance; in your book were written, every one of them, the days that were formed for me, when as yet there was none of them" (Ps 139:13, 16). Samson was to "be a Nazirite to God from the womb" (Judg 13:5). The servant of God is called and formed "from the womb" (Isa 49:1, 5). Jeremiah was already chosen as a prophet before his birth (Jer 1:5), as was Paul (Gal 1:15), and John the Baptist was to "be filled with the Holy Spirit, even from his mother's womb" (Luke 1:15). Of Jesus,

---

[43] Gushee, https://cbhd.org/content/sanctity-life (accessed March 17, 2020).

[44] Ibid.

[45] In a similar vein, Bruinsma, 78, maintains, "We worship the Giver of life, not life itself." This is partially true and partially not, because—as shown in this study—the Father, the Holy Spirit, and especially Jesus are identified with life. Jesus is "the Way, and the Truth, and the Life" (John 14:6). The problem with such a statement is that it may make human life dispensable. The author does not directly say this, although he states that "as a result of sin life has in many instances lost some of its beauty and has in some extreme cases lost virtually all of its attractiveness" (ibid.).

the angel Gabriel explained to Mary, "Therefore the child to be born will be called holy—the Son of God" (Luke 1:35). In His incarnation Jesus Himself experienced the human prenatal period, and yet was recognized as the Messiah and Son of God soon after His conception (Luke 1:39–45).[46]

God is not only the Creator of the unborn—even though humans pro-create—but His ideal for each child is also to know Him and serve others. To each human being, including each child, is offered the opportunity to attain eternal life through faith in Christ, at least when self-awareness sets in. Therefore, God will try to influence him or her to recognize this purpose of life. In any case, the not-yet-born has a firm place with God. The Bible attributes to the unborn child joy (Luke 1:44) and even rivalry (Gen 25:21–23). It shows continuity between pre-and postnatal life. There is no break in the development of life.

An aside may be in order here. In the case of abortion—that is, the death of the unborn—the issue may not just be his or her loss of life here and now (although some children survive late-term abortions and may be left dying in a morgue), but also the unborn's eternal life. But we do not know how God will treat an aborted embryo. Will God consider him or her to be exempt from the possibility of either being saved or lost? Or will he or she be saved automatically? Scripture does not seem to address these questions. Nevertheless, thinking about these matters should make us extremely careful. Depending on the situation, an aborted, unborn child may not only be robbed of life as we experience it but may never have the option to live eternally with Jesus in His kingdom. If this is so, then abortion is an even more serious issue.

Now we return to the discussion of the unborn as being fully human. Scripture is opposed to a dualistic understanding of human life. The human being is a wholistic being who cannot be divided into body and soul—or body, soul, and spirit (Gen 2:7). Therefore, the question of when the fertilized egg receives the soul and thus becomes a human being is irrelevant. According to Scripture, the unborn is a human being at each and every stage.

Why is this important to the discussion? It seems that the debate about life has at least partially moved away from the question of when life begins to the question of whether or not the new life is human, and whether the fetus is a human person. It is difficult to deny that after the

---

[46] David Gunn, "The Bible on the Ethicality of Abortion," The 1024 Project, January 31, 2014, http://1024project.com/2014/01/31/the-bible-on-the-ethicality-of-abortion/ (accessed March 17, 2020). Gunn points out that this is an insightful passage because it refers to a "post-conception meeting" of Mary and Elizabeth, in which Elizabeth's son leaps for joy, which may indicate "some level of consciousness." This is not a random movement, "but comes in direct response to Mary's arrival."

fusion of egg and sperm the zygote, as a new entity with a full genetic code, is alive. Certainly, it needs to implant into the uterus and thereby become a blastocyst, later an embryo, and finally a fetus in the narrow sense. But all the way through this process, we are dealing with life. Bellinger affirms, "The human embryo develops itself into a baby, a toddler, an adult, rather than into a frog or a sparrow, because its humanity is not 'potentiality' but an 'actuality.'"[47] This is so because of the human genome that the zygote possesses.[48] Therefore, as early as 1973 Paul Römhild maintained that there is life right from the beginning. In addition, he postulated that this life is human life:

> From the fertilized egg, which, according to our current biological knowledge, must be regarded as a human being in the single cell stage, the person, the "I" is on the move. Everything that belongs to "being" is provided . . . the human does not become human, but is human, in every phase of his development . . . so in the fertilized human egg we are dealing with the "smallest form of human appearance" . . . , and from then on we must not speak of an emerging human life, but of human life that is unfolding and growing. . . . May we now presume to determine the time from which God loves or has to love the human being—from the third month onward, from the fifth month of his/her prenatal period onward or from a later date, for instance, from his birth onward?[49]

[47] Bellinger, 85. On the other hand, Tim Crosby, "Abortion: Some Questionable Arguments," in Larson, 61, holds "that the very earliest the line of personhood could be drawn on the continuum of life would be late in the second month of pregnancy." Until then, he argues, the organism is dead according to the Harvard criteria of death issued in 1968. But this raises the questions if death should define the beginning of life, and if Harvard's definitions are the most accurate ("lack of response to external stimuli, lack to deep reflex action, lack of spontaneous movement and respiratory effort, and lack of brain activity" [p. 61]). Sakala, 12, suggests that implantation may mark "the beginning of potential personhood."

[48] "Human genomes include both protein-coding DNA genes and noncoding DNA. Haploid human genomes, which are contained in germ cells (the egg and sperm gamete cells created in the meiosis phase of sexual reproduction before fertilization creates a zygote) consist of three billion DNA base pairs, while diploid genomes (found in somatic cells) have twice the DNA content. While there are significant differences among the genomes of human individuals (on the order of 0.1% due to single-nucleotide variants and 0.6% when considering indels), these are considerably smaller than the differences between humans and their closest living relatives, the bonobos and chimpanzees (~1.1% fixed single-nucleotide variants and 4% when including indels)" (Wikipedia, s.v. "Human genome," last modified February 15, 2020, https://en.wikipedia.org/wiki/Human_genome [accessed March 17, 2020]).

[49] Paul Römhild, *Vom Ursprung des Lebens und vom Beginn des Menschseins - Auch der Unge-borene ist unser Nächster*, Die weiße Reihe 2, Beiträge zu Fragen der Lebensführung und Seelsorge (Kassel: Verlag des Weißen Kreuzes, 1973/74), 10–12 (translated by the author).

Robert Dunn states, "I believe that the embryo or zygote at the moment of conception fulfills this definition of a person. . . . This is a passive phase in the life of a person, but it makes him no less a person."[50]

However, as mentioned, a number of people deny the fetus the status of full humanity. This may be due to their acceptance of an a priori pro-abortion position. "Modern society has learned, largely from Jesus, that children have full human rights, and their vulnerability makes us especially responsible for looking after them. However, somehow we've managed to concede that a fetus is not a child, so it's not due the same legal protection."[51] Nevertheless, it is still difficult to talk about the termination of the life of a human person. It is easier and more acceptable for people to kill "non-human" life. Their suggested criteria of self-consciousness, rationality, and the ability to feel are supposed to determine who can be called a human person and who cannot. However, are these proposed criteria the correct criteria for determining the personhood of the unborn? Carsten Johnsen has a point when he speaks about "the poor faltering human creature's own subjective notion of right and wrong," which "is bound to be the only judgement throne for deciding the matter in the last analysis."[52] In the end the conclusion may be correct that

> the divergent views of abortion . . . are found to be due to one thing: the lack of a consistent anthropology. . . . The Bible knows when human life begins and when it ends. It knows everything worth knowing about man. And it is not stingy in setting forth its knowledge in front of you and me, in order that we may have those very clear and concise notions we need regarding essential questions for the guidance of our lives.[53]

---

[50] Robert H. Dunn, "The Nature of Man in the Early Stages of Life and Our Responsibility," quoted in Johnsen, 159, who himself notes, "The fact that a loving Creator has given life, even personal life, and the personal destiny which inevitably goes along with that, to a human sprout, can only signify that it has exactly the same amount of humanity at every stage of its development, and exactly the same right to be granted protection and a continuation of life. . . . The creature must have been given by God the tremendous honor of possessing a human destiny. And that is certainly an attribute the foetus possesses from the very moment when the zygote is an accomplished fact."

[51] Instone-Brewer, 43–44.

[52] Johnsen, 148. By the way, Bellinger, 75–76, suggests "that 'science' has no competence whatsoever in defining a word such as 'person,' any more than it has competence to define 'liberty,' or 'rights,' or 'wisdom,' or 'truth,' or 'the Beloved Community.' 'Person' is not a scientific concept, but a philosophical and religious one." He continues, "Culturally created, the value of life rests on social meanings, and, importantly, on sexual politics. Fetal life has value when people with power value it. Thus, inquiry into the value of potential life cannot objectively resolve the question of abortion."

[53] Johnsen, 147. When Johnsen talks about the end of human life, he may refer to death, not

Hays makes an interesting point about the fetus as a person:

> When we ask, "Is the fetus a person?" we are asking the same sort of limiting, self-justifying question that the lawyer asked Jesus: "Who is my neighbor?" Jesus, by answering the lawyer's question with this parable [of the good Samaritan], rejects casuistic attempts to circumscribe our moral concern by defining the other as belonging to a category outside the scope of our obligation. To define the unborn child as a nonperson is to narrow the scope of moral concern, whereas Jesus calls upon us to widen it by showing mercy and actively intervening on behalf of the helpless.[54]

Third Principle: The Will of God as Expressed in the Ten Commandments and Elaborated by Jesus in the Sermon on the Mount

The Decalogue was given to God's covenant people and is to guide our lives and protect us even today. Its commandments are absolutes, valid for all human beings at all times. Individuals and churches have no right to change them. Scripture even warns against a power that would dare to change God's law (Dan 7:25), while the remnant people remain faithful to God's will (Rev 12:17). The psalmist praises God's law (e.g., Ps 119) and Paul calls it holy, righteous, and good (Rom 7:12).[55] The sixth commandment states, "You shall not kill" (Exod 20:13). God calls for the preservation of human life. Since being human begins with the fusion of egg and sperm, and since prenatal life is of immense value to God, abortion falls under the legislation of the sixth commandment. According to the book of Exodus, the innocent and most vulnerable (Exod 22:22–23) in particular must not be abused or killed (Exod 23:7). Proverbs 6:16–17 states that God hates those who shed innocent blood; the unborn child is the most innocent and vulnerable of all, and therefore must be protected. Revelation 21:8 warns that "the cowardly, the faithless, the detestable, as for murderers, the sexually immoral, sorcerers, idolaters, and all liars" will not have a place in the new Jerusalem (Rev 22:15).

As previously pointed out, the argument that the unborn is not yet fully human but only has the potential of becoming human because he/she has not yet self-awareness, rationality, and other traits would also

---

in the medical sense but in the sense that life does not continue beyond death in a kind of intermediate stage or as an immortal soul.

[54] Hays, 450.

[55] Mark 7:9–13 presents the case in which Jesus accuses Pharisees and scribes of invalidating the fifth commandment by the use of their manmade traditions. Jesus stands for the Ten Commandments as the Word of God against human interpretations that change their intended meaning.

apply to the newborn. Neither self-awareness nor usefulness defines the value of human life. Aborting the life of an unborn child on the basis of his or her self-awareness or abilities would also allow for infanticide and the extermination of mentally handicapped people, individuals in a coma, and seniors who suffer, for instance, from severe forms of dementia. There is no significant difference between a fetus shortly before birth and a newborn after birth that would allow abortion in the first case and prohibit infanticide in the second. Once the door has been opened to the killing of unborn children, it may affect wider circles of society.

It is dangerous to let humans decide which life is valuable and which is not. History is full of horrid examples of the killing of not only unborn and newborn children, but also females of various ages, seniors and sick people, supposedly inferior races and individuals, so-called heretics, and others.[56] Their lives were deemed worthless. Niels-Erik Andreasen points out that "when the value of life is depreciated near the borders of human existence . . . no life is really safe anywhere, even well within those borders."[57] The cases mentioned here are not only a transgression of the sixth commandment, but also of the commandment to love one's neighbor as oneself (Lev 19:18; Mark 12:31), which summarizes the second table of the Ten Commandments.

Jesus has reinforced and broadened the commandment not to kill in Matthew 5:21–22. According to Him, killing is not only the taking of someone's life, but begins even with derogatory, inflammatory speech and angry, insulting words—what we today call hate speech. If the sixth commandment can be transgressed even by how we communicate with each other, how much more is it defied by acts of violence and actual killing? The sixth commandment is given for the preservation of human life, whether or not we consider such life worthwhile. Thus, human life

---

[56] Here is an example from "Unworthy to Live," Holocaust and Human Behavior, Facing History and Ourselves, https://www.facinghistory.org/holocaust-and-human-behavior/chapter-8/unworthy-live (accessed March 17, 2020): "As Adolf Hitler consolidated his power at home in anticipation of war, he moved not only against Jews, Sinti, and Roma but also against those Aryans whom he considered 'unworthy of life'—people with epilepsy, alcoholism, birth defects, hearing loss, mental illnesses, and personality disorders, as well as those who had vision loss or developmental delays or who even suffered from certain orthopedic problems. Hitler viewed them as 'marginal human beings' who had to make a case for their own survival at a time when the nation was preparing for war. The first to be eliminated were too young to speak on their own behalf. In fall 1938, the parents of a severely disabled infant petitioned Hitler for the right to kill their child. He granted the petition and saw in the request an opportunity to encourage what he called 'mercy killings' or 'euthanasia.' In fact, according to science historian Robert N. Proctor, the goal was not to provide mercy to the victims but to improve the 'Aryan' race and make hospital beds and personnel available for the coming war."

[57] Andreasen, 53.

is not measured by individuals' abilities or their effectiveness, but by the value that God's sacrificial love has placed on it. It is protected by God.

The English-speaking reader may wonder why cite the sixth commandment as "You shall not kill" instead of "You shall not murder," as found in most of the recent English translations. Wilma Ann Bailey[58] has examined the shift from "You shall not kill" (ASV, CEB, GNV, KJV, NAB, RSV, NJB) to "You shall not murder" (ESV, NIV, NKJV, NASB, NET, NLT, NRSV) in Protestant translations, a process that may have started approximately in the middle of the twentieth century. There is no new manuscript evidence demanding such a shift, and Bailey shows that linguistically and theologically "You shall not kill" is the better translation. But "You shall not murder" is much more limited than the broader "You shall not kill." "Murder" is premeditated killing for reasons considered unlawful by governments, but leaves the door open for killing in combat and in other cases. On the other hand, the term "killing" refers to all cases in which the life of a human being is terminated—even cases of accidental killing with no intention to hurt or take a life. The manslayer in Numbers 35:6–33 is designated with the same Hebrew term "to kill" that is used in the sixth commandment, even though in his case the issue is clearly not murder but accidental killing. Still, if a human being were to be killed accidentally, the manslayer ought to run for his life to a city of refuge, where his case would be investigated and where he would need to stay permanently if proven innocent. This case shows how serious even unintentional killing was in Israel. When in the Sermon on the Mount Jesus showed the deeper meaning of the sixth commandment, He must have had "killing" in mind and not "murdering." Jiří Moskala affirms that an English translation of the sixth commandment should use the verb "to kill."[59]

So why the change? In a historical section, Bailey traces several faith traditions, showing that for Evangelicals the desire to become mainstream churches, the growing connection to militarism, and the influence of culture led to a change of the wording of the sixth commandment as well as a change in practice. Therefore, if she is right, it was not the biblical text but an implicit agenda that led to the change of translation. This change is also more favorable to abortion than the prohibition of killing is. In a somewhat provocative way, Bailey states, "People want to kill people, and they want biblical permission to do so."[60]

---

[58] Wilma Ann Bailey, *"You Shall Not Kill" or "You shall Not Murder"? The Assault on a Biblical Text* (Collegeville, MN: Liturgical Press, 2005).

[59] Jiří Moskala, "'You Shall not Kill' or 'You Shall not Murder'? The Meaning of Ratsakh in the Sixth Commandment," *Reflections* 67 (July 2019): 1–6.

[60] Bailey, 52.

But there is another issue: the question of whether or not the Ten Commandments are to be taken as absolutes, and how an absolute understanding of the sixth commandment relates to the wars and killings of the Old Testament. As we ask ourselves if individual commandments of the Decalogue need to be kept in even exceptional cases, we have to remember that exceptions can be understood at least in two ways: 1) Humans take the liberty of making exceptions that are recorded in Scripture (these are descriptive and occur often in narratives) but they are not legitimized by God. 2) God provides exceptions to some teachings of Scripture, sometimes due to the hardness of human hearts (Matt 19:3–8). They may be limited in time. Some Old Testament permissions are revoked in the New Testament so that the original will of God is evident again (e.g., Deut 24:1–4; Matt 5:31–32). In any case, the issue of killing in the Old Testament may at times be more complex than at first thought, and needs to be handled carefully. These two types of exceptions are different and should not be confused. Real exceptions are the ones permitted by God. So we will take a quick look at God's moral law, the Decalogue.

The first three commandments (Exod 20:3–7) prohibit having rival gods to God, manufacturing and worshipping images of God, and blaspheming God. Like them, commandment five—to honor one's parents—and seven through ten—prohibiting adultery, falsehood, stealing, and coveting—have no exceptions mentioned in Scripture. Their reinforcement in the Old and New Testaments,[61] and the willingness of believers to bear disadvantages or risk their lives by keeping them at all costs,[62] indicates that they have to be understood as absolutes.

The Sabbath commandment (Exod 20:8–11) differs from the other commandments. It is phrased positively as "remember," "keep holy," "labor six days," and "the seventh-day is the Sabbath." Only then comes "you shall not do any work" for God created, rested on, blessed, and made holy the Sabbath day. The issue is the definition of work. An "exception" to working on the Sabbath were Old Testament priests (Matt 12:5), although even they would be able to remember God and His mighty deeds while being involved in sacred work. Jesus also explains the Sabbath commandment in the sense that healing and doing good deeds do not militate against the prohibition of work (Matt 12:12). On the other hand, the command against buying and selling on the Sabbath is reinforced in Nehemiah 13 because these activities are considered

---

[61] E.g., Proverbs 30:9; Hosea 4:2; Mattew 5:37; Mark 7:10–13; Acts 5:1–11; Revelation 14:5; 19:10; 21:8; 22:15.

[62] E.g., Genesis 39:6–10; Daniel 3:1–18; Revelation 13:15–17; 14:3–5.

"work." The definitions of work or so-called exceptions were divinely given, and are not a human encroachment on God's will.

We return to the sixth commandment and its exceptions. This topic deserves a serious and extensive treatment that cannot be pursued in this study.[63] Some preliminary answers to the question of why God allowed for killing in the Old Testament must suffice.

First, it is true that one can find expressions of stark violence as well as horrific imagery in some biblical texts. This must be acknowledged, but we must also try—as much as possible—to understand the times and culture, and to avoid using stereotypes or considering brutal and violent behavior as an excuse for our own decisions and conduct. When, for instance, in the narratives of the book of Job, his friends share with him their theology, this theology is not necessarily God's view of reality. When people in the Bible, under distress, cry out for justice in ways we today may consider inappropriate, this is not necessarily the best possible manner to describe God's view of justice.[64] In other words, the reader must be fair enough not to attribute to God the voice of humans portrayed in Scripture.[65] Not all human speech in Scripture reflects God's will and His intentions. The inspired speech of God's prophets does.

Second, Scripture has a so-called "dark side," because it is actually humans and evil powers who have a dark side, resorting to violence and all kinds of evil. Scripture does not paint a wonderful picture of the goodness of the human race, but honestly portrays how humans really are. Even Genesis, the first book of Scripture, is revealing: right after the fall, Cain commits the first murder. The fratricide of Abel is one of the most heinous sins, remembered negatively even in the New Testament (Heb 11:4; 1 John 3:12; Jude 11). After this bad start outside of the garden of Eden, one finds idolatry, deceit and falsehood, polygamy and incest, prostitution and homosexuality, mob violence and slavery. When it comes to killing in the Old Testament, most instances were likely not

---

[63] For some literature dealing directly or indirectly with the topic, see, e.g., Barna Magyarosi, *Holy War and Cosmic Conflict in the Old Testament: From the Exodus to the Exile*, Adventist Theological Society Dissertation Series (Berrien Springs, MI: Adventist Theological Society Publications, 2010) and Philip E. Friesen, *The Old Testament Roots of Nonviolence: Abraham's Personal Faith, Moses' Social Vision, Jesus' Fulfillment, and God's Work Today* (Eugene, OR: Wipf and Stock, 2010). Gregory A. Boyd, *Cross Vision: How the Crucifixion of Jesus Makes Sense of Old Testament Violence* (Minneapolis, MN: Fortress, 2017) also has some valuable insights, although we would not support his approach completely.

[64] See, e.g., Ángel M. Rodriguez, "Inspiration and the Imprecatory Psalms," *Journal of the Adventist Theological Society* 5, no. 1 (1994): 40–67, who notes, "If this is true, we could argue that in the imprecatory passages we find an example of divine condescension" (62).

[65] This is not to deny that Scripture as a whole and individual biblical books are inspired. Even difficult passages, if not just approached with a surface reading, reveal that, for instance, authors of the Psalms did not attempt to take vengeance into their own hands.

part of God's plan. God clearly disapproved of the very first murder. According to Joshua 22, a misunderstanding happened among the tribes of Israel, which almost led to a civil war. Fortunately, this was prevented by talking to each other.

Third, during the centuries before the first coming of Christ, believers in Yahweh were affected by other peoples and ancient Near Eastern cultures and customs of a violent nature. To some extent they became accustomed to the pagan lifestyle and philosophy of life—as we, unfortunately, are to our cultures today.[66] Revenge for a crime was common, the *lex talionis* prevalent. When the Babylonians smashed Jewish children against walls, the defeated Jews cried out for justice according to the *lex talionis*, which would call for the Babylonian children to be dashed against the rock (Ps 137:8–9). While in court the *lex talionis* did not allow a crime to be avenged by a greater crime, but rather insisted that the penalty had to be commensurate with the crime, and while at least in the Old Testament the principle was intended to stop the spiral of violence, in everyday life that may not have been the case (see Matt 5:38–39).

Fourth, God made accommodations for the situations His people were in but constantly tried to elevate them to a higher level. Therefore, one finds in the Old Testament that patriarchalism is curbed by a higher view and responsibility of women in society. There are female heroes. Slavery is mitigated by relevant laws. Religious myths of ancient Near Eastern societies, often also associated with violence and killing, are criticized and rejected. The ability of the rich to oppress the poor is reduced by the introduction of the sabbatical year and the Year of Jubilee. Divine accommodation can, for example, be seen with the law of divorce, which was later changed to be stricter.

Fifth, killing is, at times, also associated with God. As part of His judgment, God allowed people to die, for instance, in the flood, in the catastrophe of Sodom and Gomorra, and in the Red Sea. However, in all these cases God gave people sufficient warning and time to abandon their evil ways and turn to Him. God's interventions may have been necessary for the fulfillment of the proto-gospel in Genesis 3:15, the coming of the Messiah. God may have had to stop utmost corruption, otherwise all humanity would have been perverted to such an extent that God could not have revealed His true character in the incarnation of His Son. This is part of the cosmic conflict in which God functions "as

[66] We are so used to "solutions" of problems by violence that we usually cannot see other options; consider current world politics, Hollywood movies, and even the games that our children play. The so-called "solutions" of war, oppression, threat, etc. constantly breed new threats.

the Judge of the universe" who administers justice.[67] The only one who can create life, who also has the right to take life, is God.

Sixth, at times God used human instruments for His judgments: Israel (Exod 23:23–24),[68] the Assyrians (Isa 10:12, 15), the Babylonians (Jer 25:9), Cyrus (Isa 44:28), and others. Cyrus is even called "His anointed" (Isa 45:1). Barna Magyarosi calls it "Israel's involvement as a second-best solution."[69] Nevertheless, it is stressed that the battle would be the Lord's (Exod 14:14; 1 Sam 17:47; 2 Chr 20:15). Gregory Boyd notes, "Unfortunately, while the Israelites had no problem trusting Yahweh to help them use their swords to conquer enemies, they had great trouble trusting Yahweh, instead of their swords."[70] On top of this, these human instruments, which God had to use, often went too far. Israel was engaged in wars that God did not want to happen (1 Kgs 15:6–7, 16, 32; 2 Chr 35:20–24).[71] The Assyrians and Babylonians came to the point where God had to judge them for their pride and blasphemy, their atrocities and excessive violence (Isa 10:12–19; Jer 51:11, 24, 47). In spite of all this, God's ideal was to give His people rest and peace (Josh 11:23; 14:25).

Seventh, the people of God during Old Testament times and after the exodus from Egypt was Israel, a nation. Today, God's people consists of all those truly committed to Jesus and following Him, a people dispersed among almost all nations and people groups. Israel was a direct theocracy and later a monarchial theocracy. As such, it needed state laws, order, and organization different from a worldwide church. This may, to some extent, explain the conquest of Palestine and some situations of self-defense. Nevertheless, God repeatedly promised He would protect them when they were being attacked. Thus, it was also a matter of Israel trusting God.[72]

---

[67] Barna Magyarosi, "Violence and War in the Old Testament," in *Adventists and Military Service: Biblical, Historical, and Ethical Perspectives*, ed. Frank Hasel, Barna Magyarosi, and Stefan Höschele (Madrid: Editorial Safeliz, 2019), 16.

[68] Still the Lord repeatedly affirmed that He would "drive out before [them] the Amorites, the Canaanites, the Hittites, the Perizzites, the Hivites, and the Jebusites" (Exod 34:11). See also Exodus 23:28; 33:2. In addition, this was not necessarily a wholesale genocide. Uriah, Bathsheba's husband and an officer in David's army, was a Hittite who obviously feared God (2 Sam 11:9–12; 23:29). Ruth as a Moabite (Ruth 4:5) was accepted in Israel and incorporated into Jesus' genealogy, although the Moabites were generally excluded (Deut 23:3). Individuals could escape by seeking God (see Rahab of Jericho, Josh 6).

[69] Magyarosi, "Violence and War in the Old Testament," 21.

[70] Boyd, 113.

[71] 2 Samuel 11:1 seems to imply that there was war annually in the season best suited for it. This sounds almost like today, when nations are constantly involved in some kind of warfare.

[72] Magyarosi, "Violence and War in the Old Testament," 35, states, "God's initial plan concerning holy war did not include involvement of Israel in warfare. Human participation in holy war

In some cases, God is shown as making less-than-ideal accommodations for His people to some extent, which may have been necessary because they were not yet where God's people ought to have been (for example, in their desire to have a visible king, a human ruler, rather than the heavenly King directly).

Eight, it would be wrong to paint only a violent picture of the Old Testament and God's people at that time. There were periods of peace, for instance, under Solomon's rule when foreigners came to learn from him. Hezekiah did not have to defend his people against the Assyrians because the Lord took care of the situation (Isa 37). When Judah under Jehoshaphat was attacked by a coalition of kings, he placed in front of his army a choir that praised God. Jehoshaphat's army did not need to engage in war (2 Chr 20). There were instances when retaliation was not sought. The Arameans, who had come for war and were struck with blindness, were not slain, but a meal was prepared for them instead. This act of hospitality prevented the attackers from coming against Israel later (2 Kgs 6).

Ninth, we notice a marked difference between the Old Testament and the New Testament when it comes to the sixth commandment. Capital punishment, occasionally executed in Israel, has no place in the New Testament church. Church members may be disfellowshipped with the purpose of finding their way back to church again, but there is no longer capital punishment.[73] Therefore, there is no mandate for the church to get involved in the death penalty. Jesus' approach to the woman caught in adultery may have been programmatic. Whenever forms of violence are upheld by Christians, these are justified with the Old Testament, and the New Testament is eclipsed. In the New Testament there is no place for killing, warfare, genocide, abortion, infanticide, etc.

Tenth, with the incarnation of Jesus a new eon has dawned, a new covenant was established (still in continuity with former covenants, and yet different because the Messiah had come, having revealed the true nature of God). Jesus came as the prince of peace. The shepherds in the fields heard the heavenly choir sing about peace. When Jesus was tempted in the wilderness, He "had to decide whether to be the king of kings the people wanted, or the king of king Moses' tradition described. . . . Jesus had decided to skip the violent revolution."[74]

---

should have been of a spiritual nature only, the battle belonging to God. However, on account of her unbelief, and as a result of divine accommodation, participation in war became both the test of Israel's faithfulness and the means of fostering their trust in God. . . . Israel was always reminded that the outcome of the battle was exclusively in God's hands." On page 36 he addresses the fact that Israel was a theocracy. For the latter, see also Johannes Kovar, "War and Non-Violence in the New Testament," in Hasel, Magyarosi, and Höschele, 38.

[73] In order for Christians to kill Christian "heretics," the church had to resort to the Old Testament.

[74] Friesen, 84–85.

> Jesus never courted earthly power and never needed it. This is still a lesson we need to learn as his followers. Politics is the art of the possible, and is conducted by compromise to maintain a delicate and always precarious balance of power. Faith is the art of the impossible that overturns the balance of power, and was exercised flawlessly by Jesus without compromise.[75]

In the Sermon on the Mount, He blessed those who would be peace-makers (Matt 5:9). These are the true children of God. With Jesus, the kingdom of God has come. It is here among us, and yet we still expect its full revelation. But the kingdom is here. The King has been enthroned. This kingdom of Jesus is different from the world and also partially different from what we encounter in the Old Testament. In this kingdom, violence and killing no longer have a place.[76] While the two Greek terms for killing, *apokteinō* and *anairō*, appear frequently in the New Testament, nowhere are they used to indicate that Jesus' followers are involved in killing. It is time Christians stop resorting to the Old Testament in order to defend violence and death, and start recognizing that we live in the New Testament era with Christ, the Life, as Lord. Exceptions to the sixth commandment are not found in the New Testament, although worldly entities still practice killing.[77] Rather, the vision is one in which war and killing will be abandoned. Even the prophetic visions of the Old Testament foresaw a time when military tools would be converted into agricultural instruments, swords into ploughshares (Isa 2:4; Joel 3:10; Mic 4:13). In the New Testament the commandment not to kill, as it pertains to followers of Christ, is absolute. Robert Brimlow insists, "Surprisingly again, the gospel means exactly what it says. No amount of softening or interpretation that weakens these sayings is appropriate, nor can we hide behind notions of cultural or historical differences."[78] "We have a problem with the message of the gospel, but the problem is with us and not with the message itself."[79] Still, there is no place for abortion, infanticide, euthanasia, active

---

[75] Friesen, 88.

[76] See Kovar, 41–50, where he discusses non-violence in the teachings of Jesus.

[77] They occur almost a hundred times in the New Testament. A brief look at the Gospel of Matthew shows that there they are found to describe the attempt to kill Jesus, which eventually was successful, and the persecution of God's people.

[78] Brimlow, 182.

[79] Ibid., 168.

involvement in warfare, and whatever actively contributes to death.[80] The church stands for life and peace.

Fourth Principle: God Is the Owner of Life, and We Are Stewards

Scripture teaches that God owns everything (e.g., Ps 50:10–12), but humans like to defraud and play a role that is not theirs to play. With His incarnation Jesus came into "his own" (John 1:11) but was not accepted. The context tells us that He is the real owner, because He is our Creator and Savior (John 1:3, 29). So, the Godhead has a dual claim on us: we are God's because He has created us, and our Creator is also our owner. We are also His because He is our Redeemer, who has bought us by the highest possible price—His own life (1 Cor 6:19–20).

This means we are stewards of whatever God has entrusted to us, including our own lives, the lives of our children, and the lives of the unborn. The concept of stewardship allows us to work together with God. Ideally, the relationship between an owner and a steward is characterized by respect and trust, harmony, and a measure of freedom. It also includes responsibilities on the steward's part. Stewards may decide to take good care of the owner's property or, on the other hand, may waste it to their own detriment (Matt 25:14–30), but faithful stewards enjoy cooperation with the owner and some freedom in making decisions. Yet they accept that their freedom is ultimately limited by the owner's will. Since God is the giver and owner of life, we have neither final control over ourselves nor the right to take life. It simply does not belong to us.[81]

Stewardship affects not only individuals, but also the church. The issue of abortion is a matter that involves the church in guiding people, caring for them, supporting them, and loving them deeply—not only when they make the sometimes hard decision to keep an unborn child under difficult circumstances, but also after they have made a serious mistake. Like individuals, churches can also make good and bad choices.

Since stewardship is associated with some measure of freedom, we must reflect for a moment on the freedom to choose. Freedom of choice is one of the greatest privileges God has given humanity. That this choice is not an illusion is evident when we consider the biblical imperatives—for instance, the call to repent and return to God (Matt 4:17) and the call to fear God and give Him glory (Rev 14:7)—and the conditional promises in Scripture—for instance, the promises of forgiveness (1 John 1:9) and the gift of abundant life (John 10:10) and eternal life (John 3:36; 1 John 5:12–13). Freedom of choice is also linked to our ability to love. True love

---

[80] Unfortunately, Brimlow, 169, mentions, "Antisemitism, violence, warfare, strife, hatred, and intolerance have been and continue to be acceptable practices for Christians—usually in the name of politics, nationalism, and even religious truth."

[81] See Hays, 12.

presupposes free decision, and all the more so if it is not only based on emotions but on principles. Forced love is not love. We are invited to love God because He loved us first. But since God is love and He loves us, He wants us to voluntarily love Him. This makes choice a necessary given. He has given us the freedom to choose. Consequently, He did not create us as robots or mere biological machines. God does not manipulate us. We are free agents because we can reflect on Him, our lives, our future, and on other issues and then choose what to believe and how to act.

However, this also means that we can choose what is good and right or choose what is detrimental and evil. As mentioned above, with this freedom comes responsibility for our choices. We can choose to be either the wise or foolish virgins of Jesus' parable (Matt 25:1–13). We can use our talents responsibly or we can waste them (Matt 25:14–30). We can care deeply for others or we can neglect and even harm them (Matt 25:31–46), and then reap the consequences. Frank Hasel shows how far this freedom of choice reaches:

> It is remarkable that the divine sacredness of life is not exempt from the power of human choice. As creaturely beings, we have the ability to actually terminate life that, biblically speaking, God has given and only God has the right to end. This pertains to our own life as well as the life of other human beings—born or not yet born. . . . There is a remarkable and fascinating paradox in our ability of choice: by choosing to terminate life, we are free to decide to eliminate even the very freedom to choose, which God has given. And the effect of such a decision remains with us as something that is permanent and irreversible. It seems as if God knew about such drastic consequences of our creaturely freedom and therefore provided very strict boundaries to safeguard the sanctity of human life and the freedom it carries.[82]

While we enjoy the freedom of choice and conscience, we are not absolutely free. Absolute freedom is a phantom—impossible in a world shared with others. Paul indicates that by nature we are slaves of sin, and our liberty is limited to the freedom of choice. Our own experience affirms this assessment. We can choose to be enslaved to sin or be servants of righteousness, servants of God (Rom 6:6–23), thereby continuing to enjoy not only freedom of choice but also freedom from sin (as master of our lives), freedom from the law (as a way of salvation that does not work), and freedom from death (in the sense that we have eternal life

---

[82] Frank Hasel, "The Power of Choice and Life: A Short Theological Reflection," *Reflections* 67 (July 2019): 8.

even if we experience the first death, which is followed by resurrection to eternal life). While choosing God brings humans the greatest possible freedom, it also brings obedience to God's will.

In 1 Corinthians Paul describes freedom in the following way: liberty includes some latitude, liberty includes limitations, and liberty means carrying responsibility. With 1 Corinthians 9 Paul provides a personal example of what real liberty is all about. In verse 1 he states the principle that he is free. And indeed, he is free in what he can eat and drink (1 Cor 9:4). He is free in regard to marrying or not marrying (1 Cor 9:5). He is free in his work (1 Cor 9:6) and he is free in regard to accepting or not accepting remuneration for his service (1 Cor 9:7–18). Yet Paul voluntarily delimits this freedom because he has a goal: serving fellow humans (1 Cor 9:19–22) and participating in the gospel (1 Cor 9:23). According to Paul, genuine liberty consists of the ability to let go. Its predominant motif is love (1 Cor 13). Liberty means living with God, doing His will, and becoming a servant for the sake of others (1 Cor 9:19). Paul does not intend to be saved by the law; neither does he negate the law.

> Our true freedom does not consist of the unfettered power to direct our lives independently of God. Rather, it lies in our loving faith relationship with God as He has intended it to be. . . . For if we are free, we do not belong to ourselves (1 Cor 16:19; 9:19; 1 Pet 2:16), but to God who has set us free (Rom 6:18, 22; Gal 5:1). . . . Without loving relationships life would not exist, and outside a relationship with God no life will ultimately succeed. Living and existing in relationships, however, also limits the boundaries of our freedom. . . . Biblically speaking, our freedom to choose is never autonomous freedom. . . . This means that in biblical thought freedom is understood as a state of being where we are rescued from the coercive power of sin that enslaves us in order to be free to live in obedience to God.[83]

So, Christians must learn what true freedom is, not what society praises as true liberty and self-determination. According to Scripture, society's concept of freedom is slavery—slavery to the fashions, fads, and opinions of certain leaders and peers, as well as slavery to one's own self.

What does this imply for our discussion on abortion? Crosby is right when he states, "However, once a man or woman has freely chosen to enter into a sexual relationship, he or she cannot freely choose to

---

[83] Hasel, 8–9.

reject the responsibility that comes with that privilege."[84] But this is not the whole picture. Even when he rightly talks about disrespect, it is not all that needs to be said:

> Again, why do civilized people go to such lengths to dispose of a dead body in an honorable way? Why not toss it out with the garbage? Because there is a symbolic content that goes well beyond the literal content. To treat a corpse—or a fetus—with casual disrespect is to cheapen and debase humanity. We sink to the level of savages. . . . I believe that the vast majorities of abortions done today are wrong. I do not believe church institutions should have any part in this cheapening of life.[85]

While we have freedom of choice and may decide to use it by taking life, we have no right to do so.[86] Life does not belong to us, but to God, and it is not up to us to terminate life. "Freedom of conscience does not include the right to physically harm, let alone kill, another human being."[87] It also means that while the church must recognize and teach that humans have the immense privilege of freedom of choice and that in the end each person is responsible for how he or she lives and acts, the church must also clearly state the will of God as expressed in Scripture and especially the Ten Commandments, as they are interpreted and exemplified by Jesus. The church has the duty not to leave this issue open-ended. If the church through its teaching does not keep the delicate balance between the teaching of freedom of choice, which all humans have, and the proclamation of God's clear will as expressed in His commandments, people may take any fuzziness in these matters as a license to do whatever they want to do, and to do this even in the name of the church. This would not only be detrimental to the individuals involved, but also to the church and her witness in the world.

Therefore, if in official documents the church speaks about freedom of choice, choice must be understood and explained in terms of how Scripture portrays it. There is personal and institutional choice, and

---

[84] Crosby, 65.

[85] Ibid., 65–66.

[86] Johnsen, 162, writes, "With what 'sovereign authority' does any creature in this world make decisions about his own life? We have seen what Christian ethics says about that 'sovereignty.' It is an illusion. God is the Sovereign One—nobody else."

[87] James Standish, "Communist's Confessions: What Adventists Can Learn About Abortion from China," *The Compass Magazine*, October 7, 2019, https://thecompassmagazine.com/blog/communists-confessions-what-adventists-can-learn-about-abortion-from-china (accessed March 17, 2020).

there are clear limitations of that choice if we call ourselves Christians. Again, if choice as a concept is used in official documents but the limits of Christian freedom are not spelled out, then the concept may become misleading, because freedom of choice may—in the mind of the audience, influenced by the surrounding culture—become a license to do whatever our sinful hearts desire to do, independent of God's will.

Fifth Principle: Care for the Weak and the Vulnerable

Scripture teaches that God cares especially for those who are disadvantaged and oppressed. He "shows no partiality nor takes a bribe. He administers justice for the fatherless and the widow, and loves the stranger, giving him food and clothing" (Deut 10:18; cf. Jas 1:27). God's children, who are also Jesus' disciples, have a mandate to help vulnerable and suffering people and ease their lot (Ps 82:3–4; Acts 20:35), even to "rescue those who are being taken away to death," to "hold back those who are stumbling to the slaughter" (Prov 24:11).[88] In the city of Ephesus, Paul admonished the elders of the church with the words, "We must help the weak." And Jesus speaks of the least of His brothers (Matt 25:40), for whom we are responsible, and of the little ones who should not be lost (Matt 18:10–14). The very youngest—namely, the unborn—are to be counted among them.

According to Ezekiel 18:20, God does not punish children for the sins of their fathers. God expects His children to do the same. The unborn child is not responsible for the way and the circumstances under which he or she was conceived, whether wanted or not. His or her life is to be protected, as is the life of an adult.

In a certain sense, we need the disabled and the sick, the young and the old, the depressed and the downtrodden. What would human society be without such people? A society consisting only of the young and beautiful, the healthy and the brilliant, the well-to-do and the famous? It is likely that such a utopic society would not understand the concepts of mercy, gratitude, sacrifice, or overcoming selfishness. Just as parents grow and mature through caring for and raising their children, so we become more mature and balanced individuals by helping and supporting these people (Isa 58:7–11).

In addition, we should never forget that one day we may be among the disadvantaged, the forgotten, and the undesirable. Life is not only about

[88] An action taken in the case of injustice and in favor of innocent people cannot be a violent action. This would be opposed to Jesus' teachings and His own lifestyle. However, this does not mean that nothing can or should be done. We have to give up the notion that only violence can solve problems and become creative and ingenious in trying to solve problems. We also have to overcome cowardice (Rev 21:8) and be courageous: "Be strong and (very) courageous" as Joshua was (Josh 1:6–7, 9).

money, fame, and beauty. Life in a sinful world and with a human nature inclined to sin can be messy. Whether we like it or not, suffering is part of human life and, in spite of all human techniques and advances, cannot be completely eradicated from our lives (Rom 8:18; Jas 5:10, 13). Therefore, we are better off accepting suffering, learning to handle it with God's help, and thus growing by alleviating the suffering of others.

However, there is a divine promise for those who get involved with and work for the weak and vulnerable. The psalmist calls "blessed" those who intervene for others (Ps 41:1), and Jesus states, "It is more blessed to give than to receive" (Acts 20:35).[89]

Sixth Principle: God's Grace

God's grace promotes and protects life. But God is also willing to forgive our sins and deal with our shortcomings: our transgression of His commandments, our materialistic and self-centered attitudes, our worries about our future and the future of our children, and the inner pain that consumes us. We can bring all of this to God and find rest in the Lord. In gratitude we accept forgiveness, salvation, peace, and strength and decide to live according to His will.

Summary

After having discussed the biblical principles concerning the issue of abortion, we repeat them here in summary: abortion of human life militates against 1) the divinely given value and sacredness of human life; 2) the biblical understanding of the unborn child as being fully human in each and every stage of development, and therefore deserving of protection; 3) the will of God as expressed in the sixth commandment ("You shall not kill") and elaborated by Jesus in the Sermon on the Mount; 4) the fact that God is the owner of life, and that we are stewards with no right to take life; 5) God's care for the weak and the vulnerable, which is a mandate for us to do the same; and 6) God's grace, which promotes and protects life but also grants forgiveness for sins committed, if we repent and ask for forgiveness.

Difficult Cases[90]

There is no question that there are very difficult cases of pregnancy. Although statistically they are a small number, for mothers or parents facing one of these issues it is devastating. Difficult cases include pregnancies

---

[89] This is one of the so-called *agrapha*, a statement of Jesus not found in the canonical Gospels but here in Acts. It must have been of special importance to Luke, who has incorporated it in the book of Acts. This saying can be a motto for our life.

[90] For this section, see esp. Feinberg and Feinberg, 124–141.

due to rape or incest, pregnancies that would lead to a handicapped child, and pregnancies that threaten the mother's life.

All pregnancies involve at least two lives: the life of the mother and the life of the child (or children, if multiple eggs have been fertilized and the mother is bearing more than one child). Both lives, the mother's and the child's, have the right to exist and flourish. In each of these cases, as in all regular pregnancies, "the fetus has no choice than to grow, just as it had no choice in its conception or its blond hair and blue eyes."[91] So the fetus's choice is limited or essentially nonexistent because he or she just grows. The mother, however, has several choices under normal circumstances, and more limited choices in difficult cases. Under normal circumstances, she can 1) practice sexual abstinence and avoid pregnancy, or 2) use contraceptives. And once pregnant she can 3) decide to carry the child to term or allow for the newborn's adoption. In other words, she may choose life for herself and the fetus.[92] However, she may also choose to 4) abort the child, which, according to our previous discussion, would be a questionable choice, terminating human life. With difficult pregnancies, the mother's/parents' choices are more limited. For instance, in the case of rape she was violently forced to have intercourse, which led to a pregnancy. Her subsequent choice is limited to keeping or aborting the child. This is also true for the other extreme cases. On the other hand, the fetus is dependent on the mother's choice and has no choice of his or her own.

Rape and Incest

Incest can happen for two reasons. It can be consensual, and in this case it is not much different from other forms of sexual immorality. Incest can also be non-consensual. In this case it would be incestuous rape. Therefore, incest does not need to be treated separately. However, we recognize that in the case of incestuous rape, the danger of physical or mental defects in the fetus are increased. It should be noted that "conception in case of rape is very rare" for various reasons, among them that "the emotional trauma of the act may prevent ovulation."[93]

Rape is a horrible and inexcusable crime[94] that may damage the victim in many ways—physically, emotionally, and spiritually. The problem of rape is even increased if the raped woman becomes pregnant. The question then arises: is abortion justified under such heinous conditions?

---

[91] Feinberg and Feinberg, 124.

[92] Ibid.

[93] Ibid., 127.

[94] There is no excuse for a man raping a woman. There may be forgiveness, but there is no justification—no matter what the circumstances were when the rape happened.

We need to reflect on this situation for a moment without immediately following our gut feeling. In any case, the raped woman needs all our compassion and support.

Arguments put forth in favor of an abortion are the following: A pregnancy adds to the tremendous burden the abused woman is already carrying. If she is forced to keep the child, she becomes a victim at least twice. The child may also constantly remind her of the crime committed against her. She should not be forced to bear an unwanted child.

What about reasons against abortion? It is no question that a terrible crime has been committed against the victim of rape and that she needs to be able to articulate her fears, anger, and trauma with trusted persons of her choice. However, an abortion may lead to other complications for the mother, including psychological problems. The child is innocent and cannot be blamed for what happened. He or she also has a right to live. To take the child's life is to respond to one evil with another, and may lead to even more trauma for the mother. While the child may be unwanted in the beginning, this may not remain so, and he or she may become a blessing to the mother. Statistics suggest that "up to 85% of the women who become pregnant through rape or incest [in the United States] choose to have their children."[95] Besides, the child can be put up for adoption after birth, which would be a responsible decision. It is necessary to keep the child's best interests in mind, and not focus on the personal pain of the mother alone. Hays writes,

> It is inappropriate to set up the issue of conflict of "rights": the rights of the woman versus the rights of the unborn child. . . . No one has a presumptive claim on it. Nor, on the other hand, do any of us—male or female—have a "right" to control our bodies autonomously . . . (1 Cor. 6:19–20). We are always accountable to God for our decisions and actions.[96]

While those who might opt for abortion in the case of rape may be seeking alleviation of the pain and the shame that go along with it, they should not forget that this may not work as desired. In the past, women confronted with such a difficult situation have made different decisions. There were some who decided to abort the fetus caused by rape, and there were many others who decided to keep the child. A mother should not be forced into such a decision with irreversible consequences, but should receive all the support that would help her make an

[95] "18 Shocking Abortion Statistics Rape Victims," Health Research Funding, https://healthresearchfunding.org/18-shocking-abortion-statistics-rape-victims (accessed March 17, 2020).

[96] Hays, 454.

informed decision that reflects the previously discussed biblical principles. The choice to keep the child alive is a real option, even under such difficult circumstances.

Medical Conditions in the Unborn

Modern prenatal diagnostics can be a blessing in that the unborn may be treated even in the mother's womb. It can also be a kind of curse. It forces parents to make a choice about life and death where in the past this was not possible, and nature just took its course. Some babies died right after birth, and the parents were able to say goodbye to them, mourn their death, and bury them with grief and an aching heart. Today the slightest abnormalities can be detected. Yet they are not always diagnosed with absolute certainty. Still, such a diagnosis may put a tremendous burden on the parents.[97]

How to deal with these issues? First, some of the diagnosed medical conditions are mild, and the child can live with them without major challenges. Others are moderate, and in this case it may also be possible to continue life with them—for instance, some forms of Down syndrome and spina bifida (split spine).[98] "Spina bifida is a birth defect in which there is incomplete closing of the spine and membranes around the spinal cord during early development in pregnancy."[99] Some forms of spina bifida are milder. Getting enough folate before and during the pregnancy may, in many cases, prevent such a condition. Prenatal and postnatal treatments are also available, though not all effects may disappear.

Among the severe conditions are, for example, hydrocephaly and anencephaly. "Hydrocephalus is a condition in which an accumulation of cerebro-spinal fluid (CSF) occurs within the brain. This typically causes increased pressure inside the skull. . . . Hydrocephalus can occur due to birth defects or be acquired later in life."[100] "Anencephaly is the absence of a major portion of the brain, skull, and scalp that occurs during embryonic development. . . . With very few exceptions, infants with this

---

[97] See also Hays, 456.

[98] Sakala, 20, urges, "Abortion of the fetus with lesser degrees of abnormality should be managed as the normal fetus." While on the one hand, he limits abortions to threats to the mother, fetuses who cannot survive outside the mother's body, and severely impaired fetuses with no chance of gaining self-consciousness, on the other hand, he considers abortions for psychosocial threats to the mother as legitimate (ibid., 19–20). This sounds a bit ambivalent.

[99] Wikipedia, s.v. "Spina bifida," last modified March 12, 2020, https://en.wikipedia.org/wiki/Spina_bifida (accessed March 17, 2020).

[100] Wikipedia, s.v. "Hydrocephalus," last modified February 25, 2020, https://en.wikipedia.org/wiki/Hydrocephalus (accessed March 17, 2020).

disorder do not survive longer than a few hours or possibly days after their birth."[101]

The distinction of milder and more severe cases, as well as the fact that some disabilities occur before birth or develop later in life, should make us cautious. Typically, we would not kill a person who develops hydrocephaly later in life. Why, then, should we abort an unborn child with this condition? The Feinbergs suggest,

> The desire to cure or avoid diseases should not so consume us that we destroy those among us who have disabilities. . . . Self-sacrifice for the good of another is not very popular today. . . . Moreover, it is easy to forget that there are at least two parties to be considered in the matter, the parents and the handicapped child. It is important not to pit the parents' needs against the child's. . . . The proper response to crippling diseases and disabilities isn't eugenic abortions. Rather it is compassion on the sick and those who care for them, along with a renewed awareness of the enormity of the consequences of sin.[102]

Ulrich Eibach is clearly opposed to the abortion of healthy children, handicapped children, and even incurable children. Yet he writes, "This is not to say that there are no serious conflict situations in which abortion is the only possible solution."[103]

Again, there are parents who decide to abort their child who suffers from incurable disease, while others keep him or her even under these most severe conditions and allow the child to die after birth. While such decisions have to be thought through, the mother/parents need to experience the tangible love of the church family. However, abortion should not be understood as a convenient way of avoiding pain.

The Mother's Life

There are situations where it seems that only one life can be saved, either the mother's life or the child's life. These situations are heart-wrenching. The threat to the mother's life can come from the child (e.g., ectopic or tubal pregnancies) or from a disease that the mother has attracted independent of the child (e.g., late cancer). Regardless of the

---

[101] Wikipedia, s.v. "Anencephaly," last modified February 16, 2020, https://en.wikipedia.org/wiki/Anencephaly (accessed March 17, 2020).

[102] Feinberg and Feinberg, 134, 136–137.

[103] Ulrich Eibach, "Vorgeburtliche Diagnostik und Selektion unheilbar kranken und behinderten Lebens: Kritische Würdigung des Beitrags der 'Kammer für Öffentliche Verantwortung der Evangelischen Kirche in Deutschland' (EKD)," *Informationsbrief 316* (Bekenntnisbewegung "Kein anderes Evangelium"), June 2019, 11 (translated by the author).

decision made, to consider the child's life only as a potential human life and the mother's life as an actual human life can have far-reaching ethical implications. Feinberg and Feinberg warn against such an argumentation: "If the unborn baby's rights as a potential person are outweighed by those of actual persons, then regardless of the mother's situation (medical or otherwise) this line of reasoning seems to reopen the door to abortion for any reason, including convenience."[104]

They also mention the example of a mother who decided to die so that her child may live.[105] This is a heroic example of how far some mothers are willing to go, but not all mothers would do that, nor can it be required. They need to be cared for by the community of believers.

Result

All difficult cases together amount to about seven percent of all abortions, representing a slim minority. Still, they have to be taken seriously. In our short deliberations we tried to show that even difficult cases come in different categories of severity and do not automatically allow for abortion. Some of them can be treated. Actually, even in the most extreme cases abortion coincides with the commandment not to kill. While in our fallen world we may not see other options and have only partial knowledge of a situation, killing an unborn child—even for the best human reasons—incurs guilt, just as the manslayer in the Old Testament, who accidentally killed another person, was still responsible for his act.

Remwil Tornalejo may be on target when he writes that "abortion regardless of the cause of pregnancy reason has moral and ethical culpability."[106] This would mean that even in the most adverse dilemma, when abortion seems to be the only option and mothers/parents allow for it to happen, they may need to seek divine forgiveness.

Implications and Conclusion

In this article, we have shown that abortion is a serious issue. It affects at least the unborn, the mother, the father, immediate and extended family members, and the church family, and often with even long-term consequences and trauma.

---

[104] Feinberg and Feinberg, 139.

[105] Ibid. report that in 2004–2005 the pregnant Rita Fedrizzi, with full awareness that she may die, delayed her cancer treatment to save her child. A healthy baby was born, but it was too late for her cancer treatment to save her. "She literally gave her life for that of her child."

[106] Tornalejo, 126.

We have also seen that the Bible is not silent about abortion. While it does not address it with a commandment such as "You shall not abort a child," it provides enough principles to guide us in our decisions. Scripture does not support abortion, but calls believers to trust God and follow His will for them, because He has their best interests in mind. Christianity has to do with faith in the almighty Lord and love for Him and all His human sons and daughters. Again, the issue of abortion is also a faith and trust issue. We must allow God to grow our faith and, in conjunction with it, our love.

Brimlow reminds us, "We are called to live the kingdom as he [Jesus] proclaimed it and be his disciples, come what may."[107] In a prayer addressed to the Lord, he writes, "Here is the joy that is born of our faith, and here is the joy that underlies the hardship and distress. Your love for us is what makes all of us worthy of love. To deny it for anyone is to deny it for myself; to affirm it for everyone is also to affirm it for myself." And later, "While I am not sure that great love brings with it a desire to suffer, I do think that great love does not count the cost and that the cost of loving greatly may well include suffering."[108] Faith/trust and love, active in good works, may include suffering; yet they have great rewards (Matt 10:47; Col 3:23–24; Heb 10:32–35).

Abortion also affects the community of believers. The church stands for life, not for death. As the church seeks to support women and couples who are confronted with the possibility of abortion, its members are challenged to create an atmosphere of true love, enlist the help of well-functioning and committed families, and educate them to provide care for struggling individuals, couples, and families,[109] encouraging church members to open their homes to those in need, including single parents, and supporting in various ways pregnant women who decide to keep their unborn children.[110] The imitation of Jesus "suggests that we should act in service to welcome children, both born and unborn, even when to do so is obviously difficult and may cause serious hardship.... this call is a charge laid upon the church as a whole.... If this proposal sounds

---

[107] Brimlow, 151.

[108] Ibid., 173, 190. While he does not write directly in the context of abortion, but rather pacifism, it certainly also applies to the present issue.

[109] Seibold writes, "What I like to see? A group of people ... who pour out their lives for at-risk-families. Who made sure that troubled families have opportunities and guidance beyond what they'd get in their own social context. As for unwanted babies: what if every church were an orphanage, rather than a gathering of the righteous," https://spectrummagazine.org/article/column/2009/12/18/why-i%25E2%2580%2599m-neither-pro-life-nor-pro-choice (accessed May 7, 2020).

[110] Hays, 457, states, "My own judgment in this case is that the New Testament summons the community to eschew abortion and thus to undertake the burden of assisting the parents to raise the handicapped child."

impractical, that is merely a measure of how far the church has drifted from its foundation in the New Testament."[111] Michael Pearson observes,

> If we think it morally desirable that one of our sisters should go through with an unwanted pregnancy rather than seek an abortion, then we the church have to be prepared to offer the emotional, financial and social support that would make carrying the baby to term seem a possible option. To the extent that we withhold that support, remain content to be judgmental, and fail to generate an ambience of concern, we bear some measure of responsibility for those abortions which take place in our midst.[112]

In addition, while not condoning abortion, the church still cares deeply for those who have aborted a child for various reasons, or who were forced to have it done, and may be hurting physically, emotionally, and/or spiritually. We must never forget the terrible plague of human trafficking, forced prostitution, and rape in many countries around the globe today. All those affected need the help of the church—especially women who got pregnant and had an abortion or who were forced by their husbands, male friends, or relatives to have an abortion done, whether for perceived shame upon the family or other reasons. The church must be a safe haven for those hurting and must provide the service of qualified and loving people who can listen, challenge, console, and initiate healing. Instone-Brewer may have a point when he writes:

> Perhaps the way to change society's view about abortion is not by demanding stronger laws but by continuing to provide adoption agencies and accommodations, care, and advice for those who are facing the crisis of an unplanned pregnancy. Often these are the most vulnerable in society. . . . if we can show Jesus' love to

---

[111] Hays, 452–453. On page 452, he is quite definite: "How does the story [Acts 4:32–35] illuminate the issue of abortion? It suggests that the community should assume responsibility for the care of the needy. Thus, within the church, there should be no justification for abortion on economic grounds or on the ground of the incapacity of the mother to care for her child. . . . Sharing, not abortion is the answer. . . . The church's confusion on the issue of abortion is a symptom of its more fundamental unfaithfulness to the economic imperatives of the gospel. . . . The fact that abortion is usually treated as a 'woman's issue' shows how disastrously the general culture has allowed males to abdicate responsibility for children. . . . A man who has fathered an unborn child should be required and helped, within the fellowship of the church, to take responsibility for supporting the pregnant woman both emotionally and financially and to assume continuing responsibility for the child after birth. . . . The community of faith should provide whatever support is necessary for both man and woman to assume their roles as parents. This would entail not only financial support but also support of friendship, counsel, and prayer."

[112] Pearson, 152.

> them and their unborn children, society will hopefully realize that life itself is precious, even before it is born.[113]

The issue of abortion challenges all believers, but it gives individuals and the church as a whole, on a local level and on a wider level, the opportunity to be what we claim to be: the fellowship of brothers and sisters, the community of believers, the family of God.

---

[113] Instone-Brewer, 44.

CHAPTER 14

Child Sexual Abuse

Antonio Estrada, Nisim Estrada, and Stephen Bauer

> Hello, I don't know if I should call you uncle, or wannabe uncle, because I don't feel any type of affection for you. Do you want to know what I feel for you? Anger, resentment, and contempt. If you were right here I would want to slap you because that is what you deserve. I hate you so much that I don't know if I can ever forgive you. . . When I was 7 years old you made me see life in a different light. I want you to remember that what you did to me was nothing funny or humorous. If you are so ignorant as to not know, what you tried to do was an attempt to rape me. I can finally say that without crying. —Lizeth

Child sexual abuse is a moral evil that seems to flourish in a vacuum of silence in both the church and society. One significant challenge is a level of confusion over what constitutes child sexual abuse. For example, some people who were abused as children do not believe that they were actually abused. Sometimes, even the parents or other adults responsible for such children do not accept that what their children experienced was a form of abuse. This may be partly due to believing that child sexual abuse only occurs when there has been penetrative sex with the child.

Mental health professionals offer a clearer and more comprehensive definition of child sexual abuse, based, in part, on the evidence of harm produced by a variety of abusive actions. For this chapter, therefore, we borrow the following definition of child sexual abuse:

> Child sexual abuse is the involvement of a child in sexual activity that he or she does not fully comprehend, is unable to give informed consent to, or for which the child is not developmentally prepared and cannot give consent, or that violates the laws or social taboos of society. Child sexual abuse is evidenced by this

> activity between a child and an adult or another child who by age or development is in a relationship of responsibility, trust or power, the activity being intended to gratify or satisfy the needs of the other person.[1]

The vast majority of experts in the field consider sexual abuse to be any type of sexual activity that occurs between an adult and a minor, in part due to the fact that the adult is in a position of power over the minor.[2] However, it is not the age difference between the perpetrator and the child that is the central marker of sexual abuse. Rather, as Enrique Echeburúa and Paz de Corral explain, "it is the asymmetry of those involved in the relationship and the presence of co-action, implicit or explicit."[3] Such asymmetry may exist between siblings without clear correlations to age differences, and thus an individual may perpetrate an act of child sexual abuse on a fellow sibling.

To more precisely categorize types of abuse and the associated levels of traumatization, some researchers are very clear in specifying a diver' sity of behaviors that may or may not include physical contact by the aggressor towards the targeted child. Two large categories are non-contact offenses and physically intrusive offenses.

In the first category, the modality of noncontact offenses—or sexual abuse without physical contact—encompasses a wide variety of behaviors ranging from exhibitionism in its various forms (e.g., exposing the genitals intentionally towards the child), voyeurism (e.g., watching the child undress, or taking pictures when they are naked), or verbal seduction.

The second modality is called physical intrusiveness, or sexual aggression. In this modality there may be physical contact from the aggressor towards the victim, but without the intent of rape (e.g., caressing of the body or touching of the child's genitals, without the intent of anal or vaginal penetration). What is commonly understood as rape is also included in this modality; rape behavior would include the sexual act with the child or the use of objects to abuse the child.[4]

---

[1] World Health Organization, "Child Sexual Abuse," chap. 7 in *Guidelines for Medico-Legal Care of Victims of Sexual Violence* (Geneva: World Health Organization, 2003), https://www.who.int/violence_injury_prevention/resources/publications/en/guidelines_chap7.pdf.

[2] Sandra P. Thomas et al., "Childhood Experiences of Perpetrators of Child Sexual Abuse," *Perspectives in Psychiatric Care* 49 (March 2012): 187–201.

[3] Enrique Echeburúa and Paz de Corral, "Secuelas emocionales en víctimas de abuso sexual en la infancia," *Cuadernos de Medicina Forense* 12 (January–April 2006): 76.

[4] Lisa Bunting, "Dealing With a Problem That Doesn't Exist? Professional Responses to Female Perpetrated Child Sexual Abuse," *Child Abuse Review* 16 (2007): 252–267. Bunting, 257, notes that some perpetrators of child sexual abuse are women, listing several examples of their abuse

Finally, a specialized subcategory of child sexual abuse modalities includes sexual exploitation—that is, the use of children for monetary profit through trafficking and pornography. In these types of abusive behaviors, children are considered "merchandise"—sexual objects used to make a profit. This type of "business" is very lucrative and is perpetrated by international mafias that use sophisticated ways of covering up their "business," utilizing the internet, social media, and tourist trips.

No matter how one views child sexual abuse, it seems obvious that it is fundamentally predatory and exploitative. It would seem, therefore, that there should be an instinctive abhorrence and rejection of the practice. For many this is indeed true. In a sinful world, however, while the universality of human moral corruption does not logically entail that child sexual abuse must occur, it does increase the probability that some individuals—even professed Christians—will target children in order to satisfy their immoral desires.

On this basis, then, this chapter has four basic aims. First, it establishes the moral foundations for evaluating child sexual abuse. Second, it highlights the biblical principles that render child sexual abuse unacceptable and provide a foundation for dealing with this alarming issue. Third, it discusses the extent of the problem of child abuse in general and within the church, with special focus on definitions, prevalence, and consequences of child sexual abuse. Fourth, it describes the role of the church by providing examples of how church members and leaders can respond to child abuse through preventive measures, as well as by boosting protective factors that can facilitate resilience and healing for survivors. With these purposes in mind, we shall briefly survey several biblical foundations for addressing child sexual abuse.

Moral Foundations for Evaluating Child Sexual Abuse

Helping professions such as the clergy, psychology, counseling, and social work regularly produce data on the rates of child sexual abuse and how it damages children emotionally and physically. A potential problem with this is that such advocates for children may assume a common moral foundation with their readers or listeners. The first impression is that the ethical standard used to determine the moral wrongness of such abuse is a form of the harm-benefit criterion.While it is true that the apostle Paul lends some credence to this ethical approach—"Love does no harm to a neighbor" (Rom 13:10, ESV)[5]—a key

---

to children in both modalities as follows: frequent vaginal exams, forcing a child to intimately bathe and wash the perpetrator, and being watched by their mother while bathing or dressing.

[5] All biblical quotations are from the New King James Version, unless otherwise indicated.

problem is that it is not uncommon for child molesters to claim they are not harming the children they molest.

Perhaps no better example of pedophiles denying they are harming children can be found in the 1994 documentary *Chicken Hawk*. Several men who find boys sexually attractive assert, in varying ways, that there is a difference between true "man-boy love" and child molestation, claiming they would never molest a child. They also tend to deny the negative effects observed in children who have been sexually engaged with adults, hinting that children are natural sexual beings who are oppressed by current societal moral norms and that their man-boy relationships are "consensual"—age and childhood being mere social constructs—and a loving place for children to discover and develop their sexuality. Hence, the men in the documentary may have sincerely believed they would not be molesting or harming boys if they have sex with them.[6]

Furthermore, there may be local subcultures that mimic the moral standards of ancient Greece, for example, where pederasty was viewed as a morally acceptable, or even desirable, form of interpersonal relationship.[7] As Mariah Cavanaugh observes, "from the Greek's perspective, pederasty was not pedophilia, but an important part of growing up in classical Greece, and in the context of Greek culture it was not believed to be harmful or damaging to the boys involved. If anything, it was the normal path that nearly all young Greek men followed."[8] Note that the Greeks saw no harm in these pederastic relationships between men and

---

[6] *Chicken Hawk: Men Who Love Boys*, directed by Adi Sideman, released 1994. This documentary is available to view at the following websites: part 1, https://www.dailymotion.com/video/xgii60; part 2, https://www.dailymotion.com/video/xgii63; part 3, https://www.dailymotion.com/video/xgii69; part 4, https://www.dailymotion.com/video/xgii6a (all accessed June 21, 2021). Most of the men featured in this documentary claim to not practice their desires for fear of legal consequences, but one especially was very open about having sexual relationships with boys, suggesting that the boys actually seek him out, not the reverse. For more background on NAMBLA, see also Benoit Denizet-Lewis, "Boy Crazy," *Boston*, May 15, 2006, https://www.bostonmagazine.com/2006/05/15/boy-crazy/ (accessed June 28, 2021); Mike Pearl, "Whatever Happened to NAMBLA?," *Vice*, March 24, 2016, https://www.vice.com/en/article/7bd37e/whatever-happened-to-nambla (accessed June 28, 2021); and Mary deYoung, "The World According to NAMBLA: Accounting for Deviance," *The Journal of Sociology and Social Welfare* 16, no. 1 (March 1989): 111–126, https://scholarworks.wmich.edu/cgi/viewcontent.cgi?article=1885&context=jssw&httpsredir=1&referer= (accessed June 28, 2021). The article by deYoung has several quotations from NAMBLA "bulletins" that are extremely disturbing.

[7] For a brief overview of ancient pederasty, see Wikipedia, s.v. "Pederasty in Ancient Greece," last modified April 25, 2021, https://en.wikipedia.org/wiki/Pederasty_in_ancient_Greece (accessed April 30, 2021).

[8] Mariah Cavanaugh, "Ancient Greek Pederasty: Education or Exploitation?," STMU History Media, December 3, 2017, https://stmuhistorymedia.org/ancient-greek-pederasty-education-or-exploitation/ (accessed April 30, 2021).

early-teen boys. Thus, it seems apparent that a cultural context holding similar views of pederasty would dismiss as irrelevant our arguments that such pederasty harms children. Perhaps they might concede that erotic interaction with prepubescent children is harmful.

This raises the problem of who determines what is harmful and what is beneficial. It becomes entirely possible that "adults" determine that their actions do not harm the child, thus justifying erotic contact with the child while rejecting others' opinions. Thus, while the harm-benefit standard can be useful, it seems too easily subverted by personal desire, which can exploit ignorance, to be consistently effective as universal moral guide.

In the discipline of ethics, the harm-benefit criterion is an outgrowth of ethical hedonism—from Epicurus through Hobbes—where pain is self-evidently evil and pleasure (i.e., the lack of pain) is axiomatically good. The hedonistic moral standard is a foundational principle to Egoistic ethics—hence the ease with which the molester can justify his or her actions as a matter of his or her self-interest. Hedonism is also the basis of utilitarian ethics (greatest benefit to the greatest number), which explains how in some parts of the world, families may sell one child, usually a daughter, into sexual slavery and daily sexual abuse. They sacrifice one child to save the family, much as Caiaphas reasoned "that it is better for you that one man should die for the people, not that the whole nation should perish" (John 11:50, ESV). In such cases, a "moral" duty is imposed onto the child to endure Children Sexual Abuse for the greater good of the family.

It seems painfully obvious, then, that without a higher, transcendent, universally recognized moral authority to define harm and benefit, the consequentialist foundations for determining right and wrong have potentially crippling limitations that can allow some forms of child sexual abuse. In spite of such challenges with consequentialist ethics, most people resonate with the harm-benefit moral criterion and would affirm their belief that child sexual abuse is, from a moral perspective, grossly wrong.

While it is true that differing moral worldviews may achieve agreement on an issue like child sexual abuse, it is important as Seventh-day Adventist Christians to be sure that we provide a biblically based rationale. We believe there are biblical principles that, if taken seriously and submitted to, make child sexual abuse impossible to justify in any form, while also providing an overarching, higher authority able to keep hedonistic moral reasoning from running amok.

Biblical Principles and Child Sexual Abuse

We have just asserted that child sexual abuse, from a moral perspective, is grossly wrong. In this section we seek to lay biblical foundations that support this claim. We shall present our case in a way that builds from foundational principles to a capstone argument in support of our claim that such abuse is absolutely immoral.

The Divine Design for Sexuality

In the garden of Eden, God created two adult humans who jointly were made in the image of God (Gen 1:26–27). In these verses, both "man" (*adam*, "humankind") as well as God are referenced with the plural pronouns "us" or "them" and the singular pronoun "him." This shows us that humans, as the image of God, are made to experience a plurality-in-oneness that appears to mimic or image the same feature in our Triune God. This oneness is described as the new couple becoming "one flesh" (Gen 2:24), which is clearly understood by Paul to include sexual union (1 Cor 6:16).

Since the Trinity is comprised of three equal persons in a permanent relationship based on self-sacrificial love—exemplified by Christ in His sacrifice for us (Phil 2:5–8)—it strongly suggests that Adam and Eve were made by God to be united with each other in a similarly intimate, equal, lifelong relationship. It is no accident, then, that in Scripture the sexual union is always described as properly belonging in the context of a monogamous heterosexual marriage. For example, Proverbs 5 declares, "Drink water from your own cistern, and running water from your own well. Should your fountains be dispersed abroad, streams of water in the streets? Let them be only your own, and not for strangers with you" (Prov 5:15–17). But who (or what) is this personal cistern or well? The passage continues, "Let your fountain be blessed, and rejoice with the wife of your youth. As a loving deer and a graceful doe, let her breasts satisfy you at all times; and always be enraptured with her love" (Prov 5:18–19). The exclusivity God intends for the sexual relationship, within marriage, is clearly expressed in this passage.

An adult having sex with a child violates this divine design for sexual expression on several fronts. First, in most cases of abuse, the adult is not married to the child. This is also true when one sibling sexually abuses another sibling. Often the abused child is underage so cannot be legally married. Adult-child sex, as well as sibling sexual abuse, is therefore fundamentally evil because it is a violation and perversion of God's purpose for sexual expression. The sexual activity is outside of the marital context for which it was designed. As such, the perpetrator of child sexual abuse is breaking the seventh commandment prohibiting adultery (Exod 20:14), the legislation against incest if the perpetrator is a relative (Lev 18:6–17; 1 Cor 5:1), or the legislation against homosexuality if victim and perpetrator share the same sex (Lev 18:22; Rom 1:26–27) and is tacitly supportive of the contemporary drive for unbridled sexual freedom without reference to monogamous heterosexual marriage.

Second, a child is not capable of entering into the peer-to-peer, covenantal-marital relationship that is a prerequisite to the sexual union. In the case of adults who erotically target children, there is a fundamental power inequality that makes a proper peer-to-peer marital relationship impossible. Children are fundamentally to be under the watchful care and supervision of responsible adults and thus cannot be in a peer relationship with adults. This is why a specialized form of child sexual abuse, child-to-adult marriage (which occurs in some cultures, basically with the child being forced into the arrangement), is also morally problematic and a distortion of God's Edenic ideals for marital relationships. The marital oneness God purposed in creation is not achievable in an adult-child marriage.

Additionally, it can be argued that in sibling sexual abuse—usually an older sibling abusing a younger one—there is a reasonable chance that *neither* child has developed a level of maturity capable of entering into a covenantal-marital relationship. Furthermore, the power inequity between the older and younger sibling mimics the power imbalance between a child and adult. This disqualifies both the abusing sibling and the abused survivor from being able to enter into the kind of covenant in which God intended sexual intimacy to occur, and so God's purpose for sexual union is perverted and thwarted.

The Intrinsic Value of the Child

An alternate Edenic angle reminds us that children are also made in the image of God, and thus possess intrinsic personal value as a gracious gift from God. In Genesis, each creature was to reproduce "according to its kind" (Gen 1:24–25). It follows that as the offspring of the image of God, children are also the image of God. The question of whether post-fall humans are still viewed as being made in God's image is answered in the affirmative in Genesis 9:6.

In Genesis 9:6, we observe that after the flood (which is clearly after the fall), killing a human is prohibited based on the intrinsic quality of that individual being the image of God. A fellow human or an animal that kills a human is commanded to be punished, implying that taking human life somehow violates an intrinsic value that is identified with being the image of God. Jesus likewise affirms this idea of intrinsic human worth when He declares that humans are of much greater value than "many sparrows" (Matt 10:31). Thus, even after the fall, children continue to be the image of God just in the same manner as adults, and thus are endowed with the same intrinsic value. To treat the image of God as a non-person, as an object of consumption or piece of property for personal pleasure, is to violate their intrinsic value as a person made in the image of God. Child sexual abuse treats children as objects for consumption, not as sacred life created in the image of God.

Child Sexual Abuse and Biblical Law

Biblical law reinforces these theological foundations by codifying prohibitions of sexual activity between the types of sexual engagements that can include child sexual abuse. Leviticus 18 and 20 spell out prohibitions for sexual contact between near kin that cover many forms of sexual abuse relationships. While written mostly in the form of a male "uncovering the nakedness" of a female, we can infer that a female being the initiator of such activity would be equally prohibited. Actually, Leviticus 18 and 20 depict a three-generational level of potential abuse: sibling-to-sibling (or sibling-to-half-sibling), parent-to-child (or uncle/aunt-to-niece/nephew), and grandparent-to-grandchild sexual relations. It becomes entirely possible for one individual (often male) to abuse three generations in a single family!

It should be noted that Leviticus 18 and 20 do not clearly specify whether or not these prohibited relationships are consensual. This lack of specificity reminds us that there can be consensual cases of incest that would not seem to qualify as child sexual abuse. First Corinthians 5 records an example of consensual incest between legal adults by confronting the church for tolerating a Corinthian church member who was in a sexual relationship with his father's wife, presumably his stepmother. The way Paul holds the member and the church accountable lends credence to this being a consensual relationship.

On the other hand, it is precisely the broad and open language of Leviticus 18 that allows child sexual abuse with its nonconsensual dimension to be included in these prohibitions. Furthermore, Leviticus 18:24–28 shows us that these prohibitions are universal moral laws that applied to the Gentile nations being displaced by Israel. These nations were declared to be under divine judgment through being "vomited out" the land. God warns Israel they will receive the same judgment if they engage in these same practices. Additionally, Leviticus 18:29 prescribes that individual Israelites who are caught in such activities are to be expunged from the Israelite covenantal community. Thus, child sexual abuse is cast as having negative effects on the perpetrator's eternal salvation.[9]

Since these laws were regularly read to the congregation of Israel, these sexual norms would be publicly proclaimed in a periodic yet regular rhythm.[10] This would incorporate these laws into the

---

[9] Leviticus 20 has specific penalties for violating these sexual norms. These judgments would seem to assume that both parties are of accountable age to answer for their own actions and would apply to consensual cases. Thus, a consenting couple having sex outside of marriage could be executed (Deut 22:24), but in the case of rape, only the rapist would be punished (Deut 22:25). In like manner, consenting adults would be subject to the punishments of Leviticus 20, but not non-consenting victims.

[10] In Deuteronomy this would likely be during the covenant renewal every seven years. Some

moral consciousness of the people. Thus, when Amnon sexually propositioned his half-sister Tamar, Tamar knew these laws and vigorously argued against Amnon to his face that "no such thing should be done in Israel" (2 Sam 13:12). Amnon ignored her moral argument and overpowered her physically, raping her. While Tamar was likely at an age that contemporary Western culture would consider to be a child, she appears to have been of marriageable age in her cultural context. In a broad sense, while Tamar's plight does not appear to be fully analogous to our cases of child sexual abuse today, there is some similarity in the arena of consent. Since children cannot properly consent to sexual advances, this would imply that child sexual abuse is a specialized subcategory of rape.

Furthermore, the lifelong damage caused by rape, whether in adult-to-adult or in child abuse cases, is well illustrated in Tamar's sad story. As she publicly mourns her traumatization, her brother Absalom apparently brushes off her suffering. She is then reported to live desolated (or appalled) in his house, with no clear resolution of her trauma with the resulting stigma (2 Sam 13:20). Minimizing or dismissing the significance of the wounds caused by child sexual abuse further intensifies the traumatization of the abused child. Additionally, the Amnon-Tamar story points us towards another moral issue linked to child sexual abuse —namely, the misuse of personal power to exploit or oppress the weak and vulnerable.

Moral Duty to the Weak and Vulnerable

Isaiah 58 is a famous passage that condemns the exploitation and oppression of the powerless and vulnerable in the strongest of terms.[11] Isaiah 58 counters the problem of oppressive exploitation with true Sabbath observance. According to the Sabbath commandment (Exod 20:8–11; Deut 5:12–15), those in power are to honor their subordinates' —including animal laborers—rights to Sabbath rest even though they have the power to force those under their control to work as on any other day. Based on Isaiah 58 and the commandment itself, one may rightly conclude that the Sabbath calls every individual to the non-exploitation of the weak and vulnerable. Certainly, child sexual abuse is the moral opposite of the Sabbath commandment and Isaiah's expansion of it as a call to treating the exploitable justly, without exploiting their weakness. Child

---

synagogues will read the entire First Testament (OT) approximately every three years.

[11] Other texts in the Old Testament also show that God condemns oppression of the weak and vulnerable while also advocating caring for them (Prov 14:31; 17:5). Individuals are not to abuse widows, orphans, and other vulnerable people (Exod 22:22; Mal 3:5), but to please God by caring for them (Deut 6:7; Ps 78:4–6; Prov 4:3, 19:17; 22:6; 31:8–9). Likewise, if someone violated or took advantage of a young woman, the perpetrator would be harshly punished (Exod 22:16). The New Testament maintains the same principles (Matt 25:31–46; Jas 1:27; 5:1–11).

sexual abuse is fundamentally predatory, with perpetrators plotting how to entrap vulnerable victims to satisfy desires deviating from the divine norms for sexual expression.

A pair of especially egregious, but related, forms of such exploitation are child pornography and human trafficking of children for sexual exploitation. It is not just traffickers and pimps who abuse and exploit these children. Consumers of child pornography and customers of traffickers enable the sexual abuse of these children by providing a market demand for such exploitative practices. These children are powerless to understand, protest, and resist what is happening to them. By consuming child pornography or enslaving children through human trafficking, these customers directly contribute to deep and disturbing levels of child sexual abuse, and thus are as morally culpable as the pimps, producers, and traffickers. There is, however, an even more disturbing aspect to preying on vulnerable children, which provides the capstone in our case that declares child sexual abuse to be not merely evil, but grossly evil.

The Bible commands a moral duty to parents, as well as other adults, to care for and nurture children. "Fathers [and mothers], do not provoke your children to anger, but bring them up in the discipline and instruction of the Lord" (Eph 6:4). Jesus gives a strong warning about harming "little ones" in Matthew 18:6, 10, 14:

> Whoever causes one of these little ones who believe in Me to sin, it would be better for him if a millstone were hung around his neck, and he were drowned in the depth of the sea. . . . Take heed that you do not despise one of these little ones, for I say to you that in heaven their angels always see the face of My Father who is in heaven. . . . Even so it is not the will of your Father who is in heaven that one of these little ones should perish.

To nurture children is a moral duty of parents and adults, and sexual abuse in no way can be construed as nurturing children. For an adult to exploit a child they have a moral duty to nurture and protect from harm is egregiously evil. It betrays the trust of the child, engendering extreme difficulties in the child's abilities to trust others, including God. This destruction of the ability to trust impacts future abilities to form a healthy, whole intimate relationship, especially in the context of seeking marriage. The scars of child sexual abuse undermine the sanctity of future marriages and families. The dysfunctions engendered in the abused bleed over to harm their children, and even grandchildren, in a chain reaction. One abuser can harm a sequence of three or four generations.

In addition, the unresolved sense of injustice experienced by many survivors—because they have no legal ability or recourse to take action against the abuser—often creates anger issues that add to the toxicity already undermining healthy intimacy with a future spouse, future children, friends, and even God. Professionals frequently witness such phenomena as they counsel survivors of child sexual abuse. Such generally unresolvable issues may lead to depression and suicidal tendencies.

We contend that child sexual abuse is grossly evil not only because it violates God's designs for sexual expression, not only because it disregards the inherent value of the child, and not only because it is predatory and oppressive, utterly contrary to the character of God Himself as demonstrated in Christ's incarnation and death on the cross. These factors all contribute to such a conclusion. What clinches the case, however, is that in child sexual abuse, the abuser betrays the sacred responsibility and moral duty to nurture and protect children. Sexual abuse is an act of treachery against the child and against future children and future families. For this reason, child sexual abuse is not merely evil, but is utterly immoral because the treacherous treatment of a child is perpetrated by someone who should be protecting the child from any form of mistreatment. It is an immoral use of personal power that exploits a vulnerable child.

The issue of how one uses personal power brings us full circle back to humankind being the image of God. Humans are thus called to imitate the character of God: "but as He who called you is holy, you also be holy in all your conduct, because it is written, 'Be holy, for I am holy'" (1 Pet 1:15–16).[12] What is the character of holiness we are to imitate? Paul articulates an ethics of personal power rooted in the example of sacrificial love demonstrated by Christ.

Christ and the Use of Personal Power

In Philippians 2:5–8 Paul gives us a vision of Christ as one who by nature is God and who is equal with God. Thus, the pre-incarnate Christ had all the powers and prerogatives of Deity. But Christ did not cling to His equality with God and His rights as Deity; instead He emptied Himself of those powers and prerogatives to take on the form and function of a servant. He did so to die on the cross to save His enemies (Rom 5:6–8). Theologians have labeled this self-emptying of Christ as *kenosis*. Michael Gorman rightly argues that the logic of this passage is telling us that Christ acted in *character* as God through this self-emptying. As Deity, Jesus was not acting unexpectedly out of character, but rather acting out precisely who God is.[13]

Amazed by Christ's kenosis, Paul builds an ethics based on the principle of a self-emptying love that is willing to relinquish personal rights for

---

[12] Peter is quoting Leviticus 11:44.

[13] Michael J. Gorman, *Inhabiting the Cruciform God: Kenosis, Justification, and Theosis in Paul's Narrative Soteriology* (Grand Rapids, MI: Eerdmans, 2009), 27–28.

the redemption of others. Thus, in 1 Corinthians 8–9, as Paul addresses the controversy over eating food offered to idols, he appeals to the "strong"—those who felt free to eat—to be willing to give up their right to eat if that is what it takes to keep a weaker person from falling away from Christ. Paul even declares he would "never again eat meat, lest I make my brother stumble" (1 Cor 8:9–13).

Paul continues in 1 Corinthians 9 by grounding this ethical call on how to relate to the weaker brother by using Barnabas and himself as exemplifying the same principle. He makes a moral and legal argument that as apostolic figures, he and Barnabas had the right to be paid for gospel ministry without having to work a regular job like others do. In spite of having the right to be paid, he declares, "Nevertheless we have not used this right, but endure all things lest we hinder the gospel of Christ," and again, "But I have used none of these things, nor have I written these things that it should be done so to me" (1 Cor 9:12, 15). Instead of risking being perceived as exploiting the Corinthians, Paul and Barnabas relinquish their apostolic rights to compensation in order to more effectively evangelize Corinthian residents to Christ. Self-emptying sacrifice for salvific purposes becomes a driving ethical value impacting personal choices. Such choices should be modeled after the character of Christ, as exemplified by Paul and Barnabas.

Child sexual abuse seems fundamentally opposed to the kenotic character demonstrated by Christ and imitated by Paul. It is predatory, not self-sacrificial. Instead of sacrificing oneself to ensure the well-being and safety of the child, the perpetrator of sexual abuse sacrifices the well-being of the child for personal pleasure and self-gratification. Child sexual abuse is utterly incompatible with both Christ's kenotic example and Paul's ethics of personal power based on the self-emptying example of Christ demonstrated in the incarnation and cross.

Furthermore, several survivors of child sexual abuse, including a former colleague, have told us how it can seriously undermine trust in God as well as adult authority. "If God did not protect me from this abuse, why should I trust Him to guide or manage my life now?" Such testimonies remind us of Jesus' stern warning: "Whoever causes one of these little ones who believe in me to sin, it would be better for him if a great millstone were hung around his neck and he were thrown into the sea" (Mark 9:42). Those who erotically engage with children demonstrate a moral character utterly at odds with God's self-sacrificial love. They sacrifice children for their pleasure instead of practicing the godly virtue of self-emptying, self-sacrificial love designed to protect such children from the destructive, sinful use of their own personal power.

It is in this theological context that we need to consider the negative consequences of child sexual abuse. It is wrong—not merely because it causes emotional pain and suffering, but also because by causing that suffering for selfish sexual consumption, the molester fundamentally is forming a moral character diametrically opposite to the character of God, and thus defaces the divine image, both in himself (or herself) and damages the image of God in the one injured by the abuse. Additionally, God's purpose for sexual union is severely violated while also impacting the future marital dynamics of the abuse survivors in ways potentially detrimental to God's purposes for erotic love. These spiritual-moral elements go far beyond mere hedonistic harm-benefit criteria to establish a moral foundation less susceptible to the abuses of self-power over children made through spurious reasoning that no real harm is being done. It is in this larger spiritual context that we can best analyze and understand the effects of child sexual abuse.

The Extent of the Problem

For many people, particularly Christians, talking about sexual abuse towards children may sound somewhat alarmist. Nevertheless, accepting the reality of it is not an overreaction. It is a reality that tells us that incest, sexual abuse, and sexual exploitation exist in all parts of the world. It is a global problem. There is not a single country or culture that is exempt of this problem. "Sexual abuse occurs at alarmingly high rates in our society"[14] and the "reported prevalence of CSA [child sexual abuse] continues to be disturbingly high . . . in most nations for both girls and boys."[15]

> A recent meta-analysis found high levels of victimisation in most nations for both girls and boys; globally, 1 in 8 children (12.7%) had suffered CSA, with rates of 18% for girls and 7.6% for boys (Stoltenborgh et al. 2011). Even in the USA, where substantial efforts have been dedicated to prevention for several decades, and where there is some evidence to indicate a decline in recent years, the most recent national study found that 21.7% of all 14- to 17-year-olds reported experiencing some form of sexual victimisation in their childhood, and in the past year, 16.4% of girls and 9.4% of boys aged 14–17 reported such an experience (Finkelhor et al. 2015). These data included 12.9% of girls and 5.1% of boys aged 14–17 reporting they had experienced attempted or completed rape. A national study from 2006 in the USA found

---

[14] Katie Edwards et al., "Predictors of Victim-Perpetrator Relationship Stability Following a Sexual Assault: A Brief Report," *Violence and Victims* 27, no. 1 (2012): 25.

[15] Ben Mathews, *New International Frontiers in Child Sexual Abuse: Theory, Problems and Progress*, Contemporary Issues in Research and Policy 7, ed. Jill E. Korbin and Richard D. Krugm (New York: Springer, 2018), vii.

4.5% of participants reported experiencing contact CSA by a parent or adult caregiver, before sixth grade (Hussey et al. 2006).[16]

However, these numbers do not tell us the full reality because they only represent the cases that have been reported. It is well understood that sexual abuse is an underreported crime. That is why it is difficult to know the real prevalence of sexual abuse towards children.

Again, sexual abuse against children is not just specific to one country or culture. It is well understood that child sexual abuse does not differentiate between cultures, economic status, ethnicities, borders, or religions.[17]

The Victim

When we talk about child sexual abuse, it is important to first think about the victims. Who are they? What leads a child to be exposed to this type of behavior from adults? Who are the most vulnerable? Answering these questions is a priority because it is the best way to prevent future cases of abuse. Preventive actions can be taken to help potential victims as well as their parents, adults, or organizations that can safeguard the children's well-being.

What we have to make very clear is that no child is exempt from the threat of being victimized. It is paramount that we challenge the myth that "it can happen to others, but not to my child." This myth results in many children becoming victims of child sexual abuse every year.

A second myth to debunk is that "it can happen to girls but not to boys." Both girls and boys are susceptible to sexual abuse. However, research shows that more girls than boys suffer abuse. Raúl Onostre Guerra found that 95% of sexual abuse victims are female.[18] The Crimes Against Children Research Center reports that one in five girls and one in twenty boys have been victims of child sexual abuse.[19]

The third myth to refute is that "perpetrators only abuse children of a certain age." The reality is that perpetrators do not respect age. Two and three-year-old girls have been abused,[20] and even very young infants. Other studies reveal that the average age of those who have been abused

---

[16] Mathews, *New International Frontiers in Child Sexual Abuse: Theory, Problems and Progress*, vii.

[17] Philip A. Gilligan and Shamin Akhtar, "Cultural Barriers to the Disclosure of Child Sexual Abuse in Asian Communities: Listening to What Women Say," *British Journal of Social Work* 36, no. 8 (2006): 1361–1377, https://www.jstor.org/stable/23721422 (accessed April 30, 2021).

[18] Raúl Onostre Guerra, "Abuso sexual en niñas y niños: consideraciones clínicas," *Revista Chilena de Pediatría* 71, no. 4 (2012): 368–375.

[19] David Finkelhor, "Current Information on the Scope and Nature of Child Sexual Abuse," *Future of Children* 4, no. 2 (1994): 31–53.

[20] Guerra, 27.

is nine years old. However, more than 20% of children are sexually molested before the age of eight.[21]

The fourth myth to rebut is that "children from poor, at-risk families are those getting abused." As previously mentioned, sexual abuse perpetrators do not respect gender or socio-economic status. Children from all socio-economic levels and ethnic and racial groups may become victims of sexual abuse.[22]

Are children from Christian or religious families exempt from this danger? The stark reality is that children born in Christian families have been abused, even by professedly Christian parents and other family members.[23] It appears, therefore, that religious profession does not ensure prevention of sexual abuse. Diana Elliot states that "women raised in a conservative home where there was little emphasis on incorporating religious values (i.e., low intrinsic religiosity) reported higher rates of sexual abuse than women raised in a Christian home with higher integration of religious values (high intrinsic religiosity)."[24]

Of greater concern is the fact that some of these children were abused by religious leaders. In these cases, apart from all the negative effects that other victims experience, one must add that these victims may experience a loss of spirituality, distrust of religious institutions, and anger and distrust towards God.[25] As Leon J. Podles expresses, the abuse perpetrated by a priest towards a minor should be considered a sacrilege.[26]

Even if the abuse is not perpetrated by a religious leader, a child abused in the context of religiosity can experience a profoundly negative impact on their spiritual life. As one victim shares, "How can I trust a God who did not protect me from this abuse?" When professed believers

---

[21] "Child Sexual Abuse Facts & Resources," The Children's Assessment Center, https://cachouston.org/prevention/child-sexual-abuse-facts/ (accessed June 28, 2021).

[22] Kimberly Renk et al., "Prevention of Child Sexual Abuse: Are We Doing Enough?," *Trauma, Violence, and Abuse* 3, no. 1 (January 2002): 68–84.

[23] Ruard Ganzevoot, "Violence, Trauma, and Religion," paper presented at the 2006 Conference of the International Association for the Psychology of Religion, Leuven, August 28–31, 2006, http://www.ruardganzevoort.nl/pdf/2006_Violence_Trauma_and_Religion.pdf (accessed April 30, 2021). See also Diana M. Elliott, "Impact of Christian Faith on the Prevalence and Sequelae of Sexual Abuse," *Journal of Interpersonal Violence* 9 (March 1994): 95–108; and Joseph J. Guido, "A Unique Betrayal: Clergy Sexual Abuse in the Context of the Catholic Religious Tradition," *Journal of Child Sexual Abuse* 17 (2008): 255–269.

[24] Elliot, "Impact of Christian Faith," 38.

[25] F. Walker et al., "Christian-Accommodative Trauma-Focused Cognitive-Behavioral Therapy for Children and Adolescents," in *Evidence-Based Practices for Christian Counseling and Psychotherapy* (Westmont, IL: IVP Academic, 2013), 105.

[26] Leon J. Podles, *Sacrilege: Sexual Abuse in the Catholic Church* (Baltimore, MD: Crossland Press, 2008).

perpetrate sexual abuse on a child, it can seriously interfere with their ability to trust in and love God.

One important factor that may place children at future risk of sexual abuse is spending a lot of unsupervised time by themselves. Especially vulnerable are children with low self-esteem, children whose parents or teachers did not educate them about not allowing anyone to touch their bodies without their consent, children who live in precarious conditions, and children whose families are isolated (emotionally or physically) from their community and where a dominant authority figure exists.

Other factors include family environments with low family support, parental substance abuse, low parental education, domestic violence, homelessness, physical disabilities, mental health problems, child labor, and adolescent motherhood.[27]

Who Is the Abuser?

Although there is not a unique profile of those who perpetrate abuse, it is important to share what is known about those who abuse children and why they do it. It is important to know who is a potential offender in order to prevent future cases of abuse. An important factor in breaking the cycle of abuse is not just teaching the children to be careful, but whom to be careful about.

Male or Female

The vast majority of people think that males are the only ones who abuse children, completely discarding the notion of a female perpetrator. Sexual abuse is not an exclusively male problem. Women also sexually abuse children.[28] However, it is true that perpetrators are most commonly male. It may be more difficult to identify the cases of sexual abuse committed by women because the victims do not report them with the same frequency or do not know how to identify the abusive actions committed by women. Female abusers' actions and behaviors are often confused with expressions of affection. On the other hand, some do not identify the hygiene and grooming behaviors conducted by women as sexual abuse behaviors. In this way, "sexual abuse can be disguised as childcare."[29] Under these circumstances both parents and guardians should be aware that women can also commit sexual abuse, and children should be taught this.

---

[27] Laura K. Murray, Amanda Nguyen, and Judith A. Cohen, "Child Sexual Abuse," *Child and Adolescent Psychiatric Clinics of North America* 23, no. 2 (2014): 321–337.

[28] Safiye Tozdan, Peer Briken, and Arne Dekker, "Uncovering Female Child Sexual Offenders —Needs and Challenges for Practice and Research," *Journal of Clinical Medicine* 8, no. 3 (2019): 401, https://www.mdpi.com/2077-0383/8/3/401 (accessed June 28, 2021).

[29] Bunting, 252.

Studies reveal that the perpetrator can be the child's mother, grandmother, sister, babysitter, teacher, or neighbor. However, there is a presupposition that abuse perpetrated by women is not as damagin g as that committed by men. It is obviously a myth that the type of abuse that is committed by women is "softer" and thus not as aggressive as the abuse perpetrated by men. A study by Myriam S. Denov states that both myths are false, revealing that women practice three levels of abuse, which the study classifies as severe, moderate, and mild. Severe sexual abuse comprises intercourse, vaginal and/or anal penetration (with objects or fingers), cunnilingus, and fellatio. Moderate sexual abuse consists of genital contact or fondling (without penetration), and simulated intercourse. Mild sexual abuse includes acts such as kissing in a sexual way and sexual invitations.[30] We should note that the classification of "mild" is not meant to minimize or legitimize any forms of sexual abuse. Rather, these three categories are attempting to recognize that while all child sexual abuse is deeply harmful, some forms are more deeply harmful than others.

A Relative or a Stranger

The prevalent view of the general public is that perpetrators of sexual abuse are strangers. In reality, in the majority of cases the perpetrator is a family member. It may be difficult for some to accept that family members might commit abuse because there is a supposition that no one would intentionally hurt members of their own family. Most of us share the fundamental belief that family members are there to protect each other. Moreover, it becomes unfathomable that a father or mother would be capable of such a despicable act. We tend to idealize our homes as safe places for children. We idealize the family as the source of love, safety, and protection.

Unfortunately, that is not always the case. Child abuse occurs inside the doors of our homes. We need to take off the blindfolds and recognize that an overwhelming amount of evidence shows that the perpetrator is usually a member of the family or an individual who is very close to the family and/or victim. Research shows that in 70–90% of cases, the victim knows the perpetrator.[31] Research also shows that the most likely "perpetrators of child sexual abuse or assault are usually family members (34.2%) or acquaintances (58.7%) of the child or family."[32] This data aligns

---

[30] Myriam S. Denov, "The Long-Term Effects of Child Abuse by Female Perpetrators," *Journal of Interpersonal Violence* 19, no. 10 (2004): 1143, http://jiv.sagepub.com/content/19/10/1137.refs (accessed April 30, 2021).

[31] Daniel Whitaker et al.,"Risk Factors for the Perpetration of Child Sexual Abuse: A Review and Meta-Analysis," *Child Abuse & Neglect* 32 (2008): 529–548.

[32] Tanya Hinds and Angelo P. Giardino, *Child Sexual Abuse: Current Evidence, Clinical Practice,*

well with our earlier exploration of Leviticus 18 and 20 and its focus on intra-familial sexual deviancy. Mimicking familial ties, sometimes the sexual abuse perpetrator is a friend or acquaintance of the child or the family (acquaintances of the family such as a babysitter, Sunday School teacher, scoutmaster, older schoolmate, playmate, or neighbor). The aggressor is described as follows:

> In more than 90% of the cases, it's a male. In 70% of the cases they are 35 years or older. They can be very qualified professionals. With frequency, they seek employment in environments that will allow them to be close to children. Their social skill level can be average to above average. In 75% of the cases, they do not have prior criminal backgrounds. Their recidivism level is very high, even after being discovered, prosecuted and convicted. They tend to not be conflictive in jail and they exhibit good behavior. They do not accept the facts or take responsibility for them. They are usually head of a household, and they frequently have young children.[33]

Why They Abuse

We know now that the perpetrator can be male or female, young or old, with low academic background or with a graduate degree. But what makes them abuse children? What motivates these behaviors? There have been numerous studies seeking to understand what goes on in the minds of the perpetrators—what is their history, and do they share common backgrounds? None of these studies have been able to come up with a unique profile. That is why we also talk more about the risk factors that can lead a person to become a child abuser.

A large percentage of perpetrators have a history of physical abuse and neglect by their parents or guardians. They also commonly present a series of childhood traumas and psychiatric problems.[34] Even though their personal and family background as well as their victimization as children place them at greater risk of committing these crimes towards other children, it does not excuse them from carrying them out.

---

and Policy Directions, Springerbriefs in Public Health (Cham: Springer, 2020), 8.

[33] Ana G. Sacroisky et al., "Qué hacer cuando se sospecha que un niño es abusado sexualmente," *Archivos Argentinos de Pediatría* 105, no. 4 (2007): 357–367, http://www.scielo.org.ar/scielo.php?script=sci_arttext&pid=S0325-00752007000400014 (accessed April 30, 2021).

[34] Polly A. Hulme and Monte R. Middleton, "Psychosocial and Developmental Characteristics of Civilly Committed Sex Offenders," *Issues in Mental Health Nursing* 34, no. 3 (2013): 141–149, https://www.doi.org/10.3109/01612840.2012.732193 (accessed April 30, 2021).

That is why it is important to teach children that no one should touch their body without their consent, touch them in a way that makes them feel uncomfortable, or force them to keep a secret. We should also teach them to respond to such situations by going directly and telling someone they trust.

Consequences

CSA should be prevented and, if at all possible, eradicated because of the terrible damage it causes. The scars and damages the victims carry throughout their lives depend on the age of the victim at the time of the abuse, the frequency of the abuse, the type of abuse, and the relationship with the abuser. Victims who do not experience symptoms immediately after the incident of abuse will almost undoubtedly experience an onset of symptoms during adulthood. Not all victims will experience the same symptoms, nor will they experience them with the same intensity or duration.

The symptoms related to child sexual abuse may be organized in the following manner: "internalizing symptoms, externalizing behavioral problems, trauma-specific symptoms and sexually inappropriate behavior."[35] One study states that "traumatic experiences can alter people's psychological, biological, and social equilibrium to such a degree that the memory of one particular event comes to taint all other experiences."[36]

Scholars list the following symptoms as damaging effects reported by victims of abuse: anxiety disorders, depression, sleep disorders, substance abuse, post-traumatic stress disorder, a large number of abusive occurrences, confusion about sexual identity, antisocial behaviors, suicidal ideation/behavior, interpersonal disfunctioning, avoidance of people, dissociation from the abuse, psychological stress, and greater risk for experiencing intimate partner violence. Sexual assault victims may experience the following feelings as well: shame, self-blaming and self-condemnation, fear, confusion, doubt that they are worthy of anything good, rage, guilt, and humiliation.[37]

This is what the research has revealed. The numbers are cold and impersonal. They may be unconvincing to some. Maybe a reader is

---

[35] Justin Misurell et al., "Game-Based Cognitive-Behavioral Therapy Individual Model (GB-CBT-IM) for Child Sexual Abuse: A Preliminary Outcome Study," *Psychological Trauma: Theory, Research, Practice, and Policy* 6 (2014): 250–258.

[36] Bessel A. Van Der Kolk and Alexander C. Mcfarlane, "The Black Hole of Trauma," in *Traumatic Stress: The Effects of Overwhelming Experience on Mind, Body, and Society,* ed. Bessel A. Van Der Kolk, Alexander C. Mcfarlane, and Lars Weisaeth (New York: Guilford Press, 2007), 4.

[37] John Briere and Diana M. Elliott, "Prevalence and Psychological Sequelae of Self-Reported Childhood Physical and Sexual Abuse in a General Population Sample of Men and Women," *Child Abuse and Neglect* 27 (2010): 1205–1222.

wondering if all this really happens to a child sexual abuse victim. If the preceding research information is not sufficient, here are testimonies from survivors of child sexual abuse, shared with their permission:

> It's really horrible to know that I was abused. I hate it! I hate it! I hate it! Please somebody listen to me, I just want somebody to listen even if they don't say anything back. . . . I don't have any more strength to continue shouting; I feel that I'm like suffocating and might die. I would like to feel dead, forever asleep. That my eyes could remain shut, my lips to remain quiet . . . my heart without any feelings, then, I can stop being afraid. —Anabertha

> In my relationship with my boyfriend I was concerned all the time about him liking me, because he would check on me 24/7. Because he did not like the things that I did, the only solution was to deny myself. Because he didn't like it if I spoke to other people, I stopped talking to my friends. If he wanted more intimate contact, I also had to want them. My relationship with him can be summarized as me stopping being myself. —Cristina

> It was my father who abused me. . . . I found refuge in solitude, which was my only friend. Knowing that I had been abused, I felt used, defenseless. I felt like a sexual object, worthless. In the first couple of days of therapy I felt weak, tired, I wanted to hide from everyone and just cry. The memory of the abuse would not leave my head. —Anabel

> Even though I was close to people, I felt completely alone, like I was in a dark tunnel all by myself, without knowing if the light of the train would appear or even wondering if a big train would run me over. I carry on my shoulders a tremendous weight that seems impossible to carry. . . . If I try to look at the future it's like looking at something that is never going to come. If I look around me to those people who surround me, I feel inferior to them. I could describe my life as always waiting for the worst to happen to me, I could never believe that I'm worth anyone's friendship. If I look at the present, I feel unhappy, in pain, angry, sad, afraid, alone, and pessimistic. If I look at the past, I see myself as a maggot that was maltreated and that needs to continually find a way to protect itself. This is how my life has been for the past eleven years. I want to fall asleep and never wake up. —Sussy

How to Know if a Child Is Being Abused

In general, we know that few children will speak up and tell us that they are being abused. Children may not speak up because they feel a lot of shame; they think it is their fault. Or perhaps they are confused and scared. In many instances the perpetrator forces the child to keep it a secret by threats and blackmail. Nevertheless, children give us certain clues with the intention of having parents and adults question them about it so that they may receive the protection they are seeking. Sometimes they may ask questions in an indirect manner. These questions typically occur during bath time, when they are being changed for bed.

Marked Behavioral Change

We use the phrase "behavioral indicators" with an understanding that the behaviors described here do not necessarily confirm the presence of abuse. They are simply indicators of possible abuse. Therefore, parents and adults should react with caution.

Young children and elementary-age school children may imitate adult sexual behavior (not to be confused with sexual games that children often display at this age). Their games may be highly eroticized. They may display knowledge or interest in sexual topics far beyond their age. They may use sexual terminology that is not appropriate for a child their age.

They may display a radical change in behavior and emotions, may have reoccurring nightmares, and there might be an unexpected drop in their academics. They may become very isolated, frequently cry, be afraid of being alone, and become depressed.

Another type of behavior that should be monitored is wanting to avoid certain places or people, not wanting to be left alone at home, not wanting to go to a particular relative's house, or not wanting to be left alone with that person. In other instances, the child may not want to enter a room to change clothes alone (it may be at home or school). They may be receiving frequent gifts or money that cannot be easily explained.

Physical Indicators

Physical indicators may be more easily detectable and understood. For girls one should look for the presence of vaginal infection or irritation that is frequent or unusual. For boys one should look for inflammation or infection of their penis or scrotum. Look for the presence of unusual objects around the genitals or anus. Look at the child's clothes and see if there are any stains that can come from blood, semen, or dirt.

Above everything else, we must learn how to "read between the lines" when they tell us, "I don't want to stay at my uncle's house," "I don't want to be alone with Dad," "I don't want to go to grandpa's house," "I don't want to go to school," or "I don't want to be in the club anymore."

In the case of adolescents, if the abuse occurs at home, they will display intentions of leaving home without any apparent logical reason. They may want to go live with another relative or friend. Some feel a lot of fear and anger. Others feel very sensitive or uncomfortable around sexual topics. At the opposite side of the spectrum, some start exhibiting promiscuous behaviors, displaying very seductive behaviors in front of other adults. Both boys and girls will show an inclination to use drugs or present more aggressive and self-destructive behaviors. Their behaviors and thoughts can become more compulsive or obsessive. Others manifest severe difficulties in being able to concentrate in school. Some feel depressed all the time, while others have suicidal thoughts.

Responding to Child Sexual Abuse

Some Practical Guidance

If you observe any of the above indicators, look closely at the child's behavior and start asking questions. Do not wait until you can find the perpetrator; it could be too late. Act immediately! Protect your child from further abuse! It must be noted, however, that depending on the country in which one resides, there may be differing government regulations on how to intervene and report. Furthermore, in some cultures, survivors of child sexual abuse may be stigmatized and maltreated, so navigating cultural and legal complexities requires great wisdom combined with responsible preparations. In addition, in some parts of the world field of the Seventh-day Adventist Church, unions and conferences have very specific guidelines and policies for both seeking to prevent child sexual abuse and for managing the intervention and reporting process in cooperation with appropriate authorities. Therefore, if abuse is suspected, one should consult appropriate authorities in the church and in society for guidance on how to proceed.

With these legal and policy caveats in mind, we offer the following guidelines to inform responses to suspected child sexual abuse. We note that while the ensuing language often assumes parental identity as the primary perspective, the fact that parents can be key perpetrators of child sexual abuse strongly suggests that the reader keep the broader perspective of any adult confronted with suspected child sexual abuse.

If a child reveals to you that he or she has been abused, you need to believe the child. Children rarely lie about such experiences.[38] Young children do not have the knowledge or vocabulary to describe these types of behaviors. Above all, please take into consideration how descriptive

[38] Luis Villareal, "Counseling Hispanics," in *Healing for the City: Counseling in the Urban Setting* (Eugene, OR: Wipf and Stock, 2002), 293.

they are about the behaviors or the name they use for their genitals. Let appropriate authorities determine if there was abuse or not. In these cases, being indifferent or passive hurts even more than the abuse itself.

Furthermore, the adult to whom the child reports needs to stop and think carefully before acting. The emotions felt could be overwhelming and they can affect one's judgment. Indignation can make a parent lose their equanimity, but reacting in an intense manner might accentuate the trauma and cause the child to become afraid. It is necessary to first sympathize with the child, listen to them, and pay attention to their feelings. Make them aware that you are there to protect them and you will not allow this to happen again.

Once you have given the proper attention to the child to ensure safety and protection during the process of intervening, a mental health professional should conduct a proper evaluation. It may be necessary to take the child to the hospital for a medical assessment. Depending on the laws in your country, if the abuse is confirmed, the professional conducting the evaluation may be required to report it to the authorities. In places where this is not mandated, it is your responsibility to report it, if it is safe for the child. If you do not, your child will think that you are siding with the abusing party. In some countries, a parent or relative who is aware there is abuse going on and does not report it to the authorities is considered an accomplice.

Having carried out the preceding steps, your responsibility as a parent or caring adult does not end. Now it is your responsibility to remove the child from the proximity of the perpetrator. The child by no means should be near or in the presence of the offender. It is the perpetrator who must leave, not the child. It would be a serious mistake to send the child to another relative so he or she can be protected from the offending relative. In cases where this becomes complicated, if the child must leave the house, the child should leave accompanied by the parent who is providing the protection.

Finally, seek professional mental health treatment. This provides access to tools that can help a child process the aftere ffects of abuse in therapeutic ways. Child sexual abuse is a traumatic experience for everyone. Do not assume that with time children will forget. They do not need to forget; they need to work towards recovery from this experience in an appropriate manner.

Prevention and Treatment

The academic community is committed to working on behalf of children who have been abused. The idea is to reduce and hopefully eradicate this damaging evil. What should be the Christian response to this social problem? Our Christian worldview about humans being a divine creation puts us on the vanguard of protecting every child against abuse.

One of the many ways in which we can unite our voices and efforts to help stop children from becoming victims of abuse is to advocate for prevention and treatment. The treatment aspect can be left in the hands of professionals. Several therapeutic models have been developed to counteract the negative effects of sexual abuse. Some recommend following the trauma-focused interventions, others suggest a narrative or cognitive strategies,[39] and others advocate for the use of cognitive-behavioral therapy,[40] using cognitive appraisal, rational thinking, expression of thoughts and feelings, cognitive reframing, and support seeking.

One proposed model[41] uses game-based cognitive-behavioral therapy, which may alleviate "a number of symptoms and behavioral difficulties, and enhance children's knowledge of abuse and personal safety skills." Another program, called "HEALTH," has promising and satisfactory results.[42] This model's principal foundations form its acronym:

> **H**aving a supportive therapist,
> **E**nsuring personal safety,
> **A**ssisting with daily functioning,
> **L**earning to manage core PTSD
> [Post Traumatic Stress Disorder] symptoms,
> **T**reating complex PTSD symptoms, and
> **H**aving patience and persistence to enable ego strengthening.

A model called "SAFER"[43] consists of developing fundamental skills that help maintain supportive relationships, developing self-care strategies, coping with symptomatology, improving functioning, and establishing a positive self-identity. Discussing or advocating for a specific and detailed treatment plan is beyond the scope of this article.

At the same time, the entire community can become involved with prevention. Prevention is always less costly and more efficient than the treatment. There is room for all of us to have an active role in one way or another. In order for the preventive methods to be efficient, it is

---

[39] Valery A. Simon, Candice Feiring, and Charles M. Cleland, "Early Stigmatization, PTSD, and Perceived Negative Reactions of Others Predict Subsequent Strategies for Processing Child Sexual Abuse," *Psychology of Violence* 6, no. 1 (2016) 112–123, https://www.ncbi.nlm.nih.gov/pmc/articles/PMC5604874/ (accessed June 28, 2021).

[40] Thanomjit Phanichrat and Julia Townshend, "Coping Strategies Used by Survivors of Childhood Sexual Abuse on the Journey to Recovery," *Journal of Child Sexual Abuse* 19, no. 1 (2010): 71.

[41] Misurell et al., 251.

[42] Pam K. Connor and Daryl J. Higgins, "The HEALTH Model—Part 1: Treatment Program Guidelines for Complex PTSD," *Sexual and Relationship Therapy* 23, no. 4 (November 2008): 297.

[43] Connor and Higgins, 298.

recommended that one follow the Bronfenbrenner ecological model,[44] which includes the children, parents, professionals, and the public.[45]

Include the Children

This model encompasses empowering children with skills that can help them identify places or situations that may be especially dangerous. They should also be encouraged to report any intent of abuse to an authority figure (school, home, church, etc.). This model is known as the three Rs: Recognize, Resist, and Report.[46]

Involve the Parents

Since parents are the closest people of authority to the children, they have the primary responsibility for the child's well-being and safety. What parents need to know is that no child is exempt from possible abuse, no place totally safe or free of abuse. They should also be trained to recognize (without creating a paranoid attitude) possible aggressors or dangerous situations. Some experts find that parental participation in prevention workshops helps both in prevention and also in knowing how to handle those instances of abuse.[47] It also helps them discuss sexual topics with their children in a more open and honest manner. The parents are able to detect with greater ease the cases of sexual abuse and they know how to easily break the secrecy that typically surrounds cases of sexual abuse.[48]

Involve the Professionals

The professionals who need to be involved are all those who are stakeholders in the child's life. Among them we should include teachers, social workers, and local, state, and federal authorities responsible for the well-being of children and the subsequent investigation cases. All who play a decisive role in this work should be involved. The primary role of these professionals is in developing programs and conducting research and workshops that bring more information for the children, parents, and local community. Their responsibility is to provide consultations and to inform the parents on the best practices when it comes to the child's well-being.

---

44 Urie Bronfenbrenner, "Toward an Experimental Ecology of Human Development," *American Psychologist* (July 1997): 513–531.

45 Wurtele, 7–11.

46 Ibid., 4.

47 Martine Hébert, Francine Lavoie, and Nathalie Parent, "An Assessment of Outcomes Following Parents' Participation in a Child Abuse Prevention Program," *Violence and Victims* 17, no. 3 (June 2002): 355–372, http://psycnet.apa.org/psycinfo/2002-17413-006 (accessed April 30, 2021).

48 Renk et al., 68–84.

Involve the Public

Each one of those institutions (civic organizations and community agencies, churches, schools) in their sphere can help demystify the notion that abuse is a private family matter and help the community at large realize that it is a social issue all of us should be concerned with. We must work to develop not only a culture in which all cases of abuse are reported and offenders are judged, but also a culture with active pre-ventive measures to attempt to stop the development of new offenders. As Sandy K. Wurtele[49] says, "it is time to shift the focus from potential victims to potential offenders. Our task must be to stop the development of the next generation of molesters." We need a culture where governments establish laws that protect children, and where children and their caregivers are afforded the professional help they deserve when and where they need it.

The Seventh-day Adventist Church, as part of the Christian community with its various organizations at different levels, has a great opportunity to work appropriately in the prevention and eradication of sexual abuse.[50] Leaders at all levels have a great opportunity to practice a healing ministry in favor of children not only from their own Church, but also in favor of children from the entire community.

The first step in all of this is to eliminate the myth that children from Christian families are not exposed to these dangers. Let us remember that there is no such thing as a "safe place zone." All leaders of the Church at every level, at all organizations, and all local churches around the world—even in the most remote areas—should be made aware of the document approved by the General Conference regarding sexual abuse. Mechanisms should be put into place so that every church institution (schools, churches, hospitals, community agencies, etc.) can become a "molester-free environment."[51]

Our seminaries and universities should dedicate specific workshops to train future church leaders to recognize and help prevent child abuse. All leaders should know their local government's legislation as well as the Church's guidance in regards to how to proceed in cases of abuse. They should also know the legal and denominational consequences that offenders must face. Child sexual abuse should no longer be a taboo subject in our church's organizations and institutions.

---

[49] Wurtele, 14.

[50] "Child Sexual Abuse," statement voted during the Spring Meeting of the General Conference of Seventh-day Adventists' Executive Committee on Tuesday, April 1, 1997, in Loma Linda, CA, https://www.adventist.org/official-statements/child-sexual-abuse/ (accessed April 30, 2021). See the appendix for the full statement.

[51] "Child Sexual Abuse."

Conclusion

In this chapter, we have laid a biblical moral foundation that leads us to conclude that child sexual abuse is a grave moral evil to which the Seventh-day Adventist Church should voice its prophetic opposition. First, from the foundations of the creation story, we saw that God designed erotic expression and sexual intimacy to occur between equals in a proper,[52] consenting, loving marriage. Sexual contact is an exclusive privilege of the marital relationship. Child sexual abuse violates these divine designs and is thus fundamentally evil.

Second, adult-to-child sexual abuse lacks the ability for proper consent due to the power inequity inherent between an adult and a child. This form of sexual abuse is fundamentally an abuse of personal power. In a slightly differing way, sibling-to-sibling sexual abuse is also an abuse of personal power because of absence of consent to such activity and one dominating the other into victimhood.

Third, children are made in the image of God. This is not just an adult human status. As the image of God, children have inherent value and worth, which means they should not be treated as objects for consumption and disposal. Child sexual abuse violates a child's very being by failing to respect the child as being the image of God, reducing a child to a commodity for the abuser to consume.

Fourth, most child sexual abuse occurs within family or close friend circles. This seems directly addressed by having the majority of intra-familial child sexual abuse possibilities depicted in the prohibitions of Leviticus 18 and 20. Further, we saw that these prohibitions applied not just to Israel, but to Gentile-pagan Canaanites as well. God brought judgment on the Canaanites for such activities and threatened judgment on Israel if they would follow suit. Thus, Scripture acknowledges the sad fact that child sexual abuse happens among the professed people of God and shows that such practices were punishable by permanent exclusion from the covenant community. The universality of this exclusion to Jew and Gentile in this passage strongly suggests that child sexual abuse perpetrators are accountable to God and in the judgment will be excluded from the cosmic community forever, if they do not repent and change their behavior.

Fifth, the Amnon-Tamar story reminds us that by regularly talking about child sexual abuse issues publicly, we can create a corporate morality in the church that can equip children to resist the aggressors, as Tamar did with Amnon. Power inequities may mean the aggressor can

[52] A proper marriage would be a heterosexual and monogamous marriage.

still overpower and victimize, but a corporate morality may help prevent some aggressors from acting out their desires.

Sixth, the Amnon-Tamar story reminds us of how easily non-victims in the church or family communities can be insensitive to child sexual abuse victims by dismissing or marginalizing their traumatic experiences. The church should be especially tender towards and supportive of those who reveal their trauma to us.

Finally, this chapter argues that child sexual abuse is utterly incompatible with the character of God as depicted in the self-emptying of Christ in the incarnation and cross. Philippians 2:5–8 depicts Christ's demonstration of the self-sacrificial love of God by yielding up His rights of divinity to become the obedient servant who sacrificially died for even His enemies (Rom 5). Paul turns this into an ethic in 1 Corinthians 8 and 9, in which the Christian is willing to relinquish their personal rights to protect the salvation of others, depicted as weaker than oneself. Thus, the strong or powerful are called to act self-sacrificially towards the weak and not in a predatory manner. Child sexual abuse is the polar opposite of God's moral character, which is grounded in self-sacrificial service to others, not in enforcing one's power and status. Being the antithesis of God's loving character, we must conclude that child sexual abuse is utterly incompatible with any true profession and practice of our biblical faith.

In addition to Scripture, we have also surveyed the tremendous emotional and spiritual damage done to children when they are sexually abused. Such fruits cannot be the result of moral actions. Those molesting children must either be blindly deluded to the fact they are harming the child, or maliciously evil predators delighting in the power they can exercise over the child regardless of the impact on the child.

Adults are God's stewards of children and are entrusted with the responsibility of protecting them. These stewards have a moral duty to do their best to provide children with a safe environment for their development. Children, who merit special care under the eyes of the Lord because they are the heirs of the covenant, impose upon the Christian church and its leaders at every level the burden of a special mission to safeguard them as little lambs of our flock. Every adult should be committed to safeguarding every one of our children—not only from sexual abuse, but also from other forms of abuse and violence.

CHAPTER 15

Queer Theology and Sexuality

Stephen Bauer

"Queer theology" is a self-designated term, originating in the revolution over definitions of marriage and sexuality starting in the 1990s. It derives from "queer theory," which is one derivative of post-modernist philosophy. Queer theory focuses on "deconstructing" social norms, arguing that these mores are tools created and designed to preserve the power of dominant social groups. This deconstructing function has been taken into the realm of theology in order to challenge the theological foundations used to support traditional Christian definitions of marriage and sexuality.

Because queer theology operates on presuppositions which radically differ from a biblically grounded worldview, and due to its complex and radical characteristics, this study will first offer a brief overview of the kinds of issues that will be discussed here. First, we shall address the complex and somewhat convoluted definition of "queer" and the problem of defining the meaning of "queer" in the current philosophical and moral setting. Next, we shall discuss how queer theology understands biblical inspiration and authority, and how it redefines the meaning of love, sin, and grace. We will then move on to how queer theology redefines God into erotic and sexualized images and metaphors. This will include how some queer theologians sexualize the Trinity and how they cast Christ in the form of varying versions of non-normative sexualities. We end on how some even make use of the Sabbath to justify non-normative sexualities. Each section will be followed by biblical analysis and evaluation. With this overview in mind, we now turn to the task of defining queer theology.

Defining "Queer"

As already stated, "queer theology" is a self-designated term, arising out of the gay and lesbian rights movement that arose at the end of the twentieth century. These activists proclaim that they have "reclaimed" the word "queer" from its original use as a pejorative slang term for homosexuals, converting it into a term of proud identity. This shift in the meaning of "queer" is not unlike how the term "Christian" was first intended to be an insult but became a positive spiritual identity. One challenge, however, is that the term "queer" does not have a single, fixed meaning. Therefore, there is some difficulty in defining it.

A leading queer theologian, Patrick S. Cheng, notes that "queer" has three primary meanings: First, it is an umbrella term which collectively includes "lesbian, gay, bisexual, transgender, intersex, questioning, and other individuals who identify with non-normative sexualities and/or gender identities." It also may include heterosexual "allies" who, while not claiming an identity under the queer umbrella, support the quest for social justice on behalf of those included under the term. In short, "queer" is often used as an umbrella or collective term to describe people with marginalized sexualities (lesbian, gay, or bisexual) as well as with marginalized gender identities (transgender) or genitalia (intersex).[1]

A second meaning of "queer" can be "transgressive action." A transgressive action takes a word or concept with negative connotations, such as "queer," and "reclaims" it by investing it with positive meaning and identity. Thus, says Cheng, it becomes a "positive label that proudly embraces all that is transgressive or opposed to societal norms, particularly with respect to sexuality and gender identity."[2] Joretta Marshall concurs, observing that "queer suggests not an identity, but a perspective and positionality that challenges hegemonic power in multiple forms. Queer becomes a verb that is meant to destabilize discourse." She then adds, "the claim of 'queer' is not restricted in its use to self-identified bisexual, lesbian, gay, or transgendered people, but is adopted by *anyone who desires to de-stabilize normativity and power.*"[3]

According to Cheng, "a third meaning of 'queer' is grounded in the academic discipline known as queer theory, which arose in the early 1990s and is indebted to the work of the late French philosopher, Michel Foucault." Of significance for this chapter, in queer theory gender identity is not an ontological quality, but a socially negotiated identity. Queer theory "challenges [this is the transgressive function] and disrupts the

---

[1] Patrick S. Cheng, *Radical Love: An Introduction to Queer Theology* (New York: Seabury Books, 2011), 3–4. See also Joretta Marshall, "Differences, Dialogues, and Discourses: From Sexuality to Queer Theory in Learning and Teaching," *The Journal of Pastoral Theology* 19, no. 2 (Winter 2009), 36–37.

[2] Cheng, 5.

[3] Marshall, 37, emphasis supplied.

traditional notions that sexuality and gender identity are simply questions of scientific fact or that such concepts can be reduced to fixed or binary categories." Thus, the third definition of "queer" centers on the action of erasing binary boundaries, especially in the arena of sexuality and gender identity.[4] In short, queer theory denies that gender is a matter of essential nature; rather, it is a social or personal construct.

The combination of the second and third definitions positions practitioners of queer thinking in opposition to generally accepted norms, especially in issues of sexuality and gender identity. Such norms appear to be viewed as communal traditions designed to ensure hegemonic power by means of marginalizing minorities—in this context, minorities who identify with or practice non-normative views of sexuality and gender. Thus, the Bible and church tradition (especially Roman Catholic tradition) are viewed as being mere societal constructs designed to preserve certain groups in positions of hegemonic power over others.

Queer Theology and the Bible

An example of asserting that the Bible is merely a societal construct is supplied by queer scholar Deryn Guest. Guest complains that Genesis 1:27—"male and female He created them"[5]—"features strongly in the Evangelical Alliance's report that reaffirms the distinctiveness of the two sexes and the inappropriateness of crossing gender boundaries." Guest notes, "The bodies that the Deity establishes in Gen 1:27 are taken as a divinely sanctioned template that should not be tampered with. Male and female humans are the final products of the Deity's *imposition of order* on the primordial elements."[6]

Guest, however, rejects the claim that Genesis 1 is depicting a divinely prescribed normative design. Rather, he makes the text human-centered by asserting that

> it is better to focus *not on the Deity,* but on the biblical writer who *creates this authoritative character* [i.e., God]. His text tells us far more about his own anxieties of the potential of the world to collapse in on itself. . . . It is he [the biblical author] who wants to hold these things at bay and *needs a powerful deity* to do so.[7]

---

[4] Cheng, 6–7.

[5] All biblical quotations are from the English Standard Version, unless otherwise indicated.

[6] Teresa J. Hornsby and Deryn Guest, *Transgender, Intersex, and Biblical Interpretation,* Semeia Studies, ed. Steed V. Davidson (Atlanta, GA: SBL Press, 2016), 36, emphasis supplied.

[7] Ibid., 37, emphasis supplied.

Thus, Guest dismisses Genesis 1 as a divinely inspired and authoritative revelation of the divine design. Instead, he surmises that the author of this passage has invented a powerful deity to preserve the social and power structures held dear by the story's author.

A decade before Guest, Virginia Ramey Mollenkott expressed a similar sentiment, declaring, "Chapters 1 and 2 of Genesis belong to the genre of creation accounts, stories intended to describe origins and *reassure people who are threatened* in an endangered world." Mollenkott later argues that at a more fundamental level, the "Hebrew repudiation of homosexuality, cross-dressing, and transgenderism is linked to its attempt to distinguish monotheistic worship from the paganism of surrounding territories." Mollenkott notes that, contrary to the neighboring nations, Israel's Deity, although referred to as "He," is not sexed. Furthermore, sexual activity is something that differentiates humans from God. Mollenkott highlights this difference, saying, "What a contrast to the goddess-worship of ancient Sumer, where 'divine vaginas bring birth and renewal.'"[8]

Based on this protectionist paradigm, Mollenkott fast-forwards to the present, contending that our current culture "is a far cry from that of the ancient Israelites trying to differentiate monotheistic worship from the polytheism of their neighbors and to that end, drawing certain religio-social boundaries." Mollenkott likewise argues that Paul's prohibition of homosexuality was motivated by the similar goal of differentiating Christianity from the contemporary pagan religions. She concludes that "in our society, both Judaism and Christianity are so well established that they need no self-protective definition. . . . So it is time to let go of the tendency to condemn homosexuality, bisexuality, and transgenderism because of historic associations with paganism."[9] In other words, Mollenkott is claiming that the moral norms of Israel were just societal constructs, formed as acts of power to self-define against identities ascribed to them by neighboring nations. They were in no way divinely commanded.

Robert Williams puts it the most succinctly. Williams cites Norman Pittenger, a gay process theologian, who quipped, "The Bible is a rather grossly overrated book."[10] Williams adds his approval by later opining,

---

[8] Virginia Ramey Mollenkott, *Omnigender: A Trans-Religious Approach,* rev. ed. (Cleveland, OH: Pilgrim Press, 2007), 106.

[9] Ibid., 107–108.

[10] Robert Williams, *Just As I Am: A Practical Guide to Being Out, Proud, and Christian* (New York: Crown Publishers, 1992), 37. Pittenger's manuscript was not available to reference, but the fact that Williams uses this phrase to make this point is sufficient for the present study. Clearly Williams believes that "the Bible is a rather grossly overrated book" and simply borrows the language from Pittenger.

> As a Queer Christian you must be bold about saying, with Pittenger, "the Bible is a rather grossly overrated book." The point is not really whether some passage in the Bible condemns homosexual acts; the point is that you cannot allow your moral and ethical decisions to be determined by the literature of a people whose culture and history are so far removed from your own. You must dare to be iconoclastic enough to say, "So what if the Bible does say it. Who cares?"[11]

Williams further asserts that the real issue is the question as to which canonical texts are authoritative and which are not. More critically, he raises the question as to the basis for making such a determination. Self-interest seems to be the final criteria.

> Clearly, you cannot simply accept the traditional wisdom on this matter, for included in the scriptures considered canonical are a number of passages that are destructive to you. . . . You must have some sort of filter, some way of determining for yourself what is canon and what is not. If you believe God is all-loving, you simply cannot call certain, violent and hate-filled passages in the Bible "the Word of God."[12]

The self-interest criterion arises again later in Williams's work: "But the canons of traditional biblical scholarship do not serve queer Christians well; in fact, they help oppress us."[13] Thus, biblical authority is rejected and the sovereign self-selects as canonical whatever matches its own preferences and desires.

With such a view of Scripture, the result is that queer theologians make very little appeal to the Bible. Instead, a key centerpiece of the queer method is to appeal to multiple and disagreeing strands of church tradition. On this basis, variation of traditions becomes a tool with which to argue that all traditions (and hence norms) are socially constructed and not divinely inspired. Thus, no tradition can lay claim to being exclusively right. As such, social constructions are adjustable over time and cannot be fixed or absolute.[14] By leveraging such differences, this allows for the idea that queer theory and the LGBTQ movement can introduce new veins of tradition that are equally valid. Hence, appeals

---

[11] Williams, 40–43.

[12] Ibid., 43.

[13] Ibid., 123.

[14] Cheng, 21.

to various corners of Christian tradition are made, building pro-LGBTQ concepts based on these exceptional cases.[15]

This same leveraging methodology is sometimes brought to bear on the biblical text. Since practitioners of queer theology have dismissed the possibility of divine revelation, it is quite rare to see them make a serious study of the biblical text. Rather, they will latch onto a concept or doctrine from the Bible and try to manipulate it to their ends. Cheng supplies an example by first attempting to transfer divine inspiration from what is recorded in the biblical text to Christ. He asserts that Christ Himself, not the Bible, is God's revelation to man (perhaps reminiscent of Karl Barth) and in particular, the incarnation is the locus of that revelation (reminiscent of T. F. Torrance). This then permits Christ to be separated from Scripture so that He can now be used as a "divine revelation" to contradict the Bible. By moving the locus of revelation from Scripture to Christ, the Bible can more easily be treated as just another negotiable tradition.[16]

By casting the incarnation as divine revelation, the transgressive lens of queer theory uses the revelation of Christ to challenge and dissolve the binary, essentialist boundary between God and man,[17] which can then be used to dissolve the binary, essentialist boundaries within sexuality. For Cheng, the incarnation is God's "coming out" from divinity into humanity, much as the LGBTQ person comes out into society. God's "coming out" dissolves the boundary between the divine and human and is the divine revelation. "The doctrine of revelation can be understood as *God's coming out as radical love*."[18] The fundamental point is that the incarnation is infused with a queer spin, apparently being "read" through the mechanism of reader-response criticism.[19] Once practitioners of queer theology apply their queer lens to the incarnation, a queered Christ is produced. On this basis, then, Christ is used as a basis to

---

[15] Cheng, 14–16, is an introduction to this approach. See also Patrick S. Cheng, *From Sin to Amazing Grace: Discovering the Queer Christ* (New York: Seabury Press, 2012). This volume is heavily built on pitting multiple Christian traditions against each other to allow for a queering of Christ, and of the definitions of sin and grace.

[16] While not directly linked to queer theology, for further background on how christological hermeneutics can undermine biblical authority by elevating human judgment over the Scriptures, see Frank M. Hasel, "Christ-Centered Hermeneutics: Prospects and Challenges for Adventist Biblical Interpretation," *Ministry*, December 2012, 6–9.

[17] Cheng, *Radical Love*, x, 9–11, 45–48.

[18] Ibid., 45, emphasis original.

[19] At the Society of Christian Ethics, Toronto, Ontario, Canada, January 2016, one presenter in the meeting on "How Queer Theory Can Help Ethics" openly stated her dependence on reader-reaction criticism and that she was not concerned with authorial intent. All "readings" become legitimate, and the goal is to bring "marginalized" readings to the main table of discussion.

legitimize non-normative, "marginalized" sexualities. This is no accident, for the goal of queer theology, according to Elizabeth Stuart, "is to liberate everyone from contemporary constructions of sexuality and gender."[20] Before pressing forward into the specific claims made by queer theologians, it seems prudent to pause and evaluate the implications of how queer theology views the Bible and its authority.

Evaluating Queer Theology's View of Scripture

Perhaps the most foundational aspect of queer theology's significance for the biblical Christian is how it views and handles the sacred Scriptures. It seems self-evident that its views stand in direct contradiction to the Seventh-day Adventist understanding of biblical inspiration and authority. Our belief that "all Scripture is breathed out by God and profitable for teaching, for reproof, for correction, and for training in righteousness" (2 Tim 3:16) is, in practice, implicitly rejected, and in some cases, openly denied. The biblical text is treated as a personal or social construct. It is even asserted that biblical authors invented a deity to protect cherished values and power structures. Such views tacitly deny the claim that "long ago, at many times and in many ways, God spoke to our fathers by the prophets" (Heb 1:1). If such statements are merely reflecting the prophet's need of a God to support his views, and are not actually messages given by God, then the biblical text is lying, and its truthfulness cannot be trusted. Biblical authority, as understood by many Christians, is destroyed.

In this same vein, we must ask another question: if the biblical messages were not given by God but are merely social constructs, should we not expect them to match the cultural systems that surrounded them? Many authors, including Mollenkott and Guest, make such claims. Yet the previously cited admissions of Mollenkott refute such claims. When Mollenkott argues that both Paul and the authors of the Israelite canon (i.e., the Old Testament) proscribe the behaviors associated with the LGBTQ identities as a means of differentiating Israel and Christianity from the surrounding cultures, she is tacitly admitting that the biblical authors were writing contrary to the views and practices of their contemporary culture. By asserting that Christianity and Judaism are now well enough established to no longer need such self-protecting differentiations, and that it is time to erase these prohibitions even though such behaviors are historically linked to pagan beliefs and liturgy, Mollenkott recognizes that these behaviors are rooted in a

---

[20] Elizabeth Stuart, *Gay and Lesbian Theologies: Repetitions With Critical Difference* (Burlington, VT: Ashgate, 2003), 89.

fundamentally pagan worldview that differs sharply from the worldviews of Judaism and Christianity. Furthermore, Mollenkott's argument implicitly admits that there is a clear, biblical teaching on these matters, and that this biblical teaching was contrary to the contemporary culture of the biblical writers.

John Oswalt likewise shows that the mythology of ancient paganism views reality in significantly differing ways than the prophetic ideal for ancient Israel. The pagans viewed reality as an interconnected, continuous whole with no meaningful ontological boundaries in the cosmos. Thus, there were no boundaries between God and man, man and nature (exemplified in art forms like the Sphinx), or nature and God. Oswalt calls this interconnectedness that lacks essentialist boundaries the law or principle of "continuity." By contrast, the Bible presents God as transcendent from nature and man, identified with neither. There are essentialist boundaries delimiting God, man, and nature as unique categories not to be mixed together.[21] As such, the Bible differs significantly from the pagan principle of continuity. How, then, are we to explain this difference?

Oswalt expounds, "Clearly if continuity is the correct explanation of reality, and if continuity is to function as we wish, then boundaries between the realms [of God, man, and nature], and even within them are not permissible."[22] It is significant that queer theorists and theologians speak much about dissolving these exact boundaries. If Oswalt is correct, then the queer rejection of essentialist categories is highly analogous to the ancient pagan views condemned by the biblical prophets. What, then, was the outcome of pagan rejection of such boundaries?

In seeking to answer this question, Oswalt declares,

> The lack of boundaries is especially seen in the sexual domain.... There can be no boundaries between parent and child (hence, incest); there can be no boundaries around marriage (hence, prostitution); there can be no boundaries between members of the same sex (hence, homosexual behavior); there can be no boundaries between humans and animals (hence, bestiality). All these practices were told and acted out in the myths.[23]

By contrast the Bible prohibits such sexual behaviors in the Ten Commandments and especially in Leviticus 18 and 20. John's opposition to Herod's marrying his brother's wife (Matt 14:3–4) and Paul's opposi-

---

[21] John Oswalt, *The Bible Among the Myths: Unique Revelation or Just Ancient Literature* (Grand Rapids, MI: Zondervan, 2009). This description is a summary of the first half of the book.

[22] Ibid., 56.

[23] Ibid., 56–57.

tion to the incest case in Corinth (1 Cor 5) demonstrate that these moral norms were still viewed by John and Paul as universally binding. This, however, has not fully answered the question about how Israel and paganism differed.

Oswalt refocuses the question: "Did Israel follow the same thought processes as did its neighbors? . . . If so, then why did they alone come out at a radically different endpoint?" Oswalt notes that from ancient Sumerians to Old Kingdom Egyptians, everyone else surrounding Israel observed the same existential realities. "Yet when it came to their perception of ultimate reality, these profound thinkers came out where they started. If the given is this world, and if any outside interpretation of that given is rejected, the final conclusions are all going to be the same."[24]

We must ask again: why, then, was Israel so different? Oswalt gives us an answer.

> If the Hebrews came out with different—radically different—conclusions about the nature of reality and the nature of human experience, they did so because they started somewhere different from everybody else. They, of course, tell us where that point was. It was in direct revelation from the transcendent One himself. Unlike the Greeks, who were willing to accept the accolades of being the world's greatest thinkers, the Israelites tell us that they were religiously retarded. . . . Their whole history is one of [one] failure after another to live up to the light recorded in their own literature. *Thus we are forced to pay attention to the Hebrew's claims to have gotten their views by special revelation. No other explanation fits the circumstances.* Their view of God and of the world is unparalleled elsewhere. If they did not get it from the source they claim, no other good candidates present themselves.[25]

Oswalt's argument is compelling. Israel, whose fault was desiring to be like the surrounding nations (Deut 18:9; Jer 10:2), is unlike them because God spoke (Heb 1:1). Queer theology fundamentally opposes such a view and like apostate Israel of old, merely paganizes the Christian church by dissolving biblical boundaries given by divine inspiration. In short, it uses Christian language to promote essentially pagan views of God.

With the impact of queer theology on biblical authority in mind, we are now ready to ask: how, then does queer theology "queer"[26] biblical

---

[24] Oswalt, 148.

[25] Ibid., emphasis supplied. The bracketed "one" is to fix an apparent omission, for clarity.

[26] Queer theorists and theologians sometimes use "queer" as a verb, in the sense of the third

doctrines to achieve its goal of "liberating people from restrictive sexual norms?" In short, its practitioners set out to redefine—in queer parlance, to "reclaim" or "reimagine"—four areas of Christian belief: 1) the definition of love, 2) the doctrine of the Trinity, 3) who Christ is, and 4) the doctrines of sin and grace. With this plan in mind we may now turn to the first issue, the redefinition of love.

Redefining Love

Before examining how queer theology redefines love, it seems prudent to begin with a biblical survey on the nature of love. While the New Testament has much to say about the nature of love, there are two fundamental definitions of note for this discussion. First, love is cast as self-sacrificial. "Greater love has no one than this, that someone lays down his life for his friends" (John 15:13). Passages such as 1 Corinthians 13 likewise emphasize the selfless, self-sacrificial nature of love, and John says we know what love is because of the death of Christ for us (1 John 3:16). The second definition of love centers in the message to Laodicea that "those whom I love, I reprove and discipline" (Rev 3:19). The author of Hebrews echoes this sentiment in saying, "For the Lord disciplines the one he loves, and chastises every son whom he receives" (Heb 12:6).

By contrast, Cheng speaks much about "radical love," even including that phrase in his book title. In his book introduction, Cheng declares, "Radical love, I contend, is a *love so extreme that it dissolves our existing boundaries*, whether they are boundaries that separate from other people, that separate us from preconceived notions of sexuality and gender identity, or that separate us from God." Cheng asserts, however, that radical love is "not about abolishing all rules or justifying antinomian existence," but rather "radical love is premised upon safe, sane, and consensual behavior. Thus, nonconsensual behavior—such as rape or sexual exploitation—is by definition excluded from radical love."[27]

The problem is that Cheng asserts the definitions of radical love without really supplying a clear basis. As seen earlier, he seems to attempt to link radical love to the incarnation, yet his explication of the incarnation seems more an illustration that assumes his own view of radical love than being an actual foundation for it. The closest one can find to some kind of basis is Cheng's personal experience. He tells of growing up gay, loving God but feeling excluded by God and church. He claims that through his relationship to his "husband" Michael, "the boundaries between myself and the outside world [were] dissolving in a way I nev-

---

definition for "queer" in the introduction to this chapter.

[27] Cheng, *Radical Love*, x; see also ibid., 44.

er experienced before." He then tells how this relationship with Michael began to dissolve the boundaries between "God and me," rekindling his love for God.[28] This makes sense in light of Cheng's claim that "from the perspective of queer theology, however, the doctrine of revelation is more than just a matter of scripture and reason. It is also a matter of experience. Specifically, the doctrine of revelation can be understood as *God's coming out as radical love*," especially through the incarnation.[29] It seems clear, then, that personal experience, filtered through the queer value of breaking existing barriers, is read into the incarnation instead of being grounded by it. As such, his foundation for radical love is highly subjective.

For Cheng, the incarnation is highly analogous to the LGBTQ experience, for just as God "came out" of heaven into humanity through Christ, so the gay and lesbian "come out" of their closets into society.[30] Likewise, Christ "came out" of the religious and societal systems of His day just as the LGBTQ people are "coming out" of current anti-LGBTQ religious teachings and prevailing societal customs.[31] On this basis, he makes the broad generalization that God is the manifestation of a love so extreme that it dissolves the traditional boundaries seen as dividing the divine and human.

> In the same way, LGBT relationships are grounded in a love so extreme that it also dissolves existing boundaries between the self and the other, as well as rigid societal boundaries as to gender roles (for example, traditionally speaking, a man can be married only to a woman, and not to another man).[32]

We note, then, that Cheng's definition of love has no relationship to the biblical themes of self-sacrifice and authoritative rebuke. Queer love seems to sacrifice perceived barriers in order to strengthen self-definition instead of fostering self-sacrificial love. It also seems to commit the same error as Eve in Eden, failing to recognize any meaningful difference between God and man. Having defined love in this transgressive, non-biblical manner, queer theology is positioned to radically redefine God and Christ to suit their personal identities.

---

[28] Cheng, *Radical Love,* ix.

[29] Ibid., 45.

[30] Ibid., 45–46.

[31] Ibid., 46.

[32] Ibid., 50.

Queer Redefinitions of God

Before presenting how queer theologians redefine God, it is important to note that this section contains an extended exploration of queer redefinitions of God—often in their own words, and with minimal critique or analysis on the part of the present study. It should be noted that in this section some queer redefinitions of God may scandalize the unprepared reader. Following this extensive excursus is a formal section of response and analysis from a biblically oriented perspective.

The Call to Reinvent God

Cheng prepares the way for redefining our view of God by contending that the traditional depiction of God as Father is inadequate because "a truly transcendent God is ultimately beyond human categories, including sex and gender. We can only talk about God through analogical language."[33] While it is true that the paternal title applied to God is analogical, not ontological, this does not logically entail that ontological facts of God must be unknowable to humans. Scripture makes ontological statements about God. Cheng, however, argues that God is so ontologically different that we have no way to truly describe Him. Therefore, all God-talk must be analogical in the sense that humans create the analogies as part of their personal reality constructions. It seems ironic that while Cheng and his allies reject the fundamental concept of ontology—that there is a fixed essential human or divine nature—he appeals to the ontology of God's transcendence to reject the adequacy of analogical language for depicting God as Father.

Cheng builds on the work of Robert Williams, who "encouraged LGBT people to 'fire' the God of their childhood, which often can be abusive and demonic. Instead, Williams argued that we must try on new models of God, including God as female, grandmother, as divine lover, and as the one who suffers with us."[34] In particular, Williams argues that the "image of God" that most of us are raised with is "not only inadequate, but downright destructive. . . . You probably got it wired up that God disapproved of you."[35] Thus, a deity who disapproves of your sexuality needs to be fired.

---

[33] Cheng, *Radical Love*, 50

[34] Ibid., 53.

[35] Williams, 86, emphasis original.

> You need to go down to that secret chamber where *he* (and it almost always *is a he*) hides, to walk right up to him and say, "You're not God. You are a cheat and a liar. You do not have my best interests at heart; you are abusive and destructive. You are a false idol, a demon, a satanic image and I renounce you. I want no more to do with you. You are fired. Get out of my heart."[36]

Note that the human self is implied to be the sole competent judge of its own best interests, and a God not perceived to align with that self's judgement of *its* best interests ought to be fired. Williams seems to do what Guest accuses the author of Genesis of doing—creating a God who aligns with one's cherished personal views. Such a God can no longer be an omnipotent authority.

Williams goes down a classic path within theodicy discussions by setting the loving goodness of God in opposition to His omnipotence, then sacrificing the omnipotence to save the loving goodness. This is partly achieved by appealing to process theology's evolving God as well as to the AIDS crisis.[37] Cheng aptly summarizes, "As an HIV-positive man, Williams rejected the view of an omnipotent and all-powerful God, which Dorothee Sölle described as 'sadomasochist' spirituality (and not in a good way).[38] Williams refused to believe that an all-powerful God could allow the horrific suffering of HIV/AIDS to exist."[39] Thus Cheng joins Williams in the call to reinvent God into a more palatable form for LGBTQ people.

In this reconstructive project, Williams cautions that all talk about God is metaphorical and should not be taken as a dogmatic, complete view of God. Yet he later opines with dogmatic certainty,

---

[36] Williams, 87.

[37] Ibid., 96–100.

[38] See Dorothee Sölle, "A Critique of Christian Masochism," chap. 1 in *Suffering*, trans. Everett R. Kalin (Philadelphia, PA: Fortress Press, 1975). Sölle contends that traditional Christian interpretations of God and suffering cast God as sending suffering to test the individual who is supposed to endure the suffering for God's glory, and perhaps attaining eternal life. "Affliction has the intention of bringing us back to a God who only becomes great when he makes us small" (ibid., 17). In an apparent reaction to Calvin's concept of Divine Decrees, she quotes Sigmund Freud: "If the believer finally sees himself obliged to speak of God's 'inscrutable decrees,' he is admitting that all that is left to him *as a last possible consolation and source of pleasure* in his suffering is an unconditional submission." Then she adds, "Submission as a source of pleasure–that is Christian masochism" (ibid., 21–22, emphasis supplied). Pages 22–28 is a section entitled "Theological Sadism." She ends the chapter with an analysis of the sacrifice of Isaac along these lines (ibid. 28–32) and asks, "Who wants such a God? Who gains anything from him?" (ibid., 32).

[39] Cheng, *Radical Love*, 53.

> One characteristic of God's nature you should affirm as an article of faith is that God's love for you is absolutely unconditional. God loves you, period. That is a given. You can do, or did do, absolutely nothing to *earn* God's love, you can do nothing to make God love you *more*; and you can do nothing to make God *stop* loving you. God, the Relentless Lover, never gives up on you. Affirm that as a creed; believe in it as strongly as you believe the sun will rise in the east tomorrow.[40]

It seems, then, that for Williams, God is so hardwired by nature to love that He has no freedom to choose not to love. God is depicted as a deterministic slave of His own nature and can do no other. Such a Deity will be unable to love or show any preference for any individual over another. In the contextual flow of his argument, however, Williams seems to define love as an approving acceptance of a person, *as they are*, without any demand for change, especially in reference to LGBTQ preferences. Thus, "unconditional love" becomes the theological tool to eliminate all divine judgment and disapproval of the self, especially in matters of sexual preferences. The sinner can now craft a God who will always approve them as they are, without any demands for change. God can have no characteristics that might induce emotional pain or distress.

It is of interest that C. S. Lewis challenged such a definition of love half a century earlier. Lewis intimates that this permissive, non-controlling view of divine love may be more rooted in popular psychology than in Scripture. He alludes to this by observing that people want a God who is a "grandfather in heaven—a senile benevolence" who merely wishes that "a good time was had by all." Lewis astutely observes that

> love and kindness are not coterminous, and when kindness . . . is separated from the other elements of Love, it involves a certain fundamental indifference to its object, and even something like contempt for it. . . . It is for people that we care nothing about that we demand happiness on any terms: with our friends, our lovers, our children, we are exacting and would rather see them suffer much than be happy in contemptible and estranging modes. If God is Love, He is, by definition, something more than mere kindness.[41]

---

[40] Williams, 89, 91–92, emphasis original.

[41] C. S. Lewis, *The Problem of Pain: How Human Suffering Raises Almost Intolerable Intellectual Problems* (New York: Macmillan, 1962), 40–41.

It is no accident, then, that with Williams' definition of love, one of the new images of God he offers as a replacement of your childhood God whom you ought to fire is God as the unconditionally accepting, approving, doting grandmother.[42]

It is ironic, however, that in the quest to redefine God into more queer-friendly terms, we find other queer scholars depicting a sexualized God in the pain-inducing and sadomasochistic terms Williams fears. Cheng assembles such material without any apparent awareness that these alternative views contradict the vision of Williams.

Sexualizing God

An alternative to firing God is found in the tactic of sexualizing the Deity. Cheng launches the depiction of this alternative by borrowing from Stuart's description of parody as a tool for queering, declaring that parody happens when an essential concept is taken, the core preserved, yet a new and creative twist is added that fundamentally changes the meaning and opens up new possibilities. According to Cheng, queer theologians parody God's traditional attribute of omnipotence by "superimposing sexual roles on God."[43]

This sexual parody is illustrated from the work of Theodore Jennings, who suggests that the Hebrew God YHWH is depicted in the Bible as being in a homoerotic relationship with David, the king of Israel, akin to that of a warrior chief and his boy companion. Since David was king of Israel, this relationship becomes representative of YHWH being in a homoerotic relationship with Israel.[44]

Jennings seems to introduce an implied masochistic relationship between God and David, for he depicts God as the initiator of the relationship who is "on top" while David is always the "bottom" who submits to the divine initiator. Furthermore, Jennings makes an extended comparison of YHWH-David with the Zeus-Ganymede homo-erotic relationship. Jennings concludes, "Both relationships, therefore, correspond to models of age or class distinctions within male, same-sex relationships, and are, in that sense, 'pederastic' or asymmetrical in structure." Jennings even says that YHWH and David had contracted a marriage and were betrothed. Cheng reinforces this metaphor of God being in a homoerotic relationship with Israel, noting that "Gerald Loughlin has written about God's phallus,

[42] Williams, 91–92.

[43] Cheng, *Radical Love,* 51–52.

[44] Theodore Jennings, "YHWH as Erastes," in *Queer Commentary and the Hebrew Bible*, ed. Ken Stone (Cleveland, OH: Pilgrim Press, 2001), 66, 68, 70–72.

which is 'often imitated, but never seen' and yet 'deflowers' each Israelite male through the act of circumcision."[45]

The sadomasochistic element in this alleged homoerotic relationship with Israel is more graphically portrayed by Ronald Boer in "YHWH as Top: A Lost Targum." In this "targum" Boer casts Moses and YHWH as gay lovers on the top of Mount Sinai discussing the construction of the tabernacle. Later on, various mythical and historic figures (such as Sigmund Freud) are brought into the conversation, which culminates in a group sadomasochistic orgy with YHWH and Moses doing the whipping.[46] Cheng remarks, "Here Boer superimposes the leather culture of bondage and discipline, domination and submission, and sadomasochism (BDSM) onto God."

In contrast to Williams and Sölle, these theologians redefine God in positive sadomasochistic terms that were rejected by Williams and Sölle. Cheng himself seems utterly blind to this contradiction. Ironically, each of these opposing sides, along with Cheng, is trying to support the same goal—namely, to provide theological support and justification for LGBTQ people. Controversial as these depictions of God may be, there are even more attempts to reimagine God in terms of non-traditional sexuality.

The Erotic Trinity

Stuart queers the Trinity in order to challenge the traditional binary view of intimate sexual relationships.[47] The major principle she derives from the Trinity is that of "passionate friendship." She notes the "difficulty Christian theologians have always had in dealing with the third person of the Trinity." Stuart explains this difficulty as follows: "I strongly suspect that Christian clumsiness in dealing with the Spirit has a lot to do with our discomfort with the concept of threeness in relationship. Our obsession with coupledom makes us incapable of dealing with a three-person relationship, even in God."

In contrast to coupledom, she sets forth *perichoresis*, the seventh-century term used to explain the intra-Trinitarian relationship as a "dynamic, non-hierarchical equal, mutual relationship" in an "unending dance." Finally, she hints at the obvious implication: "The doctrine of the Trinity conceived as three friends dancing a dance of passion serves to remind us that we are called to more than coupledom."[48] Cheng

---

[45] Cheng, *Radical Love*, 52.

[46] Ronald Boer, "YHWH on Top: A Lost Targum," in *Queer Commentary and the Hebrew Bible*, ed. Ken Stone (Cleveland, OH: Pilgrim Press, 2001), 75–77, 86–87.

[47] Cheng, *Radical Love*,.56.

[48] Elizabeth Stuart, *Just Good Friends: Toward a Lesbian and Gay Theology of Relationships* (London: Mowbray, 1995), 242–243.

more bluntly sexualizes Stuart's comments on *perichoresis,* saying that it "means an ecstatic dance or *interpenetration* of the three persons."[49] Continuing his exposition on Stuart's Trinity, Cheng concludes that the Triune relationship "is so intimate that it might be thought of in terms of a fluid-bonded polyamorous[50] three-way relationship."[51]

Gavin D'Costa queers the Trinity in a slightly differing way. D'Costa tries to build on Hans Balthasar's Trinity theology to argue that each member of the Trinity is "simultaneously supramasculine and suprafeminine in its own giving and receiving." D'Costa also asserts that "not only is the Son bisexual in ontological terms, but so is that most worrying of potential patriarchs, the Father." (It is ironic that D'Costa makes an ontological argument in a discipline that fundamentally rejects ontological essentialism.) A bit later, D'Costa continues,

> Balthasar's Trinity symbolizes divine love in terms of interpenetrating and reciprocal relationships between supramasculine and suprafeminine, suprafeminine and suprafeminine, and supramasculine and supramasculine (analogically: heterosexual, lesbian, and gay relationships), but *only in so much* as these relationships are self-giving for the wider community, as endless outpourings and sharings.[52]

Thus, queer relationships are divinely sanctioned through queering the Trinity. Cheng leverages this a step further to assert that "both transgender and 'switch' (that is versatile or both 'top' and 'bottom') relationships are at the very heart of the Trinity."[53]

Marcella Althaus-Reid likewise uses the Trinity in a similar, though perhaps even more radical, fashion than Stuart and D'Costa. Althaus-Reid captures the concept of *kenosis* to contend that the Trinity is God's self-emptying of heterosexuality and monogamy, a process she labels "omnisexual kenosis." This process is felt to reveal God as gender-fluid and polyamorous. Thus, for Althaus-Reid, "the Trinity needs

---

[49] Cheng, *Radical Love*, 56, emphasis supplied.

[50] Wikipedia, s.v. "Polyamory," last modified April 13, 2021, https://en.wikipedia.org/wiki/Polyamory (accessed April 22, 2021), defines polyamory as follows: "Polyamory is typically the practice of, or desire for, intimate relationships where individuals may have more than one partner, with the knowledge and consent of all partners." It has been described as "consensual, ethical, and responsible non-monogamy."

[51] Cheng, *Radical Love*, 57.

[52] Gavin D'Costa, "Queer Trinity," in *Queer Theology: Rethinking the Western Body*, ed. Gerard Laughlin (Malden, MA: Blackwell Publishing, 2007), 273, emphasis original.

[53] Cheng, *Radical Love*, 58.

to be understood as an orgy which breaks down the privileging binary of pair-bonded relationships." Althaus-Reid further contends that the Trinity does not support a concept of restricted polyfidelity in which the Trinity restricts its intimacy to the threesome. Rather, she says that each member of the Trinity has "his/her own closet lovers and 'forbidden desires' (for example, Jesus' relationships with Mary Magdalene and Lazarus), which in turn results in the death of the 'illusion of limited relationships."[54]

On the basis of all these theologians, Cheng concludes, "As such, the Trinity can be a model for individuals who are polyamorous because the Trinity deconstructs the binary relationship model of marriage and domestic partnerships." Based on the condition of the correctness of D'Costa's position, Cheng adds, "Then the Trinity is actually a polygendered or polysexual being in itself!"[55]

Queering Christ

Queer theologians are not satisfied with merely queering the Trinity. They also specifically focus on reimagining Christology as well. One longstanding interpretation casts Jesus and John as gay lovers. Mollenkott opines, "Far less popular attention has been bestowed on the possibility that Jesus was sexually involved with the beloved disciple. . . . [There is] considerable New Testament evidence that Jesus engaged in such intimacy."[56] In support of her assertion, Mollenkott borrows from Theodore Jennings, who asserts that "the least forced readings of the texts that concern the 'beloved disciple' is one which supports that they refer to a relationship of love expressed by physical and personal intimacy—what we might today suppose to be a homoerotic or 'gay' relationship."[57]

Robert Goss follows suit, speaking from his perspective as an ex-Jesuit:

> My sexual/spiritual awakening took place within the Jesuits. . . . My relationship with Christ was evolving. . . . The physical description of the Beloved Disciple's head on the breast of Jesus at the Last Supper attracted me. Like many gay Christians, I always intuited that Jesus and the Beloved Disciple not only expressed their love physically but celebrated it sexually. . . . I found the Eucharist to be a significant part of bodily love. It

---

[54] Marcella Althaus-Reid, *The Queer God* (New York: Routledge, 2003), 55–59.

[55] Cheng, *Radical Love*, 59.

[56] Mollenkott, 119.

[57] Theodore Jennings, *The Man Jesus Loved: Homoerotic Narratives from the New Testament* (Cleveland, OH: Pilgrim Press, 2003), 9.

> began to take on a homoerotic dimension. Jesus said, "This is my body which is given to you." Eating Jesus' body and drinking his blood were physical acts of participation, intercommunication, and sexual love-making. I was falling in love with Jesus in a new and erotic way.[58]

When officiating as a new parish priest, Goss reports an experience he had while celebrating the Eucharist with his parishioners.

> While in devotional prayer at Eucharist, I envisioned Jesus in meditation and felt sexually aroused. . . . This erotic arousal for Christ became a quantum leap in my spiritual life; I finally understood the connection between deep sexuality and deep spirituality. I finally admitted to myself that I loved Jesus because he was a male and that it was OK to love Jesus passionately and erotically as a man. I came out to God and named myself gay.[59]

Goss continues tracing the saga of how his erotic spirituality further developed, saying,

> My technique of meditative prayer was to envision Christ with me and experience him as a lover. . . . When fantasies are focused into making love with Christ, the experience opens itself to a fundamental and profound consciousness of God. My visualizations of Jesus were certainly explicit, erotically envisioning various forms of making love to Jesus the Christ. I had sexual intercourse with Jesus. . . . Jesus became the first male lover with whom I felt thoroughly comfortable.[60]

A few pages later, he adds, "I envisioned making love to Jesus, felt myself become sexually aroused, and climaxed in an orgasmic union with Jesus the Christ."[61] In queer thinking, however, Jesus is not merely

---

[58] Robert E. Goss, *Queering Christ: Beyond Jesus Acted Up* (Cleveland, OH: Pilgrim Press, 2002), 16. The subtitle is a reference to Goss, *Jesus Acted Up: A Gay and Lesbian Manifesto* (New York: HarperSanFrancisco, 1993). In 1993, Goss set out to find a gay Jesus to support gays and lesbians. In 2002, he felt that the gay-lesbian verbiage was too narrowly defining and hegemonic, so he published *Queering Christ* to go beyond *Jesus Acted Up* by broadening views of Christ to include the whole range of queer identities. Goss also publishes under a hyphenated surname, Shore-Goss.

[59] Goss, *Queering Christ*, 17.

[60] Ibid., 17–18.

[61] Ibid., 19.

gay or a gay lover in prayer. Jesus becomes reimagined into every form of the queer spectrum.

One example is found in Mollenkott's intersex Christology. Citing the work of biologist Edward Kessel, she builds off the idea that a virgin birth would require us to see Jesus as produced through parthenogenesis. This would mean that Jesus was a biological clone of Mary and thus would have no Y chromosomes in his DNA, but only the XX chromosomes from Mary. She continues, "Kessel explains that Jesus underwent a sex reversal to the male phenotype, adding that 'biologists are generally agreed that sex reversal, like parthenogenesis, may sometimes occur in human beings as it does in lower animals.'" Mollenkott then drives the point home with a quote from Kessel: "The female embryo Jesus of the Virgin Conception and Incarnation became the two-sexed infant of the Virgin Birth who was the androgynous Christ, bearing both the chromosomal identification of a woman and the phenotypic anatomy of a man." Based on this, she declares,

> I cannot help making the connection to the Genesis depiction of a God who is imaged by both male and female, yet is literally neither one nor the other. A chromosomally female, phenotypically male Jesus would come as close as a human body could come to a perfect image of such as God. . . . It seems to me that from the perspective of his [Kessel's] findings, intersexuals come closer than anybody to a physical resemblance to Jesus—unless, perhaps we grant that honor to post-operative female-to-male transsexuals[62] who remain chromosomally female after their transition to maleness.[63]

Mollenkott extends her transgender Christology by using the alleged androgyny of Jesus to further leverage her point. "In the theology and liturgy of the Orthodox Christian Church, the wound in Christ's

---

[62] Note the exclusion of the male-to-female transition from being a close representation of God or the alleged chromosomally female Jesus. Also consider how Mollenkott's view depends on the sexual binary denied by others and by herself. See Mollenkott, 99, where she herself seems to downplay the binary when she writes, "Christian scholarship has recognized that the original created being [i.e., Adam] is either hermaphroditic or sexually undifferentiated, . . . closer to a transgender identity than to half of a binary gender construct. . . . Binary gender would be a later development, not the first intention of the Creator but provided subsequently for the sake of human companionship. From this angle, hermaphrodites or intersexuals could be viewed as reminders of Original Perfection."

[63] Mollenkott, 115–116. She refers to two works of Kessel: Edward L. Kessel, "A Proposed Biological Interpretation of the Virgin Birth," *Journal of the American Scientific Affiliation* (September 1983): 129–136, and Kessel, *The Androgynous Christ*, privately printed and available only from the author. Mollenkott leverages Kessel's work to queer Christ into being intersexed.

side is analogous to female genitals, so that Christ gives birth to 'his' bride, the Church, through the wound 'in his side, just as Eve was drawn from the side of Adam.' Talk about transgenderism!"[64] Suddenly, in queer theology Jesus can now be both intersexed and transgendered.

Nancy Wilson takes Christology in yet another direction. After trying to cast the three wise men who attended Jesus' nativity as gay, she eventually focuses on "the Bethany community" of Mary, Martha, and Lazarus. She depicts Mary and Martha as possible lesbians and Lazarus as gay. Williams also suggests that Mary, Martha, and Lazarus were not biologically related but chose each other as brother and sisters, later adding Jesus into their mix, making them a family of choice. On this basis, she contends that Jesus shows us that families of choice are equally as valid as the biological nuclear family. She notes that in the story of raising Lazarus, Lazarus is called "the one whom you love" (John 11:3), and then seeks to equate Lazarus with "the disciple whom Jesus loved" in John's Gospel, who also leaned on the breast of Jesus at the Last Supper. In so doing, she portrays Jesus and Lazarus as gay lovers.

Wilson likewise suggests that there may have been more sexual complexity in Jesus' close friendship with the Bethany trio than a purely gay relationship would suggest.[65] Says Wilson,

> I believe that the most obvious way to see Jesus as a sexual being is to seem as bisexual in orientation, if not also in his actions. If our sexuality is most healthy when it is connected, not disconnected, to our values, to intimacy, to our feelings of love and connectedness with others, then the bisexual option sounds the most fair and likely.
>
> I know that saying that Jesus was bisexual in his orientation is really going to send some people into orbit (even some gay and lesbian people)! But *it is very important to deshame the fact that Jesus, as part of his humanness, part of the concept of incarnation, was sexual.*[66]

Wilson thus depicts Jesus first as gay, then as bisexual, and implicitly as polyamorous. While the previous theologians have queered Christ in a relatively limited number of classic LGBTQ identities, Goss takes the

---

[64] Nancy Wilson, *Our Tribe: Queer Folks, God, Jesus, and the Bible* (New York: HarperSanFrancisco, 1995), 116.

[65] Ibid., 131, 140–146. See also Mollenkott, 120–121, where she too briefly intersects with Mary Magdalene as a potential lover of Christ along with Lazarus to conclude that "Jesus was bisexual."

[66] Wilson., 147, emphasis original.

enterprise to a whole new level. After probing Eleanor McLaughlin's attempts to portray Christ as a transvestite (cross-dresser, drag performer),[67] Goss continues by adding,

> I would add to McLaughlin's above quotation [about the transvestite Jesus] many other obscene and queer configurations unimagined by her: the leather Christ, Christ the bottom, Christ the lesbian boy, Christ the drag queen, and so on. McLaughlin's notion of the transvestite allows for the Christ's protean solidarity with all peoples, all economic and political locations, all genders, and all sexual orientations. . . .
>
> . . . Jesus the Christ is a liminal figure, and queer postmodern representational strategies reclaim the sexuality of Jesus/Christ and play with fluid gender constructions intersected with diverse sexual attractions. The mixing and matching of signifiers of gender difference and sexual difference in representational strategies of the Christ provide an alternative way of envisioning Christ as having liberating significance for the queer community. Our queer exploration cuts the Christ from the moorings of dominant, heterosexist and patriarchal theologies while rearticulating Christ within new diverse sexualities and diverse theologies that affirm sexual and gender alternatives. . .
>
> The Ultra Christ that Althaus-Reid envisions needs a larger wardrobe to cross-dress to depict the diverse peoples and pluralistic social locations of the postmodern world.[68]

It is interesting how various theologies can make Christ simultaneously gay (such as the claim of Jesus and John being gay lovers), bisexual, transgender and intersex, and more. The original identity labels such as "gay" and "lesbian" now seem to be viewed as broadly forcing unchosen identity labels on a person. For example, a transgender woman (i.e., male anatomy but identifies as a woman) may well vehemently reject the label of "gay," and thus this person is thought to be unable to identify with a gay Jesus. Any other identity group may raise similar objections to receiving labels not self-created. Therefore, Goss seeks to open the door to a plethora of customized Christs to satisfy any nuance of self-chosen identities. It is amazing how multiple and even self-contradictory Christs can be created to support the common goal of throwing off traditional sexual morality.

---

[67] See Eleanor McLaughlin, "Feminist Christologies: Re-Dressing the Tradition," in *Reconstructing the Christ Symbol: Essays in Feminist Christology* (New York: Paulist Press, 1993), 118–149.

[68] Goss, *Queering Christ*, 181.

This survey of how queer theologians reimagine the doctrine of God and Christology helps clarify Cheng's concept of what it means to speak about God analogically. It appears that Cheng and his colleagues are searching for theological concepts of God that they believe to be analogous with the LGBTQ experience and queer theory rather than starting with actual, fixed attributes of God. Human experience is used to define God (and Christ), and the language thus used to define Deity is called "analogical." As Althaus-Reid notes, queer theologies are autobiographical, first-person oriented, and are "characterized by an 'I,' using personal experience as the grounding norm for creating new theologies about God."[69] Mollenkott's honesty must be commended when she concedes, "We human beings really do tend to create God in our own image."[70] It is clear, then, that such theological discourse inverts the biblical ideal of humans being made in God's image into humans creating a God made in their own sinful image.

Queer theology shows us that the rejection of essentialism leads one to believe that there can be no absolute concept of God as He really is. Therefore, by default, God can now be forced to fit into varying human constructs of being and reality to support human desires and agendas. To redefine God in this way, however, also requires a redefinition of sin, for sin must now be divorced from essentialism as well.

Analysis and Critique of Queer Redefinitions of God

Queer redefinitions of God stand in clear contrast to biblical theology where only God is self-defined. In biblical theology, idolatry inherently implies that the creature defines the Creator. This is seen in passages such as Isaiah 40:19–20 and 44:9–17, as well as in Romans 1:21–23. Isaiah holds the human-designed idol in contrast to the true God who created all things and who is the unmade Maker (Isa 40:18, 21–26; 44:21–24). Being unmade, God is not defined by any other being. The second commandment is meant to protect God's right to be the sole definer of Himself. Creatures are not to attempt to define God according to their desires, needs, or logic. They must receive God as self-revealed without additional definitions from humans.

In the biblical record, however, it seems that humans have a penchant for seeking to create a God in their image instead of seeking to restore the divine image in themselves. Thus, we find the divine rebuke that "you thought that I was one like yourself" (Ps 50:21)—that is, Israel was defining God instead of submitting to God's self-disclosed definition of

[69] Althaus-Reid, 8.

[70] Mollenkott, 90.

Himself. When humans define God, Deity is morally eviscerated. Thus, the pagan deities, defined by societies surrounding Israel, are depicted as engaging in all the morally evil actions of sinful humanity, including immoral erotic activity.

It seems that queer redefinitions of God paganize Him. Like idolatrous Israel and ancient paganism, queer theology anthropomorphizes God into the image of sinful man. Just as the pagan deities were depicted as practicing sexuality that deviates from biblical standards, so today, queer theologians depict the Trinity as engaging in such practices. This stands in sharp contrast to the biblical God who, as noted by Mollenkott, is not sexed. What difference does this make?

Oswalt notes that,

> because God is not sexed and does not function in sexual ways, human sexual behavior is specifically desacralized. . . . We are not permitted to conceive of the universe in sexual terms, nor are we allowed to try to affect the universe's functioning through our sexual behavior. . . . If God is not sexed, then the use of sex to express and indeed, to reinforce, our unity with God is both mistaken and positively dangerous.[71]

In direct opposition of this separation of sexuality from spirituality, queer authors such as Goss declare sexual activity to be an integral part of spirituality. Examples include Goss's claim of finding Christ during homoerotic sex and Jennings' depiction of God being in a homoerotic relationship with David and Israel. Goss's imagined sexual encounters with Christ, as well as Boer's depiction of God and Moses in a sex orgy, seem not only paganistic but downright blasphemous! It is clear, then, that the queer sexualization of God mirrors ancient paganism, not biblical theology. There is more to this, however, than mere paganistic anthropomorphizing of God.

Paul expresses condemnation on the Gentiles because they "exchanged the glory of the immortal God for images resembling mortal man," as well as animals (Rom 1:23). In so doing, Paul says that they "worshiped and served the creature rather than the creator" (Rom 1:25). In other words, the Gentiles created their own deities in place of the true God. Each deity is customizable to each worshipper. In like manner, queer theology has created a pantheon of Christs and Trinities, all envisioned according to sinful human desires. The result is a plurality of Gods and Christs: the homosexual God/Jesus, the bisexual God/Jesus, the polyamorous God/Jesus, and more. However, these are designer Gods

---

[71] Oswalt, 74–75.

and Christs, created by humans to suit human passions. As such, Paul would declare them to be "exchanging the glory of God for images resembling" (Rom 1:23) the sexual preferences and practices of our age. On this basis it can be suggested that these theologies actually promote the practice of idolatry. Queer theologians merely carve their deities out of ideas instead of wood and stone, then worship them. Their Christs and Trinities are, however, as much a human creation as was the golden calf in Exodus. Like paganism of old, God is reduced to being, at best, a super-creature. His transcendent authority over all is lost in the plurality of customizable gods and Christs. Queer theology dissolves the biblical doctrine of God, as well as biblical moral standards for marriage and sexual expression. Such redefinitions of God cannot be effectively advocated without redefining sin and grace.

Redefining Sin and Grace

In order to queer Christology and the Trinity, it is necessary to redefine the terms "sin" and "grace." Cheng introduces the question of defining sin and grace by arguing that traditional understandings of sin focus on breaking God's law, moral or natural, and the ensuing punishment deserved. Sin is disobedience.[72]

Mollenkott notes that in traditional theology, this disobedience creates a separation from God. She counters with a "creation spirituality" that asserts that "God's connection to the creation is just as unalterable as a mother's relationship to her child." She further asserts, "There is no *eternal or real* separation between the Creator and creation." She diagnoses our spiritual problems as stemming "from the human ego which has imagined itself separate from its source."[73] Mollenkott then contrasts the traditional and the new views:

> The doctrine of Original Sin interprets Genesis 3 as describing the real, objective perversion of God's original plan by human disobedience and sinfulness. . . . By contrast, Christians who believe that the goodness of God's creation could not be subverted, see Genesis 3 as describing a body-identified *imagined* separation from God.[74]

Mollenkott is denying any real "fall" from an original ideal. Once there is no God-given ideal to be realized, sin must be redefined.

---

[72] Cheng, *Radical Love*, 70–74.

[73] Mollenkott, 93.

[74] Ibid., 95.

Cheng launches into revising the meaning of sin by arguing that the doctrine of original sin, with its sexual transmission from one generation to the next, invests sex in general with shame and negativity. For Cheng, this view of sin reinforces boundaries of acceptable sex (reproduction) and all other forms, which does not meet the goal of radical love. Thus, sin is to be defined as the rejection of radical love by supporting essentialism with its erection of boundaries, especially in gender, identity, and sexuality. Since Cheng sees Christ's incarnation as having dissolved these boundaries, sin now becomes our opposition to what God has done for us in Christ.[75] Grace, then, becomes the undoing of these aspects of sin, freeing us from such boundaries and constraints.

In pursuing the sin-grace challenge, Cheng rejects a "crime-punishment" model of sin (eventually naming Anselm of Canterbury explicitly as the source) in favor of a "Christ-centered" model that is partially justified based on Peter Abelard's moral influence model of atonement. Cheng finds the crime-punishment model to be anywhere from "inadequate" to offensive. He charges that the crime-punishment model of sin has been the root of both fear of gays and lesbians—believing they will bring divine judgment on the community—and justifying violence against gays and lesbians. He seems to assume that a crime-punishment model of sin necessitates persecution of gays and lesbians without recognizing the possibility that such mistreatment would be a misuse of the penal model of sin. His assumption, in part, is built on a couple of theologians who use the scapegoat from the Day of Atonement as a symbol of the community blaming a marginalized person/population for some problem, then violently sacrificing them (i.e., they cast the scapegoat as a blood sacrifice) for the good of the community.[76] In Cheng's view, then, the fruit of violence against gays and lesbians demonstrates the inferiority of the crime-punishment model and we need to replace it with a more merciful model.

A practical example of creating a "more merciful model," cited by Cheng, is how Kathy Rudy has queered the Sodom story, a story often used to condemn homosexuality. In the traditional view, the Sodom story condemns same-sex eroticism. In the classic rebuttal, the sin of Sodom was actually not sexual immorality, but the practice of inhospitality. Rudy leverages the hospitality motif into being the master moral criterion for determining if a sexual activity is moral or immoral. Rudy proclaims,

> The people of Sodom teach us that what is ultimately pleasing to God about our sexuality is hospitality. If our sexual relations

[75] Cheng, *Radical Love*, 70–74.

[76] Cheng, *From Sin to Amazing Grace*, 105–106.

> help us to open our hearts and our homes to lost travelers and needy strangers, they are good. . . . Hospitality can be the new criterion by which we determine the morality of sexual acts. Rather than locating morality along lines of procreation, or along the lines of complementarity, we can now measure sexual morality by determining how well our sexual encounters help us welcome the stranger into our church and into our life with God.[77]

Rudy also incorporates the unitive dimension as a co-marker of moral sex, but defines that unity by how sexual relationships help unite people into the church community. She does not apply the unification principle to monogamous marriage. Between the unitive and hospitality elements, Rudy calls us to no longer view identities like homosexual as meaningful, because we are now united by the higher identity of being Christians. Also,

> there will be no way to condemn what I have described as communal sex, for all of us as Christians would understand that sexuality that is hospitable—whether it is monogamous or communal—is good. Indeed, gay male and radical sex communities might even serve as models for explicitly Christian 'experiments' in communal living and communal sex.[78]

In like manner, Nancy Wilson builds a hospitality ethic, though more oriented to one-on-one relationships than the church community. In her chapter "A Queer Theology of Sexuality," Wilson has headings such as "Promiscuous Hospitality as a Queer Gift," "Bodily Hospitality," and "Sexuality, Strangers, and Bodily Hospitality."[79] Wilson equates our bodies to being our homes.

> If my body is my home, then my decision to share my body with another person is a lot like my decision to share my home. . . . I believe that to share ourselves sexually is to give and receive bodily hospitality. . . . To share sexually with someone is literally to *make room* for them in our body and the space surrounding our bodies.[80]

---

[77] Kathy Rudy, *Sex and the Church: Gender, Homosexuality, and the Transformation of Christian Ethics* (Boston, MA: Beacon Press, 1997), 126. Her discussion of Sodom begins on p. 125.

[78] Rudy, 128.

[79] Wilson, 231–249. Wilson's chapter is more a rambling diary than a carefully crafted argument. Her stories, however, make it clear that hospitality does not have to be monogamous.

[80] Ibid., 249, emphasis original.

Thus, Wilson has constructed a queer theology of sexuality that affirms sexual promiscuity and bodily hospitality as special gifts with which many LGBTQ people are endowed. Rudy and Wilson, therefore, portray a vision of sexual freedom that Cheng endorses as more merciful than divine command ethics and its associated, traditional understanding of sin. Radical love is declared to break all traditional boundaries and replace them with something transgressive and new.

Critiquing Redefinitions of Sin and Grace

Who Defines Sin?

Given how queer theologians redefine sin, we must ask: who gets to define sin? This is an important question, for whoever has the power to define sin is, by definition, the final moral authority. In Scripture, Paul says he would not know what sin is except through God's law (Rom 7:7). Paul specifically cites the tenth commandment —"Do not covet" (Exod 20:17; James 4:2)—as an example of this law. The Ten Commandments were written by God's finger (Exod 31:18). Thus, in Scripture, it is God who defines sin. Sinners do not have the authority to define or negotiate the definition of sin. Queer theologians thus appear to usurp the prerogative of God by attempting to redefine sin on their own terms. This seems suspiciously like the quest of Lucifer to "be like the Most High" (Isa 14:14) and the propaganda campaign of the Edenic serpent, "You shall be like God" (Gen 3:5).

Additionally, in Romans 7:8–11 it becomes clear that the core characteristic of sin is to resist established rules and order. Sin is declared to have no power until there is a law to resist. Once a law is given, then sin activates to resist it. The oppositional nature of sin against set rules and norms seems suspiciously similar to the stated goal of queer theology to be "transgressive," deconstructing prescribed rules and boundaries. Thus, the quest of queer theology appears remarkably aligned with the core characteristic of sin found in Romans 7.

Another problem is that Cheng's rejection of a crime-punishment dimension to sin contradicts clear biblical data. Already in Genesis 2, God prohibits humankind from eating the fruit of one tree in the garden. God further announces a judicial penalty—"You shall surely die"—for violating that prohibition.[81] Then God conducts a trial and judgment (Gen 3). Furthermore, the regular depictions of God judging (Rom 2:3; 3:6; 2 Tim 4:8; 1 Pet 2:23; etc.) in courtroom settings (Dan 7; Rev 20),

[81] See Stephen Bauer, "Dying You Shall Die: The Meaning of Genesis 2:17," *Ministry*, December 2011, 6–9, which shows that the announcement to humankind by God, literally translated "dying you shall die," occurs nearly fifty times in the Old Testament. Except for one or two potential exceptions, it always announces a judicial penalty for breaking a royal decree or law.

the New Testament use of courtroom terminology for justification, as well as Paul's statement that "there is therefore now no condemnation for those who are in Christ Jesus" (Rom 8:1) all point to a legal-criminal dimension in the sin-salvation dynamic recorded in Scripture. Hence we are redeemed from the curse—or penalty—of the law (Gal 3:10–13) and God "will render to every man according to his works" (Rom 2:6). By rejecting the legal-criminal dimension to sin and judgment, Cheng and his cohorts lay the foundation for the autonomous sovereignty of the sinful self to redefine sin. This autonomy from God is further reinforced by the denial of an original ideal followed by the fall of man in Genesis 3. If we are no longer fallen, and the goodness of God's creation cannot be subverted by humans, then humans can lay claim to defining sin on their own terms. This is why Cheng can invert the biblical pattern by redefining sin as the acceptance of a divine design expressed in a fixed essential nature of man that places restrictions on sexual identities and activities. Ironically, in rejecting the fall according to Genesis, Cheng effectively proposes an alternative fall, a fall into essentialism that marginalizes non-normative sexualities. For Cheng, such a position needs to be redeemed and corrected. This rejection of essentialist categories raises critical questions.

Anti-Essentialism and Biblical Anthropology

The queer rejection of essentialist categories is another interesting problem to consider. First, this rejection seems to contradict the creation story in Genesis 1 where God, not a social construct, creates male and female. Maleness and femaleness are essential dimensions of the created order, to be found not only in humans but as part of animal existence as well. This means that Adam could not choose to be female nor Eve to be male. That kind of self-definition was not possible. Thus the binary of male-female is an essential characteristic by creation design. The great irony is that those decrying the sexual binary as "imagined" or as a mere societal construct are themselves the product of a binary union of twenty-three chromosomes from a male joined to twenty-three chromosomes from a female. In the Bible, therefore, we do not find societal constructs of male-female, human-animal. Instead we find divine creation responsible for these essential characteristics.

The quest to self-define against the definition chosen by one's Creator is addressed by Isaiah. He contends that the clay jar created by the potter has no right to complain that the potter forgot to put handles on it. "Woe to him who strives with him who formed him" (Isa 45:9). This means that the doctrine of creation implies that the Creator, not the creature, defines the core characteristics of the creature. Adam and Eve resisted their creaturely position, attempting to self-define into deity. They failed. Only YHWH—"I am who I am," not what you will have me be—is self-defining. All creatures are, to a great extent, defined by their creator.[82] Queer theology appears to reject any transcending authority who defines the human being while seeking to establish autonomous self-definition.

While it is true that there are essential, non-negotiable characteristics of being male and female, it is also true that individuals and societies may construct differing interpretations of what it means to be male or female. Gender identity does involve personal and societal interpretations, but those interpretations are based on the biological fact of two sexes that express essential qualities. We need to be open to analyzing and revising societal interpretations of being male and female, so long as we keep biblical essentialism in mind.

While Cheng accurately observes that some professing Christians have used the crime-punishment model to persecute and harm those in the LGBTQ demographic, this study contends that Cheng is confusing correlation with causation. It may be true that there is some correlation between believing that God will judge and condemn those engaged in or supporting such lifestyles and who wrongly believe they, as "Christians," must be the instrument of divine judgment against such people. However, belief in the divine punishment of sin, biblically understood, cannot cause such persecution. This is because in Scripture, "Vengeance is mine, I will repay says the Lord" (Rom 12:19). Only God gets to punish sin. It is especially critical to recognize that when one belongs to the body of Christ, there is a community covenant in which church discipline can be practiced. To go outside and beyond the congregational covenant and attempt to punish sin, especially with force or violence, usurps God's place as judge. Belief in biblical definitions of sin and in divine judgements on those who sin is no license to take that judgement role into human hands. To so do would be a blasphemous affront to God's sole right to punish sin. By contrast, believers are called to implement the biblical doctrine of grace, which calls us to exemplify to other sinners—for we are sinners too—the same grace we receive from God. Our understanding of grace, however, will be impacted by our understanding of sin and divine accountability. Since queer theologians change the definition of sin, what do they do with grace?

What Is Grace?

Based on his definition of sin as the support of essentialist categories, Cheng redefines grace as God's deliverance from essentialism and the

---

[82] As humans, we cannot self-define in our essential nature. But God has so defined us as to have one area of our being which we can, through conversion and new birth, self-define to a great degree. That area is our individual moral character. We cannot self-define our DNA and heredity, but we can form our own moral character.

traditional Christian sexual morality it purportedly spawns. Thus, grace is seen as the process of liberating oppressed humans from that which would curtail full personal autonomy. In the queer context, this means being set free from essentialist-based norms in gender and sexuality. But is grace a liberation from prescribed norms as asserted by Cheng?

The Bible teaches us that the saving grace of God has appeared to all men, "teaching us to renounce ungodliness and worldly passions to live self-controlled, upright and godly lives in the present age" (Titus 2:11–12). The Bible thus depicts divine grace not as an entity that liberates us from social norms to unleash our "authentic" self-defined selves, but as a power that brings restraint from the practice of natural, sinful desires. Biblical grace sets us free from being slaves of sin to become slaves of righteousness (Rom 6:17–22). It does not enable rebellion against God's government and law.

Speaking of law, one queer theologian makes a unique attempt to redefine one of the Ten Commandments to support sexual liberation under the queer umbrella. For Seventh-day Adventists, it is noteworthy that Nancy Wilson tries to link the Sabbath to the queering of sexual norms. To this we now turn.

Queering Sexuality through the Sabbath

Wilson initially shows some similarity to an Adventist understanding of the Sabbath when she expounds,

> The Sabbath was a gift. It was created so that human beings would not be crazed by work, would not enslave themselves to one another or to work or profit or even to good deeds. It was created so that they would remember that they, as part of creation, were good, and that pleasure, joy, rest, health, relationships, and relaxation were all part of what it means to live happily in union with God.[83]

However, as she progresses in her exposition, she eventually recasts the Sabbath as a symbol for reclaiming traditionally non-normative sexualities marginalization and bringing them into the mainstream.

Wilson begins this process by exploring three ways she believes that the Sabbath was perverted in the Jewish experience. First, "ordinary people gave away their own power and capacity to interpret for themselves the laws and word of God."[84] Over time they delegated the

---

[83] Wilson, 264.

[84] Ibid., 261.

task of interpretation to religious authorities, and so the Sabbath became overregulated, and supervised by "religious police." This led to the second problem: that the Sabbath became a "litmus test" of loyalty and orthodoxy. It became an identity marker to die for instead of being the experience it was meant to be. The Sabbath as an identity marker reveals what, in Wilson's view, is the third problem: that the Sabbath became an instrument of social exclusion that nurtured inequality. The Sabbath, she asserts, became viewed as something only for good, reasonably well off, upstanding Jews. It was no longer meant for the underclasses.[85]

Wilson continues by arguing that Jesus set about to reclaim the meaning of the Sabbath by flaunting His violation of Sabbath laws. The grainfield incident in Matthew 12:1–8 is her primary example of such flaunting. In her view, by directly attacking the Sabbath laws used to uphold exclusionary power structures, Jesus was restoring the Sabbath to its original and true meaning.[86] She concludes the discussion by declaring, "It is through this view of the Sabbath Controversy that I want to begin to make my case for the connection between the Sabbath and sexuality."[87]

Wilson reveals her forthcoming strategy with the ensuing subheading in the chapter: "Sexuality Was Made for Humanity, not Humanity for Sexuality." She attempts to construct a parallel between how the meaning of the Sabbath became corrupted and how God's gift of sexuality has been damaged.

> We have ruined sexuality just like we ruined the Sabbath. We've become obsessed with "doing it right." Which does not mean relating sexually in ways that are mutually pleasurable, fulfilling, healthy, balanced[88]. . . . Religious police have haunted the bedrooms of Christians for two thousand years. . . . Like the Sabbath, sexuality was intended for our mutual joy and pleasure.[89]

---

[85] Wilson., 261–262, 264.

[86] Ibid., 263–266.

[87] Ibid., 266.

[88] This quote appears to have some punctuation and grammatical errors, but seems to be saying that the obsession with "doing it right" focuses on who gets to have sex with whom, who is not allowed to have sex, etc. In Wilson's view, people should be encouraged to relate to one another "sexually in ways that are mutually pleasurable, fulfilling, healthy, balanced," without being confined to specific relational structures such as marriage.

[89] Ibid., 267.

Wilson presents a lengthy excursus in which she cites various examples of what she believes to be an overwrought Christian oppression of sexualities that do not conform to its norms, and its accompanying religious policing. In other words, she is asserting that Christian religious leaders have corrupted sexual norms in a way similar to how the Jewish leadership distorted the Sabbath.

Continuing in this same trajectory, she contends that, as with the Sabbath, Christ would strip away these religious oppressions in order to emancipate sexuality so that it might achieve the mutual pleasure and fulfillment it was originally intended to provide. She clinches her point by declaring, "The Sabbath was made for us, not us for the Sabbath. Sexuality is a gift for us; we were not created to serve an outdated, oppressive, sick sexual ethic. How can we, in the spirit of Jesus, restore and reform sexuality, as he attempted to do with the Sabbath?"[90] In the ensuing nine pages, she outlines the contours of such "reform" by casting a vision that sets aside heteronormativity as being oppressive and creating inequality, while championing the cause of alternative sexualities, especially gay and lesbian. Thus, Wilson gives us an example of how even the Sabbath can be queered to support the elimination of traditional Christian sexual norms.

Evaluation of Wilson's Sabbath-to-Sexuality Position

For the Seventh-day Adventist, Wilson's leveraging of the Sabbath to justify the deregulation of sexuality is both intriguing and concerning. Wilson actually has some good explanations on the meaning of the Sabbath—how it helps break our addiction to work, provides rest, and promotes relationships and connectedness. She may be partially correct in suggesting that some religious leaders have overregulated sex and gender as they overregulated the Sabbath. However, her work with the Sabbath falls short on several fronts.

First, Wilson shows no recognition that there is a divine origin for the Sabbath. She treats it as a communal or social development that evolved over time, eventually becoming controlled and regulated by the religious experts. As such, then, she makes no distinction between what God actually commanded and those Sabbath laws that were human additions. For Wilson, therefore, all Sabbath laws, whether biblical or rabbinic are lumped together without differentiation. Hence, Wilson believes that Jesus was disobeying and subverting all Sabbath regulations, not just the rabbinic elements. She then translates this comprehensive view to sexual morality. For Wilson, then, heteronormative moral

---

90 Wilson, 271.

positions are socially constructed, not divinely commanded, and thus can be challenged as Jesus did with the Sabbath.

It is true that humans have sometimes overregulated divine commands. We cannot correct this error, however, by discarding all the content of the divine commandments. By failing to make a distinction between divine commands and human regulations that interpret the divine commands, Wilson essentially makes both the Sabbath and human sexuality morally meaningless. This is because if these commands are merely created by the community, without divine prescription, then any such norm or rule can be overturned or modified by that same community. If this is the case, however, morality de facto degenerates into a "might makes right" dynamic, and institutions such as the Sabbath become so malleable they lose their moral significance. There can be no moral stability because the "morals" can change rapidly with public opinion or transitions in ruling power. When there is no higher, transcendent moral authority that is external to the community, there can be no moral reform; only moral revolutions. Personal moral conviction is easily marginalized or even persecuted in such a societal structure. Wilson's approach to the Sabbath represents a moral philosophy that endangers moral and social stability.

In contrast to the inherent moral instability engendered by queer theology, biblical morality is grounded in the moral authority of one who transcends and supersedes any societal construct. We believe God has "shown thee O man what is good" (Mic 6:8). Because the "word of the Lord endures forever" (Isa 40:8), divine revelation provides a stable and secure moral foundation to guide our ethical decision making. The divine basis of morality, combined with the doctrine of personal accountability to God in the final judgement, bestows freedom on the individual to morally evaluate and critique social structures without authorization from the community. This is what makes moral reform possible without launching a power-seizing political revolution. Even if a community is morally unstable, the biblical believer—and the biblical church community—can find a sure and stable moral anchor point in Scripture. Wilson's morality is unable to provide this kind of moral stability.

Summary of Queer Theological Themes

This study has explored and analyzed the views of queer theology, tracing some of its key contours in relation to human sexuality. A short review of those main contours is now in order. This study has shown that in queer theology, the Bible is not the inspired Word of God, but rather was written to preserve moral and power structures and is the product of authorial insecurities. The author of Genesis is charged with inventing a God because he needs such a God to give moral authority to cherished beliefs under threat of collapse. Thus, in their view, the Bible can have no universal spiritual or moral authority.

Another key component of queer theology is the rejection of essentialism and the ensuing belief that sex and gender are not essential, objective qualities, but are societal constructs made by those in power to preserve the existing power structures of patriarchy and heteronormativity. Reality itself is viewed as a social construct, without an objective foundation. Thus, whoever gets the most power in society gets to create the societal constructions of right and wrong. Moral good and evil are relativized to who holds power.

Further, queer theology has been shown to significantly alter the doctrine of God. This was seen in both its reinterpretation of the Trinity and in its newly invented Christologies. Part of this reimagining of the divine is the sexualizing of God, within the eternal Triune relationships, and the sexualization of the human Jesus. Both the Trinity and Jesus are cast as homosexual, bisexual, transgendered, transvestites, intersexed, promiscuous, polyamorous, and more. God becomes created in the image of modern man rather than man being an image of who God is. Additionally, it was noted that queer theology redefines sin as holding onto essentialist beliefs that marginalize others. Sin is no longer defined by the Ten Commandments or other divine laws, but simply by our lack of inclusiveness rooted in clinging to essentialist views of gender and sexuality.

Finally, this study observed Wilson's attempt to use Jesus' challenges to Jewish Sabbath laws enforced by "religious police" as a parallel to challenging heteronormative policing by society and the church. Thus, in her view, Jesus sets for us an example of overturning repressive laws, which can inspire us today to do likewise.

Summary of Critiques and Responses to Queer Theology

In response to these views, this study showed how queer theology undermines any traditional understanding of biblical authority. By relocating divine revelation from the Bible to the incarnation of Christ, it becomes possible to place Christ in opposition to the Bible. Additionally, moral authority is relocated from Scripture to coalitions or individuals who hold political or religious power. The resulting moral relativism undermines social and moral stability, for morality becomes a matter of political might: whoever gets power can force their morality on others, but if a new political movement takes the reins of power, morality may undergo severe changes.

This study also argued that queer theology undermines God's role as sovereign ruler, Judge, and Creator. Only God can self-define in the fully autonomous sense. We further revealed how queer theology creates paganized views of the biblical God by sexualizing God for the purpose of legitimizing sexualities that do not conform to standard Christian norms. This study charged that queer theologians are effectively creating idols—carved not from wood or stone, but crafted from human ideas. Thus, they manufacture versions of God crafted in the image of sinful humans, instead of seeking to bring humans back into the image of a holy God.

We examined how queer theologians redefine sin, and we argued that only God can define sin, for the right to define sin makes one the highest moral authority. In Scripture, God defines sin through revelation, especially the Ten Commandments. In the Bible, sin does have a criminal-legal dimension, a view which queer theologians reject as valid. By defining sin as advocacy of essentialism, rejection of essentialism becomes the new norm. But this is problematic in relation to the Bible. The Bible depicts God as creating Adam and Eve as male and female. Neither Adam or Eve had the power to self-define by changing their sex. Creatures are not capable of full self-definition, and thus are not entirely autonomous. By contrast, queer theology consistently depicts humans as fully autonomous, self-defining creatures.

We explored how queer theology redefines grace so that it enables liberation from and opposition to norms and rules. The trait of systematic opposition to established norms seems highly similar to Paul's depiction of the nature of sin in Romans 7. It also stands in sharp contrast with Paul's depiction of grace to Titus, in which God's grace is a moral restraint against immorality and ungodliness, not a liberation from social and moral norms.

Finally, we contested Wilson's use of the Sabbath to promote a sexual revolution. Wilson fails to distinguish between the divinely prescribed aspects of Sabbath observance, and the human additions created by the rabbis. In so doing, she creates a logically illegitimate analogy to suggest that as Christ overthrew Sabbath norms, we are to overthrow sexual norms. What are we to make of this as biblical Christians?

Conclusion

It seems safe to conclude that the worldview expressed in queer theory, and by the queer theologians who apply it, is fundamentally at odds with the biblical worldview. Its view of human nature, moral evil and good, and the plasticity of Deity seem utterly at odds with biblical norms and thinking. The ability of queer theology to leverage any biblical doctrine or church teaching into excessively inventive interpretations belies a deeper issue—namely, the ability of a sinful human to find any way possible to justify any and all desires of the sinful heart. The queer theological universe is a place of moral anarchy where anything can be justified, dissolving the moral stability of the Bible into nothingness. In addition, the revisions of the doctrines of the Trinity and of Christ can rightly be called heretical. Human theologians recreate God into the image of sinful man instead of sinful man being reclaimed into the image of God. In short, queer theology undermines the essentials of biblical faith as we know it. In spite of this fundamental disagreement with sound biblical exposition and Christian tradition, might it be possible that encountering queer theology provides limited opportunities for the biblical Christian to engage in useful reflection which is rooted in Scripture, without endangering one's faith?

One possible area for useful reflection can come from the claim leveled by queer theology that a traditional Christian view of sexual morality and the meaning of gender are tools for exercising oppressive power. In certain cases, it is possible that overzealous Christians may have defined gender roles more rigidly that what is found in the scope of Scripture. Thus, queer theology may unwittingly help biblical Christians perceive how they may be negatively influenced by the contemporary sinful cultures in which they reside. The church should beware of usurping the Creator's role in defining His creatures by creating definitions that go beyond the scope of Scripture. While disagreeing with the positions advocated by queer theologians, it is possible that well-intentioned Christians may make the same kind of mistake as that made by advocates of queer theology—elevating our own definitions of God and of ourselves to an authoritative position above God's definitions as found in Scripture. In the end, both the biblical church and queer theologians need to avoid encroaching upon the Creator's right to define Himself and to define His creatures. Queer theology openly rejects Creator-based definitions and replaces them with human self-definition. As believers in the Genesis creation, the Seventh-day Adventist believer should surrender in faith to the Creator's definitions of who they are, and to His designs for human life.

In reflecting biblically on queer theology, one may come to a sobering conclusion that queer theology unabashedly and openly demonstrates the logical consequences and trajectory that result when biblical authority is abandoned in favor of advocating human autonomy to define one's self and one's morality. As such, it reminds us that ideas have consequences, and that accepting a non-biblical idea or set of ideas —a worldview—will, sooner or later, lead to the subversion of biblical truth and morality. The great controversy involves an attack on God's government by subverting the truth about who God is. In the paganistic sexualizing of God in queer theology, there seems to be a broad and systematic undermining of who God is. Biblically committed Christians should reflect with care and prudence on such contemporary views so as to clearly discern the spiritual and moral consequences of the ideas we encounter in engaging the world around us.

CHAPTER 16

Homosexuality and Scripture

Ekkehardt Mueller

Homosexual behavior is often discussed in the media. While some countries have laws requiring the population to accept homosexual partnerships and the adoption of children by homosexual couples—even prohibiting public questioning of homosexual practices and imposing non-discriminatory hiring—other governments persecute homosexuals. This political-cultural situation influences the position of church members on the issue of homosexuality and challenges Christian churches and other faith communities which take a biblical approach to the issue. In the meantime, the public acceptance of a homosexual lifestyle has opened the door to other alternative sexual lifestyles such as incest, polygamy, etc. Although the topic of homosexuality can be addressed from several perspectives, this study deals with some important biblical passages relevant to the topic and draws implications for the church. But first, this study will define the concept of homosexuality and note the diversity of interpretations of the biblical data.

Defining Homosexuality

Homosexuality has been understood differently and may include different phenomena. E. A. Malloy suggests understanding the homosexual as a "person, male or female, who experiences in adult life a steady and nearly exclusive erotic attraction to members of the same sex, and who is indifferent to sexual relations with the opposite sex."[1] In his opinion, certain persons are not true homosexuals even if they are involved in homosexual acts—namely, teenagers, adults who are bored with heterosexuality and get involved with members of the same sex—also called "contingent homosexuals," and so-called "situational homosexuals" who

[1] E. A. Malloy, *Homosexuality and the Christian Way of Life* (Lanham, MD: University Press of America, 1981), 11.

for the lack of heterosexual encounters "resort to homosexual outlets."[2] Malloy's definition fits "constitutional homosexuals" or "inverts," whose homosexuality is said to be permanent.

On the other hand, it has been suggested that different people are found in different places between the two poles of heterosexuality and homosexuality.[3] Some are closer to heterosexuality with some homosexual tendencies, while others are almost exclusively found close to one pole or the other.

J. W. Paris, an anthropologist notes, "Like heterosexuality, homosexuality is an idea that has a history. It may be quickly becoming history insofar as *homosexual* has been replaced by more specific terms such as lesbian, *gay* and *bisexual*."[4] She prefers to speak about "age-structured same-sex relationships," "gender-structured same-sex relationships," "profession-based same-sex relationships," and "egalitarian same-sex relationships,"[5] but also seems to be content with acronyms such as LGBT, LGTBQ, and even longer versions that are preferred in many circles.[6]

> Increasingly, people are refusing to pick sexual identity categories for themselves. Psychologist Lisa M. Diamond interviewed a number of same-sex-attracted women every few years for ten years, and in that time, more than two-thirds of the women in her study had changed their identity labels at least once, some more than once. Though all had some degree of same-sex attraction, some women shifted from calling themselves lesbian to calling themselves heterosexual. . . . Others shifted from bisexual to lesbian, from lesbian to bisexual, or from lesbian, bisexual or heterosexual to unlabeled.[7]

Already in 1987 P. Caplan made an interesting comment: "What people want, and what they do, in any society, is to a large extent what

---

[2] Ronald M. Springett, *Homosexuality in History and the Scriptures* (Silver Spring, MD: Biblical Research Institute of the General Conference, 1988), 2.

[3] A. C. Kinsey, W. B. Pomeroy, and E. E. Martin, *Sexual Behavior in the Human Male* (Philadelphia, PA: W. B. Saunders, 1965), 650–651. See Springett, 26–27.

[4] Jenell Williams Paris, *The End of Sexual Identity: Why Sex Is Too Important to Define Who We Are* (Downers Grove, IL: IVP Academic, 2011), 57. On page 63 she declares that homosexuality is "a social label and role based on a same-sex-oriented sexual identity."

[5] Ibid., 64–69.

[6] Ibid., 72.

[7] Ibid., 73.

they are made to want, and allowed to do. Sexuality . . . cannot escape its cultural connection."[8]

Homosexual acts can find expression in pederasty, rape, violence, prostitution, and promiscuity, to name some, or in a life committed to one partner of the same sex. This chapter uses the term "homosexuality" to describe same-sex attraction and same-sex activity. However, it focuses on activity, acknowledging that a difference should be made between homosexual orientation/attraction and homosexual actions/lifestyle.

Homosexuality in History

Various forms of homosexual behavior were known and present in most, if not all, cultures of the ancient Near East.[9] Such practices were not always exploitative and violent. Nevertheless, many cultures were ambivalent regarding various forms of homosexual behavior. While it may have been tolerated under certain circumstances—for instance, in the cult—it was not the norm in everyday life and was not necessarily accepted by the vast majority of the population who upheld the value of heterosexual marriage and family relationships in which children played an important role.

While family relations were treasured in Egypt, pederasty seems to have occurred too. Homosexual relations may not have been "considered wrong as long as they were based on mutual consent."[10] On the other hand, in the *Book of the Dead* a deceased man who "appears before the judge in the next world" says, "I have not had sexual relations with a boy. I have not defiled myself. . . . I have not been perverted."[11]

The situation may have been similar in Mesopotamia. The goddess Ishtar/Inanna, as the deity of love and war, was an ambiguous figure, sometimes acting like a female and sometimes like a male. She "was worshiped as a lovely maiden but also as a bearded warrior."[12] A Sumerian hymn claims that Ishtar had the power to turn men into women and

---

[8] Pat Caplan, "Introduction," in *The Cultural Construction of Sexuality*, ed. Pat Caplan (London: Routledge, 1987), 25.

[9] For a longer treatment, see Ekkehardt Mueller, "Homosexuality in History," https://adventistbiblicalresearch.org/wp-content/uploads/Homosexuality-in-History-1.pdf (accessed February 22, 2021).

[10] Donald J. Wold, *Out of Order: Homosexuality in the Bible and the Ancient Near East* (Grand Rapids, MI: Baker Books, 1998), 59.

[11] Ibid., 57–58.

[12] Saana Teppo, "Sacred Marriage and the Devotees of Ištar," in *Sacred Marriages: The Divine-Human Sexual Metaphor from Sumer to Early Christianity*, ed. Marti Nissinen and Risto Uro (Winona Lake, IN: Eisenbrauns, 2008), 76.

women into men.[13] No wonder her devotees, the *assinnus*, the *kurgarrûs*, and the *kulu'us* or galas exhibited the same pattern. "It seems that all three groups of cultic functionaries were born as men (or hermaphrodites), but . . . their appearance was either totally feminine, or they had both male and female characteristics."[14] ". . . it seems possible that the devotees sometimes participated in same-sex relations."[15] However, these practices related to the cult and may not reflect accurately what was commonly happening.

Homosexuality was prevalent in Greek society, undoubtedly due "to the narcissistic character of Greek life and the influence of its religion. The gods practiced it (e.g., Zeus with Ganymede, Heracles with Iolaus or Hylas, and Apollo with Hyacinth), so people were justified to pursue it."[16] Widely prevalent was pederasty, but homosexuality was not limited to it. "Greek homosexuality was diverse: pederasty, adult male and female, and male prostitution. It was characterized by mutuality and permanency, as well as rape and infidelity. . . . Homosexuality became institutionalized in the military, in education, in the home, and in laws."[17]

The Romans received widespread homosexuality from the Greeks but "fashioned several law codes over several centuries to legislate homosexuality in various ways."[18]

The approach taken toward homosexuality was different with Israel. The Old Testament has not only clear prohibitions against homosexuality (Lev 18:22; 20:13), but also relates instances in which homosexuality occurred. However, such occurrences are treated negatively. Homosexuality is an abomination and will be punished. The Old Testament Apocrypha and Pseudepigrapha are opposed to homosexuality, as are the Mishnah and Talmud. *Mishnah Sanhedrin* 8:7 "places homosexuality with the clearly universal crimes of murder and adultery and not with the 'ritualistic' offenses."[19]

Following the unique biblical position, Jewish and Christian societies rejected any type of homosexual activity for centuries and even

---

[13] Teppo, 85.

[14] Ibid., 77.

[15] Ibid., 81. Kathleen McCaffrey, "Reconsidering Gender Ambiguity in Mesopotamia: Is a Beard Just a Beard?" in *Sex and Gender in the Ancient Near East: Proceedings of the 47th Rencontre Assyriologique Internationale*, ed. Simo Parpola and Robert Whiting (Helsinki: Neo-Assyrian Text Corpus Project, 2002), 379–391, argues that these males who took on a female role should be considered a third gender in their society.

[16] James B. De Young, *Homosexuality: Contemporary Claims Examined in the Light of the Bible and Other Ancient Literature and Law* (Grand Rapids, MI: Kregel, 2000), 252.

[17] De Young, 252–253.

[18] Cf. ibid., 257.

[19] Ibid., 246.

millennia. Only recently some churches, following the approach of various cultures and secular governments, have made provisions for a homosexual lifestyle of their members, while others respect homosexuals as persons of equal value and as people who need to be protected against violence without, however, advocating or condoning their lifestyle.

The Diversity of Interpretations of the Biblical Data

Homosexuality is mentioned in the Bible. But interpreting the Bible depends on presuppositions. The way people view Scripture, culture, science, tradition, and the human being will influence their approach to interpreting the Bible.[20]

For instance, contemporary historicism—not to be confused with the historicist interpretation of apocalyptic prophecy—stresses that there is no absolute or timeless truth, that there is no divine revelation, and that revisions and reformulations of older beliefs are necessary to fit the prevalent culture. Theology is understood merely as a cultural analysis and critique investigating the evolution of religion.[21]

Among various views it is held that "biblical pronouncements on homosexuality [are] incomplete and even erroneous"[22] and that Scripture does not address the position of monogamous, permanent same-sex relationships.[23] It is also argued that the "Christological principle" is in

---

[20] See the excellent discussion in Michael Lefebvre, ed., *The Gospel and Sexual Orientation: A Testimony of the Reformed Presbyterian Church of North America* (Pittsburgh, PA: Crown and Covenant, 2012), 29–35.

[21] See Sheila Greeve Davaney, *Historicism: The Once and Future Challenge for Theology*, Guides to Theological Inquiry (Minneapolis, MN: Fortress Press, 2006), 160–164. Walter Wink, "Homosexuality and the Bible," in *Homosexuality and Christian Faith: Questions of Conscience for the Churches,* ed. Walter Wink (Minneapolis, MN: Fortress Press, 1999), 47, holds, "Where the Bible mentions homosexual behavior at all, it clearly condemns it. I freely grant that. The issue is precisely whether that biblical judgment is correct." Daniel A. Helminiak, *What the Bible Really Says About Homosexuality* (Estancia, NM: Alamo Square Press, 2000), devotes an entire chapter to the issue of how to interpret Scripture (29–41), opts for the historical-critical method, and concludes, "The Bible does not condemn gay sex as we understand it today" (131).

[22] De Young, 10–11, lists a number of views held in favor of a homosexual lifestyle. See also Springett, 49–51. Marion L. Soards, *Scripture and Homosexuality: Biblical Authority and the Church Today* (Louisville, KY: Westminster John Knox, 1995), 55, cautions, "Our cultural perspective is not inherently superior to the worldview(s) and attitude(s) of biblical culture(s)." Phyllis A. Bird, "The Bible in Christian Ethical Deliberation Concerning Homosexuality: Old Testament Contributions," in *Homosexuality, Science, and the Plain Sense of Scripture,* ed. David L. Balch (Grand Rapids, MI: Eerdmans, 2000), 144–145, calls the Bible "pluriform and multivocal" as well as "incomplete and biased."

[23] See Springett, 50; Vincent J. Genovesi, *In Pursuit of Love: Catholic Morality and Human Sexuality,* 2nd ed. (Collegeville, MN: Liturgical Press, 1996), 277, 296. Ellen F. Davis, "Reasoning with Scripture," *Anglican Theological Review* 90, no. 3 (2008): 518. Jack Rogers, *Jesus, the*

conflict with certain biblical statements and[24] the "concept of moral logic"[25] underlying biblical teachings should be utilized. According to the same logic, the church or the individual moved by the Holy Spirit can accept or reject divine laws,[26] and that "the primary question before us today is not whether a sexual deed is right or wrong, but whether the relationship of which it is a part is right or wrong."[27] D. O. Via maintains, "I have tried to show that if we look at a number of biblical themes in the light of contemporary knowledge and experience, we can justifiably override the unconditional biblical condemnations of homosexual practice."[28] Furthermore, it is assumed that the sexual drive in humans must be lived out and cannot be controlled.[29] Therefore, there is no

---

Bible, and Homosexuality: Explode the Myths, Heal the Church (Louisville, KY: Westminster John Knox, 2009), 89, talks about "the wonder . . . that so many lesbian and gay people have formed long-term monogamous partnerships."

[24] Cf. Rogers, 15, 53–55. He notes that the Bible contains eight texts dealing with the topic of homosexuality, "Together they cover a maximum of twelve pages in the Bible. None of these texts is about Jesus, nor do they include any of his words" (ibid., 66). See also Wink, "Homosexuality and the Bible," 47–48. William Sloane Coffin, "Liberty to the Captives and Good Tidings to the Afflicted," in Wink, *Homosexuality and Christian Faith*, 107, points out, "Not everything biblical is Christlike."

[25] James V. Brownson, Bible, *Gender, Sexuality: Reframing the Church's Debate on Same-Sex Relationships* (Grand Rapids, MI: Eerdmans, 2013), 259, writes, "When interpreting scriptural commands or prohibitions, we must ask not only what is commanded or prohibited but *why*. The reason for asking why emerges when we attempt to apply the commands and prohibitions of Scripture in new and diverse contexts." "One must read biblical commandments and prohibitions in terms of their underlying forms of moral logic."

[26] Cf. Soards, 17; Wink, "Homosexuality and the Bible," 42–44; James A. Forbes Jr., "More Light from the Spirit on Sexuality," in Wink, *Homosexuality and Christian Faith*, 6–8; Ken Sehested, "Biblical Fidelity and Sexual Orientation: Why the First Matters, Why the Second Doesn't," in Wink, *Homosexuality and Christian Faith,* 59; and Richard Rohr, "Where the Gospel Leads Us," in Wink, *Homosexuality and Christian Faith,* 85–88.

[27] David R. Larson, "Christian Sexual Norms Today: Some Proposals," in *Christianity and Homosexuality: Some Seventh-day Adventist Perspectives*, ed. David Ferguson, Fritz Guy, and David R. Larson (Roseville, CA: Adventist Forum, 2008), part 5:6, 8.

[28] Dan O. Via and Robert A. J. Gagnon, *Homosexuality and the Bible: Two Views* (Minneapolis, MN: Fortress Press, 2003), 38. Benjamin Sargent, "The Ghosts of the Past: Hermeneutical Reflections on Historical Criticism Within a Shared Conversation on Human Sexuality," *The Expository Times* 128, no. 2 (2016a): 75–76, mentions that Loveday Alexander "similarly agrees that the biblical texts discussed in this debate condemn homosexual sex when understood within their historical and linguistic contexts. However, Alexander highlights the historical distanciation of the ancient text from the contemporary reader: that the scriptural texts cannot speak directly to a context and society which has undergone a revolution in its understanding of human sexuality."

[29] Springett, 25, stresses that human sexuality is different from "the instinctive reflexive mating of animals," meaning "that human beings can control and are, therefore, responsible for their sexual expression." They have a choice. Sherwood O. Cole, "Biology, Homosexuality, and the Biblical

problem with premarital sexual relations,[30] divorce and remarriage,[31] adultery, and polygamy.[32] In addition, it is held that the "virulent biblical abhorrence to incest . . . and its explicit horror of homosexuality"[33] is shocking. Representatives of a theistic evolutionary approach claim that God has "created" homosexuals as such and that homosexuality is a gift of God, not a consequence of the general fallenness of humanity.[34]

On the other hand, the Adventist Church accepts the self-testimony of Scripture and regards the Bible as reliable revelation of God's will. Although written by human beings, it is not only the word of humans, but also the Word of God. Principles of interpretation have to be derived from Scripture and should not be forced upon it. Deductions from the fields of philosophy, psychology, and sociology that contradict Scripture have to be rejected. In addition, tradition and natural sciences should not be allowed to determine matters of faith.[35]

It is generally acknowledged that the real issue in the homosexuality debate is the nature, authority, and interpretation of Scripture.[36] W. Wink correctly states, "The real issue here, then, is not simply homosexuality, but how Scripture informs our lives today."[37] And M. L. Soards reminds us that "the decision one makes about the validity of homosexual behavior for members of the Christian community is effectively a decision about the authority of the Bible in the life of the church."[38] R. M. Davidson argues that at stake are the authority of Scripture and "*the sola scriptura principle*," "*the tota scriptura principle*," "the unity and harmony of Scripture," plus biblical doctrines such as the doctrine of creation,

---

Doctrine of Sin," *Bibliotheca Sacra* 157 (July–September 200): 360, notes, "Any attempt to reduce people to genetic or biological entities distorts human identity from a biblical perspective."

[30] Cf. Larson, part 5:13, who states, "The guideline of 'nothing before' and 'everything after' is neither realistic nor wise. . . . We should not ask whether to allow loving heterosexual and homosexual unions to exist; they already do. . . . We should do everything we can to sustain them and to support people who are in them. . . . We should also find ways to honor them in appropriate Christian ceremonies."

[31] Rogers, 43–44.

[32] Ibid., 82 and Richard Treloar, "'Come Out and Stay Out!' Hermeneutics, Homosexuality, and Schism in Anglicanism," *Anglican Theological Review* 90, no. 1 (2008): 50.

[33] Treloar, 51, referring to Regina Schwartz, *The Curse of Cain: The Violent Legacy of Monotheism* (Chicago, IL: University of Chicago Press, 1997), 107.

[34] Rogers, 81.

[35] Also, Scripture is its own interpreter. There is agreement, harmony, and clarity in Scripture. Clear texts may shed light on difficult texts. The Holy Spirit is needed in the process of interpretation, but the Holy Spirit does not simply override previous revelations.

[36] Cf. Rogers, 1–65; Helminiak, 29–41; Soards, 1–14; and Via and Gagnon, 2.

[37] Wink, "Homosexuality and the Bible," 33.

[38] Soards, 73.

biblical anthropology, "the theology of marriage and family," the doctrines of the fall and of sin, ecclesiology, "the gospel in the setting of the three angels' messages of Revelation 14," and "the great controversy worldview and the character of God."[39]

This paper tries to interpret the biblical texts in the light of an understanding of Scripture as the authoritative Word of God written by human authors but communicated through the processes of divine revelation and inspiration.

Homosexuality in Scripture

Homosexuality in the Old Testament[40]

The Old Testament contains several texts that refer to homosexuality directly. Indirect references are also found.[41] Among the direct references to homosexuality, two or three passages occur in legal material, whereas the others are found in narratives/historical accounts.

Israel did not live in isolation, but was surrounded by other nations, some of which were mentioned previously. These nations were idolatrous and practiced fertility cults in which sacred prostitution played an important role. This involved promiscuity, homosexuality between consenting partners, transvestite behavior, bestiality, and incest.[42] However, the Old Testament challenged all these practices.

Old Testament Narratives

Genesis 1–2

> God created man in His own image, in the image of God He created him; male and female He created them (Gen 1:27).[43]
> The man said, "This is now bone of my bones and flesh of my flesh. She shall be called woman, because she was taken out of Man."

---

[39] Richard M. Davidson, "Homosexuality and the Bible: What Is at Stake in the Current Debate," in *Homosexuality, Marriage, and the Church: Biblical, Counseling, and Religious Liberty Issues*, ed. Roy E. Gane, Nicholas P. Miller, and H. Peter Swanson (Berrien Springs, MI: Andrews University Press, 2012), 187–208.

[40] See Richard M. Davidson, "Homosexuality in the Old Testament," in *Homosexuality, Marriage, and the Church: Biblical, Counseling, and Religious Liberty Issues*, ed. Roy E. Gane, Nicholas P. Miller, and H. Peter Swanson (Berrien Springs, MI: Andrews University Press, 2012), 5–52.

[41] Cf. Springett, 69–88.

[42] See, e.g., Richard M. Davidson, *Flame of Yahweh: Sexuality in the Old Testament* (Peabody, MA: Hendrickson, 2007), 134–142; Robert A. J. Gagnon, *The Bible and Homosexual Practice: Texts and Hermeneutics* (Nashville, TN: Abingdon Press, 2001), 44–56; Springett, 33–48; Wold, 43–61; and William J. Webb, *Slaves, Women & Homosexuals: Exploring the Hermeneutics of Cultural Analysis* (Downers Grove, IL: InterVarsity, 2001), 81.

[43] All biblical quotations are from the NASB.

> For this reason a man shall leave his father and his mother, and be joined to his wife; and they shall become one flesh (Gen 2:23).

Although the creation account (Gen 1–2) does not talk about homo-sexuality, it sets the standard for sexual relationships. God created the first male and the first female, Adam and Eve, and joined them in marriage. Obviously, the creation account points not only to the beginning of marriage, but also portrays the ideal for sexual relations among humans.

Authors supporting homosexual partnerships suggest that the male-female combination was chosen because the multiplication of the human race was divinely commanded (Gen 1:28) and was necessary in the beginning. Yet, because the situation has changed and overpopulation is rampant, it is claimed that homosexual partnerships are even more in tune with the needs of the world today than are heterosexual relationships,[44] and therefore, supposedly, Genesis 1 and 2 cannot be used to proscribe only one form of human sexuality.

The problem with this argument is that heterosexual relationships are reduced to the function of procreation only. This is not what Genesis 1 and 2 portray. Man and woman are created in the image of God. It seems likely that the image of God has to do with humanity being God's representative on earth as well as standing in an intimate relationship with God. In addition, Genesis 5:1–3 may also suggest that the image of God included a resemblance of human faculties and the entire human being with the Lord of the universe. This image of God is found in both genders who are blessed (Gen 5:2), and is expressed in different kinds of relationships—not only procreation. R. M. Springett states, "Mankind as male and female are not created simply for the purpose of procreation. Procreative ability is carefully removed from God's image and shifted to a special word of blessing."[45]

The creation account is also interested in the concept of complementation. When Adam noticed his lack of a companion, God created for him the woman "suitable to him." Adam and Eve complemented each other. This complementation is holistic because God is holistic. Its expression is found in heterosexual marriage.

Jesus affirmed the creation account and the permanence of marriage, thus understanding Genesis 1 and 2 not only as a historical account but also as a text which is normative for humanity at all times, disapproving all homosexual relationships (Matt 19:4–8; Mark 10:2–12). Genesis 1

---

[44] Wink, "Homosexuality and the Bible," 4, suggests, "In an age of overpopulation, perhaps same sex-orientation is especially sound ecologically!"

[45] Springett, 53.

and 2 remain the foundational text to describe divinely ordained human sexual relationships.

Genesis 19 and Judges 19

> Before they lay down, the men of the city, the men of Sodom, surrounded the house, both young and old, all the people from every quarter; and they called to Lot and said to him, "Where are the men who came to you tonight? Bring them out to us that we may have relations with them [know them]" (Gen 19:4–5).

> While they were celebrating, behold, the men of the city, certain worthless fellows, surrounded the house, pounding the door; and they spoke to the owner of the house, the old man, saying, "Bring out the man who came into your house that we may have relations with him [know him]" (Judg 19:22).

While narratives that deal with homosexuality, such as the Sodom narrative (Gen 19:4–10) and the outrage in Gibeah (Judg 19:22–25), are sometimes interpreted in such a way as to avoid homosexual connotations, homosexuality is read into other passages such as the stories of Ham's sin (Gen 9:20–25),[46] the friendship of David and Jonathan (1 Sam 18, 20; 2 Sam 1), and the mother-in-law/daughter-in-law relationship between Ruth and Naomi (Ruth 1).

It has been suggested that the story dealing with Sodom is about a lack of hospitality[47] rather than homosexuality, and that the phrase "to know them" means "to get acquainted with them" rather than "to have coitus with them." However, "to have relations with them" is the meaning required by the passage (cf. Gen 4:1, 17, 25)—especially verse 8, where "to know" occurs and refers to having sexual relations,—the context of Genesis with the various sexual problems, and the intertextual connections with Judges 19 and Ezekiel 16.[48] This is also recognized by various translations.[49]

While it is true that the inhabitants of Sodom were charged with many sins, not only homosexual practice, and that the city was destroyed because of these many and grievous sins, homosexuality was one of those sins. The issue emerges in the New Testament again, and "the authors of Jude and 2 Peter undoubtedly understood a key offense of Sodom

---

[46] For a discussion of this incident, see Davidson, *Flame of Yahweh*, 142–145; and Wold, 65–76.

[47] See Rogers, 67; and Helminiak, 43–50.

[48] Wold, 89.

[49] See NASB, NIV, NJB, NKJV.

to be men desiring to have sex with males."[50] Today a number of practicing homosexuals admit that the problem with Sodom and Gibeah was a violent type of homosexual gang. But they would claim that true "covenant" homosexuality is legitimate.[51]

Alleged Homosexual Relationships

> But Ruth said, "Do not urge me to leave you or turn back from following you; for where you go, I will go, and where you lodge, I will lodge. Your people shall be my people, and your God, my God. Where you die, I will die, and there I will be buried. Thus may the LORD do to me, and worse, if anything but death parts you and me" (Ruth 1:16).

> Now it came about when he had finished speaking to Saul, that the soul of Jonathan was knit to the soul of David, and Jonathan loved him as himself. . . . Then Jonathan made a covenant with David because he loved him as himself. Jonathan stripped himself of the robe that was on him and gave it to David, with his armor, including his sword and his bow and his belt (1 Sam 18:1, 3–4).

> I am distressed for you, my brother Jonathan; you have been very pleasant to me. Your love to me was more wonderful than the love of women (2 Sam 1:26).

To interpret David's relation to Jonathan or Ruth's relation to her mother-in-law as a beautiful expression of homosexuality is far-fetched.[52] Men embracing and kissing each other and holding hands is common even today in the Near East. This has nothing to do with homosexuality.

> In this context it is not out of place to suggest that the word love has political rather than sexual overtones. The transfer of clothes from Jonathan to David has royal overtones suggesting a legal

[50] Via and Gagnon, 59.

[51] For a more detailed discussion of both passages, see Davidson, *Flame of Yahweh*, 145–149, 161–162; James R. White and Jeffrey D. Niell, *The Same Sex Controversy* (Minneapolis, MN: Bethany House, 2002), 40–51; and Andreas J. Köstenberger, *God, Marriage, and Family: Rebuilding the Biblical Foundation* (Wheaton, IL: Crossway Books, 2004), 204–208. Davidson, *Flame of Yahweh*, 149, concludes his passage on Sodom by saying "that the opprobrium attached to the Sodomites' intended activity involved not only rape but the inherent degradation of same-sex intercourse is confirmed by the intertextual linkages between Ezekiel and the sexual 'abominations' mentioned in Levitical legislation."

[52] See Davidson, *Flame of Yahweh*, 164–167.

> symbolism relegating the privilege of succession willingly to David. In this setting Jonathan moves beyond personal feelings of a friendly disposition and makes a solemn "covenant."[53]

Scholars are aware that arguments from silence may be extremely weak and should be used in exceptional cases only. Nevertheless, F. Guy not only speculates about physical intimacy between David and Jonathan, but also about the Roman military officer who asked Jesus to heal his boy, suggesting that the boy was a valuable slave and his sexual partner, and about the Ethiopian eunuch as a potential homosexual.[54] He adds, "These possible instance are, of course, highly conjectural. . . None of the stories contains an explicit recognition, much less an endorsement, of same sex love."[55] But then he asserts that "statistically it is highly probable that some of the figures in the scriptural narratives were participants in same-sex erotic relationships."[56] Even if that were true, such an approach tends to read homosexuality into texts that do not provide the slightest hint for it.[57]

The Mosaic Laws
Leviticus 18 and 20

> You shall not lie with a male as one lies with a female; it is an abomination (Lev 18:22).

> If there is a man who lies with a male as those who lie with a woman, both of them have committed a detestable act; they shall surely be put to death. Their blood-guiltiness is upon them (Lev 20:13).

Leviticus contains these two texts that clearly deal with homosexuality. Leviticus 20:13 goes further than Leviticus 18:22 by warning against the penalty of homosexual activities.

---

[53] Springett, 73. This is supported by Webb, 102. Susannah Cornwall, *Theology and Sexuality*, SCM Core Texts (Norwich: SCM Press, 2013), 129–131, has a section called "Gay-Friendly Texts?" in which she first is careful not to read too much into the texts and then seems to claim them at least partially for the lesbian and gay community.

[54] Fritz Guy, "Same-Sex Love: Theological Considerations," in *Christianity and Homosexuality: Some Seventh-day Adventist Perspectives*, ed. David Ferguson, Fritz Guy, and David R. Larson (Roseville, CA: Adventist Forum, 2008), part 4:52–53.

[55] Ibid., part 4:54.

[56] Ibid.

[57] Davidson, *Flame of Yahweh*, 165, speaks about speculation.

Suggested Interpretations. It has been suggested that "the Old Testament limits the prohibitions against same-gender sexual behavior in Leviticus 18 and 20 to the ritual or cult of Israel. . . . These passages have no impact on the New Testament/Christian moral code."[58] J. Rogers talks about "culturally conditioned law" and claims that "when these texts in Leviticus are taken out of their historical and cultural context and applied to faithful, God-worshiping Christians who are homosexual, it does violence to them."[59] Another author asserts that "the single text in the Hebrew Scriptures that talks about homogenitality forbids it—but precisely because it is 'unclean,' not because it is wrong in itself. The Christian Scriptures insist that cleanness and uncleanness do not matter."[60]

The Context. The book of Leviticus seems to consist of three major parts that can be further subdivided. The first part instructs God's people on how to approach the presence of God in the sanctuary: by being cleansed from sin—that is, justified (Lev 1–15). The center of the book is the Day of Atonement (Lev 16), pointing to the final and complete solution of the sin problem. The rest of Leviticus teaches believers how to live in the presence of God (Lev 17–27). This third part, especially chapters 18–20, deals with holiness.[61] It is in this part that texts on homosexual behavior are found.

So it is true that in the immediate and larger context, terms referring to purity and holiness as well as idolatry occur. Still, the question must be asked as to whether or not these references limit the warning against homosexuality to specific situations. We do not think so.

Although these texts are found in the context of holiness and purity, they have a moral quality, as seen, for example, by their usage in the New Testament. W. Kaiser states, "There is a category of temporary ceremonial laws, but I do not agree that homosexuality is among them. Nothing in its proscription points to or anticipates Christ, and the death penalty demanded for its violation places it in the moral realm and

---

[58] De Young, 10.

[59] Rogers, 69. In the context of Leviticus 18 and 20 and the discussion on homosexuality, Helminiak, 66–67, calls people to break away from conventions and taboos because they are "unreasonable and oppressive."

[60] Helminiak, 72.

[61] While outlines of the book vary, there is much agreement on the general structure and subdivisions of the text. Cf. John E. Hartley, *Leviticus*, vol. 4, Word Biblical Commentary (Dallas, TX: Word, 1998), xxxiv; Eugene H. Merrill, "The Pentateuch," in *Holman Concise Bible Commentary*, ed. David S. Dockery (Nashville, TN: Broadman and Holman, 1998), 38; Francis D. Nichol, ed., *The Seventh-Day Adventist Bible Commentary*, vol. 1 (Hagerstown, MD: Review and Herald Publishing Association, 1978), 696–697; Mark F. Rooker, *Leviticus*, vol. 3A, The New American Commentary (Nashville, TN: Broadman and Holman, 2000), 79; and Gordon J. Wenham, *The Book of Leviticus*, The New International Commentary on the Old Testament (Grand Rapids, MI: Eerdmans, 1979), 3–4.

not in temporary legislation."[62] R. E. Gane shows that there is a difference between ritual impurity, which can be done away with by ritual purification, and moral impurity, which is not remediable.

> The impurity of homosexual practice was not ceremonial, but moral... The laws of Leviticus 18 and 20 are not like circumcision, the temporary ethnic covenant marker. This is confirmed by the fact that in Acts 15, which releases Gentile Christians from circumcision, the "Holiness Code" prohibitions against meat offered to idols, sexual immorality (*porneia;* not only adultery), and meat from which the blood is not drained at the time of slaughter (vol. 20, 29; compare Lev 17–20) remain in force for Gentiles.[63]

"Any attempt to draw hard distinctions between sin and impurity is doomed to failure. Indeed, one of the hallmarks of the Holiness Code is that it incorporates ethics under the rubric of purity; that is, sin and impurity merge"[64] (Lev 18:24–30; Ezek 18:22, 26).

The context of the law against homosexual activity in Leviticus 18 and 20 includes, to some extent, Leviticus 19. In Leviticus 19:18, the commandment to love one's neighbor as oneself is found. This commandment is not abolished, although others in the immediate context are or may be (Lev 19:21–25, 27). Neighborly love is stressed again and again in the New Testament. Therefore, when a decision has to be made as to whether or not a specific regulation is still normative for Christians, it has to be made on an individual basis and by consulting the New Testament. The law against homosexuality cannot be discarded easily.

W. J. Webb provides a reason for the inclusion of child sacrifice in the list of seventeen intercourse prohibitions in Leviticus 18. He argues that the fifteen prohibited sexual relations preceding child sacrifice may all produce offspring; the following two, homosexuality and bestiality, do not. The chapter is concerned with appropriate sexual boundaries between male and female. "Such a structural perspective speaks against any type of homosexuality today."[65]

---

[62] Quoted in Rooker, 247. Similarly Webb, 177.

[63] Roy E. Gane, "Same-Sex Love in the Body of Christ?" in *Christianity and Homosexuality: Some Seventh-day Adventist Perspectives*, ed. David Ferguson, Fritz Guy, and David R. Larson (Roseville, CA: Adventist Forum, 2008), part 4:67–68.

[64] Via and Gagnon, 66. Wold, 119, adds, "The sex crimes of Leviticus 18, with the possible exception of Molech worship, were not cultic in nature. . . . the term *tôʿēbâ* [abomination] shows no distinction between intrinsic wrong and ritual impurity as suggested by Boswell."

[65] Webb, 200. See also ibid., 197–200.

The laws of the Holiness Code extended beyond the Israelite community and were also applicable to the stranger (Lev 18:26).[66] Furthermore, the lists of Leviticus 18 and 20 together with other vice and virtue lists "reflect transcultural values."[67] They are also based on the creation order and therefore not limited to the people of Israel.[68]

The Text. These two texts describe and condemn male homosexual activity.[69] No exceptions are mentioned. The first text is especially opposed to any homosexual activity.[70] However, it is very likely that both texts also included lesbianism. "The Mosaic legislation in general is considered from a man's (male's) perspective. Even the Decalogue is addressed in the masculine singular, but this certainly does not mean that it applies only to the male gender. The masculine singular is the Hebrew way to express gender-inclusive ideas."[71]

The second text reveals that homosexual activity was not limited to exploitative situations. The two persons involved in these acts of immorality are men (or women), obviously not an adult and a boy (or a girl). Both of them were to be punished because both of them were responsible for their acts. They are an abomination.[72] Obviously, both were involved in this activity by mutual consent.[73]

"The reason why male-male intercourse is wrong is implicit in the proscription itself: 'lying with a male as though lying with a woman.' Male-male intercourse puts a male in the category of female so far as sexual intercourse is concerned. Because sexual intercourse is about sexual completion, it requires complementary sexual others."[74] In addition, people should not have "sex with too much of an 'other' (bestiality) or too much of a 'like' (incest, male-male intercourse), and not disrupting the one-flesh bond of a legitimate sexual union (adultery)."[75] The violation of this law is

---

[66] See Davidson, *Flame of Yahweh*, 154–155; and White and Niell, 68.

[67] Webb, 196. See also ibid., 192–196.

[68] See Wold, 130.

[69] William Loader, *Sexuality in the New Testament: Understanding the Key Texts* (Louisville, KY: Westminster John Knox, 2010), 9–11, points to various interpretations of Leviticus 18:22 "sometime between the mid-first centuries BCE and CE."

[70] Cf. Springett, 63.

[71] Davidson, *Flame of Yahweh,* 150.

[72] The term *bdelygma* is discussed by Wold, 118.

[73] See Davidson, *Flame of Yahweh*, 149; and Lefebvre, 44.

[74] Via and Gagnon, 64–65.

[75] Ibid., 65.

an abomination. In "the entire Pentateuch, the only forbidden sexual act to which the word *tôʿēbâ* is specifically attached is homosexual intercourse."[76]

It bears noting that in Romans 1:26–27 and 1 Corinthians 6:9–10, Paul alludes to Leviticus 18 and 20 and makes his own statement about homosexuality. The law was still valid in Paul's time, and Paul did not indicate that it was abolished.

A specific case of fornication—namely, incest—is related in 1 Corinthians 5. The act of having sexual intimacy with one's stepmother is called *porneia*. The case of 1 Corinthians 5:1 is clearly spelled out in Leviticus 18:8. Leviticus 18 discusses unlawful sexual relations. First of all, it is evident that Paul considered Leviticus 18, or at least parts of it, as still valid for Christians. So do many Christians in the case of incest and bestiality as well as child sacrifice. Secondly, the term *porneia* clearly stands for incestuous relations and may include all unlawful sexual activities spelled out in Leviticus 18—that is, different forms of incest, sexual relations with a woman during her period, sexual relations with the wife of another man, homosexuality, and sexual relations with animals.[77] As incest is still to be shunned, so is homosexuality.

The issue of fornication was discussed and decided upon at the Jerusalem Council (Acts 15:20, 29; 21:25). Gentile Christians were ordered to abstain from fornication. Obviously, the Jerusalem Council did not discuss the validity of the Decalogue. The term they dealt with was *porneia*, whereas the Ten Commandments use the verb *moicheuō* (LXX). The other three items from which the Gentile Christians had to abstain were things polluted by idols, what has been strangled, and blood. All four activities that were to be avoided by Gentile Christians are reminiscent of similar prohibitions for Israelites and strangers in Leviticus 17:8–15 and 18:24–27.[78] It seems quite certain that the delegates to this Council, and especially James, had Leviticus 18 in mind.[79] Paul then followed the decisions of the Council of Jerusalem in the case of the

---

[76] Davidson, *Flame of Yahweh*, 151.

[77] Ibid.

[78] Oftentimes, the New Testament, when it alludes to or quotes an Old Testament text, does not only refer to the specific text but also to the entire context. When, e.g., in Revelation 12:5 the male child is mentioned who is to rule all the nations with a rod of iron, it is not just referring to Psalm 2:9 but the entire second Psalm. This principle, so often found in the New Testament, may apply also to 1 Corinthians 5:1 and its Old Testament source, Leviticus 18.

[79] Cf. C. K. Barrett, *The Acts of the Apostles*, Vol. II, The International Critical Commentary (London: T&T Clark International, 2006), 734; Darrell L. Bock, *Acts*, Baker Exegetical Commentary of the New Testament (Grand Rapids, MI: Baker Academic, 2007), 506–507; and I. Howard Marshall, *Acts,* Tyndale New Testament Commentaries, rev. ed. (Grand Rapids, MI: Eerdmans, 1991), 253.

Corinthian man. *Porneia* was referring to a broad range of sexual deviations, including incest, prostitution, and homosexuality.

Deuteronomy 23

> None of the daughters of Israel shall be a cult prostitute, nor shall any of the sons of Israel be a cult prostitute. You shall not bring the hire of a harlot or the wages of a dog into the house of the LORD your God for any votive offering, for both of these are an abomination to the LORD your God (Deut 23:17–18)

Springett suggests that homosexuality may have been referred to in the terms used in these verses. The crucial terms in these verses are the words translated "cult prostitute," "harlot," and "dog."[80] The terms *qedeshah* (female cult prostitute) and *qadesh* (male priest or cult prostitute) in verse 17 may be parallel to the "prostitute" and the "dog" in verse 18. "So-called cultic prostitution was widespread among the fertility cults of the ancient Near Eastern world . . . Nowhere was this more commonly practiced than among the peoples of Syria and Canaan, hence the special need to warn Israel against it."[81]

The term "dog" may, in contrast to the female cult prostitute, describe male prostitution (including homosexuality). It is also used in extra-biblical material. The devotees of Ishtar are called "'man-woman' or literally 'dog-woman' ('dog' represents masculinity in the negative sense)."[82] Davidson points out that the passage "is found in the section of Deuteronomy that elaborates upon the seventh commandment; this indicates that any homosexual activity is a violation of the Decalogue."[83]

Summary

The Old Testament contains clear texts, especially in the legal material, rejecting any form of homosexual activity. These texts were referred to in the New Testament and considered binding. Other texts are not as clear, and one should be careful not to read wishful thinking into Old Testament narratives and exploit texts, which may say nothing about homosexual activities. However, D. J. Wold is correct to affirm, "All the references to homosexual acts in the Old Testament are negative—whether

[80] Cf., Springett, 63–65.

[81] Eugene H. Merrill, *Deuteronomy*, The New American Commentary (Nashville, TN: Broadman and Holman, 1994), 313.

[82] Teppo, 81.

[83] See Davidson, *Flame of Yahweh*, 160.

in narrative (Gen 9:20–27; 19; Judg 19) or law (Lev 18; 20)—and carry heavy sanctions."[84]

Homosexuality in the New Testament

The New Testament contains about three explicit texts dealing with the issue of homosexuality, and some texts that refer to it in passing. Before approaching them, let us take a look at the position of Jesus.

Jesus and Homosexuality

Although Jesus has not made a direct statement dealing with homosexuality, His position on the issue is recognizable.[85]

Jesus and the Law

Jesus did not abolish the law but pointed out its real meaning and its implications. Jesus' Sermon on the Mount in Matthew 5 contains a long section on the law (Matt 5:17–48). The passage on the law begins with an introduction that stresses the indissolubility of the law (Matt 5:8–20). The law is to be taught and kept. The first two of the six so-called antitheses discuss in an exemplary way the Decalogue. Jesus did not relativize the Ten Commandments—including the seventh commandment, the commandment regarding sexual sin—but rather intensified them, revealing their intended meaning. However, He modified the subsequent Mosaic regulations and rejected the unbiblical statement to hate one's enemy (Matt 5:43). According to Matthew 23:23 He talked about the "weightier matters of the law" but did not nullify the principle and practice of tithing. R. A. J. Gagnon makes an interesting comment on Mark 7:

> The saying in Mark 7:15–19 about what defiles a person is often cited as proof that Jesus abolished the food laws. It is more likely that Jesus intended a hyperbolic contrast: what counts most is not what goes into a person but what comes out . . . If Jesus did not abrogate even such things as food laws and meticulous tithing, then it is impossible that he would have overturned a proscription of sexual immorality as serious as that of male-male intercourse.[86]

---

[84] Wold, 162.

[85] Gagnon devotes a number of pages to Jesus and the issue of sexuality. Cf. Via and Gagnon, 68–74. Wold, 161–175, devotes an entire chapter to "Christ and the Homosexual."

[86] Via and Gagnon, 69.

Jesus and Sexuality

Jesus did not approve of sexual relationships outside of a marriage covenant between a male and a female. Although He mingled with sinners and cared for them, He did not condone their behavior. This becomes quite clear in the cases of the three women who had committed sexual sins. One of them is the sinful woman of Luke 7:36–50 who anointed Him. The other two were the Samaritan woman of John 4—who had six husbands and presently cohabited with another man—and the woman caught in adultery in John 8:3–11 who was told, "Go. From now on sin no more" (John 8:11). In the Sermon on the Mount Jesus presented two antitheses on sexual issues in which He deepened the law. Adultery would already begin with our thought processes. He abolished the bill of divorce, and for Him divorce and remarriage were no longer options, except in cases of sexual immorality. According to Matthew 19:18 and Mark 10:19, Jesus again confirmed the seventh commandment. In fact, "Jesus was virtually without peer in his radical insistence on limiting the number of lifetime partners to one."[87]

Jesus and Same-Sex Sexual Relations

According to Matthew 19 and Mark 10, Jesus had a discussion with the Pharisees on the question of divorce. In this context He referred back to the creation account and quoted Genesis 1:27 and 2:24. Two human beings, male and female, become one flesh. In the Hebrew text the term "two" is missing. It is found in the LXX. By stressing that only two beings and beings of the opposite sex become one, Jesus rejected polygamy as well as homosexuality. Obviously, for Jesus the creation account was not only descriptive but prescriptive. Then, Jesus mentioned three groups of eunuchs (Matt 19:12): 1) those who are eunuchs from birth,[88] 2) those who have been made eunuchs by men, and 3) those who for the sake of the kingdom of heaven have made themselves eunuchs. The last group probably does not refer to literal eunuchs but to people such as John the Baptist, who remained unmarried for the sake of his ministry. This would imply that humans have the ability to postpone sexual intercourse indefinitely, which is true for persons with either heterosexual or homosexual inclinations. According to Matthew 19:1–12 Jesus allowed

[87] Via and Gagnon, 71.

[88] Some attempt to read into this phrase the issue of homosexuality. Rogers, 78–79, refers to M. Nissinnen who "suggests that in our contemporary context those who are eunuchs from their mother's womb might well include people who are homosexuals, because they simply lack sexual desire for people of the opposite sex." This statement seems to be carefully crafted, not claiming that in biblical times eunuchs included homosexuals. The emphasis seems to fall on the "contemporary context" in which some people would like to include homosexuals with the eunuch. But there is no evidence that this is the biblical usage of "eunuch."

for two alternatives only: being married to a person of the opposite sex or staying single. For Jesus, divorce was and is not an option, and neither is homosexuality.

In Mark 7:21–23 Jesus says that out of the heart comes evil, and He specifies, among other sins, three sexual transgressions—namely, *porneia* (fornication), *moicheia* (adultery), and *aselgeia* (sensuality, licentiousness, wantonness).[89] *Porneia* has a wide range of meanings as mentioned previously, including homosexuality. "No first-century Jew would have spoken of *porneiai* (sexual immoralities) without having in mind the list of forbidden sexual offenses in Leviticus 18 and 20, particularly incest, adultery, same-sex intercourse, and bestiality."[90] Jesus also mentions Sodom (Matt 10:15; Luke 10:12).[91]

Jesus is concerned with keeping the commandments—that is, exhibiting a Christian lifestyle, which includes proper sexual relationships. Indirectly, homosexuality is addressed and rejected. Soards concludes, "Thus, judging from both Jesus' words and actions, we may conclude that marital heterosexual unions and abstinence from sexual involvement are the options for human sexual behavior that accord with the will of God."[92]

Paul and Homosexuality

The three major Pauline texts dealing with homosexuality are Romans 1:26–27; 1 Corinthians 6:9; and 1 Timothy 1:10.

Romans 1

> For this reason God gave them over to degrading passions; for their women exchanged the natural function for that which is unnatural, and in the same way also the men abandoned the natural function of the woman and burned in their desire toward one another, men with men committing indecent acts and receiving in their own persons the due penalty of their error (Rom 1:26–27).

Suggested Interpretations. While a number of Christians hold that these texts describe homosexuality, which they reject in all its forms, others acknowledge that while the text deals with homosexuality, the issue for Paul is idolatry or pederasty, and that Paul could not have

---

[89] Wold, 167–170, shows that *aselgeia* may include homosexuality.

[90] Via and Gagnon, 73.

[91] However, his use of the term "dogs" in Matthew 7:6, although reminding us of the dogs of Deuteronomy 23:17–18, that is, homosexuals, does not seem to refer to homosexuals in this context.

[92] Soards, 29.

taken into account sexual orientation as we know it today.[93] Supposedly, he did not know about inverted homosexuals and permanent loving homosexual relations. Furthermore, it is argued that the reference to nature should be understood in the following way:

> In describing homosexuality as 'against nature' (Rom. 1:26 KJV), Paul does not condemn homosexual orientation or any committed mutual relationship. Instead, he condemns perversion of what comes naturally. It is 'against nature' for homosexuals to practice heterosexuality or for heterosexuals to practice homosexuality. Paul does not condemn people for having been born homosexual, nor does he condemn the homosexual orientation (inversion).[94]

Therefore, the issue is whether or not Paul talks about homosexuality at all and whether or not homosexuality in Romans 1 includes all forms of homosexuality and has a universal scope. The context and the text itself help us find an answer.

Recently, it has been suggested that the passage dealing with homosexuality is not Paul's own voice but the voice of a Jewish interlocutor who slanders the Gentiles.[95] This issue will not be discussed here because this paper is just a short summary of the biblical texts dealing

---

[93] Cf. Everett R. Kalin, "Romans 1:26–27 and Homosexuality," *Currents in Theology and Mission* 30 (2003): 423–432. Robin Scroggs, *The New Testament and Homosexuality* (Minneapolis, MN: Fortress Press, 1983), 121–122, states: "Only in Romans 1 is there a negative judgment made on both female as well as male homosexuality which could be considered a general indictment. Even here, the entire cumulative evidence we have looked at throughout this book suggests that despite the general language Paul, with regard to the statement about male homosexuality, must have had, *could only have had,* pederasty in mind. That Paul uses here the argument from nature might, mean, of course, that he would have made the same judgment about *any* form of homosexuality. No one can legitimately conclude, however, that he would have done so. We just do not know." This is a remarkable statement by a scholar who obviously superimposes the Greco-Roman culture on Paul and still has to acknowledge that Romans 1:26–27 sounds like "a general indictment." Wold, 185–186, briefly summarizes the "revisionist interpretations" and draws his own conclusions which differ widely from Scroggs' conclusions. Similar but more elaborate is Springett, 121–122. Soards, 48, asserts: "Yet Scroggs' contention that pederasty was the only model of homosexuality known in antiquity is simplistic and misleading." Wink, "Homosexuality and the Bible," 36, claims: "No doubt Paul was unaware of the distinction between sexual orientation, over which one has apparently no choice, and sexual behavior, over which one does." Cf. John R. Jones, "'In Christ There Is Neither . . .': Toward the Unity of the Body of Christ," in *Christianity and Homosexuality: Some Seventh-day Adventist Perspectives,* ed. David Ferguson, Fritz Guy, and David R. Larson (Roseville, CA: Adventist Forum, 2008), part 4:23.

[94] De Young, 10. Cf. Rogers, 74.

[95] See, e.g., Sigve K. Tonstad, *The Letter to the Romans: Paul among the Ecologists* (Sheffield: Sheffield Phoenix Press, 2016), 88–114.

with homosexual behavior and the issue requires an extended discussion. The author of the present study deals with this issue elsewhere, and maintains that while Paul uses certain literary devices, Romans 1b is clearly his own voice and argument, and it is integrated in his theological approach.[96]

The Literary Context. The larger context in Romans is universal in nature. While Romans 1 shows that all Gentiles are sinners—Paul presents a catalogue of vices (Rom 1:21–32)—and Romans 2 points out that the Jews are also sinners, Romans 3 concludes that all people are sinners and all are dependent on God's grace as revealed in Christ's sacrifice on our behalf. Romans 5 elaborates on the fact that all of us have been slaves to sin but in Jesus are free from it. Also, the fall is clearly referred to in Romans 5:12–19. Paul's argument is not limited to humanity in the first century AD, but encompasses people at all times while dealing with creation, the fall, sin, and salvation.[97] Therefore, the list of vices, including homosexuality, should not be limited to a special period of time either but should still be applicable today.[98]

In the immediate context of Romans 1, Paul's background for the discussion of idolatry and homosexuality is creation.[99] Romans 1:20

---

[96] See Ekkehardt Mueller, "Same Sex Sexual Relationships in Romans 1:26–27," unpublished paper, 2017.

[97] Cf. Springett, 124.

[98] James R. White and Jeffrey D. Niell, *The Same Sex Controversy* (Minneapolis: Bethany House Publishers, 2002), 134, note, "The basis of Paul's discussion in Romans 1 . . . gives us no hint that the author intends his words to be limited geographically or temporally. The concepts he presents reach back to creation itself, apply over and beyond all cultural boundaries, and speak to men and women at the very level of their existence, not merely in their cultural climate."

[99] Rogers, 76, argues that "Paul's condemnation of immoral sexual behavior is not appropriately applied to contemporary gay or lesbian Christians who are not idolaters." Even if idolatry should be the overarching theme of Romans 1, the statements on homosexuality have to be taken seriously and cannot be discarded. Furthermore, it would be wrong to contend that "idolatry, the worship of statues or images, is the *necessary* prerequisite for homosexuality," as Gagnon, *The Bible and Homosexual Practice*, 285, points out. Although idolatry may find an expression in homosexual activity, sinful passion does not need to grow out of idolatry. It comes out of humanity's sinful nature. The problem is that some advocates of a homosexual lifestyle deny that the Fall occurred or that the Fall is related to homosexuality. Rogers, 77, points to homosexual animals and claims that "examples from the animal kingdom seem to show that God pretty clearly did intend to create homosexual animals. Furthermore, the best scientific evidence also seems to show a genetic influence on sexual orientation, as well as biological differences between homosexual and heterosexual people. This data suggests that homosexuality is indeed part of God's created order" (ibid., 81). Genesis 2:20 indicates that the cattle, the birds, and the beast of the fields had "helpers," while Adam did not have "a helper suitable to him." For Adam this "suitable helper" was Eve, the missing female partner. Similarly, the Flood story mentions male and female animals only: "You shall take with you [into the ark] of every clean animal by sevens, a male and his female; and of the animals that are not clean two, a male and his female" (Gen 7:2). Genesis does not indicate that God created homosexual beings. D. Martin, "Heterosexism and the Interpretation of Romans 1:18–32," *Biblical Interpretation* 3

refers to the creation of the world and God's created works. Evidently Paul's argument is that God can be known through creation. But although the Gentiles "knew God, they did not honor him as God" (Rom 1:21). They "exchanged the glory of the incorruptible God for an image in the form of corruptible man and of birds and four-footed animals and crawling creatures" (Rom 1:23). God was replaced by gods that were nothing more than images of created beings, whether humans or animals. The list of animals, the mention of humans, and the concept of "likeness" or "image" suggest that Romans 1:23 echoes Genesis 1:24–26. In addition, Romans 1:25 points out that the Gentiles worshipped created things instead of the creator. Furthermore, Romans 1:26–27 seems to echo Genesis 1:27 by concentrating on the same terms—namely, "male" (*arsēn*) and "female" (*thēlu*) in the Septuagint, instead of using the terms "man" and "woman."[100] Since creation is so clearly referred to in the preceding verses, homosexuality must be understood in the context of creation. "Idolatry and same-sex intercourse together constitute an assault on the work of the Creator in nature"[101] no matter which form of homosexuality it is. The creation account points out God's intention for man and women, which is monogamous heterosexual marriage.

The Historical Context. When it comes to the historical context, we have to ask whether or not it is possible that the ancients may have had an idea of inverted homosexuality. If the number of inverted homosexuals among the general population amounts to somewhere between three to ten percent[102] and "has remained relatively constant for hundreds, even

---

(1995): 338, complains: "Modern scholars read the Fall into Romans 1 because it renders the text more serviceable for heterosexist purposes." Although the Fall is not directly mentioned in Romans 1, creation is, and the Fall's mention in Romans 5 reveals that it forms part of the background of Paul's theology, even in Romans 1.

[100] See also Robert A. J. Gagnon, "The Scriptural Case for a Male-Female Prerequisite for Sexual Relations: The New Testament Perspective," in *Homosexuality, Marriage, and the Church: Biblical, Counseling, and Religious Liberty Issues,* ed. Roy E. Gane, Nicholas P. Miller, and H. Peter Swanson (Berrien Springs, MI: Andrews University Press, 2012), 109. Peter Stuhlmacher, *Paul's Letter to the Romans: A Commentary* (Louisville, KY: Westminster John Knox, 1994), 37, states, "With every indication of his loathing, the apostle now pictures how the Gentiles profane themselves (in a sinful reversal of Gen. 1:27f.) in lesbian love and sodomy. . . . What the Gentiles do is contrary to creation and characteristic of their fallen state of guilt."

[101] Via and Gagnon, 78.

[102] See Ben Kemena, "Biological Determinants of Homosexual Orientation," in *Christianity and Homosexuality: Some Seventh-day Adventist Perspectives,* ed. David Ferguson, Fritz Guy, and David R. Larson (Roseville, CA: Adventist Forum, 2008), part 2:10; and Aubyn Fulton, "Response, Science and Sexual Orientation," in *Christianity and Homosexuality: Some Seventh-day Adventist Perspectives,* ed. David Ferguson, Fritz Guy, and David R. Larson (Roseville, CA: Adventist Forum, 2008), part 2:48.

thousands of years,"[103] as it is claimed, it would be quite strange if loving and caring homosexual relationships were formed only in the twentieth and twenty-first centuries and that the ancients were completely ignorant of this phenomenon.[104]

As we have seen at the beginning of this article, references to homosexuality have not only been found in extra-biblical sources dating back centuries before Christ, but also in Greco-Roman society and in the church fathers. The ancients did not only know what has been called "contingent homosexuality" and most probably "situational homosexuality," but most likely had some idea or concept of "constitutional homosexuality."

At least the notion that a person is attracted to the same sex because of his or her constitution is found in Plato's androgynous man-woman myth, summarized by Springett:

> In this myth Plato explains that primal man was dual. He had four hands, four feet, two faces and two privy parts, that is, like two people back to back–the faces opposite directions. Some of these dual, primal creatures were male in both parts, others were female in both parts and yet others (a third sex) part male and part female. These primal creatures were so strong that they became insolent, attacking the gods. Because of their continued insolence, Zeus divided these dual four-legged creatures into two-legged creatures. A dual male became two males, a dual female two females and the male-female (androgynous) became a male and a female. On this basis he accounts for the differing sexual desires apparent in society, for each creature searches out its own or opposite kind, according to its original orientation. When dual parts encounter each other they fall in love. By the creation of this myth Plato attempts to explain the attraction some men and women have for persons of the same sex.[105]

It is hardly possible that Paul, who was an educated man and who even quoted Greek authors in his speeches and writings (e.g., Acts 17:28; Titus 1:12), would not have known Plato's myth and the concept of

---

[103] Mitchell F. Henson, "Ministering to Gays Within the Church Community," in *Christianity and Homosexuality: Some Seventh-day Adventist Perspectives,* ed. David Ferguson, Fritz Guy, and David R. Larson (Roseville, CA: Adventist Forum, 2008), part 5:27.

[104] Cf. White and Niell, 128–129.

[105] Springett, 97–98. Cf. Gagnon, *The Bible and Homosexual Practice*, 353–354. Anthony C. Thiselton, *The First Epistle to the Corinthians,* The New International Greek Testament Commentary (Grand Rapids, MI: Eerdmans, 2000), 452, declares, "Paul witnessed around him *both* abusive relationships of power or money *and* examples of 'genuine love' between males. We must not misunderstand Paul's 'worldly' knowledge."

innate homosexuality.[106] "Ancient Greek and Roman artifacts and literature show long-term, loving, same-sex sexual relationships between social equal."[107] Therefore, to suggest that Paul was referring only to violent or exploitative homosexuality or pederasty but not to permanent, caring, one-partner same-gender relationships because they supposedly were not known at his time, cannot be shown.[108]

Although Paul lived hundreds of years after the giving of the law through Moses, obviously this law is—in his opinion—still applicable during New Testament times. The mention of the adult-adult homosexual intercourse in Romans 1:27 is dependent on and has as its background Leviticus 18:22 and 20:13.[109] Leviticus 18 and 20 are in view in Acts 15 and were declared binding for gentile Christians by the Jerusalem Council. Paul refers to Leviticus 18:8 when he sharply criticizes incest in the church of Corinth (1 Cor 5), indicating that for him Leviticus 18 and 20 are still valid. He goes even a step further by directly mentioning female same-gender activity (Rom 1:26), which was not directly spelled out in the Old Testament texts, though it was included with male homosexuality.[110]

The Text. As he deals with the suggestion that Romans 1 "identifies a temporary Jewish purity rule rather than a universal moral principle," De Young remarks, "God cannot consign the Gentiles to punishment for breaking a Jewish purity law."[111] Since he does bring about punishment or permits negative consequences (Rom 1:27), the laws of Leviticus 18 and 20 must have a moral quality and be universal in nature.

---

[106] White and Niell, 128–129, state: "Therefore, the assumption that he [Paul] did not know of people who professed to be homosexual as their primary 'orientation' is simply farfetched unless one is willing to say that in essence no one really 'knew' about this until the past few decades or centuries. . . . Plato's writings make reference to male homosexuality, lesbianism, the claims of some to be born as a willing mate of a man, the concept of mutuality, permanency, gay pride, pederasty, 'homophobia,' motive, desire, passion, etc. One would have to assume Paul a very poor student *and* a very poor observer of the culture around him to be unaware of these things."

[107] Paris, 68. Gagnon, "The Scriptural Case," 113, declares, "A conception of caring, mutually loving homoerotic unions already existed in Paul's cultural environment and yet even these were rejected by some Greco-Roman moralists." He develops this statement on the next pages.

[108] See Via and Gagnon, 81.

[109] These chapters are also found in a kind of universal context. See Leviticus 18:24–30; 20:2, 23.

[110] James D. G. Dunn, *Romans 1–8*, Word Biblical Commentary 38A (Dallas, TX: Word Books, 1988), 76, notes "that Paul simply takes it for granted that the Jewish abhorrence of Gentile sexual license is still the appropriate ethical response of the Gentile believer in Christ means that he recognizes at least one distinctive element of Israel's covenant righteousness which remains unchanged within the wider freedom of the new covenant."

[111] De Young, 159.

This is what J. Jones denies. He strongly argues for Leviticus 18 and 20 to be culturally and nationally bound and overcome in Jesus.[112] He also distinguishes between a level of "moral evil" and a level of "ceremonial impurity" in Romans 1, assigning verses 24–27—the passage dealing with homosexuality—to the ceremonial level. He builds his argument on the use of *adikia* (unrighteousness), *ponēria* (evil), and *asebeia* (godlessness, wickedness) in Romans 1:18, 29[113] and *akatharsia* (uncleanness) in Romans 1:24, reasoning that the former three terms have a moral quality, while *akatharsia* is ceremonial in nature. His point seems to be that homosexuality belongs to the level of ceremonial impurity, not to the level of sin. It does not affect Paul's original audience, and it does not affect us today, because Paul uses a rhetorical device. He speaks with a pre-Christian voice in order to drive his point home with the Jews—that is, to help them realize that they are also sinners.[114]

In a review of Jones' article, Gane points to the problem of defining impurity as cultic or ceremonial only. Already in the Old Testament impurity had at times a moral quality.[115] However, a closer look at the New Testament reveals that *akatharsia* (impurity) is found next to terms such as *anomia* (lawlessness, Rom 6:19), *aselgeia* (licentiousness, Eph 4:19), and *porneia* (fornication, Eph 5:3). According to 2 Corinthians 12:24 people should have repented of their *akatharsia*. The deeds of the flesh include, among others, idolatry, sorcery, enmities, strife, jealousy, outbursts of anger, and also *porneia, akatharsia,* and *aselgeia* (Gal 5:19–20). "Those who practice such things will not inherit the kingdom of God" (Gal 5:21). A similar list occurs in Colossians 3:5 and includes *akatharsia*. "For it is because of these things that the wrath of God will come upon the sons of disobedience" (Col 3:6). Thus, *akatharsia* has a moral dimension in Paul's writings. Christians are called to stay away from it, because a lifestyle of practiced *akatharsia* excludes people from the kingdom of God (see also 1 Thess 4:7).[116] Even the larger context in Romans makes it very clear that the issue is sin, not ceremonial impurity.[117]

---

[112] Jones, part 4:4–7.

[113] These terms are found in a longer list of vices, but are not a heading or summary of these other vices.

[114] Jones, part 4:13–22.

[115] See discussion above. See also Gane, part 4:66–68.

[116] White and Niell, 120, add, "The fact that a 'penalty' or 'punishment' is attached to the 'error' of performing these 'shameful deeds' reinforces the understanding that these are sinful deeds . . ."

[117] See Gagnon, "The Scriptural Case," 97; Richard B. Hays, *The Moral Vision of the New Testament: Community, Cross, New Creation—A Contemporary Introduction to New Testament Ethics* (San Francisco, CA: HarperCollins, 1996), 387.

The argument that the phrase "the natural intercourse" and its opposite "against/contrary to nature" (*para physin*) in Romans 1:26–27 are describing what is natural to an individual is unsubstantiated.[118] Nowhere is the term *physis* used in such a sense. In Romans itself the noun is found seven times;[119] however, the phrase *para physin* just twice (Rom 1:26; 11:24). In Romans 11:24 Paul uses the metaphor of a wild olive tree "by nature" (*kata physin*). From this wild olive tree, branches were cut off and "against nature" (*para physin*) grafted into the cultivated olive tree. *Kata physin* means to exist in harmony with the created order. On the other hand, *para physin* refers to what is in contrast to the order intended by the Creator.[120] This corresponds with Romans 1, where creation is clearly the background for the discussion of idolatry, homosexuality, and other vices. Here, activities and behavior described as being "against nature" imply a negative moral judgment because "homosexual practice is a violation of the natural order (as determined by God)."[121] Obviously, this includes all forms of homosexuality.[122] Jones' attempt to explain what is natural on "conventional grounds"—namely, what was located in the

---

[118] Hays, 387, states: "There are abundant instances, both in the work of Greco-Roman moral philosophers and in literary texts, of the opposition between 'natural' (*kata physin*) and 'unnatural' (*para physin*) behavior. . . . In particular, the opposition between 'natural' and 'unnatural' is very frequently used (in the absence of convenient Greek words for 'heterosexual' and 'homosexual') as a way of distinguishing between heterosexual and homosexual behavior. The categorization of homosexual behavior as 'contrary to nature' was adopted with particular vehemence by Hellenistic Jewish writers . . . 'The Law recognizes no sexual connections,' writes Josephus, 'except for the natural [*kata physin*] union of man and wife . . . But it abhors the intercourse of males with males, and punishes any who undertake such a thing with death.' In Paul's time, the categorization of homosexual practices as *para physin* was a commonplace feature of polemical attacks against such behavior, particularly in the world of Hellenistic Judaism."

[119] Romans 1:26; 2:14, 27; 11:21, 24 (three times).

[120] Joseph A. Fitzmyer, *Romans*, The Anchor Bible, vol. 33 (New York: Doubleday, 1992), 286, suggests that "in the context of vv 19–23, 'nature' also expresses for him [Paul] the order intended by the Creator, the order that is manifest in God's creation or, specifically in this case, the order seen in the function of the sexual organs themselves, which were ordained for an expression of love between man and woman and for the procreation of children. Paul now speaks of the deviant exchange of those organs as a use *para physin*." Wold, 182, concurs: "According to Paul, nature is the created order of male and female in the image of God, regulated by conscience and law." Cf. De Young, 156–157, and Köstenberger, 48.

[121] Dunn, 74. Cf. Via and Gagnon, 79–80. Gagnon, "The Scriptural Case," 99, also points to Philo and Josephus and how they in the first century A.D. used the phrase "contrary to nature" to describe homosexual activity.

[122] Springett, 130–131, declares, "If homosexual acts could gain divine approval in any sense, surely Paul would have indicated how and drawn the distinction. . . . An interpretation of his words that allows homosexual activity would have to allow also any sin in the list of vices which follows."

Greco-Roman world of the first century AD,[123] does not fit well with the argument of Paul, who reasons biblically rather than from the perspective of the Greco-Roman culture. The same is true for J. Boswell's effort to explain "unnatural" as unexpected or unusual but not as immoral behavior.[124] Gagnon suggests, "Paul in effect argues that even pagans who have no access to the book of Leviticus should know that same-sex eroticism is 'contrary to nature' because the primary sex organs fit male to female, not female to female or male to male."[125] He also says that "Paul was thinking of 'nature' not as 'the way things are usually done' (i.e., cultural convention) but rather as 'the material shape of the created order.'"[126]

The fact that Paul adds lesbianism to male homosexuality supports the previous point. "Lesbian intercourse in antiquity normally did not conform to the male pederast model or entail cultic associations or prostitution."[127] It was not exploitative. Therefore, non-exploitative but caring homosexual partnerships are included in the sins mentioned in Romans 1. However, there are those who hold that Romans 1:26 does not talk about lesbianism. Rogers writes, "The text does not say that women had sex with other women. They could have been condemned for taking the dominant position in heterosexual intercourse, or for engaging in non-procreative sexual acts with male partners."[128] D. A. Helminiak suggests that Romans 1:26, referring to

> female sexual relations that are "beyond the ordinary," could mean many things. It might mean sex during menstruation,

---

[123] Jones, part 4:17. Lewis B. Smedes, "Exploring the Morality of Homosexuality," in *Homosexuality and Christian Faith: Questions of Conscience for the Churches,* ed. Walter Wink (Minneapolis, MN: Fortress Press, 1999), 80–81, first seems to argue for a cultural understanding of "unnatural," but then admits "to be a traditionalist; I do believe that having babies is the teleological bent of sexuality. And my traditionalism leads me to suppose that homosexuality is a product of nature sometimes gone awry. But this, in turn, leads me to assume that God wants gay people to make the best life they can within the limits of what errant nature gives them. . . . Would not God also see same-sex partnerships as a morally worthy improvisation on the 'unnatural'?"

[124] John Boswell, *Christianity, Social Tolerance, and Homosexuality* (Chicago, IL: University of Chicago Press, 1980), 112.

[125] Gagnon, *The Bible and Homosexual Practice*, 254. Cf. Gane, part 4:65.

[126] Gagnon, The Bible and Homosexual Practice, 256, shows that this conclusion is valid by elaborating on the context in Romans 1. Discussing Romans 1:18–20, he reasons, "In other words, visual perception of the *material* creation that God has made . . . should lead to a mental perception about the nature of God and God's will. Similarly, the reader should expect that the appeal to nature in 1:26–27 has to do, at least primarily, with the visual perception of male-female bodily complementarity" (257). See also the section "What is 'natural' and 'unnatural' according to Paul?," in Loader, 23–29.

[127] Via and Gagnon, 80.

[128] Rogers, 75.

> sex with an uncircumcised man, oral sex, heterosexual anal sex, having sex while standing up, or anything that would not be considered the standard way of having sex. . . . There is no need to read homogeniality into the para physin of verse 26.[129]

In other words, according to these authors Romans 1:26 may describe any sexual deviation, but not lesbianism. However, verse 26 is linked to verse 27 by the term "likewise," and the homosexual male behavior is compared to the female behavior. The case is quite clear.[130] As there are gay males in verse 27, so there are lesbians in verse 26. In order to avoid this conclusion, the term "likewise" has to be reinterpreted. Gagnon has dealt with this issue extensively.[131] But even Helminiak himself concedes that his interpretation may not be correct: "But even if this interpretation is wrong, even if verse 26 is a reference to lesbian sex, the general conclusion argued below must still apply: Romans may refer to same-sex acts, but it intends no ethical condemnation of them."[132] This study argues that he is even wrong in his last assertion. "Brooten has shown through her extensive survey of Greco-Roman and Jewish literature, as well as magical, astrological and medical texts, that the phenomenon of female-female sexual relations was known and amost universally condemned as abhorrent."[133] This perfectly fits Paul's description in Romans 1.

That Paul was hardly concerned or not concerned with coercion in a homosexual relationship can be derived from Romans 1:27: "Men . . . burned in their desire toward one another, men with men committing indecent acts and receiving in their own persons the due penalty of their error." Obviously in such a homoerotic union, both partners lust

---

129 Helminiak, 87.

130 Cf. White and Niell, 117.

131 Gagnon, *The Bible and Homosexual Practice,* 297–299. James E. Miller, "The Practices of Romans 1:26: Homosexual or Heterosexual?" *Novum Testamentum* 37 (1995): 1–11, has argued that "likewise" in Romans 1:27 does not force us to parallel male same-sex intercourse with lesbianism. He quotes T. *Naph.* 3:4–5 in order to show that "likewise" can be used in a loose way (pp. 3–4): ". . .[do] not become like Sodom, which changed the order of their nature. And likewise also . . . the Watchers changed the order of their nature." The inhabitants of Sodom engaged in homosexual behavior, the angels in heterosexual. But Gagnon, *The Bible and Homosexual Practice,* 298–299, correctly points out that "neither clause [in T. *Naph.*] specifies what the 'order of nature' was changed for, which makes possible a loose comparison. However, Romans 1:27 is quite explicit about what "the natural use of the female" was exchanged for: sex with members of the same sex. For the 'likewise' of 1:27 to be appropriate, both the thing exchanged and the thing exchanged *for* must be comparable."

132 Helminiak, 90.

133 Loader, 18.

for each other.[134] Both of them consent to the homosexual relationship, both are responsible for their actions, and both of them receive the penalty.[135] God is not unfair that He would punish a boy who has been abused in a homosexual relationship, whether by being raped or by being forced into a pederast relationship.[136] However, if Paul is even opposed to a relationship of consenting adults, it can safely be assumed that he would be opposed to all other homosexual relationships.[137]

Homosexuality in Romans 1 is not limited to a certain time, culture, or to certain homosexual forms only. Paul understands it as sinful behavior. But this is not the only sinful behavior (Rom 1:29–31). All humans are sinners and need salvation. They "are justified by his grace as a gift, through the redemption that is in Christ Jesus" (Rom 3:24). While sin remains sin, sinners have to be careful in how they treat each other.

1 Corinthians 6

> Or do you not know that the unrighteous will not inherit the kingdom of God? Do not be deceived; neither fornicators, nor idolaters, nor adulterers, nor effeminate, nor homosexuals, nor thieves, nor the covetous, nor drunkards, nor revilers, nor swindlers, will inherit the kingdom of God (1 Cor 6:9–10).

Suggested Interpretation. Again it is claimed that Paul does not refer to monogamous homosexual relationships of mutual respect but condemns pederasty, homosexual prostitution, and exploitative and dehumanizing forms of homosexuality.[138] If this is true, not all male-male intercourse would be prohibited.[139] However, this does not seem to be the case. We will not go in detail in this section because similar arguments have already been discussed in the passage dealing with Romans 1.

---

[134] Wink, "Homosexuality and the Bible," 36, claims, "Likewise the relationships Paul describes are heavy with lust; they are not relationships between consenting adults who are committed to each other as faithfully and with as much integrity as any heterosexual couple."

[135] Loader, 23, supports that the issue was "mutuality rather than exploitation."

[136] Cf. Via and Gagnon, 80–81; and De Young, 158.

[137] Köstenberger, 217, argues, "There was a clear and ambiguous Greek word for pederasty, the term *paiderastēs.* We have every reason to believe that if Paul had wished to condemn, not homosexuality at large, but only pederasty, he would have used the appropriate Greek term for this practice. . . . The attempt to limit Paul's condemnation to pederasty . . . is contradicted by Paul's reference to the male partner's *mutual desire for one another* in Romans 1:27 ('consumed with passion for one another')."

[138] Cf. the examples listed by Köstenberger, 216.

[139] Cf. De Young, 10–11.

The Context. The immediate context of 1 Corinthians 6:9–10 is 1 Corinthians 5–7, dealing with the issue of human sexuality. In chapter 5 Paul mentions a case of incest in Corinth. Paul accepts as binding Leviticus 18, which discusses incest and homosexuality, and urges the Corinthian church to disfellowship the church member involved in an incestuous relationship with his stepmother. Toward the end of chapter 5 he presents a short list of four different categories of people involved in vices (v. 10), the first one being fornicators. This list is enlarged in the next verse by two additional groups of people. Christians must separate from church members who practice such vices. In 1 Corinthians 6:9–10 Paul expands this list to ten groups of people.[140]

The following outline of 1 Corinthians 6:9–10 indicates that the "unrighteous [who] will not inherit the kingdom of God" are the same as the subsequent ten groups of evildoers, neither of whom "will inherit the kingdom of God." It is possible that the ten groups in verses 9b–10 can be divided into two major parts, because four of the first five evildoers are committing sexual sins.

"Or do you not know
that the unrighteous *will not inherit the kingdom of God?*

Do not be deceived;
- neither fornicators,
- nor idolaters,
- nor adulterers,
- nor effeminate,
- nor homosexuals,
- nor thieves,
- nor the covetous,
- nor drunkards,
- nor revilers,
- nor swindlers

} *will inherit the kingdom of God.*

The first five groups of people are idolaters and sexual offenders, discussed in 1 Corinthians 5–7. In this section, two groups seem to be involved in heterosexual misconduct, while the next two groups refer to people engaged in homosexual misconduct. "Adulterers" applies to married people, while "fornicators" may refer to singles, unless the term is used in its broader sense encompassing all other groups, who are involved in sexual misbehavior. The rest of chapter 6 warns against a relationship with a prostitute. In 1 Corinthians 6:16 another creation

---

[140] In all these lists *porneia* is mentioned first.

text is quoted—namely, Genesis 2:24. And 1 Corinthians 7 goes on to describe heterosexual marriage, singleness, and divorce.[141] In order to avoid *porneia*, "each man is to have his own wife, and each woman is to have her own husband" (1 Cor 7:2). There is no room for homosexuality. If people "do not have self-control, let them marry; for it is better to marry than to burn with passion." Paul is clearly referring to heterosexual marriage.

The Text. The textual unit of 1 Corinthians 6:9–10 draws on Leviticus 18, the creation account, and Jesus' exposition of it. Although the Corinthian church with its problems pertaining to sexuality is addressed, the issue is broader. The interconnectedness of chapters 5 through 7 as well as its Old Testament background imply a universal dimension, again not limited only to time, culture, or certain forms of homosexuality only. The entire passage is prescriptive and not just descriptive. Therefore, A. C. Thiselton suggests that 1 Corinthians 6:9–10 is "an even more important and foundational passage than Romans 1."[142] Homosexual practices exclude people from the kingdom of God, as do any of the other vices mentioned by Paul.

The two terms dealing with homosexuality in 1 Corinthians 6:9 are *malakoi* and *arsenokoitai*.[143] *Malakoi* has been rendered "effeminate," "those who make women of themselves," "boy/male prostitutes," "(pervert) homosexuals," and "catamites." The term normally means "soft" or "luxurious" and appears four times in the New Testament (Matt 11:8—twice; Luke 7:25; 1 Cor 6:9). The two Gospel references depict the same event and describe persons in soft clothes. Jones points to later Christian literature where the term *malakos* describes an unworthy person.[144] However, he admits, "None of this, of course, negates the possibility that the term *malakos* included male homosexual behavior."[145] Those called *malakoi* are not just soft, mild, or weak men. The majority of the interpreters agrees that in 1 Corinthians 6:9 the term refers to homosexuals, especially to partners who play the female role in a homosexual

---

[141] Cf. Thiselton, 447, 451; and Via and Gagnon, 84–87.

[142] Thiselton, 447.

[143] These terms have been hotly debated. E.g., David F. Wright, "Homosexuals or Prostitutes: The Meaning of ARSENOKOITAI (1 Cor 6:9; 1 Tim 1:10)," *Vigiliae Christianae* 38, no. 2 (1984): 125–153, has shown that John Boswell's claim in *Christianity, Social Tolerance, and Homosexuality* that *arsenokoitai* means male prostitutes, not male homosexuals, is groundless. William L. Petersen, "Can ARSENOKOITAI Be Translated by 'Homosexuals'? (I Cor. 6.9; I Tim. 1.10)," *Vigiliae Christianae* 40, no. 2 (1986): 187–191, has responded to Wright. Basically, he holds that the modern concept of homosexuality does not correspond with the one prevalent in antiquity.

[144] Jones, part 4:9.

[145] Ibid, part 4:10.

relationship.[146] In verse 9 *malakoi* is surrounded by other terms referring to sexual and homosexual behavior, which makes it clear that this word in this context also has a sexual meaning and must be understood as a kind of homosexual behavior.[147] Gagnon sees this confirmed in extra-biblical literature—for instance, Philo of the first century AD.[148] However, to restrict the *malakoi* to children and the issue to pederasty is not only speculative but untenable.[149]

The term *arsenokoitai* helps to define the *malakoi*. It is a unique term used only by Paul,[150] who may actually have invented it by joining together the terms *arsēn* and *koitē* found in Leviticus 18:22 and 20:13 (LXX).[151] A literal translation would describe a man lying with a man in bed, that is, homosexual intercourse. Its meaning is not restricted to pederasty.[152] The *arsenokoitai* in 1 Corinthians 6:9 may be the active partners in a homosexual relationship.[153]

The severe penalty for being a *malakos* or an *arsenokoitēs*—namely, exclusion from the kingdom of God—indicates that the two terms refer to

---

146 Cf. Fitzmyer, *Romans*, 287; Joseph A. Fitzmyer, *First Corinthians*, The Anchor Bible 32 (New Haven: Yale University Press, 2008), 255–258; and Springett, 134. Leon Morris, *The First Epistle of Paul to the Corinthians: An Introduction and Commentary*, Tyndale New Testament Commentaries, rev. ed. (Grand Rapids, MI: Eerdmans, 1993), 93, understands *malakoi* and *arsenokoitai* as "the passive and active partners in homosexuality."

147 Loader, 30, mentions that "the word group appears in sexual contexts."

148 Gagnon, "The Scriptural Case," 84

149 Cf. Thiselton, 449.

150 De Young devotes an entire chapter to the discussion of the term (pp. 175–214).

151 Cf. Köstenberger, 216.

152 Gagnon, "The Scriptural Case," 87, states, "Indeed, there is no evidence in ancient Israel, Second Temple Judaism, or rabbinic Judaism that any limitation was placed in the prohibition of male-male intercourse."

153 Cf. Thiselton, 448–450; and Via and Gagnon, 83. Springett, 136, suggests, "If Paul was condemning only a crude form of homosexual activity here, by implication allowing other types, he surely would have been more explicit." Paul comes from a Jewish background, and the Jewish verdict on homosexuality is unequivocal. On the other hand, Jones, part 4:12, acknowledges that *arsenokotoi* "almost certainly" has to do with homosexuality, however, "of an exploitive sort." David E. Malick, "The Condemnation of Homosexuality in 1 Corinthians 6:9," *Bibliotheca Sacra* 150 (1993): 479–492, summarizes his article on page 492 by saying: "While Paul's choice of the words ἀρσενοκοῖται and μαλακοί allows for an application to the abuse of pederasty in his day, the words actually denote a broader field of reference including all men who have sexual relations with men. The illogical presuppositions that (a) all sexual relationships are equal before God, (b) Paul's descriptions are of excessive practices, and (c) homosexuality is a biblically approved expression of sexuality, are necessary prerequisites to the popular conclusion that Paul was discussing only 'abuses' in homosexual behavior. The Apostle Paul condemned all homosexual relationships in his vice-list in 1 Corinthians 6:9 as he addressed the need for the Corinthians to judge those within their midst."

adult males who of their own free will, whether by innate orientation or not, have homosexual intercourse with each other.[154]

Because 1 Corinthians 6 reverberates with creation and the laws of sexual morality in Leviticus 18 and 20, not to mention the other reasons noted above, homosexuality in this passage most likely includes all forms of homosexual activity and transcends an application limited only to the Corinthian church.[155]

1 Timothy 1

> But we know that the law is good, if one uses it lawfully, realizing the fact that law is not made for a righteous person, but for those who are lawless and rebellious, for the ungodly and sinners, for the unholy and profane, for those who kill their fathers or mothers, for murderers and immoral men and homosexuals and kidnappers and liars and perjurers, and whatever else is contrary to sound teaching (1 Tim 1:8–10).

The same term found in 1 Timothy 1:10, *arsenokoitai*, has already occurred in 1 Corinthians 6. The same background of Leviticus 18 and 20 is prevalent. This time, however, the term seems to be broader than in 1 Corinthians 6 because the *malakoi* are not mentioned. A distinction between passive and active partners is not made. Probably, the *arsenokoitai* are all those who are involved in any type of homosexual activity.[156]

The contribution of 1 Timothy to our discussion is that homosexuality is set in the context of the law, and this law is still binding. Furthermore, "homosexuals" are part of one of the longest vice lists in the New Testament, consisting of fourteen vices. Of these fourteen vices, eight form four pairs of two, while the remaining six describe

---

[154] Cf. Via and Gagnon, 82. De Young, 192, states, "Such researchers as Wright and Henry Mendell have definitely shown that *arsenokoitai* must be defined broadly. One cannot limit *arsenokoitai* to pederasty or to active male prostitution. It also includes same-gender orientation, condition, and mutuality."

[155] Thiselton, 452, writes, "On the basis of the distance between the first and twentieth centuries, many ask: 'Is the situation addressed by the biblical writer genuinely comparable to our own?' The more closely writers examine Greco-Roman society and the pluralism of ethical traditions, the more the Corinthian situation appears to resonate with our own. . . What is clear from the connection between 1 Corinthians 6:9 and Romans 1:26–29 and their Old Testament backgrounds is Paul's endorsement of the view that idolatry, i.e., placing human autonomy to construct one's values above covenant commitments to God, leads to a collapse of moral values in a kind of domino effect."

[156] Cf. Via and Gagnon, 87.

individual categories of sinners.[157] "On closer analysis, the organization of the vices on this list is determined by the order of the precepts of the Decalogue."[158] At least the last half of the list of vices corresponds clearly with the Ten Commandments: "those who kill their fathers or mothers," fifth commandment; "murderers," sixth commandment; "immoral men and homosexuals," seventh commandment; "kidnappers," eighth commandment; and "liars and perjurers," ninth commandment.[159] The phrase "whatever else is contrary to sound teaching" may relate to those commandments that are not directly referred to. Understood in this way, homosexuality is also a violation of the seventh commandment. Gagnon notes, "The seventh commandment against adultery, which was aimed at guarding the institution of marriage, served as a summary of all biblical sex laws, including the prohibition of male-to-male intercourse."[160]

The study of the Pauline passages dealing with homosexuality show that homosexuality is not limited to violent and promiscuous activity, nor is it restricted to pederasty. This is even supported by scholars who allow for covenantal homosexuality today: "The Pauline texts . . . do not support this limitation of male homosexuality to pederasty."[161]

All homosexual activity is against the creation order and against divine law and is therefore sin, which needs to be repented of, forgiven, and abandoned. Both the Old Testament and New Testament address our present situation.

Other New Testament Texts on Homosexuality

There are a number of other New Testament texts that may allude to homosexual activity. Although not as explicit as the previous texts, they deserve a brief comment at this point. One of them is 2 Peter 2:6–10 which mentions the destruction of Sodom and Gomorrah and their sins. Lot is referred to, who suffered because of the lifestyle of the inhabitants of Sodom. Interestingly, licentiousness, lawlessness, and corrupt desires are listed in this passage, obviously encompassing all sexual sins, including homosexuality.[162]

Another passage is Jude 7–8 where the Sodom episode is referred to again. The inhabitants of Sodom and Gomorrah "indulged in gross immorality and went after strange flesh. . . . Yet in the same way these

---

157 Cf. Raymond F. Collins, *I & II Timothy and Titus*, The New Testament Library (Louisville, KY: Westminster John Knox, 2002), 31.

158 Collins, 30.

159 Cf. Via and Gagnon, 87.

160 Gagnon, "The Scriptural Case," 89.

161 Via and Gagnon, 11.

162 Cf. Springett, 142–144.

men [the heretics of Jude's time], also by dreaming, defile the flesh, and reject authority, and revile angelic majesties." Again, homosexuality seems to be included.[163]

A final text is Revelation 22:14–15, which mentions "dogs" among those who will not enter the gates of the New Jerusalem. "Dogs" may refer to gentiles (Matt 15:26), Judaizers (Phil 3:2), heretics (2 Pet 2:22), or male prostitutes (Deut 23:18).[164] D. E. Aune suggests that "It may be that κύων, 'dog' . . . is used more specifically here for male homosexuals, pederasts, or sodomites since the term on the parallel vice list in 21:8 . . . is ἐβδελυγμένοι, 'those who are polluted.'"[165]

Rogers compares the numbers of references to the concern for the poor and oppressed in Scripture with those on homosexuality, finding that while the first category contains several thousand references, homosexuality has only a few and none of them supposedly refers to contemporary Christian homosexuals.[166] By the use of such an argument several authors suggest that the topic "homosexuality" is more or less irrelevant. Indeed there are not very many direct references to homosexuality in Scripture, but this statement is misleading. Biblical doctrines are not determined by the number of direct references to them. There is no biblical principle that would require a certain number of texts to be reached, before the issue becomes relevant. Foot washing and the millennium occur clearly only once each in Scripture. This does not prevent us from practicing foot washing and accepting the concept of the millennium. Although statistically few, the references to homosexuality in Scripture suffice to make clear God's teaching and will on this matter.

Summary

The situation in the New Testament is comparable to that of the Old Testament. The two parts of Scripture agree with each other. Both Old Testament and New Testament texts clearly address homosexual behavior in ways that are not limited in scope, time, or culture. Indeed, the Bible conveys a clear assessment of all homosexual activity at all times and makes clear that homosexual behavior is a sin that needs to be repented of and forgiven.

---

[163] Cf. Springett, 144–148.

[164] Cf. David E. Aune, *Revelation 17–22*, Word Biblical Commentary 52C (Nashville, TN: Thomas Nelson, 1998), 1223; Robert H. Mounce, *The Book of Revelation*, rev. ed., New International Commentary on the New Testament (Grand Rapids, MI: Eerdmans, 1998), 408; and Grant R. Osborne, *Revelation,* Baker Exegetical Commentary on the New Testament (Grand Rapids, MI: Baker, 2002), 701; and Springett, 148–150.

[165] Aune, 1222.

[166] Rogers, 86.

In connection with one of his warnings against the homosexual lifestyle (see 1 Cor 6:9–10 above), Paul adds an encouraging statement: "Such were some of you; but you were washed, but you were sanctified, but you were justified in the name of the Lord Jesus Christ and in the Spirit of our God" (1 Cor 9:11). Thus, after having presented his list of vices, Paul concludes that some of the Corinthian church members have been involved in these sinful activities, including homosexuality, but they have given that up and began to live a different life. Does that mean that change from a homosexual to a heterosexual orientation can happen? R. B. Hays states:

> On the one hand, the transforming power of the Spirit really is present in our midst; the testimonies of those who claim to have been healed and transformed into a heterosexual orientation should be taken seriously. . . . On the other hand, the 'not yet' looms large; the testimony of those . . . who pray and struggle in Christian community and seek healing unsuccessfully for years must be taken with no less seriousness. Perhaps for many the best outcome that is attainable in this time between the times will be a life of disciplined abstinence, free from obsessive lust. (Exactly the same standard would apply for unmarried persons of heterosexual orientation.)[167]

In other words, change can come in different ways: complete change in sexual orientation, partial change, or change of behavior and attitude even if the orientation remains. God is willing to bless and strengthen us in each situation. And it is true: "sexual gratification is not a sacred right, and celibacy is not a fate worse than death."[168]

Implications for the Church

Suggestions

There is a biblical teaching regarding sexuality including non-acceptable forms of sexual practices as there is a biblical teaching regarding the Sabbath. Both of them go back to the creation account. Both of them are indispensable. We have noticed that the Bible contains texts that are clearly opposed to homosexual activity, and the biblical teaching on this matter is not limited in scope and includes all homosexual acts at all times. Scripture makes clear that homosexual behavior is sin that needs to be repented of and forgiven. This biblical teaching is even clearer than

---

[167] Hays, 402–403.

[168] Ibid., 401.

the Sabbath doctrine insofar that there are no biblical texts that seem to militate against it. This raises the question of how we will relate to it. Where should the church go from here?

A. J. Köstenberger makes the following suggestions for the Christian church in general:

> To be sure, the church's clear proclamation of the biblical teaching on homosexuality must be coupled with the proclamation of God's love for all people, including homosexuals. . . . Homosexuality is not the unpardonable sin, and forgiveness is always available (1 Cor. 6:11). But forgiveness implies repentance, and repentance implies admission of wrong.[169]

R. Rice lists five different possibilities and discusses their problems, pointing out that options 2 and 5 do not correspond to the clear biblical witness against homosexual activity:

> 1. Same-sex relations are sinful and so is same-sex attraction. People with same-sex orientation should seek to reverse it.
> 2. Same-sex relationships are perfectly natural. They fulfill the essential purpose of sexuality just as well as heterosexual relationships do. . . . The Church should welcome into membership people who are involved in loving, committed same-sex relationships.
> 3. Although the Church must condemn same-sex behavior, it should not exclude people simply because they have a same-sex orientation. To the contrary, it should welcome them into membership and open to them positions of leadership, with the important proviso, however, that they remain celibate. . .
> 4. Homosexuality is not part of the order of things that God intended, and the Church cannot give to same-sex relationships the official approval it gives to heterosexual marriage. Nevertheless, people in committed relationships should not be excluded from Christian fellowship . . .
> 5. . . . let's affirm each other as fellow believers and together pursue a clearer understanding of this difficult issue.[170]

He comes to the conclusion that approach 3 "may have the widest appeal in the Church" and regards approaches 4 and 5 as a middle course,

---

[169] Köstenberger, 223.

[170] Richard Rice, "Is the Church Ready for Same-Sex Sex?," in *Christianity and Homosexuality: Some Seventh-day Adventist Perspectives*, ed. David Ferguson, Fritz Guy, and David R. Larson (Roseville, CA: Adventist Forum, 2008), part 4:82–83.

although it may leave those opposed and those affected unsatisfied.[171] The author of the present study contends, however, that approach 3 comes the closest to the Adventist position as spelled out in the two official statements of the Seventh-day Adventist Church on homosexuality.[172]

Adventists and Homosexuals

Some persons may argue that their sexual lifestyle is their own choice and the church should stay out of the debate on sexual ethics. But this is not the biblical position. While individuals choose what they want, the church is affected, and therefore the church must react and uphold biblical principles. The argument that sexual lifestyles should not matter to the church mistakenly assumes that morality is a private matter only. Hays clearly points out that

> the biblical strictures against homosexual behavior are concerned not only for the private morality of individuals but for the health, wholeness, and purity of the elect community. . . . Sin is like an infection of the body; thus, moral action is not merely a matter of individual freedom and preference. . . . The New Testament never considers sexual conduct a matter of purely private concern between consenting adults. According to Paul, everything that we do as Christians, including our sexual practices, affects the whole body of Christ.[173]

So the church needs to get involved, and Adventists do that. They urge members and societies to respect all people, whether heterosexuals or homosexuals. They acknowledge that all human beings are creatures of the heavenly Father, whom He loves and whom they also have decided to love. Each person is extremely valuable in God's sight. Therefore, the Seventh-day Adventist Church is opposed to hating, scorning, or abusing homosexuals. There is a distinction between homosexual orientation and homosexual activity,[174] and the Church supports those who are struggling. While upholding the biblical teaching on sexual morality, Adventists

---

[171] Rice, "Is the Church Ready for Same-Sex Sex?," 84–85.

[172] See Seventh-day Adventist Church, "Same Sex Unions," October 17, 2012, http://www.adventist.org/information/official-statements/statements/article/go/0/same-sex-unions/(accessed February 21, 2021); and "Homosexuality," Seventh-day Adventist Church, October 17, 2012, http:/www.adventist.org/information/official-statements/statements/article/go/0/homosexuality/ (accessed February 21, 2021).

[173] Hays, 391–393.

[174] Thus, Adventists reject the first option listed by R. Rice.

do not condone the sin of homosexual activity.[175] At the same time, they also follow the Bible in treating each individual with respect and compassion. We are all sinners and dependent on God's grace. We are also called to serve Christ, follow His example, and separate from sin.

175 Adventists reject the second option listed above.

CHAPTER 17

Transgenderism: Reflections from a Biblical Perspective

Elias Brasil de Souza and Larry L. Lichtenwalter

This study considers from a biblical perspective some significant topics relevant to the issue of transgenderism. In doing so, it explores the theoretical foundations of contemporary transgender studies. Since it has been suggested that the duality of male and female is a social construct, not a universal given, this study surveys the notion of sexual complementarity in the Old and New Testaments. It also examines the basics of biblical anthropology, as an understanding of biblical anthropology is necessary in order to address the dichotomy between the self and the body that is claimed to affect transgender people.

To accomplish these purposes, this study is divided into four main sections. First, it looks into the theory underlying contemporary transgender studies. Second, it provides some background information by contrasting the worldview of the ancient Near East with that of the Bible, particularly in the area of sexuality. Third, it addresses the biblical perception of sexual complementarity as grounded in creation and thus assumed throughout the biblical canon. Finally, it surveys the biblical understanding of humans as wholistic beings whose psychosomatic unity cannot be split between soul/self and body.

Theory in Transgender Studies

Some claim to have been born with the body of the opposite sex or "a gender identity not matching their sexual anatomy."[1] In other words, a transgender person is "a female trapped in a male's body" or "a male

---

[1] Cary Gabriel Costello, "Intersex and Trans* Communities: Commonalities and Tensions," in *Transgender and Intersex: Theoretical, Practical, and Artistic Perspectives*, ed. Stefan Horlacher (New York: Palgrave Macmillan, 2016), 101.

entity . . . somehow imprisoned in a female body."[2] Transgenderism can be conceptualized within at least three basic frameworks.[3] First, the approach designated as the "integrity framework" understands transgenderism against the backdrop of the integrity of maleness or femaleness intended by God at creation. From this perspective, transgenderism is considered to be sinful because it violates the creation order.[4] Second, the "disability framework" understands gender dysphoria as a kind of mental health problem, whose ultimate cause lies in the fact that we live in a fallen world.[5] This approach tends to draw its insights from the Bible and from modern science. The third approach, called the "diversity framework," sees transgenderism as something to be fostered, honored, and celebrated.[6] This last approach has gained considerable ground with contemporary society and has become the normative way of looking at transgenderism. Because of its obvious disregard of and conflict with the authority of Scripture, the following paragraphs offer an overall description of its main tenets.

In order to ground transgenderism in a theological/ideological foundation, some transgender theorists resort to neo-paganism while others turn to a reinterpretation of classical Christian theology. Some studies show significant influence of pagan spirituality on modern perceptions of the self and gender. Old pagan gnostic ideas have been revamped to suit modern tastes.[7]

We should keep in mind that one of the basic tenets of pagan religions that has found its way into Gnosticism is that gender distinctions do not matter and hence should be obliterated. *The Gospel of Thomas*, a gnostic work, says, "And that you might make the male and the female be one and the same, so that the male might not be male nor the female be female . . . then you will enter [the kingdom] (Saying 22)."[8] Thus it is not surprising that one of the most prominent modern proponents of Gnosticism, C. G. Jung, asserts, "The self is a circle whose center is

---

[2] Susan Stryker and Stephen Whittle, *The Transgender Studies Reader* (New York: Routledge, 2006), 367.

[3] See Mark A. Yarhouse, *Understanding Gender Dysphoria: Navigating Transgender Issues in a Changing Culture* (Downers Grove, IL: InterVarsity, 2015), 46–53.

[4] Ibid., 46–48.

[5] Ibid., 48–50.

[6] Ibid., 50–53.

[7] See Peter Jones, *The God of Sex: How Spirituality Defines Your Sexuality* (Colorado Springs, CO: Victor, 2006).

[8] Bentley Layton, *The Gnostic Scriptures: A New Translation With Annotations and Introductions* (New Haven, CT: Yale University Press, 1987), 384.

everywhere and whose circumference is nowhere."[9] Consequently, as one author states, the "ultimate metaphysical secret, if we dare to state it so simply, is that there are no boundaries in the universe. Boundaries are illusions, products not of reality but of the way we map and edit reality."[10] Interestingly, the first boundary to be obliterated is that of sexual distinctions. The ideal for a pagan or gnostic-oriented person is to become, in this life, spiritually and ritually androgynous—"a radical refusal of sexual differentiation, as presented in the Genesis account."[11]

Mircea Eliade, a researcher and proponent of a new spirituality, explains androgyny as "a symbolic restoration of 'Chaos,' of the undifferentiated unity that preceded the Creation, and this return to the homogeneous takes the form of a supreme regeneration, a prodigious increase of power."[12] Androgyny thus becomes a mystical ideal in which one can completely integrate the spirit world: all contraries are collapsed. Hence the distinctions between the sexes are erased since male and female merge into an androgynous whole. The joining of the opposites, as one author describes, dissolves the creational distinctions and thus allegedly "brings a 'liberating' recognition that the real self is 'uncreated.'"[13] To heal our anxiety, one feminist author recommends the sacred marriage, the hieros gamos, of the ego and the self, which gives birth to "a divine child."[14] In other words, "a woman gives birth to herself as a divine androgynous being, autonomous, and in a state of perfection in the unity of the opposites. She is whole."[15] As Louis Dupré points out, the mystical goal believed to be in all religions is "a state in which all distinctions disappear."[16]

Unsurprisingly, radical feminism provides full support to the neopaganism underlying some perceptions of transgenderism. A case in point is the feminist criticism that the most basic problem of the Bible is not its

---

[9] See Miguel Serrano, *C. G. Jung and Hermann Hesse: A Record of Two Friendships*, trans. Frank MacShane (New York: Schoken, 1968), 50, 55.

[10] Peter Jones, "Androgyny: The Pagan Sexual Ideal," *Journal of the Evangelical Theological Society* 43, no. 3 (2000): 447.

[11] Ibid.

[12] Mircea Eliade, *The Two and the One (Mephistopheles and the Androgyne)* (Chicago, IL: Chicago University Press, 1965), 114, 199, 122, quoted by Wendy Doniger and Mircea Eliade, "Androgynes," in *Encyclopedia of Religion* (Detroit, MI: Thomson Gale, 2005), 1:337.

[13] Jones, "Androgyny," 447.

[14] Maureen Murdock, *The Heroine's Journey: Woman's Quest for Wholeness* (Boston, MA: Shambala, 1990), 160.

[15] Ibid.

[16] Louis Dupré, "Unio Mystica: The State and the Experience," in *Mystical Union in Judaism, Christianity and Islam: An Ecumenical Dialogue*, ed. Moshe Idel and Bernard McGinn (New York: Continuum, 1996), 7.

reflection of a patriarchal society, but rather its assumption of a divinely ordained order of creation. From this perspective, the celebrated statement of Genesis 1:27, "male and female he created them," is not only problematic but oppressive because it has the effect of relegating whole categories of people (homosexual, transgender) to a status of abnormality. "If one has any sympathy at all with the feminist enterprise, one will have to admit that the Bible is not an infallible guide, and that it is often very problematic."[17]

In the same vein,

> Rebecca Alpert, a lesbian feminist rabbi, argues that the Genesis account of creation "introduces a rigid binary identity" that inculcates "painful and prejudicial societal attitudes" toward intersexuals, lesbians, gays, transgendered individuals—in short, anyone who deviates from the "compulsory heterosexuality" entailed in the biblical call to become "one flesh" (Gen 2:24).[18]

In the same vein, feminist scholar Margaret D. Kamitsuka argues "that a sex binarism is problematic because of its link to heteronormativity (the notion that heterosexuality is the only legitimate form of sexual desire) and thus to heterosexism."[19] So she proposes "how to deconstruct that male-female sex binarism, in light of Judith Butler's poststructuralist theory of how selfhood (including gender and sex) is constituted performatively within a nexus of disciplinary cultural discursive conventions."[20]

On the other hand, some radical scholars attempt to ground trans-genderism in the biblical text itself. Theodore W. Jacob Jennings, for example, claims to have found instances of transgendering in prophetic treatments of "Israel" or members thereof as metaphorical "women," including a transgendering in relation to YHWH. Jennings likewise points to Joseph, especially in Genesis 37 and 39, as a (wo)man, a "queer" figure mediating gender as well as other life divisions.[21] Other theorists reinterpret classical Christian doctrines in light of transgenderism and other contemporary perceptions of sexuality. Thus, according to

---

[17] John F. Brug, "Review of *The Bible After Babel: Historical Criticism in a Postmodern Age* by John J. Collins," *Wisconsin Lutheran Quarterly* 104 (2007): 230.

[18] Quoted by Margaret D. Kamitsuka, *Feminist Theology and the Challenge of Difference*, Reflection and Theory in the Study of Religion Series, ed. James Wetzel (Oxford: Oxford University Press, 2007), 67.

[19] Ibid., 64.

[20] Ibid.

[21] Theodore W. Jennings, *Jacob's Wound: Homoerotic Narrative in the Literature of Ancient Israel* (New York: Continuum, 2005), 147, 177–198.

Marcella Althaus-Reid, the Trinity needs to be understood as an orgy, which breaks down the privileging of binary or pair-bonded relationships. Initially, the Trinity appears to be an example of "restricted polyfidelity" in which the three persons of the Godhead are themselves in a closed, or faithful, sexual relationship. However, Althaus-Reid argues that each person of the Trinity has his/her own closet of lovers and "forbidden desires" (for example, Jesus' relationships with Mary Magdalene and Lazarus), which in turn results in the death of the "illusion of limited relationships." Althaus-Reid further contends that the Trinity reminds us that men and women are not limited to "dyadic" or "fixed" sexual identities, but rather "multitudes."[22]

In this connection, we should note that the so-called transgender experience may fall under three distinct categories, which Rogers Brubaker defines as "trans of migration," "trans of between," and "trans of beyond."[23] Trans of migration are transgender people who feel dysphoric and want a surgical correction to align their biological sex with their gender identity. The trans of between are transgender people who feel happy to live somewhere in between the male and female genders. The trans of beyond designates transgender persons who desire to transcend gender as a binary category and express their sexuality in absolutely different ways. More akin to the latter group is the postmodern claim that gender distinctions are oppressive.[24]

Space limitations do not allow further interaction with all the complexities of theoretical approaches underlying transgenderism as anideology. However, this brief analysis should suffice to indicate that current pleas for a new understanding of sexuality, particularly transgenderism, comes with a very heavy philosophical and critical baggage. Indeed, in some aspects transgender theory seems to resort to ideas found in ancient Near Eastern religions. Some of the foregoing perspectives on human nature/sexuality have been both challenged and rejected by the Bible's unique understanding of reality, as will be discussed.

---

[22] Patrick S. Cheng, *Radical Love: An Introduction to Queer Theology* (New York: Seabury Books, 2011), 59, Kindle.

[23] Rogers Brubaker, *Trans: Gender and Race in an Age of Unsettled Identities* (Princeton, NJ: Princeton University Press, 2016), 72.

[24] Alain Beauclair, "The Power of Seduction," in *New Philosophies of Sex and Love: Thinking Through Desire*, ed. Sarah LaChance Adams, Christopher M. Davidson, and Caroline R. Lundquist (London: Rowman and Littlefield, 2017), 235–256. See also Lauren Swayne Barthold, *A Hermeneutic Approach to Gender and Other Social Identities* (New York: Palgrave Macmillan, 2016).

Ancient Near Eastern Background

Biblical writers faced different challenges than those put forth by modern conceptions of sexuality such as fluid perceptions of gender, gender as an individual choice, and the so-called "gender identity disorder."[25] Nonetheless, the Scriptures came into being amidst a process of interaction with and reaction to an environment often characterized by diversity of sexual mores.[26] In this process, the Bible produced a worldview that, despite some superficial similarities, differs profoundly from the thought world of the ancient Near East.[27]

Understanding the worldview reflected in the Bible is essential for sound exegesis and hermeneutics. In this area, scholars falter between two opinions: whereas some tend to emphasize the similarities, others focus on the distinctions between the Bible (particularly the Old Testament) and its ancient Near Eastern environment. As a representative of the former view, Mark S. Smith has produced three provocative tomes emphasizing the ancient Near Eastern background of the Bible's religious ideas.[28] More recently, from a conservative perspective, John H. Walton has produced an impressive work emphasizing the similarities between the Bible and the "cognitive environment" of the ancient Near East. Walton argues that "the Old Testament and New Testament were located firmly in the cognitive environment of the ancient world" and that "the Early Christians did as well, is patently obvious in the text and logically mandated."[29]

John Oswalt, from another standpoint, though recognizing similarities, points out specific areas of contrast between the Bible and the ancient Near East.[30] Among other items, Oswalt stresses the principle of continuity, according to which everything that exists is in continuity

---

[25] John W. Kennedy, "The Transgender Moment: Evangelicals Hope to Respond With Both Moral Authority and Biblical Compassion to Gender Identity Disorder," *Christianity Today* 52, no. 2 (February 1, 2008): 54–58.

[26] For example, around 2400 BC, a Sumerian list of human professions mentions prostitutes, priests, male prostitutes and transsexuals (Peter N. Stearns, *Sexuality in World History*, Themes in World History [London: Routledge, 2009], 24).

[27] See John N. Oswalt, *The Bible Among the Myths: Unique Revelation or Just Ancient Literature?* (Grand Rapids, MI: Zondervan, 2009).

[28] See Mark S. Smith, *The Origins of Biblical Monotheism: Israel's Polytheistic Background and the Ugaritic Texts* (New York: Oxford University Press, 2001); Smith, *The Early History of God: Yahweh and the Other Deities in Ancient Israel*, The Biblical Resource Series, 2nd ed. (Grand Rapids, MI: Eerdmans, 2002); and Smith, *The Memoirs of God: History, Memory, and the Experience of the Divine in Ancient Israel* (Minneapolis, MN: Augsburg Fortress, 2004).

[29] John H. Walton, *The Lost World of Scripture: Ancient Literary Culture and Biblical Authority* (Downers Grove, IL: InterVarsity, 2013), 293–294, emphasis original.

[30] Oswalt.

with everything else.[31] As indicated, for example, in the creation myth Enuma Elish, Marduk fashioned the world from the carcass of Tiamat and made humans from the blood of the god Qingu.[32] In some other ancient Near Eastern creation myths, procreation explains the origin of all things. Ancient Near Eastern religion, therefore, rests on the assumption of continuity—namely, that there is a continuous flow between the human world and the world of the gods.

The divine world was thought to be formed by a variety of gods who came into being primarily through sexual means. These gods represented different domains of reality, such as natural phenomena, geographic locations, or cosmic entities. In addition, the gods were not bound to moral principles and did not exist within the constraints of ethical demands. Therefore, notions of right and wrong were not reflected in the character of the gods, but rather existed for practical reasons—namely, to make society work and be in harmony with an impersonal cosmic order. This view of reality precludes universal moral standards binding for either humans or deities. Indeed, ancient Near Eastern literature portrays the gods experiencing moral failures, unjustified anger, and sexual drives. In other words, ancient Near Eastern deities were large-scale humans.

Nonetheless, since absolute reality is impersonal, even the gods were trapped in a chain of circumstances over which they had no control; some of them would die and rise again according to the fate ultimately determined by impersonal cosmic powers. Within such a worldview, humans and gods alike are trapped within the unbreakable chain of destiny and impersonal forces. Humans can cope with life by ritual or magical manipulation of the gods and the cosmic order.

According to this worldview, religion functions to maintain the cycles of existence with minimum disruption. This may help explain somewhat the sexual mores, magical procedures, and other practices such as cultic prostitution and human sacrifices. As everything is continuous with everything else, magical and ritual actions performed upon the human level of reality had the power to interfere and alter the course of the ultimate reality. But, since ultimate reality is impersonal, material, and eternal, there can be no eschatological hope. Furthermore, as noted, the multiplicity of deities with different ethical standards precludes the establishment of an absolute morality.

As a result of a worldview that conceives continuity between human and divine spheres, ancient Near Eastern texts ascribe to the gods

---

[31] Oswalt, 47–61.

[32] William W. Hallo and K. Lawson Younger, eds., *The Context of Scripture*, vol. 1 (New York: Brill, 1997), 390–401.

the same sexual attributes that humankind has. So, the gods have come into existence through procreation and are often portrayed as sexually aroused. In Mesopotamia, for example, the "descent of generations of human beings has its equivalent in the sphere of divine beings and the forces of nature."[33] And "the sexuality of the youthful gods is wholly preoccupied with phallic displays and impregnation as proof of virility."[34] Interestingly, the "most popular deity of ancient Mesopotamia" was the goddess Inanna/Ishtar. She "represented the power of sexual attraction and the carnal pleasure that proceeds from it. Focused on the immediate gratification of her own sensual needs, she was neither a goddess of marriage nor of childbirth. Her sexual appetite was inexhaustible and her relationships with men short term."[35]

Egyptians also conceived of their deities as sexually involved in a variety of ways. Sexual intercourse between a deity (the god Amun) and a woman brought the king into existence.[36] Deities could be involved in homoerotic activity, as indicated in the story of Horus and Seth. However, condemnation of same-sex intercourse applied only to the passive partner.[37] There were also rumors of a pharaoh nurturing sexual desire for one of his generals.[38] Additional connections between worldview and sexuality emerge in the representation of deities with an erect penis. This so-called "celebration of the phallus," as Edward Bleiberg says,

> appears to be directly related to the Egyptians' concerns with the creation (and sustaining) of the universe, in which the king was thought to play a significant role—which was no doubt one of the reasons the Egyptian state would have been concerned to ensure that the ithyphallic figures continued to be important elements of many cults.[39]

In Canaan—as much as the Ugaritic texts may represent the general context of the religious ideas of the larger area—deities were also depicted as sexually involved with one another. Since the processes of nature stood in continuity with the divine world, the relations of the gods and

---

[33] Gwendolyn Leick, *Sex and Eroticism in Mesopotamian Literature* (London: Routledge, 1994), 12.

[34] Ibid., 55.

[35] Stephen Bertman, *Handbook to Life in Ancient Mesopotamia* (New York: Oxford University Press, 2005), 120.

[36] Ian Shaw, *Ancient Egypt: A Very Short Introduction* (Oxford: Oxford University Press, 2004), 93.

[37] Edward Bleiberg, *Ancient Egypt, 2615–332 B.C.E*, World Eras 5, ed. Anthony J. Scotti Jr. (Detroit, MI: Gale Group, 2002), 192.

[38] Ibid.

[39] Ibid., 133.

goddesses determined the fertility of the land. In times of drought, for example, the Canaanites would engage in cultic prostitution to move Baal to pour the rain upon the earth. They understood the rain as the sperm of Baal poured from heavens to bring fertility to the land. Thus, "according to Canaanite fertility cult theology, when the divine sex activity of the god is emulated at the earthly high place (a place of worship usually set on a hill, sometimes a high or large altar), that same activity is further stimulated through sympathetic magic."[40]

As the ancient worldview conceived of sexuality as the driving power of creation, all means should be used to harness that force. Sex, then, naturally was integrated with the ancient Near Eastern cultic and ritual system. Given this perception of reality, ethics became compromised and consequently no absolute norms could be established to regulate sexual behavior. Although some law codes included some norms of sexual conduct, they claimed no absolute foundation because the multiplicity of gods precluded any claim to an absolute and universal ethical norm.

Some particular instances of what may be called transgenderism are attested in the ancient Near East. A glaring example comes from Egypt. It is reported that Pharaoh Hatshepsut (ca. 1478/1472–1458 BC), after seizing power, had herself depicted as male. It is difficult to explain such behavior; as "there was no specific reason why a woman could not be pharaoh and Hatshepsut was not the first woman to take the throne (the last ruler of the Twelfth Dynasty, Sobeknofru, was a woman), Hatshepsut's assumption of masculine traits and iconography was exceptional."[41] Other indications of transgender behavior come from the court of Akhenaten (1353–1336 BC), where the "king is often depicted with feminine hips and his wife Nefertiti with the crown normally reserved for the pharaoh; the meaning of this iconography is still unclear."[42]

Another possible indication of transgender behavior may be noted in the actual practice of cross-dressing from Canaan and Mesopotamia. Harold Torger Vedeler notes that mainly in cultic settings, "there are numerous terms for individuals whose gender does not appear to have been specifically male or female, including *assinnu, kulu'û,* and *kurgarrû* in Akkadian and *sag-ur-sag, gala, and pi-li-pi-li* in Sumerian."[43] Some of these individuals were of ambiguous gender or were men who had been

---

[40] Richard M. Davidson, *Flame of Yahweh: Sexuality in the Old Testament* (Peabody, MA: Hendrickson, 2007), 93, emphasis original.

[41] Harold Torger Vedeler, "Reconstructing Meaning in Deuteronomy 22:5: Gender, Society, and Transvestitism in Israel and the Ancient Near East," *Journal of Biblical Literature* 127, no. 3 (2006): 465.

[42] Ibid.

[43] Ibid.

changed into women.[44] Involved in the worship of Inanna-Istar, they "mimic her gender ambiguity in that they themselves cross-dress in ritual performances, strangely donning female clothes on their right side and male garments on the left."[45] It has been speculated that these cult personnel may have been eunuchs or hermaphrodites.[46] Interestingly, Innana was the goddess of sexuality and her personality spans the roles of both genders. One of her better-known epithets was "the one who can change woman into man and man into woman."[47] As S. Tamar Kamionkowski summarizes, "Ishtar represents not only the spectrum of gender expressions, but also the fluidity of such gender roles. Today's woman may be tomorrow's man. A man in one setting may have a different gender assignment in another setting."[48] Thus "gender multiplicity and fluidity are given a divinely sanctioned place in the ordered universe."[49] In contrast and opposition to such ideas, the Old Testament affirms sexual polarity as grounded in creation as noted in the following section.

Sexual Complementarity in the Bible

Old Testament

In contrast to the ancient Near Eastern perception of sexuality and its modern offshoots in neo-paganism and neo-Gnosticism, the Old Testament indicates discontinuity between the divine and human worlds. Creation came into being by the sovereign Word of God that peacefully brought the created order into existence and established boundaries and distinctions within it. For example, God differentiated the firmament from the waters below, the dry land from the seas, the sun from the moon, male from female. As for humans, although created in God's image, they remain distinct from God.

Some laws demanded respect for the boundaries established by God in the created order. The law against cross-dressing reads, "A woman shall not wear anything that pertains to a man, nor shall a man put on a

---

[44] See Martti Nissinen, *Homoeroticism in the Biblical World: A Historical Perspective* (Minneapolis, MN: Fortress, 1998), 28–36.

[45] Nili Sacher Fox, "Gender Transformation and Transgression: Contextualizing the Prohibition of Cross-Dressing in Deuteronomy 22:5," in *Mishneh Todah: Studies in Deuteronomy and Its Cultural Environment in Honor of Jeffrey H. Tigay*, ed. Nili Sacher Fox, David A. Glatt-Gilad, and Michael J. Williams (Winona Lake, IN: Eisenbrauns, 2009), 54.

[46] Ibid.

[47] S. Tamar Kamionkowski, *Gender Reversal and Cosmic Chaos: A Study on the Book of Ezekiel*, Journal for the Study of the Old Testament Supplement Series 368 (New York: Sheffield Academic Press, 2003), 81.

[48] Ibid.

[49] Ibid., 81–82.

woman's garment, for all who do so are an abomination to the Lord your God" (Deut 22:5).[50]

The wearing of clothes designed for the opposite sex is attested in ancient Near Eastern texts and artifacts. However, only in Israel was cross-dressing forbidden. And since it is an "abomination" (*tōʿēbāh*), it belongs to the same category as idolatry and homosexual lifestyle (Deut 7:25; 18:12; Lev 18:22; 20:13). Most commentators understand this law as a reaction against foreign cults in which men dressed as females and acted as cult prostitutes in fertility rituals.[51] Although at first glance this hypothesis may seem plausible, the evidence that the Deuteronomic prohibition of cross-dressing was a reaction to such practices is meager.[52] Indeed, the law under consideration makes no mention of magical rites or cultic practices associated with cross-dressing. Although such practices were attested in the surrounding cultures, they do not seem to provide the ultimate rationale for the law. Most likely, the underlying motivation for the law lies in the Bible's perception of sexual complementarity and its aversion to mixtures and confusion in the natural and social orders. Therefore, since dress functions as a mark of gender distinctions,[53] it seems likely that this legislation intended to preserve the gender differentiation established at creation. As one critical scholar recognizes, "Israel's two-gender system, at least in its idealized biblical form, allowed no room for fluidity of identity for any member of society regardless of his or her role or status."[54]

That said, we conclude that the rationale and purpose of the legislation against cross-dressing surpasses the immediate historical circumstances allegedly associated with magic rites and pagan cults. This regulation enforces respect for boundaries as a creation principle. As Walter Kaiser aptly says, the "maintenance of the sanctity of the sexes established in the

---

[50] All biblical quotations are from the NKJV, unless otherwise indicated.

[51] See, e.g., Samuel Rolles Driver, *A Critical and Exegetical Commentary on Deuteronomy*, International Critical Commentary, 3rd ed. (Edinburgh: T&T Clark, 1902), 250–251; and Peter C. Craigie, *The Book of Deuteronomy*, New International Commentary on the Old Testament (Grand Rapids, MI: Eerdmans, 1976), 288. Another view has been advanced by Harry Hoffner, "Some Contributions of Hittitology to Old Testament Study," *Tyndale Bulletin* 20 (1969): 48–51, who suggests that this legislation was a reaction against the magical practices involving gendered clothing and objects.

[52] See Fox, 66.

[53] According to Vern L. Bullough and Bonnie Bullough, *Cross Dressing, Sex, and Gender* (Philadelphia, PA: University of Pennsylvania Press, 1993), viii, "dress traditionally has been a ubiquitous symbol of sexual differences, emphasizing social conceptions of masculinity and femininity. Cross dressing, therefore, represents a symbolic incursion into territory that crosses gender boundaries."

[54] See Fox, 71.

created order was the foundation of this legislation. The tendency to obliterate all sexual distinctions often led to licentiousness and promoted an unnaturalness opposed to the created order."[55] And insofar as clothes are an indication of one's sex, these boundaries ought to be respected.[56]

Other regulations proscribe various kinds of unlawful mixtures:

> You shall not sow your vineyard with different kinds of seed, lest the yield of the seed which you have sown and the fruit of your vineyard be defiled. You shall not plow with an ox and a donkey together. You shall not wear a garment of different sorts, such as wool and linen mixed together. (Deut 22:9–11)

> You shall keep My statutes. You shall not let your livestock breed with another kind. You shall not sow your field with mixed seed. Nor shall a garment of mixed linen and wool come upon you. (Lev 19:19)

Although concerns with improper mixing of animals, plants, or clothing belongs to the ceremonial system, the most likely rationale for these laws is creation—that is, God issued these prescriptions to Israel as pedagogical devices to help the Israelites learn to respect the boundaries of creation.[57] In relation to Deuteronomy 22:9–11, as Victor Hamilton observes,

> the remainder of the chapter (Deut 22:13–30) is about sexual relations, or more accurately, the violation of those relations. Perhaps the three brief laws about not mixing (two kinds of seeds, the ox and the ass, wool and linen [Deut 22:9–11]) serve as a prelude to these laws on chastity, which also deal with unlawful mixing at the sexual level.[58]

---

[55] Walter C. Kaiser Jr., *Toward Old Testament Ethics* (Grand Rapids, MI: Zondervan, 1983), 198.

[56] See Jackie A. Naudé, "Sexual Ordinances," in *New International Dictionary of Old Testament Theology & Exegesis*, ed. Willem VanGemeren, vol. 4 (Grand Rapids, MI: Zondervan, 1997), 1210.

[57] As suggested by George Bush, *Notes, Critical and Practical, on the Book of Leviticus* (New York: A. McFarren, 1852), 206, "This might perhaps have been forbidden in order to impress the Israelites with a greater abhorrence of the crime of bestiality, or at least to afford them among the brute creation no example of those unnatural commixtures which were prohibited in the foregoing chapter, v. 22." "The people are first reminded that holiness is about being set apart and that in every area of life they were to be a holy, separated people for God. Unnatural mixtures were seen as out of keeping with the creation order that everything was made 'according to its kind' (Gen 1:21, 24–25)" (Philip H. Eveson, *The Beauty of Holiness: The Book of Leviticus Simply Explained*, Welwyn Commentary Series [Darlington: Evangelical Press, 2007], 261).

[58] Victor P. Hamilton, *Handbook on the Pentateuch*, 2nd ed. (Grand Rapids, MI: Baker Academic, 2005), 426.

In the same vein, Hamilton suggests that "the Numbers version of the tassel law (Num 15:37–41; cf. Deut 22:12) says that the purpose of these ornaments is to remind the Israelites of God's commands so that they will not 'prostitute' themselves by pursuing the 'lusts' of their own heart and eyes (Num 15:39)."[59] As for Leviticus 19:9, it may be noted that these laws also belong to a cluster of instructions related to sexual matters, which in context (Lev 19:18, 20) required respect for boundaries—notably sexual boundaries established at creation.[60]

A distinctive aspect of the biblical worldview lies in its perception of sexuality. As reported in Genesis 1 and assumed throughout Scripture, God created the sexual polarity as an essential constituent of humans. God, however, remains outside and above the sexual distinctions given to creation. As recorded in Genesis 1, in the beginning God made humankind as male and female (Gen 1:27) and evaluated this creative act as "very good" (Gen 1:31). With the graphic words *zākār* (male) and *nĕkēbâ* (female), the Bible expresses the sexual duality of humanity.

As a specific term to designate the male gender, *zākār* is etymologically related to the male organ[61] and occurs in several passages related to circumcision, a rite undergone only by male Israelites (Gen 17:10, 12, 14, 23; 34:15, 22, 24; Exod 12:48). It is instructive to note that *nĕkēbâ*, the counterpart of *zākār*, "derives from the root *nqb*, 'bore, pierce,'" which seems

---

[59] Hamilton, 426.

[60] Hermeneutical questions seem unavoidable at this juncture. Are these laws still binding on Christians today? If not, how can we safely say that the laws pertaining to sexual purity still retain normative force for the contemporary church? Although space does not allow for a full-fledged exposition of the hermeneutical issues involving the Pentateuchal laws, some brief considerations may be in order. First, we should hold in mind that for the ancient Israelites the entirety of the law was obligatory. They would not have made a clear-cut distinction between moral and ceremonial law. Second, some aspects of the law, although binding upon the Israelites, are no longer binding upon the church today. The purpose of the latter laws was to function as pedagogical devices to guide the ancient people of God to a clearer understanding of moral principles and action. An example that may illustrate this situation is the centralization of the cult so clearly established in the book of Deuteronomy. For the Israelites, the one place of worship and the one God were inextricable connected. As part of God's pedagogy, the people were required to worship in a central place in order to better grasp the reality of God. Later, in the course of salvation history, the one place was abrogated, but the one God remained as crucial as ever. It seems that in regard to the laws against unlawful mixtures, God wanted to make a related point. By avoiding certain kinds of mixtures, the people were taught to preserve certain boundaries established by God at creation—namely, illegitimate sexual relationships. Although later the regulations on cloth, seeds, and animals lost their force, the principle to which they pointed remains as binding as ever.

[61] See Ludwig Koehler, Walter Baumgartner and Johann Stamm, *The Hebrew and Aramaic Lexicon of the Old Testament* (New York: Brill, 1999), 270–271; and Francis Brown, Samuel Rolles Driver, and Charles Augustus Briggs, *Enhanced Brown-Driver-Briggs Hebrew and English Lexicon* (Oxford: Clarendon Press, 1977), 271.

to be a clear "sexual reference"[62] to the female sexual organ. Although such terminology may seem crude to modern standards, its etymology underscores the anatomic complementarity created by God.

Genesis 2 likewise indicates that the sexual complementarity was God's intention. He created the man and the woman to enjoy sexual intimacy, which, according to the order of creation, requires two beings capable of complementing each other as man and woman. As recounted in Genesis 2, when the Lord introduces the woman to the man, the man immediately recognizes that the woman has the attributes to complement the man:

> This is now bone of my bones
> And flesh of my flesh;
> She shall be called Woman [*ʾiššâ*],
> because she was taken out of Man [*ʾîš*]. (Gen 2:23)

In this poetic expression Adam makes two crucial recognitions. First, he recognizes his obvious affinity with the woman by using the phrase "bone of my bones and flesh of my flesh." Some scholars contend that this expression is a mere affirmation of kinship with the woman, not sexual complementarity.[63] However, similar expressions in the Old Testament not only convey the notion of kinship, but also function as a declaration of loyalty (e.g., Gen 29:14; Judg 9:2; 2 Sam 5:1; 19:12–13). "Adam thus composed the first marriage vows in which he declared his loyalty to this mate regardless of the circumstances."[64] Second, Adam also makes a crucial distinction between them. In the wordplay *ʾiššâ/ʾîš*, Adam recognizes that man and woman bear the same essential human dignity with all its entailments; however, in the same breath, this poetic expression indicates the sexual complementarity that allows the man (*ʾîš*) and the woman (*iššâ*) to complement each other. As the narrative unfolds, sexual complementarity emerges as the precondition for man and woman to become one flesh:

> Therefore a man [*ʾîš*] shall leave his father and mother
> and be joined to his wife [*ʾiššâ*]
> and they shall become one flesh [*bāsār ʾeḥād*]. (Gen 2:24)

---

[62] R. E. Clements, "זָכָר" *Theological Dictionary of the Old Testament*, ed. G. Johannes Botterweck and Helmer Ringgren, trans. David E. Green (Grand Rapids, MI: Eerdmans, 1980), 4:83.

[63] James V. Brownson, *Bible, Gender, Sexuality: Reframing the Church's Debate on Same-Sex Relationships* (Grand Rapids, MI: Eerdmans, 2013), 32–34. See also Gordon J. Wenham, *Genesis 1–15*, Word Biblical Commentary 1 (Dallas, TX: Word, 1998), 70.

[64] James E. Smith, *The Pentateuch*, Old Testament Survey Series, 2nd ed. (Joplin, MO: College Press, 1993), Genesis 2:22b–25.

Consequently, the sexual complementarity established by God at creation provides a foundation to regulate sexual relationships. Any deviation from this norm meets with divine disapproval and judgment since it is regarded as a violation of the created order.

Some scholars understand the biblical narrative to portray *'ādām* at first as an androgynous creature from which the man and the woman were created.[65] This view—attested in some gnostic gospels[66] and voiced by Samuel bar Nahman, a third-century rabbi—may ultimately be indebted to Plato, who talks about the creation of gendered beings out of androgynous creatures.[67] Interestingly, some myths and figurines of late antiquity also depict gods with androgynous traits.[68] A close examination of the biblical narrative yields strong reasons to dismiss such a position. First, the expression "male and female He created them" (Gen 1:27) points to two individual creatures. Second, the loneliness of *'ādām* described in the creation account (Gen 2:18–20) can hardly be attributed to an androgynous being.[69] Such a creature would be incapable of feeling the need for a sexual counterpart. Third, the parallel between *'dam* and *'îššâ* (Gen 2:25) points back to the parallel between "man" (*'îš*) and "woman" (*'îššâ*) (Gen 2:23). This indicates that Adam was not an androgynous creature, subsequently split into "man" and "woman," but a "man" out of which the "woman" was derived.[70] Fourth, the woman comes into being by an act of "construction" (*banah*) by God, not by an act of separation from an original androgynous creature (Gen 2:22).[71]

---

[65] See Robert A. J. Gagnon, *The Bible and Homosexual Practice: Texts and Hermeneutics* (Nashville, TN: Abingdon, 2010), 60 n. 44.

[66] According to the *Gospel of Thomas*, Adam was neither male nor female but an androgynous creature (Sayings 4, 11, 16, 22–23, 49, 75, 106). See Kathleen E. Corley, "Salome and Jesus at Table in the Gospel of Thomas," *Semeia* 86 (1999): 91. Anne W. Stewart, "Eve and Her Interpreters," in *Women's Bible Commentary*, ed. Carol A. Newsom, Jacqueline E. Lapsley, and Sharon H. Ringe, rev. ed. (Louisville, KY: Westminster John Knox, 2012), 48, says that the *Gospel of Philip* (63) "suggests that death came into the world not when Adam ate the apple but when Eve was created from Adam's side. It suggests that the first human was an androgynous being, and when Eve and Adam were separated from a single body, death entered."

[67] See Brownson, 27.

[68] See, e.g., Marie Delcourt, *Hermaphrodite: Myths and Rites of the Bisexual Figure in Classical Antiquity* (London: Studio Books, 1961); and Kathlyn M. Cooney, "Androgynous Bronze Figurines in Storage at the Los Angeles County Museum of Art," in *Servant of Mut: Studies in Honor of Richard A. Fazzini*, ed. Sue D'Auria, Probleme der Äegyptologie 28 (Leiden: Brill, 2008), 63–72.

[69] William C. Williams, "Sexuality, Human," in *Evangelical Dictionary of Biblical Theology*, Baker Reference Library, ed. Walter A. Elwell (Grand Rapids, MI: Baker Book House, 1996), Logos.

[70] See Brevard S. Childs, *Old Testament Theology in a Canonical Context* (Philadelphia, PA: Fortress, 1989), 190.

[71] Interestingly, the Greek words for "from the man" in Genesis 2:23 used in the Septuagint are also gendered (*ek tou andros*) rather than androgynous. This makes it improbable that Paul,

Another approach contends that rather than conveying the "*complementarity* of male and female," Genesis 2 focuses on "the *similarity* of male and female," also understood as a "kinship bond."[72] Since space limitations do not permit a detailed critique of this view, it shall suffice to say that the similarity and kinship bond that characterize each sexual gender do not preclude sexual complementarity. Indeed, both the similarities and the sexual differentiation stand on the biological substratum that according to the biblical worldview identifies every human being as either male or female.

That said, it seems evident that sexual complementarity is reaffirmed throughout the Bible. Hence, the male is consistently identified on the basis of external genitalia. As a sign of His covenant with Abraham, God established the rite of circumcision. In doing so, God explicitly defines the marker of a male: "This is My covenant which you shall keep, between Me and you and your descendants after you: Every male child among you shall be circumcised; and you shall be circumcised in the flesh of your foreskins, and it shall be a sign of the covenant between Me and you" (Gen 17:10–11). Instructively, God's covenantal relationship with His people was indicated by a sign that affirmed the distinction between male and female. In addition, we should also note some passages that employ the expression "that urinates against the wall" to designate the male (1 Sam 25:22, 34; 1 Kgs 14:10; 16:11; 21:21; 2 Kgs 9:8, AKJV). In alluding to the urination of the male penis, this idiom makes clear that a male is someone who has a penis. Most English versions euphemistically but correctly translate the expression as "male." This further indicates that the Old Testament defines the male according to the external genitalia, thus making clear that "male" and "female" are distinguished on an anatomical basis.

New Testament

In keeping with the foregoing perspective of the Hebrew Scriptures in contrast to ancient Near Eastern, neo-pagan, and neo-gnostic perceptions of human sexuality, the New Testament likewise assumes sexual polarity as an essential constituent of humans. The New Testament also demonstrates that sexual complementarity was the Creator's intention. The sexual differentiation and complementarity of the sexes is reiterated by Jesus and Paul.

Sexual polarity is evidenced in the unequivocal distinction of "male and female" and "male or female": "And He answered and said to them,

---

who also used the Septuagint, would have viewed the creation of woman as the division of an androgynous *'adam*. In 1 Timothy 2:11–15 Paul describes the formation of the man with the verb ἐπλάσθη eplasthē ("was formed"), which comes from the Septuagint (Gen 2:7).

[72] Brownson, 26.

'Have you not read that He who made them at the beginning made them male and female'" (Matt 19:4); "But from the beginning of creation, God made them male and female" (Mark 10:6); "There is neither male nor female; for you are all one in Christ Jesus" (Gal 3:28). The words are unambiguous: *arsēn* ("male")[73] and *thēlu* ("female").[74] They are used for sexual differentiation and unity in human couples.[75] For Genesis 1:27, the LXX translates the Hebrew *zākār ûnĕkēbâ* of the creation of male and female in the image of God with the phrase *arsēn kai thēly*, "male and female."[76]

The male/female differentiation Jesus refers to is no mere social construct. Rather, it is rooted in God's creation intent where "male" and "female" have essential physical, mental, emotional, moral, spiritual, personhood, and social characteristics in relation to the realities of human nature created in the image of God.[77]

Jesus affirms that God's purposeful design was the creation of two distinct and complementary sexes—male and female (*ho ktisas apo arsēn kai thēlu epoiēsen autos*, Matt 19:4)—that designate a fundamental distinction, which the Creator has embedded in the very biology of the human race (cf. *arsēn kai thēlu epoiēsen autos*, Gen 1:27 LXX).[78]

---

[73] "Etymologically related to old Indic *árṣati* ("it flows"; cf. Lat. ros), ἄρσην (*arsēn*) . . . literally means that which discharges sperm and therefore male offspring, male child" (Horst Robert Balz and Gerhard Schneider, *Exegetical Dictionary of the New Testament* [Grand Rapids, MI: Eerdmans, 1990], 1:158). The word "*arsēn* occurs some 54 times in the LXX canonical and uncanonical writings, chiefly for the Heb. *zāḵār*" (C. Brown, "Ἄρσην," in *New International Dictionary of New Testament Theology*, ed. Lothar Coenen, Erich Beyreuther, and Hans Bietenhard (Grand Rapids, MI: Zondervan, 1986), 562.

[74] Etymologically related to θῆλυς (*thēlys)* which signifies 'breast feeding' (related to θῆσθαι (*thēsthai*), from θηλή (*thēlē*), mother's breast . . .). It designates the female among animals, people, and gods. It is connected with ἄρσην (*arsēn*) in Genesis 1:27 (LXX) and Mark 10:6; Matthew 19:4 (Balz and Schneider, 147).

[75] Ibid.

[76] Brown, 562.

[77] Differentiation is a hallmark of established creation boundaries: light from darkness (Gen 1:4), firmament from the waters below (Gen 1:6–7), the dry land from the seas (Gen 1:9–10), the day from night (Gen 1:14–15), the sun from the moon (Gen 1:16–17), male from female (Gen 1:27), etc. In particular, the "male/female" differentiation continues to be identified for both human beings and animals up through the flood narrative (Gen 1:27; 5:2; 6:19; 7:2–3, 9, 16).

[78] Brownson, 260–280, incorrectly argues that we need to unearth the wider biblical "moral logic" that "undergirds" passages like these and then translate that logic into our own cultural practice. But his hermeneutic in doing so incorrectly determines that gender complementarity is nowhere "explicitly portrayed or discussed" in Scripture. In particular, Brownson argues that Genesis 2:24, the primary text to which the appeal to establish gender complementarity is directed, is not speaking primarily of the difference between male and female—and thus gender complementarity. Rather, in his opinion, it is speaking of their sameness in which male and female form a "kinship bond." The "flesh of my flesh" idiom in Genesis 2:23 thus functions the same way it functions elsewhere in the Old Testament—to denote kinship, not sexual,

Thus, gender—male and female—is linked to corresponding anatomy. Within the biblical worldview, there is no discussion of gender apart from anatomy.[79]

Furthermore, and in keeping with the Genesis narrative, Jesus' reference to the creation narrative suggests an ontological gender-based sexual nature of male and female. Human physical sex distinctions together with gender converge in a full view of personhood reflecting God's image (Gen 1:26–28). The New Testament Scripture thus provides a high view of a distinct and observable human male/female identity and sexuality as intended. This male/female differential essentially upholds the entire human person rather than merely locating one's identity in their sexual organs or functions. One cannot separate the two—body or being, whether male or female.[80] This affirms how gender serves as the basic identity foundation for all mankind.[81]

Gender is among the first elements of self-knowledge. Together with race and family, it is one of the three major factors of individual, personal identification.[82] Nevertheless, gender "stands as the most important factor for personal identity."[83] It governs social, ethical, and spiritual

---

anatomical "fit." Adam needs one who is like him, rather than unlike him (Gen 2:18–20). Therefore, God creates a woman to be such a "like" partner (Gen 2:20). In Brownson's view, the Old and New Testament rejection of same-sex erotic behavior is based not on commitment to "gender complementarity," but rather fear of cultic prostitution (in Leviticus), idolatry (1 Cor 6), or an "excess of desire" (Rom 1). Exploitation, abuse, and lust are the watchwords here. Brownson's argument, however, disconnects procreation and children from human sexuality. It also disconnects human sexuality from materiality and actual human bodies.

[79] The anatomic characteristics/differentiation of both male and female are nuanced etymologically in both Hebrew (as already noted) and Greek terms respectively (male—*zākār*, female—*nĕkēbā*; male—*arsēn*, female—*thēlu*)—that is, connoting the male sexual organ as circumcised and issuing semen, etc., or the female sexual organ as "pierced through" (hole). See Victor P. Hamilton, "זָכָר" (*zākār*), in VanGemeren, 1106; J. B. Bauer, "ἄρσην, *arsēn*," in Balz and Schneider, 158; and Brown, 562–571.

[80] David E. James, *God's Truth About Gender: Unraveling the Lies of Modern Human Sexuality, Behavior and Identity* (Sisters, OR: VMI Publishers, 2008), 86, suggests that "gender is a transcendent concept" that we, as created beings, reflect in our physical natures as man and woman. He does not mean to suggest that God is male or female, but rather that gender was a basis for which human beings were to bear God's likeness and, in doing so, reflect divine qualities of interpersonal relationship and balance within diversity.

[81] Ibid., 74.

[82] Ibid., 70.

[83] James, notes that "without a clear understanding of one's gender status, an individual will be at loss as to where he or she fits in relationship to the rest of the world. Gender identity determines one's behaviors and interactions with other humans. This is true in regard to how one relates to individuals of his or her own gender as well as the opposite one. When one speaks of an individual personality, it is impossible to describe the person without acknowledging his or her gender" Ibid.

behavior patterns.[84] This knowledge encompasses an internal sense of self and, often, a preference for external behaviors in keeping with one's inner-orienting gender identity.[85] That is why a gender identity crisis is the most severe form of identity crisis known to humans.[86]

Paul's distinction of "male nor female" (*arsēn kai thēlu*) maintains the clarity of the forgoing biblical creation gender realities of "male and female" while at the same time focuses on the essential new and transcending identity one finds in Jesus Christ: "There is neither Jew nor Greek, there is neither slave nor free man, there is neither male nor female; for you are all one in Christ Jesus" (Gal 3:28).

Later traditions under the influence of Gnosticism have been read into Paul's statement that in Christ there is "neither male nor female."[87] During the second century, the "neither male nor female" formula of Galatians 3:28 was picked up in a number of gnostic documents and became a major feature in the teaching of this heretical movement.[88] The ideal for the gnostic was to become sexless. It posited a radical refusal of sexual differentiation and a complete confusion of sexual identity in God's intended role.[89] The "neither male nor female" formula was understood as a call for "eliminating gender distinctions and the unique aspects of masculine and feminine personhood derived from them."[90] Not only was the elimination of sexuality taken as a prerequisite for salvation, but just as circumcision was for the Judaizers of Galatia, gender reversal became obligatory for the Gnostic heretics.[91] "For the Gnostics, creation and the material world were inherently evil. Since sexuality was an obvious carrier of this fallenness, it had to be reversed or neutralized in order to achieve release from the constricting 'prison house of matter.'"[92]

But Paul does not abolish sexual differences, as is proposed in gnostic writings. Nor does he allow for an undifferentiated unity, androgynous Adam, or androgynous mystical ideal.

---

[84] James, 137.

[85] Andrew Solomon, *Far From the Tree: Parents, Children, and the Search for Identity* (London: Random House, 2014), 607.

[86] James, 74.

[87] E.g., *The Gospel of Thomas* 22, 114.

[88] Timothy George, *Galatians,* New American Commentary 30 (Nashville, TN: Broadman and Holman, 1994), 290–291.

[89] John MacArthur, *Different by Design*, MacArthur Study Series (Wheaton, IL: Victor Books, 1996), 26–27.

[90] George, 290–291.

[91] Ibid.

[92] Ibid.

While their self-identity is radically altered when people come to Jesus Christ, this new identity does not negate or change either race or gender. "In the new creation, men remain men, and women remain women. The categorization of the community by race, social status, and gender, leading to patriarchal hierarchies, no longer exists. The community now receives its constitutive identity from Christ."[93] Consequently, Paul affirms males and females in their personhood and worth.

According to Romans 1, reversing, circumventing, or aiding nature in matters of sexuality is like trying to put together discordant entities.[94] Paul links the reversal of the created order in worship with the reversal of the created order in sexuality (Rom 1:21–23, 25). The context for Romans 1:21–32 is universal in nature.[95] According to Paul, the existential roots of homosexuality are in the turning of the face from God.[96] It is unnatural within God's creation.[97] As has been shown, sexual polarity is an essential constituent of humans and sexual complementarity in God's purposeful design. It is significant that here Paul again uses the creation order distinction of "male" and "female" (*arsēn* and *thēlu*) rather than generic terms for man and woman. In doing so he maintains the clear creation gender realities of "male and female" as found in the Genesis narrative and the teachings of Jesus.[98]

A key concept Paul uses is "exchange": they exchanged the glory of the immortal God (Rom 1:23); they exchanged the truth about God (Rom 1:25); they exchanged natural intercourse (Rom 1:26). Men and women exchanged the natural for the unnatural. Swapping God for idols entailed

---

[93] Charles B. Cousar, *Reading Galatians, Philippians, and 1 Thessalonian: A Literary and Theological Commentary*, Reading the New Testament Series (Macon, GA: Smyth and Helwys, 2001), 67.

[94] D. F. Wright, "Sexuality, Sexual Ethics," in *Dictionary of Paul and His Letters*, ed. Gerald F. Hawthorne, Ralph P. Martin, and Daniel G. Reid (Downers Grove, IL: InterVarsity Press, 1993), 872.

[95] In outlining the universal nature of sin and divine judgment, Paul includes Gentiles, Jews, and all of humanity through the ages (Rom 1–3). All alike are dependent on God's grace as revealed in Christ's sacrifice on our behalf. See Ekkehardt Mueller, "Homosexuality in Romans 1:26–27," Biblical Research Institute, https://adventistbiblicalresearch.org/wp-content/uploads/homosexuality-in-rom.pdf (accessed May 14, 2021).

[96] This may not be so with every homosexual or lesbian, however. Paul's focus is sexual behavior in terms of choice in relation to God's creative purpose rather than sexual orientation.

[97] See discussion in Robert A. J. Gagnon, "The Scriptural Case for a Male-Female Prerequisite for Sexual Relations: A Critique of the Arguments of Two Adventist Scholars," in *Homosexuality, Marriage, and the Church: Biblical, Counseling, and Religious Liberty Issues*, ed. Roy E. Gane (Berrien Springs, MI: Andrews University Press, 2012), 153 n. 102.

[98] Genesis 1:26–27; Matthew 19:4. Paul's focus on gender difference—rather than the alleged

a denial of God's true nature.[99] Swapping natural intercourse for unnatural male/male or female/female intercourse entailed a fundamental denial of one's own true nature and self. This in no way suggests, however, that Paul's focus is merely idolatry rather than human sexuality—and homosexuality in particular.[100] We must not misunderstand Paul's "worldly knowledge" in terms of the confusion of human sexuality within his contemporary cultural context, which included both abusive relationships of power or money and examples of "genuine love" between members of the same sex.[101] He is well aware of what he is talking about. Paul uses the term *para physin* ("against nature") to communicate clearly that homosexual or lesbian practice is a violation of the natural order as determined by God.[102] The order intended by God includes the function of the sex organs themselves. The deviant exchange of those organs is seen as a use that is against nature.[103] This positions the use of one's body in its sexual dimensions clearly in view as an instrument of self in relation to God.

Paul further links homosexuality with humanity's turning away from the Creator to images of their fellow creatures. The actions of the sinful human being itself have an ironic element—difference is exchanged for sameness.[104]

---

presence of "exploitation" or an "excess of desire" in homosexual unions as per Brownson—would explain his denunciation of same-sex erotic behavior in Romans 1:26–27.

[99] Miroslav M. Kiš, "Return to Innocence," in *Homosexuality, Marriage, and the Church: Biblical, Counseling, and Religious Liberty Issues*, ed. Roy E. Gane (Berrien Springs, MI: Andrews University Press, 2012), 179.

[100] Mueller, "Homosexuality in Romans 1:26–27." "The issue is hardly whether or not Paul in Romans 1:26–27 addresses homosexuality and considers it to be sin; this can be taken for granted. The issue is whether or not homosexuality in Romans 1 includes all forms of homosexuality and has a universal scope" (ibid., 1).

[101] Anthony C. Thiselton, *The First Epistle to the Corinthians* (Grand Rapids, MI: Eerdmans, 2000), 452.

[102] Mueller, "Homosexuality in Romans 1:26–27," 2.

[103] Joseph A. Fitzmyer, *Romans*, Anchor Bible 33 (New York: Doubleday, 1992), 286, suggests that "in the context of vv 19–23, 'nature' also expresses for him [Paul] the order intended by the Creator, the order that is manifest in God's creation or, specifically in this case, the order seen in the function of the sexual organs themselves, which were ordained for an expression of love between man and woman and for the procreation of children. Paul now speaks of the deviant exchange of those organs as a use *para physin*."

[104] Simon Gathercole, "Sin in God's Economy: Agencies in Romans 1 and 7," in *Divine and Human Agency in Paul and His Cultural Environment*, ed. Simon J. Gathercole and John M. G. Barclay (London: T&T Clark, 2007), 162.

The key correspondence between idolatry on the one hand and homosexual behavior on the other

> lies in the fact that both involve turning away from the "other" to the "same." . . . Humanity should be oriented toward God but turns in on itself (Rom 1:25). Woman should be oriented toward man, but turns in on itself (Rom 1:26). Man should be oriented toward woman, but turns in on itself (Rom 1:27).[105]

"The meta-sin of suppression or exchange" results in a cascade of sins (plural), in physical degradation in general (Rom 1:24), and in female and male homosexuality (Rom 1:26–27). This then is expanded to the entire sphere of doing "those things which are not fitting" (NKJV) and to a whole host of sins that emerge in the list of vices depicting the social chaos of a world in rebellion against God (Rom 1:28–31). Such rebellion violates the sexual polarity, as expressed in the creation gender realities of "male and female" found in the Genesis narrative and the teachings of Jesus.

Wholistic Anthropology of the Bible

Old Testament

Some transgender theorists make a dichotomy between sex and gender. Susan Stryker says,

> This set of cultural beliefs and practices about what biological sex means can be called 'gender.' It can feel confusing at first to try to think analytically about the difference between sex and gender, and the relationship between them, because one of our strongest unexamined cultural beliefs is that gender and sex are the same thing, which is why most people tend to use sex and gender interchangeably in everyday speech. A good rule of thumb to keep in mind is that sex is generally considered biological, and gender is generally considered cultural, and that you should use the words male and female (rather than man and woman) to refer to sex.[106]

Such a claim presupposes a dualism between sex and gender that is at odds with biblical anthropology and its wholistic view of human nature and its perception of the body.

---

[105] See Gathercole, 158–172, esp. 163–164.

[106] Susan Stryker, *Transgender History: The Roots of Today's Revolution*, 2nd ed. (New York: Seal Press, 2017), 32.

It is important to note that in contrast to the ancient Near Eastern thought, the body and what we do with it remains crucial to biblical ethics. Given its wholistic anthropology, the Bible portrays the body as intimately intertwined with the divine breath and thus an indispensable element for humans to exist as living souls. As shown in the creation narratives, the dignity of the body emerges from the concept of *imago dei*, which, by including the whole human being as God's image, gives the body unparalleled dignity. In addition, God's special involvement in bringing into existence the body—or the whole human person, for that matter—further underscores the significance of the body. Thus, whether from the clay of the earth or from a rib of man, the fact remains that the Creator became personally and intimately involved in fashioning the human body and the whole human person. It is instructive to note that God continually guides the coming into being of every person. The psalmist confesses with wonder,

For You formed my inward parts;
You covered me in my mother's womb.
I will praise You, for I am fearfully and wonderfully made;
Marvelous are Your works,
And that my soul knows very well.
My frame was not hidden from You,
When I was made in secret,
And skillfully wrought in the lowest parts of the earth.
Your eyes saw my substance, being yet unformed.
And in Your book they all were written,
The days fashioned for me,
When as yet there were none of them. (Ps 139:13–16)

Another poem thus describes God's involvement with the engendering of the human body:

Remember, I pray, that You have made me like clay.
And will You turn me into dust again?
Did You not pour me out like milk,
And curdle me like cheese,
Clothe me with skin and flesh,
And knit me together with bones and sinews?
You have granted me life and favor,
And Your care has preserved my spirit. (Job 10:9–12)

From this perspective, we can better understand why the Bible emphasizes the holiness and purity of the body. Being shaped by God and brought into this world by the loving oversight of the Creator, the body ultimately derives its value from God Himself, who in the ritual system prescribes holiness and purity for the body. Therefore, holiness, as God's requirement from His people, includes that we take appropriate care of our bodies.

The Old Testament conceives of the human being as an indivisible unity of body and breath of life.[107] A close look at the anthropological language of the Old Testament indicates that the body, mind, and other aspects of the human being form a single entity that cannot be separated. Thus, the term *nĕpĕš*, which carries the literal meaning of "throat" or "neck," indicates desire, soul, life, person, and could even function as a pronoun. Similarly, the term *bāśār,* which literally means "flesh" or "body," also serves to convey the notion of relationship and sometimes indicates human weakness. The term *rûaḥ*, which carries the primary notion of "wind," is used to designate breath, vital powers, spirit, feelings, and the will. In regard to *lēb*, "heart," it must be pointed out that it conveys the notions of feelings, wish, reason, or decision of will. Interestingly, the blood conveys the life of the body and the internal organs such as bowels, liver, and kidneys are the seat of conscience (Jer 12:2), emotions (Pss 16:9; 30:12; 57:8; 108:1; Lam 2:11), and wisdom (Prov 14:33).[108]

Significantly, terms used to designate parts of a person can also refer to the whole person, and can in fact be replaced by personal pronouns, as the following parallelism indicates:

> When wisdom enters your heart [*lēb*],
> And knowledge is pleasant to your soul [*nĕpĕs*],
> Discretion will preserve you;
> Understanding will keep you. (Prov 2:10–11, emphasis supplied)

Thus, speaking about your "heart" and "soul" is tantamount to speaking about "you." The Old Testament conceives of the human being as a unity. As Charles H. H. Scobie notes, the Old Testament "does not make a twofold division into 'body' and 'soul,' nor a threefold division into 'body,' 'mind,' and 'spirit.' Rather, each of the major anthropological

[107] See Richard M. Davidson, "The Nature of the Human Being from the Beginning: Genesis 1–11," in *"What Are Human Beings That You Remember Them?": Proceedings of the Third International Bible Conference, Nof Ginosar and Jerusalem, June 11–21, 2012*, ed. Clinton Wahlen (Silver Spring, MD: Biblical Research Institute, 2015), 11–42; and Paul B. Petersen, "'Unwholly' Relationships: Unity in a Biblical Ontology," in Wahlen, 235–248.

[108] Hans Walter Wolff, *Anthropology of the Old Testament*, trans. Margaret Kohl (London: SCM Press, 1974), 7–79.

terms describes the whole person from one particular aspect."[109] It follows from this that the body cannot be separated from the self, since one cannot be conceived apart from the other. As noted, "the metaphorical use of parts of the body shows that man is regarded as a psycho-physical being whose life can manifest itself by extension or concentration in all parts of the body."[110] Furthermore, the human being "is always seen in his totality, which is quickened by a unitary life. The unity of human nature is not expressed by the antithetical concepts of body and soul but by the complementary and inseparable concepts of body and life."[111]

It should be noted at this point that the wholistic anthropology of the Old Testament entails a perception of personal identity and selfhood that differs in significant aspects from modern perceptions. Charles Taylor shows that the idea of an autonomous self and the "sense of ourselves as beings with inner depths, and the connected notion that we are 'selves'" comes from Plato via Neoplatonism through Augustine, Descartes, and Montaigne.[112] Such perception of an inner and "autonomous self"[113] is at odds with the biblical perception of individual identity. According to the Old Testament, personal identity is embodied, heteronomous, and rooted in social identity. Thus, it is not possible to speak of the self as an autonomous entity lodged in the inner recesses of the body. In addition, one's identity is deeply rooted in the social life of the community. Old Testament anthropology conceives of the human being as a wholistic entity and therefore cannot conceive of a separation between sex and gender or a dichotomy between the self and the body.

New Testament

The New Testament likewise conceives of the human being as an indivisible unity of body and breath of life.[114] Its five major anthropological

---

[109] Charles H. H. Scobie, *Ways of Our God: An Approach to Biblical Theology* (Grand Rapids, MI: Eerdmans 2002), 656–657.

[110] Gerhard Kittel, Geoffrey W. Bromiley, and Gerhard Friedrich, eds., *Theological Dictionary of the New Testament* (Grand Rapids, MI: Eerdmans, 1964), 631.

[111] Ibid., 631.

[112] Charles Taylor, *Sources of the Self: The Making of the Modern Identity* (Cambridge, MA: Harvard University Press, 1989), x.

[113] See James P. Eckman, *The Truth About Worldviews: A Biblical Understanding of Worldview Alternatives* (Wheaton, IL: Crossway Books, 2004), 9–10. Not all postmoderns would accept the idea of an "autonomous self." Some currents of postmodern thought are at odds with the notion of an autonomous self. However, in doing so they open a door to relativism. See Lisa Blackman, *The Body: The Key Concepts* (Oxford: Berg, 2008), 70, 76, 91, 111, who speaks about the "fiction of the autonomous self."

[114] See Ekkehardt Mueller, "The Nature of the Human Being in the New Testament," in Wahlen, 133–163; Samuele Bacchiocchi, *Immortality or Resurrection? A Biblical Study of Human Nature and Destiny* (Berrien Springs, MI: Biblical Perspectives, 1997); Joel B. Green, *Body, Soul, and*

terms—*sōma, psychē, pneuma, sarx,* and *kardia*—each has reference to the human being as a whole person, not just a part.[115] Wholeness of being is a given; it goes without saying. It is a multidimensional unity.[116] No part of the human self exists by itself or for itself. The whole person is under the sovereignty of the Creator, Redeemer God.[117] The inner man's very nature demands the body.[118]

New Testament anthropology thus excludes the Greek dualism of body and soul and any notion of an immortal soul as one's inner life "imprisoned" in their body awaiting liberating death. In the New Testament, death is an enemy, not a great liberator (1 Cor 15:26).

Furthermore, the body is not evil, but rather "a temple of the Holy Spirit" (1 Cor 6:19). As cardinal doctrines of New Testament faith, the incarnation of Jesus and the resurrection

> give significance to the body and in turn to the belief in the wholeness of man. The incarnation of Jesus Christ gives a forceful significance to the indivisibility of man. If some part of man had not needed redemption, or if man was not a "whole," God would

---

Human Life (Grand Rapids, MI: Baker Academic, 2008); Oscar Cullmann, *Immortality of the Soul or Resurrection of the Dead?* (London: Epworth Press, 1964); and V. Norskov Olsen, "Man's Wholeness of Being," in *Man, the Image of God: The Diviner Design—The Human Distortion* (Hagerstown, MD: Review and Herald, 1988), 141–152.

[115] Mueller, "Nature of the Human Being," 145–162.

[116] An example can be found in Revelation 18:13 where the word "soul" (*psychē*) is placed alongside the book's only use of the word "body" (*sōma*)—that is, "and bodies and souls of men." Many translations gloss over this evocative connection altogether when either interpreting bodies as "slaves" or implying bodies are separate and distinct from the human soul. The NIV reads "and bodies and souls of men." The NLT reads "and bodies—that is, human slaves." Interestingly, Revelation uses the word "corpse" (*ptōma*) three times when referring to dead bodies (Rev 11:8–9), suggesting that in Revelation 18:13 a living body is in view and that the concepts of "bodies" and "human souls" are synonymous. In other words, as the text refers to the exploitation of "bodies," John envisions the entire person (human soul). As an obvious epexegetical *kai*, Revelation 18:13 would better be translated "bodies—that is, human souls" (i.e., "human beings"). While the notion of "slaves" is evident from the context (or, perhaps, prostitution), the anthropological implications of the phrase's construction moves the attentive reader beyond the moral dysfunction of exploitation itself to nuancing the ontological reality of human beings in their essence—an embodied being. It focuses the reality of the organic unity of the body and human soul as well. When you sell the body, you sell the human soul—the person. This human soul/person includes whom she or he is in her/his desires, emotions, feelings, thinking, and inner self. Thus, when one speaks of the human soul, body is assumed and vice versa. See Larry Lichtenwalter, "Souls Under the Altar: The 'Soul' and Related Anthropological Imagery in John's Apocalypse," *Journal of the Adventist Theological Society* 26, no. 1 (2015): 57–93.

[117] Olsen, 142.

[118] Cullmann, 32–33.

not have needed to be incarnated. The resurrection of Christ testifies to the same.[119]

The reality is that the fall has affected every part of humans' being and action. It touches each aspect of human life, including human sexuality and gender identity: "all our experience of sexual life is conditioned by the fall."[120] As a result of the fall, "the sexuality which we know from human experience does in fact bear witness to a vast rent which runs right through human nature," creating "a shame which cannot be overcome, and a longing which cannot be satisfied."[121] This biblical understanding of the human predicament and its impact on human sexuality finds contemporary expression in the kind of deep emotional distress evidenced in transgender people who honestly, yet painfully, grapple with their personal gender identity—trying to find or be their true selves. The wholistic anthropology of the Bible informs a more realistic understanding of these painful realities.

While one's essential self-identity is radically altered when they come to Christ, this new identity does not negate or essentially alter either race or gender. Gender, race, and family are three immutable birth-related personal identity factors. One cannot choose, change, or alter his or her gender, race, or family.[122] One can choose Christ, however, and in doing so receive a new identity into which other realities of one's identity (race and gender) find new wholeness.[123] Paul thus affirms both males and females in their worth and personhood. His use of the words *arsēn* and *thēlu* to designate the male and female distinction occurs only here in the context of gospel implications and then again in Romans 1:26–27 in a creation order context. Elsewhere Paul uses the generic terms of "man" and "woman" for cultural/ethical/role related issues.[124]

For the apostle Paul, "sexual intercourse is uniquely expressive of our whole being":[125] "Every sin that a man does is outside the body, but he who commits sexual immorality sins against his own body" (1 Cor 6:18). This is a distinctive anthropology in which the body is no mere external expression or instrument of the true person that resides in some

---

[119] Olsen, 149.

[120] S. L. Jones, "Sexuality," in *Baker Encyclopedia of Psychology & Counseling*, ed. David G. Benner and Peter C. Hill (Grand Rapids, MI: Baker Books, 1999), 1108.

[121] Emil Brunner, *Man in Revolt* (Philadelphia, PA: Westminster John Knox, 1979), 348.

[122] Ibid., 70.

[123] See ibid.

[124] 1 Corinthians 7:1–2; 11:3, 7–12; 1 Timothy 2:12.

[125] Gagnon, "Scriptural Case for a Male-Female Prerequisite for Sexual Relations," 77.

inner sense.[126] A human being *is* a body, rather than *having* a body. Sexual activity embodies the whole person. What one does with one's sexuality touches his or her entire person. The body cannot be separated from the self. One cannot be conceived without the other.

Thessalonian believers living in a first-century culture of immorality—with its confusion of human sexuality and identity—were reminded of the organic link between their sexuality and their experience of God's gracious gift and work of holiness:

> This is—the will of God—your holiness: that you—abstain from sexual immorality; that each of you—know how—to control his (her, your) body; in holiness and honor, not in passion of lust like the Gentiles who do not know God; that none—transgress (exploit)—his or her brother (or sister) in this matter. . . . The calling of God is not to impurity but to the most thorough holiness, . . . It is not for nothing that the Spirit God gives us is called the Holy Spirit. (1 Thess 4:3–8)[127]

The injunction to holiness concentrates on the matter of sexual morality. This is not the whole of holiness, but it is an important aspect of it.[128] It is a complex passage. There are five infinitive clauses whose meanings and relationships to each other are often difficult to disentangle, but the point is clear—holiness and sexuality connect in a profound spiritual/moral dynamic and way of life that should honor God (1 Thess 4:1–2).[129]

The manner in which the theme of "holiness" is developed here is intriguing. Although the concern of the entire passage is the will of God, the specific theme of 1 Thessalonians 4:3–8 is a call to experience divine holiness (*hagiasmos*). A concern for holiness (*hagiasmos*, 4:3a; *hagion*, 4:8b) brackets the specific injunctions (4:3b–8a). The literary inclusio opens with the divine will for holiness and closes with the Holy Spirit who alone enables such a calling. The repetition of the *hagios* word group throughout is evident in the Greek.

While sexual immorality (*porneia*) occurs here only once,[130] the *hagios* word group occurs four times. Yet the sexual overtones dominate "and

---

[126] Wright, 872.

[127] Paraphrase by the authors of the present study.

[128] F. F. Bruce, *1 and 2 Thessalonians* (Dallas, TX: Word, 1998), 83.

[129] Jacob W. Elias, *1 and 2 Thessalonians* (Scottdale, PA: Herald Press, 1995), 137.

[130] The word "immorality" (*porneia*) was used frequently in Judeo-Christian literature, where it could refer to premarital or extramarital intercourse, prostitution, incest, and any other type of sexual impropriety. See D. Michael Martin, *1, 2 Thessalonians*, New American Commentary 33 (Nashville, TN: Broadman and Holman, 1995), 123.

so the sanctification of one's sexual self deserves to be highlighted."[131] Various aspects of sexual activity are presented in these verses. First Thessalonians 4:3b presents a broad general statement linking holiness with sexual integrity. First Thessalonians 4:4–5 addresses sexuality in relation to oneself (assuming *skeuos* means "body").[132] This contrasts holiness and honor with "passions of lust."[133] First Thessalonians 4:6 looks outside the self, and warns against immorality as an offense against both God and others.[134] Finally, 1 Thessalonians 4:8 places human sexuality in all its facets and expressions in relation to the work of the Holy Spirit in one's life. The Holy Spirit's continued presence and transforming power is dependent on one's choices and behavior with regards to their sexuality. Sexual permissiveness leads ultimately to rejecting the Holy Spirit's voice to one's soul. Spiritual discernment and sexual purity appear to go together.

If the human body in its sexual dimensions is indeed connoted here,[135] then one's physical sexual self—that is, gender with his or her genitalia (anatomical sex)—are included together with identity and desire. The envisioned self-control over one's "passions of desire" is in relation to these physical sexual dimensions, compelling sexual emotion/desire, and gender identity realities (1 Thess 4:4–5). One is to act with holiness and honor with respect to both the sexual dimensions of his or her body and his or her inner self as a sexual being.

The "holiness and honor" include three critical points of reference: 1) one's physical and emotional self as a sexual being (1 Thess 4:4), 2) other human beings who may be sexual partners or exploited sexual objects (1 Thess 4:6), and 3) God who has created him or her as a sexual

---

[131] Martin, 129.

[132] The exegetical problems in 1 Thessalonians 4:3–6 defy a satisfactory solution. Three English translations of 1 Thessalonians 4:4 illustrate just one of the problems in the text: "that each one of you know how to take a wife for himself in holiness and honor" (RSV); "that each one of you know how to control your own body in holiness and honor" (NRSV); "each of you guarding his member [genitalia] in sanctity and honor" (NAB). Is the meaning of *skeuos* "wife," "one's own body," or "one's genitalia"? Weighing the evidence, major exegetes and commentators usually settle for either "wife" or "body" in its sexual dimensions. See discussion in Elias, 139–140; and Charles A. Wanamaker, *The Epistles to the Thessalonians: A Commentary on the Greek Text* (Grand Rapids, MI: Eerdmans, 1990), 152–153. Given the problems attached with understanding this passage as referring to a wife, it seems better to understand *skeuos* as connoting the human body in its sexual dimensions (Wanamaker, 152; and Bruce, 83).

[133] The phrase "passion of desire" (*pathei epithumias*) in 1 Thessalonians 4:5 reflects the deep inner reality of sexual drive and struggle for expression and mastery over the self and self-honor, as outlined in this study.

[134] Martin, 131–132.

[135] See discussion in the present study of *skeuos* as "body" (in its sexual dimensions) rather than "wife."

being with entwined physical, emotional, psychological, and spiritual dimensions (1 Thess 4:3, 7–8; cf. Gen 1:27; Matt 19:4). There is no severing of the body from one's sexual self and/or his or her desires. The complete sexual self is in view in relation to what holiness and honor before God entail.

This profound organic relationship between human sexuality (with its entwined physical, emotional, psychological, personhood, and spiritual dimensions) and divine holiness (*hagiasmos*) is one of the clearest demonstrations in the New Testament of the extent to which human sexuality is included in God's redemptive purpose of restoring men and women in His image. It is significant that the biblical concept of the "holy" first appears in relation to creation, during which God created human sexuality with all its profound dimensions when He made male and female in His image.[136] The sustained biblical appeal for human beings to be holy as God is holy (Lev 11:44–45; 1 Pet 1:15–16) repeatedly includes the phenomena and expressions of human sexuality (Lev 18:1–19:2; 1 Pet 1:14–15; 1 Thess 4:1–8).

If biblical correctives and counsel regarding the confusion of human sexuality are ultimately placed in the context of being holy as God is holy, we can assume that contemporary issues of transgenderism can be rightly placed there as well. In the final analysis, the reference points towards wholeness in gender dissonance, and the quest for gender change lies in God's original and ultimate purpose as well as our restoration to His holy image with respect to human sexuality and our core identity as one in His image.

If also, as the passage under discussion here seems to imply, both the anatomical and inner dimensions of human sexuality are in view with regards to moral choice and holiness, then human beings (transgender people included) do have real freedom of control over our bodies. We have freedom to do with our bodies whatever we choose in response to our experiences of strong inner sexual desire, emotion, and perception of identity (for self and the other). And yet, "holiness and honor" in

[136] Genesis 1:26–28; 2:18–25; cf. Matthew 19:4. Genesis 2:1–4; cf. Exodus 20:8–11. While this first reference to "holy" is in the context of the creation Sabbath, it nevertheless appears between the narrative inclusion of the creation of human beings as male and female (Gen 1:26–28; 2:7, 18–25). See Mathilde Frey, "The Creation Sabbath: Theological Intentionality of the Concept of Holiness in the Pentateuch" (paper presented at 2008 ETS/ATS Annual Meeting, Providence, Rhode Island, 2008), 1–11. Genesis places the Sabbath as the final and climactic act of God's creation on the seventh day, "placing human beings in a vivid mutual relationship with their Holy Creator, worshiping Him" (Jiří Moskala, "The Sabbath in the First Creation Account," *Journal of the Adventist Theological Society* 13, no. 1 [Spring 2002]: 55–66). It is human beings as male and female who experience such a vivid mutual relationship with their holy Creator. See also Kenneth A. Strand, "The Sabbath," in *Handbook of Seventh-day Adventist Theology*, ed. Raoul Dederen (Hagerstown, MD: Review and Herald, 2000), 493–495.

relation to one's sexual self, others' sexuality, as well as God's holy image and purpose remain the truest backdrop and norm for how human beings are to both view their body and what they should do with its physical gender markers. Anything else is to follow the values and norms of contemporary culture (the *ethnē*) that does not know God (1 Thess 4:5).

These insights would place human sexuality and our questions of gender identification against an objective moral frame of reference. Scripture vividly reminds us that "all our experience of sexual life is conditioned by the fall."[137] God's gracious invitation to holiness is the truest pathway to sexual and gender wholeness. The text's reference to "not in passion of desire" (*mē en pathei epithumias*, 1 Thess 4:5) need not be read as totally carnal, but can include one's genuine human struggle with his or her sexuality—however it entices or compels from deep within.[138] It can include the deep emotional distress evidenced in transgender people who painfully struggle with their personal gender identity, trying to be their true selves.

The holiness towards which this passage directs human sexuality and behavior is no philosophical or abstract concept. It is toward a person—God who alone is holy and who graciously extends the very power of His holy being and nature to us in the person of the Holy Spirit and in the merits of His Son's redemptive work.

In the beginning God assigned male and female with respective sex anatomy. Neither Adam nor Eve chose their gender and its implied roles. There was completeness, wholeness. There was equilibrium of body in its sexual dimensions together with a sense and experience of maleness or femaleness. What now, when, because of our fallen condition, there is such an experience as gender dissonance? Do we change our body to match our inner sense of self? Or do we invite God through His Holy Spirit to bring change within our inner self to either match our body or be patient with where we are? How do we faithfully live between the "already" and "not yet"?

According to the New Testament witness, the implications of this self/body/sex phenomenon assert that there is no essential fragmentation or alienation of one's body and his or her inner person, as appears in secular Platonic and psychological views of the human being.[139] According

---

137 Jones, "Sexuality," 1108.

138 The word *paschō* in such contexts means "to experience strong physical desires," usually of a sexual nature. The word group reflects nuances of trouble, suffering, emotion, and appetite. This need not be shameful (as in Rom 1:26) or necessarily sinful (as per Rom 7:5). But it can reflect moral confusion because of our fallen sinful nature (Gal 5:24) as well as genuine human sexual need and desires (1 Tim 5:11), which can in themselves bring emotional trouble and suffering deep within because of a loss of perceived or real wholeness with respect to one's sexuality.

139 See Nancy Pearcey, *Saving Leonardo: A Call to Resist the Secular Assault on Mind, Morals, & Meaning* (Nashville, TN: Broadman and Holman, 2017), 49–66.

to New Testament Scripture, essential selfhood cannot be split from human sexuality, nor are matters of sexuality mere social constructs.

The New Testament vision of the human body is positive. It unfolds a theology of the body that places the human body in the context of worship and how we can best serve and please God (Rom 12:1–2; 1 Cor 6:19–20). Corporeal action has moral significance. It is an instrument of activity in both time and space. There can be no human activity that does not involve the body. Whatever life one lives is lived out in one's body.[140] Presenting the body to God as a living holy sacrifice includes everything one would do with and to one's body. Our bodies rightly belong to God alone. Because of that our bodies acquire a distinctive value. Our stewardship of the body arises from the obligatory claim of God upon our bodies. In simplest terms, our bodies do not belong to ourselves! In the whole range of what pertains to the body, we encounter God's presence and God's claim on our very selves.[141]

Conclusion

Scripture's wholistic anthropology affirms the body's primary and secondary sex characteristics as undeniable gender markers to be taken seriously in gender identity issues: It informs us that what one either chooses or does with his or her body's sexual dimensions can have profound implications for one's emotional, moral, and spiritual well-being. It warns against any existential disconnect between sexual identity and sexual activity, which can lead to behaviors that both profoundly disappoint and hurt emotionally and spiritually. It asserts that there is no room for a dichotomy between the self/soul and the body with respect to sexuality. It maintains the creation distinction between sexes and challenges notions that one's real self is uncreated and thus dependent on what one may choose to be. It underscores that how one thinks with regard to one's gender and sex relates directly to both behavior and the interior self. It underscores gender as among the first elements of self-knowledge and as the most important factor for personal identity—an identity that governs social, ethical, and spiritual behavior patterns. It reveals how gender serves as the basic identity foundation for all mankind.

On the other hand, the biblical witness of human sexuality allows for the phenomena of painful gender dissonance because of fallen nature. It rests on the Scriptures' overarching creation, fall, redemption, and final consummation narrative. Within this framework, gender dissonance is

---

[140] Klaus Berger, *Identity and Experience in the New Testament* (Minneapolis, MN: Fortress, 2003), 65.

[141] Ibid., 67.

viewed as a result of living in a fallen world in which experiencing it seems to be a non-moral reality that should be related to with compassion.[142]

Within this creation-consummation narrative, both the Old and New Testaments manifest a profound sensitivity towards those whose lives may be filled with ambiguity, guilt, shame, loneliness, anxiety, fear, and hopelessness because of sex- or gender-related experiences. It offers the hope of finding a new wholeness in Christ while living in the ambiguity of the "already" and "not yet" of redemption and final consummation. It gives assurance of divine empowerment through the Holy Spirit as one relates to one's sexuality and God's gracious invitation to wholeness and holiness. Its vision of human sexuality is reflected in divine exhortation, compassion, and redemptive purpose. Individuals are invited to reflect on God's original plan. They are not free to do or be whatever they want with respect to their body temple ("You are not your own," 1 Cor 6:19). They are slaves of the Lord Jesus Christ in every aspect of their being. They are invited to wait on God while they are offered divine compassion and grace in the interim.

Biblical anthropology and the creation-consummation narrative can help orient transgender people to the biblical ideal as they make difficult choices regarding their experience and options towards finding wholeness. But these two perspectives can also nurture compassionate care and understanding in the body of Christ as God's people come alongside transgender people as a truly redemptive community.

[142] Yarhouse, 48–50.

CHAPTER 18

Towards an Adventist Approach to Transgenderism

Kwabena Donkor

Christian thought has traditionally identified the foundation of biblical sexuality in the principle that sexual differentiation is of critical relevance for the complementary sexual merging of two persons into one.[1] The male-female binary has been an integral component of this foundational principle. Karl Barth reflects this traditional viewpoint when in referring to the image of God in man as true *humanum* ("human essence") he observes,

> Man can and will always be man before God and among his fellows only as he is man in relationship to woman and woman in relationship to man. And as he is one or the other he is man. And since it is this and nothing else that makes him man, he is distinguished from the beast and every other creature, existing in the free differentiation and relationship in which God has chosen, willed and created him as His partner. The fact that he was created man and woman will be the *great paradigm of everything that is to take place between him and God, and also of everything that is to take place between him and his fellows.*[2]

The rise of certain intellectual currents and values in contemporary cultures of the world has led to the argument that traditional truth claims about sexuality may not be so reified. Among these currents are historical-critical analysis of the Bible, postmodernism,

---

[1] K. J. Vanhoozer et al., eds., "Sexuality," in *Dictionary for Theological Interpretation of the Bible* (Grand Rapids, MI: Baker Academic, 2005), 739–740.

[2] Karl Barth, *Church Dogmatics*, G. W. Bromiley, and T. F. Torrance, vol. 3, part 1 (New York: T&T Clark, 2004), 186, emphasis supplied.

deconstructionist ideas, and absolutist versions of pluralism, diversity, andtolerance.[3] The increasing impact of these cultural values on human sexuality is profound and revolutionary. It has led to the questioning of traditional marital and sexual paradigms, leading to arguments in favor not only of homosexuality, lesbianism, bisexuality, transgenderism, and several alternative sexualities, but also a call to end "heterosexism." The issue with transgenderism is part of a larger cultural sexual phenomenon and should be approached as such. Among Seventh-day Adventists, homosexuality appears to have received quite a bit of attention, but the issue of transgenderism demands no less consideration. Contemporary culture's openness towards sexuality has brought the issues surrounding transgendered persons to the fore.

How should this phenomenon be evaluated? What should be the Seventh-day Adventist Church's response both in theory and practice? Here we provide a modest attempt to initiate discussion on the matter. It is evident that differing positions on sexuality are rooted in varying ideas on what it means to be human. Our approach here is primarily to explore what biblical ideas may contribute to clarifying the Adventist response to transgenderism, although the intellectual currents in today's culture that were alluded to previously will not be completely bypassed. But before we get bogged down with facts and figures and ideas, it is important to provide a set of "contemporary" definitions with which to place transgenderism on the contemporary landscape of sexuality. The following definitions are adapted from the "Comprehensive* List of LGBTQ+ Vocabulary Definitions."[4]

Biological sex: the chromosomal, hormonal, and anatomical characteristics that are used to classify an individual as female, male, or intersex.

Bisexual: a person who has romantic attraction, sexual attraction, or sexual behavior toward both males and females, or romantic or sexual attraction to people of any sex.

Cisgender: a person whose gender identity and biological sex at birth align.

Gender binary: the idea that there are only two genders—male/female or man/woman—and that people must be gendered as one or the other.

Gender identity: the internal perception of one's gender and how they label themselves—man, woman, genderqueer, trans, etc.

Heterosexism: behavior that treats heterosexuality as better or more "right" than other sexualities.

---

[3] Vanhoozer et al., 739.

[4] See "Comprehensive* List of LGBTQ+ Vocabulary Definitions," It's Pronounced Metrosexual, http://itspronouncedmetrosexual.com/2013/01/a-comprehensive-list-of-lgbtq-term-definitions/(accessed October 21, 2020).

Heterosexual: a person primarily emotionally, physically, and/or sexually attracted to members of the opposite sex. Also known as "straight."

Homosexual: a person primarily emotionally, physically, and/or sexually attracted to members of the same sex/gender.

Intersex: someone whose combination of chromosomes, gonads, hormones, internal sex organs, and genitals differs from the two expected patterns of male or female.

Lesbian: a term used to describe women attracted romantically, erotically, and/or emotionally to other women.

Sexual orientation: the type of sexual, romantic, emotional/spiritual attraction one feels for others.

Sex reassignment surgery (SRS): a term used by some medical professionals to refer to a group of surgical options that alter a person's biological sex.

Third gender: a term for a person who identifies not with either "man" or "woman," but with another gender.

Transgender: a broad term to denote the many ways in which people may experience, express, or present their gender identity in a way that is different from people whose gender identity and biological sex are congruent.

Transsexual: a person who identifies psychologically as a gender/sex other than the one to which they were assigned at birth. Transsexuals often wish to transform their bodies to match their inner sense of gender/sex.

Transvestite: a person who dresses as the binary opposite gender expression ("cross-dresses") for any one of many reasons, including relaxation, fun, and sexual gratification.

"Transgender," then, is the term used to describe the state of a person who believes that their experience of gender is different than that suggested by their biological sex. With such a state, a person's primary and secondary sex characteristics are consistent with their formal status as either male or female. In other words, both the genetic/gonadal/hormonal and genital aspects of sex appear to be consistently male or female, as the case may be. The inconsistency or incongruence, for which reason a person's state may be denoted transgendered, consists in gender identity (one's internal perception of gender).[5] For example, a person who is biologically male and transgendered would claim a sense of desire to be a girl and adopt roles that are typically and culturally identified with females. While some transgendered persons may be indifferent or content with their state, there are those who find in this apparent contradiction between body and gender identity a source of discomfort and stress—

[5] Hessel Bouma, "The Nature of Gender: Gender Identity in Persons Who Are Intersexed or Transgendered," *Journal of Psychology and Theology* 33, no. 3 (2005): 166, https://doi.org/10.1177/009164710503300302 (accessed October 21, 2020).

hence, the association of the phrase "gender dysphoria" with transgenderism. A person in this state of dysphoria, believing that he or she was born in a "wrong" body and wishing to transition or has already transitioned through hormonal treatment and sex reassignment surgery is termed "transsexual."[6]

The controversy surrounding transgenderism boils down to whether it is a legitimate way of expressing human sexuality. On the one hand, there are those who issue calls for inclusion, arguing in favor of transgenderism as legitimate categories of human sexuality/gender and appealing for its integration into the human understanding of gender. On the other hand, there are others who hold a dichotomous, binary view of human sexuality and gender as male/female, and consider alternative sexualities as aberrations at best. Each of these positions has significant implications for the Church and society with regards to individuals' participation in certain cultural and ecclesial roles.[7] From the point of view of the Church, questions such as these are raised: Should gender status be an obstruction to an individual's participation in the community of faith? Is sex reassignment surgery an acceptable treatment for transsexual persons?[8] What about the church recognizing or even solemnizing marriages or other unions of transsexual persons? The answers to such questions cannot be pursued in a vacuum because underlying them are one's conception of human nature. As Paul McHugh has correctly said in the context of surgical sex, "without any fixed position on what is given in human nature, any manipulation of it can be defended as legitimate."[9] We contend that the Bible provides a fixed position on what is given in human nature, from which decisions may be made regarding what may or may not be done with and/or to it.

Biblical Perspectives on Human Sex and Gender

The search for biblical perspectives on sex and gender requires a comprehensive view that takes into account not only God's creative intentions, but also aberrations to those purposes that are recognized in the Bible as a result of sin.

[6] Mark A. Yarhouse, *Understanding Gender Dysphoria* (Downers Grove, IL: IVP Academic, 2015), 20.

[7] Bouma, 166.

[8] Victoria S. Kolakowski, "Toward a Christian Ethical Response to Transsexual Persons," *Theology and Sexuality* 6 (1997): 10.

[9] Paul R. McHugh, "Surgical Sex: Why We Stopped Doing Sex Change Operations," *First Things*, November 2004, http://www.firstthings.com/article/2004/11/surgical-sex (accessed October 21, 2020).

Perspectives from Creation

Seventh-day Adventists take the Genesis creation account of humanity as the foundational text from which every discussion on sex and gender proceeds. In adopting this stance, the church treats the biblical creation account as not simply a metaphor or mythical story, but as a reliable historical account of the origins of humans. The crucial passage is Genesis 1:27: "God created mankind in His own image, in the image of God He created them; male and female He created them."[10]

The phenomenon of separation and differentiation in God's creative work as presented in the Genesis account is readily evident. The firmament is differentiated from the waters below (Gen 1:7), the dry land is separated from the sea (Gen 1:9), the light for the day is differentiated from the light of the night (Gen 1:16), and humans are "qualitatively and absolutely differentiated from non-human beings."[11] As beings created in the "image of God," humans are in a qualitative sense *formally* different from the rest of creation. God's act of differentiation in regard to humans, however, moves beyond their formal differentiation from non-human beings. It would seem that being completely human required a *material* aspect of differentiation within the life. This material differentiation within human life took effect in the narrative that culminates in the creation of Eve as Adam's companion (Gen 2:18–25). Ray S. Anderson explains,

> The differentiation which constitutes human being as "co-humanity" is the primary differentiation, from which the formal differentiation of human/non-human is derived. It would appear that the purpose of Genesis 2 is to teach that very truth. The original statement regarding creation of the human in the likeness of God expresses first of all the material differentiation: "male and female he created them" (Gen. 1:27). Only thereafter is the formal differentiation between the human and non-human made clear.[12]

The Genesis creation account is, therefore, instructive on human nature, firstly, by showing that human differentiation at creation is intrinsically sexual. So Nathan Jastram observes, "God created man as male and female, in two sexes, and any attempt to find a human nature that is not enfleshed in one of the two sexes is unbiblical."[13] Bipolarity of

---

[10] All biblical quotations are from the New International Version, unless otherwise indicated.

[11] Ray S. Anderson, *On Being Human: Essays in Theological Anthropology* (Pasadena, CA: Fuller Seminary Press, 1991), 28.

[12] Ibid., 37.

[13] Nathan Jastram, "Man as Male and Female: Created in the Image of God," *Concordia Theological Quarterly* 68, no. 1 (2004): 64.

the sexes and the distinction between male and female originated with God as creaturely endowment of what it means to be human.[14] Secondly, the creation account is informative in regards to the intricate connection between sex and gender. This connection has to be sought from the radical or essential sexual nature of humans, as previously noted. The narrative—from the animals being brought to Adam in order for him to acquaint himself, to the creation of Eve as Adam's wife (Gen 2:19–25)—entails the existential development of Adam's insight into himself as human. The process, beginning with the naming of the animals, led to the thought that "there was not found a help meet for man."[15] C. F. Keil and F. Delitzsch capture the thrust of the narrative:

> Before the creation of the woman we must regard the man (Adam) as being neither male, in the sense of complete sexual distinction, nor androgynous as though both sexes were combined in the one individual created at the first, but as created in anticipation of the future, with a preponderant tendency, a male in simple potentiality, out of which state he passed, the moment the woman stood by his side.[16]

The essential sexual nature of humans at creation therefore had a *telos* that envisioned the genders of masculinity and femininity in the final state of Adam and Eve as husband and wife. Quite clearly, God's telic design in the creation of Eve was discerned by Adam in his evocative response after awaking from sleep and seeing the woman. It is remarkable that this discovery is not brought to Adam by revelation, but he realizes in the woman, "bone of his bones and flesh of his flesh," an *anticipation* of the relation described in the last part of the text: "she shall be called Woman, because she was taken out of Man" (Gen 2:23). Keil and Delitzsch notes quite helpfully that the words of Genesis 2:24, "That is why a man leaves his father and mother and is united to his wife, and they become one flesh," are the utterance of revelation to embody the truth of "marriage as the deepest corporeal and spiritual unity of man and woman."[17] Here, the

---

[14] See Richard M. Davidson, *Flame of Yahweh: Sexuality in the Old Testament* (Peabody, MA: Hendrickson, 2007), 19–21, for a full discussion, including his arguments against the view of an ideal androgynous or hermaphroditic being that was later differentiated into two sexes.

[15] C. F. Keil and F. Delitzsch, *Commentary on the Old Testament*, vol. 1 (Peabody, MA: Hendrickson, 2011), 55.

[16] Ibid.

[17] Ibid., 56.

biblical account speaks past Adam and Eve to all humanity.[18] God's verdict after all of this was that the creation was "very good."

The foregoing observations on the intricate connection between sex and gender at creation may be expressed theologically. Our sexual nature orients us towards a divinely ordained goal in which our differentiation as males and females is "completed in a perfect modality of personal being. This is the basis for what—in psychological terms—is called gender identity."[19] To grant the fact that at creation gender was tied closely to sex is to take an essentialist[20] approach to biblical reality. Anderson expresses this connection well.

> The gender identity which is expressed in terms of male or female personal being must be seen as an "ontological" rather than a pragmatic or social distinction. That is, to be male or female in terms of gender identity is to know oneself in the essential differentiation which constitutes personhood itself. We are committed then to hold that sexuality, as intrinsic to the image of God, also entails that gender identity is rooted in an ontological determination of personal being.[21]

Partial Evaluation and Conclusion

The biblical creation account presents a strong, inseparable connection between sex and gender. We may, therefore, conclude that in God's design at creation, the elements of physiology and psychology that contemporary studies on sex and gender have exposed were in congruence. That is, both Adam and Eve's chromosomes, gonads, sexual anatomy, and secondary sexual characteristics were properly aligned with their respective senses of gender identity, sexual orientation, and gender roles. Clearly, the

---

[18] Donald E. Gowan, *Genesis 1–11: From Eden to Babel* (Grand Rapids, MI: Eerdmans, 1988), 49, writes, concerning Genesis 2:24, "This is one of the most obvious indicators of J's awareness that he is writing our story and not just the story of two unique, primordial individuals, for 2:24 does not apply to them at all: they had no parents. J is not even interested in the customs of his own patriarchal culture, in which the woman left her household to join the man, but is speaking of something more fundamental about the relationship of man and woman."

[19] Anderson, 109.

[20] Essentialism is the view that for any specific kind of entity, there is a set of characteristics or properties, all of which any entity of that kind must possess. Therefore, all things can be precisely defined or described. In this view, it follows that terms or words should have a single definition and meaning.

[21] Anderson, 109. Anderson brings clarity to this issue by noting the centrality of the concept of *imago Dei* in the discussion. In his view, "it is not necessary that gender identity itself be intrinsic to creaturely sexuality, only that it be intrinsic to the *imago Dei* which is experienced as creaturely sexuality" (ibid., 111).

biblical creation account shows that creaturely sexuality comprised of an ontological bipolarity of biological[22] sexes in anticipation of gender as masculine in the case of Adam and feminine in the case of Eve.

The case we are making for biblical bipolarity of the sexes should not be confused with the case that others have made for a "dipolar" view of the sexes. The latter argues for the masculine and feminine as two poles of human sexuality with a wide range of in-between variations.[23] The difficulty with this argument has been noted.[24]

> A case can certainly be made at the psychological level for a dipolar opposition rather than a dimorphic one. It can, that is, be argued that *masculinity* and *femininity* are matters of relatively more or less rather than either-or. But it cannot be argued that this is the case with maleness and femaleness, the biological endowment from which the psychological and behavioral possibilities arise. It is generally well known that the starting point for dimorphic differentiation is already present at the conception of a child in the presence or absence of a "Y" chromosome, the effect of which is to differentiate the development of a male from the female gonadal structure with which all embryos begin.

The inextricable connection between sex and gender also leads us to conclude that anatomy (physiology) is determinative of gender but not exclusively. Similarly, the mind (psychology) is also determinative of gender but not exclusively. This conclusion is consistent with the general biblical understanding of the wholistic, integrated nature of the human being. One may not indulge in dualistic thinking in a way that privileges anatomy over psychology or vice versa. In this sense, the practice of sex

---

[22] Oliver O'Donovan, "Transsexualism and Christian Marriage," *Journal of Religious Ethics* 11, no. 1 (1983): 143, remarks insightfully, "The Christian understanding of marriage, which relates to the dimorphism of human biology, is not out of tune with modern medical understanding. One can express the Christian perspective like this: the either-or of biological maleness and femaleness to which the human race is bound is not a meaningless or oppressive condition of nature; it is the good gift of God because it gives rise to possibilities of relationship in which the polarities of masculine and feminine, more subtly nuanced than the biological differentiation, can play a decisive part. Through masculinity and femininity, we claim the significance of maleness and femaleness for relationship and give it, through relationship, an interpretation which can express our individuality as persons. But this enjoyment of masculinity and femininity in relationship always evokes biological maleness and femaleness, and only as that biological opposition is taken up into a structure of life which fully exploits its capacity for enabling relationship, can masculinity and femininity be more widely enjoyed without fear of degeneration and exploitation."

[23] Ibid., 142.

[24] Ibid.

reassignment surgery for transgendered persons seems to be grounded in a philosophical privileging of mind over body which may be Platonic and gnostic in orientation. Conversely, to privilege body over mind reflects a dualistic mode of thinking that, at best, fails to capture the biblical sense of personhood as originally intended by God at creation.

Perspectives from the Fall

Unlike critical scholars who prefer to see Genesis 1–11 not as history but an etiological myth, Seventh-day Adventists take these accounts as real historical record of origins and early human history.[25] Genesis 3 provides the foundation for the traditional view of what is termed "the fall." The narrative describes Adam and Eve as beginning their existence in an idyllic, perfect state that was subsequently disrupted by their choice to disobey God's instructions: "But you must not eat from the tree of the knowledge of good and evil, for when you eat from it you will certainly die" (Gen 2:17). The account proceeds to show the consequences of the first family's fatal choice, noting the effect on humanity but also referring to God cursing the ground as an outcome of Adam's sin (Gen 3:14–19). In the New Testament, Paul presents a cosmic sense of the fall (Rom 8: 20–22). The particular quality or character of these consequences, paying special attention to the human situation, needs careful theological reflection in order to draw out their implications for sex and gender after the fall.

Debilitation

The sense of enfeeblement of the human being is hinted at in God's pronouncement on the woman after the fall. "To the woman he said, 'I will make your pains in childbearing very severe; with painful labor you will give birth to children'" (Gen 3:16). Bearing children and bringing them forth was part of God's creation design (Gen 1:22). What is new after the fall is the reality that henceforth she would bear children in pain. In Keil's and Delitzsch's view, "the punishment consisted in an *enfeebling of nature* in consequence of sin."[26] In the New Testament Paul alludes to the fall account in Romans 8:20-22, and describes its impact in terms of subjecting the creation to futility. His depiction of the fall's effect is captured cogently by James D. G. Dunn:

> Here, the primary allusion is to the Adam narratives: *ματαιότης [mataiotes]* in the sense of the futility of an object which does

---

[25] Beginning with the European Enlightenment, reason gained primacy over revelation. Together with the rise of critical approaches to the Bible and the spread of evolutionary theory, the doctrine of the fall came under serious questioning. The result has been a general symbolic interpretation of Genesis 3.

[26] Keil and Delitzsch, 64, emphasis supplied.

> *not function as it was designed to do* (like an expensive satellite which has malfunctioned and now spins uselessly in space), or, more precisely, which has been *given a role for which it was not designed* and which is unreal or illusory.[27]

To the extent that all creation, including human nature, is impacted by this futility, Paul's comment is quite instructive. Dunn's reflection on Paul's use of the term "futility" would seem to qualify the case of the intersex and transgendered as manifestations of the futility with which human sexuality has been dealt on account of the fall.

Enslavement

One of the ways in which the cosmic effect of the fall on the human condition may be expressed is in terms of the imagery of enslavement. Paul resorts to the use of this metaphor in his writings to describe the pre-conversion state of persons (Rom 6:16–20; Eph 2:1–3). The biblical term "enslavement" depicts the human condition to be in a state where it finds itself in the grasp of an alien power or force. The Reformation concept of the "Bondage of the Will," prominent in the work of Martin Luther and John Calvin, comes close to expressing the same biblical idea of enslavement. Luther wrote that "the Scripture sets before us a man who is not only bound, wretched, captive, sick and dead, but who, through the operations of Satan his lord, adds to his miseries that of blindness, so that he believes himself to be free, happy, possessed of liberty and ability, whole and alive."[28] Whereas the concept entails the notion of spiritual blindness and death as well as the overbearing power of sin and Satan over a person, our interest here is in the nature of moral freedom in humans after the fall. In our state of enslavement, human moral choices are neither neutral nor autonomous. In making moral choices we are already predisposed. Stanley Grenz expresses the problem quite pertinently in the context of God's design for human life:

> The opposite of the bondage of the will is the freedom of the will. In the context of the human destiny, this term means not merely the ability to choose from among options, but the ability to live in accordance with our design as given by God. Such freedom is exactly what we lack. As a result of sin, we are in bondage, for by our strength we simply cannot live according to

---

[27] James D. G. Dunn, *Romans 1–8*, Word Biblical Commentary 38A (Dallas, TX: Word, 1988), 470, emphasis supplied.

[28] Martin Luther, *De Servo Arbitrio*, 162, quoted in James A. Nestingen, "Biblical Clarity and Ambiguity in the Bondage of the Will," *Logia* 22, no. 1 (2013): 32.

> God's design (Isa 64:6). All our lives we live under bondage to the power of sin which holds us in its grasp, even though we —like the Pharisees—might think we are free (John 8:33–34). Consequently, we must be set free from bondage in order to live out our God-given destiny.[29]

The irony of the human situation, as both Luther and Grenz point out, is that though we are enslaved, we think ourselves to be free and autonomous. Indeed, the essence of the temptation in the garden that precipitated the fall was a deceptive aspiration for autonomy. Thus, associated with our enslavement is a measure of self-deception.

Depravity

The two previously discussed effects of the fall on human nature belong together. Humans are enslaved (specifically, morally predisposed in their choices) as a direct result of the fall and its debilitating effect on their nature. As a consequence of our enslavement, we are materially predisposed to do evil. In this sense, we may depict humans as depraved, meaning "marked to do evil." Theologically, however, depravity has been related more closely to human inability or powerlessness to alleviate our critical situation. In this sense, the Reformed doctrine of total depravity was designed to stand in contrast to medieval Roman Catholic teaching on the freedom of human will. Medieval scholastics distinguished the "likeness of God" from "the image of God" and maintained that the fall resulted only in the loss of the likeness of God as a gift that Adam received from God, without impairing the image of God (natural human powers, especially reason). Calvin in particular countered the Catholic position with the doctrine of total depravity to deny any freedom to the unregenerate will except the freedom to sin.

Without entering into a discussion of the merits of both the Catholic and Reformed notions of human depravity, we can affirm that the Bible depicts fallen humanity as unable, on their own, to alter their life situation by determination, exercise of will power, or self-reformation. The deleterious effects of the fall and sin have left neither the body (Rom 6:6, 12; 7:24), the mind (Rom 1:21; 2 Cor 3:14–15; 4:4), nor the emotions (Rom 1:6–27; Gal 5:24; 2 Tim 3:2–4) unscathed. Paul speaks of the believer's experience as being dead and made alive by God (Eph 2:1–5; Col 2:13). But what are the practical effects of this fallen human condition?

Fallen Human Condition, Temptation, and Sin

Defective bodies, minds, and emotions predispose humans to temptation and sin. A question that has emerged with renewed emphasis in the

[29] Stanley J. Grenz, *Theology for the Community of God* (Grand Rapids, MI: Eerdmans, 1994), 211.

context of the contemporary debates on human sexuality is whether these constituent aspects of fallen human nature, qua structural inclinations, are sinful in themselves. The position has been defended, in the context of Jesus' temptation, that "temptation is not sinful when it comes to us from the outside. . . . But when the enticement comes from our own sinful nature, that is an entirely different matter. In that case, the temptation *itself* is sinful."[30] This is a challenging conclusion, but before taking it up, the point should be made at the outset that the issue here is not to defend the Pelagian view that somehow human nature is inwardly disposed to do good. Our discussion on the effects of the fall clearly denounces such a position. Still, the position is challenging on a few theological fronts. First, Denny Burk and Heath Lambert locate temptation in internal human predisposing factors to sin and they judge those predispositions *themselves* to be sinful. By this we understand the authors to be saying that the internal manifestations of these inclinations involve one in something that is immoral. This is the authors' conclusion from the discussion of Augustine's notion of concupiscence.[31] If such is the nature of temptation, then the temptation of Jesus becomes an issue since He, having no internal inclination to sin, was still tempted. The authors' solution is to posit that Jesus' temptation was solely from external sources, since His "impeccability" meant "not merely that he never sinned but that it was impossible for him to sin."[32] This dichotomy, even in the case of Jesus between internal and external sources of temptation, is rather artificial. Body, mind, and emotions respond to external stimuli to produce occasions of temptation and sin. "Temptation is never simply a problem with the object of desire. Temptation entices or lures us by

---

[30] Denny Burk and Heath Lambert, *Transforming Homosexuality* (Phillipsburg, NJ: P&R, 2015), 53.

[31] Ibid., 42–43.

[32] Ibid. This matter raises questions about different understandings of the human nature of Christ that we cannot discuss here. Ellen G. White, *The Desire of Ages* (Mountain View, CA: Pacific Press, 1898), 48–49, observes that "Jesus accepted humanity when the race had been weakened by four thousand years of sin. Like every child of Adam, He accepted the results of the working of the great law of heredity. What these results were is shown in the history of His earthly ancestors. He came with such a heredity to share our sorrows and temptations, and to give us the example of a sinless life." In what on the surface appears to be a contradictory statement, White, *Testimonies for the Church*, vol. 2 (Mountain View, CA: Pacific Press, 1868), 508, also notes, "He was a mighty petitioner, not possessing the passions of our human, fallen natures, but compassed with like infirmities, tempted in all points even as we are. Jesus endured agony which required help and support from His Father." In the latter passage, "passion" relates to "nature," as carefully shown by Erwin R. Gane, "Christ and Human Perfection," supplement, *The Ministry* (October 1970, repr. August 2003): 16, to deal with *His spiritual nature*, as distinct from the physical and intellectual nature of man. In this, Christ is different from us. On the other hand, Christ was like us in our *infirmities*, which in this case must be what is left of human nature when the *spiritual* is taken out—namely, the physical.

our own appetite or imaginative relation to the object of desire."[33] Fur-ther-more, granting that Jesus was the only begotten Son of God, "He took upon Himself human nature, and was tempted in all points as human nature is tempted. *He could have sinned; He could have fallen*, but not for one moment was there in him an evil propensity."[34] Thus, the idea that it was impossible for Jesus to sin would seem to make His temptation in the wilderness a docetic charade that is unsustainable in Adventist theological thinking.

Second, it seems that failure to distinguish a little bit more carefully the use of the term "sin" or "sinful" may lead to some theological confusion. In the context of Burk and Lambert's discussion, this particular confusion has to do with what happens to those fallen, internal predisposing faculties when a person is saved. This issue will be taken up subsequently, but Burk and Lambert quote Augustine to defend the thesis of the sinfulness of temptation *itself* when it is internally caused.

> This lust [desire/concupiscence] is not, you see—and this is a point you really must listen to above all else: you see, this lust is not some kind of alien nature. . . . It's our debility, it's our vice. It won't be detached from us and exist somewhere else, but it will be cured and not exist anywhere at all [in the resurrection].[35]

The question Augustine's quotation raises in the same breath is this: If this concupiscence, this internal predisposition to temptation, in *itself* is sinful, and it will not be cured until the resurrection, then what is the situation of the sinner? Is he or she really saved this side of eternity? Paul also knew about salvation in the context of the fallen human condition. R. H. Mounce comments:

> What I am by nature is in constant conflict with what I aspire to be as a child of God in whom the Spirit of God dwells. That conflict will never be settled until, seeing God, we shall be like him (1 John 3:2). Caught up in this spiritual warfare, Paul cried out: What a wretched man am I! Who is able to free me from the "clutches of my own sinful nature?" (Phillips). The "body of death" was like a corpse that hung on him and from which he was unable to free himself. It constantly interfered with his desire

---

[33] K. A. Richardson, *James*, New American Commentary 36 (Nashville, TN: Broadman and Holman, 1997), 81.

[34] Francis D. Nichol, ed., *Seventh-Day Adventist Bible Commentary*, vol. 5 (Hagerstown, MD: Review and Herald, 1980), 1128.

[35] Quoted in Burk and Lambert, 43.

> to obey the higher impulses of his new nature. Who is able to rescue the believer crying out for deliverance? The answer is, Thanks be to God, there is deliverance through Jesus Christ our Lord (v. 25). Through the death and resurrection of Christ, God has provided the power to live in the freedom of the Spirit (cf. 8:2).[36]

In spite of Paul's doxology about deliverance through Christ, he does not suggest anywhere that the struggle ceases for the believer.

The view that when the enticement comes from our own sinful nature the temptation *itself* is sinful is challenging for Adventists also because of the settled conviction among many that "temptation is not sin; the sin lies in yielding."[37]

Partial Evaluation and Conclusion

The earth as God created it has suffered a fall that has impacted all reality. Human nature as a whole has suffered debilitation, enslavement, and depravity. In the area of human sexuality, although the Bible teaches that God created man dimorphically as male and female, as we have shown, there are those whose experiences preclude them from making a definite either/or identification. Such is the experience of the group collectively identified as "intersex," whose sexual conditions may involve "abnormalities of the external genitals, the internal reproductive organs, sex chromosomes, and/or sex-related hormones."[38] Although the case of the transgendered is different, as explained in the introduction, it presents no less a case of human sexual anomaly.[39]

---

[36] R. H. Mounce, *Romans*, New American Commentary 27 (Nashville, TN: Broadman and Holman, 1995), 169–171.

[37] Ellen G. White, *Counsels to Parents, Teachers, and Students* (Mountain View, CA: Pacific Press, 1913), 218.

[38] Scott E. Stiegemeyer, "How Do You Know Whether You Are a Man or a Woman," *Concordia Theological Quarterly* 79 (2015): 23.

[39] According to the American Psychiatric Association, *Diagnostic and Statistical Manual of Mental Disorders: DSM-5* (Washington, DC: American Psychiatric Association, 2013), 452, quoted in Stiegemeyer, 31, "transgender or gender dysphoria (the current clinical terminology) is diagnosed to be experienced as (A). A marked incongruence between one's experienced/expressed gender and assigned gender, of at least 6 months' duration, as manifested by at least two of the following: 1. A marked incongruence between one's experienced/expressed gender and primary and/or secondary sex characteristics (or in young adolescents, the anticipated secondary sex characteristics). 2. A strong desire to be rid of one's primary and/or secondary sex characteristics because of a marked incongruence with one's experienced/expressed gender (or in young adolescents, a desire to prevent the development of the anticipated secondary sex characteristics). 3. A strong desire for the primary and/or secondary sex characteristics of the other gender. 4. A strong desire to be of the other gender (or some alternative gender different from one's assigned

What should be made of these sexual incongruities? The critical issue is whether the discovery of a particular confusing body should lead us to question our categories of "normal" and "abnormal" sexuality. The contemporary disdain for metanarrative and metaphysics seems to be reflected in the discussion. So, Hessel Bouma wonders whether the diversity of gender and gendered behaviors across species and the diversity of traits within genders among humans are all the consequences of sin, pondering whether God's creational intent was monolithic females and males. She is led to speculate, "Perhaps intersexed and transgendered persons are a powerful reminder that gender, while itself a good gift of God, contains within it great diversity that we tend to forget or ignore in our focus on definitions or prototypes for gender categories."[40]

Our conclusion is that human nature as we see and experience it today is not the same as human nature as it came forth from the Creator's hands. The biblical depictions of the fall and its consequences lead us to this conclusion. Therefore, particular or individual human sexualities may not necessarily reflect God's creative intentions.[41] Physiological anomalies and physical deformities, while not *immoral*, are not *desirable* and therefore we should not talk about them as if they are unproblematic. They remain constitutional problems of the human condition that, for the believer, may either become manageable through the Lord's grace ("My grace is sufficient for you," 2 Cor 12:9) or healed through His divine touch, but ultimately removed when the corruptible puts on the incorruptible (1 Cor 15:53–54).

Biblical Perspectives on Salvation and Brokenness

So far, we have examined the good creation of God in regard to human sexuality and gender as well as the impact the fall has had on it. We have also suggested that the situation of the intersex and transgendered may be a manifestation of the futility introduced into God's good creation with regard to human sexuality. We concluded that such human imperfections, while not *immoral*, are not *desirable* and therefore should

gender). 5. A strong desire to be treated as the other gender (or some alternative gender different from one's assigned gender). 6. A strong conviction that one has the typical feelings and reactions of the other gender (or some alternative gender different from one's assigned gender). (B). The condition is associated with clinically significant distress or impairment in social, occupational, or other important areas of functioning."

[40] Bouma, 175. These considerations are motivated by the views of theologians such as Stanley Grenz, whose interpretation of Genesis 1:26–31 focuses on relationality rather than scientific descriptions of the biological and psychological character of gender.

[41] For a general discussion, see Christopher R. Seitz, "Human Sexuality: Viewed from the Bible's Understanding of the Human Condition," *Theology Today* 52, no. 2 (1995): 236–246.

not be treated as if they are unproblematic. The question we face now is the following: what should we make of a *believer* who claims to be transgendered and experiences the incongruence of sex and gender associated with it? In other words, is it possible for someone who has truly been born again to continue to have gender dysphoria? Theologically, this question juxtaposes the experiences of conversion/salvation/redemption and human brokenness. More specifically, does conversion/salvation/redemption in the Bible involve total restoration—physical and psychological? Is it acceptable to talk about Christian "identity in brokenness," which might mean "redemption in brokenness"? What exactly does salvation accomplish?

Salvation After the Fall

The fall of Adam and Eve did not take God by surprise. The Bible speaks about a plan of redemption that had been put in place before the founding of the world (1 Cor 2:7). Although humans fell, the Bible presents God as Savior (1 Chr 16:35, Hab 3:18; Luke 1:47; Titus 1:3), the one who comes to save and deliver His people. Theologically, salvation is a broad concept that encompasses many ideas including repentance, conversion, justification, sanctification, righteousness, reconciliation, and regeneration. The Old Testament employs many words that correspond with the idea of salvation, but the most extensive term is *yasha'*, denoting the basic idea of being brought from unfavorable to favorable circumstances where life flourishes.[42] The New Testament also has several terms to signify salvation, although *sozo* seems to be greatly favored. The word emphasizes salvation in its spiritual, moral, and eschatological senses.

Our interest in salvation for this study, however, is a very specific one. One dimension of the concept of salvation that we consider particularly relevant for our topic is the notion of new creation (2 Cor 5:17). What does it mean that when a person is in Christ he/she *is* a new creature? Helpfully, Ulrich Leupold raises this issue by asking, "What is the 'isness' of salvation? What force has the copula in the sentence 'I am saved'?"[43] The aspect of salvation directly related to this question is the notion of regeneration. The concept describes the inner renewal by the Spirit of God that occurs when a person becomes a Christian.[44] The idea is expressed in several places in the Bible. Although there is no specific word for it in the Old Testament, regeneration is expressed by the notion of "circumcision of heart" (Deut 30:6; Jer 4:4). Regeneration is also reflected in

---

[42] Ivan T. Blazen, "Salvation," in *Handbook of Seventh-day Adventist Theology*, ed. Raoul Dederen (Hagerstown, MD: Review and Herald, 2000), 272.

[43] Ulrich S. Leupold, "Regeneration in the Theology of Paul," *Lutheran Quarterly* 17, no. 3 (1965): 241.

[44] H. Burkhardt, "Regeneration," in *New Dictionary of Theology*, ed. Sinclair B. Ferguson and David F. Wright (Downers Grove, IL: InterVarsity, 1988), 574.

the idea of God giving His people a new heart (Ezek 11:19) and writing His laws on their hearts (Jer 31:33). In the New Testament, regeneration is expressed by the idea of being born not by human processes but by the will of God (John 1:13; cf. 3:3, 6). In Titus 3:5, regeneration is described by the phrase "washing of regeneration," where the words *palingenesia* (*palin*, "again"; *genesia*, "birth" or "genesis") and *anakainosis* ("to be new again") are used. The language in Ephesians 4:22–24 is perhaps even more vivid, for believers are urged to put off the old man and put on the new. In this case, the word "created" is used in connection with the new man, seemingly alluding to the Genesis creation account. First Peter 1:3 is equally rich in describing the believer's new experience as a new birth (1 Pet 1:3, 23).

We are interested in the concept of regeneration in connection with transgenderism because with its idea of new creation and new birth, we wish to know what tangible changes, if any, may accompany it. The notion of regeneration is tantalizing in this regard because it shows that salvation is no mere abstract concept (such as a mere forensic act), but one that has ontic[45] relevance. Paul's dynamic notions of salvation such as "baptized in Christ's death" (Rom 6:3), "planted together in the likeness of his death" (Rom 6:5) or the idea of "a new creature. . . . The old has passed away . . . the new has come" (2 Cor 5:17) express a relationship "of an ontic transformation."[46] Granting that salvation (regeneration) involves ontic transformation, we may rightly inquire about the extent of this transformation. Specifically, knowing that transgenderism involves an issue of health where a person's biological sex is in conflict with their sense of masculinity or femininity, *must* regeneration as "new creation" resolve this tension? The question canvasses the wider issue of whether salvation *must* be accompanied with the elimination of all physical, psychological, and other internal human states or conditions that may be a source of perturbance or stress for the believer. On the one hand, Werner Foerster considers New Testament *soteria* in relation to later Judaism, the Greek world, and Gnosticism and concludes that

> NT *soteria* does not refer to earthly relationships. Its content is not, as in the Greek understanding, well-being, health of body and soul. Nor is it the earthly liberation of the people of God from the heathen yoke, as in Judaism. It does not relate to any circumstances as such. It denotes neither healing in a religious

[45] The word "ontic" is used here to describe something that has the character of real existence.

[46] Leupold, 246.

> sense, nor life, nor liberation from satanic or demonic power. It has to do solely with man's relationship to God.[47]

On the other hand, Donald E. Gowan sets about to challenge Foerster's conclusion, charging that by basing his definition of *soteria* on the Pauline use of the term, Foerster dismisses the evidence from the Synoptic Gospels and Acts.[48] For Foerster,

> each of us has a "disability" of some kind which faith in Christ has the power to heal, but the overcoming of those disabilities, physical, psychological and spiritual may often be compared with the stroke victim learning to move his fingers or take a few steps again. When Paul speaks of the Christian being freed from the power of sin, born again to a new life, but still struggling with temptation and frequently failing (Romans 6 and 7) he is talking about real healing which has made a radical change in life, making it possible to function in a healthy way, but like other healings it is not complete to the extent of giving us a body like Superman's or a soul like Christ's.[49]

It is important to note that Gowan appears to define healing in the qualified way of "real healing," which makes people triumph in the midst of their suffering. For indeed he recognizes that while we must work at healing the body, "until the eschaton pain will still afflict us."[50]

The Bible seems to acknowledge that some believers will have less than perfect bodies. When Jesus speaks about the three categories of eunuchs in the context of the permanence of marriage (Matt 19:12), His phrase "the one who is able to accept it" would seem to suggest that there would be those in the kingdom "whom God grants (Matt 19:11) the ability to accept non-marriage."[51] It is significant what may be said about those eunuchs in the first category.

---

[47] Werner Foerster, "*sozo, soteria, soter, soterios*," in *Theological Dictionary of the New Testament*, ed. Gerhard Kittel and Gerhard Friedrich, vol. 7 (Grand Rapids, MI: Eerdmans, 1971), 1002.

[48] Donald E. Gowan, "Salvation as Healing," *Ex Auditu 5* (1989): 1–19.

[49] Ibid., 15.

[50] Ibid., 16. He observes, "Others are destroyed by these afflictions, but the church has a gift to offer them which might enable them to triumph, as Christians we know have been able to triumph in the midst of their sufferings. Do not misunderstand me; I do not advocate the gospel as a painkiller, taking the place of vigorous action on behalf of health, peace, and justice from oppression or pain we are striving for. That does not have to mean we have totally failed, however, if we do not forget that God heals in various ways" (ibid).

[51] D. A. Hagner, *Matthew 14–28*, Word Biblical Commentary 33B (Dallas, TX: Word, 1998), 550.

> Eunuchs by birth at the beginning of the list make it quite clear, however, that Matthew has lack/loss of male potential in view. As now, children were occasionally born with defective genitals and subsequently would fail to develop male secondary characteristics as they grew up.[52]

In Paul's discussion of resurrection in 1 Corinthians 15:42–49, he contrasts the "body that is sown" with the "body that is raised." In the several contrasting ideas he introduces, he notes in verse 43 regarding the earthly body, "It is sown in dishonor, it is raised in glory; it is sown in weakness, it is raised in power." It is generally understood that by sowing and raising, Paul is not merely contrasting a dead body with a resurrected body. Rather,

> to describe the pre-resurrection *sōma* as **sown in weakness** expresses Paul's realism about the *frailty, fragility, vulnerability,* and constraints of human existence (including that of Christians) without diminishing the power of the cross, which is the presupposition for the triumph of the resurrection mode of existence[53] (emphasis original).

To characterize a person's post-conversion experience of such fragility and vulnerability as *sinful in itself* seems to be an inaccurate depiction at best.

That true believers may have to endure medical or psychological challenges does not take away from the fact that in some cases believers may experience healing through the power of God. The Bible recounts numerous stories of persons who were healed from both physiological and psychological ailments (e.g., Mark 5:1–20; Luke 5:12–15). In some instances, individuals who were so healed were described as having been saved. Luke, in fact, speaks of being saved by faith several times, when the salvation received is healing of the body (Luke 8:48, 50; 17:19; 18:42).

---

[52] John Nolland, *The Gospel of Matthew: A Commentary on the Greek Text* (Grand Rapids, MI: Eerdmans, 2005), 778.

[53] A. C. Thiselton, *The First Epistle to the Corinthians: A Commentary on the Greek Text* (Grand Rapids, MI: Eerdmans, 2000), 1274. See also S. J. Kistemaker and W. Hendriksen, *Exposition of the First Epistle to the Corinthians*, New Testament Commentary 18 (Grand Rapids, MI: Baker Book House, 2001), 572: "It is sown in corruption, it is raised in incorruption." Paul writes that the whole creation has been subjected to futility. Because of man's sin and God's subsequent curse it is in bondage of decay (refer to Rom. 8:19–21). This world tainted by corruption will not be annihilated at the consummation but renewed. Then it will be restored in incorruption. In this life, the physical *bodies of believers endure the ravages of corruption*, but at the resurrection these bodies will be raised in incorruption" (emphasis supplied).

Partial Evaluation and Conclusion

The fall dealt a severe blow to God's creation, but the situation was not altogether hopeless because God already had a plan in place for the salvation of the creation. The Bible is in fact a record of God's salvific relation with His creation. The first promise of this plan was announced in Genesis 3:15 and culminated in the incarnation, life, death, and resurrection of Jesus Christ. For the human experience, salvation has many components. But because of our interest in transgender issues, we have focused on the aspect of regeneration due to its ontic transformational significance. Regeneration brings about a new creation; indeed, recipients are described as "born again." Yet, our discussion shows that the Christian new birth experience may not necessarily remove the believer's physiological challenges in the present life. We conclude, therefore, that transgendered and intersexed persons may have genuine salvation experiences and still continue to be dogged by the dysphoria associated with the condition. It may be that the transgendered person's experience of salvation may mean that he or she experiences regeneration as *tri-um-phing* under the suffering of dysphoria. Obviously, we may also not rule it out as an impossibility that transgendered persons may receive the healing touch of the Lord.

Christian Frameworks for Approaching Transgenderism

Based on the conclusions we have drawn so far in the discussion, we may say that transgenderism is an expression of one form of human brokenness that may manifest itself not only in the world, but also in the Christian community. Much of how these persons are approached in the church will depend on the framework through which they are viewed.

Mark Yarhouse distinguishes three frameworks as lenses through which transgendered persons are viewed: integrity, disability, and diversity. We will evaluate each of these frameworks in the context of the principles we have outlined in our discussion so far.

The Integrity Framework

The integrity framework evaluates transgenderism from the point of view of the creation ideal of the male-female binary that we previously discussed. The framework seeks to preserve the stamp of maleness and femaleness as sacred, and it is concerned that transsexuality threatens it. Yarhouse identifies Robert Gagnon with this framework, based on his comment that "transsexuality is in some respects an even more extreme version of the problem of homosexuality: an explicit denial of the integrity of one's own sex and an overt attempt at marring the sacred image of maleness or femaleness formed by God."[54] It appears that biological sex as a key component of one's personhood plays a major role in the integrity framework.

On the basis of our discussion on biblical perspectives on sex and gender from the creation point of view, there is little to disagree with on what the integrity framework affirms. A few clarifications, however, need to be made. First, while Gagnon is concerned with transsexuality, we are concerned with transgenderism (a genuine physiological and not a chosen state). We are concerned with the ethics of transgenderism as a state in which a person finds himself or herself. Our view is that as a manifestation of the fall, the transgender state, where no choices have been made in response to the dysphoria, though not *immoral*, is *not desirable*. It appears that the integrity model alone is incomplete because it focuses only on the creation ideal and does not factor in the fall as an aspect of the biblical perspective on sex and gender. Second, we too would be unfavorably inclined towards transsexuality, especially where sex reassignment surgery is involved, but on slightly different grounds. As argued earlier, while we accept the immutable role of biological sex in the determination of gender, we recognize that it is not the sole determining factor because of our wholistic understanding of personhood. Anatomy is determinative of gender but not exclusively. The mind is also determinative of gender but not exclusively.

The Disability Framework

While the integrity framework focuses on the creation ideal of human sexuality, the disability framework emphasizes sexuality after the fall. Proponents of the disability framework are convinced about two things. First, the situation of the transgendered person is what it was *not* supposed to be. Second, there are in operation real, unchosen causal pathways to the transgendered situation. In other words, these proponents take seriously both the Bible (special revelation) as well as science and the related research on transgenderism (general revelation).[55] From the point of view of the science of it, transgenderism, whether it is traced to brain malfunctions or other multiple factors, is thought about along the lines of such health conditions as eating disorders, depression, and schizophrenia. By seeking to understand the science and related research on transgenderism,

---

[54] Robert A. Gagnon, "Transsexuality and Ordination," http://www.robgagnon.net/articles/TranssexualityOrdination.pdf (accessed October 21, 2020), 3–4, suggests that "here it is not just a case of a self-affirmed attraction and behavior that has the practical effect of compromising the integrity of one's sex as male or female. It is a decisive complaint or rebellion against God for having created oneself as male or female."

[55] Yarhouse, 49.

proponents are able to affirm the non-moral nature of the phenomenon with confidence.

Our analysis of the biblical perspective on sex and gender in the context of the fall is in basic harmony with the disability framework. The disability classification, however, seems to create a certain attitudinal response. Positively, it evokes a compassionate and caring reaction. However, to categorize as "disabled" is to resign to a certain destiny. Yarhouse correctly detects the result of such attitudinal positioning. While proponents of the framework may accept the sanctity of creation's male-female differentiation, "the openness to palliative care and inter-vention that allows for cross-gender identification may not be a sufficient response to adherents of the integrity framework."[56] Heather Looy points to what may be a more acceptable position: "While the fall into sin has created distortions in how femaleness and maleness are experienced and expressed, living in the time of grace means that we must seek to redeem gender and sexuality in harmony with God's intentions."[57]

The Diversity Framework

The diversity framework calls for the celebration of extant sexual diversities within cultures. As Yarhouse correctly points out, proponents of this strong form of diversity framework are influenced by the scholarship of scholars who stand in the hermeneutical tradition of Michael Foucault.[58] In this tradition, where scholars like Hans Georg Gadamer, Paul Ricoeur, and Jacques Derrida also stand, the Bible has lost its traditional epistemological privilege. Ontologically, this means that its view of human nature based on the Genesis creation narrative is no longer definitive. Two anthropological trajectories result, particularly on the issue of human sexuality. First, there are those who embrace an essentialist view of human nature but in a way that is not rooted in the *imago Dei* as discussed above. These rely, among others, on the binaries of male/female and homosexual/heterosexual, presuming that sex and sexuality are essential characteristics and that sexuality is something natural, God-given, and not subject to change.[59] But, essentialism in this sense is defined with reference to a person's manner of birth. Therefore, a person born with whatever sexual tendencies has an essential nature that is natural, God-given, and not subject to change—just as a person born

[56] Yarhouse, 49.

[57] Heather Looy, "Male and Female God Created Them: The Challenge of Intersexuality," *Journal of Psychology and Christianity* 21, no. 1 (2002): 17, quoted in Yarhouse, 49.

[58] Yarhouse, 51.

[59] Laurel C. Schneider and Carolyn Roncolato, "Queer Theologies," *Religion Compass* 6, no. 1 (2012): 2.

with heterosexual tendencies also has an essential nature that is natural, God-given, and not subject to change.

The second anthropological trajectory is represented by queer theory. Queer theory is against sex/gender classifications that are based on essential, natural divisions between male and female, gay and straight. Queer theory has roots in the liberation theology movement, but it is particularly traced to the 1990s when

> the protean diversity of human sexual practices and preferences made universal claims about sexual orientation increasingly difficult to sustain. An academic and political divide had emerged between "essentialists" who claim a universal "nature" to sexual identity and "social constructionists" who argue from anthropological, historical, and sociological observation that sexual identity is historically conditioned and constructed.[60]

The tendency here is also to separate the notion of sex as a physiological phenomenon from gender, considered to be a social construct of femininity or masculinity that may vary from culture to culture.[61]

Rooted as it is in the foregoing ideological principles, the diversity framework represents postmodern epistemology where all human knowledge, it is claimed, is historically contextual, local, and particular, yielding what has been called the "contextual thesis."[62] In the view of Diogenes Allen, with an embargo on all metanarratives, the conclusion is inevitable that "every understanding of reality is a function of history and culture."[63] Furthermore, Allen observes, "this relativism is so potent that not only do we construct reality differently in different eras and societies, but it appears that there is little, if anything, to stop each individual from constructing reality in his or her own way."[64]

The principles of the diversity framework stand contrary to the biblical view on sexuality and therefore cannot point a way forward for us on the matter at hand. The integrity and disability frameworks present only partial views but also lack the eschatological dimension. We will, therefore, bring our final concluding thoughts together by considering what

---

[60] Schneider and Roncolatod, 3.

[61] Holger Szesnat, "In Fear of Androgyny," *Journal of Theology for Southern Africa* 93 (1995): 34.

[62] Keith Yandell, "Modernism, Post-Modernism, and the Minimalist Canons of Common Grace," *Christian Scholars Review* 27 (1997): 19.

[63] Diogenes Allen, "Christianity and the Creed of Postmodernism," *Christian Scholars Review* 23, no. 2 (1993): 120.

[64] Ibid.

we think is a more comprehensive framework to approach the issue of transgenderism: the great controversy theme.

Conclusion: The Great Controversy Framework

The great controversy theme in Adventist theology depicts a cosmic conflict that commenced in heaven when Lucifer, a created being endowed with freedom of choice, exalted himself to become Satan, God's adversary. He led a portion of the heavenly angels into a rebellion that subsequently introduced the spirit of rebellion into this world when he led Adam and Eve into sin. The consequence of human sin has been the distortion of the image of God in humanity, and the disordering of the created world. At the core of this controversy between Christ and Satan is the character of God, His law, and His sovereignty over the universe.

At the same time, the theme represents a philosophy of history, a metanarrative that provides meaning to the origin of evil and its eventual destruction as well as the restoration of God's original purpose for this world. Comprehensive in scope and breadth, the theme illumines every aspect of human and creaturely life and encompasses the past, present, and eternity. Tracing the earthly phase of the conflict to the sin of Adam and Eve in the garden of Eden, the theme takes the creation and fall stories of Genesis as trustworthy accounts of human history. It takes a high view of Scripture and sees in the histories and teachings of canonical books of the Bible the unfolding of God's purposes for His creation.

Considered as a metanarrative, the great controversy theme, like the three frameworks previously discussed, may be called into service to shed light on the issue of transgenderism. Indeed, the above discussion of biblical perspectives on sex and gender, both from the point of view of creation and the fall as well as the discussion on salvation, are vignettes on the theme. Furthermore, our evaluation of the three frameworks has been done from the point of view of the great controversy theme. The question for us now is how these broad themes inform the specific issues of transgenderism.

The first foundational issue is the truth about the nature of human sexuality. Our analysis above, which is also the great controversy view, shows that the male-female binary is the foundation of God's intention on human sexuality. The mirroring of the image of God in this structure of human sexuality cements its enduring nature. Furthermore, the constituent components of this binary were fitted for the harmonious working out of God's purposes. It was all very good (Gen 1:31). From this perspective, transgenderism represents a departure from God's creaturely intentions with regard to the outfitting of human bodily and psychological faculties for binary sexuality.

The second foundational issue is the truth about how human sexuality turned out to be the way it is today. The great controversy motif attributes the current situation to the outworking of forces against God's purposes for creation. To bring about His creative intentions, God established laws, both physical and moral, for the created order. Since the fall, there has been a frontal attack on these laws by Satan whereby creation groans in futility (Rom 8:20–22). For intelligent beings in particular, God's moral law has been brought into disfavor. Predicting an intensification of this situation towards the end of earth's history, Jesus used the word *anomia*, meaning "lawlessness" (Matt 24:12; cf. 2 Thess 2:3–9). The great controversy theme, therefore, understands all the deviations in God's creation, including aberrations in sexuality, as springing from this basic intrusion of lawlessness into the created order. In contemporary times this lawlessness is paraded as freedom, whereas loyalty to the law of God is enjoined on all people at this very time (Rev 12:17; 14:12). Meanwhile, we should be ever mindful of the debilitation, enslavement, and depravity of the human condition.

The third foundational issue is the truth about why human sexuality, as an aspect of the creation order and its laws, is being called into question. The encounter between Eve and the serpent in the garden of Eden is instructive here. The crux of the temptation was Satan's attempt to lead the woman to distrust the goodness of God's expressed will for herself and Adam, and to suggest a substitute. Withholding their hand from the fruit was not in their best interest, the serpent suggested. The alternative of eating the fruit was the option that Satan offered through the serpent. Ultimately, the issue boils down to questioning the character of a God who would keep the best away from His creatures. Alternative sexualities, and the outfitting of human bodily and psychological faculties to facilitate them (such as transgenderism represents), may be seen as one aspect, in the area of human sexuality, of the ongoing strategy of the enemy to question God's character. Indeed, we may speak of a broader scheme of imitations and counterfeits. Ekkehardt Mueller provides an outline of imitations and counterfeit in the big picture of the great controversy as depicted in the book of Revelation.[65]

The final foundation issue is the truth about human sexuality in the interim, while the conflict rages on. The great controversy theme foresees a time when the conflict will come to a close. Satan, the archenemy of God, was defeated on the cross, but his final elimination and the complete restoration of order in God's universe awaits the second coming of Christ. In the interim those who suffer deviations in bodily and psychological functions, such as transgender people, are promised continuous victory

---

[65] Ekkehardt Mueller, "Evil Powers and Occult Practices in the Apocalypse," in *Church, Culture, and Spirits*, ed. Kwabena Donkor (Silver Spring, MD: Biblical Research Institute, 2011), 108–109.

in Christ over their circumstances. In the interim the dysphoria of transgenderism may or may not be entirely eliminated, but the promise of grace to live, in this case sexually, in accordance with God's will (law), is extended to all. Here again, Paul's discussion of the realities of living in the flesh (Rom 7:13–25) until the quickening (Rom 8:11) or redemption (Rom 8:23) of our mortal bodies keeps the interim dimension in view. Dunn is correct in his view that "the force of σάρξ [*sarx*] is precisely that it denotes an unavoidable attachment and tie to this age which must perish before redemption can be complete (Rom 8:11, 23), and which therefore denotes not merely a pre-Christian state."[66] Furthermore, the contrast between willing and doing that Paul sets forth (Rom 7:18–19) "is the contrast between on the one hand the renewed heart and enlightened mind (5:5; 6:17; 12:2; contrast 1:21, 28; 2:5), and on the other the yet unredeemed mortal body (8:11, 23)."[67]

Finally, what is the practical implication of all of this discussion for transgender people in the Adventist Church? Specifically, can transgender people be members of the church family? To begin, we wish to be absolutely clear that this question relates to individuals who sincerely embody in their experience a conflict between their biological sex and their sense of gender, prior to any response that may have moral implications. It is our view, based on the biblical discussion undertaken in this study, that the experience of incongruence by *itself* cannot be a barrier to church membership. This conclusion is based in part on our disagreement with the view that the internal experience of the transgendered person's dysphoria is sinful in *itself*. Transgender people can be members who through grace *may* experience divine healing and go on to live a heterosexual life pleasing to God; or they may, through that same grace, live *in this life* with their dysphoria in a manner that is not contrary to God's will on sexual expression. They may be legitimate subjects of loving and compassionate pastoral care, this side of eternity. The great controversy framework assures us, however, that the day is coming when

> sin and sinners are no more. The entire universe is clean. One pulse of harmony and gladness beats through the vast creation. From Him who created all will flow life, and light, and gladness, throughout the realms of unlimited space . . . and from the minutest atom to the greatest world, all things, animate and inanimate, in their unshadowed beauty and perfect joy will declare that God is love.[68]

---

[66] Dunn, 391.

[67] Ibid.

[68] Ellen G. White, *The Great Controversy* (Mountain View, CA: Pacific Press, 1950), 678.

CHAPTER 19

Cybersex and Robotic Sex: Social, Psychological, and Biblical Issues

Vanderlei Dorneles

Now, more than ever before, people of all ages enjoy an unprecedented communicative and interactive experience. Using computers, the internet, and social networking, adults and children alike are communicating and interacting with one another with increased intensity. As such, the concepts of connection, interactivity, relationships, and communication are used in the context of new technologies.

The life-changing effects of new technologies, however, go beyond facilitating communication. We live in a time when presuppositions, truths, principles, and habits are undergoing rapid transformation.[1] In the context of the internet and social networking, probably the most evident change has to do with principles and habits related to sexuality. Nowadays, over the internet, people are finding and choosing companion-ship without regard to location, age, social level, or religious orientation. The ease of finding sexual partners is proportional to the fluidity of these relationships. At the same speed as messages are exchanged by internet users, their feelings can be aroused and broken. The internet and social networking offer an outlet through which people can express their sexual impulses as never before. Additionally, there are available a great number of instruments and gadgets to extend and facilitate sexual experiences —from sex toys to intelligent and seductive robots.

---

[1] French philosopher Pierre Lévy, *Les Technologies de l'intelligence: L'avenir de la pensée à l'ère informatique* (Paris: La Découverte, 1990), 18, writes, "We live one of those rare moments when, through a new technical configuration, that is, through a new relationship with the cosmos, a new style of humanity is being invented."

As Christians, we need to analyze our postmodern age and its transformations in terms of ideas, practices, and instruments that can affect our lives, our families, and the church as well. More importantly, we need to evaluate those changes in light of the Word of God, which gives us clear principles and practices related to family and sexuality.

This chapter, after some introductory remarks on postmodernism and sexuality, addresses two kinds of postmodern sexual practices related to the internet and new technologies—cybersex and robotic sex—and provides an evaluation of such practices according to biblical principles.

Postmodernism and Sexuality

Postmodernism has been defined as a new condition in which the mass media has abolished distance and turned human society into a global village. This worldview does not recognize absolute truths and considers everything in culture to be human creations.[2] From this viewpoint, religion, marriage, and family are no longer considered to be pre-established values and principles, but only human structures and social organizations. These changes have caused great transformations in lifestyle.[3]

At the center of these transformations lies a new sexuality.[4] Internet and social networking are major instruments in the promotion of the current "sexual revolution"[5] and thus are changing the patterns of social communication and interpersonal relationships. Indeed, researchers demonstrate that sex is the most frequently searched-for topic on the internet, and over half of the time people spend on the internet is related to

---

[2] See Stanley J. Grenz, *A Primer on Postmodernism* (Grand Rapids, MI: Eerdmans, 1996). For basic definitions of postmodernism, see also Perry Anderson, *The Origins of Postmodernity* (New York: Verso, 2002); Jean-François Lyotard, *The Postmodern Condition: A Report on Knowledge* (Minneapolis, MN: University of Minnesota Press, 1984); and Vanderlei Dorneles, *Cristãos em Busca do Êxtase* (Tatuí: Casa Publicadora Brasileira, 2014), 13–44.

[3] Since postmodernists do not accept the pre-established principles and values, they tend to demolish every structure and pattern of behavior and consider them to be mere traditions. In terms of sexuality, postmodernists tend to see every kind of sexual experience as natural, useful, and good. Because of this, the deconstructionist concept behind Alfred Kinsey's words, "The only unnatural sexual act is that which you cannot perform" (Susan Ratcliffe, ed., *Oxford Treasury of Sayings and Quotations* [New York: Oxford University Press, 2011], 417), is quite widespread nowadays.

[4] Sasha Reseneil, "Toward an Understanding of Postmodern Transformation of Sexuality and Cathexis," January 21, 2000, http://www.leeds.ac.uk/cava/papers/wsp8 (accessed December 16, 2015).

[5] Jill C. Manning, "The Effects of Pornography on Marriage: Dealings with a Spouse's Sexually Addictive and Compulsive Behaviors," in *The Family in the New Millennium: World Voices Supporting the "Natural" Clan*, ed. A. Scott Loveless and Thomas B. Holman, vol. 2 (Westport, CT: Praeger, 2007), 374–375.

sexual activity.[6] British psychologist Mark D. Griffiths, who researches behavioral addictions, says that "the convenience of online pornography and adult chat sites provides an immediately available vehicle to easily fall into compulsive patterns of online use."[7] Michael W. Ross, a behavioral science professor at the University of Texas, says that "the Internet becomes a new form of the expression of the self (or selves), and a non-traditional social and sexual setting."[8]

Postmodern behavior is usually connected to liberation, emancipation, and discovery. As traditional and modern attitudes of discipline and contention are discarded, new forms of sexual practices take their place. According to the controversial French philosopher Michel Foucault,[9] modern social life is characterized by the emergence of "disciplinary power," which is able to mold human nature, especially in terms of sexuality. In the 1970s he wrote, "The success of disciplinary power derives no doubt from the use of simple instruments; hierarchical observation, normalizing judgment and their combination in a procedure that is specific to it, the examination."[10] However, nowadays the internet is eliminating the structures of social observation and vigilance. It changes power relations by allowing people to hide themselves while getting satisfaction for their sexual impulses. The internet transfers power to individuals—who are now able to change their "form, age, gender, position, or sexual orientation"[11]—and sets them free from the traditional power of regulation.

Thus, the technology of the internet and social networking lies at the center of the postmodern sexual revolution because it not only propagates pornography and sexual narratives, but also creates new forms to manifest sexual impulses. One of these forms is cybersex.

---

[6] Mark D. Griffiths, "Sex on the Internet: Observations and Implications for Internet Sex Addiction," *The Journal of Sex Research* 38, no. 4 (November 2001): 333.

[7] Griffiths, 333.

[8] Michael W. Ross, "Typing, Doing, and Being: Sexuality and the Internet," *The Journal of Sex Research* 42, no. 4 (November 2005): 342.

[9] Michel Foucault (1926–1984) was a French historian, philosopher, philologist, and literary critic. Part of his scholarly production has to do with sexuality and the traditional means to repress it. He is one of the most influential writers of the post-World War II period. Under the influence of the German philosopher Friedrich Nietzsche and the psychoanalyst Sigmund Freud, Foucault himself defined his own work as a critical history of modernity. He died of AIDS in Paris.

[10] Michel Foucault, *Discipline and Punish: The Birth of Prison* (New York: Vintage Books, 1995), 170.

[11] Ross, 343.

Cybersex: Consequences and Evaluation

"Computer sex," "netsex," "mudsex," and, colloquially, "cybering" are other terms for cybersex. They refer to a situation in which two or more people connected remotely via a computer network exchange sexually explicit messages describing a sexual experience in a virtual sexual encounter to stimulate feelings and fantasies. The goal of cybersex is to reach emotional and physical satisfaction.[12] The messages exchanged arouse the imagination and can produce a high level of sexual excitement.[13]

Cybersex may be practiced by lovers who are geographically separated or among individuals who have no prior knowledge of one another and who meet each other in cyberspace. It may involve the use of only typed words or may include voice and images via webcam. Sometimes people express their fantasies only in a cybersex conversation, without physical satisfaction, but "these text-based interactions may be accompanied by masturbation."[14] Thus it can also be considered a form of assisted sexual stimulation. If the virtual encounter does not lead to physical satisfaction, it remains at least a shared fantasy.

Several factors make online encounters or cybersex potentially seductive and even addictive. The remote distance and possibility of secrecy give users a sense of complete liberty. Both timidity and the sensation of doing something wrong seem to disappear. Thus, the internet permits an anonymous manifestation of the self. In fact, the internet provides a "kind of missing link" between fantasies and the desire for intimacy. It removes social cues and enables the "crystallization of fantasy."[15]

The internet tends "to keep actual behavior at a distance."[16] Restricting sexual impulses to fantasy gives users the false sense of doing something without *truly* engaging in the act. The use of expressions like "virtual reality," "second life," and "virtual love" to describe activities and relationships carried on through the internet and social networking suggests that a "cyber-encounter" is not "real." However, though the encounter is not physical, the feelings and sensations are real and can involve the whole being or body. The mind receives high levels of stimulation, which expands the imagination and produces the sensation of a real encounter.

---

[12] Ross, 342.

[13] Meenakshi Gigi Durham, *Technosex: Precarious Corporealities, Mediated Sexualities, and the Ethics of Embodied Technics* (London: Macmillan, 2016), 41–59.

[14] Griffiths, 335.

[15] Ross, 344.

[16] Ibid.

Imagination and fantasy are the keys to this kind of experience.[17] The satisfaction comes from a concentration of lustful thoughts.

Social and Psychological Consequences

Psychologists consider sexuality to be an integral and essential component of the self and identity. But it is also one of the most difficult aspects of the self for an individual to express, explore, and balance. This happens because there are constraints such as social sanctions, embarrassment, and fear of negative reactions that may hinder an individual from expressing and practicing his or her sexuality. Some psychologists see the emergence of the internet, networking, and chat sites as new channels by which an individual can freely explore and express aspects of sexuality securely and without fear.[18]

However, despite this optimistic view, many people who engage in virtual relationships or cybersex, after eliminating some fears and restrictions, progress to physical encounters with partners they met through the internet. Both men and women relate new and more liberating sexual behavior, not only in meeting virtual partners physically, but also in adopting unsafe sexual practices.[19] In addition, other researchers express concerns about cybersex because of the addictive behavior associated with it. Addiction to internet sex is a reality, defined as "an extremely potent addiction that must be treated as such." Additionally, counselors and therapists are seeing an increasing number of children and teens with problems associated with online sexual activities.[20]

---

[17] Elizabeth M. Reid, "Text-Based Virtual Realities: Identity and the Cyborg Body," in *High Noon on the Electronic Frontier: Conceptual Issues in Cyberspace*, ed. Peter Ludlow (Cambridge, MA: MIT Press, 1999), 327–328, argues that in a virtual encounter the self of each partner is not a person in the real sense, but a symbol constructed by language. The identity of the players constantly changes according to the context. "All of these phenomena place gender, sexuality, identity and corporeality beyond the plane of certainty" (ibid.). The second life or second self is very fluid and mutable. With the self physically freed, it is possible to "bypass the boundaries delineated by cultural constructs of beauty, ugliness and fashion" (ibid.). So, this body belongs to the dimension of symbolism.

[18] Katelyn Y. A. McKenna et al., "Demarginalizing the Sexual Self," *The Journal of Sex Research* 38, no. 4 (November 2001): 302, highlight some issues of social and emotional safety related to cybersex, including sexually transmitted diseases and pregnancy.

[19] Julie M. Albright, "Sex in America Online: An Exploration of Sex, Marital Status, and Sexual Identity in Internet Sex Seeking and Its Impacts," *The Journal of Sex Research* 45, no. 2 (June 2008): 176, reports some research that shows the negative consequences or even addictive quality of seeking sex online. According to her, many of those who have experienced cybersex report "serious adverse consequences" because of their partner's involvement in sex online, including "18% reporting that erotic chat online had turned into an offline sexual affair." There is also evidence that those who seek sexual partners online may also engage in other high-risk sexual behaviors, including having multiple sexual partners, anal sex, and exposure to sexual diseases.

[20] Griffiths, 339.

From the viewpoint of emotions and feelings, a study by Arizona Community Physicians showed that those married to individuals with sexual addictions and compulsivity often report feelings of hurt, betrayal, rejection, loneliness, shame, humiliation, jealousy, anger, and loss of self-esteem. They also "felt that online affairs were as emotionally painful to them as live or off line affairs."[21]

Although some psychologists and sexologists consider the internet and social networking to be a positive channel for expressing sexuality, cybersex has also been defined as a real, albeit not physical, relationship and a potentially addictive behavior. Its effects on emotions and feelings can be very painful and destructive.

In order to broaden the evaluation of this practice, it is helpful to consider what is virtual in the context of the internet.

The word "virtual" has become very common in recent decades, especially in the context of the internet and social networking, but it is not necessarily well understood. "Virtual" is often wrongly used in contrast with "real" or "true." For many, "virtual reality" is something that does not necessarily exist.

Currently, the word "virtual" has at least three meanings: 1) a technical meaning associated with information in the field of technology or computers, 2) a philosophical meaning, and 3) a contemporary meaning. Pierre Lévy ascribes the fascination with virtual reality, to a large extent, to a confusion of these three meanings. He explains that, in the philosophical sense, virtual is "that which exists potentially rather than actually," like expected problems that are solved through actualization.[22] From a philosophical viewpoint, "virtual" is also an important dimension of reality, an idealistic reality that is not accessible or possible.[23] However, as currently used, the word "virtual" often signifies "unreality," as opposed to reality defined as a material embodiment or tangible presence. In this last definition, something "virtual" happens or exists independent of space. According to Lévy, "any entity [person or thing] is virtual if it is deterritorialized."[24]

From this perspective, "virtual" stands for a specific kind of reality. Even though we cannot assign it any spatial coordinates, the virtual

---

[21] William David Spencer, "Digital Adultery, 'Meta-Anon Widows,' Real-World Divorce, and the Need for a Virtual Sexual Ethic," in *Human-Robot Personal Relationships,* ed. Maarten H. Lamers and Fons J. Verbeek (Leiden: Leiden University, 2010), 102. See also Manning, 377.

[22] Pierre Lévy, *Cyberculture*, trans. Robert Bononno (Minneapolis, MN: University of Minnesota Press, 2001), 29.

[23] See Gilles Deleuze, *Bergsonism*, trans. Hugh Tomlinson and Barbara Habberjam (New York: Zone, 1991), 96–98.

[24] Lévy, *Cyberculture*, 29.

is nonetheless real. "The virtual exists without being anywhere."[25] Thus, "virtual" refers to the specific space of the internet or cyberspace,[26] rather than the non-existent or unreal in themselves.

In fact, by creating cyberspace, the internet has created new kinds of experiences, businesses, and relationships that are nearly independent of geographic location and temporal co-occurrence. The extension of cyberspace through the expansion of the internet accompanies and accelerates a general virtualization of the economy and society.[27] Technology in general has extended our abilities, skills, and even our bodies to unthinkable dimensions.[28] By using vehicles, we can travel farther distances than using only our feet. By using computers, we can memorize and organize more information than our minds are able to do. Cyberspace in particular, which is a deterritorialized space, has extended our skills and actions in different ways. One can do things outside the territorial space and afterward feel as though one did not do them at all. In other words, something virtual, therefore, is something that exists and is real, even though it is not present in terms of physical space and corporality.

A Biblical Evaluation

From the above, the question emerges about the ethical aspects of virtual sex. Considering that the virtual is no less real in the context of the internet, one must evaluate virtual sex in light of the biblical concept of sin.[29]

According to the Bible, sin is not committed only when we touch something with our hands or bodies. Indeed, sin belongs not only to the realm of practical and corporal actions, but can also happen in the mind. Therefore, one can be contaminated and stand condemnable before God through lustful thoughts and imagination like those proper to cybersex. Biblically, the heart or mind is not only the point where sin starts, but also the sphere where sin can be committed and fully realized.

---

[25] *Cyberculture*, 30.

[26] On the concept of "cyberspace," see M. Graham, "Geography/Internet: Ethereal Alternate Dimensions of Cyberspace or Grounded Augmented Realities?," *The Geographical Journal* 179, no. 2 (2013): 177–188; Lance Strate, "The Varieties of Cyberspace: Problems in Definition and Delimitation," *Western Journal of Communication* 63, no. 3 (1999): 382–412; and Morten T. Hojsgaard and Margit Warburg, eds., *Religion and Cyberspace* (New York: Routledge, 2005).

[27] Lévy, *Cyberculture*, 31.

[28] The Canadian philosopher Marshall McLuhan, *The Medium Is the Message* (New York: Penguin, 1969), considers technologies to be "extensions" of the human body and senses.

[29] See Hossein Bidgoli, ed., *The Internet Encyclopedia*, vol. 1 (Hoboken, NJ: Wiley, 2004), s.v. "cybercrime"; and David Wall, ed., *Crime and the Internet: Cybercrimes and Cyberfears* (New York: Routledge, 2001).

Inner Sin in the Old Testament

In addition to its many commands prohibiting wrong actions (e.g., Exod 20; Deut 5), the Old Testament clearly talks about sin in terms of thoughts or feelings. Leviticus 19:17 says, "You shall not hate your brother in your heart."[30] Deuteronomy 15:9 adds, "Beware lest there be a wicked thought in your heart." The Hebrew word *lebab* ("heart") occurs 249 times in the Old Testament, including fifty-one in Deuteronomy alone, and refers to one's intimate feelings.[31]

From a positive perspective, the Bible talks about serving and obeying God with the "heart," which suggests the mind, thoughts, or inner being. Moses said that the people of Israel would seek the Lord and find Him if they did so with their "heart" and with all their "soul" (Deut 4:29). They should also "love" God with their "heart" and "strength" (Deut 6:5), and keep the law in their "heart" (Deut 6:6; cf. 11:18). Joshua also warned them to "serve" the Lord with "all [their] heart and with all [their] soul" (Josh 22:5). It also bears noting David's warning to Solomon: "Know the God of your father, and serve him with a loyal heart and with a willing mind; for the Lord searches all hearts and understands all the intent of the thoughts" (1 Chr 28:9). These passages indicate that a relationship with God involves the whole being—especially the "heart" and "soul," the inner dimensions of the self. They are part of that which is created and redeemed by God. According to the Bible, the heart can be "pure" (Ps 24:4; 73:1) and upright (Ps 119:7), or even "perverse" (Ps 101:4). This clearly indicates that sin occurs at the level of the "heart," thoughts, and imagination. "All sin, not least sexual sin, begins with the imagination."[32]

Furthermore, the tenth commandment expresses a specific prohibition against covetousness (Exod 20:17; Deut 5:21) that goes "beyond what people do" to include "their minds and desires." The sin prohibited here has to do with "the set of one's soul," "one's intentions," "one's

---

[30] All biblical quotations are from the NKJV, unless otherwise indicated.

[31] The alternative Hebrew word *leb* occurs 596 times. The Hebrew word *lebab*, translated as "heart," in general refers to affect, desire, and will. When used in relation to the human heart, *leb/lebab* designates "personal identity," "vital center," "affective center," "elemental emotions," "noetic center," "voluntative center," and "religious and ethical realm" (see G. Johannes Botterweck, Helmer Ringgren, and Heinz-Josef Fabry, eds., *Theological Dictionary of the Old Testament*, vol. 7 [Grand Rapids, MI: Eerdmans, 1995], 412–430). The heart represents the "center of emotions, feelings, moods, and passions" (Douglas R. Edwards, "Heart," *The HarperCollins Bible Dictionary*, ed. Paul Achtemeier [New York: HarperCollins, 1996], 408).

[32] D. A. Carson, *Matthew, Mark, Luke, The Expositor's Bible Commentary*, vol. 8 ed. Frank E. Gaebelein (Grand Rapids, MI: Zondervan, 1990), 151. The tenth commandment "represents a decided advance beyond the morality of any other ancient code. Most codes went no further than the deed, and a few took speech into account, but none proposed to regulate the thoughts" (Nichol, 1:607).

motivations," and "one's heart."[33] By touching the source of sin (the heart), the tenth commandment becomes "the capstone of the Decalogue."[34]

The Hebrew verb *khamad*, translated as "covet," occurs twenty-one times in the Old Testament, with both positive and negative connotations. It can also connote the idea of "pleasant" (Gen 2:9; 3:6), "desired" (Ps 19:10), "desirable" (Prov 21:20), and "precious" (Isa 44:9). The general idea of the root *khamad* is "to desire earnestly," "to take pleasure in," "to long after," or "to covet."[35] In the second reading of the law (Deut 5:21), it occurs in parallel with *tit'awweh*, which means "to set one's desire" on somebody or something. The commandment, therefore, deals with "man's inner heart" and "every inner instinct."[36]

As a sinful desire, *khamad* is distinct and separate from actually taking possession of the desirable thing. That is clear in Deuteronomy 7:25, where the verbs *khamad* ("covet") and *laqakh* (to "take," "get," or "receive") represent distinct kinds of attitude. The same occurs in Achan's report. He says, "When I saw among the spoils a beautiful Babylonian garment . . . I coveted [*khamad*] them and took [*laqakh*] them" (Josh 7:21). The same sequence appears in Proverbs 6:25 in relation to the harlot: "Do not lust [*khamad*] after her beauty in your heart, nor let her allure [*laqakh*] you with her eyelids." In a similar sequence, Micah distinguishes the sin of "coveting" from that of "taking" (Mic 2:2), which indicates two specific kinds of sin.

Thus, the goal of the tenth commandment is not only avoiding the theft of another's wife or possessions, but purity of thought and imagination.

The prohibition against coveting teaches us that God sees and judges the heart and is "concerned less with the outward act than with the thought from which the action springs."[37] The tenth commandment also establishes the principle that "the very thoughts of our hearts come under the jurisdiction of God's law."[38] However, besides that, "this basic com-mandment reveals the profound truth that we are not the helpless slaves of our natural desires and passions."[39] We have a force, the will, which, "under the power of Christ, can submerge every unlawful desire

[33] Earl S. Kalland, *Deuteronomy*, *The Expositor's Bible Commentary*, vol. 3 ed. Frank E. Gaebelein (Grand Rapids, MI: Zondervan, 1990), 60.

[34] Simon J. Kistemaker, *1 Corinthians*, New Testament Commentary (Grand Rapids, MI: Baker Academic, 1973, 2007), 329.

[35] Walter C. Kaiser, *Exodus*, *The Expositor's Bible Commentary*, vol. 2 ed. Frank E. Gaebelein (Grand Rapids, MI: Zondervan, 1990), 435.

[36] Ibid., 436.

[37] Nichol, 1:607. Cf. 1 Samuel 16:7; 1 Kings 8:39; 1 Chronicles 28:9; Hebrews 4:13.

[38] Nichol, 1:607.

[39] Ibid.

and passion."[40] This commandment "sums up the Decalogue by affirming that man is essentially a free moral agent."[41]

Thus, according to the Bible, to imagine, desire, or dwell on a sinful thought or fantasy is tantamount to a sinful act. This inner and hidden sin can contaminate the soul and defile the person. Independent of what is tied to the lustful thought and imagination—a person connected through the internet and thus not physically accessible, a porn image, or just a tale or story that arouses lustful feelings—such an experience is a violation of the tenth commandment or its underlying principle. On the other hand, with pure thoughts and feelings we serve and honor God. By maintaining our hearts and minds pure[42] and free from dwelling on lustful fantasies, we offer our whole being a sanctuary fit for the Holy Spirit.

Inner Sin in the New Testament

In contrast to those who considered sin an external act, unrelated to thought and motivation,[43] Jesus emphasized the inner nature of sin, especially in the Sermon on the Mount. In the Beatitudes, Jesus promises that those "pure in heart" will see God (Matt 5:8), and no one has the right to expect that vision without this qualification.[44] It is significant that Jesus delivered the beatitude about purity just before talking about the inner nature of sin (Matt 5:21, 27, 33). So when Jesus talks about adultery, He points to the purity of heart, which should underlie the righteousness of the actions.

In Matthew 5, every time Jesus says, "But I say to you" (Matt 5:22, 28, 32, 34, 39, 44), He corrects the misinterpretation of the law promoted by human tradition. Jesus equates angry and lustful thoughts to a transgression of the spirit of the law. Thus, "whoever looks at a woman to lust for her has already committed adultery with her in his *heart*" (Matt 5:28, emphasis supplied). Interestingly, Jesus uses here the same word for "adultery," *moicheuō* (Exod 20:13, Deut 5:17), occurring in the seventh commandment as translated by the Septuagint. This usage of the verb *moicheuō* indicates that for Jesus the sin of lustful imagination

---

[40] Ibid., 1:607.

[41] Ibid.

[42] On "to be pure in heart," see the next section.

[43] According to Matthew Henry, *Matthew Henry's Commentary on the Whole Bible*, vol. 5, *Matthew to John* (Peabody, MA: Hendrickson, 1991), 49, "The Pharisees, in their expositions on this command [the seventh], made it to extend no further than the act of adultery, suggesting that if the iniquity was only regarded in the heart, and went no further, God would not hear it." See also William Hendriksen, *Matthew*, New Testament Commentary (Grand Rapids, MI: Baker Academic, 1973, 2007), 302.

[44] Leon Morris, *Hebrews*, *The Expositor's Bible Commentary*, vol. 12 ed. Frank E. Gaebelein (Grand Rapids, MI: Zondervan, 1981), 139.

(Matt 5:28)is a transgression of both the tenth and seventh commandments, and this is committed *in* the heart.[45] According to Jesus, the seventh commandment, which prohibits adultery, includes every kind of sexual sin.[46] "We are here taught, that there is such a thing as *heart-adultery*, adulterous thoughts and dispositions, which never proceed to the act of adultery or fornication."[47] Thus, in contrast to the Pharisees, Jesus views "the evil lust of the heart as adultery, just as he views the hatred of the heart as murder."[48]

Although Jesus also consistently uses the verb *moicheuō* in reference to the seventh commandment (Matt 19:18; Mark 10:19; Luke 18:20), He also uses the Greek *porneia* to describe the sin that makes room for divorce (Matt 19:9).[49] Thus from Jesus' perspective, "adultery does not consist [only] in physical intercourse with a strange woman; it is present already in the desire which negates fidelity."[50]

In describing the kind of looking that is sinful, Jesus uses the Greek verb *epithumeō* ("lust," Matt 5:28). Its meaning is "to set one's heart upon [a thing]," "to long for," "to covet," "to desire."[51] This Greek word translates the Hebrew word *khamad*, in the tenth commandment. To lust for a thing is "to experience an intense, eager desire for it." Like *khamad*, the verb *epithumeō* is used in both a positive and negative sense. Jesus told the twelve that He had "desired" *(epithumeō)* to eat the last Passover with them (Luke 22:15; in its positive sense it appears also in Matt 13:17; Luke 17:22; Heb 6:11; 1 Pet 1:12).

It bears noting that Jesus uses the concept of pure "heart" *(Gk. kardia)* already established in Deuteronomy 6:5 and 15:9. The purity that Jesus has in mind is the same one already expected in the Old Testament. The Greek word *kardia* in Matthew 5:28 refers to "the intellect, the affections, and the will." Christ points out that "character is determined, not so much by the outward act, as by the inward attitude that motivates the act."[52]

---

[45] Spencer, 101, argues that Christ established a new standard, in relation to the Pharisees' view, according to which "hatred in the heart was akin to actual murder" and "lust in the heart was akin to actual adultery." On that basis, he says that Christians need to consider that "virtual sin is sin."

[46] Both Paul and James also use the verb *moicheuō* in reference to the seventh commandment (see Rom 13:9; Jas 2:11).

[47] Henry, 5:49.

[48] Hendriksen, 302.

[49] Richard M. Davidson, "Divorce and Remarriage in the Old Testament: A Fresh Look at Deuteronomy 24:1–4," *Journal of the Adventist Theological Society* 10, no. 1 (1999): 2–22.

[50] Friedrich Hauck, "Μοιχεύω, Μοιχάω, Μοιχεία, Μοῖχος, Μοιχαλίς," in *Theological Dictionary of the New Testament*, ed. Gerhard Kittel, Geoffrey W. Bromiley, and Gerhard Friedrich, (Grand Rapids, MI: Eerdmans, 2006), 734.

[51] Nichol, 5:336.

[52] Ibid., 5:336.

He considers that sin is, first and above all else, "an act of the higher powers of the mind the reason, the power of choice, the will."[53] Jesus' teaching about the lustful imagination includes "all forms of sexual relations outside marriage," since the "desire has the same nature as the action."[54]

The meaning of being pure in heart has been viewed, especially in Matthew, as "inner moral purity" in contrast with "merely external piety or ceremonial cleanness."[55] This is a key theme in Matthew, especially in Jesus' confrontation with the Pharisees (Matt 15:19–20; 23:25–28). In Jesus' view, purity defines people who "think, speak, and act without hypocrisy." So "sincerity, honesty, the condition of being without guile"[56] is emphasized in Matthew 5:8. In 1 Timothy 1:5 "pure" is a synonym for "unfeigned" (KJV) or "sincere." Thus, Jesus' viewpoint on purity has to do with obeying God's commandments even at the level of our thoughts and feelings and not merely in an external manner as the Pharisees understood. By using the concept of pure in heart, "Jesus speaks of obedience."[57] However, complete purity in one's whole life, including the heart, is possible only by the blood of Jesus.[58]

It is remarkable that nurturing lustful imagination and desire for a person who is before our eyes or far away, connected by the internet or social networking, whether this person is married or single, constitutes a transgression of the seventh commandment and defiles the heart. Jesus indicates that both married and single person can commit adultery by desiring either a married or single person.

The same dimension of sin in terms of thought and imagination echoes in the apostles' writings. In 1 Corinthians 10:6 Paul recollects the

---

[53] Ibid.

[54] D. Guthrie and J. A. Motyer, eds., *The New Bible Commentary,* 3rd ed. (Grand Rapids, MI: Eerdmans, 1993), 823.

[55] Carson, 134.

[56] Hendriksen, 276.

[57] Kittel, 3:425.

[58] The Greek word used for "pure" in Matthew 5:8 is *katharos*, which means "clean." The concept of *"cleansing"* is very strong in the Scriptures. In the Old Testament, things and people got defiled or impure both ceremonially and morally because of contact with impure animals, blood, death, sexual fluids, and sin in general (Lev 5:2; 11:43; 12:2; 15:2; Num 19:13). The blood of the sacrifices at the temple provided the cleanness (Lev 5:6; 14:19; 16:16). In this context, according to Kittel, 3:426, "cleansing and remission are synonymous." However, the New Testament emphasizes moral instead of ceremonial cleanness, and the blood of Jesus is the only way to obtain purity. "The purity of the NT community is personal and moral by nature. It consists in full and unreserved self-offering to God which renews the heart" (ibid., 425). John says the disciples were clean by their relationship with Jesus, the Spirit, and the Word of God (John 13:10; 15:2; 17:17–19; 1 John 1:7, 9). Complete purity by the blood of Jesus is the status of the redeemed before God (Rev 15:6; 19:8, 14; cf. 22:14), but uncleanness is the condition of those who will be outside the holy city (Rev 21:27; 22:11, 15).

history of Israel: "Now these things became our examples, to the intent that we should not lust after evil things as they also lusted [*epithumeō*]." In 1 Corinthians 10:8, he uses *porneuō*, the common New Testament verb for "committing sexual immorality."[59] He adds, in 1 Thessalonians 4:3, 7, "For this is the will of God, your sanctification: that you should abstain from sexual immorality; . . . For God did not call us to uncleanness, but in holiness." Here the apostle exhorts them to "personal consecration and purity, especially in sexual relations."[60] Christians have been called out of the world to be separate from uncleanness and to sanctification, "which the Holy Spirit . . . is performing in their hearts."[61] In a similar vein, 1 Thessalonians 5:23 says, "Now may the God of peace himself sanctify you completely; and may your whole spirit, soul, and body be preserved blameless at the coming of our Lord Jesus Christ." By using the Greek *holotelēs*,[62] "completely," Paul indicates that sanctification encompasses the whole being, including the skills of the mind and "knowledge" (*pneuma*, "spirit"), the "will and emotions" (*psychē*, "soul"), and "strength or physical dimension" (*sōma*, "body").[63]

In the same line, Peter calls Christian converts to be pure in mind and heart. "As obedient children, not conforming yourselves to the former lusts, as in your ignorance; but as he who called you *is* holy, you also be holy in all *your* conduct" (1 Pet 1:14–15). He is calling the Christians "to exercise mental diligence and moral discipline."[64] Edwin Blum points out that the passive imperative participle *syschēmatizomenoi* ("not conforming," found only here and in Romans 12:2) would be well translated as "Don't let the world around you squeeze you into its own mold, but let God remold your minds from within." Thus Peter is exhorting Christians "to control their desires rather than to be controlled by them."[65]

The basic idea of holiness is separation from everything that is impure and profane and setting oneself apart for God's purpose. Peter exhorts Christians to be separate and sanctified by citing the code of holiness

---

[59] W. Harold Mare, *1 Corinthians*, *The Expositor's Bible Commentary*, vol. 10 ed. Frank E. Gaebelein (Grand Rapids, MI: Zondervan, 1981), 249.

[60] Guthrie and Motyer, 1158.

[61] William Hendriksen and Simon J. Kistemaker, *Thessalonians, the Pastorals, and Hebrews*, New Testament Commentary (Grand Rapids, MI: Baker Academic, 1973, 2007), 101.

[62] As noted by A. T. Robertson, quoted by ibid., 141, this Greek word is used only here in the New Testament and its literal meaning is "the whole of each of you, every part of each of you."

[63] Robert L. Thomas, *1 & 2 Thessalonians*, *The Expositor's Bible Commentary*, vol. 11 ed. Frank E. Gaebelein (Grand Rapids, MI: Zondervan, 1981), 295.

[64] Guthrie and Motyer, 1240.

[65] Edwin A. Blum, *1 & 2 Peter*, *The Expositor's Bible Commentary*, vol. 12 ed. Frank E. Gaebelein (Grand Rapids, MI: Zondervan, 1981), 223.

given by the holy God in Leviticus 11, 18–20.[66] As God is sinless and totally separate from sin, He "expects that whatever we do, say, or think is holy."[67]

While holiness can elevate and rescue human nature from the condition of sin, the fantasy and lustful imagination that accompany cybersex and pornography are "powerful instrument[s] in debasing manhood and womanhood to the level of a mere sex object."[68] Those kinds of sexual experiences center on one's own self and stimulate sexual satisfaction without "interpersonal relationship or mutual respect."[69] Sex was created by God as part of a male-female relationship in order to expand and deepen mutual love.

Some of Jesus' contemporaries limited their definition of sin to physical acts, but Jesus made clear that sin does occur in the form of thoughts, desires, imagination, concupiscence, and other unclean thoughts and feelings. This kind of inner sin is committed when one dwells persistently on lustful imagination, desire, or covetousness for any person. In light of the Sermon on the Mount, Christians need to understand the nature of sin in terms of contamination and degradation of thoughts and feelings.

Both the commandment against "coveting" and Jesus' explanation about desiring a person focus on the thoughts. This sin can be committed even apart from touching the desired person—just by the imagination and feelings common in cybersex.

In cybersex, sinful thoughts are nurtured by virtual images and/or texts. Sinful feelings can also be aroused by a computerized image, which can provoke emotions and produce a transitory satisfaction.

Robotic Sex: Consequences and Evaluation

If cybersex through computers is a practice that requires a Christian answer, what might one say about computerized bodies or the development of humanlike machines able to enter into emotional relationships with human beings? Actually, computerized robots with human appearance and the skills to relate to and seduce human beings have become a reality in recent years, and may become more and more common and advanced as time goes by.

---

[66] The motivation that Peter gives to his exhortation, "As he who called you is holy, you also be holy," and then quoting "Be holy, for I am holy" (1 Peter 1:16), suggests that he has in mind the code of holiness in Leviticus (see Lev 11:44–45; 19:2; 20:26).

[67] Simon J. Kistemaker, *Exposition of the Epistles of Peter and the Epistle of Jude*, New Testament Commentary, vol. 16 (Grand Rapids, MI; Baker Academic, 1987), 61.

[68] Miroslav M. Kiš, "Christian Lifestyle and Behavior," in *Handbook of Seventh-day Adventist Theology*, ed. Raoul Dederen (Hagerstown, MD: Review and Herald, 2001), 697.

[69] Ibid.

Robots have been used in factories and laboratories, but they can also perform domestic labor like mowing lawns, vacuuming carpets, and washing dishes and clothes. In the year 2000, about four hundred thousand domestic service robots were in use. This number had risen to about four million by 2007.[70] More recent data has shown that the market for robots has grown exponentially. As one author notes: "The number of robots in use worldwide multiplied three-fold over the past two decades, to 2.25 million. Trends suggest the global stock of robots will multiply even faster in the next 20 years, reaching as many as 20 million by 2030, with 14 million in China alone."[71]

However, the use of robots for interpersonal relationship and sexual engagement is the most startling social phenomenon. Sales of all types of entertainment and leisure robots are projected at about nine million units over the same period.

According to the most optimistic perspectives, sexual robots would permit human beings not only to enjoy them, but also to learn more about love and sex with them. Everything that human beings have developed in terms of sex and self-satisfaction would be inserted into the robots' programs, and they would teach human beings to love and have satisfactory sexual relationships.

In 2005, in his book *Robots Unlimited*,[72] the artificial-intelligence expert David Levy imagined a great revolution in the field of robotics. He believed that by 2050, with the evolution of artificial intelligence, robots would have intellectual and emotional skills. Two years later, in another book on the topic, he wrote that future robots would be like humans.[73] One source predicts that "robotic sex partners will be a commonplace" by 2025.[74]

However, some companies have already sold thousands of these kinds of robots to customers in different countries.[75] The robots do not

---

[70] William David Spencer, "Should the *Imago Dei* Be Extended to Robot: Love and Sex with Robots, the Future of Marriage, and the Christian Concept of Personhood," *Africanus Journal* 1, no. 2 (November 2009): 12.

[71] Adrian Cooper, "The Shape of Things to Come," *How Robots Change the World, Oxford Economics* (June 26, 2019), 3, available at https://www.oxfordeconomics.com/recent-releases/how-robots-change-the-world (accessed December 22, 2021).

[72] David Levy, *Robots Unlimited: Life in a Virtual Age* (Boca Raton, FL: CRC Press, 2005).

[73] Ibid., 10.

[74] Aaron Smith and Janna Anderson, "Predictions for the State of AI and Robotics in 2025," AI, *Pew Research Center, Internet & Technology* (August 6, 2014), available at https://www.pewresearch.org/internet/2014/08/06/predictions-for-the-state-of-ai-and-robotics-in-2025/

[75] For example, according to Andrea Forni, *Robots – The New Era: Living, Working and Investing in the Robotics Society of the Future* (Self-published, 2015), since 2010, the company True Companion has sold the male "Rocky" and female "Roxxxy" sexbots. Roxxxy is described as a real doll 170 centimeters tall and weighing 54 kilograms, and has "basic artificial intelligence that

yet have high performance in terms of social interaction, but research has been done to improve those skills.[76] Sexbots have been manufactured with artificial skin and sensory abilities. Researchers in Japan, Italy, and the United States are working on high-tech skin development to upgrade their attractiveness.

Human beings have reached a high level of technology and resources, and we have decided to use those things to improve our lives as we can and desire. Our contemporary culture is characterized by the belief that technology can produce intelligent machines and gadgets endowed with human intelligence, emotions, and sexuality[77]—that is, devices designed in the human image to satisfy human desires and fantasies.[78]

Dehumanization of Human Beings

The idea of sex with robots is considered strange and even perverted by many people, including Christians and non-Christians alike. How can people develop feelings for and emotional relationships with robots, knowing they are interacting with a machine programmed to talk and act like a person?

However, since sexual behavior has undergone very rapid change in recent decades, even abnormal and eccentric practices and lifestyles have become acceptable and even promoted. Sexual practices and lifestyles such as polyamory and homosexuality, which were previously considered immoral and even illegal in some places, are now perceived as normal due to the current sexual revolution.

---

allows her to recognize spoken language and formulate brief response phases based on a database of codified words." She does not have motor capacities but can "simulate pleasure and orgasm."

[76] Research on robot appearance and feelings has been done by several universities and companies and includes researchers from different fields such as psychology, robotics, and computer science (Levy, *Love + Sex with Robots* [New York: HarperCollins, 2007] 115). The area of research in which most development remains to be done is artificial intelligence, enabling robots "to think, to understand, to be creative, to be able to carry on a conversation, and to exhibit emotion, personality, consciousness, and the many other products of our brainpower" (Forni, 268).

[77] Glenda Shaw Garlock, "Loving Machines: Theorizing Human and Sociable-Technology Interaction," in *Human-Robot Personal Relationships*, ed. Maarten H. Lamers and Fons J. Verbeek (Leiden: Leiden University, 2010), 3.

[78] Long before designing robots for sexual purposes, technology had been used to facilitate sexual satisfaction through objects—such as vibrators, which have become common in recent decades. In 1976, as few as 1% of the American population used vibrators, but in 1982, only six years later, 25% of cosmopolitan people admitted to using them. The sales of vibrators are booming. The United Kingdom's leading sex shop chain, Ann Summers, sold 2.5 million in 2004. In Australia, one million are sold per year, with eight million already purchased by early 2005. Americans in 2001 were estimated to be buying 12.5 million vibrators every year, to add to an estimated fifty million plus that were already in the bedrooms of Americans at that time (cf. Levy, *Love + Sex with Robots*, 232).

Furthermore, the fact that some people may see and consider their partners as sexual objects suggests that relationships with robots that unconditionally do whatever their owners desire would be not only possible, but predictable. In addition, the feelings manifested in relation to electronic machines and pets show it is not only possible but easy to engage lovingly with something that is not a human being.[79]

Some people who own pets state that their relationship with their dogs is preferable to human beings because they are always there, "always loving, and comparatively uncritical."[80] In other words, a relationship with an animal "manages to avoid those conditional and judgmental features that are so inconvenient in human relationships."[81] In this case, "strong feelings directed toward a pet are an indication of an inadequacy in the person's relationships with humans."[82] Thus, a preference for relationships with robots, since they could demonstrate the same skills of love, care, and submission as pets, may result in experimentation with new forms of relationships.

In this context, the rise of humanized robots to satisfy the need for companionship and to provide sexual pleasure calls for consideration. Since technologies and practices are like a mirror that reflects the worldview, values, and principles of a society,[83] relationships with machines, pets, and robots can reveal some interesting trends in the current trajectory of human beings.

Sherry Turkle, a researcher at the Massachusetts Institute of Technology, has long studied human behavior in relation to computers. She highlights that the issue today is not what machines can do for us or against us, but what we are doing with ourselves. She says, "Computers are making people more machine-like while machines gain 'souls.'"[84]

---

[79] The pet phenomenon can be seen as evidence that human beings can develop feelings, including love, for other beings or objects, not only for other humans (cf. Levy, *Robots Unlimited*, 318).

[80] Levy, *Love + Sex with Robots*, 51–52, 62.

[81] Ibid.

[82] Ibid.

[83] Lévy, *Cyberculture*, 7, understands that every culture and every era has its own technology, and it reflects and determines the characteristics of that particular culture. The culture would be "conditioned" by its technologies, but not necessarily "determined." Manuel Castells, *The Rise of the Network Society* (Oxford: Wiley-Blackwell, 2009), also supports this view of technology as an extension of human society. The technology "incorporates" the society that develops and employs it. Technology and society would be one and the same reality. "Society cannot be understood or represented without its technological tools."

[84] Sherry Turkle, "'Spinning' Technology: What We Are Not Thinking About When We Are Thinking About Computers," in *Technological Visions: The Hopes and Fears that Shape New Technologies*, ed. Marita Sturken, Douglas Thomas, and Sandra J. Ball-Rokeach (Philadelphia, PA: Temple University Press, 2004), 25.

Thus the "question is not what computers will be like in the future, but what we will be like, what kind of people we are becoming."[85]

As early as the 1980s, Turkle perceived a parallel between human relationships with animals and relationships with computers. She says that "before the computer, the animals . . . seemed our nearest neighbors in the known universe. Computers, with their interactivity, their psychology, with whatever fragments of intelligence they have, now bid for this place."[86] Turkle questioned what people accustomed to computers would do in the future in terms of relationships. Actually, she predicted that people's relationship with computers would inspire the invention of "new hybrid self-images, built up out of the materials of animal, mind, and machine."[87] She said also that "the computer was gonna be like some little animal."[88]

The current sexual robots could be seen as intelligent and loving sexual objects devoid of heart and free will, built in the human image: submissive electronic pets to always be there, entirely available to their owners to satisfy their every desire without any condition or demand.

Commenting on a future with humanlike robots, the *Guardian's* editor Stuart Jeffries says that the advertising discourse on robots bears a "creeping" and "revolting" sense about "what it is to be human." He perceptively says that advertisement "offers us the ultimate dream of consumer society—the final decadence of capitalism, the seductive hope that humanity should be overcome for the sake of higher levels of customer satisfaction, the folly at the end of the road to transhumanism."[89]

This transhumanism would be a condition in which people are unable to relate to each other and accept a person like a person, and consequently preferring to relate to a computerized object or programmed body. The preference for relationships at a distance mediated by computers, in the case of cybersex, or for pets or robots instead of human persons, may reveal that this transhumanism is becoming a reality.

The rise of a society in which people prefer sexual and romantic relationships with robots over human partners is a sign that human beings are becoming unable to live and enjoy loving relationships with each other. This phenomenon suggests that some people consider the person they love and have sex with as a submissive object devoid of free will. Such a view supports the idea that sex can be maintained without any consideration

---

[85] Turkle, 'Spinning' Technology, 25.

[86] Sherry Turkle, *The Second Self: Computers and the Human Spirit*, 20th Anniversary ed. (Cambridge, MA: MIT Press, 2005).

[87] Ibid.

[88] Ibid., 118.

[89] Stuart Jeffries, "Robots Are Coming...," *The Guardian*, May 10, 2008.

for the thoughts and feelings of the other person. This behavior is being transferred to machines or computerized robots.

Technology and Reality

Optimistic predictions about a future world full of intelligent robots are based on the presupposition that technology can satisfy human expectations better than human beings. From this perspective, Joel Snell states that "robotic sex may become 'better' than human sex." According to him, "like many other technologies that have replaced human endeavors, robots may surpass human technique; because they would be programmable, sexbots would meet each individual user's needs."[90]

Why do people attribute so much power to technology in its ability to surpass human skills even in the sexual aspect? It may be said that computer technology has been able to give life to imagination and fantasy independent of the limits and boundaries of reality. In addition, this technology has allowed to reproduce imagined fantasies as the highest model of reality, giving them the status of supreme reality, as in Plato's metaphysics.[91] Moreover, technology allows immediate connection to this idealistic world of imagination, removing obstacles between the individual and the charmed life in a hyperreal world.

The imaginary is reproduced and explored in various entertainment products, among them novels, movies, stories, and games, as well as in cyberspace and in a life permeated by technology in the form of intelligent machines and robots. In this world, people prefer representation over reality and consider illusion as sacred and truth as profane.[92]

The sociologist Zygmunt Bauman considers that the technology of amusement creates an anxiety that transforms postmodern individuals into sensation-seekers and collectors of experiences, impelled to

---

[90] Joel Snell, "Predictions: Robotic Sex," in *Visions of Technology: A Century of Vital Debate About Machines, Systems and the Human World,* ed. Richard Rhodes (New York: Touchstone, 2000), 372.

[91] The Greek philosopher Plato understood that reality is divided into two dimensions: one we can see and another invisible. According to him, as noted by Hans Kelsen, *General Theory of Law and State,* trans. Anders Wedberg (Clark, NJ: Lawbook Exchange, 2009), 12, what we can see and capture with our senses is not the true reality, but only the shadows and forms of what really exists. The dimension of metaphysics would be the real world, invisible but entirely perfect and absolute, constituted by "ideas." For Plato, "the things in this visible world are only imperfect copies, shadows, so to speak, of the ideas existing in the invisible world" (ibid.). He saw a dualism between "reality and idea, an imperfect world of our senses and another perfect world," "between nature and super-nature, the natural and the supernatural, the empirical and the transcendental, the here and the hereafter" (ibid.).

[92] Quoting Ludwig Feuerbach, the French essayist Guy Ernest Debord, *The Society of the Spectacle,* trans. Donald Nicholson-Smith (New York: Zone Books, 1994), 3, proposes that spectacles and technologically produced images interfere with the individual's ability to see and interpret the world critically.

seek permanent and new ecstasies.[93] The satisfaction of this expectation requires fantasy to be reproduced as something more real than reality can offer. In order to fulfill this function, technology must be improved progressively. Thus, the image or representation of reality becomes more plausible than the original, and technlogical products tend to be more interesting and more attractive than real things. Everything is carefully planned to make grand impacts and evoke sensations. From this illusory perspective, it is not hard to understand why sexbots are advertised as able to love and give more pleasure than real human beings.

The Italian essayist Umberto Eco analyzes artificial American cities and parks, made to imitate reality, as realms of fantasy and imaginary. Those cities, through their high level of artifice, create the idea of the "absolute fake." Eco says that "Disneyland tells us that faked nature corresponds much more to our daydream demands . . . [and] tells us that technology can give us more reality than nature can."[94] This spectacular simulation of reality also creates the impression that the imitation has reached the very peak and that, from now on, reality will be less than its imitation. In the same way, sexbots are advertised as supreme bodies able to provide more love than any human person could.

This statement drives us to remember the temptation in Eden, when Satan affirmed that eating the prohibited fruit would make Adam and Eve like God (Gen 3:4). Like the fruit of knowledge of good and evil, robotic technology would have the power to attribute a high level of existence to those ready to use it. Thus, it seems that the advertising discourse of the serpent echoes in the advertisement of sexbots.

A Biblical Evaluation

As advertisements for sexbots promise a high level of pleasure and satisfaction, it is necessary to ask: What is the nature of a robot? Is it a person or a living soul? Could it be considered a sexual partner according to biblical standards? What about the Bible and this robotic technology? The ensuing paragraphs address these issues from the perspective of the biblical concept of sexuality and the divine image.

Creation and Human Companionship

The story of creation is the main source of the definition of human nature and sexuality. The manner in which God created woman to complete man's existence has much to teach us about what it means to be a human being and the pattern of relationships and sexuality in God's original plan.

---

[93] Zygmunt Bauman, *Globalization: The Human Consequences* (New York: Columbia University Press, 1998), 94.

[94] Umberto Eco, *Travels in Hyperreality* (London: Picador, 1986), 44.

In the Genesis account, God's evaluation of His creative work uses the adjective "good" (Heb. *tob*) six times (Gen 1:4, 10, 12, 18, 21, 25). The seventh time, when this adjective is used to evaluate the creation of man (male and female) as the apex of creation, God adds the adverb "very" (*me'od*, Gen 1:31). For Him, on the final day, the creation was good "in abundance."[95] It had reached its fullness with the creation of humankind as male and female. The Hebrew *tob me'od* ("very good") connotes the "quintessence of goodness, wholesomeness, appropriateness, beauty."[96]

However, the following report about the specific creation of man and woman (Gen 2:18–25) suggests that before the divine evaluation as "very good," God evaluated it as "not good" (Gen 2:18) when He saw the man alone. Thus the paradise story records a "short time" in which only one human being existed, and for this brief moment "there was no approval formula," only the reverse: "It is not good that man should be alone" (Gen 2:18).[97] After naming the animals, Adam felt himself alone because he did not have a companion like the animals (Gen 2:19–20). He was missing a female counterpart to complete the concept of *'adam* (Gen 5:1–2), the generic man. "The female as a constitutive element of the very existence of man as a collective entity (Gen 5:1–2) was not yet created. God's conclusion regarding human monosexuality is that it is 'not good' (Gen 2:18)."[98]

This additional report (Gen 2) indicates that human sexuality according to God's original plan cannot be fulfilled without a human counterpart also created in the divine image. "To be sexual creatures entails being incomplete in ourselves." The sexual nature of Adam not only reveals his incompleteness but also allows him to sense this "incompleteness."[99] This short lapse in the Genesis account with "only one *'adam*" had the purpose of showing him that "he lacked a counterpart" and "thus stood in need of a 'fit helper,' or suitable companion."[100] As one author noted, "Man is whole only in his complementarity with another being who is like himself."[101]

---

[95] Richard M. Davidson, "The Theology of Sexuality in the Beginning: Genesis 1–2," *Andrews University Seminary Studies* 26, no. 1 (Spring 1988): 11.

[96] Ibid.

[97] Aecio E. Cairus, "The Doctrine of Man," in Dederen, 209.

[98] Zoltán Szalos-Farkas, "Spirituality and Human Sexuality: A Theological and Anthropological Perspective," in *Marriage: Biblical and Theological Aspects*, ed. Ekkehardt Mueller and Elias Brasil de Souza (Silver Spring, MD: Biblical Research Institute, 2015), 126.

[99] Stanley J. Grenz, "Theological Foundations for Male-Female Relationship," *Journal of the Evangelical Theological Society* 41 (1998): 621.

[100] Cairus, 209.

[101] Richard M. Davidson, *Flame of Yahweh: Sexuality in the Old Testament* (Peabody, MA: Hendrickson, 2007), 38.

There is no doubt that the author of Genesis planned this additional report . . . highlight the creation . . . the woman as the finishing of mankind's creation. God set Adam to name the animals in order to drive him to realize his loneliness. This is clear in Genesis 2:20, where the author concludes, "But for Adam there was not found a helper comparable to him." The absence of Adam's counterpart is the reason not only for his loneliness, but also for his incompleteness as a human being. This incompleteness is resolved by the creation of the woman, also in the divine image.

The Divine Image and Human Relationship

What does the report of creation suggest about what it means to be created in God's image? What is its implication in terms of human relationship and sexuality?

The couple "man and woman" is mentioned ten times in the first five chapters in Genesis, and twice the author says "male and female [God] created them" (Gen 1:27; 5:2). Genesis 1 states that man was created in God's image as male and female, suggesting that sharing a likeness with God implies living in a male-female partnership. In the Genesis 2 report of woman's creation, the author returns to this theme to emphasize that man's creation "in God's image" also entails a "partnership" (*'ezer kenegdo*, Gen 2:18). This suggests that "the 'likeness' that the man and the woman share with God in chapter 1 finds analogy in the 'likeness' between the man and his wife in Genesis 2."[102] This likeness is expressed in the relational nature they share between themselves.

Thus, to be created in God's image points to the binitarian nature of human beings. Based on this conception, Zoltán Szalos-Farkas says that "the *binitarian* concept of the human beings is radically incompatible with the *solitarian* practice of human sexuality."[103] There is no way to fulfill the sexuality of man in the image of God except within a marriage relationship between a man and a woman created in the divine image.

The creation account thus places the function of sexuality in the "context of fellowship, intimacy, and complementation on which genuine humanity is predicated."[104] This is much higher than any other purpose like "mere procreation, re-creation, or 'release of tension' to which sexuality has often been reduced."[105]

---

[102] John H. Sailhamer, *Genesis, The Expositor's Bible Commentary*, vol. 2 ed. Frank E. Gaebelein (Grand Rapids, MI: Zondervan, 1990), 46.

[103] Szalos-Farkas, 138.

[104] Cairus, 210.

[105] Ibid.

Furthermore, the relational nature of man in God's image is emphasized by the creation formula. In creating man, God said, "Let us make . . ." (Gen 1:26). Again, six times the author of the account uses the expression "Then God said" followed by a "Let there be" or "Let the" (Gen 1:3, 6, 9, 14, 20, 24). However, the seventh time, the expression "Then God said" is followed by "Let *us* make" (Gen 1:26, emphasis supplied). The six previous creative acts are introduced by an impersonal formula in the third person, "Let there be," but the creation of man is introduced in the first person plural, "Let us make."[106] The divine creative acts culminate in the participation of the divine plurality in the creation of human plurality, in the seventh creative act.

The Bible says twice that man was created (*bara'*) in God's "image" and a third time that man was created (*bara'*) "male and female" (Gen 1:27). The same pattern is repeated in Genesis 5: "In the day that God created [*bara'*] man, he made him in the likeness of God. He created [*bara*] them male and female" (Gen 5:1b–2a). Thus, the man (*'adam*) was created as a plurality, "male and female," and this plurality reflects the plurality of God: "Let us make man in our image." "Following this clue the divine plurality expressed in Genesis 1:26 ['Let us make'] is seen as an anticipation of the human plurality of the man and woman, thus casting the human relationship between man and woman in the role of reflecting God's own personal relationship with himself [in the Trinity]."[107]

Since man, as male and female, was created in the image of God, which implies the relational nature of mankind, living in relationship is the way to fulfill the original divine purpose. Adam and Eve were created in the image of God in view of their "unique capacity for a personal relationship to God as the transcending ground of their being."[108] The image of God is a relational concept. "Ultimately we do not reflect God's image on our own but in relationship. Thus the *imago Dei* is not primarily what we are as individuals. Rather, it is present among humans in relationship."[109] Human beings contribute to God's glory because we were designed for a loving fellowship with Him (cf. Ps 100:1–4). This loving fellowship with God unfolds in a loving fellowship with one another, but especially in the sexuality of a marriage constituted by a man and a woman. According to the divine plan, "the sexual relationship between husband and wife is inextricably bound up with the spiritual unity of both man and woman with their Creator."[110]

---

[106] Sailhamer, 37.

[107] Ibid., 38.

[108] John Jefferson Davis, *The Frontiers of Science and Faith* (Downers Grove, IL: InterVarsity, 2002), 108–109.

[109] Grenz, "Theological Foundations for Male-Female Relationship," 620.

[110] Davidson, "Theology of Sexuality," 23.

Thus the image of God implies the capacity to live in fellowship with God and each other. To lose this capacity means losing the original image of the Creator. The way human beings live and express sexuality is one of the most important ways of expressing our likeness to God. Sexuality lived in solitude and in a self-centered manner, as with robots, perverts the divine original plan for human beings.

The Divine Image and Human Sexuality

When he named the animals, Adam could not find any companionship among "all cattle, to the birds of the air, and to every beast of the field" (Gen 2:20). Man is distinct from other creatures because he received the breath of God and was created in the divine image (Gen 2:7; 1:27). Man's likeness to God is shown here against the background of his distinction from the other creatures. The point of this narrative is that "there was no helper who corresponded to man among the animals," which were not created in the divine image.[111]

The relationship between human beings and other creatures and things is one of rule instead of love and sex (Gen 1:26). In fact, the Bible prohibits sexual interaction between humans and other species, as it would be a source of contamination (Lev 18:23). The only acceptable sexual relationship according to the Bible is between a male and female of the same species. A man may have sexual interaction only with a woman, for she is also created in the divine image. "Now Adam knew [*yada*'] Eve his wife" and "she conceived" a son (Gen 4:1). The Hebrew *yāda*' literally means "to know," but also "to experience," "to understand," "to care about." "It is used of sexual relations in the sense of a full knowledge and deep relation between partners."[112] This kind of relationship is possible only between two beings of the same species. Adam and Eve shared the same image of God and, because of that, could enjoy their sexuality together in a pleasurable and fruitful manner.

As creatures made in the image of God, Adam and Eve were endowed with "rational powers," "freedom of choice," "moral purity," "physical appearance," and "emotional life."[113] These features of God's image also made them compatible with each other. In this relationship man and woman can develop their characteristics as creatures in the divine image by learning and growing through love, service, help, support, and even sacrifice.

After creating man and woman in His image, God said that "man" and "his wife" should become "one flesh" (Gen 2:24) within the marriage covenant. Richard Davidson says that this experience has to do with both

---

[111] Sailhamer, 46.

[112] Calvin B. Rock, "Marriage and Family," in Dederen, 725.

[113] William Shea, "Creation," in Dederen, 424.

sexual and spiritual union, the only means to establish the "innermost mystery" of oneness and to find "fulfillment in marital relationship."[114] He explains that the Hebrew term *basar,* "flesh," in the Old Testament refers "not only to one's physical body but is a term to denote human relationship." The "one flesh" concept indicates "sexual concourse and psychological concurrence, in the full sense of the conjunction of bodies and minds, at once through eros and *agapē*."[115] This implies that being "one flesh" involves "all the physical, sensual, social, intellectual, emotional, and spiritual dimensions of life."[116]

This experience is possible because Adam and Eve were male and female—individuals with differences, but "bone of each other's bone, flesh of each other's flesh."[117] Thus, it is only possible to be "one flesh" and reach fulfillment as a human being according to God's original design with another whole person created in divine image, bone of the same bone. Any other sexual experience without flesh union between a husband and a wife, like that with robots, is outside the divine original plan. Robots have no flesh, no bones, no mind, no heart.

The so-called sexual relationship between human and robot acts against the nature of love as well as the nature of man. While in normal life love includes resignation and even sacrifice, in a relationship with robots the only thing that one expects is self-satisfaction. Resignation and sacrifice are part of love because the loved person is irreplaceable. Adam only had one Eve. One needs to care for a loved one. However, robots can be replaced at any time if they are damaged. This relationship is centered on the self, since "there will never be any need for a human to sacrifice their own life for their robot or to take a major risk on its behalf."[118]

A manufactured robot-partner in the image of man to serve him without any conditions would be the institutionalization of selfishness and sex depersonalization, since its love and sex are the results of a computer program devoid of feelings and true emotions.[119] Szalos-Farkas says that "in attending to personal ends, sex unavoidably becomes depersonalized, a commodity to make 'me' happy,"[120] as is the desire of one who wants to use another for his own selfish pleasure.

---

[114] Davidson, *Flame of Yahweh,* 46.

[115] Ibid.

[116] Ibid., 37.

[117] Ibid., 38.

[118] Levy, *Robots Unlimited,* 132.

[119] Spencer, "*Imago Dei,*" 17.

[120] Szalos-Farkas, 133.

William Spencer argues that a Christian response to the issue of sexbots needs to consider the notion of the "image of God in humanity and its ultimate function as a didactic means to teach us to love someone other so that we can learn to love the One Great Wholly Other than us: the Triune God."[121] A so-called love relationship with a robot manufactured in the image of man, but without the breath of God, is a counterfeit of God's original plan.

The advertisements for some female robots say that they will be "programmed to be totally obedient, always alluring and ready for coitus female sex slaves, engineered to be [the] so-called 'perfect woman'" and demand nothing.[122] The impulse expressed in such a relationship is only erotic and has nothing authentically romantic. The impulse of *eros* is not interested in the needs or feelings of the other person. "It does not have any regard for the entirety of the human self, of which personhood is an essential aspect. Such attitude goes against the scriptural understanding of the human being" as the image of God.[123]

Every kind of sexual technique and skill could be input into a computerized robot, but it would never be a being created in the divine image. Le Trung, a designer who programmed and made a femdroid named "Aiko," says, "But one thing I will never be able to give her is true emotion or a soul [like a sensible mind or heart]."[124]

Therefore, sex with robots must be seen as a deviation of human sexuality and a wrong use of those skills divinely designed to be a means of pleasure and union for marriage partners. It is also a source of contamination for the soul in light of the Bible's view of the purity of heart.

Conclusion

In the postmodern context, people have become more and more interested in knowing and experimenting with sexual satisfaction as if it were the most important aspect of life. The main factor in the contemporary sexual revolution is technology. By using computers, the internet, and social networking, people are seeking and finding love and sexual companionship as they find things or commodities to satisfy physical needs. Love and sex tend to lose their spiritual nature and become a mere convenience.

Nowadays, traditional values and principles have been discarded in favor of a liberal and self-centered lifestyle. As secularized people lose the

[121] Spencer, "*Imago Dei,*" 6.

[122] Ibid., 18.

[123] Szalos-Farkas, 139.

[124] Quoted in Spencer, "Digital Adultery," 103.

spiritual and biblical principles of love, sex, and what it is to be human, different kinds of sexual practices are adopted as if they were acceptable and natural. Among those are the widespread practice of cybersex, or computer sex, and the startling use of sexbots. These practices have been the cause of concern, pain, sorrow, and addictive behaviors.

According to the biblical perspective, cybersex and sex with robots are not acceptable because God designed sexuality to be experienced by a man and woman created in the divine image, within the intimacy of a holy marriage. Additionally, the lustful feelings and emotions inherent in these kinds of sexual experiments constitute what the Bible clearly defines as adultery in the heart or a perversion of the original sexuality.

Sexuality is "very good" when it fulfills the divine plan, which requires that it be enjoyed between a man and a woman created in the divine image. It should be not merely functional, but also relational.[125] Thus sexuality is not only a means of pleasure and procreation, but a didactic means of fulfilling human nature in the divine image at that high level of existence designed by God at creation. The postmodern sexual revolution suggests that human beings tend to distance themselves from the divine image and lose the capacity to live in love and fellowship according to God's plan for marriage.

Cybersex, robotic sex, and any other sexual experience of a similar type must be seen as an artificial and selfish experience that cannot fulfill God's plan for human beings. Indeed, sexuality is a pleasurable and fruitful experience that fulfills human nature when it occurs in a loving marriage between a male and female created in the divine image. By improving the spirit of love and sacrifice, such a partnership points out the divine origin of humanity and contributes to elevating and redeeming human beings from selfishness.

---

[125] Szalos-Farkas, 128.

CHAPTER 20

The Seduction of Forbidden Intimacy

Alberto R. Timm

Seductive attractions between two people not married to each other can vary significantly in nature, form, and intensity, but they are far more common than people typically admit. The Normal Bar, the world's most extensive survey of people's sexual and emotional lives, shows that "61% of women and 90% of men fantasize sexually about people they meet."[1] But such fantasies can easily escalate from mere thoughts to enchanting imagination, overwhelming desires, irreversible decisions, and high-risk actions. Some people simply choose to have an intimate physical affair outside of marriage, regardless of the consequences it might have. Others take a more cautious approach, preferring to nourish a less perceivable emotional affair.

The Sexual Intelligence Project discovered that forty-five percent of those who cheated on their partners did so without forethought. In other words, the affair was not planned—it "just happened." They were driven by their sexual feelings without fully understanding the toll the affair would take on them and the important relationships in their lives. In hindsight, many cheating spouses would have rather kept their sexual feelings under control than to see "the full impact of their infidelity on their partner—the terrible pain, the sense of betrayal, the loss of trust."[2] Some people who cheated on their partners or were cheated by them even qualify infidelity as a pain worse than death.

---

[1] Chrisanna Northrup, Pepper Schwartz, and James Witte, *The Normal Bar: The Surprising Secrets of Happy Couples and What They Reveal About Creating a New Normal in Your Relationship* (New York: Harmony, 2013), 214. See also http://www.thenormalbar.com (accessed October 18, 2021).

[2] Sheree Conrad and Michael Milburn, *Sexual Intelligence: The Groundbreaking Study that Shows You How to Boost Your "Sex IQ" and Gain Greater Sexual Satisfaction* (New York: Crown, 2001), 259, 261–262.

Several helpful books address this extremely important and complex issue.[3] Some try to help those who are hurt by an affair.[4] Others are intended to build healthy relationships that are able to withstand seductive temptations.[5] This article examines the subject of sex outside of marriage from a biblical–moral perspective. Scriptural teachings and stories provide helpful suggestions on how to build affair-resistant relationships.

Biblical Moral Perspective

The Bible deals with the matter of sex outside of marriage by intermingling moral commands with practical counsels on how to live a life of moral integrity. Almost all the commands and counsels surround the foundational moral commandment, "You shall not commit adultery" (Exod 20:14; Deut 5:18; cf. Matt 5:27; 19:18; Rom 13:9).[6] The phrase "commit adultery" (Heb. *na'ap*; LXX and Gk. *moicheuō*) has been defined in different ways. For example, one author applies it only to "sexual intercourse between a man, married or not, and a married woman who is not his wife." So for this author, "a married man is free to cohabit with whomever he likes, provided he does not infringe on another man's conjugal rights."[7]

By contrast, James K. Bruckner sees this commandment as bearing a much broader meaning. He argues,

> The prohibition against adultery generally defends the integrity and emotional stability of the family for the sake of the children, wife, and husband. It preserves the trust that is foundational to healthy family relationships. The integrity of the family protects

[3] Some suggest the existence of five kinds of affairs ("5 Different Types of Extramarital Affairs," http://www.affairhandbook.com/index.php/different-types-marital-affairs [accessed June 15, 2016]); others suggest six (Douglas LaBier, "Having An Affair? There Are Six Different Kinds," https://www.psychologytoday.com/blog/the-new-resilience/201004/having-affair-there-are-six-different-kinds [accessed June 15, 2016]); and some even seventeen (Mira Kirshenbaum, *When Good People Have Affairs: Inside the Hearts & Minds of People in Two Relationships* [New York: St. Martin's Press, 2008], 35-74) kinds of affairs.

[4] E.g., Douglas K. Snyder, Donald H. Baucom, and Kristina C. Gordon, *Getting Past the Affair: A Program to Help You Cope, Heal, and Move On—Together or Apart* (New York: Guilford, 2007); Kirshenbaum; Janis A. Spring and Michael Spring, *After the Affair: Healing the Pain and Rebuilding Trust When a Partner Has Been Unfaithful*, 2nd ed. (New York: William Morrow, 2012).

[5] E.g., J. Allan Petersen, *The Myth of the Greener Grass* (Wheaton, IL: Tyndale, 1983); E. Michael Lillibridge, *The Love Book for Couples: Building a Healthy Relationship* (Atlanta, GA: Humanics, 1984); Conrad and Milburn; Willard F. Harley, Jr., *His Needs, Her Needs: Building an Affair-proof Marriage*, rev. exp. ed. (Grand Rapids, MI: Revel, 2011).

[6] All biblical quotations are from the NIV, unless otherwise noted.

[7] William H. C. Propp, *Exodus 19–40*, The Anchor Bible 2A (New York: Doubleday, 2006), 179.

the most vulnerable in society, the children, whose emotional security is always at risk.[8]

Yet Carol Meyers points out how to unfold that meaning: "This succinct precept proscribes sex outside of marriage. But for whom? The prohibition of adultery does not specify, and it is only by looking at other biblical texts that the range of adulterous behaviors can be ascertained."[9]

Undeniably, the adultery prohibition assumes a much broader scope and a far richer meaning if understood in light of the other moral instructions of the Pentateuch. For instance, Leviticus 18 outlines the boundaries of biblical sexuality by condemning not only incest and sexual relations with close relatives (Lev 18:6–17) but also polygamy (Lev 18:18), adultery (Lev 18:20), homosexuality (Lev 18:22), and bestiality (Lev 18:23).[10] Deuteronomy 22 highlights virginity and condemns premarital sex (Deut 22:13–21), adultery with another's man wife (Deut 22:22), fornication with a betrothed woman (Deut 22:23–24), rape (Deut 22:25–29), and incest (Deut 22:30).[11]

Some of the most eloquent warnings against physical and emotional infidelity are found in Proverbs 5–7. In these chapters seduction is associated with physical beauty, eyelids, special clothing and perfume, voice inflection, and persuasive words. Warning against a seductress, the author states, "Do not lust in your heart after her beauty or let her captivate you with her eyes" (Prov 6:25), and keep "from your neighbor's wife, from the smooth talk of a wayward woman" (Prov 6:24) "for the lips of the adulterous woman drip honey, and her speech is smoother than oil" (Prov 5:3). After a passionate kiss (Prov 7:13), she will use religious language to disarm you with her seductive speech:

Today I fulfilled my vows,
and I have food from my fellowship offering at home.
So I came out to meet you;
I looked for you and have found you!
I have covered my bed
with colored linens from Egypt.
I have perfumed my bed

[8] James K. Bruckner, *Exodus*, New International Bible Commentary 2 (Peabody, MA: Hendrickson, 2008), 190.

[9] Carol Meyers, *Exodus*, The New Cambridge Bible Commentary (New York: Cambridge University Press, 2005), 175.

[10] Richard M. Davison, *Flame of Yahweh: Sexuality in the Old Testament* (Grand Rapids, MI: Baker Academic, 2007), 149–159, 174, 193–198, 200–201, 346, 434–443.

[11] Ibid., 354–361.

> with myrrh, aloes and cinnamon.
> Come, let's drink deeply of love till morning;
> let's enjoy ourselves with love!
> My husband is not at home;
> he has gone on a long journey.
> He took his purse filled with money
> and will not be home till full moon (Prov 7:14–20).

Despite the allure, the extramarital affair is considered "a highway to the grave, leading down to the chambers of death" (Prov 7:27). The one who has an extramarital affair is compared to a gazelle in the hand of the hunter, a bird in the snare of the fowler (Prov 6:5), an ox that goes to the slaughter, "a deer stepping into a noose" (Prov 7:22), someone struck in the liver by an arrow, and "a bird darting into a snare" (Prov 7:23). Thus, the natural conclusion is that "a man who commits adultery has no sense; whoever does so destroys himself" (Prov 6:32).

In addition to those warnings, the author also recommends at least four practical strategies to preserve moral purity. One is to strengthen the romantic love of one's own marriage. The author states:

> May your fountain be blessed,
> and may you rejoice in the wife of your youth.
> A loving doe, a graceful deer—
> may her breasts satisfy you always,
> may you ever be intoxicated with her love.
> Why, my son, be intoxicated with another man's wife?
> Why embrace the bosom of a wayward woman? (Prov 5:18–20).

Another strategy is to maintain physical distance from a seductive temptation. The author warns, "Keep to a path far from her [the seductress], do not go near the door of her house" (Prov 5:8), and do not "stray into her paths" (Prov 7:25). A third strategy is to exercise emotional control. "Do not let your heart turn to her ways," he cautions (Prov 7:25). "Keep your heart with all vigilance, for from it flow the springs of life" (Prov 4:23, NRSV). The last but not least strategy is to be always aware of God's divine presence. The author affirms, "For your ways are in full view of the Lord, and he examines all your paths" (Prov 5:21).

Noticeably, the prophet Malachi underscores faithfulness to the marriage vow, acknowledging God Himself as the true witness to the marriage covenant. First, the prophet declares, "The Lord is the witness between you and the wife of your youth. You have been unfaithful to her, though she is your partner, the wife of your marriage covenant" (Mal 2:14). And then he warns, "So be on your guard, and do not be unfaithful to the wife of your youth" (Mal 2:15). Although this passage explicitly admonishes the husband to be faithful to his wife, the same principle is also applicable to the wife, who must be likewise faithful to her husband.

In His Sermon on the Mount, Christ revealed the mental and emotional dimensions of the "You shall not commit adultery" commandment (Exod 20:14). He stated, "You have heard that it was said, 'You shall not commit adultery.' But I tell you that anyone who looks at a woman lustfully has already committed adultery with her in his heart" (Matt 5:27–29). This statement is both a fulfillment of the messianic promise, "I will put my law in their minds, and write it on their hearts" (Jer 31:33; cf. Heb 8:10; 10:16), and a recognition of the mental source of moral infidelity—"for it is from within, out of a person's heart, that evil thoughts come—sexual immorality, theft, murder, adultery, greed, malice, deceit, lewdness, envy, slander, arrogance and folly. All these evils come from inside and defile a person" (Mark 7:21–23; cf. Matt 15:19–20). Since thoughts generate emotions that result in actions, the battle for moral purity (see Jas 4:7–10) has to be fought at the mental level in order to prevent sinful actions from taking place.

The apostle Paul speaks of true Christians as those who imitate Christ (1 Cor 11:1) and have "the mind of Christ" (1 Cor 2:16). Mental purity is also implied in Philippians 4:8:

> Finally, believers, whatever is true, whatever is honorable and worthy of respect, whatever is right and confirmed by God's word, whatever is pure and wholesome, whatever is lovely and brings peace, whatever is admirable and of good repute; if there is any excellence, if there is anything worthy of praise, think continually on these things [center your mind on them, and implant them in your heart] (Phil 4:8, AMP).

Paul suggests another elucidative perspective of extramarital affairs while referring to the human body as a "sanctuary of the Holy Spirit" (1 Cor 6:19) and a member of Christ (1 Cor 6:15). Recognizing that through sexual intimacy two people "become one flesh" (Gen 2:24), Paul explains that extramarital affairs not only unlawfully unite the bodies of those involved in such affairs, but also destroy their own relationship with the Lord. He argues forcefully,

> Do you not know that your bodies are members of Christ himself? Shall I then take the members of Christ and unite them with a prostitute? Never! Do you not know that he who unites himself with a prostitute is one with her in body? For it is said, "The two will become one flesh." But whoever is united with the Lord is one with him in spirit (1 Cor 6:15–17).

These concepts provide a helpful moral framework to better understand the illicit affairs described in the Bible—case studies, if you will, that "were written down as warnings for us" (1 Cor 10:11).

Biblical Illustrative Cases

The Bible catalogs a range of affair-related cases that tend to escalate within a thought-imagination-desire-decision-action affair-progression model. In other words, thoughts escalate to imagination, then to desire, subsequently to decision, and finally to action. One author explains, "Sex is all in our heads, quite literally. Our brains are involved in all steps of sexual behavior and in all its variations, from feelings of sexual desire and partner choice, to arousal, orgasm and even post-coital cuddling."[12] No wonder the biblical concept of true "repentance" (Gk. *metanoia*) implies a proactive change of mind that stops sinful thoughts from escalating into sinful actions.

This section deals specifically with three eye-opening case studies—Potiphar's wife and Joseph (Gen 39:6–18), King David and Bathsheba (2 Sam 11), and Amnon and Tamar (2 Sam 13). From the perspective of the aforementioned affair-progression model, one can easily see that all three aggressors aimed to materialize their sensual imaginations into sexual affairs, but their respective victims did not have the same intentions.

Potiphar's Wife and Joseph

The classic example of overcoming sexual temptation at the thought level is Joseph's persistent rejection of the seductive entreaties of Potiphar's wife, as described in Genesis 39:6–18. "This was not a one-and-done event, or some impetuous suggestion she may have regretted later." It was indeed "a daily temptation, not easily dismissed."[13]

Almost all the circumstances in this story favored an affair between Joseph and Potiphar's wife. On one side was Joseph, a handsome, single young man living in a foreign country far away from his family.[14] Undoubtedly, Joseph had his own emotional and physical needs, and no one from his family circle was overseeing his private life. On the other hand was his master's wife casting "longing eyes" (Gen 39:7, NKJV)

---

[12] Carla Clark, "Brain Sex in Men and Women—From Arousal to Orgasm," http://brainblogger.com/2014/05/20/brain-sex-in-men-and-women-from-arousal-to-orgasm (posted May 20, 2014; accessed June 15, 2016).

[13] Bill T. Arnold, *Genesis*, The New Cambridge Bible Commentary (Cambridge: Cambridge University Press, 2009), 332.

[14] Helpful insights into the psychosocial vulnerability of migrants are provided in Mike Donalds-on et al., eds., *Migrant Men: Critical Studies of Masculinities and the Migration Experience*

and "day after day" trying to seduce him "to go to bed with her" (Gen 39:10). But one day when they were alone, the temptation came "so sudden, so strong, so seductive"[15] that "she caught him by his cloak and said, 'Come to bed with me!'" (Gen 39:12). Without any excuses or rationalizations, "he left his cloak in her hand and ran out of the house" (Gen 39:12). How was Joseph able to overcome temptation under such alluring and compelling circumstances?

The Bible narrative provides helpful insights that answer this question. First, Joseph went into the house "to attend to his duties" (Gen 39:11), without exposing himself voluntarily to temptation. Second, when Potiphar's wife began seducing him, Joseph explained to her that he would never ever have such an affair, which would mean not only betrayal of his master—her husband—but also betrayal and "sin against God" (Gen 39:8–9). His "answer was quick, well reasoned, and decisive, but it also needed to be persistent."[16] Joseph's emotional faithfulness allowed him to remain physically faithful at that most crucial moment. Had he allowed his mind to become sensualized, he would have been morally vulnerable and without the needed strength to overcome temptation.

As in many love stories—the story of Joseph and Potiphar's wife included—passion and hate are never far from each other. Frustrated by unrequited love, the emotional pendulum of the seductress moved rapidly from extreme passion for Joseph to extreme hate for him, eventually falsely accusing Joseph for her own immoral behavior (Gen 39:13–18). Joseph could have avoided that constraining situation by returning her amorous entreaties, but it would most certainly have ended his career in Egypt, not to mention that such an offense could incur the death penalty.[17] Undeniably, the Joseph narrative is an inspiring story of loyalty and moral purity in the midst of the most compelling circumstances and tragic consequences.

King David and Bathsheba

In contrast to the inspiring story of Joseph, 2 Samuel 11 describes the scenario of King David's disgraceful affair with Bathsheba. One author suggests this incident is part of a literary triad including Bathsheba (2 Sam 11–12), Tamar (2 Sam 13), and the woman of Tekoa (2 Sam 14),

---

(New York: Routledge, 2009); Oliva M. Espín, *Women Crossing Boundaries: A Psychology of Immigration and Transformations of Sexuality* (New York: Routledge, 1999).

[15] E. G. White, *Patriarchs and Prophets* (Battle Creek, MI: Review and Herald, 1890), 217.

[16] Arnold, 332.

[17] For more detailed assessments of how ancient Egyptians punished sexual affairs with married women, see James B. Reynolds, "Sex Morals and the Law in Ancient Egypt and Babylon," *Journal of Criminal Law and Criminology* 5/1 (1914): 21–22; Charlotte Booth, *In Bed with the Ancient Egyptians* (Gloucestershire: Amberley, 2015), 74–89.

and ends up fulfilling Samuel's warning that a king would "take your daughters" to serve him (1 Sam 8:13).[18]

> Bathsheba's coming to the king in obedience to his command results in a sexual encounter not because she is initiating a sexual encounter, but because he has already initiated it, using his power as king to send and to take her, a combination of power acts which is often associated with the use of force to make people do what they do not want to do. Ironically, Bathsheba is an honorable Israelite woman who should have been able to expect the king to do justice to use his power to protect her from violation, both physical and moral. Kings are supposed to keep the people safe, especially loyal subjects such as Uriah, Eliam, and Bathsheba.[19]

But instead of protecting Bathsheba, King David adulterously exploited her. Second Samuel 11 tells us that one evening David went to the roof of his palace, from where he saw a very beautiful woman bathing (2 Sam 11:2). Instead of averting his gaze and thereby checking his emotions, David proceeded down the affair continuum to desire, decision, and eventually action. First, he tried "to find out about her" and was informed that she was the daughter of Eliam and the wife of Uriah the Hittite (2 Sam 11:3). Taking advantage of the fact that her husband was away on a military campaign, David requested that she be brought to his palace, where he slept with her and even got her pregnant (2 Sam 11:4–5).

In an attempt to cover up his shameful deed David ordered that Uriah return home from the battlefield. He then personally tried to convince Uriah to go home and spend some time with his wife. Having been away for quite some time, David assumed that Uriah most certainly would end up having sex with his wife, which could justify her recent pregnancy. But the strategy did not work out as planned, and "Uriah slept at the entrance to the palace with all his master's servants" (2 Sam 11:6–9), insisting that he would never go home to eat, drink, and "make love" to his wife while his colleagues were "camped in the open country" (2 Sam 11:10–11). David would not be deterred by Uriah's integrity. David urged him to stay one more day, and even "made him drunk," surmising that the inebriated soldier would instinctively go home and have sex with his wife. But even under such conditions,

[18] April D. Westbrook, *'And He Will Take Your Daughters…': Woman Story and the Ethical Evaluation of Monarchy in the David Narrative* (London: Bloomsbury, 2015), 113–116, 121.

[19] Ibid., 129.

Uriah remained faithful to his commitment (2 Sam 11:12–13). Drink could not dull his reasoning power or sense of honor.

Frustrated with his failed attempts, David sent Uriah back to the battlefield carrying with him a letter containing his own death sentence. Addressed to commander Joab, David's letter requested that Uriah be placed at the very frontline of the battle to "be struck down and die" (2 Sam 11:14–15). The request was carried out, and the news of Uriah's death pleased the king (2 Sam 11:16–25). When Bathsheba "heard that her husband was dead, she mourned for him," after which "David had her brought to his house, and she became his wife" (2 Sam 11:26–27). But the biblical record says that "the thing David had done displeased the Lord" (2 Sam 11:27), and his sinful misbehavior was punished by the death of the son he had with Bathsheba (2 Sam 12:1–25).

Several lessons can be learned from this sad story. First, we should never forget that tiny sparks can become very destructive fires. This whole sad episode began with David's uncontrolled sensual imagination. Second, one never knows exactly how such a story will end. In this specific case, the unpredictable path David followed led to an unexpected pregnancy, a horrific murder, and the destruction of a marriage. A third lesson to be learned is that sin has a destructive domino effect. The transgression of any moral commandment opens the door to other forms of moral disobedience. In the process of transforming Bathsheba into a desirable sexual idol, David continually made immoral choices—coveting his neighbor's wife, committing adultery with her, trying to lie about her pregnancy, betraying the confidence of her husband, and then—frighteningly—ordering him to be murdered (cf. Exod 20:3, 13–17). This tragic sinful path undermined David's moral leadership within his own family, and the nation at large.

Amnon and Tamar

The Bible record states that David married several wives (1 Sam 18–19; 2 Sam 3:2–5; 5:13; 2 Sam 11:1–17; 1 Chr 3:1–3) and had many children with them (1 Chr 3:1–9). The oldest of them was Amnon, son of Ahinoam of Jezreel (1 Chr 3:1). The only daughter mentioned by name is Tamar, sister of Absalom (2 Sam 13:1), both of whom were children of Maakah (1 Chr 3:2). Thus, Amnon and Tamar were David's children by different wives.

Second Samuel 13 explains that Amnon fell in love with his beautiful and virgin half sister Tamar, and became so obsessed with her that "he made himself ill" (2 Sam 13:1–2). Poorly advised by his cousin Jonadab, Amnon laid down and pretended to be ill. When David came to see him, Amnon requested to be served by Tamar. She prepared some food and brought it to the house of Amnon, who was lying down. Requesting that everyone else should leave the place, Amnon asked Tamar to bring the food into his bedroom to eat from her own hand. But when she was close to him, he grabbed her and said, "Come to bed with me, my sister" (2 Sam 13:3–11).

Tamar was a woman of moral principle. She replied,

> No, my brother! . . . Don't force me! Such a thing should not be done in Israel! Don't do this wicked thing. What about me? Where could I get rid of my disgrace? And what about you? You would be like one of the wicked fools in Israel. Please speak to the king; he will not keep me from being married to you (2 Sam 13:12–13).

But Amnon did not care about her, and "since he was stronger than she, he raped her" (2 Sam 13:14).

When the act was over, Amnon "hated her more than he had loved her," and simply sent her away (2 Sam 13:15). Tamar even pleaded with him, "No! . . . Sending me away would be a greater wrong than what you have already done to me" (2 Sam 13:16). But he did not listen to her, and asked his personal servant to put her out and bolt the door after her. She then put ashes on her head, tore the ornate robe she was wearing, and went away—weeping aloud—to live in her brother Absalom's house as a desolate woman (2 Sam 13:16–20). The biblical record says that David "was furious" about what happened, but did not do anything about it. Yet her brother Absalom, although never saying a word to Amnon, did not forgive him for having disgraced Tamar's life (2 Sam 13:21–22). Two years later, Absalom organized a sheepshearers' celebration in which his men killed Amnon for what he had done to Tamar (2 Sam 13:23–39).

One of the sobering lessons of this story is that passionate love can very easily morph into irrational hate. In many cases, romantic dating and passionate interludes remain intoxicating up to the moment when that which is forbidden takes place. Then, feelings of guilt and revulsion take over. Another lesson to be learned is that unforgiven sins (and sometimes even forgiven ones) have their respective wages that sooner or later have to be paid (cf. Gen 4:7; Rom 6:23). Two years after raping his own sister, Amnon unexpectedly paid those wages with his own life. Undoubtedly, David could have provided a better moral example for his family had he not followed the path of polygamy and had he not committed that abhorrent adultery with Bathsheba.

Not all love stories have such seductive appeals as Potiphar's wife to Joseph, or have such a disastrous end as David's adultery with Bathsheba or Amnon's rape of Tamar. Regardless of its intensity and consequences, every affair outside of marriage is a departure from God's moral standards and bears its own negative consequences. Sometimes both partners are able to keep a mutual pledge to conceal an affair for the rest of their respective lives, but in many cases one of them ends up revealing the affair to a third party. Even if this does not happen, an affair typically negatively affects the participants' relationships with their spouses. In other cases, the affair is discovered and disclosed by someone else. Regardless of what may be the final outcome, never forget that though you may run away from others you can never run from yourself. According to the well-known French proverb, "There is no pillow so soft as a clear conscience."

Affair-Resistant Relationships

We live in a sensualized and sexualized world with many tempting appeals, similar to those in the days of Noah (Matt 24:37–39; Luke 17:26–27). It is not surprising that evolutionary biologists and psychologists regard heterosexual monogamy as an obsolete religious taboo.[20] But we are encouraged by God's Word to live above the standards of this world (John 17:14–16; Rom 12:2), keeping our hands clean and our own hearts pure (Ps 24:4). The following eight principles can help us build strong affair-resistant relationships.

Recognize Your Own Vulnerability

Greek mythology describes the hero Achilles as having an immortalized body with a mortal heel. During the Trojan War, Achilles supposedly played a crucial role, but was fatally wounded in his heel by a poisoned arrow shot by Paris and guided to its target by the god Apollo.[21] That was the end of this "immortal" figure.

Every human being has his or her own moral "Achilles heel" that needs to be well guarded, and his or her own level of vulnerability that should never be breached. Many people fall morally by considering themselves stronger than they really are. Temptation is indeed too subtle and persuasive to be played with. In reality, "the heart is deceitful above all things and beyond cure. Who can understand it?" (Jer 17:9).

Keep Emotions Under Control

Almost all physical affairs are preceded by romantic relationships and emotional infidelity outside of marriage. Such romantic or emotional preludes can include interpersonal relations, pornographic exposure,

---

[20] E.g., Robert Wright, "Our Cheating Hearts," *Time*, International ed., Aug. 15, 1994, 26–34; David P. Barash and Judith E. Lipton, *The Myth of Monogamy: Fidelity and Infidelity in Animals and People* (New York: Henry Holt, 2001); David M. Buss, *Evolutionary Psychology: The New Science of the Mind,* 5th ed. (London and New York: Routledge, 2016), 101–191; Debra Soh, *The End of Gender: Debunking the Myths about Sex and Identity in Our Society* (New York: Phreshold, 2020).

[21] "Achilles," http://www.greekmythology.comMyths/Heroes/Achilles/achilles.html (accessed January 5, 2015).

internet dating, sensual fantasies, or anything else that makes the individual emotionally vulnerable.

For this reason we are warned, "Keep your heart with all vigilance, for from it flow the springs of life" (Prov 4:23, NRSV). Job declared, "I made a covenant with my eyes not to look lustfully at a young woman" (Job 31:1). The Stoic philosopher Epictetus (AD 55–135) alerted, "Chastise your passions, that they may not chastise you."[22] Ellen White declares,

> Strength of character consists of two things—power of will and power of self-control. Many youth mistake strong, uncontrolled passion for strength of character; but the truth is that he who is mastered by his passions is a weak man. The real greatness and nobility of the man is measured by his power to subdue his feelings, not by the power of his feelings to subdue him.[23]

> You should keep off from Satan's enchanted ground, and not allow your minds to be swayed from allegiance to God. Through Christ you may and should be happy, and should acquire habits of self-control. Even your thoughts must be brought into subjection to the will of God, and your feelings under the control of reason and religion. Your imagination was not given you to be allowed to run riot and have its own way, without any effort at restraint or discipline. If the thoughts are wrong, the feelings will be wrong; and the thoughts and feelings combined make up the moral character.[24]

Avoid Risky Places and Circumstances

In the Garden of Eden, Eve exposed herself to temptation by going to the tree of the knowledge of good and evil, and even conversing with the serpent (Gen 2:15–17; 3:1–7). One of the most precarious situations is when one is alone with someone who seems more interesting and attractive than others, and when one shares parts of one's private life with him or her. Such situations might include a close relationship at the workplace, going out together for a meal, a business trip, a carpool, or even taking a simple ride together.

---

[22] The Works of Epictetus: *His Discourses, in Four Books, the Enchiridion, and Fragments*, new rev. ed., trans. Thomas W. Higginson (New York: Thomas Nelson and Sons, [1890]), 248 (Fragments IV), https://archive.org/stream/theworksofepicte00epicuoft#page/n7/mode/2up (accessed June 15, 2016).

[23] Ellen G. White, *Counsels to Parents, Teachers, and Students Regarding Christian Education* (Mountain View, CA: Pacific Press, 1943), 222.

[24] Ellen G. White, *Testimonies for the Church* (Mountain View, CA: Pacific Press, 1948), 5:310.

In the article "8 Things Married People Should Never Do … If They Want to Stay Married!," number 1 reads, "Never ride in a car alone with someone of the opposite sex." Based on his own experience, the author says "car rides are times when we tend to lighten up and open up. We feel safe, and we start sharing things. You're isolated from the world, and it gives opportunity for all kinds of trouble."[25] Many cases of romantic and even sexual infidelity grow spontaneously out of a too-close friendship between two couples from different family circles. Doing many family activities together, the male spouse of one couple and the female spouse of the other can easily develop an attraction for each other.

Set Borders and Limits for Those Who Do Not Have Them

In the stories of Joseph and Tamar, the victims revealed high moral principles and the aggressors were driven by uncontrolled passions, but the outcomes were completely different. Joseph was stronger than Potiphar's wife and escaped from her. Tamar was more fragile than Amnon and was raped by him. Despite such contrasts, there is another important similarity: both cases occurred within family circles with people one would trust the most. Unfortunately, many cases of child sexual abuse happen within those circles as well.

Our world is full of people with unrestrained sexual impulses, sensualized minds, and unsatisfied emotional needs who do not always respect the moral borders and limits of healthy social relationships. Such people should be helped—not by meeting their expectations and satisfying their seductive desires, but by limiting their invasive behavior and helping them develop higher moral values. Joseph stated clearly to Potiphar's wife that any kind of affair between them would mean the betrayal of his master and a "sin against God" (Gen 39:8–9). Likewise, Tamar argued forcefully with Amnon that his sexual advances were wicked and inappropriate behavior that would bring complete shame and disgrace on her life (2 Sam 13:12–13).

Value Mature Love Over Romantic Love

One author suggests that couples usually experience three stages of love.[26] The first is romantic love (falling in love with) in which a couple kisses each other and goes out to see the sunset. Some have described this as a sort of Hollywood love. Lasting only for some three to six months, this stage tends to give place to disappointment and disillusionment.

---

[25] Sean Chandler, "8 Things Married People Should Never Do … If They Want to Stay Married!" http://www.modernministryblog.com/?s=Things+Married+People+Should+Never+Do+(posted November 5, 2013; accessed June 15, 2016).

[26] Lillibridge, 7–14.

In the next stage, which can last several months or more, one begins to notice more clearly the faults and foibles of the other person. The third stage is mature love (being in love with), which means the acceptance of the whole person with his or her strengths and assets, faults and foibles.

Assuming that "the grass is always greener on the other side of the fence," some people confuse their own mature love with fading love, and a new romantic love with genuine love. By finding someone else who awakens the romantic love already gone from their own marriage, many people believe that they are rediscovering true love and end up replacing their old partner with this new, more seductive person. They simply forget that the new romantic love will not last forever either! The best antidote to such illusion is to understand, value, and nourish the mature love of our own marriages. As stated in Proverbs 5:18, "May your fountain be blessed, and may you rejoice in the wife of your youth."

Realize That You Are to Some Extent Responsible for the Feelings of Others

The three provocative individuals mentioned above—Potiphar's wife, King David, and Amnon—were egocentric people who did not care about the feelings of their respective desired partners. Potiphar's wife ended up blaming Joseph for her own immoral behavior. King David did not want to assume Bathsheba's pregnancy, and even destroyed her marriage. Amnon hated Tamar after he raped her. Such practices are typical of evil societies where people are simply used for pleasure, but they are absolutely reprehensible from a biblical perspective.

History has proven time and again that too much freedom for some means lack of freedom for others. As Christians we are responsible for those who suffer from social injustices (Jas 1:27; 5:4), as well as for the feelings of others (Matt 18:6). We should never ever play irresponsibly with other people's emotions. Some people may come out of an extra-marital romantic relationship or sexual affair without much guilt and remorse, but others may be emotionally damaged for the rest of their lives, feeling betrayed by a professed Christian who should have behaved like the Master (Matt 10:25). How different would our society and world be if we would develop more empathy for others and care for them as brothers and sisters in Christ.

Ask God to Replace Your Selfish Love With His Altruistic Love

According to one writer, marriage is in crisis today to a large extent because it has "lost its social function to become a source of self-gratification."[27] Undoubtedly, our modern competitive culture has generated a

---

[27] Terezinha Féres-Carneiro, quoted in Thaís Oyama and Lizia Bydlowski, "Até que o casamento os separe," *Veja* (Brazil), March 22, 2000, 120–125.

society of self-centered individuals. But the real problem derives from our selfish hearts (Matt 15:19; Mark 7:21–23; Gal 5:19–21), which need to be transformed by the power of God (2 Cor 5:17; Gal 5:22–24). Only a real conversion experience can bring into our lives a new perspective driven by altruistic love (Matt 5:43–48; John 13:34–35; 1 John 4:20).

White insightfully suggests,

> Picture a large circle, from the edge of which are many lines all running to the center. The nearer these lines approach the center, the nearer they are to one another.
>
> Thus it is in the Christian life. The closer we come to Christ, the nearer we shall be to one another. God is glorified as His people unite in harmonious action.[28]

Genuine Christians are filled with God's altruistic love. Instead of using people for their own sake and pleasure, they try to uplift people for this life and for eternity. Their healthy social behavior is always marked by the motto, "Because I love you in Christ I respect you, and I'm willing to help you overcome your own weaknesses and temptations."

Never Lose Sight of the Great Cosmic-Historical Controversy Between Good and Evil

The Bible declares that we are in a spiritual battle in which God wants us to live in harmony with His moral standards, and Satan is trying to convince us to live according to our own cheating hearts (cf. Eph 6:10–18; Jas 4:7). God observes not only our visible social behavior but also our most private thoughts and emotions (Ps 7:9; Jer 17:10; Rom 8:27). The apostle Paul says that "we have been made a spectacle to the whole universe, to angels as well as to men" (1 Cor 4:9). And David reasoned,

> Where can I go from your Spirit?
> Where can I flee from your presence?
> If I go up to the heavens, you are there;
> if I make my bed in the depths, you are there.
> If I rise on the wings of the dawn,
> if I settle on the far side of the sea,
> even there your hand will guide me,
> your right hand will hold me fast (Ps 139:7–10).

Regrettably, many professed Christians today are so involved with, and so enchanted by, "the fleeting pleasures of sin" (Heb 11:25) that they

---

[28] Ellen G. White, *The Adventist Home* (Washington, DC: Review and Herald, 1980), 179.

are no longer conscious of this spiritual-moral battle. White explains very clearly,

> Men who do not repent will not fail to receive according to their works. Sin may be concealed, denied, covered up from father, mother, wife, children, and associates. No one but the guilty actors may cherish the least suspicion of the wrong; but it is laid bare before the intelligences of heaven. The darkness of the darkest night, the secrecy of all deceptive arts, is not sufficient to veil one thought from the knowledge of the Eternal.[29]

By keeping this cosmic-historical reality in mind, one's cheating tendencies may lose their seductiveness and power. In addition, concentrating on Jesus and loving Him as our Savior motivates believers to do His will and follow His example of living a pure life.

Conclusion

The Bible provides abiding moral commands and helpful practical counsels on how to live a life of moral integrity. From a biblical perspective, sexual intercourse should be restricted only to monogamous, heterosexual marriages. This implies that premarital, homosexual, and extramarital sexual affairs are transgressions of God's moral standards. Christ's interpretation of the seventh commandment, "You shall not commit adultery" (Exod 20:14), condemns even the sensual thoughts that precede the sexual act (Matt 5:27–29). Both physical and mental purity are also implied in the question-answer statement of Psalm 24:3–4: "Who may ascend the mountain of the Lord? Who may stand in his holy place? The one who has clean hands and a pure heart."

The three seductive individuals mentioned above—Potiphar's wife, King David, and Amnon—remind us that extramarital affairs can have unpredictable and disastrous consequences. But even without such devastating outcomes, every affair outside of marriage tends to generate family/social problems, weakens one's moral strength, and opens the door to the transgression of other moral commandments of the Decalogue.

In these morally degraded last days of human history (2 Tim 3:1–7), we are encouraged by God's Word to "live holy and godly lives" (2 Pet 3:11–12). Our affair-resistant relationships can be strengthened by (1) recognizing our own vulnerability, (2) keeping our emotions under control, (3) avoiding risky places and circumstances, (4) setting borders and limits for those who do not have them, (5) valuing mature love over

---

[29] Ellen G. White, "Nothing Is Hidden," *Review and Herald*, March 27, 1888, 193.

romantic love, (6) realizing that we are responsible for the feelings of others, (7) asking God to replace our own selfish love with His altruistic love, and (8) never losing sight of the great cosmic-historical controversy between good and evil. But these eight points need to be undergirded by a past that has been forgiven and resolved with God.

A Brazilian Parnassian poet, judge, and magistrate wrote an introspective poem titled "Secret Evil" (Mal Secreto). In this poem he says that if we could see through the mask of the face the "pain that dwells in man's soul and destroys all dreams," perhaps "so many people who now make us envious, would then move us to pity!"[30] In reality, many human hearts are bleeding from moral wounds that refuse to heal. But we have the wonderful promise that "if we confess our sins, he is faithful and just and will forgive us our sins and purify us from all unrighteousness" (1 John 1:9). And then "the peace of God, which transcends all understanding, will guard your hearts and your minds in Christ Jesus" (Phil 4:7). May this saving experience become a reality in our own lives, now and forever!

---

[30] Raimundo Correia, "Secret Evil," trans. Carlos Alberto Santos, http://interlingua.wikia.com/wiki/Mal_secrete_en (accessed January 9, 2016).

APPENDIX

This appendix includes various documents voted by committees of the General Conference of Seventh-day Adventists and documents voted by the Biblical Research Institute Ethics Committee (BRIEC). They have been released over the years and reflect issues that are also addressed in this second volume of the Biblical Research Institute Studies in Biblical Ethics series.

A word about these documents is in order. Official "statements" of the Seventh-day Adventist Church and excerpts from the *General Conference Working Policy 2020–2021* have the highest authority among these documents, followed by official "guidelines" and "documents." The "statements" or "opinions" of the BRIEC, a committee of the General Conference, are worth considering but have not been voted by the world church—although some have led to official church statements. Also, the BRIEC has been asked to prepare statements that were adopted with slight modifications by the world church. These include the "Statement on the Biblical View of Unborn Life and Its Implications for Abortion" and the "Statement on Transgenderism."[1]

The documents presented here are arranged in reverse chronological order, from most recent to oldest; they are not in any way organized according to their categorization as "statements," "guidelines," "documents," etc. Therefore, the reader is advised to note the category and name of the document, the body that voted it, and the date of publication. This information is provided with each document.

The appendix attempts to provide for the reader a vista into the theological-ethical thinking of the Seventh-day Adventist Church regarding crucial and pressing ethical issues. Statements are by nature short and cannot be argued extensively. However, the chapters of this volume have provided deeper insights. Therefore, it is advisable to study both the chapters in the main body of this work as well as the documents in the appendix.

The reader may also notice that the content of some chapters is not reflected in official statements. One reason is that some issues represent

---

[1] Most of the official statements can be found on the General Conference website: "Official Statements," Seventh-day Adventist Church, https://www.adventist.org/official-statements/ (accessed February 8, 2022).

more recent developments. In addition, the church does not attempt to address each and every current issue in an official statement. Basic Adventist theology is presented in the 28 Fundamental Beliefs[2] so that it is not necessary to deal with all subject matters. Still, the collection of documents found in this volume is valuable.

§

[2] See "Official Beliefs of the Seventh-day Adventist Church," Seventh-day Adventist Church, https://www.adventist.org/beliefs/ (accessed February 8, 2022).

Polygamy[1]

2021–2022

It is clearly God's plan that man should live in a state of monogamy, that a man should have only one living wife. Any contravention of this plan results in confusion and the lowering of the moral standards that should govern human society, and especially the Church. The practice of polygamy on the part of many non-Christian peoples for whom we are laboring is in itself a challenge to Christian principles and constitutes a ground of compromise if permitted in the Christian church. The denomination has therefore adopted the following policy:

1. A man found living in a state of polygamy when the gospel reaches him shall upon conversion be required to change his status by putting away all his wives save one before he shall be considered eligible for baptism and church membership.
2. Men thus putting away their wives shall be expected to make proper provision for their future support, and that of their children, as far as it is within their power to do so.
3. We recognize that the message finds people in certain countries living in a state of polygamy, where tribal customs subject a wife who has been put away to lifelong shame and disgrace, even to the point of becoming common property, her children also becoming disgraced thereby. In all such cases the church is to cooperate with the former husband in making such provision for these wives and children as will provide for their care and protect them from disgrace and undue suffering.
4. We recognize the right of a wife who has been put away by a polygamous husband to marry again.
5. Wives of a polygamist, who have entered into the marriage in their heathen state, and who upon accepting Christianity are still not permitted to leave their husbands because of tribal custom, may upon approval of the local and union committees become baptized members of the church. However, should a woman who is a member of the church enter into marriage as a secondary wife, she shall be disfellowshipped and shall not be readmitted to the church unless she separates from her polygamous husband.

§

[1] C 70 Polygamy - *GC Working Policy 2020-2021* - Division Administration, 159.

Statement on the Biblical View of Unborn Life and Its Implications for Abortion[1]

2019

VOTED, To adopt the document, Statement on the Biblical View of Unborn Life and Its Implications for Abortion, which reads as follows:

Statement on the Biblical View of Unborn Life and Its Implications for Abortion

Human beings are created in the image of God. Part of the gift that God has given us as humans is procreation, the ability to participate in creation along with the Author of life. This sacred gift should always be valued and treasured. In God's original plan every pregnancy should be the result of the expression of love between a man and a woman committed to each other in marriage. A pregnancy should be wanted, and each baby should be loved, valued, and nurtured even before birth. Unfortunately, since the entrance of sin, Satan has made intentional efforts to mar the image of God by defacing all of God's gifts—including the gift of procreation. Consequently, individuals are at times faced with difficult dilemmas and decisions regarding a pregnancy.

The Seventh-day Adventist Church is committed to the teachings and principles of the Holy Scriptures which express God's values on life and provide guidance for prospective mothers and fathers, medical personnel, churches, and all believers in matters of faith, doctrine, ethical behavior, and lifestyle. The Church while not being the conscience of individual believers has the duty to convey the principles and teachings of the Word of God.

This statement affirms the sanctity of life and presents biblical principles bearing on abortion. As used in this statement, abortion is defined as any action aimed at the termination of a pregnancy and does not include the spontaneous termination of a pregnancy, known also as a miscarriage.

Biblical Principles And Teachings Relating To Abortion

As the practice of abortion must be weighed in the light of Scripture, the following biblical principles and teachings provide guidance for the community of faith and individuals affected by such difficult choices:

1. *God upholds the value and sacredness of human life.* Human life is of the greatest value to God. Having created humanity in His image (Genesis 1:27; 2:7), God has a personal interest in people. God loves them and

---

[1] This statement was voted by the General Conference of Seventh-day Adventists Executive Committee at the Annual Council Session in Silver Spring, Maryland on October 16, 2019. htt–://www.adventist.org/official-statements/statement-on-the-biblical-view-of-unborn-life-and-its-implications-for-abortion/ (accessed January 11, 2022).

communicates with them, and they in turn can love and communicate with Him.

Life is a gift of God, and God is the Giver of life. In Jesus is life (John 1:4). He has life in Himself (John 5:26). He is the resurrection and the life (John 11:25; 14:6). He provides abundant life (John 10:10). Those who have the Son have life (1 John 5:12). He is also the Sustainer of life (Acts 17:25–28; Colossians 1:17; Hebrews 1:1–3), and the Holy Spirit is described as the Spirit of life (Romans 8:2). God cares deeply for His creation and especially for humankind.

Furthermore, the importance of human life is made clear by the fact that, after the Fall (Genesis 3), God "gave His only begotten Son, that whoever believes in Him should not perish but have everlasting life" (John 3:16). While God could have abandoned and terminated sinful humanity, He opted for life. Consequently, Christ's followers will be raised from the dead and will live in face-to-face communion with God (John 11:25–26; 1 Thessalonians 4:15–16; Revelation 21:3). Thus, human life is of inestimable value. This is true for all stages of human life: the unborn, children of various ages, adolescents, adults, and seniors—independent of physical, mental, and emotional capacities. It is also true for all humans regardless of sex, ethnicity, social status, religion, and whatever else may distinguish them. Such an understanding of the sanctity of life gives inviolable and equal value to each and every human life and requires it to be treated with the utmost respect and care.

2. *God considers the unborn child as human life.* Prenatal life is precious in God's sight, and the Bible describes God's knowledge of people before they were conceived. "Your eyes saw my substance, being yet unformed. And in Your book they all were written, the days fashioned for me, when as yet there were none of them" (Psalms 139:16). In certain cases, God directly guided prenatal life. Samson was to "be a Nazirite to God from the womb" (Judges 13:5). The servant of God is "called from the womb" (Isaiah 49:1, 5). Jeremiah was already chosen as a prophet before his birth (Jeremiah 1:5), as was Paul (Galatians 1:15), and John the Baptist was to "be filled with the Holy Spirit, even from his mother's womb" (Luke 1:15). Of Jesus the angel Gabriel explained to Mary: "therefore the child to be born will be called holy—the Son of God" (Luke 1:35). In His Incarnation Jesus Himself experienced the human prenatal period and was recognized as the Messiah and Son of God soon after His conception (Luke 1:40–45). The Bible already attributes to the unborn child joy (Luke 1:44) and even rivalry (Genesis 25:21–23). Those not-yet-born have a firm place with God (Job 10:8–12; 31:13–15). Biblical law shows a strong regard for protecting human life and considers harm to or the loss of a baby or mother as a result of a violent act a serious issue (Exodus 21:22–23).

3. *The will of God regarding human life is expressed in the Ten Commandments and explained by Jesus in the Sermon on the Mount.* The

Decalogue was given to God's covenant people and the world to guide their lives and protect them. Its commandments are unchanging truths which should be cherished, respected, and obeyed. The Psalmist praises God's law (e.g., Psalms 119), and Paul calls it holy, righteous, and good (Romans 7:12). The sixth commandment states: "You shall not kill" (Exodus 20:13), which calls for the preservation of human life. The principle to preserve life enshrined in the sixth commandment places abortion within its scope. Jesus reinforced the commandment not to kill in Matthew 5:21–22. Life is protected by God. It is not measured by individuals' abilities or their usefulness, but by the value that God's creation and sacrificial love has placed on it. Personhood, human value, and salvation are not earned or merited but graciously granted by God.

4. *God is the Owner of life, and human beings are His stewards.* Scripture teaches that God owns everything (Psalms 50:10–12). God has a dual claim on humans. They are His because He is their Creator and therefore, He owns them (Psalms 139:13–16). They are also His because He is their Redeemer and has bought them with the highest possible price—His own life (1 Corinthians 6:19–20). This means that all human beings are stewards of whatever God has entrusted to them, including their own lives, the lives of their children, and the unborn.

The stewardship of life also includes carrying responsibilities which in some ways limit their choices (1 Corinthians 9:19–22). Since God is the Giver and Owner of life, human beings do not have ultimate control over themselves and should seek to preserve life wherever possible. The principle of the stewardship of life obligates the community of believers to guide, support, care for, and love those facing decisions about pregnancies.

5. *The Bible teaches care for the weak and the vulnerable.* God Himself cares for those who are disadvantaged and oppressed and protects them. He "shows no partiality nor takes a bribe. He administers justice for the fatherless and the widow, and loves the stranger, giving him food and clothing" (Deuteronomy 10:17–18, cf. Psalm 82:3–4; James 1:27). He does not hold children accountable for the sins of their fathers (Ezekiel 18:20). God expects the same of His children. They are called to help vulnerable people and ease their lot (Psalm 41:1; 82:3–4; Acts 20:35). Jesus speaks of the least of His brothers (Matthew 25:40), for whom His followers are responsible, and of the little ones who should not be despised or lost (Matthew 18:10–14). The very youngest, namely the unborn, should be counted among them.

6. *God's grace promotes life in a world marred by sin and death.* It is God's nature to protect, preserve, and sustain life. In addition to the providence of God over His creation (Psalms 103:19; Colossians 1:17; Hebrews 1:3), the Bible acknowledges the wide-ranging, devastating, and degrading effects of sin on the creation, including on human bodies. In Romans 8:20–24 Paul describes the impact of the Fall as subjecting the creation

to futility. Consequently, in rare and extreme cases, human conception may produce pregnancies with fatal prospects and/or acute, life-threatening birth anomalies that present individuals and couples with exceptional dilemmas. Decisions in such cases may be left to the conscience of the individuals involved and their families. These decisions should be well-informed and guided by the Holy Spirit and the biblical view of life outlined above. God's grace promotes and protects life. Individuals in these challenging situations may come to Him in sincerity and find direction, comfort, and peace in the Lord.

Implications

The Seventh-day Adventist Church considers abortion out of harmony with God's plan for human life. It affects the unborn, the mother, the father, immediate and extended family members, the church family, and society with long term consequences for all. Believers aim to trust God and follow His will for them, knowing He has their best interests in mind.

While not condoning abortion, the Church and its members are called to follow the example of Jesus, being "full of grace and truth" (John 1:14), to (1) create an atmosphere of true love and provide grace-filled, biblical pastoral care and loving support to those facing difficult decisions regarding abortion; (2) enlist the help of well-functioning and committed families and educate them to provide care for struggling individuals, couples, and families; (3) encourage church members to open their homes to those in need, including single parents, parentless children, and adoptive or foster care children; (4) care deeply for and support in various ways pregnant women who decide to keep their unborn children; and (5) provide emotional and spiritual support to those who have aborted a child for various reasons or were forced to have an abortion and may be hurting physically, emotionally, and/or spiritually.

The issue of abortion presents enormous challenges, but it gives individuals and the Church the opportunity to be what they aspire to be, the fellowship of brothers and sisters, the community of believers, the family of God, revealing His immeasurable and unfailing love.

§

Statement on Transgenderism[1]

2017

The increasing awareness of the needs and challenges that transgender men and women experience and the rise of transgender issues to social prominence worldwide raise important questions not only for those affected by the transgender phenomenon but also for the Seventh-day Adventist Church. While the struggles and challenges of those identifying as transgender people have some elements in common with the struggles of all human beings, we recognize the uniqueness of their situation and the limitation of our knowledge in specific instances. Yet, we believe that Scripture provides principles for guidance and counsel to transgender people and the Church, transcending human conventions and culture.

The Transgender Phenomenon

In modern society, gender identity typically denotes "the public (and usually legally recognized) lived role as boy or girl, man or woman," while sex refers "to the biological indicators of male and female."[2] Gender identification usually aligns with a person's biological sex at birth. However, misalignment may happen at the physical and/or mental-emotional levels.

On the physical level ambiguity in genitalia may result from anatomical and physiological abnormalities so that it cannot be clearly established whether a child is male or female. This ambiguity of anatomical sexual differentiation is often called hermaphroditism or intersexualism.[3]

On the mental-emotional level misalignment occurs with transgender people whose sexual anatomy is clearly male or female but who identify with the opposite gender of their biological sex. They may describe themselves as being trapped in a wrong body. Transgenderism, formerly clinically diagnosed as "gender identity disorder" and now termed "gender dysphoria," may be understood as a general term to describe the variety of ways individuals interpret and express their gender identity differently from those who determine gender on the basis of biological sex.[4] "Gender dysphoria is manifested in a variety of ways, including strong desires to be treated as the other gender or to be rid of one's

---

[1] Guidelines for the Seventh-day Adventist Church, April 11, 2017.

[2] Diagnostic and Statistical Manual of Mental Disorders, 5th ed. (DSM-5TM), edited by the American Psychiatric Association (Washington, DC: American Psychiatric Publishing, 2013), 451.

[3] Those born with ambiguous genitalia may or may not benefit from corrective surgical treatment.

[4] See DSM-5TM, 451–459.

sex characteristics, or a strong conviction that one has feelings and reactions typical of the other gender."[5]

Due to contemporary trends to reject the biblical gender binary (male and female) and replace it with a growing spectrum of gender types, certain choices triggered by the transgender condition have come to be regarded as normal and accepted in contemporary culture. However, the desire to change or live as a person of another gender may result in biblically inappropriate lifestyle choices. Gender dysphoria may, for instance, result in cross-dressing,[6] sex reassignment surgery, and the desire to have a marital relationship with a person of the same biological sex. On the other hand, transgender people may suffer silently, living a celibate life or being married to a spouse of the opposite sex.

Biblical Principles Relating to Sexuality and the Transgender Phenomenon

As the transgender phenomenon must be evaluated by Scripture, the following biblical principles and teachings may help the community of faith relate to people affected by gender dysphoria in a biblical and Christ-like way:

1. God created humanity as two persons who are respectively identified as male and female in terms of gender. The Bible inextricably ties gender to biological sex (Gen 1:27; 2:22–24) and does not make a distinction between the two. The Word of God affirms complementarity as well as clear distinctions between male and female in creation. The Genesis creation account is foundational to all questions of human sexuality.
2. From a biblical perspective, the human being is a psychosomatic unity. For example, Scripture repeatedly calls the entire human being a soul (Gen 2:7; Jer 13:17; 52:28–30; Ezek 18:4; Acts 2:41; 1 Cor 15:45), a body (Eph 5:28; Rom 12:1–2; Rev 18:13), flesh (1 Pet 1:24), and spirit (2 Tim 4:22; 1 John 4:1–3). Thus, the Bible does not endorse dualism in the sense of a separation between one's body and one's sense of sexuality. In addition, an immortal part of humans is not envisioned in Scripture because God alone possesses immortality (1 Tim 6:14–16) and will bestow it on those who believe in Him at the first resurrection (1 Cor 15:51–54). Thus, a human being is also meant to be an undivided sexual entity, and sexual identity cannot be independent from one's body. According to Scripture, our gender identity, as designed by God, is determined by our biological sex at birth (Gen 1:27; 5:1–2; Ps 139:13–14; Mark 10:6).

---

[5] This sentence is part of a succinct summary of gender dysphoria provided to introduce DSM-5TM that was published in 2013 (accessed April 11, 2017).

[6] Cross-dressing, also referred to as transvestite behavior, is prohibited in Deuteronomy 22:5.

3. Scripture acknowledges, however, that due to the Fall (Gen 3:6–19) the whole human being — that is, our mental, physical, and spiritual faculties — are affected by sin (Jer 17:9; Rom 3:9; 7:14–23; 8:20–23; Gal 5:17) and need to be renewed by God (Rom 12:2). Our emotions, feelings, and perceptions are not fully reliable indicators of God's designs, ideals, and truth (Prov 14:12; 16:25). We need guidance from God through Scripture to determine what is in our best interest and live according to His will (2 Tim 3:16).
4. The fact that some individuals claim a gender identity incompatible with their biological sex reveals a serious dichotomy. This brokenness or distress, whether felt or not, is an expression of the damaging effects of sin on humans and may have a variety of causes. Although gender dysphoria is not intrinsically sinful, it may result in sinful choices. It is another indicator that, on a personal level, humans are involved in the great controversy.
5. As long as transgender people are committed to ordering their lives according to the biblical teachings on sexuality and marriage they can be members of the Seventh-day Adventist Church. The Bible clearly and consistently identifies any sexual activity outside of heterosexual marriage as sin (Matt 5:28, 31–32; 1 Tim 1:8–11; Heb 13:4). Alternative sexual lifestyles are sinful distortions of God's good gift of sexuality (Rom 1:21–28; 1 Cor 6:9–10).
6. Because the Bible regards humans as wholistic entities and does not differentiate between biological sex and gender identity, the Church strongly cautions transgender people against sex reassignment surgery and against marriage, if they have undergone such a procedure. From the biblical wholistic viewpoint of human nature, a full transition from one gender to another and the attainment of an integrated sexual identity cannot be expected in the case of sex reassignment surgery.
7. The Bible commands followers of Christ to love everyone. Created in the image of God, they must be treated with dignity and respect. This includes transgender people. Acts of ridicule, abuse, or bullying towards transgender people are incompatible with the biblical commandment, "You shall love your neighbor as yourself" (Mark 12:31).
8. The Church as the community of Jesus Christ is meant to be a refuge and place of hope, care, and understanding to all who are perplexed, suffering, struggling, and lonely, for "a bruised reed He will not break, and smoking flax He will not quench" (Matt 12:20). All people are invited to attend the Seventh-day Adventist Church and enjoy the fellowship of its believers. Those who are members can fully participate in church life as long as they embrace the message, mission, and values of the Church.

9. The Bible proclaims the good news that sexual sins committed by heterosexuals, homosexuals, transgender people, or others can be forgiven, and lives can be transformed through faith in Jesus Christ (1 Cor 6:9–11).
10. Those who experience incongruity between their biological sex and gender identity are encouraged to follow biblical principles in dealing with their distress. They are invited to reflect on God's original plan of purity and sexual fidelity. Belonging to God, all are called to honor Him with their bodies and their lifestyle choices (1 Cor 6:19). With all believers, transgender people are encouraged to wait on God and are offered the fullness of divine compassion, peace, and grace in anticipation of Christ's soon return when all true followers of Christ will be completely restored to God's ideal.

§

Guidelines for the Seventh-day Adventist Church in Responding to Changing Cultural Attitudes Regarding Homosexual and Other Alternative Sexual Practices[1]

2014

VOTED, To adopt the Guidelines for the Seventh-day Adventist Church in Responding to Changing Cultural Attitudes Regarding Homosexual and Other Alternative Sexual Practices, which read as follows:

The Divine Ideal of Sexuality and Marriage

Issues related to human sexuality and marriage can be seen in their true light as they are viewed against the background of the divine ideal for humanity. God's creative activity culminated in making humankind in His own image as male and female and instituting marriage. Marriage as a wonderful divine gift to humanity is a covenant-based union of the two genders physically, emotionally, and spiritually, referred to in Scripture as "one flesh." Jesus Christ affirmed marriage to be both monogamous and heterosexual, a lifelong union of loving companionship between a man and a woman. In addition, throughout Scripture such heterosexual union in marriage is elevated as a symbol of the bond between Deity and humanity.

The harmonious relation of a man and a woman in marriage provides a microcosm of social unity that is time-honored as a core ingredient of stable societies. The Creator intended married sexuality not only to serve a unitive purpose but also to provide joy, pleasure, and physical completeness. At the same time, it is to a husband and wife whose love has enabled them to know each other in a deep sexual bond that a child may be entrusted. Their child, a living embodiment of their oneness, thrives in the atmosphere of married love and unity and has the benefit of a relationship with each of the natural parents.

While the monogamous union in marriage of a man and a woman is affirmed as the divinely ordained foundation of the family and social life and the only morally appropriate locus of intimate sexual expression,[2] singleness and the friendship of singles are within the divine design as well. Scripture, however, places a distinction between acceptable conduct in friendship relations and sexual conduct in marriage.

Unfortunately, human sexuality and marriage have been corrupted by sin. Therefore, Scripture does not focus only on the positive aspects

---

[1] These guidelines were voted by the General Conference of Seventh-day Adventists Executive Committee at the Spring Meeting session in Silver Spring, Maryland, 2014

[2] See the Seventh-day Adventist Church's Official Statements about "Same-Sex Unions" and "Homosexuality."

of human sexuality but also on wrong expressions of sexuality and their negative impact on people and society. It warns humans of destructive sexual behaviors such as fornication, adultery, homosexual intimacies, incest, and polygamy, (e.g., Matt 19:1–12; 1 Cor 5:1–13; 6:9–20; 7:10–16, 39; Heb 13:4; Rev 22:14–15) and calls them to do what is good, healthy, and beneficial.

The Seventh-day Adventist Church adheres without reservation to the divine ideal of pure, honorable, and loving sexual relations within heterosexual marriage, believing that any lowering of this high view is detrimental to humanity. It also believes that the ideals of purity and beauty of marriage as designed by God need to be emphasized. Through the redemptive work of Christ, the original purpose of marriage may be recovered, and the delightful and wholesome experience of matrimony may be realized by a man and a woman who join their lives in a lifelong marriage covenant.

The Church and Society

The Seventh-day Adventist Church believes that it has been called into existence by God to proclaim the everlasting gospel to the entire world, and to invite persons everywhere to be ready for the second coming of Jesus. The Church pursues God's mission around the globe, currently teaching, preaching, caring, and serving in more than 200 nations. The Seventh-day Adventist Church has no creedal statement: it believes that its teachings rest on the authority of the Bible alone. It summarizes those beliefs, however, in a Statement of Fundamental Beliefs, currently 28 in number. Central to the Church's understanding of God's plan for ordering human society is its teaching on "Marriage and the Family."[3]

Because Seventh-day Adventists live, work, and minister in every part of the world, individual Seventh-day Adventists and the institutions by which the Church pursues God's mission relate to and interact with all levels of human government. The Bible instructs Christians to be obedient to the laws enacted by civil government, and wherever morally possible, Seventh-day Adventist members and Church organizations will seek to be subject to the governing authorities, even as they seek counsel about how to respond when the claims of government conflict with the truths of the Bible and the Fundamental Beliefs of the Church.

The Church's Relationship to Civil Legislation About Heterosexuality and Alternative Sexual Behaviors

The Word of God is replete with instruction and illustration bearing on the believer's relationship to the authority and jurisdiction of civil government. Because the Seventh-day Adventist Church values the entirety of

---

[3] Fundamental Beliefs of Seventh-day Adventists, "Marriage and Family," No. 23.

the Word of God as its ultimate authority for truth, doctrine, and way of life, it always seeks to reflect in its teaching and practice the full message of Scripture regarding appropriate interaction with civil government. To that end, the Church periodically offers counsel to individuals, leaders, and church institutions when the claims of civil government and the teachings of the Bible appear to be in conflict. This document focuses on the growing divide between the enactments of some civil governments and the beliefs of the Seventh-day Adventist Church about acceptable sexual behaviors.

The following principles, though not comprehensive, undergird the Church's consistent application of biblical truths to the societies and cultures in which it operates and the governments to which it responds. These principles will be especially important in framing, for a Church ministry or organization, an appropriate response to any level of civil government that may attempt to impose on the Church its perceptions of legally and morally acceptable sexual practices.

1. *All human governments exist through the provision and allowance of God.* The apostle Paul clearly instructs both individual Christians and the Church to place themselves willingly in submission to human governments that have been ordained by God to preserve God-given liberties, promote justice, preserve social order, and care for the disadvantaged (see Rom 13:1–3). Insofar as they act in concert with the values and principles articulated in the Word of God, civil governments deserve the respect and obedience of individual believers and the corporate Church. Wherever possible, individual Seventh-day Adventists and Church organizations in a given state or nation will seek by their behavior and statements to be understood as loyal citizens, participating in the rights and responsibilities of citizenship. Additionally, believers are instructed to pray for those in civil authority (1 Tim 2:1–2) so that believers may practice the virtues of God's kingdom.
2. *Although the authority of human government is derived from the authority of God, the claims and jurisdictions of human governments are never ultimately definitive for either individual believers or the Church. Both individual believers and the Church owe supreme allegiance to God Himself.* On those occasions when the claims of civil government directly conflict with and contradict the teaching of the Word of God as understood by the Seventh-day Adventist Church, both the Church and its members are bound by that same Word of God to obey its precepts rather than those of human government (Acts 5:29). This expression of a higher allegiance is specific only to the claim of government that is in contradiction to the Word of God, and does not otherwise diminish or remove the obligation of either the Church or individual believers to live in submission to civil authority on other matters.

3. *Because individual believers and the organized Church enjoy the rights and liberties given them by God and ratified by civil government, they may fully participate in the processes by which societies organize social life, provide for public and electoral order, and structure civil relationships.* This may include a clear articulation of the Church's beliefs in such things as (1) the preservation of liberty of conscience; (2) the protection of the weak and disadvantaged; (3) the values of God-given health principles and practices in building up the social and economic welfare of the state. Neither individual Seventh-day Adventists nor the congregations, institutions, and entities through which they engage in their God-given mission should surrender their privileges and rights as a result of opposition to their allegiance to biblical teaching. With its long history of defending religious liberty and freedom of worship around the globe, the Seventh-day Adventist Church defends the rights of all persons, of whatever faith, to follow the dictates of their conscience and to engage in the religious practices to which that faith compels them.
4. *Because the Seventh-day Adventist Church believes and practices a wholistic understanding of the gospel of Jesus Christ, its evangelistic, educational, publishing, medical, and other ministry organizations are integral and indivisible expressions of its fulfillment of the commission given by Jesus, "Go therefore and make disciples of all nations, baptizing them in the name of the Father and of the Son and of the Holy Spirit, teaching them to observe all that I have commanded you"* (Matt 28:19–20, ESV). While Seventh-day Adventist congregations, publishing and media ministries, educational institutions, hospitals and medical centers, and ministry organizations appear to share certain similarities with other social and cultural institutions, they have historically been organized and continue to be organized on a faith and missional basis. They exist for the express purpose of communicating the saving knowledge of Jesus Christ through their multiform methods and initiatives, and to advance the mission of the Seventh-day Adventist Church, and should enjoy all the privileges and liberties accorded to the religious organization of which they are essential parts. The Seventh-day Adventist Church vigorously asserts and defends the nonseparability of its various forms of mission, and urges all civil governments to accord to each of its organizations and entities the rights of conscience and freedom of religious practice asserted in the United Nations Declaration of Human Rights and guaranteed in the constitutions of most world states.
5. *In their interface with civil governments and societies, both the Church and individual Seventh-day Adventists must conduct themselves as representatives of the kingdom of Christ, exhibiting His characteristics of love, humility, honesty, reconciliation, and commitment to the*

truths of the Word of God. Each human being, of whatever gender, race, nationality, social class, faith, or sexual orientation, deserves to be treated with respect and dignity by the Seventh-day Adventist Church and the entities and organizations through which it pursues God's mission. Because it defines itself as the body of Christ, who "died for us" "while we were yet sinners" (Rom 5:8), the Church holds itself to the highest standards of speech and conduct toward all human beings. Recognizing that God is the ultimate Judge of all persons, the Church believes in the opportunity of all persons to be included in the kingdom of heaven as they acknowledge and forsake their sinfulness, confess Christ as Lord, accept His righteousness in place of their own, seek to obey His commandments, and live His life of service. The Church affirms its right to describe some behaviors, ways of living, and the organizations that promote them as contrary to the Word of God. The Church is also responsible, however, to differentiate clearly between its critique of those beliefs and behaviors, and its respect for the persons expressing those beliefs and behaviors. The Church does not condone and will not allow its public statements on matters of social concern to be characterized as contempt or verbal humiliation of those with whom it disagrees. In exercising its freedoms, the Church's public speech must exhibit the grace always seen in Jesus. All Seventh-day Adventist entities and organizations, as well as individual members of the Church, are urged to express their respect for individuals or groups of persons with whose behavior and opinions they are compelled to disagree because of allegiance to the Word of God. The Church earns the credibility to participate in difficult social and national issues by its clear identification of itself as a redemptive entity.

In light of the above principles derived from the Word of God, the Seventh-day Adventist Church seeks to offer counsel to congregations, church organizations and entities, and those who lead church organizations and entities. The complex issues surrounding civil governments' responses to the reality of homosexuality and alternative sexual practices in contemporary society underscore the importance of this counsel.

The Challenges of State Legislation

In a growing number of nations, governments enact special legislative or judicial protection to prevent what they consider discriminatory behavior. Those protections sometimes appear to impair the religious-freedom rights of Seventh-day Adventist pastors, leaders, and Church organizations to employ persons, perform weddings, offer employment benefits, publish missional material, make public statements, and provide education or educational housing on the basis of the Seventh-day Adventist teaching about the sinfulness of sexual behaviors prohibited by Scripture.

Conversely, in a number of nations, homosexual or alternative sexual practices result in harsh penalties imposed by law. While Seventh-day Adventist institutions and members may appropriately advocate for preserving the unique and God-given institution of heterosexual marriage in their societies and legal codes, it is the position of the Church to treat those practicing homosexual or alternative sexual behaviors with the redemptive love taught and lived by Jesus.

The Moral and Religious Freedoms of the Church

The Seventh-day Adventist Church will encourage all its congregations, employees, ministry leaders, organizations, and entities to uphold church teachings and faith-based practices in Church membership, employment, education, and marriage ceremonies, including officiating at weddings. These teachings and faith-based practices, built upon the Bible's instructions about human sexuality, are equally applicable to heterosexual and homosexual relationships. It is inconsistent with the Church's understanding of scriptural teaching to admit into or maintain in membership persons practicing sexual behaviors incompatible with biblical teachings. Neither is it acceptable for Adventist pastors or churches to provide wedding services or facilities for same-sex couples.

In upholding these Scriptural standards, the Church relies upon the faith-based exemptions usually and customarily extended by civil government to religious organizations and their affiliated ministries to organize themselves according to their understanding of moral truth. The Church will also attempt to provide legal counsel and resources to Church leaders, organizations, and entities so that they operate in harmony with its biblical understanding of human sexuality.

Congregational leaders, Church employees, ministry leaders, and institutions are advised to review carefully the Church's existing policies with regard to membership, employment, and education to ensure that local practices are in harmony with the Church's expressed teachings about sexual behavior. Consistent expression and application of organizational policies and teachings regarding such behavior will be a key feature of maintaining the faith-based exemptions customarily allowed by civil governments.

Faith-Based Decision Making in Emplyment and Enrollment

The Seventh-day Adventist Church asserts and reserves the right for its entities to employ individuals according to Church teaching about sexual behaviors compatible with the teaching of Scripture as understood by the Seventh-day Adventist Church. While each institution and ministry operates in its own society and legal climate, each also expresses the worldwide belief system and teachings of the global Church. The Church maintains the right of these ministries and institutions to make decisions based on the teaching of Scripture and will provide legal review of relevant law and ordinances.

Wherever possible and feasible, the Church will continue to advocate, both legislatively and in courts of law, for faith-based preferential hiring and enrollment practices for itself and its ministries.

The Church and Public Speech

The Church asserts the right to express its commitment to biblical truth through the communication it makes available to its members and to various publics, as well as to defend the free-speech rights of its employees to express the Church's teaching about sexual behavior in public environments, including worship services, evangelistic meetings, educational classrooms, and public forums. Church leaders accept the responsibility to keep themselves and Church employees informed about government regulations regarding acceptable speech, and to invite periodic legal review of how those regulations should affect the Church's mission. Those responsible for the Church's official communication and those who preach and teach should emphasize the importance of surrendering all behavior, including sexual behavior, to the transforming power of Jesus Christ. The standard for both published material and public statements about sexual behaviors must be that they are widely understood as both "clear and respectful," expressing biblical truth with the kindness of Jesus Himself.

The Church's Commitment to Training and Legal Review

To achieve a consistent application of a "clear and respectful" standard in its ministries, the Church urges all its ministries, including pastoral and evangelistic ministries, educational ministries, publishing and media ministries, and health and medical ministries, among others, periodically to provide training and counsel to employees who interface with the public through media and public presentations. This training should include a review of current national or community law pertaining to public speech about sexual behaviors, and examples of appropriate ways to communicate the Church's beliefs and teachings.

§

Sex-Change Surgery: A Current Position[1]

2014

The rise of transgender issues to social prominence raises important questions for the Seventh-day Adventist Church. In particular, the question of sex-change surgery (also called sex reassignment surgery) challenges the Church with sensitive questions. Although the transgender question is important, the scope of this document is limited to providing some guidance regarding sex-change surgery. We acknowledge that questions related to sex-change surgery are not merely clinical, but involve human beings who are experiencing deep emotional distress as they try to grapple with their personal gender identity. These people need our love, prayers, support, and guidance. There are two areas of questions for believers in reference to sex-change surgery. The first is whether those who are already members of the church but experience gender identity tensions should have sex-change surgery. The second regards those who first have had sex-change surgery and then come to Christ and the Church.

Believers and Sex-Change Surgery

Gender identification usually aligns with one's birth sex. Sometimes, however, genetic, chromosomal, hormonal, and intrauterine influences may result in ambiguity of anatomical sexual differentiation. In these situations, anatomical development of genitalia can result in a spectrum of disorders spanning the gamut from definitely female to overtly male. Those born with ambiguous genitalia may well benefit from corrective surgical treatment. There is another group of persons whose anatomical gender identity is clearly male or female but who identify with the opposite gender of their biological sex. Such individuals sometimes request surgical intervention to change their genitalia into that approximating the opposite sex. They are the focus of the following considerations.

(1) While the struggles and challenges of those identifying as transgender have some elements in common with the struggles of all human beings, we recognize the uniqueness of their existential situation and the limitation of our knowledge in such issues.

(2) As Christians we look to the Word of God for guidance. First, from a biblical perspective the human being is a psychosomatic unity. This means that sexual identity cannot be entirely independent from one's body as is frequently asserted. In fact, in Scripture, our gender identity is, to a significant extent, determined by our birth sex with God being the author of gender identity (Gen 1:27; 5:1–2; Mark 10:6; Ps 139:13–14). Second, the

---

[1] The BRI Ethics Committee is indebted to Ángel M. Rodríguez on whose work this statement is based, e.g., https://adventistbiblicalresearch.org/sites/default/files/pdf/sex-change%20surgery.pdf (accessed January 11, 2022).

Bible reminds us that each person with his/her mind and psyche is part of the creation that is corrupted by sin (Rom 3:9; 7:17; 8:20–23; Jer 17:9; Gal 5:17) and needs to be renewed by God (Rom 12:2). Our emotions, feelings, and perceptions are not fully reliable indicators of God's designs, ideals, and truth (Prov 14:12; 16:25). We need guidance from God, through Scripture, to determine what is in our best interest (2 Tim 3:16).

(3) A human is meant to be an undivided sexual entity. The claim that some individuals experience a psychological sexual identity incompatible with their biological sex reveals a serious type of psychological dichotomy. Such psychological disturbance or brokenness is an expression of the damaging effects of sin on humans. It remains unclear, however, if this disturbance or brokenness can be overcome through sexchange surgery. Such treatment may disturb the patient even more.

(4) So far, sex-change surgeries are irreversible. Persons undergoing these procedures have to use hormones for the rest of their lives, which indicates that an integrated sexual identity is not achieved through surgery. Surgery does not solve the problem completely. What aggravates the situation is that while surgery is irreversible, people may change psychologically as they grow and mature, seeking again a new identity.

(5) In some cases, sex-change surgery may be motivated by a sophisticated desire for homosexual activity. Undergoing sex-change surgery in order to satisfy the homosexual urge to have sex with a person of the same sex would violate the ethical and moral biblical principle of sexual activity being limited to heterosexual marriage.

(6) The Scriptures call humans to manage their emotions and passions by bringing them under the lordship of Christ (Gal 5:24; Jas 4:7). Sexual drives and identities are not to be satisfied on the grounds that, since they are considered to be normal or natural, we should let nature run its course. Sin and evil have corrupted human nature, including gender identity and sexuality. While self-discipline is indispensable in bringing both into harmony with biblical values and principles, God has promised the Holy Spirit to help us face our sinful impulses and our attraction to sin.

(7) Since surgery does not solve the situation, a person is more likely to find wholeness and healing by learning to live with his or her sexual condition of a real or perceived dichotomy in sexual identity while leaning on the Lord for constant help. For these reasons the BRI Ethics Committee strongly cautions against such a radical and irreversible procedure and urges pastors and church members to demonstrate care and regard toward those who struggle with this challenging issue. Should individuals seek to use sex-change surgery as a way of circumventing biblical principles addressing human sexuality and the proper way to satisfy such desires, they would be acting against God's revealed will. The Church must remain loyal to its commitment to the will of the risen Lord as revealed in the Scriptures and therefore display love for all.

New Converts with Pre-Conversion Sex-Change Surgery

The situation becomes even more complex in the case of persons who underwent sex-change surgery before coming to know Jesus as their personal Savior and Lord. How should the Church deal with them when they ask to become members of the community of believers? To answer this crucial question we make the following recommendations:

(1) That we treat these persons with love and respect, demonstrating our serious interest in their wellbeing. Those involved in the conversation should do their utmost to avoid aggravating the new converts' emotional condition. Adding pain to persons who have been hurting most of their lives is not an expression of Christian love.

(2) That we recognize that God called them to salvation in the state in which they were found by Him, lacking wholeness, and that they accepted the call to salvation.

(3) That we do not coerce these persons to reverse their surgery. It could be argued that although the Lord finds us in a state of fragmentation, He wants to transform and restore us, and that, therefore, new believers should begin a process of medical reversal that will take them back as close as possible to their pre-surgery physical condition. Such an attempt would create significant problems because complete surgical reversal remains impossible, and even a partial reversal may seriously endanger the health of the persons involved.

(4) That we do not deny church membership to persons who have undergone sex-change surgery but are committed to the Lord and His will. The only thing that we can biblically require is what the Bible requires from all of us: to allow the Spirit of the Lord to bring inner healing to us and to live a life of moral and sexual purity while looking forward to the moment when the Lord will restore wholeness to all of us. The irreversible nature of sex-change surgery, the fact that the Lord touches the hearts of transgender persons and accepts them as His children, as well as the recognition that all of our bodies have not yet been redeemed (Rom 8:23), makes us very cautious when interacting with them. Our respect and care for these persons follows Christ's example of serving others while being fully committed to God and His revealed will.

§

Marriage of Persons who Have Experienced Sex-Change Surgery: A Current Position

2014

The question of whether marriage should be considered by transgender people who have experienced sex-change surgery[1] or whether it should be discouraged by the Adventist Church is a delicate question.[2] Oftentimes the affected persons have suffered emotionally and spiritually because of their feelings of gender incongruity and rejection by others. So they need all our love and respect. However, if marriage of transgender persons is being considered, a few considerations are in order.

(1) The Bible teaches clearly that according to God's plan and design only one male and one female can be joined together in marriage. In strongest terms Jesus upheld heterosexual marriage and ruled out polygamy as well as homosexual relations. These biblical norms are binding for humanity at all times and under all circumstances. Therefore, they need to be adhered to when pondering marriage of transgender people.

(2) The Biblical Research Institute Ethics Committee currently works with the assumption that a male to female surgically-changed transgender person should be considered female and a female to male surgically-changed transgender person male, even though the new state is not perfect as constant dependence on hormone therapy indicates. If a transgender person has not had a sex-change surgery, the committee would consider that person to be male or female according to his/her biological sex, even if that person has adopted a first name associated with the sex opposite of his/her biological sex.

(3) This would mean that a marriage between a non-transgender male and a transgender male or between a non-transgender female and a transgender female would be understood as a homosexual relationship,[3] prohibited by Scripture.

(4) A transgender person may be attracted to the same sex but may dislike sexual relations, for instance, as a male with another male and therefore may seek sex-change surgery, which would open the way to have sex with a male now as a female. Such behavior appears to be a

---

[1] Other designations are sex reassignment surgery, gender reassignment surgery, sex affirmation surgery, gender confirmation surgery, or sex realignment surgery.

[2] For the question of whether the BRI Ethics Committee would recommend or discourage sex change, see the statement on sexchange surgery.

[3] See the two official statements of the Adventist Church on homosexuality: http://www.adventist.org/information/officialstatements/statements/article/go/0/homosexuality/vitality/service/ and http://www.adventist.org/information/officialstatements/statements/article/go/0/same-sex-unions/beliefs/en/ (accessed January 11, 2022).

sophisticated form of homosexual behavior that would also militate against the biblical perspective of homosexuality.

(5) Regarding the question of whether a surgically changed transgender person should attempt to reverse the prior surgery, we do not expect persons who have undergone sex-change surgery to attempt to revert to their former state, because presently sex-change surgery is irreversible. Under this assumption it would theoretically be possible for a transgender female to marry a male and a transgender male a female unless the sex-change surgery was undertaken for homosexual desires. Yet even if marriage would be potentially possible, we believe that transgender persons who have had a sex-change surgery should abstain from seeking it.

(6) A marriage between a transgender person and a non-transgender person can be a tremendous challenge, especially if total transparency is lacking. The non-transgender partner would need to know that the future spouse originally had the same biological sex that the other partner still has. Some partners might be able to live with such a situation, while others may find it challenging or impossible to live in a marriage relationship with a transgender person. In addition, the issues of sexual relations and having children would need to be raised between the partners that want to marry. For instance, a male to female transgender person cannot bear children naturally.

(7) Even if both partners were transgender persons, reasons for getting married, issues of sexuality, having children, forming a family, etc. would militate against such a marriage.

(8) As much as heterosexual marriage of non-transgender partners is a blessing, it also means work and adjustment of the partners to each other. This does not end after an initial period of a few months or even several years but continues for as long as a marriage exists. Today some heterosexual marriages are ending in divorce even after thirty or forty years because the spouses can no longer stand each other's idiosyncrasies and standard behavioral attitudes. If this is true for marriages that are entered into by persons who have not had their gender identities compromised in any way, it is an even greater challenge for persons who come into a marriage relationship with strong psychological burdens as a consequence of feeling trapped in the body of the other sex. Marriage is not a way to bring psychological healing to individuals struggling with gender identity issues. For these reasons we strongly caution transgender people against a transgender getting married. However, even if the Church would not approve of a couple's choice to marry, the local pastor should still minister to those entrusted to his care.

§

Homosexuality[1]

2012

The Seventh day Adventist Church recognizes that every human being is valuable in the sight of God, and we seek to minister to all men and women in the spirit of Jesus. We also believe that by God's grace and through the encouragement of the community of faith, an individual may live in harmony with the principles of God's Word.

Seventh-day Adventists believe that sexual intimacy belongs only within the marital relationship of a man and a woman. This was the design established by God at creation. The Scriptures declare: "For this reason a man will leave his father and mother and be united to his wife, and they will become one flesh" (Gen 2:24, NIV). Throughout Scripture this heterosexual pattern is affirmed. The Bible makes no accommodation for homosexual activity or relationships. Sexual acts outside the circle of a heterosexual marriage are forbidden (Lev 18:5–23, 26; Lev 20:7–21; Rom 1:24–27; 1 Cor 6:9–11). Jesus Christ reaffirmed the divine creation intent: "'Haven't you read,' he replied, 'that at the beginning the Creator "made them male and female," and said, "For this reason a man will leave his father and mother and be united to his wife, and the two will become one flesh?" So they are no longer two, but one'" (Matt 19:4–6, NIV). For these reasons Seventh-day Adventists are opposed to homosexual practices and relationships.

Jesus affirmed the dignity of all human beings and reached out compassionately to persons and families suffering the consequences of sin. He offered caring ministry and words of solace to struggling people, while differentiating His love for sinners from His clear teaching about sinful practices. As His disciples, Seventh-day Adventists endeavor to follow the Lord's instruction and example, living a life of Christ-like compassion and faithfulness.

§

[1] This statement was voted during the Annual Council of the General Conference Executive Committee on Sunday, October 3, 1999 in Silver Spring, Maryland. Revised by the General Conference Executive Committee, October 17, 2012.

Same-Sex Unions[1]

2012

Over the past several decades the Seventh-day Adventist Church has felt it necessary to clearly state in various ways its position in regard to marriage, the family, and human sexuality. These subjects are at the heart of many pressing issues facing society. That which for centuries has been considered to be basic Christian morality in the marriage setting is now increasingly called into question, not only in secular society but within Christian churches themselves.

The institutions of marriage and family are under attack and facing growing centrifugal forces that are tearing them apart. An increasing number of nations are not only debating the topic of "same-sex unions," but some have already passed various pieces of legislation, thus making it a world issue. The public discussion has engendered strong emotions. In light of these developments, the Seventh-day Adventist Church is clearly restating its position.

We reaffirm, without hesitation, our long-standing position as expressed in the Church's Fundamental Beliefs: "Marriage was divinely established in Eden and affirmed by Jesus to be a lifelong union between a man and a woman in loving companionship."[2] Though "sin has perverted God's ideals for marriage and family," "the family tie is the closest, the most tender and sacred of any human relationship," and thus "families need to experience renewal and reformation in their relationships" (An Affirmation of Family, 1990). God instituted "marriage, a covenant-based union of two genders [male and female] physically, emotionally, and spiritually, spoken of in Scripture as 'one flesh.'" "The monogamous union in marriage of a man and a woman is . . . the only morally appropriate locus of genital or related intimate sexual expression." "Any lowering of this high view is to that extent a lowering of the heavenly ideal" (An Affirmation of Marriage, 1996).[3]

Homosexuality is a manifestation of the disturbance and brokenness in human inclinations and relations caused by the entrance of sin into the world. While everyone is subject to fallen human nature, "we also believe that by God's grace and through the encouragement of the community of

---

[1] This document was approved and voted by the General Conference of Seventh-day Adventists Executive Committee, October 17, 2012.

[2] Seventh-day Adventists Believe: An exposition of the fundamental beliefs of the Seventh-day Adventist Church, Doctrine 23 on 'Marriage and the Family."

[3] Public Statement, An Affirmation of Family, released July 5, 1990, at the General Conference Session, Indianapolis, IN.

faith, an individual may live in harmony with the principles of God's Word" (Seventh-day Adventist Position Statement on Homosexuality, 2012).

We hold that all people, regardless of their sexual orientation, are loved by God. We do not condone singling out any group for scorn and derision, let alone abuse. Still, God's Word that transcends time and culture does not permit a homosexual lifestyle. The Bible's opposition to same-sex unions/marriage is anchored in God's plan at creation for marriage (Gen 1:26–28; 2:20–24), in divine legislation (Lev 18:22; 20:13; 1 Cor 6:9–11), and in Jesus' explicit confirmation of a permanent, monogamous, and heterosexual marriage relationship (Matt 19:4–6).

§

Ending Violence against Women and Girls[1]

2010

We, the members of the Seventh-day Adventist Church, speak up and join with others to bring an end to violence against women and girls. Global statistics indicate that in all societies women and girls are more frequently the victims of violence. Actions or threats likely to result in physical, sexual, or psychological harm or suffering are incompatible with biblical ethics and Christian morality. Such actions include, but are not limited to, family violence, rape, Female Genital Mutilation (FGM), honor killings, and dowry murders. Manipulation, denial of personal liberty, and coercion are also acts of abuse and violence. To such behaviors the Seventh-day Adventist Church says, "Let's end it now!"

Seventh-day Adventists recognize that creation in God's image bestows dignity and worth on every individual. The measure of that worth is seen in the sacrificial death of Jesus Christ to provide eternal life for everyone. The love and compassion that characterized the earthly life of Jesus sets an example for all His followers in their relationship with others. Christ-like behavior leaves no room for violence against family members or persons outside the family.

The Bible counsels Christians to view the body as the temple of God. Bringing intentional harm to another person desecrates that which God honors and is therefore sinful behavior. Seventh-day Adventists commit themselves to being leaders in breaking the cycle of violence perpetrated against women and girls. We will speak out in defense of victims and survivors through teaching, preaching, Bible study, and advocacy programs.

The Seventh day Adventist Church seeks and welcomes partnerships and collaboration with others in addressing this global issue. The collective voice of many can save tens of thousands of women and girls from the harm and suffering that result from abuse and violence.

§

---

[1] This statement was approved and voted by the Executive Committee of the General Conference of Seventh-day Adventists on June 23, 2010, and released at the General Conference Session in Atlanta. Georgia, June 24-July 3, 2010.

Statement of Consensus Concerning Female Genital Mutilation[1]

2000

As part of their mission to the entire world, Seventh-day Adventists have a firm commitment to provide health care that preserves and restores human wholeness. By wholeness we mean the harmonious development of the physical, intellectual, social, and spiritual dimensions of a person's life, unified through a loving relationship with God and expressed in generous service to others. Because Adventists believe that each human being is created in God's image as a unified person, rather than as a duality of body and soul, we believe in a ministry of grace that affects all aspects of human life, including physical and emotional well-being.

Ministry to the entire person leads Seventh-day Adventists to be concerned about the widespread practice of female genital mutilation.[2] Often referred to as "female circumcision" or, more recently, "female genital cutting," such practices currently affect scores of millions of living women and girls, with additional millions of girls disfigured annually. These estimates do not account for the young girls who die as a result of the more radical forms of genital mutilation. These practices range from excision of the clitoral prepuce to complete removal of the vulva with closure of the vaginal opening. Our central concern, expressed in this statement of principles, is for all forms of female genital injury that lead to physical dysfunction or emotional trauma. Moreover, such procedures are often done with unclean instruments, without anesthesia, on forcibly held young girls between the ages of four and twelve. Hemorrhage, shock, infection, incontinence, damage to surrounding organs, and massive scarring are frequent results. In addition to this physical devastation, genital mutilation is also emotionally traumatic.

Women who have been subjected to genital mutilation are also often afflicted with a variety of long-term gynecological health problems,

---

[1] This statement was received by the General Conference of Seventh-day Adventists Administrative Committee (ADCOM) on April 4, 2000 and recommended for use by departments and services.

[2] "Currently, the different types of female genital mutilation known to be practiced are classified as follows: Type I Excision of the prepuce, with or without excision of part or all of the clitoris Type II Excision of the clitoris with partial or total excision of the labia minora Type III Excision of part or all of the external genitalia and stitching/narrowing of vaginal opening (infibulation) Type IV Unclassified: includes pricking, piercing or incising of the clitoris and/or labia; cauterization by burning of the clitoris and surrounding tissue; scraping of tissues surrounding the vaginal orifice [angurya cuts] or cutting of the vagina [gishiri cuts]; introduction of corrosive substances or herbs into the vaginato cause bleeding or for the purposes of tightening or narrowing it; and any other procedure that falls under the definition of female genital mutilation given above." This classification is taken from Female Genital Mutilation: A Joint WHO, UNICEF, UNFPA Statement. Published by World Health Organization, Geneva, 1997.

including fistulas, chronic infections, and problems with menstruation. Upon entering marriage, intercourse is usually a painful, traumatic event, often necessitating reopening of the scarified vaginal opening. Childbirth may also be impeded due to rigid scarring of the tissues. At times, maternal and fetal deaths also result.

In the cultures where female genital mutilation is prevalent, the practice is considered justified for a variety of reasons. It is believed, for example, that such mutilation will preserve virginity in unmarried women, assist in controlling their sexual drive, strengthen sexual faithfulness for married women, and increase sexual pleasure for their husbands. It is also believed that removal of all or part of female genitalia improves cleanliness, is cosmetically desirable, and makes childbirth safer for the infant. Because of these beliefs, women who have not undergone such procedures may be considered unsuited for marriage. Despite evidence against such reasons, and despite the efforts of numerous human rights organizations, the practice of female genital mutilation continues in a variety of cultures, with a prevalence exceeding 90 percent in some countries.

In some cultures, female genital mutilation is defended as a form of religious practice. While Seventh-day Adventists strongly advocate protection of religious liberty, Adventists believe that the right to practice one's religion does not vindicate harming another person. Thus, appeals to religious liberty do not justify female genital mutilation.

Biblical Principles

The Adventist Church's opposition to female genital mutilation is based on the following biblical principles:

1. Preservation of life and health. The Bible presents the goodness of God's creation, including the creation of human beings (Gen 1:31; Ps 139:13–14). God is the Source and Sustainer of human life (Job 33:4; Ps 36:9; John 1:3–4; Acts 17:25, 28). God calls for the preservation of human life and holds humanity accountable for its destruction (Gen 9:5–6; Ex 20:13; Deut 24:16; Jer 7:3–34). The human body is "the temple of the Holy Spirit," and followers of God are urged to care for and preserve their bodies, including the Creator's gift of sexuality, as a spiritual responsibility (1 Cor 6:15–19). Because female genital mutilation is harmful to health, threatening to life, and injurious to sexual function, it is incompatible with the will of God.
2. Blessing of marital intimacy. Scripture celebrates the divinely ordained gift of sexual intimacy within marriage (Eccl 9:9; Prov 5:18–19; Song of Sol 4:16–5:1; Heb 13:4). The practice of female genital mutilation should be renounced because it threatens the Creator's design for the experience of joyful sexuality by married couples.
3. Healthful procreation. For married couples, the gift of sexual union may be further blessed by the birth of children (Ps 113:9; 127:3–5;

128:3; Prov 31:28). The fact that successful childbirth is threatened by female genital mutilation is additional grounds for opposition to this practice.

4. Protection of vulnerable persons. Scripture prescribes that special efforts be made to care for those who are most vulnerable (Deut 10:17–19; Ps 82:3–4; Ps 24:11–12; Isa 1:16, 17; Luke 1:52–54). Jesus taught that children should be loved and protected (Mark 10:13–16; Matt 18:4–6). The genital mutilation of young girls violates the biblical mandate to safeguard children and protect them from harm and abuse.
5. Compassionate care. Love for the neighbor prompts Christians to provide compassionate care to those who have been injured (Luke 10:25–37; Isa 61:1). Christians are called to care with compassion for those who have experienced physical and emotional trauma caused by female genital mutilation.
6. Sharing truth. Christians are called to overcome error by expressing the truth in a loving manner (Ps 15:2–3; Eph 4:25). The fundamental truth of the gospel is intended to liberate people from all types of bondage to falsehood (John 8:31–36). Thus, Christians should join in sharing accurate information about the harm of female genital mutilation and the beliefs that underlie this practice.

Respect for cultures. Christians should be sensitive to and respectful of cultural differences (1 Cor 9:19–23; Rom 12:1–2). At the same time, we believe that God's principles transcend cultural traditions (Dan 1:8–9; 3:17–18; Matt 15:3; Acts 5:27–29). The fundamental principles of Scripture provide a basis for the transformation of cultural practices. While we acknowledge that female genital mutilation is firmly entrenched in many cultures, we find this practice to be incompatible with divinely revealed principles.

Conclusion

Because female genital mutilation threatens physical, emotional, and relational health, Seventh-day Adventists are opposed to this practice. The Church calls on its health care professionals, educational and medical institutions, and all members along with people of good will to cooperate in efforts to eliminate the practice of female genital mutilation. Through education and loving presentation of the gospel, it is our hope and our intention that those threatened by this practice will find protection and wholeness and that those who have been subjected to this practice will find solace and compassionate care.

§

Birth Control: A Seventh-day Adventist Statement of Consensus[1]

1999

Scientific technologies today permit greater control of human fertility and reproduction than was formerly possible. These technologies make possible sexual intercourse with the expectation of pregnancy and childbirth greatly reduced. Christian married couples have a potential for fertility control that has created many questions with wide-ranging religious, medical, social, and political implications. Opportunities and benefits exist as a result of the new capabilities, as do challenges and drawbacks. A number of moral issues must be considered. Christians who ultimately must make their own personal choices on these issues must be informed in order to make sound decisions based on biblical principles.

Among the issues to be considered is the question of the appropriateness of human intervention in the natural biological processes of human reproduction. If any intervention is appropriate, then additional questions regarding what, when, and how must be addressed. Other related concerns include:

- likelihood of increased sexual immorality which the availability and use of birth control methods may promote;
- gender dominance issues related to the sexual privileges and prerogatives of both women and men;
- social issues, including the right of a society to encroach upon personal freedom in the interest of the society at large and the burden of economic and educational support for the disadvantaged; and
- stewardship issues related to population growth and the use of natural resources.

A statement of moral considerations regarding birth control must be set in the broader context of biblical teachings about sexuality, marriage, parenthood, and the value of children and an understanding of the interconnectedness between these issues. With an awareness of the diversity of opinion within the Church, the following biblically based principles are set forth to educate and to guide in decision making.

1. **Responsible stewardship.** God created human beings in His own image, male and female, with capacities to think and to make decisions (Isa 1:18; Josh 24:15; Deut 30:15–20). God gave human beings dominion over the earth (Gen 1:26, 28). This dominion requires overseeing and caring for nature. Christian stewardship also requires taking responsibility for human procreation. Sexuality, as

[1] This statement was voted during the Annual Council of the General Conference Executive Committee on Wednesday, September 29, 1999 in Silver Spring, MD.

one of the aspects of human nature over which the individual has stewardship, is to be expressed in harmony with God's will (Exod 20:14; Gen 39:9; Lev 20:10–21; 1 Cor 6:12–20).

2. **Procreative purpose.** The perpetuation of the human family is one of God's purposes for human sexuality (Gen 1:28). Though it may be inferred that marriages are generally intended to yield offspring, Scripture never presents procreation as an obligation of every couple in order to please God. However, divine revelation places a high value on children and expresses the joy to be found in parenting (Matt 19:14; Ps 127:3). Bearing and rearing children help parents to understand God and to develop compassion, caring, humility, and unselfishness (Ps 103:13; Luke 11:13)
3. **Unifying purpose.** Sexuality serves a unifying purpose in marriage that is God-ordained and distinguishable from the procreative purpose (Gen 2:24). Sexuality in marriage is intended to include joy, pleasure, and delight (Eccl 9:9; Prov 5:18–19; Song of Sol 4:16–5:1). God intends that couples may have ongoing sexual communion apart from procreation (1 Cor 7:3–5), a communion that forges strong bonds and protects a marriage partner from an inappropriate relationship with someone other than his or her spouse (Prov 5:15–20; Song of Sol 8:6–7). In God's design, sexual intimacy is not only for the purpose of conception. Scripture does not prohibit married couples from enjoying the delights of conjugal relations while taking measures to prevent pregnancy.
4. **Freedom to choose.** In creation—and again through the redemption of Christ—God has given human beings freedom of choice, and He asks them to use their freedom responsibly (Gal 5:1, 13). In the divine plan, husband and wife constitute a distinct family unit, having both the freedom and the responsibility to share in making determinations about their family (Gen 2:24). Married partners should be considerate of each other in making decisions about birth control, being willing to consider the needs of the other as well as one's own (Phil 2:4). For those who choose to bear children, the procreative choice is not without limits. Several factors must inform their choice, including the ability to provide for the needs of children (1 Tim 5:8); the physical, emotional, and spiritual health of the mother and other care givers (3 John 2; 1 Cor 6:19; Phil 2:4; Eph 5:25); the social and political circumstances into which children will be born (Matt 24:19); and the quality of life and the global resources available. We are stewards of God's creation and therefore must look beyond our own happiness and desires to consider the needs of others (Phil 2:4).
5. **Appropriate methods of birth control.** Moral decision making about the choice and use of the various birth control agents must

stem from an understanding of their probable effects on physical and emotional health, the manner in which the various agents operate, and the financial expenditure involved. A variety of methods of birth control—including barrier methods, spermicides, and sterilization—prevent conception and are morally acceptable. Some other birth control methods may prevent the release of the egg (ovulation), may prevent the union of egg and sperm (fertilization), or may prevent attachment of the already fertilized egg (implantation). Because of uncertainty about how they will function in any given instance, they may be morally suspect for people who believe that protectable human life begins at fertilization. However, since the majority of fertilized ova naturally fail to implant or are lost after implantation, even when birth control methods are not being used, hormonal methods of birth control and IUDs, which represent a similar process, may be viewed as morally acceptable. Abortion, the intentional termination of an established pregnancy, is not morally acceptable for purposes of birth control.

6. **Misuse of birth control.** Though the increased ability to manage fertility and protect against sexually transmitted disease may be useful to many married couples, birth control can be misused. For example, those who would engage in premarital and extramarital sexual relations may more readily indulge in such behaviors because of the availability of birth control methods. The use of such methods to protect sex outside of marriage may reduce the risks of sexually transmitted diseases and/or pregnancy. Sex outside of marriage, however, is both harmful and immoral, whether or not these risks have been diminished.
7. A redemptive approach. The availability of birth control methods makes education about sexuality and morality even more imperative. Less effort should be put forth in condemnation and more in education and redemptive approaches that seek to allow each individual to be persuaded by the deep movings of the Holy Spirit.
8. Some current examples of these methods include intrauterine devices (IUDs), hormone pills (including the "morning after pill"), injections, or implants. Questions about these methods should be referred to a medical professional.

§

Meeting the Challenges of Sexually Transmitted Diseases[1]

1998

The contemporary world is confronted by grave ethical, medical, and social problems resulting from increasing sexual permissiveness and associated promiscuity. Because Christians are a part of the larger social community, these attitudes and behaviors have infiltrated the Seventh-day Adventist Church as well, demanding that we address them.

So serious are the challenges presented by sexually transmitted diseases (STDs) that the United Nations, in conjunction with most of the world's governments, the healthcare community, religious, political, and economic leaders, has instituted a series of major research and health education programs that focus on prevention and treatment. The goal is to prevent, cure, and minimize the effects—or at least slow the spread—of these diseases.

At particular risk are youth entering puberty at increasingly younger ages, when they are especially vulnerable to peer pressure and a barrage of media and peer messages that treat casual sex outside marriage as acceptable and normal. Many youth are sexually active early in their teen years and soon become well established in patterns of sexual activity.

Correlated with increased sexual activity is a dramatic increase in STDs associated with serious physical and emotional problems.

- Advances have been made along several lines:
- research has provided more accurate data;
- benefits of using condoms to reduce unwanted pregnancy and the spread of STDs have been documented;
- dangers of promiscuity have been recognized;
- more effective treatment has reduced the spread and progression of many STDs;
- risk of long-term emotional damage resulting from casual sex has been recognized; and
- support has grown for the position that abstinence from extra-marital sex preserves sexual and emotional health.

These advances, despite their limitations, have proved beneficial and should be encouraged for their positive effects. Seventh-day Adventist care givers should be encouraged to participate in promoting such efforts and deserve the support of church members as they do so. A pragmatic approach to dealing with these serious problems and the use of appropriate interventions should by no means be interpreted as endorsement or encouragement of sexual activity outside marriage or of unfaithfulness

[1] This statement was voted during the Annual Council of the General Conference Executive Committee on Sunday, September 27, 1998, in Iguacu Falls, Brazil.

within marriage. Instead, these efforts must be seen as compassionate attempts to prevent or reduce the negative consequences of detrimental sexual behaviors.

At times, family members, and pastors, teachers, counselors, physicians, and others in helping professions may find themselves working with individuals who, despite strong counsel, refuse to turn from sexual decadence and live by God's high standard of morality. In such cases, those entrusted with ministry may, as a last resort, counsel specific individuals to use contraceptive and prophylactic methods such as condoms in an attempt to prevent pregnancy and reduce the risk of spreading life-decimating STDs. Utmost care should be taken when making such an intervention to make it clear to the individual(s) and members of the community involved that this extreme measure should in no way be misconstrued as a scriptural sanction for sexual intimacy outside marriage. Such action on the part of professionals should be considered interim and utilized only in individual cases. Though such interventions may provide a little time for grace to do its work in human hearts, they do not provide a viable long-term solution. The Church must remain committed to making the most of every opportunity to reinforce the wisdom of God's design for human sexuality and to calling men and women to the highest standard of moral conduct.

Biblical Principles:

Although the efforts described above are in many ways beneficial, they are only a response to existing situations created by the impact of sin. In the Scriptures, God has set out a superior plan to guide our use of His gift of sexuality. Built upon a series of guiding principles, it presents in practical terms God's ideal for His people who must live in a sin-stricken world.

1. Sexual intimacy is reserved for marriage. Sexuality is a loving gift of the Creator to humanity (Gen 1:26–27). The gospel calls believers to an appreciation for and stewardship of their sexuality in harmony with the divine purposes (1 Cor 3:16–17; 6:13–20; Eph 5:1–8; Phil 1:27; 1 Thess 4:3–7). In God's plan, sexual intimacy is reserved for a man and a woman within the bounds of the marriage covenant (Gen 2:24, 26; Exod 20:14; Prov 5; Song of Sol 4:12; 8:8–10; 2:6–7; 3:5; 8:3–4; Hos 3:3; Heb 13:4). Sexual fidelity within marriage is crucial to convey a full understanding of God's metaphor comparing marriage to His relationship with His people (Isa 54:5; Hos 2:14–23; 2 Cor 11:2; Rev 19:6–9; 21:9).

2. Sexual intimacy outside of marriage is immoral and harmful. Such intimacy has detrimental effects on individuals (Lev 18:6–3; Rom 1:24–27; 1 Cor 6:18), as well as on the marriage relationship (Prov 5:1–23). It is identified by Scripture as part of the sinful life (Gal 5:19; Col 3:5).

3. God recognizes human frailty. His divine will for human beings and His intent for creation are unchangeable (Mal 3:6; Matt 5:17–20;

Acts 20:27). His absolute love for human beings and His redemptive intent are equally unchangeable (John 3:16; Rom 5:8; 8:35–39; Eph 1:1–14; 3:14–19; 1 John 4:7–10). The gospel message, centered in Jesus Christ, binds these truths together (Ps 85:10; 1 John 2:1–2).

God's grace is the only hope for fallen humanity (Rom 3:23–24; 5:1–2, 20; Eph 2:1–5). He is patient and long-suffering with human frailty (Num 14:18–19; Ps 86:15; 103:13–14; Hos 11:8–9; Jonah 3:1; 4:10–11; Matt 23:37; 1 Tim 1:15–16). Though God's grace does not give license to sin (Rom 6:1–2), it is through such grace that God accomplishes His redemptive intent in the circumstances resulting from sin (Rom 5:12–21). God's practical dealings in cases of divorce (Deut 24:1–5; Ezra 10:10–11; Matt 19:7–8), polygamy (Exod 21:10; Deut 17:17; 21:15–17; Matt 19:4–5), the introduction of flesh foods (Gen 1:11–12, 29–30; 9:3; Lev 3:17; 11:47), and provision for an earthly monarch (1 Sam 8:7; 10:19; Hos 13:11) offer examples of interventions short of God's ideal. Through such cases, we see His grace and mercy at work in a world deformed by sin.

4. The Church conducts its mission in a fallen world. Existing conditions contrast sharply with God's ideal. Both believers and unbelievers are vulnerable to sexual immorality as one of the tragic results of sin (John 17:15; 1 John 2:15). The Church is called to minister to believers and unbelievers alike, reaching and reclaiming sinners (Matt 28:19; Mark 2:17; 2 Cor 5:20–21), nurturing the growth of believers (Eph 2:19–22; 4:11–13, 15; 1 Thess 5:11; 2 Peter 3:18), uplifting the infinite worth of each individual (Isa 43:3–4, 7; Matt 12:12; Luke 12:7; 15:1–32; 1 Peter 1:18–19), protecting the weak and vulnerable (Rom 15:1; 1 Thess 5:14; Heb 13:3), promoting and preserving life and health (John 10:10; 1 Cor 6:19; 3 John 2), and calling men and women to take up their lofty position as God's chosen and holy people (Eph 4:1; 5:8; 1 Peter 1:15–16; 2:5, 9). The ministry of the Church is both to meet individuals where they are (1 Cor 3:1–2; 7:1–28), and to call them to a higher standard (Luke 19:5–10; John 8:3–11; Acts 17:18–34).

5. A spiritual development process is anticipated in the Christian life. Change for the Christian involves both conversion (John 3:3, 7; Acts 3:19; Rom 12:2; 2 Cor 5:17) and growth (Prov 4:18; Luke 2:52; Eph 3:17–19; 4:11–15; 2 Peter 3:18). At conversion, believers accept Christ's perfect life as their own by faith and experience a Spirit-led transformation of values (John 3:5; Gal 2:20). Both external and internal forces may provoke relapses in thought or conduct (Gal 5:16–18; 1 John 3:20), but commitment to grace-induced progress in the Christian life (1 Cor 15:10; Phil 3:12–14; Col 1:28–29) and reliance upon God-provided resources (Rom 8:5–7; Gal 5:24–25) will produce growth toward Christlikeness (Gal 5:22–25; Eph 5:1).

The Scriptures call for human beings to progress morally and spiritually throughout their lives (Luke 2:52; 1 Cor 13:11; 14:20). Planning for and facilitating such growth is integral to fulfilling the gospel commission (Matt 28:20; Eph 3:14–24). It is the task of religious education to attend to individual development and to present truth in ways that hearers can understand (Matt 11:15), causing them to stretch but not to stumble (Rom 14:1–21; 1 Cor 8:9–13). Though some allowance may be made for the unlearned or immature (Matt 13:34; John 16:12; Acts 17:30; 1 Cor 3:1–2), over time individuals should progress toward a more complete understanding of God's will (John 16:13) and a fuller expression of love for God and one another (Matt 22:37–39; John 13:35; 8:9; 13:11; 1 John 3:14; 4:11–12). Under God's blessing, the clear presentation of the gospel and careful attention to the disciple-making process will bear spiritual fruit, even among those who have been involved in sexual sin (1 Cor 6:9–11).

Implications:

1. The Church affirms the biblical view of sexuality as a wholesome attribute of human nature created by God to be enjoyed and used responsibly in marriage as part of Christian discipleship.

2. The Church is committed to sharing a biblical view of human sexuality in an intentional and culturally sensitive manner. Emphasis is placed on appreciating and understanding the human body and its functions, upholding sexual chastity outside and fidelity within marital relationships, and developing skills for decision making and communication about sexual behavior. The Church is committed to conveying the truth that the misuse of one's own sexuality and the abuse of power in relationships are contrary to God's ideal.

3. The Church calls people to dedicate themselves before God to sexual abstinence outside the marriage covenant and sexual faithfulness to one's spouse. Apart from the wholesome expression of sexual intimacy in marriage, abstinence is the only safe and moral path for the Christian. In any other context, sexual activity is both harmful and immoral. This high standard represents God's intention for the use of His gift, and believers are called upon to uphold this ideal, regardless of the prevailing standards in the culture around them.

4. The Church recognizes the sinfulness of humanity. Human beings make mistakes, use poor judgment, and may deliberately choose to engage in sexual practices that are contrary to God's ideal. Others may not know where to turn for help to live sexually pure lives. Nothing, however, can spare such individuals from the consequences of departing from the divine plan. Emotional and spiritual wounds left by sexual activity that violates God's plan inevitably leave scars. But the Church extends Christ's ministry of mercy and grace by offering God's forgiveness, healing, and restorative power. It must seek to provide the personal, spiritual, and emotional support that will enable the wounded to lay hold of the gospel's resources. The Church must also help persons and families identify and access the full network of professional resources available.

5. The Church recognizes as morally acceptable the use of contraceptive measures, including condoms, by married couples who seek to control conception. Condoms in particular may be indicated in some marital circumstances—for example, when one partner has been exposed to or has contracted a sexually transmitted disease, thus putting the spouse at high risk for infection.

On the other hand, the premarital or extramarital use of condoms—either in an attempt to lower the risk of unwanted pregnancy or to prevent the transmission of a sexually transmitted disease raises moral concerns. These concerns must be considered in the context of the divine plan for human sexuality, the relationship between God's creative intent and His regard for human frailty, the process of spiritual growth and moral development within individuals, and the nature of the Church's mission.

Though condoms have proved to be somewhat effective in preventing pregnancy and the spread of disease, this does not make sex outside of marriage morally acceptable. Neither does this fact prevent the emotional damage that results from such behavior. The Church's appeal to youth and adults alike, believers and nonbelievers, is to live lives worthy of the grace extended to us in Christ, drawing as fully as possible upon divine and human resources to live according to God's ideal for sexuality.

6. The Church acknowledges that in cases where a married person may be at risk for transmitting or contracting a sexually transmitted disease such as Human Immunodeficiency Virus (HIV) from his or her marriage partner, the use of a condom is not only morally acceptable but also strongly recommended if the husband and wife decide to continue having sexual intercourse. Users of condoms must be alerted to the importance of using them properly and to the limits of their effectiveness in preventing the transmission of HIV infection.

Appeal:

We are facing a crisis that threatens the lives and well-being of many people, including church members. Both youth and adults are in peril. The Church must develop, without delay, a comprehensive strategy of education and prevention. The resources of health, social services, educational, ministerial, and other professionals, both within and without the Church, must be mobilized. This crisis demands priority attention—using every legitimate resource and method at the Church's disposal to target the home, school, church, and community. The destiny of an entire generation of human beings is at stake, and we are in a race against time.

Research indicates that condoms, when correctly used, have about a 97 percent success rate in prevention of pregnancy and about an 85 to 90 percent success rate in prevention of virus transmission, as used by the general population. In those groups who use them consistently and correctly, the effectiveness is about 97 percent.

§

Child Sexual Abuse[1]

1997

Child sexual abuse occurs when a person older or stronger than the child uses his or her power, authority, or position of trust to involve a child in sexual behavior or activity. Incest, a specific form of child sexual abuse, is defined as any sexual activity between a child and a parent, a sibling, an extended family member, or a step/surrogate parent.

Sexual abusers may be men or women and may be of any age, nationality, or socio-economic background. They are often men who are married with children, have respectable jobs, and may be regular churchgoers. It is common for offenders to strongly deny their abusive behavior, to refuse to see their actions as a problem, and to rationalize their behavior or place blame on something or someone else. While it is true that many abusers exhibit deeply rooted insecurities and low self-esteem, these problems should never be accepted as an excuse for sexually abusing a child. Most authorities agree that the real issue in child sexual abuse is more related to a desire for power and control than for sex.

When God created the human family, He began with a marriage between a man and a woman based on mutual love and trust. This relationship is still designed to provide the foundation for a stable, happy family in which the dignity, worth, and integrity of each family member is protected and upheld. Every child, whether male or female, is to be affirmed as a gift from God. Parents are given the privilege and responsibility of providing nurture, protection, and physical care for the children entrusted to them by God. Children should be able to honor, respect, and trust their parents and other family members without the risk of abuse.

The Bible condemns child sexual abuse in the strongest possible terms. It sees any attempt to confuse, blur, or denigrate personal, generational, or gender boundaries through sexually abusive behavior as an act of betrayal and a gross violation of personhood. It openly condemns abuses of power, authority, and responsibility because these strike at the very heart of the victims' deepest feelings about themselves, others, and God, and shatter their capacity to love and trust. Jesus used strong language to condemn the actions of anyone who, through word or deed, causes a child to stumble.

The Adventist Christian community is not immune from child sexual abuse. We believe that the tenets of the Seventh-day Adventist faith require us to be actively involved in its prevention. We are also committed to

[1] (The above statement is informed by principles expressed in the following scriptural passages: Gen 1:26–28; 2:18–25; Lev 18:20; 2 Sam 13:1–22; Matt 18:6–9; 1 Cor 5:1–5; Eph 6:1–4; Col 3:18–21; 1 Tim 5:5–8.) This statement was voted during the Spring Meeting of the General Conference Executive Committee on Tuesday, April 1, 1997, in Loma Linda, California. https://www.adventist.org/official-statements/child-sexual-abuse/ (accessed January 11, 2022).

spiritually assisting abused and abusive individuals and their families in their healing and recovery process, and to holding church professionals and church lay leaders accountable for maintaining their personal behavior as is appropriate for persons in positions of spiritual leadership and trust.

As a Church we believe our faith calls us to:

1. Uphold the principles of Christ for family relationships in which the self-respect, dignity, and purity of children are recognized as divinely mandated rights.
2. Provide an atmosphere where children who have been abused can feel safe when reporting sexual abuse and can feel that someone will listen to them.
3. Become thoroughly informed about sexual abuse and its impact upon our own church community.
4. Help ministers and lay leaders to recognize the warning signs of child sexual abuse and know how to respond appropriately when abuse is suspected or a child reports being sexually abused.
5. Establish referral relationships with professional counselors and local sexual assault agencies who can, with their professional skills, assist abuse victims and their families.
6. Create guidelines/policies at the appropriate levels to assist church leaders in:
    1. Endeavoring to treat with fairness persons accused of sexually abusing children,
    2. Holding abusers accountable for their actions and administering appropriate discipline.
7. Support the education and enrichment of families and family members by:
    1. Dispelling commonly held religious and cultural beliefs which may be used to justify or cover up child sexual abuse.
    2. Building a healthy sense of personal worth in each child which enables him or her to respect self and others.
    3. Fostering Christlike relationships between males and females in the home and in the church.
8. Provide caring support and a faith-based redemptive ministry within the church community for abuse survivors and abusers while enabling them to access the available network of professional resources in the community.
9. Encourage the training of more family professionals to facilitate the healing and recovery process of abuse victims and perpetrators.

§

Pornography[1]

1990

Diverse courts and cultures may debate the definitions and consequences of pornography (the literature of sexual deviance), but on the basis of eternal principles, Seventh-day Adventists of whatever culture deem pornography to be destructive, demeaning, desensitizing, and exploitative.

It is *destructive* to marital relationships, thus subverting God's design that husband and wife cleave so closely to each other that they become, symbolically, "one flesh" (Genesis 2:24).

It is *demeaning*, defining a woman (and in some instances a man) not as a spiritual-mental-physical whole, but as a one-dimensional and disposable sex object, thus depriving her of the worth and the respect that are her due and right as a daughter of God.

It is *desensitizing* to the viewer/reader, callousing the conscience and "perverting the perception," thus producing a "depraved person" (Romans 1:22. 28, *NEB*).

It is *exploitative*, pandering to prurience, and basally abusive, thus contrary to the Golden rule, which insists that one treat others as one wishes to be treated (Matthew 7:12). Particularly offensive is child pornography. Said Jesus: "If anyone leads astray even one child who believes in me, he would be better off thrown into the depths of the sea with a millstone hung around his neck!" (See Matthew 18:6).

Though Norman Cousins may not have said it in Biblical language, he has perceptively written: "The trouble with this wide open pornography . . . is not that it corrupts but that it desensitizes; not that it unleashes the passions but that it cripples the emotions; not that it encourages a mature attitude, but that it is a reversion to infantile obsessions; not that it removes the blinders, but that it distorts the view. Prowess is proclaimed but love is denied. What we have is not liberation but dehumanization." –*Saturday Review of Literature*, Sept. 20, 1975.

A society plagued by plunging standards of decency, increasing child prostitution, teenage pregnancies, sexual assaults on women and children, drug-damaged mentalities, and organized crime can ill afford pornography's contribution to these evils.

Wise, indeed, is the counsel of Christianity's first great theologian: "If you believe in goodness and if you value the approval of God, fix your

---

[1] This public statement was released by the General Conference president, Neal C. Wilson, after consultation with the 16 world vice presidents of the Seventh-day Adventist Church, on July 5, 1990, at the General Conference session in Indianapolis, Indiana.

minds on the things which are holy and right and pure and beautiful and good" (Phil 4:8–9, *Phillips*). This is advice that all Christians would do well to heed.

§

Statement on Aids[1]

1990

Acquired immunodeficiency syndrome (AIDS) and associated conditions are spreading rapidly around the world. On the basis of statistical studies, it is estimated that in the near future, in many countries of the world, every church congregation numbering 100 or more will include at least one member who has a friend or relative with AIDS.

AIDS is transmitted through two major sources: sexual intimacy with an infected person, and introduction of HIV (human immunodeficiency virus) contaminated blood into the body either through injections with unsterile needles and syringes or through contaminated blood products. AIDS can be prevented by avoiding sexual contact before marriage and maintaining a faithful monogamous relationship with an uninfected person in marriage, and by avoiding the use of unsterile needles for injections and assuring the safety of blood products.

Adventists are committed to education for prevention of AIDS. For many years Adventists have fought against the circulation, sale, and use of drugs, and continue to do so. Adventist support sex education thatincludes the concept that human sexuality is God's gift to humanity. Biblical sexuality clearly limits sexual relationships to one's spouse and excludes promiscuous and all other sexual relationships and the consequent increased exposure to HIV.

The Christlike response to AIDS must be personal — compassionate, helpful, and redemptive. Just as Jesus cared about those with leprosy, the feared communicable disease of His day, His followers today will care for those with AIDS. James advised, "What good is there in your saying to them, 'God bless you! Keep warm and eat well!"—if you don't give them the necessities of life?" (James 2:16, TEV).

§

[1] This public statement was released by the General Conference president, Neal C. Wilson, after consultation with the 16 world vice presidents of the Seventh-day Adventist Church, on July 5, 1990, at the General Conference session in Indianapolis, IN.

Sexual Behavior[1]

1987

In His infinite love and wisdom God created mankind, both male and female, and in so doing based human society on the firm foundation of loving homes and families.

It is Satan's purpose, however, to pervert every good thing; and the perversion of the best inevitably leads to that which is worst. Under the influence of passion unrestrained by moral and religious principle, the association of the sexes has, to a deeply disturbing extent, degenerated into license and abuse which results in bondage. With the aid of many films, television, video, radio programs, and printed materials, the world is being steered on a course to new depths of shame and depravity. Not only is the basic structure of society being greatly damaged but also the breakdown of the family fosters other gross evils. The results in distorted lives of children and youth are distressing and evoke our pity, and the effects are not only disastrous but also cumulative.

These evils have become more open and constitute a serious and growing threat to the ideals and purposes of the Christian home. Sexual practices which are contrary to God's expressed will are adultery and premarital sex, as well as obsessive sexual behavior. Sexual abuse of spouses, sexual abuse of children, incest, homosexual practices (gay and lesbian), and bestiality are among the obvious perversions of God's original plan. As the intent of clear passages of Scripture (see Exod 20:14; Lev 18:22–23, 29 and 20:13; Matthew 5:27–28; 1 Cor 6:9; 1 Tim 1:10; Rom 1:20–32) is denied and as their warnings are rejected in exchange for human opinions, much uncertainty and confusion prevail. This is what Satan desires. He has always attempted to cause people to forget that when God as Creator made Adam, He also created Eve to be Adam's female companion ("male and female he created them" Gen 1:24, NEB). In spite of the clear moral standards set forth in God's Word for relationships between man and woman, the world today is witnessing a resurgence of the perversions and depravity that marked ancient civilizations.

The degrading results of the obsession of this age with sex and the pursuit of sensual pleasure are clearly described in the Word of God. But Christ came to destroy the works of the devil and reestablish the right relationship of human beings with each other and with their Creator. Thus, though fallen in Adam and captive to sin, those who turn to Christ in repentance receive full pardon and choose the better way, the way to complete restoration. By means of the cross, the power of the Holy Spirit in the

[1] This statement was approved and voted by the General Conference of Seventh-day Adventists Executive Committee at the Annual Council session in Washington, D.C., October 12, 1987.

"inner man," and the nurturing ministry of the Church, all may be freed from the grip of perversions and sinful practices.

An acceptance of God's free grace inevitably leads the individual believer to the kind of life and conduct that "will add luster to the doctrine of our God and Saviour" (Titus 2:10, NEB). It will also lead the corporate church to firm and loving discipline of the member whose conduct misrepresents the Saviour and distorts and lowers the true standards of Christian life and behavior.

The Church recognizes the penetrating truth and powerful motivations of Paul's words to Titus: "For the grace of God has dawned upon the world with healing for all mankind; and by it we are disciplined to renounce godless ways and worldly desires, and to live a life of temperance, honesty, and godliness in the present age, looking forward to the happy fulfilment of our hope when the splendor of our great God and Saviour Christ Jesus will appear. He it is who sacrificed himself for us, to set us free —from all wickedness and to make us a pure people marked out for his own, eager to do good."—Titus 2:11–14, NEB. (See also 2 Peter 3:11–14.)

§

Scripture Index

Extrabiblical Literature Index